THE MODERN WORLD

1650–1850

Western Society: Institutions and Ideals

McGRAW-HILL BOOK COMPANY *New York   St. Louis   San Francisco*
                                      Toronto   London   Sydney

Peter H. Amann

Associate Professor of History
State University of New York at Binghamton

VOLUME III

THE
MODERN
WORLD

1650-1850

THE MODERN WORLD 1650–1850, Volume III

Copyright © 1967 by McGraw-Hill, Inc. All Rights Reserved.
Printed in the United States of America. This book, or
parts thereof, may not be reproduced in any form without
permission of the publishers.
Library of Congress Catalog Card Number 67–10884

1 2 3 4 5 6 7 8 9 0   HD   7 4 3 2 1 0 6 9 8 7

*The following articles or selections have been reprinted in this volume with
the permission of the publishers:*

Hornick, "Austria over All if She Only Will," from EARLY ECONOMIC
THOUGHT, edited by A. E. Monroe. Harvard University Press, 1924.

Selection from IMMANUEL KANT'S CRITIQUE OF PURE REASON,
translated by Norman Kemp Smith. St. Martin's Press, Inc., Macmillan &
Co., Ltd.

Selection from NAPOLEON SELF-REVEALED, edited and translated by
J. M. Thompson. Houghton Mifflin Co., Boston and New York, 1934. Canada
permission from Basil Blackwell, Oxford.

To MARIAN WILSON, friend, critic, and secretary extraordinary

Preface

This anthology grew out of a college freshman course in Western Institutions and Social Ideas taught by a staff that used original sources as materials for discussion and analysis. To keep a discussion course stimulating and exciting to teacher and student alike, we found ourselves supplementing existing anthologies with new documents. This anthology is the logical end product of these efforts. On the basis of our experience in discussing original documents in an introductory course, we determined that three principles should characterize our anthology.

First, we asked that an anthology have a range sufficient to allow real flexibility. A useful anthology should permit the revamping of a course from year to year, if only to prevent the instructors from going stale. In theory, our four volumes at well over one million words could include enough selections to suppy a two-year discussion course meeting four days a week. Attractive as some of us might find such a prospect, most Western civilization courses meet for a single academic year and, at that, for one or two weekly discussion sessions. We would expect most courses to use less than half of the anthologized documents in any one year. Consequently, this anthology should provide every instructor (or staff) with ample leeway to assign material to fit his particular students.

Our arrangement of the readings within each of the four volumes is topical as well as chronological. Although we have grouped together documents that are likely to be discussed together (or that provide a common pool from which to choose one reading) and have put them in what seems to us a sensible sequence, our organization in no way impinges upon the freedom of the instructor to rearrange as he sees fit.

Second, we felt that a useful anthology should have definite limits and a point of view; otherwise flexibility might dissolve into chaos. Our limits are explicit: we selected documents either to portray ideas about Western society or to illustrate Western political, economic, religious, or other institutions. We did not seek to present historical events as such, leaving this task to a text or to the discretion of the instructor. By focusing on institutions and social ideas, we excluded "pure" philosophy (such as linguistic analysis) and "pure" science (such as the Quantum Theory) on the one hand and literature and art for their own sakes on the other. Selections from Chaucer's *Canterbury Tales* and Dostoevski's *The Brothers Karamazov* appear in this collection because in our judgment they illustrate certain values and institutions better than other available documents. It is in any case obvious that with the availability of primary works in paperback, an instructor who so wishes can easily pick supplementary literary works. By focusing on the West, we have deliberately excluded documents from cultures like the Byzantine or Islamic that are related, yet raise complex questions of affiliations best handled in text or lecture.

Third, we relied on our classroom experience for selecting documents that by their content and format lend themselves to fruitful and interesting discussion. By choosing selections of from ten to twenty pages, we have been able to include many documents in full and others in excerpts substantial enough to permit the author's line of argument and point of view to emerge. Athough almost every conceivable type of document—from philosophical treatise to personal diary—is represented, we have been sparing in the use of legal and constitutional texts that tend to appeal to professional historians, but are too technical for undergraduate discussion. In making our selections, we have tried neither to draw up a catalogue of familiar names nor to stock a museum of esoterica. We have tried to find and edit the most interesting and significant documents that illustrate major ideological and institutional trends. Some two dozen documents have been specially translated into English for this anthology. Our guidelines throughout have been significance, intrinsic interest, and discussability.

Our introduction preceding the documents attempt to provide just enough background to permit intelligent reading, without prejudging issues by means of capsule summaries or leading questions. They make no claim to provide continuity or depth. We consider it more constructive to suggest to the student—in the short introductory essay following the Table of Contents—the kinds of questions by which he can learn to come to grips with original sources for himself.

From its half-conscious inception to its final form, this four-volume anthology has been a collective venture on the part of three historians and one philosopher. Not only did all the editors participate in the detailed planning of each volume, but each of us has contributed selections and introductions to each of the four volumes. Our overriding concern has been to produce a collection of readings that would be interesting, unhackneyed, and enjoyable to use. We can only hope that we have succeeded.

Peter H. Amann

Richard J. Burke, Jr.
Melvin Cherno
Gerald M. Straka

Contents

IV IMPRESSIONS OF THE AGE

V THE REVOLUTIONARY EPOCH

On Reading
Original Sources

A generation ago the historian Carl Becker shocked an after-dinner audience with a speech entitled, "Every Man His Own Historian." His audience was made up of members of the American Historical Association who had come to honor and hear their newly elected president. Yet Becker upset their mental equilibrium—and their digestion—by suggesting that history was not some secret art to be passed on to a cloistered initiate who would emerge years later from behind ivy walls with eyesight impaired and a Ph.D. to his name. Becker's point was that man's attempt to make sense of his own past was a natural and universal concern; that since no two men were alike, every man had to deal with the past—to be his own historian—in terms meaningful to himself. Yet Becker did not imply that all men were equally qualified for the task. Though the past is always seen through human eyes—by someone with interests, predilections, prejudices, and blind spots—there is nonetheless something like 20/20 vision in history as opposed to the myopia that results from lack of training. There are *some* tricks to the trade, and they can be learned.

One of the aims of any course using an anthology such as this is to provide you with some critical insight into the unavoidable job of being your own historian. All your life you will have to come to terms with the past, whether it be yesterday's personal encounter or the international roulette wheel stopping at your number. Even most family arguments boil down to historical controversy.

In dealing with the readings in this anthology, your first objective should be to master the technique of being your own *competent* historian. Here you are asked to make sense of a cultural tradition by analyzing documents illustrating different aspects of that tradition. The variety of documents that you will face is enormous. They may be roughly classified as follows:

1 History, biography, autobiography
2 Letters, journals, memoirs
3 Philosophical and scientific treatises
4 Speeches, sermons, manifestoes, public debates
5 Articles in periodicals
6 Essays, dialogues, poetry
7 Legal and constitutional documents
8 Diplomatic reports

You may best begin your analysis by following some rather basic considerations. Every one of these documents may be studied from various perspectives: each will have (1) an author, (2) a social and cultural context, (3) a purpose or function, (4) a subject matter, (5) a structure and method, and (6) relationship with and affiliations to other documents. You can make each of these "dimensions" of a document a focus for analysis, either by yourself or in class discussion. Each is a *direction* in which you can strike out; each suggests a *question* or a cluster of questions that you can raise about the document. If you learn to ask these questions habitually while reading, you are well on your way toward a critical understanding of history, even in its more difficult social and intellectual aspects.

Dimension 1: The Author.   You may read a document as an expression of the author's point of view. A presidential message to Congress, for instance, is an expression of presidential policy on a given problem or problems. You may raise the question of the author's background, of his values and biases. In most cases this is a straightforward enough question. Sometimes this may be a crucial question, although at other times it is of minor importance or even altogether irrelevant.

Dimension 2: The Historical Context.   You may read a document as reflecting the social and cultural milieu out of which it comes. When a Chinese leader makes a statement of national policy, for example, to what extent do his ideas and the way in which he puts them reflect the historical experience of China on the one hand, of the Chinese Communist movement on the other? This kind of question is related to the previous one, yet it is broader: it involves the ideas and values held during whole historical eras. You should learn to move back and forth between textbook and documents, evaluating the textbook interpretations of the Protestant Reformation or of the Industrial Revolution in terms of generalizations you have drawn from your original readings for each period.

Dimension 3: The Purpose.   Not all documents aim simply to tell the truth, the whole truth, and nothing but the truth. Many of them, through the use of rhetorical devices, are designed to win a case, whether in an actual court, in formal debate, or in a wider forum of opinion. Many are pitched to a special audience to get some particular point across, for instance, a speech of Adolf Hitler's addressing a Nazi party rally. Some are justifications of actions already taken, others exhortations for the future. Clearly, all written documents are intelligible only in terms of the purpose or function they intended to serve and of the audience they attempted to reach.

Dimension 4: The Subject Matter.   This may be the obvious question, yet it may not always be easy to answer. What is the reading about? You should practice summarizing documents in your own words and as briefly as possible, particularly when this is difficult to do. You may have to summarize ideas that have been advanced or to characterize institutions that have been described or exemplified. In historical or biographical narratives, subject matter is normally central. What were the ancient Germans like? What sort of man was Leonardo da Vinci? What was the structure of the ancient Roman Republic? What was life like at the court of Louis XIV of France?

Dimension 5: Structure and Method.   This is the *internal* dimension. How does a document hang together? What is the relation of the parts to the whole? *How* does the President present his case for certain legislation to Congress? In a straightforward historical narrative or a list of grievances, these internal relationships may be very simple; in a philosophical treatise or in a tragedy the internal structure may be very complex and artful. If a document presents an *argument,* then the question of its validity is perfectly in order, as is the question of the truth of its premises.

Dimension 6: Relationships to Other Documents.   In this broad category fall all the questions about the influence of earlier writers on later ones and about similarities, contrasts, "climates of opinion," and traditions. How does the foreign policy statement of our Chinese Communist leader compare with earlier such announcements? With announced Russian Communist aims, recent and in Lenin's day? With the way non-Communist countries justify and announce their policy? Does our Chinese Communist seem to follow the guidelines for holding on to power suggested by Machiavelli in the sixteenth century? You may consider a given document as an effect of earlier developments and as a cause of subsequent ones. It may be combined with others of its own period to form a trend. It may be grouped in countless ways. As editors, we have already done some grouping by dividing the readings into four volumes and by choosing an arrangement within the volumes that is partly topical. Your instructor, by assigning some readings and not others, will have made yet another such grouping.

All this may seem very abstract and remote, until you really get down to cases. Take, as an example, the Declaration of Independence of July 4, 1776 (see Vol. III, pages 327–330). This document is at least vaguely familiar to most Americans, yet it reveals its full significance—as well as a nest of controversial issues—only when analyzed in terms of the six dimensions that have been suggested.

The Declaration of Independence was drafted chiefly by Thomas Jefferson, revised by a committee that included Benjamin Franklin and John Adams, and signed by all fifty-six delegates to the Second Continental Congress, the representatives of the "Thirteen" United States of America. Who, then, was its *author?* Does it really represent the views of all the inhabitants of those thirteen states? A majority of them? How were the delegates elected?

The social and cultural *context* of the document was the eighteenth-century Enlightenment, with its appeal to "self-evident truths" characteristic of that period's buoyant confidence in the power of human reason to apprehend objective fact. Could such an appeal carry any force today, after modern psychology has revealed the numberless ways in which we all deceive ourselves and after the history of modern wars and totalitarian regimes has demonstrated the folly of calling man the "rational animal"?

The *purpose* of the Declaration, as we are told explicitly, is to justify the revolution of the thirteen colonies against their mother country. But what is "justification"? Is it only a convenient cover-up for what they had undertaken? Was it an attempt to win support from other countries, perhaps from France?

As for its *subject matter,* most of it seems to be about the actions of "the present

King of Great Britain." (This is puzzling in itself, for did not the Glorious Revolution of 1688–1689 establish the supremacy of Parliament over the King?) On closer examination, however, these actions all have one thing in common: they are allegedly violations of the "rights" of the colonists. With this as a clue, we see that the opening and closing sections of the document also deal with the concept of rights.

This leads to a consideration of the *structure* of the Declaration of Independence, which proves to be that of a "hypothetical syllogism": *if* any government fails to protect the rights of its citizens to life, liberty, and the pursuit of happiness, *then* such a government forfeits all claim to their allegiance; the English government *has* failed to protect our rights (the long list of grievances is intended to prove this); *therefore* we owe the English government no allegiance. This is Jefferson's argument reduced to its essentials. In form it is a logical argument: if x is true, then y is true; but x *is* true: therefore y is true. If its premises are also true—and this is quite another question—then its conclusion must be accepted. But what are these premises? How can we tell whether they are true?

Finally, the Declaration of Independence reveals the strong *influence* of John Locke's Second Treatise of Civil Government (see Vol. III, pages 44–64) and in turn the Declaration of Independence had an undoubted *effect* on the great French Revolution that broke out only thirteen years later. Did the Declaration also serve as the basis for the United States Constitution, or was that latter document founded on different philosophical premises? Did the Declaration establish political democracy? Did it have anything to say about capitalism? Have the principles set forth in the Declaration played any part in the current wave of colonial wars of independence in Africa and Asia?

Not all these dimensions are equally important in every document. Even so, you would do well to cultivate the habit of asking yourself all six questions about every document you encounter, before deciding which are the most significant in each particular case. In time this becomes second nature, yet to do this is to cultivate the critical faculty that is an essential part of an educated man.

THE MODERN WORLD

1650–1850

~§ *Part One*

Seventeenth Century
Statecraft

❧ RELIGION AND ALLEGIANCE

Roger Manwaring

The divine-right-of-kings theory evolved from two primary traditions: first, the Roman Caesaro-Papist legacy that Caesar united in his person the sacred offices of emperor and supreme priest, although joining the gods after death; and second, the Christian interpretation of the state's religious character as broadly formulated by St. Paul, which held that all governments are empowered by God to carry out the tasks of keeping the peace. Order was one of God's injunctions, and even those pagan rulers who maintained it could be considered "God's ministers."

From the fifth to the twelfth centuries this semidivinity of the king was accepted as fact, though not until the time of Gregory VII, when monarchs made claims to God-given absolutism rivaling those of the Pope, was much written on the subject. Later, early in the sixteenth century, Protestant leaders and laymen championed the doctrine that the king is responsible only to God for his people's well-being, especially where it concerned the right of Protestant princes over Church lands and over the jurisdiction of the objectionable ecclesiastical courts. From the Reformation into the eighteenth century, divine-right monarchy held full sway, its continuing strength stemming as much from the pious acceptance of the common man as from its position in public law.

The following sermon on the subject was give in 1627 by Roger Manwaring (1590–1653), one of the chaplains of King Charles I of England. Manwaring was later impeached by the Long Parliament for his displeasing views, and his book was publicly burned. Yet divine right was nevertheless held to be a primary tenet of Anglicanism well into the eighteenth century. In countries like Prussia, Austria, and Russia, the doctrine propped up thrones throughout the nineteenth and even into the twentieth century.

Unity is the foundation of all difference and distinction; distinction the mother of multitude; multitude and number infer relation; which is the knot and confederation of things different by reason of some respect they bear unto each other. These relations and respects challenge duties correspondent according as they stand in distance or nearness, afar off or near conjoined.

Roger Manwaring, *Religion and Allegiance* (London: 1710), pp. 3–13, 35–40. Rendered into modern English by Gerald Straka.

Of all relations the first and most original is that between the creator and the creature whereby that which is made depends upon the maker thereof, both in constitution and preservation: for which the creature doth ever owe to the creator, the actual and perpetual performance of that which to its nature is most agreeable, which duty is called natural. And sometimes also is the creature bound to submit in those things that are quite . . . against the natural, both inclination and operation thereof, if the Creator's pleasure be so to command it, which dutiful submission is called by the divines an obediential capacity in that which is made, by all means to do homage to Him that made it of mere nothing.

The next is that between husband and spouse, a respect which even ethnic antiquity called and accounted sacred, the foul violation of which sacred bed and bond of matrimony was ever counted heinous and justly recompensed with that wound and dishonor that could never be blotted out, Prov. 6. 33.

Upon this followed that third bond of reference which is between parents and children, where, if dutiful obedience be not performed by them that received to them that gave their being, the malediction is no less than this, that "their light shall be put out in obscure darkness," Prov. 20. 20. "The ravens of the valleys to pick out their eyes, and the young eagles to eat them up," Prov. 30. 17.

In the fourth place did likewise accrue that necessary dependence of the servant on his lord, God having so ordained "that the eyes of servants should look unto the hand of their masters and the eyes of the hand-maid unto the hand of her mistress," Ps. 123. 2.

From all which forenamed respects there did arise that most high, sacred, and transcendent relation which naturally grows between the Lord's anointed and their loyal subjects, to, and over whom, their lawful sovereigns are no less than fathers, lords, kings, and gods on earth.

Now as the duties comporting with all these several relations if they shall be answerably done are the cause of all the prosperity, happiness, and felicity which doth befall them in their several stations, so is it in the world the only cause of all tranquility, peace, and order, and those things which distinction, number, and disparity of condition have made different, it most effectually reduceth to union, that, as of one, there arose many, so by this means do multitudes become to be made one again, Acts 4. 32. I Cor. 10. 17. Which happy reunion nature doth by all means much affect but the effecting thereof is the main and most gracious work of religion. Which the wisdom of Solomon well seeing, and the spirit that was in him well searching into, he sends forth the sententious dictates of his divine and royal wisdom, fenced with no less reason than the fortress of religion, in these words following, "I counsel thee to keep the king's commandment, and that in regard of the oath of God."

This is God's text and the king's, and for the sake of all kings was it written, and as the king is the sacred and supreme head of two bodies, the one spiritual, the other secular, so this high and royal text contains in it two parts correspondent: 1. the one civil, which is a counsel of state, or a politic caution, "I counsel thee to keep the king's commandment," 2. the other spiritual, which is a devout or religious reason, and that in regard of the oath of God. The first part is founded upon the second, the second is the ground of the first: religion the stay of polity, which, if it be truly taught, devoutly followed, and sincerely practised, is the root of all virtues, the foundation of all well-ordered commonweals, and the well-head from whence all, even temporal felicity, doth flow. The zeal and fervor of which religion, if at any time it fall into a wane or declination, contempt, or derision, portends evermore the ruin and desolation of that state and kingdom where the service and worship of Him who sits in Heaven is set at naught and fills the world with terrible examples of God's revenging justice and most ireful indignation. . . .

. . . Now, all things that work and have any operation must of necessity work by some power or ability which is in them. All power is either such as is created and derived from some higher cause, or such as is uncreated and independent. Of this last kind is that power which is in God alone who is self-able in all things and most puissant of Himself, and from and by no other. All powers created are of God, "no power, unless it be given from above," John 19. 11. And all the powers that are of this sort, "are ordained of God," Rom. 13. 1. Among all the powers that be ordained of God the regal is most high, strong, and large: kings above all, inferior to none, to no man, to no angel, to no order of angels. For tho' in nature, order, and place, the angels be superior to men, yet to powers and persons royal they are not, in regard of any dependence that princes have of them: their power then the highest. No power in the world, or in the hierarchy of the church, can lay restraint upon these supremes, therefore theirs the strongest. And the largest it is, for that no parts within their dominions, no persons under their jurisdictions (be they never so great) can be privileged from their power, nor be exempted from their care, be they never so mean. To this power the highest and greatest peer must stoop and cast down his coronet at the foot-stool of his sovereign. The poorest creature which lieth by the wall or goes by the highway-side is not without sundry and sensible tokens of that sweet and royal care and providence which extendeth itself to the lowest of his subjects. The way they pass by is the king's high-way. The laws which make provision for their relief take their binding force from the supreme will of their liege-lord. The bread that feeds their hungry souls, the poor rags which hide thir nakedness, all are the fruit and superfluity of that happy plenty and abundance caused by a wise and peaceable government: whereas, if we should come to hear the dreadful and confused noise of war, . . . if plough-shares should be turned into swords and scythes into spears, then famine of bread, and cleanness of teeth, and dearth of all good things would be the just and most deserved punishment of all, both their and our sins.

Now to this high, large, and most constraining power of kings, not only nature, but even God Himself gives from Heaven most full and ample testimony and that this power is not merely human, but super-human, and indeed no less than a power divine. Tho' majesty (saith Herodotus) be shrouded under mortality, yet is it endowed with such a power from above as bears no small resemblance with the deity. For if it were of men, or if that power which is dispersed in communities and multitudes were collected and settled in the king, then might this power be thought human and to rise from men, but because God would have men to conceive quite otherwise of regal sovereignty, therefore Himself pronounceth this of them who wear crowns on their heads, sit upon thrones, and with scepters in their hands rule nations, "I said ye are gods," Ps. 82. 6.

That sublime power therefore which resides in earthly potentates is not a derivation or collection of human power scattered among many and gathered into one head, but a participation of God's own omnipotency, which He never did communicate to any multitudes of men in the world but only and immediately to his own vicegerents. And that is His meaning when He saith, "by me kings reign," Prov. 8. 15. Kings they are by His immediate constitution, and by Him also do they rule and exercise their so high and large authority.

This therefore may be well conceived to be the cause wherefore God doth plead in scripture, and that so mainly, not only for the sovereignty, but also for the security of His anointed, "I said ye are gods". . . .

The power of princes then is both natural and divine, not from any consent or allowance of men . . . not therefore in any consent of men, not in grace, not in any municipal law, or local custom, nor in any law national, nor yet in the law of nations, which consent of men and tract of time hath made forcible, not, finally, in the pope, or any people, is regal pre-eminency founded: for Adam had dominion settled in him before ever there was either pope or people; neither popes nor populous multitudes have any right to give or take in this case. So that royalty is a pre[-eminency] wherein monarchs are invested immediately from God, for by Him do they reign. And likewise sacred to God Himself, "for he who toucheth them, toucheth the apple of God's own eye," and therefore, "touch not mine anointed."

Supreme also it is, and independent [of] any man, men, or angels; and for this, saith He, they are gods, whose glorious and dreadful names must not be meddled with by any wicked tongues or pens nor mingled with any lewd, perverse, or depraving thoughts, and for this, "curse not the king in thy thought". . . .

Now then, a commandment is an act descending from three most eminent faculties of this human soul. First, from the understanding; finding out by exact discourse, advice, and counsel, what is to be done, by which extensions of reason the intellectual part draws to practice. Secondly, from the judgment, decreeing and resolving what is the meetest to be done amongst many particulars. And, lastly, from the imperial sway of the will which fastens a command on all other powers to do their parts for the dispatch of such designs as reason hath found out and judgment thought meet or necessary to be done.

To draw then towards some conclusion of the point in hand, all the significations of a royal pleasure are, and ought to be, to all loyal subjects, in the nature and force of a command: as well, for that none may, nor can search into the high discourse and deep counsels of kings, seeing their hearts are so deep by reason of their distance from common men even as the heavens are in respect of the earth. Therefore, said He, who was wise in heart and deep in counsel, "the heavens for height, and the earth for depth, and the heart of a king is unsearchable," Prov. 25. 3. As also, for that none may dare to call in question the judgment of a king, because the heart of a king is in the hand of God and He turneth it which way He pleaseth. Who then may question that which God doth proclaim from heaven to be in His hands and at His guidance? And for His sovereign will, (which gives a binding force to all His royal edicts, concluded out of the reasons of state and depth of counsel) who may dare resist it without incurable . . . breach of conscience? Seeing the apostle speaks under terms of so great terror, that he who resists commits a sin done with an high hand, "for he resists the ordinance of God," Rom. 13. and so contracts an heinous guilt and incurs likewise the heaviest punishment, for to his own soul doth he receive damnation.

Nay, tho' any king in the world should command flatly against the law of God, yet were his power no otherwise at all to be resisted, but for the not doing of his will in that which is clearly unlawful, to endure with patience whatsoever penalty his pleasure should inflict upon them, who in this case would desire rather to obey God than man. By which patient and meek suffering of their sovereign's pleasure they should become glorious martyrs; whereas, by resisting of his will, they should forever endure the pain and stain of odious traitors and impious malefactors.

But, on the other side, if any king shall command that which stands not in any opposition to the original laws of God, nature, nations, and the gospel, (tho' it be not correspondent in every circumstance to laws national and municipal) no subject may, without hazard of his own damnation, in rebelling against God, question or disobey the will and pleasure of his sovereign. For, as a father of the country, he commands what his pleasure is out of the counsel and judgment: as a king of subjects, he enjoins it; as a lord over God's inheritance, he exacts it; as a supreme head of the body, he adviseth it; as a defender of the faith, he requires it as their homage; as a protector of their persons, lives, and states, he deserves it; and, as the sovereign procurer of all the happiness, peace, and welfare, which they enjoy who are under him, he doth most justly claim at their hands. To kings, therefore, in all these respects nothing can be denied (without manifest and sinful violation of law and conscience) that may answer their royal state and excellency, that may further the supply of their urgent necessities, that may be for the security of their royal persons, (whose lives are worth millions of others) that may serve for the protection of their kingdoms, territories, and dominions, that may enable them to yield relief, aid, and succour to their dear and royal confederates and allies, or that may be for the defence and propagation of that sacred and precious truth, the public profession whereof they do maintain by their laws and prerogatives royal.

Obedience is a willing and understanding act of an inferior, done at the command and to the honor of a superior. Reasonable then, and willing must it be; violenced duties, forced and extorted actions, are not within the compass of true obedience. Voluntary service is that which pleaseth God and man, and so well doth this suit with the nature of God (to whom all things ought to yield most willing obedience) that He pronounceth it "better than sacrifice, and to hearken, better than the fat of rams," I Sam. 15. 22.

Every will, therefore, and inclination that is in the creature is charged with the duty of obedience toward the maker of it. To this end God hath planted a double capacity and possibility in the creature to submit to His pleasure. The one is natural, by which the creature in all its actions that follow and flow from its form doth actually and perpetually serve the Creator, as the heavens in moving, the earth in standing still, the fire in burning, the air and water in refreshing, cooling, and flowing.

The other capacity is called obediential, whereby the creature is ever ready to do that which is contrary to its own nature if the Maker's pleasure be to command it so. And with this obedience did the earth fearfully shrink and fall asunder, Num. 16. 32.

to swallow up those rebels against God and the king, so to give them a sudden and ready passage into hell by a direct and straight diameter. Thus did the waters stand in heaps, Exod. 14. 20. and leave the channel dry that God's people might find a marvelous way and His enemies a strange death, Wisd. 19. 5. Thus did stones yield to be lifted up against their nature into the air that they might fall back and recoil with greater violence to bruise and brain the enemies of His people, Josh. 10. 11. Thus did the fire of the Babylonian furnace refresh the three children, Dan. 3. 27. And thus, in fine, did the sun stand still in Gibeon and the moon in the Valley of Ajalon, Josh. 10. 20. to give the longer light and lesser heat to them who fought for Him that made both sun and moon.

Now, this power which God hath over, and this kind of subjection which He receives from the creature, is a privilege and prerogative which God hath reserved only to Himself and not communicated at any time to any king or Caesar to have or to receive regularly, but only by way of impetration and extraordinary dispensation for dispatch of some miraculous work, as it was in Moses and Joshua.

All the obedience therefore that man can challenge from man is in part natural as agreeable and convenient to their inclinations, and in part moral, in as much as it is free and willing. And this, of right, may every superior exact of his inferior as a due debt and every inferior must yield it unto his lawful superior for the same reason. Children to parents in discipline and domesticals; servants to their lords in their respective and obliged duties; soldiers to their commanders in martial affairs and feats of arms; people to their pastors in conscientious duties and matters of salvation; subjects to their lawful sovereigns in the high concernments of state and policy. And this is that obedience wherewith we are all charged in this text by the word of God and wisdom of Solomon. . . .

And this is a truth so solid and fundamental that it hath the clear and express text and testimony of holy writ, is grounded on the perpetual practice of all the primitive saints and martyrs, hath the consent of all the holy bishops and Catholic writers. Never any good or learned men taught or thought the contrary till the Devil of late infused it into the heads of those two fiery and entailed foxes of the world, the Roman Jesuits, and German Puritans.

To put an end then to this whole matter, it may clearly (by what hath been already spoken) appear unto all of indifferent and impartial judgment how many are the paradoxes which they run themselves into, who (in this case) do in so stiff a manner refuse obedience to supreme authority.

For, first, what a paradox is it in divinity to opine that religion is an orat[or] to persuade rebellion or disobedience to sacred and anointed kings? This being the weapon wherewith St. Augustine did ward the blows of heathenish objections made against the Christians: give us, if you can, such consuls, such provincials; such husbands, such wives; such parents, such children; such masters, such servants; such debtors, such creditors; such judges, such officers; such kings, such people or subjects; such publicans, such tribute-payers as Christians are and the doctrine they profess teacheth them to be. And indeed impossible it is that of religion, which is the mistress of obedience, any man should learn the evil lesson of disobedience.

Again, what a paradox is this in nature to think that the part should not conform itself to the whole, nature having stampt this law, and it being the very impress of nature's light that every part ought in right to comply with the whole or greater part. So in all the counsels of the church and parliaments of the world hath it ever been since the world began, without which yielding of the lesser to the greater side or number no laws could ever have been agreed upon nor the world or the church ever enjoyed any peaceable or happy days. Now, these refusers of obedience have quite forgotten their very yielding to the major part, for what a handful are they, compared with almost two hundred thousand men which have willingly submitted and lead the way of most dutiful obedience towards his Majesty? And therefore these Recusants * must of necessity follow them in so good a rule and precedent unless they will have men to think that the very light of natural illumination is damped in them.

Thirdly, what a paradox is this in point of policy to imagine that a part of the republic (tho' the greater) should submit their shoulders to the burden of the whole? For in every well ordered commonwealth, as by distributive justice, each person hath a share in the profits and honors therein, so, by the same justice ought he to bear a part in the taxes and burdens thereof: for it hath the ground from that rule that every commodity that passeth unto any man carries with it a certain burden correspondent. Nay, this is founded expressly on the apostle's words, where he teacheth, (and that from the very sense of nature) "that the members ought to have the same care one of another," I Cor. 12. 25. much more of the whole or greater part. For any member therefore in this case to enjoy a privilege, is to prejudice the whole, and so to extinguish and overthrow the safety and welfare as well of the natural, as of the politic corporation, and the sacred constitution of both.

Fourthly, what a paradox is this in loyalty (and that very foul) so far to depress supreme authority and to tie the hands and clip the wings of sacred kings and to attempt the keeping of them within such strait and intolerable bounds as not to be able to command that from their subjects which the laws of God and nature do most plentifully allow them; yea, though it be for the singular behoof, benefit and advancement of the commonwealth, as at this time and in this case it is clearly manifest? . . .

Lastly, what a paradox is this in point of patience for any man to disobey the commandments of a king requiring but what by scripture and nature is allowed him, and for disobedience to resolve to suffer, and in so suffering, to think themselves martyrs? By whom such impressions as these are made in their minds is not hard to conjecture. . . .

The schoolmen have a maxim and they take it from the scriptures that the will of man being cross and unhappy in itself becomes then most right and equal when it receives motion or direction from the will of God revealed in his word. This word then, which is the seed of religion, is the rule of direction too. A dangerous thing therefore it is to suffer men in any Christian commonwealth to drink in that fanatical and erroneous spirit which teacheth them to relinquish those clear and common rules of nature's light and supernaturally revealed truth by which all men ought to be guided, and to reduce all things to the dictates of a private conscience and (enthusiast-like) so

* [English Catholics who refused to attend Anglican services or recognize the authority of the Church of England. (*Ed.*)]

pertinaciously to adhere thereunto that they cannot be beaten from them neither by any force of human reason, nor by any ground or fortress of religion, nor by the weight and greatness of any royal injunction, nor by the representation of any (be they never so great) urgencies of state, neither by mercy received, nor by justice inflicted, nor by the most laudable and religious examples of those who have [showed] unto them the way of most dutiful submission in this kind.

Regard it also we must as a reason that ought ever to be most potent and able to persuade us, for this was the very style and character of the ancient saints which they did professedly both believe and practice, that for their most blessed Lord's sake, who is eternal in the heavens, they did yield all reverence and obedience unto their temporal lords and kings on earth, reigned they never so despotically, nay never so tyrannically, or with never so little clemency. . . .

Look we then (and that seriously) to our rule, to our reason, to our religion, to the oath of God, to the commandments of God, to the counsel of God, to God Himself, to our own conscience toward all these, to God's wrath and vengeance threatened to the condemners of all, or any of these, . . . so shall we be good and faithful servants unto God, and to His anointed king most dutiful and obedient subjects (the one whereof can in no wise be without the other). And so we being restored to the paths of our dutiful obedience we shall be (in God's good time) rendered at the gates of eternal paradise.

And so, *vivat rex,* and *vincat veritas* [may the king live and may truth conquer]. The blessing of life and peace be upon the head of his most sacred majesty that he may live long and . . . reign glorious over us, and triumph victoriously over his enemies, and so become an invincible defender of this faith, religion, and truth, and so, this truth, faith, and religion, may defend him in his most sacred person, in his imperial power, and in his royal posterity for evermore.

And let all those who love God and the king say "Amen," even so "Amen, amen."

₰ THE CITIZEN

Thomas Hobbes

Political theorists from Aristotle to Machiavelli have often considered themselves "scientific." That Thomas Hobbes (1588–1679) should make a similar claim was nothing new. What had altered was the concept of "science"; Hobbes was a pioneer in seeking to apply the new methods perfected in his own day to the study of political organization. In the knowledge that Bacon, Galileo, and Descartes (see pages 87–88) had already begun to redefine nature in mechanistic terms, Hobbes saw the possibilities of a comprehensive redefinition of man and of his social organization. Man was to be regarded as subject to the laws of mechanics, his motion like that of a machine, his complexity an engineering problem. If the primal cause of social behavior could be ascertained, the source of human motivation would be understood at every level—individual, family, community, and national. Hobbes thus began with a description of the workings of matter, applied his conclusion to single individuals, and gradually built, in a series of studies, a broad social structure, the functioning of which could be explained by a single principle.

Hobbes was paradoxical in marshaling the revolutionary insights of the "new science" in behalf of an ancient and traditional form of politics: his support of absolutism seemed to derive from his scientific analysis. If a single cause affected all human interaction, then there would be a single solution to social problems. In such a world there must be a unitary and monolithic ruler representative of that law's intent and responsible for its administration. As much as Hobbes claimed scientific detachment, his overwhelming stress on order makes him a deliberate partisan of absolutism. His contemporary critics hounded him with this charge, and he had to admit that his argument sprang in part from a deep-seated need for security. As an old man, he himself once explained that his mother bore him prematurely because of her fear of the Spanish Armada then approaching the English coast. "She brought forth twins," he said, "myself and fear."

More prosaically, Hobbes was no doubt influenced by the troubled times in which he lived. When the clouds of rebellion billowed over England in 1640, he fled to France where he remained eleven years, until the English civil wars were over. There he wrote The Citizen *(1642) and his more famous* Leviathan *(1651) to justify for himself, if not so successfully to the rebels, the overriding necessity of obedience. Whether Hobbes was personally afraid of anarchy or objectively dedicated to political science, he was an innovator of great influence, one of the most important thinkers of the modern era.*

THE AUTHOR'S PREFACE TO THE READER

Reader, I promise thee here such things, which ordinarily promised do seem to challenge the greatest attention, (whether thou regard the dignity or profit of the matter

Thomas Hobbes, "Philosophical Elements of a True Citizen," in W. Molesworth, ed., *Hobbes's Works* (London: J. Bohn, 1839–1845), II, ix–xvii, 5–11, 14, 16–18, 20–26, 29–30, 36–48, 63–66, 68–71, 149–158, 163–164.

treated, or the right method of handling it, or the honest motive and good advice to undertake it, or lastly the moderation of the author,) and I lay them here before thine eyes. In this book thou shalt find briefly described the duties of man: first, as men; then as subjects; lastly, as Christians. Under which duties are contained, not only the elements of the laws of nature and of nations, together with the true original and power of justice; but also the very essence of Christian religion itself, so far forth as the measure of this my purpose could well bear it.

Which kind of doctrine, excepting what relates to Christian religion, the most ancient sages did judge fittest to be delivered to posterity, either curiously adorned with verse, or clouded with allegories, as a most beautiful and hallowed mystery of royal authority; lest by the disputations of private men it might be defiled. Other philosophers in the mean time, to the advantage of mankind, did contemplate the faces and motions of things; others, without disadvantage, their natures and causes. But in after times, Socrates is said to have been the first who truly loved this civil science; although hitherto not thoroughly understood, yet glimmering forth as through a cloud in the government of the commonweal: and that he set so great a value on this, that utterly abandoning and despising all other parts of philosophy, he wholly embraced this, as judging it only worthy the labour of his mind. After him comes Plato, Aristotle, Cicero, and other philosophers, as well Greek as Latin. And now at length all men of all nations, not only philosophers but even the vulgar, have and do still deal with this as a matter of ease, exposed and prostitute to every mother-wit, and to be attained without any great care or study. And, which makes mainly for its dignity, those who suppose themselves to have it, or are in such employment as they ought to have it, do so wonderfully please themselves in its *idea,* as they easily brook the followers of other arts to be esteemed and styled ingenuous, learned, skilful, and what you will, except prudent: for this name, in regard of civil knowledge, they presume to be due to themselves only. Whether therefore the worth of arts is to be weighed by the worthiness of the persons who entertain them, or by the number of those who have written of them, or by the judgment of the wisest; certainly this must carry it, which so nearly relates to princes, and others engaged in the government of mankind; in whose adulterate species also the most part of men do delight themselves, and in which the most excellent wits of philosophers have been conversant. The benefit of it, when rightly delivered, that is, when derived from true principles by evident connection, we shall then best discern, when we shall but well have considered the mischiefs that have befallen mankind from its counterfeit and babbling form. For in matters wherein we speculate for the exercise of our wits, if any error escape us, it is without hurt; neither is there any loss, but of time only. But in those things which every man ought to meditate for the steerage of his life, it necessarily happens that not only from errors, but even from ignorance itself, there arise offences, contentions, nay, even slaughter itself. Look now, how great a prejudice these are; such and so great is the benefit arising from this doctrine of morality truly declared. How many kings, and those good men too, hath this one error, that a tyrant king might lawfully be put to death, been the slaughter of! How many throats hath this false position cut, that a prince for some causes may by some certain men be deposed! And what bloodshed hath not this erroneous doctrine caused, that kings are not superiors to, but administrators for the multitude! Lastly, how many rebellions hath this opinion been the cause of, which teacheth that the knowledge whether the commands of kings be just or unjust, belongs to private men; and that before they yield obedience, they not only may, but ought to dispute them! Besides, in the moral philosophy now commonly received, there are many things no less dangerous than those, which it matters not now to recite. I suppose those ancients foresaw this, who rather chose to have the science of justice wrapped up in fables, than openly exposed to disputations. For before such questions began to be moved, princes did not sue for, but already exercised the supreme power. They kept their empire entire, not by arguments, but by punishing the wicked and protecting the good. Likewise subjects did not measure what was just by the sayings and judgments of private men, but by the laws of the realm; nor were they kept in peace by disputations, but by power and authority. Yea, they reverenced the supreme power, whether residing in one man or in a council, as a certain visible divinity. Therefore they little used, as in our days, to join themselves with ambitious and hellish spirits, to the utter ruin of their state. For they could not entertain so strange a fancy, as not to desire the preservation of that by which they were preserved. In truth, the simplicity of those times was not yet capable of so learned a piece of folly. Wherefore it was peace and a golden age, which ended not before that, Saturn being expelled, it was taught lawful to take up arms against kings. This, I say, the ancients not only themselves saw, but in one of their fables they seem very aptly to have signified it to us. For they say, that when Ixion was invited by Jupiter to a banquet, he fell in love, and began to court Juno herself. Offering to embrace her, he clasped a cloud; from whence the Centaurs proceeded, by nature half men, half horses, a fierce, a fighting, and unquiet generation. Which changing the names only, is as much as if they should have said, that private men being called to councils of state, desired to prostitute justice, the only sister and wife of the supreme, to their own judgments and apprehensions; but embracing a false and empty shadow instead of it, they have begotten those hermaphrodite opinions of moral philosophers, partly right and comely, partly brutal and wild; the causes of all contentions and bloodsheds. Since therefore such opinions are daily seen to arise, if any man now shall dispel those clouds, and by most firm reasons demonstrate that there are no authentical doctrines concerning right and wrong, good and evil, besides the constituted laws in each realm and government; and that the question whether any future action will prove just or unjust, good or ill, is to be demanded of none but those to whom the supreme hath committed the interpretation of his laws: surely he will not only show us the highway to peace, but will also teach us how to avoid the close, dark, and dangerous by-paths to faction and sedition; than which I know not what can be thought more profitable.

Concerning my method, I thought it not sufficient to use a plain and evident style in what I have to deliver, except I took my beginning from the very matter of civil government, and thence proceeded to its generation and form, and the first beginning of justice. For everything is best understood by its constitutive causes. For as in a watch, or some such small engine, the matter, figure, and motion of the wheels cannot well be known, except it be taken insunder and viewed in parts; so to make a more curious search into the rights of states and duties of subjects, it is necessary, I say, not to take them insunder, but yet that they be so considered as if they were dissolved; that is, that we rightly understand what the quality of human nature is, in what matters it is, in what not, fit to make up a civil government, and how men must be agreed amongst themselves that intend to grow up into a well-grounded state. Having therefore followed this kind of method, in the first place I set down for a principle, by experience known to all men and denied by none, to wit, that the dispositions of men are naturally such, that except they be restrained through fear of some coercive power, every man will distrust and dread each other; and as by natural right he may, so by necessity he will be forced to make use of the strength he hath, toward the preservation of himself. You will object perhaps, that there are some who deny this. Truly so it happens, that very many do deny it. But shall I therefore seem to fight against myself, because I affirm that the same men confess and deny the same thing? In truth I do not; but they do, whose actions disavow what their discourses approve of. We see all countries, though they be at peace with their neighbours, yet guarding their frontiers with armed men, their towns with walls and ports, and keeping constant watches. To what purpose is all this, if there be no fear of the neighbouring power? We see even in well-governed states, where there are laws and punishments appointed for offenders, yet particular men travel not without their sword by their sides for their defenses; neither sleep they without shutting not only their doors against their fellow subjects, but also their trunks and coffers for fear of domestics. Can men give a clearer testimony of the distrust they have each of other, and all of all? Now, since they do thus, and even countries as well as men, they publicly profess their mutual fear and diffidence. But in disputing they deny it; that is as much as to say, that out of a desire they have to contradict others, they gainsay themselves. Some object that this principle being admitted, it would needs follow, not only that all men were wicked, (which perhaps though it seem hard, yet we must yield to, since it is so clearly declared by holy writ), but also wicked by nature, which cannot be granted without impiety. But this, that men are evil by nature, follows not from this principle. For though the wicked were fewer than the righteous, yet because we cannot distinguish them, there is a necessity of suspecting, heeding, anticipating, subjugating, self-defending, ever incident to the most honest and fairest conditioned. Much less does it follow, that those who are wicked, are so by nature. For though from nature, that is, from their first birth, as they are merely sensible creatures, they have this disposition, that immediately as much as in them lies they desire and do whatsoever is best pleasing to them, and that either through fear they fly from, or through hardness repel those dangers which approach them; yet are they not for this reason to be accounted wicked. For the affections of the mind, which arise only from the lower parts of the soul, are not wicked themselves; but the actions thence proceeding may be so sometimes, as when they are either offensive or against duty. Unless you give children all they ask for, they are peevish and cry, aye, and strike their parents sometimes; and all this they have from nature. Yet are they free from guilt, neither may we properly call them wicked; first, because they cannot hurt; next, because wanting the free use of reason they are exempted from all duty. These when they come to riper years, having acquired power whereby they may do hurt, if they shall continue to do the same things, then truly they both begin to be, and are properly accounted wicked. Insomuch as a wicked man is almost the same thing with a child grown strong and sturdy, or a man of a childish disposition; and malice the same with a defect of reason in that age when nature ought to be better governed through good education and experience. Unless therefore we will say that men are naturally evil, because they receive not their education and use of reason from nature, we must needs acknowledge that men may derive desire, fear, anger, and other passions from nature, and yet not impute the evil effects of those unto nature. . . .

LIBERTY

Chapter I. Of the State of Men without Civil Society

. . . **3**   The cause of mutual fear consists partly in the natural equality of men, partly in their mutual will of hurting: whence it comes to pass, that we can neither expect from others, nor promise to ourselves the least security. For if we look on men full-grown, and consider how brittle the frame of our human body is, which perishing, all its strength, vigour, and wisdom itself perisheth with it; and how easy a matter it is, even for the weakest man to kill the strongest: there is no reason why any man, trusting to his own strength, should conceive himself made by nature above others. They are equals, who can do equal things one against the other; but they who can do the greatest things, namely, kill, can do equal things. All men therefore among themselves are by nature equal; the inequality we now discern, hath its spring from the civil law.

4   All men in the state of nature have a desire and will to hurt, but not proceeding from the same cause, neither equally to be condemned. For one man, according to that natural equality which is among us, permits as much to others as he assumes to himself; which is an argument of a temperate man, and one that rightly values his power. Another, supposing himself above others, will have a license to do what he lists, and challenges respect and honour, as due to him before others; which is an argument of a fiery spirit. This man's will to hurt ariseth from vain glory, and the false esteem he hath of his own strength; the other's from the necessity of defending himself, his liberty, and his goods, against this man's violence. . . .

6   But the most frequent reason why men desire to hurt each other, ariseth hence, that many men at the same time have an appetite to the same thing; which yet very often they can neither enjoy in common, nor yet divide it; whence it follows that the strongest must have it, and who is strongest must be decided by the sword.

7   Among so many dangers therefore, as the natural lusts of men do daily threaten each other withal, to have a care of one's self is so far from being a matter scornfully to be looked upon, that one has neither the power nor wish to have done otherwise. For every man is desirous of what is good for him, and shuns what is evil, but chiefly the chiefest of natural evils, which is death; and this he doth by a certain impulsion of nature, no less than that whereby a stone moves downward. It is therefore neither absurd nor reprehensible, neither against the dictates of true reason, for a man to use all his endeavours to preserve and defend his body and the members thereof from death and sorrows. But that which is not contrary to right reason, that all men account to be done justly, and with right. Neither by the word *right* is anything else signified, than liberty which every man hath to make use of his natural faculties according to right reason. Therefore the first foundation of natural right is this, that *every man as much as in him lies endeavour to protect his life and members.*

8   But because it is in vain for a man to have a right to the end, if the right to the necessary means be denied him, it follows, that since every man hath a right to preserve himself, he must also be allowed a right *to use all the means, and do all the actions, without which he cannot preserve himself.*

9   Now whether the means which he is about to use, and the action he is performing, be necessary to the preservation of his life and members or not, he himself, by the right of nature, must be judge. For if it be contrary to right reason that I should judge of mine own peril, say, that another man is judge. Why now, because he judgeth of what concerns me, by the same reason, because we are equal by nature, will I judge also of things which do belong to him. Therefore it agrees with right reason, that is, it is the right of nature that I judge of his opinion, that is, whether it conduce to my preservation or not.

10   Nature hath given to *every one a right to all;* that is, it was lawful for every man, in the bare state of nature, or before such time as men had engaged themselves by any covenants or bonds, to do what he would, and against whom he thought fit, and to possess, use, and enjoy all what he would, or could get. Now because whatsoever a man would, it therefore seems good to him because he wills it, and either it really doth, or at least seems to him to contribute towards his preservation, (but we have already allowed him to be judge, in the foregoing article, whether it doth or not, insomuch as we are to hold all for necessary whatsoever he shall esteem so), and by the 7th article it appears that by the right of nature those things may be done, and must be had, which necessarily conduce to the protection of life and members, it follows, that in the state of nature, to have all, and do all, is lawful for all. And this is that which is meant by that common saying, *nature hath given all to all.* From whence we understand likewise, that in the state of nature profit is the measure of right.

11   But it was the least benefit for men thus to have a common right to all things. For the effects of this right are the same, almost, as if there had been no right at all. For although any man might say of every thing, *this is mine,* yet could he not enjoy it, by reason of his neighbour, who having equal right and equal power, would pretend the same thing to be his.

12   If now to this natural proclivity of men, to hurt each other, which they derive from their passions, but chiefly from a vain esteem of themselves, you add, the right of all to all, wherewith one by right invades, the other by right resists, and whence arise perpetual jealousies and suspicions on all hands, and how hard a thing it is to provide against an enemy invading us with an intention to oppress and ruin, though he come with a small number, and no great provision; it cannot be denied but that the natural state of men, before they entered into society, was a mere war, and that not simply, but a war of all men against all men. For what is WAR, but that same time in which the will of contesting by force is fully declared, either by words or deeds? The time remaining is termed PEACE. . . .

Chapter II. Of the Law of Nature Concerning Contracts

. . . the first and fundamental law of nature is, *that peace is to be sought after, where it may be found; and where not, there to provide ourselves for helps of war.* For we showed in the last article of the foregoing chapter, that this precept is the dictate of right reason; but that the dictates of right reason are natural laws, that hath been newly proved above. But this is the first, because the rest are derived from this, and they direct the ways either to peace or self-defence.

3 But one of the natural laws derived from this fundamental one is this: *that the right of all men to all things ought not to be retained; but that some certain rights ought to be transferred or relinquished.* For if every one should retain his right to all things, it must necessarily follow, that some by right might invade, and others, by the same right, might defend themselves against them. For every man by natural necessity endeavours to defend his body, and the things which he judgeth necessary towards the protection of his body. Therefore war would follow. He therefore acts against the reason of peace, that is, against the law of nature, whosoever he be, that doth not part with his right to all things.

4 But he is said to part with his right, who either absolutely renounceth it, or conveys it to another. He absolutely renounceth it, who by some sufficient sign or meet tokens declares, that he is willing that it shall never be lawful for him to do that again, which before *by right* he might have done. But he conveys it to another, who by some sufficient sign or meet tokens declares to that other, that he is willing it should be unlawful for him to resist him, in going about to do somewhat in the performance whereof he might before *with right* have resisted him. But that the conveyance of right consists merely in not resisting, is understood by this, that before it was conveyed, he to whom he conveyed it, had even then also a right to all; whence he could not give any new right; but the resisting right he had before he gave it, by reason whereof the other could not freely enjoy his rights, is utterly abolished. Whosoever therefore acquires some right in the natural state of men, he only procures himself security and freedom from just molestation in the enjoyment of his primitive right. As for example, if any man shall sell or give away a farm, he utterly deprives himself only from all right to this farm; but he does not so others also. . . .

9 But the act of two, or more, mutually conveying their rights, is called a *contract.* But in every contract, either both parties instantly perform what they contract for, insomuch as there is no trust had from either to other; or the one performs, the other is trusted; or neither perform. Where both parties perfom presently, there the contract is ended as soon as it is performed. But where there is credit given, either to one or both, there the party trusted promiseth after-performance; and this kind of promise is called a *covenant.* . . .

11 But the covenants which are made in contract of mutual trust, neither party performing out of hand, if there arise a just suspicion in either of them, are in the state of nature invalid. For he that first performs, by reason of the wicked disposition of the greatest part of men studying their own advantage either by right or wrong, exposeth himself to the perverse will of him with whom he hath contracted. For it suits not with reason, that any man should perform first, if it be not likely that the other will make good his promise after; which, whether it be probable or not, he that doubts it must be judge of, as hath been showed in the foregoing chapter in the ninth article. Thus, I say, things stand in the state of nature. But in a civil state, when there is a power which can compel both parties, he that hath contracted to perform first, must first perform; because, that since the other may be compelled, the cause which made him fear the other's non-performance, ceaseth. . . .

14 Covenants are made of such things only as fall under our deliberation. For it can be no covenant without the will of the contractor. But the will is the last act of him who deliberates; wherefore they only concern things *possible* and *to come*. No man, therefore, by his compact obligeth himself to an impossibility. But yet, though we often covenant to do such things as then seemed possible when we promised them, which yet afterward appear to be impossible, are we not therefore freed from all obligation. The reason whereof is, that he who promiseth a future, in certainty receives a present benefit, on condition that he return another for it. For his will, who performs the present benefit, hath simply before it for its object a certain good, equally valuable with the thing promised; but the thing itself not simply, but with condition if it could be done. But if it should so happen, that even this should prove impossible, why then he must perform as much as he can. Covenants, therefore, oblige us not to perform just the thing itself covenanted for, but our utmost endeavour; for this only is, the things themselves are not in our power.

15 We are freed from covenants two ways, either by performing, or by being forgiven. By performing, for beyond that we obliged not ourselves. By being forgiven, because he whom we obliged ourselves to, by forgiving is conceived to return us that right which we passed over to him. For forgiving implies giving, that is, by the fourth article of this chapter, a conveyance of right to him to whom the gift is made.

16 It is a usual question, whether compacts extorted from us through fear, do oblige or not. For example, if, to redeem my life from the power of a robber, I promise to pay him 100*l*. next day, and that I will do no act whereby to apprehend and bring him to justice: whether I am tied to keep promise or not. But though such a promise must sometimes be judged to be of no effect, yet it is not to be accounted so because it proceedeth from fear. For then it would follow, that those promises which reduced men to a civil life, and by which laws were made, might likewise be of none effect; (for it proceeds from fear of mutual slaughter, that one man submits himself to the dominion of another); and he should play the fool finely, who should trust his captive covenanting with the price of his redemption. It holds universally true, that promises do oblige, when there is some benefit received, and when the promise, and the thing promised, be lawful. But it is lawful, for the redemption of my life, both to promise and to give what I will of mine own to any man, even to a thief. We are obliged, therefore, by promises proceeding from fear, except the civil law forbid them; by virtue whereof, that which is promised becomes unlawful.

17 Whosoever shall contract with one to do or omit somewhat, and shall after covenant the contrary with another, he maketh not the former, but the latter contract unlawful. For he hath no longer right to do or to omit aught, who by former contracts hath conveyed it to another. Wherefore he can convey no right by latter contracts, and what is promised is promised without right. He is therefore tied only to his first contract, to break which is unlawful.

18 No man is obliged by any contracts whatsoever not to resist him who shall offer to kill, wound, or any other way hurt his body. For there is in every man a certain high degree of fear, through which he apprehends that evil which is done to him to be the greatest; and therefore by natural necessity he shuns it all he can, and it is supposed he can do no otherwise. When a man is arrived to this degree of fear, we cannot expect but he will provide for himself either by flight or fight. Since therefore no man is tied to impossibilities, they who are threatened either with death, (which is the greatest evil to nature), or wounds, or some other bodily hurts, and are not stout enough to bear them, are not obliged to endure them. Furthermore, he that is tied by contract is trusted; for faith only is the bond of contracts; but they who are brought to punishment, either capital or more gentle, are fettered or strongly guarded; which is a most certain sign that they seemed not sufficiently bound from non-resistance by their contracts. It is one thing, if I promise thus: if I do it not at the day appointed, kill me. Another thing, if thus: if I do it not, though you should offer to kill me, I will not resist. All men, if need be, contract the first way, and there is need sometimes. This second way, none; neither is it ever needful. For in the mere state of nature, if you have a mind to kill, that state itself affords you a right: insomuch as you need not first trust him, if for breach of trust you will afterwards kill him. But in a civil state, where the right of life and death and of all corporal punishment is with the supreme, that same right of killing cannot be granted to any private person. Neither need the supreme himself contract with any man patiently to yield to his punishment; but only this, that no man offer to defend others from him. If in the state of nature, as between two realms, there should a contract be made on condition of killing if it were not performed, we must presuppose another contract of not killing before the appointed day. Wherefore on that day, if there be no performance, the right of war returns, that is a hostile state, in which all things are lawful, and therefore resistance also. Lastly, by the contract of not resisting, we are obliged, of two evils to make choice of that which seems the greater. For certain death is a greater evil than fighting. But of two evils it is impossible not to choose the least. By such a compact, therefore, we should be tied to impossibilities; which is contrary to the very nature of compacts.

19 Likewise no man is tied by any compacts whatsoever to accuse himself, or any other, by whose damage he is like to procure himself a bitter life. Wherefore neither is a father obliged to bear witness against his son, nor a husband against his wife, nor a son against his father, nor any man against any one by whose means he hath his subsistence; for in vain is that testimony which is presumed to be corrupted from nature. But although no man be tied to accuse himself by any compact, yet in a public trial he may by torture be forced to make answer. But such answers are no testimony of the fact, but helps for the searching out of truth; so that whether the party tortured his answer be true or false, or whether he answer not at all, whatsoever he doth, he doth it by right. . . .

Chapter III. Of the Other Laws of Nature

. . . **1** Another of the laws of nature is, to *perform contracts*, or *to keep trust*. For it hath been showed in the foregoing chapter, that the law of nature commands every man, as a thing necessary, to obtain peace, to convey certain rights from each to other; and that this, as often as it shall happen to be done, is called a contract. But this is so far forth only conducible to peace, as we shall perform ourselves what we contract with others shall be done or omitted; and in vain would contracts be made, unless we stood to them. Because therefore to stand to our covenants, or to keep faith, is a thing necessary for the obtaining of peace; it will prove, by the second article of the second chapter, to be a precept of the natural law. . . .

9   The fourth precept of nature is, *that every man render himself useful unto others:* which that we may rightly understand, we must remember that there is in men a diversity of dispositions to enter into society, arising from the diversity of their affections, not unlike that which is found in stones, brought together in the building, by reason of the diversity of their matter and figure. For as a stone, which in regard of its sharp and angular form takes up more room from other stones than it fills up itself, neither because of the hardness of its matter can it well be pressed together, or easily cut, and would hinder the building from being fitly compacted, is cast away, as not fit for use: so a man, for the harshness of his disposition in retaining superfluities for himself, and detaining of necessaries from others, and being incorrigible by reason of the stubbornness of his affections, is commonly said to be useless and troublesome unto others. Now, because each one not by right only, but even by natural necessity, is supposed with all his main might to intend the procurement of those things which are necessary to his own preservation; if any man will contend on the other side for superfluities, by his default there will arise a war; because that on him alone there lay no necessity of contending; he therefore acts against the fundamental law of nature. Whence it follows, (which we were to show), that it is a precept of nature, that every man accommodate himself to others. But he who breaks this law, may be called *useless* and troublesome. Yet Cicero opposeth *inhumanity* to this *usefulness,* as having regard to this very law. . . .

11   The sixth precept of the natural law is, *that in revenge and punishments we must have our eye not at the evil past, but the future good:* that is, it is not lawful to inflict punishment for any other end, but that the offender may be corrected, or that others warned by his punishment may become better. But this is confirmed chiefly from hence, that each man is bound by the law of nature to forgive one another, provided he give caution for the future, as hath been showed in the foregoing article. Furthermore, because revenge, if the time past be only considered, is nothing else but a certain triumph and glory of mind, which points at no end; for it contemplates only what is past, but the end is a thing to come; but that which is directed to no end, is vain: that revenge therefore which regards not the future, proceeds from vain glory, and is therefore without reason. But to hurt another without reason, introduces a war, and is contrary to the fundamental law of nature. It is therefore a precept of the law of nature, that in revenge we look not backwards, but forward. Now the breach of this law is commonly called *cruelty.* . . .

13   The question whether of two men be the more worthy, belongs not to the natural, but civil state. For it hath been showed before (Chap. 1. Art. 3) that all men by nature are equal; and therefore the inequality which now is, suppose from riches, power, nobility of kindred, is come from the civil law. I know that Aristotle, in his first book of Politics, affirms as a foundation of the whole political science, that some men by nature are made worthy to command, others only to serve; as if lord and servant were distinguished not by consent of men, but by an aptness, that is, a certain kind of natural knowledge or ignorance. Which foundation is not only against reason, (as but now hath been showed), but also against experience. For neither almost is any man so dull of understanding as not to judge it better to be ruled by himself, than to yield himself to the government of another; neither if the wiser and stronger do contest, have these always or often the upper hand of those. Whether therefore men be equal by nature, the equality is to be acknowledged; or whether unequal, because they are like to contest for dominion, it is necessary for the obtaining of peace, *that they be esteemed as equal;* and therefore it is in the eighth place a precept of the law of nature, *that every man be accounted by nature equal to another;* the contrary to which law is *pride.* . . .

15   In the tenth place it is commanded by the law of nature, *that every man in dividing right to others, shew himself equal to either party.* By the foregoing law we are forbidden to assume more right by nature to ourselves, than we grant to others. We may take less if we will; for that sometimes is an argument of modesty. But if at any time matter of right be to be divided by us unto others, we are forbidden by this law to favour one more or less than another. For he that by favouring one before another observes not this natural equality, reproaches him whom he thus undervalues: but it is declared above, that a reproach is against the laws of nature. The observance of this precept is called *equity;* the breach, *respect of persons.* . . .

16   From the foregoing law is collected this eleventh, *those things which cannot be divided, must be used in common if they can, and if the quantity of the matter permit, every man as much as he lists; but if the quantity permit not, then with limitation, and proportionally to the number of the users.* For otherwise that equality can by no means be observed, which we have showed in the foregoing article to be commanded by the law of nature.

17   Also what cannot be divided nor had in common, it is provided by the law of nature, which may be the twelfth precept, *that the use of that thing be either by turns, or adjudged to one only by lot; and that in the using it by turns, it be also decided by lot, who shall have the first use of it.* For here also regard is to be had unto equality: but no other can be found but that of lot.

18   But all lot is twofold, *arbitrary* or *natural.* Arbitrary is that which is cast by the consent of the contenders, and it consists in mere chance, as they say, or fortune. *Natural* is primogeniture, . . . as it were, given by lot; or first possession. Therefore the things which can neither be divided nor had in common, must be granted to the first possessor; as also those things which belonged to the father are due to the son, unless the father himself have formerly conveyed away that right to some other. Let this therefore stand for the thirteenth law of nature.

19   The fourteenth precept of the law of nature is, *that safety must be assured to the mediators for peace.* For the reason which commands the end, commands also the means necessary to the end. But the first dictate of reason is peace; all the rest are means to obtain it, and without which peace cannot be had. But neither can peace be had without mediation, nor mediation without safety. It is therefore a dictate of reason, that is, a law of nature, that we must give all security to the mediators for peace.

20   Furthermore because, although men should agree to make all these and whatsoever other laws of nature, and should endeavour to keep them, yet doubts and controversies would daily arise concerning the application of them unto their actions, to wit, whether what was done were against the law or not, which we call the question of right; whence will follow a fight between parties, either sides supposing themselves wronged: it is therefore necessary to the preservation of peace, because in this case no other fit remedy can possibly be thought on, that both the disagreeing parties refer the matter unto some third, and oblige themselves by mutual compacts to stand to his judgment in deciding the controversy. And he to whom they thus refer themselves, is called an arbiter. It is therefore the fifteenth precept of the natural law, *that both parties disputing concerning the matter of right, submit themselves unto the opinion and judgment of some third.*

21   But from this ground, that an arbiter or judge is chosen by the differing parties to determine the controversy, we gather that the arbiter must not be one of the parties. For every man is presumed to seek what is good for himself naturally, and what is just only for peace sake and accidentally; and therefore cannot observe that same equality commanded by the law of nature, so exactly as a third man would do. It is therefore in the sixteenth place contained in the law of nature, *that no man must be judge or arbiter in his own cause.*

22   From the same ground follows in the seventeenth place, *that no man must be judge, who propounds unto himself any hope of profit or glory from the victory of either part:* for the like reason sways here, as in the foregoing law.

23   But when there is some controversy of the fact itself, to wit, whether that be done or not which is said to be done, the natural law wills that the arbiter trust both parties alike, that is, because they affim contradictories, that he believe neither. He must therefore give credit to a third, or a third and fourth, or more, that he may be able to give judgment of the fact, as often as by other signs he cannot come to the knowledge of it. The eighteenth law of nature therefore enjoins arbiters and judges of fact, *that where firm and certain signs of the fact appear not, there they rule their sentence by such witnesses as seem to be indifferent to both parts.*

24   From the above declared definition of an arbiter may be furthermore understood, *that no contract or promise must pass between him and the parties whose judge he is appointed, by virtue whereof he may be engaged to speak in favour of either part, nay, or be obliged to judge according to equity, or to pronounce such sentence as he shall truly judge to be equal.* The judge is indeed bound to give such sentence as he shall judge to be equal, by the law of nature recounted in the 15th article: to the obligation of which law nothing can be added by way of compact. Such compact therefore would be in vain. Besides, if giving wrong judgment he should contend for the equity of it, except such compact be of no force, the controversy would remain after judgment given: which is contrary to the constitution of an arbiter, who is so chosen, as both parties have obliged themselves to stand to the judgment which he should pronounce. The law of nature therefore commands the judge to be disengaged, which is its nineteenth precept. . . .

26 Perhaps some man, who sees all these precepts of nature derived by a certain artifice from the single dictate of reason advising us to look to the preservation and safeguard of ourselves, will say that the deduction of these laws is so hard, that it is not to be expected they will be vulgarly known, and therefore neither will they prove obliging: for laws, if they be not known, oblige not, nay indeed, are not laws. To this I answer, it is true, that hope, fear, anger, ambition, covetousness, vain glory, and other perturbations of mind, do hinder a man, so as he cannot attain to the knowledge of these laws whilst those passions prevail in him: but there is no man who is not sometimes in a quiet mind. At that time therefore there is nothing easier for him to know, though he be never so rude and unlearned, than this only rule, that when he doubts whether what he is now doing to another may be done by the law of nature or not, he conceive himself to be in that other's stead. Here instantly those perturbations which persuaded him to the fact, being now cast into the other scale, dissuade him as much. And this rule is not only easy, but is anciently celebrated in these words, *quod tibi fieri non vis, alteri ne feceris: do not that to others, you would not have done to yourself.* . . . .

29 *The laws of nature are immutable and eternal:* what they forbid, can never be lawful; what they command, can never be unlawful. For *pride, ingratitude, breach of contracts* (or *injury*)*, inhumanity, contumely,* will never be lawful, nor the contrary virtues to these ever unlawful, as we take them for dispositions of the mind, that is, as they are considered in the court of conscience, where only they oblige and are laws. Yet actions may be so diversified by circumstances and the civil law, that what is done with equity at one time, is guilty of iniquity at another; and what suits with reason at one time, is contrary to it another. Yet reason is still the same, and changeth not her end, which is peace and defence, nor the means to attain them, to wit, those virtues of the mind which we have declared above, and which cannot be abrogated by any custom or law whatsoever.

30 It is evident by what hath hitherto been said, how easily the laws of nature are to be observed, because they require the endeavour only, (but that must be true and constant) ; which whoso shall perform, we may rightly call him *just.* For he who tends to this with his whole might, namely, that his actions be squared according to the precepts of nature, he shows clearly that he hath a mind to fulfil all those laws; which is all we are obliged to by rational nature. Now he that hath done all he is obliged to, is a just man.

31 All writers do agree, that the natural law is the same with the moral. Let us see wherefore this is true. We must know, therefore, that good and evil are names given to things to signify the inclination or aversion of them, by whom they were given. But the inclinations of men are diverse, according to their diverse constitutions, customs, opinions; as we may see in those things we apprehend by sense, as by tasting, touching, smelling; but much more in those which pertain to the common actions of life, where what this man commends, that is to say, calls *good,* the other undervalues, as being evil. Nay, very often the same man at diverse times praises and dispraises the same thing. Whilst thus they do, necessary it is there should be discord and strife. They are, therefore, so long in the state of war, as by reason of the diversity of the present appetite, they mete good and evil by diverse measures. All men easily acknowledge this state, as long as they are in it, to be evil, and by consequence that peace is good. They therefore who could not agree concerning a present, do agree concerning a future good; which indeed is a work of reason; for things present are obvious to the sense, things to come to our reason only. Reason declaring peace to be good, it follows by the same reason, that all the necessary means to peace be good also; and therefore that modesty, equity, trust, humanity, mercy, (which we have demonstrated to be necessary to peace), are good manners or habits, that is, virtues. The law therefore, in the means to peace, commands also good manners, or the practice of virtue; and therefore it is called *moral*. . . .

DOMINION

Chapter V. Of the Causes and First Beginning of Civil Government

. . . **1**   It is of itself manifest that the actions of men proceed from the will, and the will from hope and fear, insomuch as when they shall see a greater good or less evil likely to happen to them by the breach than observation of the laws, they will wittingly violate them. The hope therefore which each man hath of his security and self-preservation, consists in this, that by force or craft he may disappoint his neighbour, either openly or by stratagem. Whence we may understand, that the natural laws, though well understood, do not instantly secure any man in their practice; and consequently, that as long as there is no caution had from the invasion of others, there remains to every man that same primitive right of self-defence by such means as either he can or will make use of, that is, a right to all things, or the right of war. And it is sufficient for the fulfilling of the natural law, that a man be prepared in mind to embrace peace when it may be had.

2   It is a trite saying, that all laws are silent in the time of war, and it is a true one, not only if we speak of the civil, but also of the natural laws, provided they be referred not to the mind, but to the actions of men. . . . And we mean such a war, as is of all men against all men; such as is the mere state of nature; although in the war of nation against nation, a certain mean was wont to be observed. And therefore in old time, there was a manner of living, and as it were a certain economy, which they called . . . living by rapine; which was neither against the law of nature (things then so standing), nor void of glory to those who exercised it with valour, not with cruelty. Their custom was, taking away the rest, to spare life, and abstain from oxen fit for plough, and every instrument serviceable to husbandry. Which yet is not so to be taken, as if they were bound to do thus by the law of nature; but that they had regard to their own glory herein, lest by too much cruelty they might be suspected guilty of fear.

3   Since therefore the exercise of the natural law is necessary for the preservation of peace, and that for the exercise of the natural law security is no less necessary; it is worth the considering what that is which affords such a security. For this matter nothing else can be imagined, but that each man provide himself of such meet helps, as the invasion of one on the other may be rendered so dangerous, as either of them may think it better to refrain than to meddle. But first, it is plain that the consent of two or three cannot make good such a security; because that the addition but of one, or some few on the other side, is sufficient to make the victory undoubtedly sure, and heartens the enemy to attack us. It is therefore necessary, to the end the security sought for may be obtained, that the number of them who conspire in a mutual assistance be so great, that the accession of some few to the enemy's party may not prove to them a matter of moment sufficient to assure the victory.

4   Furthermore, how great soever the number of them is who meet on self-defence, if yet they agree not among themselves of some excellent means whereby to compass this, but every man after his own manner shall make use of his endeavours, nothing will be done; because that, divided in their opinions, they will be a hinderance to each other; or if they agree well enough to some one action, through hope of victory, spoil, or revenge, yet afterward, through diversity of wits and counsels, or emulation and envy, with which men naturally contend, they will be so torn and rent, as they will neither give mutual help nor desire peace, except they be constrained to it by some common fear. Whence it follows that the consent of many, (which consists in this only, as we have already defined in the foregoing section, that they direct all their actions to the same end and the common good), that is to say, that the society proceeding from mutual help only, yields not that security which they seek for, who meet and agree in the exercise of the above-named laws of nature; but that somewhat else must be done, that those who have once consented for the common good to peace and mutual help, may by fear be restrained lest afterwards they again dissent, when their private interest shall appear discrepant from the common good. . . .

6   Since therefore the conspiring of many wills to the same end doth not suffice to preserve peace, and to make a lasting defence, it is requisite that, in those necessary matters which concern peace and self-defence, there be but one will of all men. But this cannot be done, unless every man will so subject his will to some other one, to wit, either man or council, that whatsoever his will is in those things which are necessary to the common peace, it be received for the wills of all men in general, and of every one in particular. Now the gathering together of many men, who deliberate of what is to be done or not to be done for the common good of all men, is that which I call a *council*.

7   This submission of the wills of all those men to the will of one man or one council, is then made, when each one of them obligeth himself by contract to every one of the rest, not to resist the will of that one man or council, to which he hath submitted himself; that is, that he refuse him not the use of his wealth and strength against any others whatsoever; for he is supposed still to retain a right of defending himself against violence: and this is called *union*. But we understand that to be the will of the council, which is the will of the major part of those men of whom the council consists.

8   But though the will itself be not voluntary, but only the beginning of voluntary actions; (for we will not to will, but to act) ; and therefore falls least of all under deliberation and compact; yet he who submits his will to the will of another, conveys to that other the right of his strength and faculties. Insomuch as when the rest have done the same, he to whom they have submitted, hath so much power, as by the terror of it he can conform the wills of particular men unto unity and concord.

9   Now union thus made, is called a city or civil society; and also a civil person. For when there is one will of all men, it is to be esteemed for one person; and by the word *one,* it is to be known and distinguished from all particular men, as having its own rights and properties. Insomuch as neither any one citizen, nor all of them together, (if we except him, whose will stands for the will of all), is to be accounted a city. A *city* therefore, (that we may define it), is *one person,* whose will, by the compact of many men, is to be received for the will of them all; so as he may use all the power and faculties of each particular person to the maintenance of peace, and for common defence.

10   But although every city be a civil person, yet every civil person is not a city; for it may happen that many citizens, by the permission of the city, may join together in one person, for the doing of certain things. These now will be civil persons; as the companies of merchants, and many other convents. But cities they are not, because they have not submitted themselves to the will of the company simply and in all things, but in certain things only determined by the city, and on such terms as it is lawful for any one of them to contend in judgment against the body itself of the sodality; which is by no means allowable to a citizen against the city. Such like societies, therefore, are civil persons subordinate to the city.

11   In every city, that man or council, to whose will each particular man hath subjected his will so as hath been declared, is said to have the *supreme power,* or *chief command,* or *dominion.* Which power and right of commanding, consists in this, that each citizen hath conveyed all his strength and power to that man or council; which to have done, because no man can transfer his power in a natural manner, is nothing else than to have parted with his right of resisting. Each citizen, as also every subordinate civil person, is called the *subject* of him who hath the chief command.

12   By what hath been said, it is sufficiently showed in what manner and by what degrees many natural persons, through desire of preserving themselves and by mutual fear, have grown together into a civil person, whom we have called a *city.* But they who submit themselves to another for fear, either submit to him whom they fear, or some other whom they confide in for protection. They act according to the first manner, who are vanquished in war, that they may not be slain; they according to the second, who are not yet overcome, that they may not be overcome. The first manner receives its beginning from natural power, and may be called the natural beginning of a city; the latter from the council and constitution of those who meet together, which is a beginning by institution. Hence it is that there are two kinds of cities; the one natural, such as the paternal and despotical; the other institutive, which may be also called political. In the first, the lord acquires to himself such citizens as he will; in the other, the citizens by their own wills appoint a lord over themselves, whether he be one man or one company of men, endued with the command in chief. . . .

Chapter XII. Of the Internal Causes Tending to the Dissolution of any Government

. . . **1**   Hitherto hath been spoken, by what causes and pacts commonweals are constituted, and what the rights of princes are over their subjects. Now we will briefly say somewhat concerning the causes which dissolve them, or the reasons of seditions. Now as in the motion of natural bodies three things are to be considered, namely, *internal disposition,* that they be susceptible of the motion to be produced; the *external agent,* whereby a certain and determined motion may in act be produced; and the *action itself:* so also in a commonweal where the subjects begin to raise tumults, three things present themselves to our regard; first, the *doctrines* and the *passions* contrary to peace, wherewith the minds of men are fitted and disposed; next, their quality and condition who solicit, assemble, and direct them, already thus disposed, to take up arms and quit their allegiance; lastly, the manner how this is done, or the *faction* itself. But one and the first which disposeth them to sedition, is this, *that the knowledge of good and evil belongs to each single man.* In the state of nature indeed, where every man lives by equal right, and has not by any mutual pacts submitted to the command of others, we have granted this to be true; nay, proved it in chap. 1. art. 9. But in the civil state it is false. For it was shown . . . that the civil laws were the rules of *good* and *evil, just* and *unjust, honest* and *dishonest;* that therefore what the legislator commands, must be held for *good,* and what he forbids for *evil.* And the legislator is ever that person who hath the supreme power in the commonweal, that is to say, the monarch in a monarchy. . . . For if private men may pursue that as good and shun that as evil, which appears to them to be so, to what end serve those words of his: *Give therefore unto thy servant an understanding heart, to judge thy people, that I may discern between good and evil?* Since therefore it belongs to kings to discern between *good* and *evil,* wicked are those, though usual, sayings, *that he only is a king who does righteously,* and *that kings must not be obeyed unless they command us just things;* and many other such like. Before there was any government, *just* and *unjust* had no being, their nature only being relative to some command: and every action in its own nature is indifferent; that it becomes *just* or *unjust,* proceeds from the right of the magistrate. Legitimate kings therefore make the things they command just by commanding them, and those which they forbid, unjust, by forbidding them. But private men, while they assume to themselves the knowledge of *good* and *evil,* desire to be even as kings; which cannot be with the safety of the commonweal. . . .

2 Whatsoever any man doth against his conscience, is a sin; for he who doth so, contemns the law. But we must distinguish. That is my sin indeed, which committing I do believe to be my sin; but what I believe to be another man's sin, I may sometimes do that without any sin of mine. For if I be commanded to do that which is a sin in him who commands me, if I do it, and he that commands me by right lord over me, I sin not. For if I wage war at the commandment of my prince, conceiving the war at the commandment of my prince, conceiving the war to be unjustly undertaken, I do not therefore do unjustly; but rather if I refuse to do it, arrogating to myself the knowledge of what is just and unjust, which pertains only to my prince. They who observe not this distinction, will fall into a necessity of sinning, as oft as any-thing is commanded them which either is, or seems to be unlawful to them: for if they obey, they sin against their conscience; and if they obey not, against right. If they sin against their conscience, they declare that they fear not the pains of the world to come; if they sin against right, they do, as much as in them lies, abolish human society and the civil life of the present world. Their opinion therefore who teach,

that subjects sin when they obey their prince's commands which to them seem unjust, is both erroneous, and to be reckoned among those which are contrary to civil obedience; and it depends upon that original error which we have observed above, in the foregoing article. For by our taking upon us to judge of *good* and *evil,* we are the occasion that as well our obedience, as disobedience, becomes sin unto us.

3   The third seditious doctrine springs from the same root, that *tyrannicide is lawful;* nay, at this day it is by many divines, and of old it was by all the philosophers, Plato, Aristotle, Cicero, Seneca, Plutarch, and the rest of the maintainers of the Greek and Roman anarchies, held not only lawful, but even worthy of the greatest praise. And under the title of *tyrants,* they mean not only monarchs, but all those who bear the chief rule in any government whatsoever; for not Pisistratus only at Athens, but those Thirty also who succeeded him, and ruled together, were all called *tyrants.* But he whom men require to be put to death as being *a tyrant,* commands either by right or without right. If without right, he is an enemy, and by right to be put to death; but then this must not be called the *killing a tyrant,* but an *enemy.* If by right, then the divine interrogation takes place: *Who hath told thee that he was a tyrant? Hast thou eaten of the tree, whereof I commanded thee that thou shouldst not eat?* For why dost thou call him a *tyrant,* whom God hath made a *king,* except that thou, being a private person, úsurpest to thyself the knowledge of *good* and *evil?* But how pernicious this opinion is to all governments, but especially to that which is *monarchical,* we may hence discern; namely, that by it every *king,* whether good or ill, stands exposed to be condemned by the judgment, and slain by the hand of every murderous villain.

4   The fourth opinion adversary to civil society, is theirs who hold, *that they who bear rule are subject also to the civil laws.* . . . that a city can neither be bound to itself, nor to any subject; not to itself, because no man can be obliged except it be to another; not to any subject, because the single wills of the subjects are contained in the will of the city; insomuch that if the city will be free from all such obligation, the subjects will so too; and by consequence she is so. But that which holds true in a city, that must be supposed to be true in a man, or an assembly of men who have the supreme authority; for they make a city, which hath no being but by their supreme power. Now that this opinion cannot consist with the very being of government, is evident from hence; that by it the knowledge of what is *good* and *evil,* that is to say, the definition of what is, and what is not against the laws, would return to each single person. Obedience therefore will cease, as oft as anything seems to be commanded contrary to the civil laws, and together with it all coercive jurisdiction; which cannot possibly be without the destruction of the very essence of government. Yet this error hath great props, Aristotle and others; who, by reason of human infirmity, suppose the supreme power to be committed with most security to the laws only. But they seem to have looked very shallowly into the nature of government, who thought that the constraining power, the interpretation of laws, and the making of laws, all which are powers necessarily belonging to government, should be left wholly to the laws themselves. Now although particular subjects may sometimes contend in judgment, and go to law with the supreme magistrate; yet this is only then, when the question

is not what the magistrate may, but what by a certain rule he hath declared he would do. As, when by any law the judges sit upon the life of a subject, the question is not whether the magistrate could by his absolute right deprive him of his life; but whether by that law his will was that he should be deprived of it. But his will was, he should, if he brake the law; else his will was, he should not. This therefore, that a subject may have an action of law against his supreme magistrate, is not strength of argument sufficient to prove, that he is tied to his own laws. On the contrary, it is evident that he is not tied to his own laws; because no man is bound to himself. Laws therefore are set for Titius and Caius, not for the ruler. However, by the ambition of lawyers it is so ordered, that the laws to unskilful men seem not to depend on the authority of the magistrate, but their prudence.

5   In the fifth place, *that the supreme authority may be divided,* is a most fatal opinion to all commonweals. But diverse men divide it diverse ways. For some divide it, so as to grant a supremacy to the civil power in matters pertaining to peace and the benefits of this life; but in things concerning the salvation of the soul they transfer it on others. Now, because justice is of all things most necessary to salvation, it happens that subjects measuring justice, not as they ought, by the civil laws, but by the precepts and doctrines of them who, in regard of the magistrate, are either private men or strangers, through a superstitious fear dare not perform the obedience due to their princes; through fear falling into that which they most feared. Now what can be more pernicious to any state, than that men should, by the apprehension of everlasting torments, be deterred from obeying their princes, that is to say, the laws; or from being just? There are also some, who divide the supreme authority so as to allow the power of war and peace unto one whom they call a *monarch;* but the right of raising money they give to some others, and not to him. But because monies are the sinews of war and peace, they who thus divide the authority, do either really not divide it at all, but place it wholly in them in whose power the money is, but give the name of it to another: or if they do really divide it, they dissolve the government. For neither upon necessity can war be waged, nor can the public peace be preserved without money. . . .

7   The seventh doctrine opposite to government, is this; *that each subject hath an absolute dominion over the goods he is in possession of:* that is to say, such a *propriety* as excludes not only the right of all the rest of his fellow-subjects to the same goods, but also of the magistrate himself. Which is not true; for they who have a *lord* over them, have themselves no *lordship.* . . . Now the magistrate is lord of all his subjects, by the constitution of government. Before the yoke of civil society was undertaken, no man had any *proper right;* all things were *common* to all men. Tell me therefore, how gottest thou this *propriety* but from the magistrate? How got the magistrate it, but that every man transferred his right on him? And thou therefore hast also given up thy right to him. Thy *dominion* therefore, and *propriety,* is just so much as he will, and shall last so long as he pleases; even as in a family, each son hath such *proper* goods, and so long lasting, as seems good to the father. But the greatest part of men who profess civil prudence, reason otherwise. We are equal, say they, by nature; there is no reason why any man should by better right take my goods from me, than I his from him. We know that money sometimes is needful for

the defence and maintenance of the public; but let them who require it, show us the present necessity, and they shall receive it. They who talk thus know not, that what they would have, is already done from the beginning, in the very constitution of government; and therefore speaking as in a dissolute multitude and yet not fashioned government, they destroy the frame.

8   In the last place, it is a great hindrance to civil government, especially monarchical, that men distinguish not enough between a *people* and a *multitude*. The *people* is somewhat that is *one*, having *one will*, and to whom *one action* may be attributed; none of these can properly be said of a multitude. The *people* rules in all governments. For even in *monarchies* the *people* commands; for the *people* wills by the will of *one man;* but the multitude are citizens, that is to say, subjects. In a *democracy* and *aristocracy*, the citizens are the *multitude*, but the *court* is the *people*. And in a *monarchy,* the subjects are the *multitude*, and (however it seem a paradox) the king is the *people*. The common sort of men, and others who little consider these truths, do always speak of a *great number* of men as of the *people*, that is to say, the *city*. They say, that the *city* hath rebelled against the *king* (which is impossible), and that the *people* will and nill what murmuring and discontented subjects would have or would not have; under pretence of the *people* stirring up the *citizens* against the *city*, that is to say, the *multitude* against the *people*. And these are almost all the opinions, wherewith subjects being tainted do easily tumult. And forasmuch as in all manner of government majesty is to be preserved by him or them, who have the supreme authority; the *crimen laesae majestatis* naturally cleaves to these opinions. . . .

13   Many men, who are themselves very well affected to civil society, do through want of knowledge co-operate to the disposing of subjects' minds to *sedition,* whilst they teach young men a doctrine conformable to the said opinions in their schools, and all the people in their pulpits. Now they who desire to bring this disposition into act, place their whole endeavour in this: first, that they may join the ill-affected together into *faction* and *conspiracy;* next, that themselves may have the greatest stroke in the *faction*. They gather them into *faction,* while they make themselves the relators and interpreters of the counsels and actions of single men, and nominate the persons and places to assemble and deliberate of such things whereby the present government may be reformed, according as it shall seem best to their interests. Now to the end that they themselves may have the chief rule in the *faction,* the *faction* must be kept in a *faction;* that is to say, they must have their secret meetings apart with a few, where they may order what shall afterward be propounded in a general meeting, and by whom, and on what subject, and in what order each of them shall speak, how they may draw the powerfullest and most popular men of the *faction* to their side. And thus when they have gotten a faction big enough, in which they may rule by their eloquence, they move it to take upon it the managing of affairs. And thus they sometimes oppress the commonwealth, namely, where there is no other faction to oppose them; but for the most part they rend it, and introduce a civil war. For *folly* and *eloquence* concur in the subversion of government, in the same manner (as the fable hath it) as heretofore the daughters of Pelias, king of Thessaly, conspired with Medea against their father. They going to restore the decrepit old man to his youth again, by the counsel of Medea they cut him into pieces, and set him in the fire to boil; in vain expecting when he would live again. So the common people, through their folly, like the daughters of Pelias, desiring to renew the ancient government, being drawn away by the *eloquence* of ambitious men, as it were by the witchcraft of Medea; divided into *faction* they consume it rather by those flames, than they reform it.

❧ IN DEFENSE AGAINST TYRANNY

The theory and practice of modern democracy evolved in part from attempts to secure independence from hostile authorities long before the belief that all men are equal or possessed of natural and inalienable rights was generally admitted. As late as the sixteenth and seventeenth centuries, Western society was essentially hierarchical, a pyramid with a king at the apex, a peasantry at the base. Yet an equality of sorts existed among men in the same station, particularly within the semi-independent communities and town corporations which, despite attempts at standardizing and absorbing them into dynastic states, still dotted Europe. Here civil rights were conferred by membership in the local guild or by residency in the town or the county; "liberty" was defined as the right to free movement and to other privileges conferred on all members of the particular community. Occasionally some of these communities exercised some democratic control through discussion, voting, and representation of one form or another, but always only for the benefit of those who were franchised members. People from other villages, towns, or professions possessed no civil status here, being "foreigners" or "outsiders," even if from adjacent areas. Indeed, from the late medieval period on, even residence did not necessarily confer a "liberty," which was increasingly restricted to a town oligarchy or patriciate.

One early inroad on this exclusivism, resulting from the Reformation, was effected by the Calvinists. For a time, far-flung communities of converts tended to adopt the rules of government outlined by Calvin, so that a Dutch Calvinist could feel reasonably at home in Geneva or in La Rochelle, France. This relative equality and popular participation never went very far or applied to such religious dissenters as Roger Williams, as his Congregationalists found out in New England. Democracy did not extend to heretics and sinners, and by the eighteenth century the Calvinist

adventure in limited democracy was over: eighteenth-century Geneva
was as rigidly stratified as other European city republics.

Vindiciae Contra Tyrannos *("In Defense of Liberty against Tyrants"),*
appearing in 1579 and widely republished in the seventeenth century, is a
product of the heyday of militant Calvinism. Of disputed authorship,
this Huguenot (that is, French Calvinist) manifesto was a ringing response
to the Saint Bartholomew's Day massacre of several thousand Reformers
seven bitter years earlier. Although the Vindiciae *upheld the claims of a*
religious faith, its assertion of the responsibility of kings to their people
and of the divine right of rebellion (in sharp contrast to Manwaring's
divine right of kings; see pages 3–10), was adaptable to other circumstances.
The Vindiciae *became a universal rallying cry for malcontents anywhere*
chafing under royal tyranny.

WHETHER SUBJECTS ARE BOUND AND OUGHT TO OBEY PRINCES, IF THEY
COMMAND THAT WHICH IS AGAINST THE LAW OF GOD

This question happily may seem at first view to be altogether superfluous and unprofitable, for that it seems to make a doubt of an axiome always held infallible
amongst Christians, confirmed by many testimonies in Holy Scripture, divers examples
of the Histories of all Ages, and by the death of all the Holy Martyrs, for it may be
well demanded wherefore Christians have endured so many afflictions, but that they
were always persuaded, that God must be obeyed simply, and absolutely, and Kings
with this exception that they command not that which is repugnant to the Law of God.
Otherways wherefore should the Apostles have answered, that God must rather be
obeyed than men, and also seeing that the only will of God is always just, and that
of men may be, and is, oftentimes unjust, who can doubt but that we must always
obey God's commandments without any exception, and men's ever with limitation.
But for so much as there are many Princes in these days, calling themselves Christians,
which arrogantly assume an unlimited power, over which God himself hath no
command, and that they have no want of flatterers, which adore them as Gods upon
earth, many others also, which for fear, or by constraint, either seem, or else do
believe, that Princes ought to be obeyed in all things, and by all men. And withal,
seeing the unhappiness of these times is such, that there is nothing so firm, certain,
or pure, which is not shaken, disgraced, or polluted; I fear me that whosoever shall
nearly, and thoroughly consider these things, will confess this question to be not only
most profitable, but also, the times considered, most necessary.

For my own part when I consider the cause of the many calamities, wherewith

[Hubert Languet or P. Duplessis-Mornay], *Vindiciae Contra Tyrannos* (London, 1689), pp.
1–4, 6–10, 12, 17, 58, 62–67, 77–79, 134–135.

Christendom hath been afflicted, for these late years, I cannot but remember that of the Prophet, *Hosea, the Princes of Judah were like them that remove the bounds: wherefore I will pour out my self like water. Ephraim is oppressed, and broken in judgment, because he willingly walked after the Commandments.* Here you see the sin of the Princes, and people dispersed in these two words. The Princes exceed their bounds, not contenting themselves with that Authority which the Almighty, and all good God hath given them, but seek to usurp that sovereignty, which he hath reserved to himself over all men, being not content to command the Bodies, and goods of their Subjects at their pleasure, but assume licence to themselves to inforce the Consciences, which appertains chiefly to Jesus Christ, holding the earth not great enough for their ambition, they will climb and conquer Heaven it self. The people on the other side walks after the commandment, when they yield to the desire of Princes, who command them that which is against the Law of God, and as it were burn incense to, and adore these earthy Gods; and instead of resisting them, if they have means and occasion, suffer them to usurp the place of God, making no conscience to give that to *Caesar,* which belongs properly and only to God. Now is there any man that sees not this, if a man disobey a Prince commanding that which is wicked and unlawful, he shall presently be esteemed a Rebel, a Traytor, and guilty of High Treason, our Saviour Christ, the Apostles and all the Christians of the Primitive Church were charged with these Calumnies. If any after the example of *Ezra,* and *Nehemiah,* dispose himself to the building of the Temple of the Lord, it will be said he aspires to the Crown, hatches innovations, and seeks the ruine of the State, then you shall presently see a million of these Minnions, and flatterers of Princes tickling their ears with an opinion, that if they once suffer this Temple to be re-builded, they may bid their Kingdom farewell and never look to raise impost or taxes on these men.

But what a madness is this? There are no Estates which ought to be esteemed firm and stable, but those in whom the Temple of God is built, and which are indeed the Temple it self, and these we may truly call Kings, which reign with God, seeing that it is by him only that Kings reign: On the contrary what beastly foolishness it is to think, that the State and Kingdom cannot subsist if God Almighty be not excluded, and his Temple demolished. From hence proceeds so many Tyrannous enterprises, unhappy and tragick death of Kings, and ruines of people. If these Sicophants knew what difference there is between *God* and *Caesar,* between the King of Kings, and a simple King, between the Lord, and the Vassal, and what tributes this Lord requires of his Subjects, and what Authority he gives to Kings over those his Subjects, certainly so many Princes would not strive to trouble the Kingdom of God, and we should not see some of them precipitated from their Thrones by the just instigation of the Almighty, revenging himself of them, in the midst of their greatest strength, and the people should not be so sack't and pillag'd, and troden down.

It then belongs to Princes to know how far they may extend their Authority, and to Subjects in what they may obey them, lest the one incroaching on that jurisdiction, which no way belongs to them, and the others obeying him which commandeth further than he ought, they be both chastised, when they shall give an account thereof before another Judge: Now the end and scope of the question propounded, whereof the Holy Scripture shall principally give the resolution, is that which followeth. The question is, if Subjects be bound to obey Kings, in case they command that which is against the Law of God: that is to say, to which of the two (God or the King) must we rather obey, when the question shall be resolved concerning the King, to whom is attributed absolute power, that concerning other Magistrates shall be also determined.

First, the Holy Scripture doth teach, that God reigns by his own proper Authority, and Kings by derivation, God from himself, Kings from God, that God hath a jurisdiction proper, Kings are his delegates: It follows then, that the jurisdiction of God hath no limits, that of Kings bounded, that the power of God is infinite, that of Kings confin'd, that the Kingdom of God extends itself to all places, that of Kings is restrain'd within the confines of certain Countries: In like manner God hath created of nothing both Heaven and Earth; wherefore by good right he is Lord, and true Proprietor, both of the one, and the other: All the Inhabitants of the Earth hold of him that which they have, and are but his tenants, and farmers; all the Princes and Governors of the World are his stipendaries and vassals, and are bound to take and acknowledge their investitures from him. Briefly, God alone is the owner and Lord, and all men of what degree, or quality soever they be, are his servants, farmers, officers and vassals, and owe account and acknowledgment to him, according to that which he hath committed to their dispensation, the higher their place is, the greater their account must be, and according to the ranks whereunto God hath raised them, must they make their reckoning before his divine Majesty, which the Holy Scripture teacheth in infinite places, and all the faithful, yea, and the wisest among the Heathen have ever acknowledged. . . .

At this day at the Inaugurating of Kings, and Christian Princes, they are called the servants of God, destinated to govern his people. Seeing then that Kings are only the Lieutenants of God, established in the Throne of God, by the Lord God himself, and the people are the people of God, and that the honour which is done to these Lieutenants proceeeds from the reverence which is born to those, that sent them to this service: it follows of necessity that Kings must be obeyed for God's cause, and not against God, and then, when they serve and obey God, and not other ways. It may be that the flatterers of the Court will reply, that God hath resigned his power unto Kings, reserving Heaven for himself, and allowing the Earth to them to Reign, and govern there according to their own fancies; briefly that the great ones of the World hold a divided Empire with God himself. . . .

God doth not at any time divest himself of his power, he holds a Scepter in one hand to repress and quell the audacious boldness of those Princes which mutiny against him, and in the other a ballance to control those that administer not justice with equity as they ought, than these there cannot be expressed more certain marks of sovereign Command. And if the Emperor in creating a King, reserves always to himself the imperial sovereignty, or a King as he of *France* in granting the Government or possession of a Province to a stranger, or if it be to his Brother or Son reserves always to himself appeals, and the knowledg of such things as are the marks of royalty and sovereignty, the which also are always understood of themselves to be excepted, although they were altogether omitted in the grant of investure, and fealty promised, with much more reason should God have Sovereign Power and Command over all Kings being his Servants and Officers, seeing we read, in so many places of Scripture, that he will call them to an account, and punish them, if they do not faithfully discharge their duties.

Then therefore all Kings are the Vassals of the King of Kings, invested into their Office by the sword, which is the cognisance of their Royal Authority, to the end, that with the sword they maintain the Law of God, defend the good, and punish the evil: Even as we commonly see, that he which is a Sovereign Lord, puts his Vassals into possession of their fee, by girding them with a sword, delivering them a buckler, and a standard, with condition that they shall fight for them with those Arms if occasion shall serve. Now if we consider what is the duty of Vassals, we shall find that what may be said of them, agrees properly to Kings. The Vassal receives his fee of his Lord with right of justice, and charge to serve him in his Wars. The King is established by the Lord God, the King of Kings; to the end he should administer justice to his people and defend them against all their Enemies. The Vassal receives Laws and Conditions from his Sovereign: God Commands the King to observe his Laws and to have them always before his Eyes, promising that he and his Successors shall possess long the Kingdom, if they be obedient, and on the contrary, that their Reign shall be of small continuance, if they prove Rebellious to their Sovereign King. The Vassal obligeth himself by Oath unto his Lord, and swears that he will be faithful, and obedient: In like manner the King promiseth solemnly to command, according to the express Law of God. Briefly the Vassal looseth his fee, if he Commit Fellony, and by Law forfeiteth all his Priviledges: In the like case the King looseth his Right, and many times his Realm also, if he despise God, if he [plot] with his Enemies, and if he Commit Fellony against that Royal Majesty, this will appear more clearly by the consideration of the Covenant which is Contrasted between God and the King, for God does that honour to his Servants to call them his Confederates. Now we read of two sorts of Covenants at the Inaugurating of Kings, the first between God, the King, and the People, that the people might be the people of God: The second between the King and the people, that the people shall obey faithfully, and the King command justly, we will treat hereafter of the second, and now speak of the first.

When King *Joas* was Crowned we read that a Covenant was Contracted between God, the King, and the People: or, as it is said in another place between *Jehojada* the High-Priest, all the People, and the King, *That God should be their Lord*. In like manner we read that *Josias* and all the people entred into Covenants with the Lord: we may gather from these testimonies, that in passing these Covenants the High-Priest did Covenant in the Name of God in express terms, that the King and the People should take order that God might be served purely, and according to his will, throughout the whole Kingdom of *Juda,* that the King should so Reign that the People were suffered to serve God, and held in obedience to his Law: That the people should so obey the King, as their obedience should have principal Relation to God. It appears by this that the King and the People are joyntly bound by promise and did oblige themselves by solemn Oath to serve God before all things. And indeed presently after they had sworn the Covenant, *Josias* and *Joas* did ruine the Idolatry of *Baal* and re-established the pure service of God. The principal points of the Covenants were chiefly these.

That the King himself, and all the people should be careful to honour and serve

God according to his will revealed in his word, which if they performed, God would assist and preserve their Estates: as in doing the contrary, he would abandon, and exterminate them, which doth plainly appear by the conferring of divers passages of holy writ. *Moses* somewhat before his death propounds these conditions of Covenant to all the people, and at the same time commands that the Law, which be those precepts given by the Lord should be in *deposito* kept in the Ark of the Covenant. After the decease of *Moses, Joshua* was established Captain, and Conductor of the people of God, and according as the Lord himself admonished, if he would have happy success in his Affairs, he should not in any sort estrange himself from the Law; *Joshua* also for his part, desiring to make the *Israelites* understand upon what condition God had given them the Country of *Canaan,* as soon as they were entered into it, after due sacrifices performed, he read the Law in the presence of all the people, promising unto them in the Lord's name all good things if they persisted in obedience; and threatening of all evil if they wilfully connived in disobedience. Summarily, he assures them all prosperity, if they observed the Law; as otherways, he expressly declared, that in doing the contrary they should be utterly ruined: Also at all such times as they left the service of God, they were delivered into the hands of the *Canaanites,* and reduced into slavery, under their Tyranny. Now this Covenant between God and the people in the times of the Judges, had vigor also in the times of the Kings, and was treated with them. After that *Saul* had been anointed, chosen, and wholly established King, *Samuel* speaks unto the people in these terms; *Behold the King whom you have demanded and chosen, God hath established him King over you, obey you therefore and serve the Lord, as well you, as your King which is established over you, otherwise you and your King shall perish.* As if he should say, you would have a King and God hath given you this here, notwithstanding think not that God will suffer any encroachment upon his right, but know that the King is as well bound to observe the Law as you, and if he fail therein, his delinquency shall be punished as severely as yours: Briefly, according to your desires *Saul* is given you for your King, to lead you in the Wars, but with this condition annexed that he himself follow the Law of God. After that *Saul* was rejected, because he kept not his promise, *David* was established King on the same condition, so also was his Son *Solomon,* for the Lord said, *If thou keep my Law, I will confirm with thee the Covenant which I contracted with David.* Now concerning this Covenant, it is inserted into the second Book of the Chronicles, as followeth. *There shall not fail thee a man in my sight, to sit upon the Throne of Israel: yet so that thy children take heed to their way to walk in my Law, as thou hast walked before me, But if they serve Idols, I will drive them from the Land whereof I have given them possession.* And therefore it was that the book of the Law was called the book of the Covenant of the Lord, (who commanded the Priests to give it the King) according to which *Samuel* put it into the hands of *Saul,* and according to the tenure thereof *Josias* yields himself . . . vassal of the Lord. Also the Law which is kept in the Ark, is called the Covenant of the Lord with the Children of Israel. Finally, the people delivered from the Captivity of *Babylon,* do renew the Covenant with God, and do acknowledge throughout that Chapter, that they worthily deserved all those punishments for their falsifying their promise to God! It appears then that the Kings swear as vassals to observe the Law of God, whom they confess to be Sovereign Lord over all. Now according to that which we have already touched, if they violate their Oath, and transgress the Law, we say that they have lost their Kingdom, as vassals lose their fee by Committing Fellony. . . .

Now although the form both of the Church, and the *Jewish* Kingdom be changed, for that which was before inclosed within the narrow bounds of *Judea,* is now dilated throughout the whole World, notwithstanding the same things may be said of Christian Kings, the Gospel having succeeded the Law, and Christian Princes being in the place of those of *Jewry.* There is the same Covenant, the same Conditions, the same Punishments, and if they fail in the accomplishing, the same God Almighty revenger of all perfidious disloyalty; and as the former were bound to keep the Law, so the other are obliged to adhere to the Doctrine of the Gospel, for the advancement whereof these Kings at their anoynting, and receiving, do promise to imploy the utmost of their means. . . .

We see that God invests Kings into their Kingdoms, almost in the same manner that vassals are invested into their sees by their Sovereign, we must needs conclude, that Kings are the vassals of God, and deserve to be deprived of the benefit they receive from their Lord if they commit Fellony, in the same fashion as rebellious vassals are of their Estates. These premises being allowed, this question may be easily resolved; for if God hold the place of Sovereign Lord, and the King as Vassal: who dare deny but that we must rather obey the Sovereign than the Vassal? If God commands one thing, and the King commands the contrary, what is that proud man that would term him a Rebel which refuseth to obey the King, when else he must disobey God. But on the contrary he should rather be condemned, and held for truly rebellious, which omits to obey God, or which will obey the King, when he forbids him to yield Obedience to God. Briefly, if God calls us on the one side to enroll us in his Service, and the King on the other, is any man so void of reason as he will not say we must leave the King, and apply our selves to God's Service: so far be it from us to believe, that we are bound to obey a King, commanding any thing contrary to the Law of God, that contrarily in obeying him we become Rebels to God; no more, nor less than we would esteem a County-man a Rebel, which for the Love he bears to some rich and ancient inferior Lord, would bear Arms against the Sovereign Prince, or which had rather obey the Writs of an Inferior Judge than of a Superior, the Commandments of a Lieutenant of a Province, than of a Prince; to be brief, the Directions of an Officer rather than the express Ordinances of the King himself. . . .

KINGS ARE MADE BY THE PEOPLE

We have showed before that it is God, that doth appoint Kings, which chooseth them, which gives the Kingdom to them: now we say that the People establish Kings, putteth the Scepter into their hands, and which with their Suffrages, approveth the Election. God would have it done in this manner, to the end, that the King should acknowledge, that after God they hold their power and Sovereignty from the people, and that it might the rather induce them, to apply and Address the utmost of their care and thoughts for the profit of the people, without being puffed with any vain imagination, that they were formed of any matter more excellent than other Men; for which they were raised so high above others: as if they were to Command our flocks of sheep, or herds of Cattle; but let them remember and know, that they are of the same Mould and Condition as others, raised from the Earth by the voice and Acclamations, now as it were upon the shoulders of the people unto their Thrones, that they might afterwards bear on their own shoulders the greatest burthens of the Commonwealth. . . .

Briefly, for so much as none were ever born with Crowns on their Heads, and Scepters in their Hands, and that no Man can be a King by himself, nor reign without People; whereas on the contrary, the People may subsist of themselves, and were long before they had any Kings, it must of necessity follow, that Kings were at the first constituted by the People; and although the Sons and Dependants of such Kings inheriting their Fathers' Virtues, may in a sort seem to have rendered their Kingdoms Hereditary to their Off-springs, and that in some Kingdoms and Countries, the Right of free Election seems in a sort buried; yet notwithstanding, in all well ordered Kingdoms, this Custom is yet remaining, the Sons do not succeed the Fathers, before the People have first as it were anew established them by their new Approbation; neither were they acknowledged in Quality, as inheriting it from the Dead; but approved and accounted Kings then only, when they were invested with the Kingdom, by receiving the Scepter and Diadem from the Hands of those who represent the Majesty of the People. One may see most evident Marks of this in Christian Kingdoms, which are at this day esteemed Hereditary; for the *French* King, he of *Spain* and *England,* and others, are commonly Sacred, and as it were, put into Possession of their Authority by the Peers, Lords of the Kingdom, and Officers of the Crown, which represent the Body of the People; no more nor less than the Emperors of *Germany* are chosen by the Electors, and the Kings of *Polonia,* by the Yawodes and Palatines of the Kingdom, where the Right of Election is yet in force. . . .

To conclude in a Word, all Kings at the first were altogether elected, and those which at this day seem to have their Crowns and Royal Authority by Inheritance, have or should have first and principally their Confirmation from the People. Briefly, although the People of some Countries have been accustomed to choose their Kings of such a Lineage, which for some notable Merits have worthily deserved it; yet we must believe that they choose the Stock it self, and not every Branch that proceeds from it; neither are they so tied to that Election, as if the successor degenerate, they may not choose another more worthy, neither those which come and are the next of that Stock, are born Kings, but created such, nor called Kings, but princes of the Blood Royal.

THE WHOLE BODY OF THE PEOPLE IS ABOVE THE KING

Now seeing that the People choose and establish their Kings, it followeth that the whole Body of the People is above the King; for it is a thing most evident, that he which is established by another, is accounted under him that hath established him, and he which receives his Authority from another, is less than he from whom he derives his Power. . . .

Furthermore, it must necessarily be, that Kings were instituted for the People's Sake, neither can it be, *that for the Pleasure of fame hundreds of men, and without doubt more foolish and worse than many of the other, all the rest were made, but much rather that these hundred were made for the Use and Service of all the other, and reason requires that he be preferred above the other, who was made only to and for his Occasion:* so it is, that for that Ship's Sail, the Owner appoints a Pilot over her, who sits at the Helm, and looks that she keeps her Course, nor run not upon any dangerous Shelf; the Pilot doing his Duty, is obeyed by the Marriners; yea, and of himself that is Owner of the Vessel, nothwithstanding the Pilot is a Servant as well as the least in the Ship, from whom he only differs in this, that he serves in a better place than they do. In a Common-wealth, commonly compared to a Ship, the King holds the Place of Pilot, the People in general are Owners of the Vessel, obeying the Pilot, whilst he is careful of the publick Good; as though this Pilot neither is nor ought to be esteemed other than Servant to the Publick; as a Judge or General in War differs little from other Officers, but that he is bound to bear greater Burdens, and expose himself to more Dangers. By the same reason also which the King gains by acquist of Arms, be it that he possesseth himself of Frontier places in warring on the Enemy, or that which he gets by Escheats or Confiscations, he gets it to the Kingdom, and not to himself, to wit, to the *People,* of whom the *Kingdom* is composed; no more nor less than the Servant doth for his Master; neither may one contract or oblige themselves to him, but by and with reference to the Authority derived from the *People.* Furthermore, there is an infinite sort of *People* which live without a *King,* but we cannot imagine a *King* without *People.* And those which have been raised to the Royal Dignity, were not advanced because they excelled other Men in Beauty and Comeliness, nor in some Excellency of Nature to govern them as Shepherds do their Flocks, but rather being made out of the same Mass with the rest of the People, they should acknowledge that for them, they as it were borrow their Power and Authority.

The ancient Custom of the *French* represents that exceeding well, for they used to lift up on a Buckler, and salute him King whom they had chosen. And wherefore is it said, *I pray you, that Kings have an infinite number of Eyes, a million of Ears, with extreme long Hands, and Feet exceeding Swift?* Is it because they are like to to *Argos, Gerien, Midas,* and divers others so celebrated by the Poets; No truly, but it is said in regard of all the People, whom the business principally concerns, who lend to the King for the good of the Common-wealth, their Eyes, their Ears, their Means, their Faculties. Let the *People* forsake the King, he presently falls to the Ground, although before his Hearing and Sight seemed most excellent, and that he was strong and in the best Disposition that might be; yea, that he seemed to triumph in all magnificence, yet in an instant he will become most vile and contemptible, to be brief, instead of those Divine Honours wherewith all men adore him, he shall be compelled to become a Pedant, and whip Children in the School at *Corinth.* Take away but the Basis to this Giant, and like the Rhodian Coloss, he presently tumbles on the ground and falls into pieces. Seeing then that the King is established in this degree by the *People,* and for their sake, and that he cannot subsist without them, who can think it strange then for us to conclude, that the *People* are above the King? Now that which we speak of all the *People* universally, ought also to be understood, as hath been delivered in the second Question, of those which in every Kingdom or Town do lawfully represent the Body of the *People,* and which ordinarily (or at least should be) called the Officers of the Kingdom, or of the Crown, and not of the King; for the Officers of the King, it is he which placeth and displaceth them at his pleasure, yea, after his Death they have no more power, and are accounted as dead. On the contrary, the Officers of the Kingdom *receive their Authority from the People in the general Assembly of the States (or at the least were accustomed so anciently to have done) and cannot be disauthorized but by them, so then the one depends of the King, the other of the Kingdom, those of the Sovereign Officer of the Kingdom, which is the King himself, these of the Sovereignty it self, that is of the People, of which Sovereignty, both the King and all his Officers of the Kingdom ought to depend, the Charge of the one hath proper relation to the Care of the Kings Person; that of the other, to look that the Common-wealth receive no Damage; the first ought to serve and assist the King, as all Domestick Servants are bound to do to their Master; the other to preserve the Rights and Privileges of the People, and to carefully hinder the Prince, that he neither omit the things that may advantage the State, nor commit any thing that may endammage the Publick. . . .*

But peradventure, some one will reply, you speak to us here of Peers, of Lords and Officers of the Crown. But I for my part see not any, but only some shews and shadows of Antiquity as if they were to be represented on a Stage I see not for the present scarce any Tract of that ancient Liberty, and Authority; nay, which is worse a great part, if not all, of those Officers take care of nothing but their particular Affairs, and almost, if not altogether, serve as Flatterers about those Kings who joyntly toss the poor people like Tennis-balls: hardly is there one to be found that hath Compassion on, or will lend a helping hand to the miserable Subjects, flea'd and scorched to the very bones, by their insolent and insupportable Oppression. If any be but thought to have such a desire, they are presently condemned as Rebels and seditious, and are constrained either to fly with much discommodity, or else must run hazard both of Life and Liberty. What can be answered to this? the business goes thus. The Outragiousness of Kings, the ignorance of the party, together with the wicked connivence of the great ones of the Kingdom, hath been for the most part such throughout the World, that the Licentious and unbridled Power wherewith most Kings are transported and which hath made them inusupportable, hath in a manner by the length of Continuance gained right of Prescription, and the People for want of using it hath intacitely quit, if not altogether lost, their just and ancient Authority. So that it ordinarily happens that what all Men's care ought to attend on, is for the most part neglected by every Man; for what is committed to the generality, no Man thinks is commended to his Custody. Notwithstanding, no such Prescription nor prevarication can justly prejudice the Right of the People: It is commonly said that the Exchequers do admit no rule of Prescription against it, much less against the whole Body of the people, whose power transcends the Kings, and in whose Right the King assumes to himself that privilege; for otherwise, wherefore is the Prince only Administrator, and the people true Proprietor of the publick Exchequer, as we will prove here presently after. Furthermore, it is not a thing resolved on by all, that no Tyrannous Intrusion or Usurpation, and continuance in the same Course, can by any length of time prescribe against lawful Liberty. If it be objected, that Kings were enthroned, and received their Authority from the people that lived five hundred years ago, and not by those now living, I answer that the Common-wealth never dies, although Kings be taken out of this Life one after another: for as the continual running of the water gives the River a perpetual Being: so the Alternative revolution of Birth and death renders the People . . . immortal.

And further, as we have at this day the same *Seine* and *Tiber* as was 1000 years ago: in like manner also is there the same People of *Germany, France,* and *Italy* (excepting intermixing of Colonies, or such like) neither can the lapse of time, nor changing of individuals, alter in any sort the right of those People. Furthermore, if they say the King receives his Kingdom from his Father, and not from the People, and he from his Grandfather, and so one from another upward.

I ask, could the Grandfather or Ancestor, transfer a greater right to his Successor, then he had himself? If he could not (as without doubt it must need be so) is it not plainly perspicuous, that what the Successor further Arrogates to himself, he may usurp with as safe a Conscience, as what a Thief gets by the High-way side. The People on the contrary have their Right of eviction entire and whole; although that the Officers of the Crown have for a time lost or left their Ranks, this cannot in any true Right prejudice the People, but rather clear otherwise; as one would not grant Audience, or show favour to a Slave which had long time held his Master Prisoner, and did not only vaunt himself to be free, but also presumptuously assumed power over the life and death of his Master; neither would any Man allow the excuse of a Thief, because he had continued in that Trade 30. years, or for that he had been bred in that course of life by his Father, if he presumed by his long continuance in that Function to prescribe for the lawfulness, but rather the longer he had continued in his wickedness, the more grievous should be his punishment: in like manner, the Prince is altogether unsupportable which because he succeeds a Tyrant, or hath kept the people (by whose Suffrages he holds the Crown) in a long slavery, or hath suppressed the Officers of the Kingdom (who should be Protectors of the publick Liberty) that therefore presumes, that what he affects is lawful for him to effect, and that his Will is not to be restrained or corrected by any positive Law whatsoever. For prescription in Tyranny detracts nothing from the Right of the people; nay, it rather much aggravates the Princes' Outrages. But what if the Peers and principal Officers of the Kingdom makes themselves parts with the King? What if betraying the publick, cause the Yoke of Tyranny upon the peoples' Neck? shall it follow, that by this prevarication and Treason the Authority is devolved into the King? Does this detract any thing from the Right of the peoples' Liberty, or does it add any licentious power to the King? Let the people thank themselves, say you, who relyed on the disloyal Loyalty of such men.

But I answer, that these Officers are indeed those Protectors whose principal Care and study should be, *that the People be maintained in the free and absolute Fruition of their Goods and Liberty.* And therefore, in the same manner as if a treacherous Advocate for a sum of Money should agree to betray the Cause of his Client, into the hands of his Adversary, which he ought to have defended, hath not power for all that to alter the course of Justice, nor of a bad Cause to make a good one, although perhaps for a time he gives some Colour of it.

In like manner this Conspiracy of the great ones combined to ruin the Inferiors cannot disanul the Right of the people; in the mean Season, those great ones incur the punishment that the same alots against Prevaricators, and for the people, the same Law allows them to choose another Advocate, and afresh to pursue their Cause, as if it were then only to begin. . . .

Furthermore, as the Prince's pleasure is not always law, so many times it is not expedient that the People doe all that which may lawfully be done: for it may oftentimes chance, that the Medicine proves more dangerous than the Disease. Therefore it becomes wise men, to try all ways before they come to blows, to use all other remedies before they suffer the Sword to decide the Controversie. If then those which represent the Body of the People, foresee any Innovation or Machination against the State, or that it be already embarqued into a course of Perdition; their duty is, first to admonish the Prince, and not to attend, that the disease by accession of time and accidents, becomes unrecoverable. For Tyranny may be properly resembled unto a Feaver Hectick, the which at the first is easie to be cured, but with much difficulty to be known; but after it is sufficiently known, it becomes uncurable. Therefore small beginnings are to be carefully observed, and by those whom it concerns diligently prevented.

If the Prince therefore persist in his violent courses, and contemn frequent admonitions, addressing his designs only to that end, that he may oppress at his pleasure, and effect his own desires without fear or restraint; he then doubtless makes himself liable to that detested crime of *Tyranny:* and whatsoever either the law, or lawful authority permits against a Tyrant, may be lawfully practised against him. Tyranny is not onely a will, but the chief, and as it were the complement and abstract of vices. A Tyrant subverts the State, pillages the people, lays stratagems to entrap their lives, breaks promise with all, scoffs at the sacred Obligations of a solemn Oath, and therefore is he so much more vile than the vilest of usual Malefactors, by how much offences committed against a generality, are worthy of greater punishment than those which concern only particular and private persons. If Thieves and those that commit Sacriledge, be declared Infamous; nay, if they justly suffer Corporal punishment by Death, can we invent any that may be worthily equivalent for so outragious a Crime?

Furthermore, we have already proved, that all Kings receive their Royal Authority from the people, that the whole people consider'd in one body, is above and greater than the King; and that the King and Emperor are only the prime and supream Governours and Ministers of the Kingdom and Empire; but the People the absolute Lord and Owner thereof. It therefore necessarily follows, that a Tyrant is in the same manner guilty of rebellion against the Majesty of the people, as the Lord of a fee, which Felloniously trangress the Conditions of his Investitutes, and is liable to the same punishment, yea, and certainly deserves much more greater than the equity of those Laws inflict on the delinquents. Therefore . . . he may either be deposed by those which are Lords in Sovereignty over him, or else justly punished according to the Law . . . which condemns those which offer Violence to the publick. The body of the people must needs be the Sovereign of those which represent it, which in some places are the Electors, Palatines, Peers; in other, the Assembly of the general Estates.

And if the Tyranny have gotten such sure footing, as there is no other means but force to remove him; then it is lawful for them to call the people to Arms, to Inroll and raise Forces, and to imploy the utmost of their power, and use against him all advantages and stratagems of War, as against the Enemy of the Common-wealth, and the Disturber of the Publick Peace. Briefly, the same sentence may be justly pronounced against him, as was against *Manlius Capitolinus* at *Rome. Thou wast to me Manlius, when thou didst tumble down the Gaules that sealed the Capitole: But since thou art now become an Enemy, like one of them, thou shalt be precipitated down from the same place from whence thou formerly tumbledst those Enemies. . . .*

ᴇᴆ TREATISE OF CIVIL GOVERNMENT

John Locke

John Locke (1632–1704) gained his reputation as a political theorist and philosopher. He made his living as the personal physician of a great English aristocrat, Lord Shaftesbury, whose Whig party fought the rising absolutism of the last two Stuart monarchs of Great Britain, Charles II and James II. Much of the Treatise of Civil Government, *the grand defense of the Whig position, was written during the 1680s when Locke had followed his patron into exile to Holland. James was overthrown in 1688 by a coalition of vested interests which, offended by royal Catholicism and absolutism, offered the crown to William of Orange, Stadtholder of the Netherlands. Locke returned to England with the triumphant Shaftesbury, and published his* Treatise *there soon after.*

Locke's rationale for representative government, though only one of literally hundreds of political pamphlets produced by the Glorious Revolution, became widely known and remained influential in both Europe and America throughout the eighteenth century. Locke's theory of the social contract may be considered an elaborate amendment to Hobbes's, yet it was Locke's analysis of property and his theory of human rights which shaped the ideas of American and French revolutionists 100 years after Locke's time.

Altogether, John Locke's interests were broad and his achievements diverse. He studied medicine and mathematics in his youth, participated in a diplomatic mission to Prussia, and assisted in drafting a constitution for Carolina. His Essay Concerning Human Understanding *and* Thoughts on Education, *which contain conclusions drawn from empirical observation, are regarded as among the earliest essays in the field now called psychology. Locke's* Reasonableness of Christianity *was a masterful attempt to correlate divine revelation and reason. He wrote works on economics and aided in the revision of England's monetary system. The total accomplishment of his life in no little way prepared England for the eighteenth century's Age of Reason.*

OF THE STATE OF NATURE

To understand political power right, and derive it from its original, we must consider what state all men are naturally in, and that is, a state of perfect freedom to order their actions and dispose of their possessions and persons, as they tnink fit, within the bounds of the law of nature; without asking leave, or depending upon the will of any other man.

A state also of equality, wherein all the power and jurisdiction is reciprocal, no one having more than another; there being nothing more evident, than that creatures of the same species and rank, promiscuously born to all the same advantages of nature, and the use of the same faculties, should also be equal one amongst another without subordination or subjection; unless the lord and master of them all should, by any manifest declaration of his will, set one above another, and confer on him, by an evident and clear appointment, an undoubted right to dominion and sovereignty. . . .

But though this be a state of liberty, yet it is not a state of licence: though man in that state have an uncontrolable liberty to dispose of his person or possessions, yet he has not liberty to destroy himself, or so much as any creature in his possession, but where some nobler use than its bare preservation calls for it. The state of nature has a law of nature to govern it, which obliges every one: and reason, which is that law, teaches all mankind, who will but consult it, that being all equal and independent, no one ought to harm another in his life, health, liberty, or possessions: for men being all the workmanship of one omnipotent and infinitely wise Maker; all the servants of one sovereign master, sent into the world by his order, and about his business; they are his property, whose workmanship they are, made to last during his, not another's pleasure: and being furnished with like faculties, sharing all in one community of nature, there cannot be supposed any such subordination among us, that may authorize us to destroy another, as if we were made for one another's uses, as the inferior ranks of creatures are for ours. Every one, as he is bound to preserve himself, and not to quit his station wilfully, so by the like reason, when his own preservation comes not in competition, ought he, as much as he can, to preserve the rest of mankind, and may not, unless it be to do justice to an offender, take away or impair the life, or what tends to the preservation of life, the liberty, health, limb, or goods of another.

John Locke, "Two Treatises of Government," *The Works of John Locke* (London: Wiotridge & Son, 1812), V, 339–343, 345–349, 351–354, 357, 361, 388–391, 394–396, 411–423, 426–430, 432–433, 464–469, 484–485.

And that all men may be restrained from invading others rights, and from doing hurt to one another, and the law of nature be observed, which willeth the peace and preservation of all mankind, the execution of the law of nature is, in that state, put into every man's hands, whereby every one has a right to punish the transgressors of that law to such a degree as may hinder its violation: for the law of nature would, as all other laws that concern men in this world, be in vain, if there were nobody that in the state of nature had a power to execute that law, and thereby preserve the innocent and restrain offenders. And if any one in the state of nature may punish another for any evil he has done, every one may do so: for in that state of perfect equality, where naturally there is no superiority or jurisdiction of one over another, what any may do in prosecution of that law, every one must needs have a right to do.

And thus, in the state of nature, "one man comes by a power over another;" but yet no absolute or arbitrary power, to use a criminal, when he has got him in his hands, according to the passionate heats, or boundless extravagancy of his own will; but only to retribute to him, so far as calm reason and conscience dictate, what is proportionate to his transgression; which is so much as may serve for reparation and restraint: for these two are the only reasons, why one man may lawfully do harm to another, which is that we call punishment. In transgressing the law of nature, the offender declares himself to live by another rule than that of reason and common equity, which is that measure God has set to the actions of men, for their mutual security; and so he becomes dangerous to mankind, the tye, which is to secure them from injury and violence, being slighted and broken by him. Which being a trespass against the whole species, and the peace and safety of it, provided for by the law of nature; every man upon this score, by the right he hath to preserve mankind in general, may restrain, or where it is necessary, destroy things noxious to them, and so may bring such evil on any one, who hath transgressed that law, as may make him repent the doing of it, and thereby deter him, and by his example others, from doing the like mischief. And in this case, and upon this ground, "every man hath a right to punish the offender, and be executioner of the law of nature."

I doubt not but this will seem a very strange doctrine to some men: but before they condemn it, I desire them to resolve me, by what right any prince or state can put to death, or punish any alien, for any crime he commits in their country. It is certain their laws, by virtue of any sanction they receive from the promulgated will of the legislative, reach not a stranger: they speak not to him, nor, if they did, is he bound to hearken to them. The legislative authority, by which they are in force over the subjects of that commonwealth, hath no power over him. Those who have the supreme power of making laws in England, France, or Holland, are to an Indian but like the rest of the world, men without authority: and therefore, if by the law of nature every man hath not a power to punish offences against it, as he soberly judges the case to require, I see not how the magistrates of any community can punish an alien of another country; since, in reference to him, they can have no more power than what every man naturally may have over another.

Besides the crime which consists in violating the law, and varying from the right rule of reason, whereby a man so far becomes degenerate, and declares himself to quit the principles of human nature, and to be a noxious creature, there is commonly injury done to some person or other, and some other man receives damage by his transgression: in which case he who hath received any damage, has, besides the right of punishishment common to him with other men, a particular right to seek reparation from him that has done it: and any other person, who finds it just, may also join with him that is injured, and assist in recovering from the offender so much as may make satisfaction for the harm he has suffered.

From these two distinct rights, the one of punishing the crime for restraint, and preventing the like offence, which right of punishing is in every body; the other of taking reparation, which belongs only to the injured party; comes it to pass that the magistrate, who by being magistrate hath the common right of punishing put into his hands, can often, where the public good demands not the execution of the law, remit the punishment of criminal offences by his own authority, but yet cannot remit the satisfaction due to any private man for the damage he has received. . . .

To this strange doctrine, viz. That "in the state of nature every one has the executive power" of the law of nature, I doubt not but it will be objected, that it is unreasonable for men to be judges in their own cases, that self love will make men partial to themselves and their friends: and on the other side, that ill-nature, passion, and revenge will carry them too far in punishing others; and hence nothing but confusion and disorder will follow: and that therefore God hath certainly appointed government to restrain the partiality and violence of men. I easily grant, that civil government is the proper remedy for the inconveniencies of the state of nature, which must certainly be great, where men may be judges in their own case; since it is easy to be imagined, that he who was so unjust as to do his brother an injury, will scarce be so just as to condemn himself for it: but I shall desire those who make this objection, to remember, that absolute monarchs are but men; and if government is to be the remedy of those evils, which necessarily follow from men's being judges in their own cases, and the state of nature is therefore not to be endured; I desire to know what kind of government that is, and how much better it is than the state of nature, where one man commanding a multitude, has the liberty to be judged in his own case, and may do to all his subjects whatever he pleases, without the least liberty to any one to question or control those who execute his pleasure? and in whatsoever he doth, whether led by reason, mistake or passion, must be submitted to? much better it is in the state of nature, wherein men are not bound to submit to the unjust will of another: and if he that judges, judges amiss in his own, or any other case, he is answerable for it to the rest of mankind.

It is often asked as a mighty objection, "where are, or ever were there any men in such a state of nature?" To which it may suffice as an answer at present, that since all princes and rulers of independent governments, all through the world, are in a state of nature, it is plain the world never was, nor ever will be, without numbers of men in that state. I have named all governors of independent communities, whether they are, or are not, in league with others: for it is not every compact that puts an end to the state of nature between men, but only this one of agreeing together mutually to enter into one community, and make one body politic; other promises and compacts men may make one with another, and yet still be in the state of nature. The promises and bargains for truck, &c. between the two men in the desert island, mentioned by

Garcilasso de la Vega, in his history of Peru; or between a Swiss and an Indian, in the woods of America; are binding to them, though they are perfectly in a state of nature, in reference to one another: for truth and keeping of faith belongs to men as men, and not as members of society. . . .

OF THE STATE OF WAR

. . . And here we have the plain "difference between the state of nature and the state of war," which however some men have confounded, are as far distant, as a state of peace, good-will, mutual assistance and preservation, and a state of enmity, malice, violence and mutual destruction, are one from another. Men living together according to reason, without a common superiour on earth, with authority to judge between them, is properly the state of nature. But force, or a declared design of force, upon the person of another, where there is no common superiour on earth to appeal to for relief, is the state of war. . . .

OF PROPERTY

Whether we consider natural reason, which tells us, that men, being once born, have a right to their preservation, and consequently to meat and drink, and such other things as nature affords for their subsistence; or revelation, which gives us an account of those grants God made of the world to Adam, and to Noah, and his sons; it is very clear, that God, as king David says, Psal. cxv. 16. "has given the earth to the children of men;" given it to mankind in common. But this being supposed, it seems to some a very great difficulty how any one should ever come to have a property in any thing. . . .

Though the earth, and all inferiour creatures, be common to all men, yet every man has a property in his own person: this nobody has any right to but himself. The labour of his body, and the work of his hands, we may say, are properly his. Whatsoever then he removes out of the state that nature hath provided, and left it in, he hath mixed his labour with, and joined to it something that is his own, and thereby makes it his property. It being by him removed from the common state nature hath placed it in, it hath by this labour something annexed to it, that excludes the common right of other men. For this labour being the unquestionable property of the labourer, no man but he can have a right to what that is once joined to, at least where there is enough, and as good, left in common for others. . . .

God gave the world to men in common; but since he gave it them for their benefit, and the greatest conveniencies of life they were capable to draw from it, it cannot be supposed he meant it should always remain common and uncultivated. He gave it to the use of the industrious and rational, (and labour was to be his title to it) not to the fancy or covetousness of the quarrelsome and contentious. He that had as good left for his improvement, as was already taken up, needed not complain, ought not to meddle with what was already improved by another's labour: if he did, it is plain he desired the benefit of another's pains, which he had no right to, and not the ground which God had given him in common with others to labour on, and whereof there was as good left, as that already possessed, and more than he knew what to do with, or his industry could reach to. . . .

And thus, without supposing any private dominion, and property in Adam, over all the world, exclusive of all other men, which can no way be proved, nor any one's property be made out from it; but supposing the world given, as it was, to the children of men in common, we see how labour could make men distinct titles to several parcels of it, for their private uses; wherein there could be no doubt of right, no room for quarrel. . . .

But because no political society can be, nor subsist, without having in itself the power to preserve the property, and, in order thereunto, punish the offences of all those of that society; there and there only is political society, where every one of the members hath quitted his natural power, resigned it up into the hands of the community in all cases that excludes him not from appealing for protection to the law established by it. And thus all private judgment of every particular member being excluded, the community comes to be umpire by settled standing rules, indifferent, and the same to all parties; and by men having authority from the community, for the execution of those rules, decides all the differences that may happen between any members of that society concerning any matter of right; and punishes those offences which any member hath committed against the society, with such penalties as the law has established, whereby it is easy to discern, who are, and who are not, in political society together. Those who are united into one body, and have a common established law and judicature to appeal to, with authority to decide controversies between them, and punish offenders, are in civil society one with another: but those who have no such common appeal, I mean on earth, are still in the state of nature, each being, where there is no other, judge for himself, and executioner: which is, as I have before showed, the perfect state of nature.

And thus the commonwealth comes by a power to set down what punishment shall belong to the several transgressions which they think worthy of it, committed amongst the members of that society, (which is the power of making laws) as well as it has the power to punish any injury done unto any of its members, by any one that is not of it, (which is the power of war and peace;) and all this for the preservation of the property of all the members of that society, as far as is possible. But though every man who has entered into civil society, and is become a member of any commonwealth, has thereby quitted his power to punish offences against the law of nature, in prosecution of his own private judgment; yet with the judgment of offences, which he has given up to the legislative in all cases, where he can appeal to the magistrate, he has given a right to the commonwealth to employ his force, for the execution of the judgments of the commonwealth, whenever he shall be called to it; which indeed are his own judgments, they being made by himself, or his representative. And herein we have the original of the legislative and executive power of civil society, which is to judge by standing laws, how far offences are to be punished, when committed within the commonwealth; and also to determine. by occasional judgments founded on the present circumstances of the fact, how far injuries from without are to be vindicated; and in both these to employ all the force of all the members, when there shall be need.

Whenever therefore any number of men are so united into one society, as to quit every one his executive power of the law of nature, and to resign it to the public, there and there only is a political, or civil society. And this is done, wherever any number of men, in the state of nature, enter into society to make one people, one body politic, under one supreme government; or else when any one joins himself to, and incorporates with any government already made: for hereby he authorizes the society, or, which is all one, the legislative thereof, to make laws for him, as the public good of the society shall require; to the execution whereof, his own assistance (as to his own degrees) is due. And this puts men out of a state of nature into that of a commonwealth, by setting up a judge on earth, with authority to determine all the controversies, and redress the injuries that may happen to any member of the commonwealth: which judge is the legislative, or magistrate appointed by it. And wherever there are any number of men, however associated, that have no such decisive power to appeal to, there they are still in the state of nature.

Hence it is evident, that absolute monarchy, which by some men is counted the only government in the world, is indeed inconsistent with civil society, and so can be no form of civil government at all: for the end of civil society being to avoid and remedy these inconveniencies of the state of nature, which necessarily follow from every man being judge in his own case, by setting up a known authority, to which every one of that society may appeal upon any injury received, or controversy that may arise, and which every one of the society ought to obey; wherever any persons are, who have not such an authority to appeal to for the decision of any difference between them, there those persons are still in the state of nature; and so is every absolute prince, in respect of those who are under his dominion.

For he being supposed to have all, both legislative and executive power in himself alone, there is no judge to be found, no appeal lies open to any one, who may fairly, and indifferently, and with authority decide, and from whose decision relief and redress may be expected of any injury or inconveniency that may be suffered from the prince, or by his order: so that such a man, however intitled, czar, or grand seignior, or how you please, is as much in the state of nature, with all under his dominion, as he is with the rest of mankind: for wherever any two men are, who have no standing rule, and common judge to appeal to on earth, for the determination of controversies of right betwixt them, there they are still in the state of nature, and under all the inconveniencies of it, with only this woful difference to the subject, or rather slave of an absolute prince; that whereas in the ordinary state of nature he has a liberty to judge of his right, and, according to the best of his power, to maintain it; now, whenever his property is invaded by the will and order of his monarch, he has not only no appeal, as those in society ought to have, but, as if he were degraded from the common state of rational creatures, is denied a liberty to judge of, or to defend his right; and so is exposed to all the misery and inconveniencies, that a man can fear from one, who being in the unrestrained state of nature, is yet corrupted with flattery, and armed with power. . . .

OF THE BEGINNING OF POLITICAL SOCIETIES

Men being, as has been said, by nature, all free, equal, and independent, no one can be put out of this estate, and subjected to the political power of another, without his own consent. The only way, whereby any one divests himself of his natural liberty, and puts on the bonds of civil society, is by agreeing with other men to join and unite into a community, for their comfortable, safe, and peaceable living one amongst another, in a secure enjoyment of their properties, and a greater security against any, that are not of it. This any number of men may do, because it injures not the freedom of the rest; they are left as they were in the liberty of the state of nature. When any number of men have so consented to make one community or government, they are thereby presently incorporated, and make one body politic, wherein the majority have a right to act and conclude the rest.

For when any number of men have, by the consent of every individual, made a community, they have thereby made that community one body, with a power to act as one body, which is only by the will and determination of the majority: for that which acts any community, being only the consent of the individuals of it, and it being necessary to that which is one body to move one way; it is necessary the body should move that way whither the greater force carries it, which is the consent of the majority: or else it is impossible it should act or continue one body, one community, which the consent of every individual that united into it, agreed that it should; and so every one is bound by that consent to be concluded by the majority. And therefore we see, that in assemblies, impowered to act by positive laws, where no number is set by that positive law which impowers them, the act of the majority passes for the act of the whole, and of course determines; as having, by the law of nature and reason, the power of the whole.

And thus every man, by consenting with others to make one body politic under one government, puts himself under an obligation, to every one of that society, to submit to the determination of the majority, and to be concluded by it; or else this original compact, whereby he with others incorporate into one society, would signify nothing, and be no compact, if he be left free, and under no other ties than he was in before in the state of nature. For what appearance would there be of any compact? what new engagement if he were no farther tied by any decrees of the society, than he himself thought fit, and did actually consent to? This would be still as great a liberty, as he himself had before his compact, or any one else in the state of nature hath, who may submit himself, and consent to any acts of it if he thinks fit.

For if the consent of the majority shall not, in reason, be received as the act of the whole, and conclude every individual; nothing but the consent of every individual can make any thing to be the act of the whole: but such a consent is next to impossible ever to be had, if we consider the infirmities of health, and avocations of business, which in a number, though much less than that of a commonwealth, will necessarily keep many away from the public assembly. To which if we add the variety of opinions, and contrariety of interest, which unavoidably happen in all collections of men, the coming into society upon such terms would be only like Cato's coming into the theatre, only to go out again. Such a constitution as this would make the mighty leviathan of a shorter duration, than the feeblest creatures, and not let it outlast the day it was born in: which cannot be supposed, till we can think, that rational creatures should desire and constitute societies only to be dissolved; for where the majority cannot conclude the rest, there they cannot act as one body, and consequently will be immediately dissolved again.

Whosoever therefore out of a state of nature unite into a community, must be understood to give up all the power, necessary to the ends for which they unite into society, to the majority of the community, unless they expressly agreed in any number greater than the majority. And this is done by barely agreeing to unite into one political society, which is all the compact that is, or needs be, between the individuals, that enter into, or make up a commonwealth. And thus that, which begins and actually constitutes any political society, is nothing, but the consent of any number of freemen capable of a majority, to unite and incorporate into such a society. And this is that, and that only, which did, or could give beginning to any lawful government in the world. . . .

OF THE ENDS OF POLITICAL SOCIETY AND GOVERNMENT

If man in the state of nature be so free, as has been said; if he be absolute lord of his own person and possessions, equal to the greatest, and subject to nobody, why will he part with his freedom? why will he give up his empire, and subject himself to the dominion and control of any other power? To which it is obvious to answer, that though in the state of nature he hath such a right, yet the enjoyment of it is very uncertain, and constantly exposed to the invasion of others; for all being kings as much as he, every man his equal, and the greater part no strict observers of equity and justice, the enjoyment of the property he has in this state is very unsafe, very unsecure. This makes him willing to quit a condition, which, however free, is full of fears and continual dangers: and it is not without reason, that he seeks out, and is willing to join in society with others, who are already united, or have a mind to unite, for the mutual preservation of their lives, liberties, and estates, which I call by the general name, property.

The great and chief end, therefore, of men's uniting into commonwealths, and putting themselves under government, is the preservation of their property. To which in the state of nature there are many things wanting.

First, There wants an established, settled, known law, received and allowed by common consent to be the standard of right and wrong, and the common measure to decide all controversies between them: for though the law of nature be plain and intelligible to all rational creatures; yet men being biassed by their interest, as well as ignorant for want of studying it, are not apt to allow for it as a law binding to them in the application of it to their particular cases.

Secondly, In the state of nature there wants a known and indifferent judge, with authority to determine all differences according to the established law: for every one in that state being both judge and executioner of the law of nature, men being partial to themselves, passion and revenge is very apt to carry them too far, and with too much heat, in their own cases; as well as negligence, and unconcernedness, to make them too remiss in other men's.

Thirdly, In the state of nature, there often wants power to back and support the sentence when right, and to give it due execution. They who by any injustice offend, will seldom fail, where they are able, by force to make good their injustice; such resistance many times makes the punishment dangerous, and frequently destructive, to those who attempt it.

Thus mankind, notwithstanding all the privileges of the state of nature, being but in an ill condition, while they remain in it, are quickly driven into society. Hence it comes to pass that we seldom find any number of men live any time together in this state. The inconveniencies that they are therein exposed to, by the irregular and uncertain exercise of the power every man has of punishing the transgressions of others, make them take sanctuary under the established laws of government, and therein seek the preservation of their property. It is this makes them so willingly give up every one his single power of punishing, to be exercised by such alone, as shall be appointed to it amongst them; and by such rules as the community, or those authorized by them to that purpose, shall agree on. And in this we have the original right of both the legislative and executive power, as well as of the governments and societies themselves.

For in the state of nature, to omit the liberty he has of innocent delights, a man has two powers.

The first is to do whatsoever he thinks fit for the preservation of himself and others within the permission of the law of nature: by which law, common to them all, he and all the rest of mankind are one community, make up one society, distinct from all other creatures. And, were it not for the corruption and viciousness of degenerate men, there would be no need of any other; no necessity that men should separate from this great and natural community, and by positive agreements combine into smaller and divided associations.

The other power a man has in the state of nature, is the power to punish the crimes committed against that law. Both these he gives up, when he joins in a private, if I may so call it, or particular politic society, and incorporates into any commonwealth, separate from the rest of mankind.

The first power, viz. "of doing whatsover he thought fit for the preservation of himself," and the rest of mankind, he gives up to be regulated by laws made by the society, so far forth as the preservation of himself and the rest of that society shall require; which laws of the society in many things confine the liberty he had by the law of nature.

Secondly, The power of punishing he wholly gives up, and engages his natural force, (which he might before employ in the execution of the law of nature, by his own single authority, as he thought fit) to assist the executive power of the society, as the law thereof shall require: for being now in a new state, wherein he is to enjoy many conveniencies, from the labour, assistance, and society of others in the same community, as well as protection from its whole strength; he is to part also, with as much of his natural liberty, in providing for himself, as the good, prosperity, and safety of the society shall require; which is not only necessary, but just, since the other members of the society do the like.

But though men, when they enter into society, give up the equality, liberty, and executive power they had in the state of nature, into the hands of the society, to be so far disposed of by the legislative, as the good of the society shall require; yet it being only with an intention in every one the better to preserve himself, his liberty and property; (for no rational creature can be supposed to change his condition with an intention to be worse) the power of the society, or legislative constituted by them, can never be supposed to extend farther, than the common good; but is obliged to secure every one's property, by providing against those three defects above-mentioned, that made the state of nature so unsafe and uneasy. And so whoever has the legislative or supreme power of any commonwealth, is bound to govern by established standing laws, promulgated and known to the people, and not by extemporary decrees; by indifferent and upright judges, who are to decide controversies by those laws; and to employ the force of the community at home, only in the execution of such laws; or abroad to prevent or redress foreign injuries, and secure the community from inroads and invasion. And all this to be directed to no other end, but the peace, safety, and public good of the people.

OF THE FORMS OF A COMMONWEALTH

. . . By commonwealth, I must be understood all along to mean, not a democracy, or any form of government; but any independent community, which the Latines signified by the word civitas; to which the word which best answers in our language, is commonwealth, and most properly expresses such a society of men, which community or city in English does not: for there may be subordinate communities in government; and city amongst us has quite a different notion from commonwealth: and therefore, to avoid ambiguity, I crave leave to use the word commonwealth in that sense, in which I find it used by king James the first: and I take it to be its genuine signification; which if any body dislike, I consent with him to change it for a better.

OF THE EXTENT OF THE LEGISLATIVE POWER

The great end of men's entering into society being the enjoyment of their properties in peace and safety, and the great instrument and means of that being the laws established in that society; the first and fundamental positive law of all commonwealths is the establishing of the legislative power; as the first and fundamental natural law, which is to govern even the legislative itself, is the preservation of the society, and (as far as will consist with the public good) of every person in it. This legislative is not only the supreme power of the commonwealth, but sacred and unalterable in the hands where the community have once placed it; nor can any edict of any body else, in what form soever conceived, or by what power soever backed, have the force and obligation of a law, which has not its sanction from that legislative which the public has chosen and appointed; for without this the law could not have that, which is absolutely necessary to its being a law, the consent of the society; over whom nobody can have a power to make laws, but by their own consent, and by authority received from them. And therefore all the obedience, which by the most solemn ties any one can be obliged to pay, ultimately terminates in this supreme power, and is directed by those laws which it enacts; nor can any oaths to any foreign power whatsoever, or any domestic subordinate power, discharge any member of the society from his obedience to the legislative, acting pursuant to their trust; nor oblige him to any obedience contrary to the laws so enacted, or farther than they do allow; it being ridiculous to imagine one can be tied ultimately to obey any power in the society, which is not supreme.

Though the legislative, whether placed in one or more, whether it be always in being, or only by intervals, though it be the supreme power in every commonwealth; yet,

First, It is not, nor can possibly be absolutely arbitrary over the lives and fortunes of the people: for it being but the joint power of every member of the society given up to that person, or assembly, which is legislator; it can be no more than those persons had in a state of nature before they entered into society, and gave up to the community: for nobody can transfer to another more power than he has in himself; and nobody has an absolute arbitrary power over himself, or over any other, to destroy his own life, or take away the life or property of another. A man, as has been proved, cannot subject himself to the arbitrary power of another; and having in the state of nature no arbitrary power over the life, liberty, or possession of another, but only so much as the law of nature gave him for the preservation of himself and the rest of mankind; this is all he doth, or can give up to the commonwealth, and by it to the legislative power, so that the legislative can have no more than this. Their power, in the utmost bounds of it, is limited to the public good of the society. It is a power, that hath no other end but preservation, and therefore can never have a right to destroy, enslave, or designedly to impoverish the subjects. The obligations of the law of nature cease not in society, but only in many cases are drawn closer, and have by human laws known penalties annexed to them, to enforce their observation. Thus the law of nature stands as an eternal rule to all men, legislators as well as others. The rules that they make for other men's actions, must, as well as their own and other men's actions, be conformable to the laws of nature, i.e. to the will of God, of which that is a declaration; and the "fundamental law of nature being the preservation of mankind," no human sanction can be good, or valid against it.

Secondly, The legislative or supreme authority cannot assume to itself a power to rule, by extemporary, arbitrary decrees; but is bound to dispense justice, and to decide the rights of the subject, by promulgated, standing laws, and known authorized judges. For the law of nature being unwritten, and so no-where to be found, but in the minds of men; they who through passion, or interest, shall miscite, or misapply it, cannot so easily be convinced of their mistake, where there is no established judge: and so it serves not, as it ought, to determine the rights, and fence the properties of those that live under it; especially where every one is judge, interpreter, and executioner of it too, and that in his own case: and he that has right on his side, having ordinarily but his own single strength, hath not force enough to defend himself from injuries, or to punish delinquents. To avoid these inconveniencies, which disorder men's properties in the state of nature, men unite into societies, that they may have the united strength of the whole society to secure and defend their properties, and may have standing rules to bound it, by which every one may know what is his. To this end it is that men give up all their natural power to the society which they enter into, and the community put the legislative power into such hands as they think fit: with this trust, that they shall be governed by declared laws, or else their peace, quiet, and property will still be at the same uncertainty, as it was in the state of nature.

Absolute arbitrary power, or governing without settled standing laws, can neither of them consist with the ends of society and government, which men would not quit the freedom of the state of nature for, and tie themselves up under, were it not to preserve their lives, liberties, and fortunes, and by stated rules of right and property to secure their peace and quiet. It cannot be supposed that they should intend, had they a power so to do, to give to any one, or more, an absolute arbitrary power over their persons and estates, and put a force into the magistrate's hand to execute his unlimited will arbitrarily upon them. This were to put themselves into a worse condition than the state of nature, wherein they had a liberty to defend their right against the injuries of others, and were upon equal terms of force to maintain it, whether invaded by a single man, or many in combination. Whereas by supposing they have given up themselves to the absolute arbitrary power and will of a legislator, they have disarmed themselves, and armed him, to make a prey of them when he pleases; he being in a much worse condition, who is exposed to the arbitarary power of one man, who has the command of 100,000, than he that is exposed to the arbitrary power of 100,000 single men; nobody being secure, that his will, who has such a command, is better than that of other men, though his force be 100,000 times stronger. And therefore, whatever form the commonwealth is under, the ruling power ought to govern by declared and received laws, and not by extemporary dictates and undetermined resolutions: for then mankind will be in a far worse condition than in the state of nature, if they shall have armed one or a few men with the joint power of a multitude, to force them to obey at pleasure the exorbitant and unlimited degrees of their sudden thoughts, or unrestrained, and till that moment unknown wills, without having any measures set down which may guide and justify their actions: for all the power the government has, being only for the good of the society, as it ought not to be arbitrary and at pleasure, so it ought to be exercised by established and promulgated laws; that both the people may know their duty, and be safe and secure within the limits of the law: and the rulers too kept within their bounds, and not be tempted, by the power they have in their hands, to employ it to such purposes, and by such measures, as they would not have known, and own not willingly.

Thirdly, The supreme power cannot take from any man part of his property without his own consent, for the preservation of property being the end of government, and that for which men enter into society, it necessarily supposes and requires, that the people should have property, without which they must be supposed to lose that, by entering into society, which was the end for which they entered into it; too gross an absurdity for any man to own. Men therefore in society have property, they have such right to the goods, which by the law of the community are their's, that no body hath a right to take their substance or any part of it from them, without their own consent; without this they have no property at all; for I have truly no property in that, which another can by right take from me, when he pleases, against my consent. Hence it is a mistake to think, that the supreme or legislative power of any commonwealth can do what it will, and dispose of the estates of the subject arbitrarily, or take any part of them at pleasure. This is not much to be feared in governments where the legislative consists, wholly or in part, in assemblies which are variable, whose members, upon the dissolution of the assembly, are subjects under the common laws of their country, equally with the rest. But in governments, where the legislative is in one lasting assembly always in being, or in one man, as in absolute monarchies, there is danger still, that they will think themselves to have a distinct interest from the rest of the community; and so will be apt to increase their own riches and power, by taking what they think fit from the people: for a man's property is not at all secure, though there be good and equitable laws to set the bounds of it between him and his fellow-subjects, if he who commands those subjects, have power to take from any private man, what part he pleases of his property, and use and dispose of it as he thinks good.

But government, into whatsover hands it is put, being, as I have before showed, intrusted with this condition, and for this end, that men might have and secure their properties; the prince, or senate, however it may have power to make laws, for the regulating of property between the subjects one amongst another, yet can never have a power to take to themselves the whole, or any part of the subject's property, without their own consent: for this would be in effect to leave them no property at all. And to let us see, that even absolute power, where it is necessary, is not arbitrary by being absolute, but is still limited by that reason, and confined to those ends, which required it in some cases to be absolute, we need look no farther than the common practice of martial discipline: for the preservation of the army, and in it of the whole commonwealth, requires an absolute obedience to the command of every superior officer, and it is justly death to disobey or dispute the most dangerous or unreasonable of them; but yet we see, that neither the serjeant, that could command a soldier to march up to the mouth of a cannon, or stand in a breach, where he is almost sure to perish, can command that soldier to give him one penny of his money; nor the general, that can condemn him to death for deserting his post, or for not obeying the most desperate orders, can yet, with all his absolute power of life and death, dispose of one farthing of that soldier's estate, or seize one jot of his goods; whom yet he can command any thing, and hang for the least disobedience: because such a blind obedience is necessary to that end, for which the commander has his power viz. the preservation of the rest; but the disposing of his goods has nothing to do with it.

It is true, governments cannot be supported without great charge, and it is fit every one who enjoys his share of the protection, should pay out of his estate his proportion for the maintenance of it. But still it must be with his own consent, i.e. the consent of the majority, giving it either by themselves, or their representatives chosen by them: for if any one shall claim a power to lay and levy taxes on the people, by his own authority, and without such consent of the people, he thereby invades the fundamental law of property, and subverts the end of government: for what property have I in that, which another may by right take, when he pleases, to himself?

Fourthly, The legislative cannot transfer the power of making laws to any other hands: for it being but a delegated power from the people, they who have it cannot pass it over to others. The people alone can appoint the form of the commonwealth, which is by constituting the legislative, and appointing in whose hands that shall be. And when the people have said, we will submit to rules, and be governed by laws made by such men, and in such forms, nobody else can say other men shall make laws for them; nor can the people be bound by any laws, but such as are enacted by those whom they have chosen, and authorized to make laws for them. The power of the legislative being derived from the people by a positive voluntary grant and institution, can be no other than what that positive grant conveyed, which being only to make laws, and not to make legislators, the legislative can have no power to transfer their authority of making laws and place it in other hands. . . .

OF THE SUBORDINATION OF THE POWERS OF THE COMMONWEALTH

Though in a constituted commonwealth, standing upon its own basis, and acting according to its own nature, that is, acting for the preservation of the community, there can be but one supreme power, which is the legislative, to which all the rest are and must be subordinate; yet the legislative being only a fiduciary power to act for certain ends, there remains still "in the people a supreme power to remove or alter the legislative," when they find the legislative act contrary to the trust respond in them: for all power given with trust for the attaining an end, being limited by that end; whenever that end is manifestly neglected or opposed, the trust must necessarily be forfeited, and the power devolve into the hands of those that gave it, who may place it anew where they shall think best for their safety and security. And thus the community perpetually retains a supreme power of saving themselves from the attempts and designs of any body, even of their legislators, whenever they shall be so foolish, or so wicked, as to lay and carry on designs against the liberties and properties of the subject: for no man, or society of men, having a power to deliver up their preservation, or consequently the means of it, to the absolute will and arbitarary dominion of another; whenever any one shall go about to bring them into such a slavish condition, they will always have a right to preserve what they have not a power to part with; and to rid themselves of those who invade this fundamental, sacred, and unalterable law of self-preservation, for which they entered into society. And thus the community may be said in this respect to be always the supreme power, but not as considered under any form of government, because this power of the people can never take place till the government be dissolved.

In all cases, whilst the government subsists, the legislative is the supreme power: for what can give laws to another, must needs be superior to him; and since the legislative is no otherwise legislative of the society, but by the right it has to make laws for all the parts, and for every member of the society, prescribing rules to their actions, and giving power of execution, where they are transgressed; the legislative must needs be the supreme, and all other powers, in any members or parts of the society, derived from and subordinate to it.

In some commonwealths, where the legislative is not always in being, and the executive is vested in a single person, who has also a share in the legislative; there that single person in a very tolerable sense may also be called supreme; not that he has in himself all the supreme power, which is that of law-making; but because he has in him the supreme execution, from whom all inferiour magistrates derive all their several subordinate powers, or at least the greatest part of them: having also no legislative superiour to him, there being no law to be made without his consent, which cannot be expected should ever subject him to the other part of the legislative, he is properly enough in this sense supreme. But yet it is to be observed, that though oaths of allegiance and fealty are taken to him, it is not to him as supreme legislator, but as supreme executor of the law, made by a joint power of him with others: allegiance being nothing but an obedience according to law, which when he violates, he has no right to obedience, nor can claim it otherwise, than as the public person invested with the power of the law; and so is to be considered as the image, phantom, or representative of the commonwealth, acted by the will of the society, declared in its laws; and thus he has no will, no power, but that of the law. But when he quits this representation, this public will, and acts by his own private will, he degrades himself, and is but a single private person without power, and without will, that has no right to obedience; the members owing no obedience but to the public will of the society.

The executive power, placed any where but in a person that has also a share in the legislative, is visibly subordinate and accountable to it, and may be at pleasure changed and displaced; so that it is not the supreme executive power that is exempt from subordination: but the supreme executive power vested in one, who having a share in the legislative, has no distinct superiour legislative to be subordinate and accountable to, farther than he himself shall join and consent; so that he is no more subordinate than he himself shall think fit, which one may certainly conclude will be but very little. Of other ministerial and subordinate powers in a commonwealth, we need not speak, they being so multiplied with infinite variety, in the different customs and constitutions of distinct commonwealths, that it is impossible to give a particular account of them all. Only thus much, which is necessary to our present purpose, we may take notice of concerning them, that they have no manner of authority, any of them, beyond what is by positive grant and commission delegated to them, and are all of them accountable to some other power in the commonwealth.

It is not necessary, no, nor so much as convenient, that the legislative should be always in being; but absolutely necessary that the executive power should; because there is not always need of new laws to be made, but always need of execution of the laws that are made. When the legislative hath put the execution of the laws they make into other hands, they have a power still to resume it out of those hands, when they find cause, and to punish for any male administration against the laws. The same holds also in regard of the federative power, that and the executive being both ministerial and subordinate to the legislative, which, as has been showed, in a constituted commonwealth is the supreme. The legislative also in this case being supposed to consist of several persons, (for if it be a single person, it cannot but be always in being, and so will, as supreme, naturally have the supreme executive power, together with the legislative) may assemble, and exercise their legislature, at the times that either their original constitution, or their own adjournment, appoints, or when they please; if neither of these hath appointed any time, or there be no other way prescribed to convoke them: for the supreme power being placed in them by the people, it is always in them, and they may exercise it when they please, unless by their original constitution they are limited to certain seasons, or by an act of their supreme power they have adjourned to a certain time; and when that time comes, they have a right to assemble and act again.

If the legislative, or any part of it, be made up of representatives chosen for that time by the people, which afterwards return into the ordinary state of subjects, and have no share in the legislature but upon a new choice, this power of choosing must also be exercised by the people, either at certain appointed seasons, or else when they are summoned to it; and in this latter case the power of convoking the legislative is ordinarily placed in the executive, and has one of these two limitations in respect of time: that either the original constitution requires their assembling and acting at certain intervals, and then the executive power does nothing but ministerially issue directions for their electing and assembling according to due forms; or else it is left to his prudence to call them by new elections, when the occasions, or exigencies of the public require the amendment of old, or making of new laws, or the redress or prevention of any inconveniencies, that lie on, or threaten the people.

It may be demanded here, What if the executive power, being possessed of the force of the commonwealth, shall make use of that force to hinder the meeting and acting of the legislative, when the original constitution, or the public exigencies require it? I say, using force upon the people without authority, and contrary to the trust put in him that does so, is a state of war with the people, who have a right to reinstate their legislative in the exercise of their power: for having erected a legislative, with an intent they should exercise the power of making laws, either at certain set times, or when there is need of it; when they are hindered by any force from what is so necessary to the society, and wherein the safety and preservation of the people consists, the people have a right to remove it by force. In all states and conditions, the true remedy of force without authority, is to oppose force to it. The use of force without authority, always puts him that uses it into a state of war, as the aggressor, and renders him liable to be treated accordingly. . . .

"Salus populi suprema lex," is certainly so just and fundamental a rule, that he, who sincerely follows it, cannot dangerously err. If therefore the executive, who has the power of convoking the legislative, observing rather the true proportion than fashion of representation, regulates not by old custom, but true reason, the number of members in all places that have a right to be distinctly represented, which no part of the people, however incorporated, can pretend to, but in proportion to the assistance which it affords to the public; it cannot be judged to have set up a new legislative, but to have restored the old and true one, and to have rectified the disorders which succession of time had insensibly, as well as inevitably introduced; for it being the interest as well as intention of the people, to have a fair and equal representative; whoever brings it nearest to that, is an undoubted friend to, and establisher of the government, and cannot miss the consent and approbation of the community; prerogative being nothing but a power in the hands of the prince to provide for the public good, in such cases, which depending upon unforeseen and uncertain occurrences, certain and unalterable laws could not safely direct; whatsoever shall be done manifestly for the good of the people, and the establishing the government upon its true foundations, is, and always will be, just prerogative. The power of erecting new corporations, and therewith new representatives, carries with it a supposition that in time the measures of representation might vary, and those places have a just right to be represented which before had none; and by the same reason, those cease to have a right, and be too inconsiderable for such a privilege, which before had it. It is not a change from the present state, which perhaps corruption or decay has introduced, that makes an inroad upon the government; but the tendency of it to injure or oppress the people, and to set up one part or party, with a distinction from, and an unequal subjection of the rest. Whatsoever cannot but be acknowledged to be of advantage to the society, and people in general, upon just and lasting measures, will always, when done, justify itself; and whenever the people shall choose their representatives upon just and undeniably equal measures, suitable to the original frame of the government, it cannot be doubted to be the will and act of the society, whoever permitted or caused them so to do. . . .

OF THE DISSOLUTION OF GOVERNMENT

He that will with any clearness speak of the dissolution of government, ought in the first place to distinguish between the dissolution of the society and the dissolution of the government. That which makes the community, and brings men out of the loose state of nature into one politic society, is the agreement which every one has with the rest to incorporate, and act as one body, and so be one distinct commonwealth. The usual, and almost only way whereby this union is dissolved, is the inroad of foreign force making a conquest upon them: for in that case, (not being able to maintain and support themselves, as one entire and independent body) the union belonging to that body which consisted therein, must necessarily cease, and so every one return to the state he was in before, with a liberty to shift for himself, and provide for his own safety, as he thinks fit, in some other society. Whenever the society is dissolved, it is certain the government of that society cannot remain. Thus conquerors' swords often cut up governments by the roots, and mangle societies to pieces, separating the subdued or scattered multitude from the protection of, and dependence on, that society which ought to have preserved them from violence. The world is too well instructed in, and too forward to allow of, this way of dissolving of governments, to need any more to be said of it; and there wants not much argument to prove, that where the society is dissolved, the government cannot remain; that being as impossible, as for the frame of a house to subsist when the materials of it are scattered and dissipated by a whirlwind, or jumbled into a confused heap by an earthquake.

Besides this overturning from without, governments are dissolved from within.

First, When the legislative is altered. Civil society being a state of peace, amongst those who are of it, from whom the state of war is excluded by the umpirage, which they have provided in their legislative, for the ending all differences that may arise amongst any of them; it is in their legislative, that the members of a commonwealth are united, and combined together into one coherent living body. This is the soul that gives form, life, and unity to the commonwealth: from hence the several members have their mutual influence, sympathy, and connexion; and therefore, when the legislative is broken, or dissolved, dissolution and death follows: for, the essence and union of the society consisting in having one will, the legislative, when once established by the majority, has the declaring, and as it were keeping of that will. The constitution of the legislative is the first and fundamental act of society, whereby provision is made for the continuation of their union, under the direction of persons, and bonds of laws, made by persons authorized thereunto, by the consent and appointment of the people; without which no one man, or number of men, amongst them, can have authority of making laws that shall be binding to the rest. When any one, or more, shall take upon them to make laws, whom the people have not appointed so to do, they make laws without authority, which the people are not therefore bound to obey; by which means they come again to be out of subjection, and may constitute to themselves a new legislative, as they think best, being in full liberty to resist the force of those, who without authority would impose any thing upon them. Every one is at the disposure of his own will, when those who had, by the delegation of the society, the declaring of the public will, are excluded from it, and others usurp the place, who have no such authority or delegation.

This being usually brought about by such in the commonwealth who misuse the power they have, it is hard to consider it aright, and know at whose door to lay it, without knowing the form of government in which it happens. Let us suppose then the legislative placed in the concurrence of three distinct persons.

1. A single hereditary person, having the constant, supreme, executive power, and with it the power of convoking and dissolving the other two, within certain periods of time.

2. An assembly of hereditary nobility.

3. An assembly of representatives chosen pro tempore, by the people. Such a form of government supposed, it is evident,

First, That when such a single person, or prince, sets up his own arbitrary will in place of the laws, which are the will of the society, declared by the legislative, then the legislative is changed: for that being in effect the legislative, whose rules and laws are put in execution, and required to be obeyed; when other laws are set up, and other rules pretended, and enforced, than what the legislative, constituted by the society, have enacted, it is plain that the legislative is changed, Whoever introduces new laws, not being thereunto authorized, by the fundamental appointment of the society, or subverts the old; disowns and overturns the power by which they were made, and so sets up a new legislative.

Secondly, When the prince hinders the legislative from assembling in its due time, or from acting freely, pursuant to those ends for which it was constituted, the legislative is altered: for it is not a certain number of men, no, nor their meeting, unless they have also freedom of debating, and leisure of perfecting, what is for the good of the society, wherein the legislative consists: when these are taken away or altered, so as to deprive the society of the due exercise of their power, the legislative is truly altered: for it is not names that constitute governments, but the use and exercise of those powers that were intended to accompany them; so that he, who takes away the freedom, or hinders the acting of the legislative in its due seasons, in effect takes away the legislative, and puts an end to the government.

Thirdly, When, by the arbitrary power of the prince, the electors, or ways of election, are altered, without the consent, and contrary to the common interest of the people, there also the legislative is altered: for, if others than those whom the society hath authorized thereunto, do choose, or in another way than what the society hath prescribed, those chosen are not the legislative appointed by the people.

Fourthly, The delivery also of the people into the subjection of a foreign power, either by the prince, or by the legislative, is certainly a change of the legislative, and so a dissolution of the government: for the end why people entered into society being to be preserved one intire, free, independent society, to be governed by its own laws; this is lost, whenever they are given up into the power of another.

Why, in such a constitution as this, the dissolution of the government in these cases is to be imputed to the prince, is evident; because he, having the force, treasure, and offices of the state to employ, and often persuading himself, or being flattered by others, that as supreme magistrate, he is uncapable of control; he alone is in a condition to make great advances toward such changes, under pretence of lawful authority, and has it in his hands to terrify or suppress opposers, as factious, seditious, and enemies to the government: whereas no other part of the legislative, or people, is capable by themselves to attempt any alteration of the legislative, without open and visible rebellion, apt enough to be taken notice of; which, when it prevails, produces effects very little different from foreign conquest. Besides, the prince in such a form of government having the power of dissolving the other parts of the legislative, and thereby rendering them private persons, they can never in opposition to him, or without his concurrence, alter the legislative by a law, his consent being necessary to give any of their decrees that sanction. But yet, so far as the other parts of the legislative any way contribute to any attempt upon the government, and do either promote, or not (what lies in them) hinder such designs; they are guilty, and partake in this, which is certainly the greatest crime men can be guilty of one towards another.

There is one way more whereby such a government may be dissolved, and that is, when he who has the supreme executive power neglects and abandons that charge, so that the laws already made can no longer be put in execution. This is demonstratively to reduce all to anarchy, and so effectually to dissolve the government: for laws not being made for themselves, but to be, by their execution, the bonds of the society, to keep every part of the body politic in its due place and function; when that totally ceases, the government visibly ceases, and the people become a confused multitude, without order or connexion, Where there is no longer the administration of justice, for the securing of men's rights, nor any remaining power within the community to direct the force, or provide for the necessities of the public; there certainly is no government left. Where the laws cannot be executed, it is all one as if there were no laws; and a government without laws is, I suppose, a mystery in politics, inconceivable to human capacity, and inconsistent with human society.

In these and the like cases, when the government is dissolved, the people are at liberty to provide for themselves, by erecting a new legislative, differing from the other, by the change of persons, or form, or both, as they shall find it most for their safety and good: for the society can never, by the fault of another, lose the native and original right it has to preserve itself; which can only be done by a settled legislative, and a fair and impartial execution of the laws made by it. But the state of mankind is not so miserable that they are not capable of using this remedy, till it be too late to look for any. To tell people they may provide for themselves, by erecting a new legislative, when by oppression, artifice, or being delivered over to a foreign power, their old one is gone, is only to tell them, they may expect relief when it is too late, and the evil is past cure. This is in effect no more than to bid them first be slaves, and then to take care of their liberty; and when their chains are on, tell them, they may act like freemen. This, if barely so, is rather mockery than relief; and men can never be secure from tyranny, if there be no means to escape it till they are perfectly under it: and therefore it is, that they have not only a right to get out of it, but to prevent it.

There is, therefore, secondly, another way whereby governments are dissolved, and that is, when the legislative, or the prince, either of them, act contrary to their trust.

First, The legislative acts against the trust reposed in them, when they endeavour to invade the property of the subject, and to make themselves, or any part of the community, masters, or arbitrary disposers of the lives, liberties, or fortunes of the people.

The reason why men enter into society, is the preservation of their property; and the end why they choose and authorize a legislative, is, that there may be laws made, and rules set, as guards and fences to the properties of all the members of the society: to limit the power, and moderate the dominion, of every part and member of the society: for since it can never be supposed to be the will of the society, that the legislative should have a power to destroy that which every one designs to secure by entering into society, and for which the people submitted themselves to legislators of their own making; whenever the legislators endeavour to take away and destroy the property of the people, or to reduce them to slavery under arbitrary power, they put themselves into a state of war with the people, who are thereupon absolved from any farther obedience, and are left to the common refuge, which God hath provided for all men, against force and violence. . . .

If a controversy arise betwixt a prince and some of the people, in a matter where the law is silent, or doubtful, and the thing be of great consequence, I should think the proper umpire, in such a case, should be the body of the people: for in cases where the prince hath a trust reposed in him, and is dispensed from the common ordinary rules of the law; there, if any men find themselves aggrieved, and think the prince acts contrary to, or beyond that trust, who so proper to judge as the body of the people, (who, at first, lodged that trust in him) how far they meant it should extend? But if the prince, or whoever they be in the administration, decline that way of determination, the appeal then lies no where but to heaven; force between either persons, who have no known superior on earth, or which permits no appeal to a judge on earth, being properly a state of war, wherein the appeal lies only to heaven; and in that state the injured party must judge for himself, when he will think fit to make use of that appeal, and put himself upon it.

To conclude, The power that every individual gave the society, when he entered into it, can never revert to the individuals again, as long as the society lasts, but will always remain in the community; because without this there can be no community, no commonwealth, which is contrary to the original agreement: so also when the society hath placed the legislative in any assembly of men, to continue in them and their successors, with direction and authority for providing such successors, the legislative can never revert to the people whilst that government lasts; because, having provided a legislative with power to continue for ever, they have given up their political power to the legislative, and cannot resume it. But if they have set limits to the duration of their legislative, and made this supreme power in any person, or assembly, only temporary; or else, when by the miscarriages of those in authority, it is forfeited; upon the forfeiture, or at the determination of the time set, it reverts to the society, and the people have a right to act as supreme, and continue the legislative in themselves; or erect a new form, or under the old form place it in new hands, as they think good.

✍️ SECRET MEMORANDUM ON THE NETHERLANDS IN 1655
Hector Pierre Chanut

During the second half of the seventeenth century, at the very time when French absolutism was held up as the model for all progressive states, the wealthiest, most densely populated and most civilized country in all Europe conformed least to the new French dispensation. After a long struggle in the late sixteenth century, the seven northern provinces of the Spanish Netherlands, organized as a confederation, had succeeded in breaking loose from the Spanish crown. Their formal independence was not internationally recognized until 1648, by which time Amsterdam had become the great commercial hub of Europe. Meanwhile, the general prosperity and enterprise of the United Provinces of the Netherlands had become the envy of their formidable English and French neighbors and competitors.

The document below is a memorandum on the politics—internal and international—of the Netherlands, drawn up for the benefit of his successor by Hector Pierre Chanut, French ambassador to the United Provinces from 1653 to 1655. Chanut, trained as a lawyer, was a high-level official of the French government, bringing many years' experience as ambassador and diplomatic negotiator to his delicate Dutch assignment. Relations with the United Provinces had been strained ever since 1648, when the Dutch broke their alliance with France to conclude a separate peace with Spain. Moreover, Chanut's immediate predecessor had compromised himself by supporting too openly the (temporarily)

*losing faction in the endless seesaw battle between the oligarchy of the
province of Holland and the would-be monarch, the Stadtholder.
The situation was further complicated by the aftermath of a naval war
which the Netherlands had just lost to Cromwell's England. In any
case, the uneasy peace between France and the United Provinces was
to be broken in 1662; fifty years of ensuing intermittent warfare were
to leave the Netherlands among the nominal victors, yet were to
undermine their commercial predominance, which passed to Great Britain.*

For the sake of order, a report on a country comprising various kinds of governments
and having diverse interests should first consider such a country in and of itself, and
then bring out more clearly its attitudes toward the other states of Europe.

To begin with the principal aspects of this republic: the conflict, or, rather, the
jealousy over authority, between the province of Holland and the six other provinces
still persists. This creates something like two factions in the Assembly of the States-
General, where the six provinces, whenever they can unite their votes, carry the
decision. Yet it is but rarely that they all join forces. Even when they do pass a resolution over all the obstacles and delays which the Hollanders put in their way, experience shows that in matters of importance nothing is carried out without the consent
of Holland. This is true for two main reasons: in the first place, the latter province
by itself contributes more than half the cost of running the state. Its taxes are paid
promptly and in full, unlike those of the other provinces, which are tardy and are
never paid up. The other reason is that there are always some private and secret interests by which Holland controls a few of the deputies from other provinces. As soon
as cooperation among the six provinces ends, the fervor with which the adopted resolution was being carried out wanes, new business comes up, and the right time for
action slips by.

To hear the deputies of the six provinces arrogantly and indignantly inveigh against
Holland, one might believe that they would humiliate her and impose their opinions
by force. The Assembly resounds with the tumult of their disputes, which are not
always as seemly as respect for the place should require. All this anger, however, is
dissipated in words, and Holland is never forced to act against her own inclinations.
There are people, well versed in the affairs of the Low Countries, who maintain
that in a showdown Holland would back down and accept the decision of the other
provinces rather than permit an open break to occur. Yet it is doubtful whether she
would ever let the others take advantage of her. Since she has so many means of

Hector Pierre Chanut, "Mémoire secret de l'état auquel se trouvaient les Provinces-Unités des
Pays-Bas sur la fin de l'année 1655," in Louis André and Emile Bourgeois, eds., *Recueil des
Instructions données aux Ambassadeurs et Ministres de France depuis les Traités de Westphalie
jusqu'à la Révolution française*, (Paris: E. de Boccard, 1922), Vol. XXI (*Hollande*), Part I,
1648–1697, pp. 159–182. Translated by Peter Amann.

avoiding the alternatives of compliance or rupture, it is almost inconceivable that she should ever find herself in these straits.

One could scarcely find a more noteworthy test of this than that abusive bill by which the Prince of Orange was ousted from all his public offices, which Holland had granted to the Protector [Cromwell] over and above the [official] peace terms, without consultation of the provinces. The latter made a noise that resounded in every city assembly of the country; there were fiery oratory, protestations, bills fulminating against certain private persons with great influence in the province [of Holland]. Nonetheless this furious battery had no effect. When the Hollanders negotiated with Prince William of Nassau in October 1655 to assuage the complaints of the provinces by a compromise, [the agreement] nonetheless failed to nullify this act of dispossession.

From all of which, dealing with the provinces, one may formulate the rule that if concerted action is sought and Holland's vote is assured, it is superfluous to court the votes of the other six provinces. Yet if it is simply a question of preventing, of opposing, of thwarting, the provinces may be very useful: each one would have considerable influence in its own area, particularly if a revolution were to divide the members of the republic.

There is a special tie between Holland and Zeeland. While occasions for complaints arise on both sides, particularly over trade and over the West India Company (in which the Zeelanders had the largest share and the ruin of which they blame on the Hollanders), nonetheless these two provinces fraternize and support each other against the others, which have fewer commercial interests.

Gelderland . . . always seems to take the leadership of the other provinces against Holland. Yet because [Gelderland] contributes little in taxes though it sends numerous deputies to the Assembly, Holland can always count on a few of them as friends and can always blame the others for proposing grand and ambitious schemes to the realization of which they would contribute precious little.

As far as Holland is concerned, Friesland is less tractable than any of the other provinces. But because for the most part it is democratically governed and because the dispositions there are naturally proud and stubborn, [Friesland] is always preoccupied with her own affairs. Her governor, Prince William of Nassau, enjoys only a precarious authority which he is barely able to maintain among the factions that divide the cities.

Utrecht rarely parts company with Holland. The city [of Utrecht], only six miles distant from Amsterdam, has close relations with the latter, the families of the two cities being allied.

The province of Overijssel had in 1633 split into two factions when the cities of Zwolle and Campen had invested Prince William of Nassau with the government of the province during the minority of the Prince of Orange, an act which [the city of] Deventer opposed. In the dissension which threatened to lead to bloodshed, Holland encouraged and supported the citizens of Deventer, while several other provinces loyal to the House of Orange upheld the other two cities. Yet by the end of the year the affair was negotiated and a compromise reached between Prince William and the governing body of Holland. As this treaty called for the former's abdication from the government of Overijssel, one part of the province owed a debt of obligation to the Hollanders, while the other part blamed the other provinces for their inadequate support.

Groningen is governed by Prince William of Nassau who is very popular there. Since it is evident that this prince, notwithstanding anything he may say, is seeking to win over the Hollanders, one may conclude that the former province under its [present] governor will not rise to challenge Holland.

Just as by the Union of Utrecht each province claims its own sovereignty and has not surrendered it to the republic, so the chief cities of each province consider themselves free and sovereign in the administration of their own affairs to the extent that they claim complete control over any troops in their territory by order of the state. They elect their own mayors; they have independent councils and fill official appointments themselves, though there are some variations according to the differing customs of the provinces. Yet all of them are alike in having rival factions that gain power by defeating their opponents and in sending the deputies that make up the Estates of each of the provinces.

Any important proposals made at the Estates-General are forwarded for discussion to the councils of each city. Therefore, in the present state of the provinces, regardless of favors granted, it is impossible to control persons who are sufficiently powerful to insure the passage of a resolution. The provincial deputies to the Estates-General change frequently, while in the cities each council is made up of many members, influence is short-lived and jealousy great. Back in the time of the Princes of Orange, who chose the mayors, distributed offices and benefices, and maintained certain persons in positions of authority, it was not difficult to gain a few [deputies] and with their aid to push through desirable legislation in the Estates. Today such expenses would be both unending and fruitless. It should therefore suffice to have a faithful friend in each of the provincial deputations in order to block and divert evil resolutions.

Save in the event of misfortunes that would overcome the Hollanders' aversion to the authority of the Princes of Orange, it is hopeless to expect these people to revert to their original republican form of government under a captain-general. It is even likely that a majority would rather suffer a king than a captain-general, at least among those who hold power in the province today, belonging as they do to the Arminian * faction. The common people, on the other hand, retain their affection for the House of Orange and would prefer the ancient authority of the princes of that name to the rather austere government of those actually in power. Yet in Holland the masses play no role whatsoever in governing the state, which is aristocratic. As long as no major disruption of public affairs occurs, it is unlikely that the people would meddle in the conduct of those who govern them. Any effort that might be made to egg them on and to rekindle their loyalty to the House of Orange would be both useless and odious and would only put the position of the prince himself in jeopardy. . . .

It is in this matter of commerce that these people are most farsighted. Their merchants are the most sophisticated in the world. By long tradition they keep all their trade secrets within the family, while the policy of the state is wholly oriented to fostering commerce, which is indeed the soul of these provinces. For this reason,

* [Moderate as against rigid Calvinists. (*ed.*)]

ever since the Treaty with Spain [1648], their maxim is to be at peace with everyone while promoting war among others. Even when they engaged in the shameful betrayal of France at Münster, those who sought peace at any price in order to disarm the Prince of Orange got their people to accept it by holding out the hope that, with France and Spain remaining at war, they alone would capture the trade of the whole world. . . . They were surprised by the war against the English which they had not anticipated. Several foreigners with funds invested with the Bank of Amsterdam and [Amsterdam] merchants have withdrawn them. The wars that have occurred in Poland have impeded the Baltic Sea trade. All together these causes have, even in the estimation of the best merchants in Amsterdam, diminished their commerce by one third; and it is reasonable to believe that it has declined even further, since it is scarcely the policy of merchants to admit their [full] losses. Since the entire government is mercantile, those who play the preponderant role in the state still orate grandly about their resources and do not tolerate any mention of this obvious commercial decline. Yet it is revealing, on the other hand, that in order to manage their finances, the rate of interest on the sum of about seventy million pounds owed to private persons has been lowered to four per cent. Indeed, if commerce were flourishing, in a country where merchandise enjoys such great honor, who would not prefer to invest his money at ten per cent with merchants rather than lending it at four per cent to the state, which, since it cannot be forced to repay, is always an unreliable debtor.

From this absolute necessity of preserving their commerce, it may be concluded that the Estates-General regards all those as enemies who disturb trade or divert it. Yet save for some very momentous reasons, they will never decide to declare war on those who are their principal trading partners, though they will always be very pleased to see their neighbors' shops closed so that their own may be the only ones open. . . .

. . . As to religion, freedom is so complete in Holland that it is even permissible to have no religion at all. As the magistrates know full well, several rich Amsterdam merchants profess to have none, attend no church—neither Calvinist, Lutheran, Anabaptist, Arminian, nor any of the places of worship of the several private sects which do not yet have fixed names; [these merchants are] not even [found] among the Unitarians, whose number is very considerable and who are scattered among all the churches.

In the midst of so many sects and of Judaism, which is publicly practiced in Amsterdam, the Catholics alone are deprived of public religious services. The tolerance which they encounter varies from province to province. Zeeland watches them closely, punishing most rigorously all those who celebrate mass at home and admit persons outside their household. Known priests are very badly treated there. In Utrecht, where the number of upper-class Catholics is greater, the magistrate is not rigorous in carrying out the ordinances, ignoring gatherings provided they are held discreetly.

In Holland the cities differ among themselves. In the larger ones, Leyden excepted, mass is held in several places. The magistrate confines himself to making an occasional effort to surprise Catholics and priests at their altar, though in return for a small bribe he secretly gives them advance warning. Amsterdam is freer than any other city. It virtually never happens that private homes are raided to break up Catholic services. In the countryside at least one third of the peasants, and among them the most prosperous, are Catholics, who meet for religious services in barns and other specially prepared places.

The reason which the Gentlemen of the Estates-General advance when reproached with this harshness toward Catholics—to whom no other crime can be ascribed than their fidelity to the religion of their fathers at a time when others accepted the new doctrine of Calvin, who gave of their goods and of their blood to win their common liberty and who live peaceably in their home districts—the pretext given for this unbearable iniquity is the supposition that all Catholics in the United Provinces are loyal to the Spaniards, that they retain in their hearts the aim of turning the country back to its former masters. This may be true; yet it is within the power of the state to prevent it. For if the Catholics were only treated as are the Jews and the Anabaptists, if they received some places where they could worship God without fear of the police . . . they would love their country and their freedom. . . .

As to the internal affairs of the United Provinces, the persons who by their birth, their offices, or their influence occupy the first ranks [of society] remain to be considered. This is an area in which private judgment is rash and foolhardy, for nothing is more difficult to know than men, nor are any subjects more changeable. Nonetheless in rendering an account to one's master, it should be permitted to report what one has heard in public and what one has gleaned in private conversation with the most important people.

As Madame the Princess-Royal, mother to the Prince of Orange, decided in 1655 to visit France, her qualities will have become known. In this connection, it should suffice to note that the partisans of the House of Orange believe that were she more careful in showing gratitude to the servants of the Prince, her son, she would encourage them and thus gain new supporters. This would be easy to do by flattering the wives of the Gentlemen of the Estates-General, who have great influence on the actions of their husbands. . . . The age of the Prince of Orange does not permit me to say anything [about him] save that one may expect of him all that we have seen in his forefathers. . . .

Prince William of Nassau, governor of the provinces of Friesland and Groningen, has great qualities. He is esteemed by all military men, though they all agree that his real character is inscrutable. Much of the time his behavior is extraordinarily wary, while at intervals he can be extremely outspoken. To judge from the complaints of his friends, he seems to blow hot and cold. By cautiously bending to the interests of the prevailing faction, he has made some of his supporters fearful of joining him in any long-range projects. . . .

Prince Maurice of Nassau, his cousin and a former governor of all the state possessions in the West Indies, is at present commander of the Horse, Grand-Master of the Order of Malta in North Germany, and governor of Cleves for the Elector of Brandenburg. Because of these last named offices, he is considered to stand somewhat aloof from the United Provinces. This prince, less involved in provincial politics because of residing abroad most of the time, spends part of his leisure in satisfying his wholesome curiosity about buildings, architectural plans, and other such things. . . .

Monsieur d'Obdam, the lieutenant-admiral, is one of the most important persons in Holland. A member of the ancient nobility of Wassanaer, he is closely linked to the party that is hostile to the House of Orange, or rather, hostile to the authority of the captain-general's office such as it had been exercised by these princes. Rumor has it that the last two princes showed little appreciation for his military talents. Even though they gave him offices that allowed him to live (his patrimony being very slender), they did nothing to enhance his reputation. He on his side indicated clearly his disapproval of their increasing power. . . .

Monsieur de Witt, the Pensionary of Holland, comes from the city of Dortrecht. By virtue of the power that Holland wields over the other provinces, and by that which he personally enjoys among the ten or twelve principal leaders of the Hollander governing faction, [de Witt] is today the most important man in the country. Considering the weight and dignity of his office, he is youthful yet has great qualities to sustain him. Insofar as can be expected from a man his age, he is competent in dealing with [state] business: he shows courage, is firm in never yielding to any fear, and has, as far as one can judge up to now, a very disinterested character. His influence fluctuates with the occasion as is true in all constituted bodies composed of many persons. Yet he always remains in full control and, even without seeming to, can turn things his way. Aside from his determintion to exclude the House of Orange and to prevent the re-establishment of the office of captain-general or some analogous authority, one cannot reproach him with pursuing any other end than the welfare of his province. Even though he personally owns little in the way of property, no one has noticed that he is making much of an effort to increase his holdings. . . .

It would be tedious and not very useful to describe the dispositions and conditions of the large number of deputies that compose the body of the Assembly of the Estates-General. Taken singly, [the deputies] wield little power and are frequently replaced. . . .

From all that has been reported about the present constitution of the United Provinces, one may see that all the parts are not so united as to be able to conspire in common with regard to the other states of Europe. Each province, seeking to safeguard its own existence as much as the common union embodied in the republic, has its own special inclination. . . .

The province of Gelderland regards the Empire as an entity which it might join in case of disaster, while retaining its liberties in the manner of the imperial cities. The province of Overijssel has the same thing in mind. Any time that an alliance with the German princes is proposed, those two provinces will back such a proposal.

Friesland has its commercial ties with Denmark and Norway and therefore takes the interests of these kingdoms to heart. Groningen, in similar circumstances, follows suit.

Zeeland, the bulk of whose trade is with France, to which she is also closer geographically, always has and continues to display on all occasions her respect for the King and her love for the Nation. After having loudly disapproved of the Peace of Münster, [Zeeland] still disclaims responsibility for this action with a permanent disavowal.

Holland has more than a single orientation, since the nature of her commerce varies and is dispersed among several cities with special attachments to the peoples with whom they do business. Haarlem, Leyden, and a few cities of North-Holland, relying as they do on France as the main outlet for their manufactures, have warm feelings for us. Rotterdam divides [its affection] between France and England, Amsterdam between France, Spain, and the northern kingdoms.

Even though these individual inclinations do carry weight in the decisions of the state as a whole, in and of themselves they are not so powerful that one may predict in advance the outcome of the deliberations of the whole Assembly in any affair regarding foreign interests. The result will always remain uncertain just as long as this republic can survive with such a formless and leaderless government. . . .

◄§ AUSTRIA OVER ALL IF SHE ONLY WILL

Philipp Wilhelm von Hornick

Mercantilism, both as a doctrine and a set of policies, paralleled the rise of the sovereign state in early modern Europe, a development that had substituted the norm of independent political entities jostling for power for the older ideal of universal church and all-embracing empire. Just as the new age accepted without question the desirability of the state's political independence in relation to other states, economic independence was considered closely related and equally vital. Although no two mercantilist theoreticians or policy makers agreed on every point, they all accepted a system of central economic regulation designed to promote maximum prosperity at home, stimulate exports to other countries, and achieve a high degree of internal self-sufficiency. Throughout the sixteenth and seventeenth centuries, mercantilists also tended to share an overriding concern in the accumulation of gold and silver—the sinews of war at a time of primitive public credit. Eighteenth-century mercantilism was less preoccupied with precious metals.

As a system of economic nationalism geared to the interests of the ruler rather than to those of the nation, mercantilism was bound to take very different forms in maritime trading states such as Great Britain or the Netherlands and in landlocked countries such as Bavaria or Austria. The following proposal, never fully put into effect, outlined a drastic mercantilist policy within the comparatively backward setting of central Europe. Philipp Wilhelm von Hornick (1638–1712), a trained lawyer and bureaucrat, published his views on Austrian economic policy in 1684. The work was widely read and reprinted for a generation.

I. NINE PRINCIPAL RULES OF NATIONAL ECONOMY

If the might and eminence of a country consist in its surplus of gold, silver, and all other things necessary or convenient for its *subsistence,* derived, so far as possible, from its own resources, without *dependence* upon other countries, and in the proper fostering, use, and application of these, then it follows that a general national *economy* (*Landes-Oeconomie*) should consider how such a surplus, fostering, and enjoyment can be brought about, without *dependence* upon others, or where this is not feasible in every respect, with as little *dependence* as possible upon foreign countries, and sparing use of the country's own cash. For this purpose the following nine rules are especially serviceable.

First, to inspect the country's soil with the greatest care, and not to leave the agricultural possibilities or a single corner or clod of earth unconsidered. Every useful form of *plant* under the sun should be experimented with, to see whether it is adapted to the country, for the distance or nearness of the sun is not all that counts. Above all, no trouble or expense should be spared to discover gold and silver.

Second, all commodities found in a country, which cannot be used in their natural state, should be worked up within the country; since the payment for *manufacturing* generally exceeds the value of the raw material by two, three, ten, twenty, and even a hundred fold, and the neglect of this is an abomination to prudent managers.

Third, for carrying out the above two rules, there will be need of people, both for producing and cultivating the raw materials and for working them up. Therefore, attention should be given to the population, that it may be as large as the country can support, this being a well-ordered state's most important concern, but, unfortunately, one that is often neglected. And the people should be turned by all possible means from idleness to remunerative *professions;* instructed and encouraged in all kinds of *inventions,* arts, and trades; and, if necessary, instructors should be brought in from foreign countries for this.

Fourth, gold and silver once in the country, whether from its own mines or obtained by *industry* from foreign countries, are under no circumstances to be taken out for any purpose, so far as possible, or allowed to be buried in chests or coffers, but must always remain in *circulation;* nor should much be permitted in uses where they are at once *destroyed* and cannot be utilized again. For under these conditions, it will be impossible for a country that has once acquired a considerable supply of cash, especially one that possesses gold and silver mines, ever to sink into poverty; indeed, it is impossible that it should not continually increase in wealth and property. Therefore,

Fifth, the inhabitants of the country should make every effort to get along with their domestic products, to confine their luxury to these alone, and to do without foreign products as far as possible (except where great need leaves no alternative, or if not need, wide-spread, unavoidable abuse, of which Indian spices are an example). And so on.

Philipp Wilhelm von Hornick, "Austria over All if She Only Will," in Arthur E. Monroe, ed., *Early Economic Thought* (Cambridge: Harvard University Press, 1924), pp. 223–243.

Sixth, in case the said purchases were indispensable because of necessity or *irremedi-able* abuse, they should be obtained from these foreigners at first hand, so far as pos-sible, and not for gold or silver, but in exchange for other domestic wares.

Seventh, such foreign commodities should in this case be imported in unfinished form, and worked up within the country, thus earning the wages of *manufacture* there.

Eighth, opportunities should be sought night and day for selling the country's super-fluous goods to these foreigners in manufactured form, so far as this is necessary, and for gold and silver; and to this end, *consumption,* so to speak, must be sought in the farthest ends of the earth, and developed in every possible way.

Ninth, except for important considerations, no importation should be allowed under any circumstances of commodities of which there is a sufficient supply of suitable qual-ity at home; and in this matter neither sympathy nor compassion should be shown for-eigners, be they friends, kinsfolk, *allies,* or enemies. For all friendship ceases, when it involves my own weakness and ruin. And this holds good, even if the domestic com-modities are of poorer quality, or even higher priced. For it would be better to pay for an article two dollars which remain in the country than only one which goes out, how-ever strange this may seem to the ill-informed.

There is no need of further elucidating these fundamental rules of a general national *economy*. Their reasonableness is obvious to every man of intelligence. I do not mean to exclude all exceptions. The circumstances of each country may allow them now and then, but only rarely. If countries and their way of looking after things are considered according to these rules, it will be easy to judge their general *economy*. I do not pre-sume to instruct anyone; but, in all modesty, I venture to say that any manager and administrator of a general national *economy,* whether of high or low degree, who judges himself according to these rules, will be able to tell easily whether he has properly administered his duties or not. They are not the *invention* of a *speculative* mind. They follow from the nature of things, reason confirms them, and in every place where riches flourish all or part of them are applied. Therefore my reader will not resent my delay-ing him somewhat with this bit of *theory;* and if he has intelligence, which I do not doubt, he will easily discover its purpose. I believe that he will gradually see the light, if he has not already done so, and realize whether the well-known scarcity of money in Austria is to be ascribed to nature, or to indolence and carelessness, that is, to human will alone. "This is an old story," many perhaps will say, "a sort of commercial or *cameral primer,* which we have known a long time." But why is such a primer in so many places unfortunately so little practised, or even learned? By this standard, then, and this touch-stone we wish to test our Austria: to investigate her natural gifts as far as possible, and then to consider how they can be developed.

II. HOW TO INSTITUTE REFORMS IN THE NATIONAL ECONOMY PROPERLY

"Good preaching," some one will reproach me. "He may well cry the loudest over the pain of a sick man who can help least. Show us what to do about it." Now I have already said that I did not intend to explain how to *apply* our rules, but to leave that to those who have general oversight of the Austrian realm, and who are in charge of its administration. If my unauthoritative ideas are desired, however, I should like to begin with the above-mentioned fifth rule, and advise the Austrians TO BE CONTENT FOR A WHILE WITH THEIR OWN GOODS, WITH THEIR OWN MANUFACTURES, HOWEVER BAD THEY MAY BE AT FIRST, AND TO REFRAIN FROM FOREIGN ONES, KEEPING THEIR GOOD GOLD AND SILVER IN THEIR POCKETS. This would fit in with all the other rules, and everything else would follow from this alone. For the ninth rule is practically included in this fifth one; and if people would use nothing but domestic *manufactures,* the children and inhabitants of the country would be compelled (most of them gladly) to turn their hands to their own *manaufactures,* and to work up the domestic raw materials. In this way the second rule would be greatly furthered. And since artisans go where they can get a living, and many foreigners would necessarily be out of work as a result of the prohibition of their *products,* and sometimes even lack our raw materials, they would be compelled to come to Austria, in order to seek work, necessary raw materials, and their living, and to settle there; thus furthering the principal part of the third rule, namely, the development of a population engaged in *manufactures.* Then foreigners, having little more of their own to give, would lose the magnet with which they attract away our gold and silver. And thus the fourth rule would be *observed,* and the money would remain in the country. Since we could not do without a few things, however, such as Indian spices, fish products, and, for a time, raw silk, &c., we would have cause, opportunity, and material to exchange our surplus domestic products with our neighbors and others, without giving the most indispensable goods for them, according to the advice of the sixth rule. We would be able to do without these all the more easily, since the erection of domestic *factories,* immigration of foreign artisans, and growth of the country's population would increase domestic *consumption;* whereby the eighth rule would be greatly furthered. And once the country had acquired a supply of cash in this way (as must certainly happen in a very few years, even if we kept only the annual product of our mines), then with the means would come the spirit, the desire, and the *perseverance* to apply the first rule, by developing *plants* hitherto lacking, and abandoned or otherwise neglected mines; the seventh, in working up foreign raw materials; and to take such further measures as may be needed under the first rule for the improvement of hitherto uncultivated tracts of land, under the third for populating the country with peasantry, under the sixth for doing our own transporting both of foreign and domestic goods, and under the eighth in various ways. Indeed I may say without shyness, and surely without joking, that Austria has certain hidden resources, which will raise the first, third, and eighth rules to a degree impossible for the other countries of Europe to attain, and will, in all probability, win for Austria a wealth and splendor such as she has never had in her history or even dared to hope for.

III. THAT THE APPLICATION OF THE FIFTH RULE IS TO BE EFFECTED BY THE PROHIBITION OF THE FOUR PRINCIPAL FOREIGN MANUFACTURES: SILK, WOOLEN, LINEN, AND FRENCH WARES

Now we come to the big question, how to go about it to induce the inhabitants of Austria to content themselves with their own domestic *manufactures;* for according to my own admission, there are very few such available, and one can hardly advise people to clothe themselves as in primitive times in untanned sheepskin. . . . my only concern is that I shall have to prescribe a bitter pill for my Austrians, who like to dress trimly and expensively, and live for their physical *comfort*. But to make some concession, I must admit that I did not mean the *abstinence* from foreign goods to be taken in a *general* sense at the beginning, intending for the time being to put only those things on our black-list, the neglect of which can bring greatest harm to the country, the proper cultivation of which will bring the greatest, quickest, and most obvious advantage, and the lack of which from abroad will be easiest to bear or most readily replaced. In this category I place first woolen *manufactures,* both woven and knit goods, with the single exception of millers' bolting-cloth, as interfering too much with the pantry, for a year, until it is supplied within the country. Second, all linen goods of all kinds. Third, silk *manufactures* of all *stages*. Fourth, everything included under the name French *manufactures* and not included in the three classes mentioned above, whether made in France itself or in Italy, or in Switzerland, or elsewhere. Quite an undertaking! but I think that even according to our description it is the right solution. For it is certain that these four *sorts* of foreign goods are the real leeches which rob us of the inmost strength of our body and suck the best blood from our veins. Certain it is that these four *manufactures* are the beasts of prey which alone take every year upwards of sixteen million *gulden* from our pockets, just as if they had never been there. I was present when it was estimated, by distinguished men well acquainted with the country, that our annual loss of money through French wares alone amounts to three million *gulden* and more. If, moreover, as the above-mentioned *Survey of Manufactures in Germany* makes certain, fifteen thousand dollars are exported every year for bolting-cloth from Saxony alone, so that at least a hundred thousand dollars must yearly take flight from Austria as a whole for it, and bolting-cloth makes up hardly a fiftieth part of the foreign wool *manufactures* imported by us: then it must follow that at least seven million *gulden* leave Austria every year for these wool *manufactures*. What I have said above about the six and a half million dollars of mere wages and business-men's *profits,* which remain every year in the city of Leyden alone, according to clear reckoning, for woolen *manufactures* in cloth, small-wares, &c. will make credible what I here allege concerning the seven million *gulden* which annually go out of Austria for such *manufactures*. Now silk *manufactures* are probably not much inferior to the woolen.

Indeed, if more than nine thousand dollars are exported annually for silk from Saxony alone, again according to the statement in the *Survey of Manufactures in Germany,* and the *author* is afraid of appearing unreasonable in placing the total at such a modest sum, should we not likewise consider a man unreasonable who put the Austrian consumption thereof only about four times higher? And yet that would make six million *gulden*. If, however, everything made of linen be added, which is also not inconsiderable, we can reckon up and see whether less than eighteen or twenty millions are sacrificed annually, simply to satisfy the unnecessary desire for display in dress, and poured into the coffers of strangers, mostly our enemies. I might say that in Vienna before the siege * there were two hundred thousand men over twelve years old, each of

* [By the Turks in 1683. (*Ed.*)]

whom on the average spent ten *gulden* a year (most of them, indeed, thirty and more, many even a hundred, and not a few several hundred and even thousands) for foreign articles of clothing. Now it is easy to show that the other capital cities of the Austrian states, also very splendid, as well as other substantial and fine towns, besides the great and lesser nobility, together with their servants and officials, the whole kingdom of Hungary, the great and lesser clergy, besides all those under twelve years of age and yet having their share of foreign goods, and finally what is spent on other forms of personal property from abroad, all taken together, must, if Vienna amounts to at least eight, reveal a loss of eighteen millions. Let no one be offended at this, or be astonished at the huge sum, as if we were only playing with millions. For a neighboring state, which is only one sixth as large as Austria, exports annually, according to clear reckoning, three million dollars, according to the above-cited *Survey of Manufactures*. We know where all this money comes from, yet the country remains in the same condition as before, and consequently is exporting just as much again. How much more credible is it, then, that Austria lets foreigners have eleven or twelve million dollars.

To guard, nevertheless, against all doubts, reasonable or unreasonable: I will reduce the figures almost a half, leaving the total ten millions net, which are thrown out the door like a penny, without any hope of their return, simply for four kinds of *manufactures*. If these ten millions were kept in Austria for only a single year, how this lifeless body would begin to move and to revive! How it would recover and gain strength! And if, as would follow anyway, these ten millions made their way into *circulation,* in addition to what is in general use even under the present bad conditions, and, like the human blood by the power of the heart, passed every year to a large extent through the prince's treasury, in a gentle, practical, and tolerable way (which is the duty of the exchequer): How all the members of the German-Austrian state would suddenly rejoice and feel strong! If, however, this were kept up ten or twenty years, or longer, and if a suitable watch were kept over these four *manufactures* and also over the other trades in this way, and in each branch as far as practicable, and if finally the foreign *consumption* of domestic raw and *manufactured* products were increased in the course of time as much as possible; what in all Europe would then equal our Austria? And what sort of *manufactures* are these, the dispensing with which from foreign sources could make us so prosperous? They would, it is true, require some oversight and pains for their development, but nowhere would they be easier to introduce than in Austria, as I will demonstrate below. We could well do without the French trumpery, without special difficulty either, and in a few years imitate them more easily and more readily than others. I will also explain that in its place.

IV. WHY NOT ADOPT OTHER MORE MODERATE MEANS THAN THE COMPLETE PROHIBITION OF FOREIGN MANUFACTURES?

Now we come to the question how to enable Austria to be content with her own domestic *products* in the often-cited four branches of *manufacture,* giving up foreign ones, and this is the real crux of the matter. Following the general course hitherto adopted, people will immediately conclude: First of all, *manufactures* should be introduced in

Austria, privileges granted for this purpose, companies established; and when they have been introduced, either heavy taxes and import duties should be put upon foreign goods coming in, so that they may not be as cheap as the domestic ones, and so will have to stay outside; or *magazines* should be established, in which foreign as well as domestic goods shall be deposited, with instructions that merchants shall not proceed to the sale of the foreign, until the domestic have all been sold; finally, in order that progress may be made with the domestic *manufactures,* foreign goods should then be forbidden through the Bank. But these ways are, in my opinion, uncertain, slow, and, in view of our German temperament, sure to come to nothing. For, in the first place, capitals will be lacking, because rich people will not want to let them out of their strong-boxes, because of lack of confidence in the project. In the second place, no spirit or *resolution* will be forthcoming, on account of equal lack of confidence in the result, and this not unreasonably. For, in the third place, because of the slowness of such *introduction,* merchants and others not well disposed toward the plan, especially foreign *factors,* will have ample opportunity to *ruin* the beginnings by a thousand kinds of devices. The desire to become rich quickly, and impatience at waiting for gains, which, on account of the uncertainty of *consumption,* are bound to be uncertain, will, in the fourth place, do a good deal of damage by itself; the long time, in the fifth place, will also take away our energy and cool our enthusiasm. Besides, in the sixth place, there would be endless smuggling under such easy and careless *administration.* The domestic goods, in the seventh place, will have to bear reproaches for this or that pretended defect, and so fall into disrepute and *discredit. Luxury,* the raging *beast,* would, in the eighth place, not be repelled by the high prices of foreign goods, but would develop all the greater passion for them. The domestic *manufactures* would, in the ninth place, never attain complete development, as long as there was hope of getting the foreign ones. To sum up: The eventual prohibition and exclusion of foreign *products* would never be achieved in this way. For our illness is too great and too dangerous to yield to such weak and slow treatment.

I therefore deal with the problem in a very different way. Other people wish to introduce domestic *manufactures,* in order to exclude foreign ones later. I, however, advise the prohibition of foreign ones, in order to introduce domestic ones later. A big program! How much *opposition* is doubtless already being *formulated* against it, almost before it has left my hand! I shall not allow myself to be misled thereby, but remain convinced that foreign *manufactures* must be *banned* in order to promote domestic ones. I only wish to restrain premature judgment, until I have set forth the arguments for my proposal, and have disposed of the objections which may be urged against it. All my life I have preferred the simplest, most effective, and most certain, though apparently somewhat strong means to over-refined methods, neither cold nor warm, and therefore subject to all sorts of attacks, and in the end to much more inconvenience than those which work rigorously. Now there is nothing simpler in *execution* than the complete prohibition of all foreign goods in our four branches of *manufactures.* For smuggling cannot take place, if only those assigned to supervise it remain faithful, through fear and hope, punishment and reward; and if domestic goods are protected against violators of the public faith by the strict taboo. Nothing easier; for a bit of paper and ink, some decrees at the custom-houses and passes, *instruction* of some officials, arrangements for inspection and paying duties, and the unavoidable and inescapable punishing of the first or second who are caught red-handed, as well as the criminal's helpers and the receivers of the smuggled goods, be they great or small, will fix everything. Nothing prompter; for in twenty-four hours, so to speak, everything can be put into operation, and within a year the *effect* will be felt throughout Austria, both in the *Treasury* of the prince and in the coffers of his subjects. Nothing surer and more vigorous; for necessity itself and the sure profit resulting from the certainty of *consumption,* will teach the country's inhabitants to devote themselves to their own *manufactures.* When the money no longer goes to foreigners, at least ten millions will remain in the country annually, and go to increase our business capital. And the above-mentioned assurance of *consumption,* and the resulting sure profit, will encourage the capitalists to release their cash. Foreign artisans will be compelled by lack of work and bread to come into Austria to seek both. A hundred other advantages besides, which may not now be thought of, are likely to appear in the course of the *execution.*

*   *   *

V. OBJECTIONS TO THE PROHIBITION OF FOREIGN GOODS ANSWERED

I now have to answer the objections. I will take them up briefly, in order that this work may not be expanded to undue proportions. Enough is said for the sensible, and more detail would be wasted on the others. The first is: HOW COULD WE GET ALONG WITH DOMESTIC GOODS, IF FOREIGN ONES WERE SO SUDDENLY BANNED, AND HOW PROVIDE SUBSTITUTES? Answer: To tell the truth, we do not need the so-called French wares at all. Hence we shall be able to do without them merely until they gradually come to be *produced* in the country, as there is already a beginning in many of them; and other branches also cannot long fail to be *stabilized,* even more promptly than the other three much more important *manufactures.* In the case of silk goods the situation is about the same. Moreover, it is only for two or three years that there will be any shortage of them in the country; in five or six years there will be plenty. In the case of linen *manufactures,* Austria would have plenty already, as far as quantity goes, if only the good people who make that their *profession,* could find enough work. And as for variety and quality, it would probably not take long to supply that. Silesia alone would suffice, where this weaving has almost no gild, and everywhere, both in distinguished and peasant houses, the loom is found in rooms and chambers, upon which everybody works, and everyone is taught, just as in spinning. In the case of cloth-making the circumstances are not much different, and I know that in many an otherwise little known town there has been almost incredible progress. If only the domestic *consumption* were assured to them, and they were provided with, say, a half-year's stock of wool, how soon the cloth-making industry, as well as wool-spinning, which is not very badly off anyway, on account of the *continual* sales to foreign countries, would expand to five or six times what it now is. The thinner stuffs might, in case of necessity, have to bear the same fate as silk-making, namely, to slow down for a short time, meanwhile replacing the wanted linings with something else, until their *fabrication* is introduced in the country. To sum up: Linen and cloth, the most necessary, we should have in sufficient supply immediately, the small-wares would be supplementary to them. With light woolens, silks, and French wares we could, in case of necessity, dispense altogether forever, as our ancestors did, and hence all the more readily for a time only.

*   *   *

WHAT IS TO BE DONE ABOUT THOSE MERCHANTS WHO ARE ENGAGED SOLELY IN THE IMPORTING BUSINESS? THEY WILL BE RUINED.—An advantage! For they are the very fellows who are impoverishing the country. It is therefore better that they should collapse than the commonwealth. They will be able to hold out, however, until they obtain *commissions* from domestic wholesalers or financiers or *credit* from them, or book-keeping with the *manufacturers,* or some other position or service (of which there will then be a hundred times as many as there are ruined merchants), or invest any *capital* they may have in domestic *manufactures.* If they do not wish to be employed by the domestic *factories,* however, and they have no *capital* to invest, then such worthless rascals, who act only to the advantage of foreigners and to the harm of Austria, and who have not been able to do any more than earn their daily bread, are no more worthy of sympathy than downright fools.

OUR AUSTRIAN MANUFACTURES WILL NOT BE AS GOOD AS THE FOREIGN ONES.— Such a claim is in many cases a delusion of the Devil, who is hostile to the prosperity of Austria. Granted, however, that this would be an unavoidable evil, still it would not be unendurable. I will cite the prohibition of Hungarian wine in Austria, Styria, and elsewhere. If you ask why wines are prohibited which are better than the domestic ones, and even cheaper, the answer will be: That the domestic gifts of Providence may be utilized and prudently *consumed,* not despised, thrown away, or ruined; that the highlands may be *benefited,* and the limited cultivation of vineyards, an important source of regalian * revenue, may not be abandoned; that thereby so much more money may stay in our pockets. It is the same with Hungarian salt, to which the Austrian is inferior. And yet the former is kept out and the latter retains control of the field. It is quite the proper thing, however, and can be applied . . . to domestic *manufactures.* For if we have such *principles* in a few things, why do we not *extend* them to the great and many? If we use them on two such necessary articles as wine and salt, why do we not apply them the more readily to the unnecessary abuse in matters of clothing? If my proposal aimed at restricting the subsistence of Austria, and cutting down her food or drink by prohibiting commodities, there might be some reason to complain that this was too hard; that the body could not suddenly give up the nourishment to which it had become accustomed; that it would be an injury to health. But there is no question here of eating and drinking, or of health and long life, or of fasting and abstaining, but whether the body should be decked with Silesian or foreign cloth, with Upper Austrian linen or Indian *bombazine,* with domestic or foreign-made silks or stockings, with Austrian or French ribbons, which has nothing to do with health or palate or stomach, but merely things of fancy, and not even becoming to the proud spirit of dis-

* [Royal. (*Ed.*)]

play. As to how domestic wares may be made as good as foreign in quality, that is, in durability as well as beauty, I will undertake to set forth my views somewhat more fully below.

*   *   *

WE CANNOT MAKE OUR PRODUCTS AS GOOD AS FOREIGN ONES, SINCE WE HAVE NEITHER SILK NOR THE SPANISH WOOL WHICH IS INDISPENSABLE FOR FINE CLOTHS.— On that point people may well ask advice of the English and Dutch, who not only have no silk at home, but have no hope of ever having any; and have little of the long wool for cloth, besides having no Spanish wool, the same as we. Where they procure such raw materials, we shall find them too. Indeed, we shall obtain Milanese and Sicilian silk and Spanish wool all the more easily, since the Spaniards will prefer to grant this to their kinsfolk and most faithful *allies* rather than to others. As for long wool, it is not only easy to develop an ample supply of that in Bohemia, as pointed out above, but our neighbors will be as glad to sell it to us for our money or other goods as to anyone else.

BUT WHAT WILL DAME FASHION, THE SOLE ARBITER OF MANUFACTURES IN MATTERS OF DRESS, SAY TO THAT: SURELY ONE MUST DRESS LIKE OTHER NATIONS.—It would be a good thing if we sent Dame Fashion to the Devil, her father. There are incomparably more *nations* in the world that keep to one kind of clothing, than vary it. Why should we, then, imitate the few and not the many? Or if we can not do without this foolish *variety,* we should be free, anyway, to be as foolish as the French, and to *invent* such things from time to time out of our own fancy, in order to remain masters of our *manufactures.* If this would not do either, then samples, both of clothing styles and cloth patterns, might be brought from France and *fabricated* here; thus remedying this misfortune also. Indeed, it would be an advantageous change for the merchants. For now, when a new fashion comes in, the goods have to be ordered from a distance. Before they arrive, the style often changes again, and the merchant suffers a loss. If the *factories* are in the country itself, however, no more will be made in the new styles than just enough, so to speak, to supply the daily demand.

WHERE ARE OUR GERMANS TO GET CLEVERNESS ENOUGH TO INVENT A NEAT CLOTH-PATTERN OR FANCY JEWELRY-DESIGN, OR EVEN TO IMITATE ONE? THEY HAVEN'T BRAINS ENOUGH.—Such sarcasm should be retracted by the lips that uttered it. For the contrary is amply demonstrated above, and there is no other reason for the backwardness of our people except that the best artists are not honored among us. So they go off to France and Holland. The artisans who stay among us are not encouraged, and know, moreover, that even if they did make something good, foreign wares would always be esteemed more highly. Nevertheless there are such people here and there. I should like to have defied the one who displayed before the old King in Augsburg a foreign-made ribbon, which he could not imitate. And even in Dresden I know a young man whose first trade was that of ribbon-maker, later, as this did not give him a living, a lackey, still later a silk weaver in the new royal silk *manufactory;* who, in everything to which he chooses to *apply* himself, equals, where he does not surpass, foreigners, and has already given so many proofs of it that he can not be accused of presumption when he says, according to his habit, that he will undertake to imitate any *lessons* given him; and to give *lessons* to others which they would not imitate.

* * *

WHERE IS THE CAPITAL FOR DOMESTIC INVESTMENT TO BE OBTAINED?—If I should answer that it is for the Prince to see to that, I should be right, perhaps, but the times will not endure it. If I should therefore pass it on to the provinces, it might not be a mistake, either, but it might nevertheless not *encounter* the same *sentiment.* Therefore let it remain as suggested above, that if ten millions stay in the country every year more than now, and the *consumption* of domestic *products* is well assured, then there will be an abundance of *capital.* Moreover, I hear of a new strange proposal for obtaining *Credit* to make a big *Capital* without any; of which it will be possible to judge, when it has been given out.

* * *

IT IS TO BE FEARED THAT WE SHALL HAVE TO LIVE AT THE MERCY OF DOMESTIC ARTISANS AND BUSINESS-MEN, SINCE THEY WILL RAISE THEIR PRICES EXCESSIVELY WHEN THEY ARE NOT RESTRAINED BY FOREIGNERS.—If the government supervises things as it should, and checks wantonness, this will not have to be feared. And if manufactures eventually become extensive, the people themselves will strive for money and bread, and make goods cheap through their plentifulness. Where foodstuffs, house-rent, and wages of servants, as well as raw materials or goods, are inexpensive, as with us, and where wares are not brought from a distance and consequently are subject to no heavy charges for freight, tolls, or risk, it is hardly possible that they should be higher-priced than foreign ones (especially if the market is certain, and the goods do not have to lie long at *interest*). It might even be said that strangers do not make us gifts of these things, either; and it would be better, after all, if something must be sacrificed, to be a victim to one's own countryman rather than to a stranger, and to console one's self with the fact, already alluded to above, that it is better, although not every peasant can understand it, to pay two dollars for a domestic article, which remains in the country, than only one for a foreign one, which is exported. For what once goes out stays out. But what remains in domestic *circulation* involves no loss to the *public,* but is an advantage in several ways. The merchant himself, who invested it, can profit by it again. The state is to be thought of as a rich man, who has his money in many purses. If he takes something out of one and puts it into the other, he becomes no poorer thereby. For, although one purse becomes lighter, the other becomes that much heavier. He is master, however, of one as well as of the other. And this must be a leading *principle* of national *economy,* or things will not go well.

BUT THOSE NATIONS WHOSE MANUFACTURES WE PROPOSE TO PROHIBIT WILL BE ANGRY, AND CUT US OFF FROM SUCH THINGS AS WE MAY STILL NEED FROM THEM; OUR DOMESTIC GOODS HITHERTO TAKEN BY THEM WILL BE LEFT ON OUR HANDS; OUR ALLIANCES AND WE OURSELVES WILL BE DESERTED IN TIME OF NEED.—Let them be angry who will. If they are enemies, we do not need to spare their feelings; if they are friends, they will excuse us if we, by eventually developing a good *economy,* get into a *position* not only to help ourselves, but also in case of need to be of more *real* service to them. We see how France is angry at the way England consigns to the flames all French wares that are discovered. And after all, let him who stands behind Job take a friendship which really aims only at plundering our purse. We have learned how much friends give us for nothing in an emergency. And other *nations* are not so foolish, either, as to refuse us their unprohibited wares out of spite on account of the prohibited ones, and to avenge and increase the forced loss by a voluntary one. The free commerce of many places, such as Hamburg, Amsterdam, &c., does not allow any buyer to be excluded. And even if all others should treat us that way, the Spaniards, at any rate, for the reasons pointed out above, and because they have almost as much interest in our prosperity as we, would be for us rather than for anyone else, and not leave us in the lurch for the best Spanish wool and Italian silk; which are the two things which we still need to import. And, after all, we could get silk through Turkey. The nations, however, from whom we must get long wool, are not among those to whom our prohibition will cause any damage. They will therefore have no reason to prohibit our buying it; and in an emergency Bohemia, as already pointed out, would have to devote herself more to the production of this long wool. So there is no danger that our goods intended for export will be left on our hands. These are: wine, grain, oxen, copper, iron, quicksilver, hides, linen, all kinds of *minerals,* &c. For those who buy these things of us are either not among those who are injured by our prohibition, or are not able to do without such goods of ours. When we have become somewhat stronger financially as a result of our *economy,* we will not only have no need of foreign alliances and assistance, but they would even offer themselves of their own accord. For much money, many *alliances,* as France shows well enough. And on the contrary: *Point d'argent, point de Suisses.** Doubtless those who will not like our good order, because hitherto they have had good fishing in troubled waters, will try all sorts of tricks in order to lead us astray. . . .

VI. HOW TO RAISE THE QUALITY OF DOMESTIC MANUFACTURES, SO THAT THEY MAY NOT BE INFERIOR TO FOREIGN ONES

Here we have to consider briefly how the quality of domestic *manufactures* is to be raised, in order that they may equal foreign ones. . . . We have the materials for work like others, hands and heads like others, tools like others. If then the *effect* is not produced, as with others, it is certainly a willful wantonness, or at least a wanton awkwardness, which the government will know how to restrain, if it understands its duties. And it has been pointed out already that foreigners take our woven cloths and linen to their countries, finish them there, and thereby *transform* them into foreign goods; which finishing, God willing, we should also be able to imitate. They likewise take out our Silesian yarns and make their linen out of them. They take out our flax, hackle it again, and prepare it in a special way; then spin it in their way. In this connection it is to be

* ["No money, no Swiss" (mercenaries). (*Ed.*)]

noted that they make two kinds of linen, the best for themselves, the poorer for us and other foreigners; and indeed for the reason that they think we do not pay for theirs according to its value. The first is made of Silesian weft, but the warp is of Dutch or similar yarns, made, however, of Silesian or other high-German flax. In the other, both warp and weft are high-German and Silesian. I have been informed, moreover, that they take our woven Silesian linen and full it in butter-milk. For let no one be surprised at the fulling of linen, since Leipzig also understands that. In this way must high-German goods be made into good foreign ones. There is nothing in all this which we Austrians could not imitate. If our minds were too dull to find it out for ourselves, then have artists from other places come here; and spare no expense, for they will pay for themselves, though they had to be bought for their weight in gold. If this is not satisfactory, then send some of our native sons thither, and have them learn it. If the Germans, as soon as they reach France or Holland, equal or even surpass the inhabitants there, as long as they are among them, they can also bring the art back with them, and do a service to their fatherland, to which they owe everything anyway. It is of no consequence that the tools may not be brought to us from France or Holland. For even if that were not possible, either whole or in pieces, it would be a simple thing for an alert *mathematical* head to grasp them and later set them up here, though it required more than one journey. I also hear from the Swiss that they now know how to make their hemp as good as the best Dutch linen. I praise them, not only for such diligence, but also because they plant their land with big high hemp rather than small flax, and yet know how to make use of it as well as the latter. Now if the Swiss can do this, why not the Austrians too? These very Swiss also furnish us with a notable example of diligence in the wool manufacture. All the world a while ago procured its bolting-cloth from France, and long believed that it would never be brought from anywhere else. But now it is made as well in Switzerland as in France, and the greater part of what is used in Germany comes from there, although the Calwische Company in Würtemberg does something along that line. How much the silk *Manufacture* is growing in Switzerland is well known, moreover. And sometimes we are so absurd as to tax these people with being a little too *materialistic,* when we doubt all the while whether we also have intelligence and cleverness enough to do what is an easy matter for them.

It would also be no small assurance of the goodness of domestic wares to erect halls, warehouses, and inspecting rooms, requiring all finished pieces of cloth of any kind, or other things, to be brought there and pass an examination. Only those passing it would be current in the warehouses and honest merchants' shops; those which did not pass it would be *excluded* from other upright wares and remain mere peddler's goods. The falsifying or misuse of the stamps put on the good wares after inspection should, on account of the great *consequences,* be punished as a *violation* of general confidence and a weakening of the general *credit* of the community; not much less severely than the counterfeiting of money and government documents and seals, even with capital punishment in some cases, like grand larceny. In this way Austrian goods would not only be kept up to proper quality and workmanship, but in a short time would also acquire great *credit* and *reputation* at home and abroad, which would promote sales greatly, since every buyer could feel assured he was not being cheated.

Furthermore, there might be established in Austria certain annual *competitions,* no master or journeyman being excluded who is either a native of the country or who plans to settle there; and providing that whoever won there should be rewarded with certain *privileges,* emoluments, or in money and other prizes, which would be easy to arrange in such a way that it would not cost the *public* anything. This would not only be an impetus to the arts among the inhabitants, but would also attract the best workmen from abroad.

≈§ Part Two

The Enlightenment

ᴥⱥ DISCOURSE ON METHOD

René Descartes

René Descartes (1596–1650), the great French philosopher, physicist, and mathematician, died in the year that formally opens this volume; his influence, however, which lay in the succeeding period, was so vast that he must be included here. Together with the Italian Galileo Galilei (1564–1642) and the Englishman Francis Bacon (1561–1626), he inaugurated an age of science: of rapid advances in the understanding of nature, and of an even-more-revolutionary spread of the influence of this knowledge to other areas of life. His Discourse on Method *(1637) was the manifesto of that revolution. Claiming to be far more radical than they actually were, Descartes's writings nevertheless struck a responsive chord in a whole generation of intellectuals, each of whom in his turn was responsible for profound innovations: Baruch Spinoza (see pages 129–130), Blaise Pascal, Nicolas Malebranche, John Locke (see pages 43–44), and Gottfried Leibniz.*

The life of Descartes is typical of the restless and stormy spirit of his time. Born into a wealthy provincial family, he received a fine education (which he disparaged later) in the new Jesuit Royal College of La Flèche in Anjou. At sixteen, he left school for "the world": first Paris, center of controversy and debauchery; then volunteer military service in the armies of Holland, Bavaria, and Hungary. At thirty-three, he retired to seclusion in Holland and began to write. He corresponded with the leading minds of his day on intellectual matters, but remained in Holland for twenty years, writing books that were hailed in some quarters and publicly burned in others. He regarded himself as a good Catholic all his life. After 1633, when Galileo had been condemned by the Holy Office and made to recant for asserting that the earth moves around the sun, Descartes—who believed this too—wrote with one eye on Rome. In Part V of the Discourse *(see pages 100–101) he tells us that he too has recanted in his way. Nevertheless, his writings were placed on the Index of Forbidden Books, where they still are today.*

The Discourse, *the full title of which is* On the Method of Rightly Conducting the Reason and Seeking Truth in the Sciences, *was originally not a separate work but the introduction to a volume of three scientific treatises: "Dioptrics," on the theory of light and vision; "Meteors," on atmospheric phenomena; and "Geometry," in which he introduced his justly famous algebraic method (analytic geometry). His new method was thus not a pious hope, but a proved instrument: these*

*three treatises alone would guarantee him an honored place in the
history of science.*

*Although Descartes is sometimes called a sceptic, this is a serious
mistake. He thought he had discovered an infallible method and a set
of self-evident first principles; and he seems to have fully believed that
man would now proceed to construct an impregnable system of knowledge
containing all (known) truth and nothing but the truth. This edifice
would be added to by succeeding generations, but the foundation would
remain as firm as that of his great model, Euclid's* Elements of
Geometry *(which had already functioned in this way for twenty centuries), because the alternatives to both systems were strictly unthinkable.*

*It took two more centuries before the alternatives to Euclid's system
were found to be thinkable, after all. Descartes' system was less fortunate:
it lasted less than a generation. More important, the whole attempt to
base science on "self-evident" first principles was soon abandoned in
favor of a basically inductive or empirical approach. But Descartes'
dream of an orderly, verified body of knowledge accessible to all men
is scarcely less inspiring today that it was 300 years ago, when it
marked the end of one era and the opening of another.*

PART I

Good sense is, of all things among men, the most equally distributed; for every one
thinks himself so abundantly provided with it, that those even who are the most
difficult to satisfy in everything else, do not usually desire a larger measure of this
quality than they already possess. And in this it is not likely that all are mistaken: the
conviction is rather to be held as testifying that the power of judging aright and of
distinguishing Truth from Error, which is properly what is called Good Sense or
Reason, is by nature equal in all men; and that the diversity of our opinions, consequently, does not arise from some being endowed with a larger share of Reason than
others, but solely from this, that we conduct our thoughts along different ways, and do
not fix our attention on the same objects. For to be possessed of a vigorous mind is
not enough; the prime requisite is rightly to apply it. The greatest minds, as they are
capable of the highest excellencies, are open likewise to the greatest aberrations; and
those who travel very slowly may yet make far greater progress, provided they keep
always to the straight road, than those who, while they run, forsake it.

For myself, I have never fancied my mind to be in any respect more perfect than

Rene Descartes, *Discourse on Method*, trans. John Veitch (Chicago: Open Court Publishing
Co., 1899), pp. 1–10, 16–23, 34–50, 59–63, 64–69.

those of the generality; on the contrary, I have often wished that I were equal to some others in promptitude of thought, or in clearness and distinctness of imagination, or in fulness and readiness of memory. And besides these, I know of no other qualities that contribute to the perfection of the mind; for as to the Reason or Sense, inasmuch as it is that alone which constitutes us men, and distinguishes us from the brutes, I am disposed to believe that it is to be found complete in each individual; and on this point to adopt the common opinion of philosophers, who say that the difference of greater and less holds only among the *accidents,* and not among the *forms* or *natures* of *individuals* of the same *species.*

I will not hesitate, however, to avow my belief that it has been my singular good fortune to have very early in life fallen in with certain tracks which have conducted me to considerations and maxims, of which I have formed a Method that gives me the means, as I think, of gradually augmenting my knowledge, and of raising it by little and little to the highest point which the mediocrity of my talents and the brief duration of my life will permit me to reach. For I have already reaped from it such fruits that, although I have been accustomed to think lowly enough of myself, and although when I look with the eye of a philosopher at the varied courses and pursuits of mankind at large, I find scarcely one which does not appear vain and useless, I nevertheless derive the highest satisfaction from the progress I conceive myself to have already made in the search after truth, and cannot help entertaining such expectations of the future as to believe that if, among the occupations of men as men, there is any one really excellent and important, it is that which I have chosen.

After all, it is possible I may be mistaken; and it is but a little copper and glass, perhaps, that I take for gold and diamonds. I know how very liable we are to delusion in what relates to ourselves, and also how much the judgments of our friends are to be suspected when given in our favour. But I shall endeavour in this Discourse to describe the paths I have followed, and to delineate my life as in a picture, in order that each one may be able to judge of them for himself, and that in the general opinion entertained of them, as gathered from current report, I myself may have a new help towards instruction to be added to those I have been in the habit of employing.

My present design, then, is not to teach the Method which each ought to follow for the right conduct of his reason, but solely to describe the way in which I have endeavoured to conduct my own. They who set themselves to give precepts must of course regard themselves as possessed of greater skill than those to whom they prescribe; and if they err in the slightest particular, they subject themselves to censure. But as this Tract is put forth merely as a history, or, if you will, as a tale, in which, amid some examples worthy of imitation, there will be found, perhaps, as many more which it were advisable not to follow, I hope it will prove useful to some without being hurtful to any, and that my openness will find some favour with all.

From my childhood, I have been familiar with letters; and as I was given to believe that by their help a clear and certain knowledge of all that is useful in life might be acquired, I was ardently desirous of instruction. But as soon as I had finished the entire course of study, at the close of which it is customary to be admitted into the order of the learned, I completely changed my opinion. For I found myself involved in so many doubts and errors, that I was convinced I had advanced no farther in all my attempts at learning, than the discovery at every turn of my own ignorance. And yet I was studying in one of the most celebrated Schools in Europe, in which I thought there must be learned men, if such were anywhere to be found. I had been taught all that others learned there; and not contented with the sciences actually taught us, I had, in addition, read all the books that had fallen into my hands, treating of such branches as are esteemed the most curious and rare. I knew the judgment which others had formed of me; and I did not find that I was considered inferior to my fellows, although there were among them some who were already marked out to fill the places of our instructors. And, in fine, our age appeared to me as flourishing, and as fertile in powerful minds as any preceding one. I was thus led to take the liberty of judging of all other men by myself, and of concluding that there was no science in existence that was of such a nature as I had previously been given to believe.

I still continued, however, to hold in esteem the studies of the Schools. I was aware that the Languages taught in them are necessary to the understanding of the writings of the ancients; that the grace of Fable stirs the mind; that the memorable deeds of History elevate it; and, if read with discretion, aid in forming the judgment; that the perusal of all excellent books is, as it were, to interview with the noblest men of past ages, who have written them, and even a studied interview, in which are discovered to us only their choicest thoughts; that Eloquence has incomparable force and beauty; that Poesy has its ravishing graces and delights; that in the Mathematics there are many refined discoveries eminently suited to gratify the inquisitive, as well as further all the arts and lessen the labour of man; that numerous highly useful precepts and exhortations to virtue are contained in treatises on Morals; that Theology points out the path to heaven; that Philosophy affords the means of discoursing with an appearance of truth on all matters, and commands the admiration of the more simple; that Jurisprudence, Medicine, and the other Sciences, secure for their cultivators honours and riches; and, in fine, that it is useful to bestow some attention upon all, even upon those abounding the most in superstition and error, that we may be in a position to determine their real value, and guard against being deceived.

But I believed that I had already given sufficient time to Languages, and likewise to the reading of the writings of the ancients, to their Histories and Fables. For to hold converse with those of other ages and to travel, are almost the same thing. It is useful to know something of the manners of different nations, that we may be able to form a more correct judgment regarding our own, and be prevented from thinking that everything contrary to our customs is ridiculous and irrational,—a conclusion usually come to by those whose experience has been limited to their own country. On the other hand, when too much time is occupied in travelling, we become strangers to our native country; and the over curious in the customs of the past are generally ignorant of those of the present. Besides, fictitious narratives lead us to imagine the possibility of many events that are impossible; and even the most faithful histories, if they do not wholly misrepresent matters, or exaggerate their importance to render the account of them more worthy of perusal, omit, at least, almost always the meanest and least striking of the attendant circumstances; hence it happens that the remainder does not represent the truth, and that such as regulate their conduct by examples drawn from this source, are apt to fall into the extravagances of the knight-errants of Romance, and to entertain projects that exceed their powers.

I esteemed Eloquence highly, and was in raptures with Poesy; but I thought that both were gifts of nature rather than fruits of study. Those in whom the faculty of Reason is predominant, and who most skilfully dispose their thoughts with a view to render them clear and intelligible, are always the best able to persuade others of the truth of what they lay down, though they should speak only in the language of Lower Brittany, and be wholly ignorant of the rules of Rhetoric; and those whose minds are stored with the most agreeable fancies, and who can give expression to them with the greatest embellishment and harmony, are still the best poets, though unacquainted with the Art of Poetry.

I was especially delighted with the Mathematics, on account of the certitude and evidence of their reasonings: but I had not as yet a precise knowledge of their true use; and thinking that they but contributed to the advancement of the mechanical arts, I was astonished that foundations, so strong and solid, should have had no loftier superstructure reared on them. On the other hand, I compared the disquisitions of the ancient Moralists to very towering and magnificent palaces with no better foundation than sand and mud: they laud the virtues very highly, and exhibit them as estimable far above anything on earth; but they give us no adequate criterion of virtue, and frequently that which they designate with so fine a name is but apathy, or pride, or despair, or parricide.

I revered our Theology, and aspired as much as any one to reach heaven: but being given assuredly to understand that the way is not less open to the most ignorant than to the most learned, and that the revealed truths which lead to heaven are above our comprehension, I did not presume to subject them to the impotency of my Reason; and I thought that in order competently to undertake their examination, there was need of some special help from heaven, and of being more than man.

Of Philosophy I will say nothing, except that when I saw that it had been cultivated for many ages by the most distinguished men, and that yet there is not a single matter within its sphere which is not still in dispute, and nothing, therefore, which is above doubt, I did not presume to anticipate that my success would be greater in it than that of others; and further, when I considered the number of conflicting opinions touching a single matter that may be upheld by learned men, while there can be but one true, I reckoned as well-nigh false all that was only probable.

As to the other Sciences, inasmuch as these borrow their principles from Philosophy, I judged that no solid superstructures could be reared on foundations so infirm; and neither the honour nor the gain held out by them was sufficient to determine me to their cultivation: for I was not, thank heaven, in a condition which compelled me to make merchandise of Science for the bettering of my fortune; and though I might not profess to scorn glory as a Cynic, I yet made very slight account of that honour which I hoped to acquire only through fictitious titles. And, in fine, of false Sciences I thought I knew the worth sufficiently to escape being deceived by the professions of an alchemist, the predictions of an astrologer, the impostures of a magician, or by the artifices and boasting of any of those who profess to know things of which they are ignorant.

For these reasons, as soon as my age permitted me to pass from under the control of my instructors, I entirely abandoned the study of letters, and resolved no longer to seek any other science than the knowledge of myself, or of the great book of the world. I spent the remainder of my youth in travelling, in visiting courts and armies, in holding intercourse with men of different dispositions and ranks, in collecting varied experience, in proving myself in the different situations into which fortune threw me, and, above all, in making such reflection on the matter of my experience as to secure my improvement. For it occurred to me that I should find much more truth in the reasonings of each individual with reference to the affairs in which he is personally interested, and the issue of which must presently punish him if he has judged amiss, than in those conducted by a man of letters in his study, regarding speculative matters that are of no practical moment, and followed by no consequences to himself, farther, perhaps, than that they foster his vanity the better the more remote they are from common sense; requiring, as they must in this case, the exercise of greater ingenuity and art to render them probable. In addition, I had always a most earnest desire to know how to distinguish the true from the false, in order that I might be able clearly to discriminate the right path in life, and proceed in it with confidence.

It is true that, while busied only in considering the manners of other men, I found here, too, scarce any ground for settled conviction, and remarked hardly less contradiction among them than in the opinions of the philosophers. So that the greatest advantage I derived from the study consisted in this, that, observing many things which, however extravagant and ridiculous to our apprehension, are yet by common consent received and approved by other great nations, I learned to entertain too decided a belief in regard to nothing of the truth of which I had been persuaded merely by example and custom: and thus I gradually extricated myself from many errors powerful enough to darken our Natural Intelligence, and incapacitate us in great measure from listening to Reason. But after I had been occupied several years in thus studying the book of the world, and in essaying to gather some experience, I at length resolved to make myself an object of study, and to employ all the powers of my mind in choosing the paths I ought to follow; an undertaking which was accompanied with greater success than it would have been had I never quitted my country or my books.

PART II

. . . I had become aware, even so early as during my college life, that no opinion, however absurd and incredible, can be imagined, which has not been maintained by some one of the philosophers; and afterwards in the course of my travels I remarked that all those whose opinions are decidedly repugnant to ours are not on that account barbarians and savages, but on the contrary that many of these nations make an equally good, if not a better, use of their Reason than we do. I took into account also the very different character which a person brought up from infancy in France or Germany exhibits, from that which, with the same mind originally, this individual would have possessed had he lived always among the Chinese or with savages, and the circumstance that in dress itself the fashion which pleased us ten years ago, and which may again, perhaps, be received into favour before ten years have gone, appears to us at this moment extravagant and ridiculous. I was thus led to infer that the ground of our opinions is far more custom and example than any certain knowledge. And, finally, although such be the ground of our opinions, I remarked that a plurality of suffrages is no guarantee of truth where it is at all of difficult discovery, as in such cases it is much more likely that it will be found by one than by many. I could, however, select from the crowd no one whose opinions seemed worthy of preference, and thus I found myself constrained, as it were, to use my own Reason in the conduct of my life.

But like one walking alone and in the dark, I resolved to proceed so slowly and with such circumspection, that if I did not advance far, I would at least guard against falling. I did not even choose to dismiss summarily any of the opinions that had crept into my belief without having been introduced by Reason, but first of all took sufficient time carefully to satisfy myself of the general nature of the task I was setting myself, and ascertain the true Method by which to arrive at the knowledge of whatever lay within the compass of my powers.

Among the branches of Philosophy, I had, at an earlier period, given some attention to Logic, and among those of the Mathematics to Geometrical Analysis and Algebra,— three arts or Sciences which ought, as I conceived, to contribute something to my design. But, on examination, I found that, as for Logic, its syllogisms and the majority of its other precepts are of avail rather in the communication of what we already know, or even as the Art of Lully, in speaking without judgment of things of which we are ignorant, than in the investigation of the unknown; and although this Science contains indeed a number of correct and very excellent precepts, there are, nevertheless, so many others, and these either injurious or superfluous, mingled with the former, that it is almost quite as difficult to effect a severance of the true from the false as it is to extract a Diana or a Minerva from a rough block of marble. Then as to the Analysis of the ancients and the Algebra of the moderns, besides that they embrace only matters highly abstract, and, to appearance, of no use, the former is so exclusively restricted to the consideration of figures, that it can exercise the Understanding only on condition of greatly fatiguing the Imagination, and, in the latter, there is so complete a subjection to certain rules and formulas, that there results an art full of confusion and obscurity calculated to embarrass, instead of a science fitted to cultivate the mind. By these considerations I was induced to seek some other Method which would comprise the advantages of the three and be exempt from their defects. And as a multitude of laws often only hampers justice, so that a state is best governed when, with few laws, these are rigidly administered; in like manner, instead of the great number of precepts of which Logic is composed, I believed that the four following would prove perfectly sufficient for me, provided I took the firm and unwavering resolution never in a single instance to fail in observing them.

The *first* was never to accept anything for true which I did not clearly know to be such; that is to say, carefully to avoid precipitancy and prejudice, and to comprise nothing more in my judgment than what was presented to my mind so clearly and distinctly as to exclude all ground of doubt.

The *second,* to divide each of the difficulties under examination into as many parts as possible, and as might be necessary for its adequate solution.

The *third,* to conduct my thoughts in such order that, by commencing with objects the simplest and easiest to know, I might ascend by little and little, and, as it were, step by step, to the knowledge of the more complex; assigning in thought a certain order even to those objects which in their own nature do not stand in a relation of antecedence and sequence.

And the *last,* in every case to make enumerations so complete, and reviews so general, that I might be assured that nothing was omitted.

The long chains of simple and easy reasonings by means of which geometers are accustomed to reach the conclusions of their most difficult demonstrations, had led me to imagine that all things, to the knowledge of which man is competent, are mutually connected in the same way, and that there is nothing so far removed from us as to be beyond our reach, or so hidden that we cannot discover it, provided only we abstain from accepting the false for the true, and always preserve in our thoughts the order necessary for the deduction of one truth from another. And I had little difficulty in determining the objects with which it was necessary to commence, for I was already persuaded that it must be with the simplest and easiest to know, and, considering that of all those who have hitherto sought truth in the Sciences, the mathematicians alone have been able to find any demonstrations, that is, any certain and evident reasons, I did not doubt but that such must have been the rule of their investigations. I resolved to commence, therefore, with the examination of the simplest objects, not anticipating, however, from this any other advantage than that to be found in accustoming my mind to the love and nourishment of truth, and to a distaste for all such reasonings as were unsound. But I had no intention on that account of attempting to master all the particular Sciences commonly denominated Mathematics: but observing that, however different their objects, they all agree in considering only the various relations or proportions subsisting among those objects, I thought it best for my purpose to consider these proportions in the most general form possible, without referring them to any objects in particular, except such as would most facilitate the knowledge of them, and without by any means restricting them to these, that afterwards I might thus be the better able to apply them to every other class of objects to which they are legitimately applicable. Perceiving further, that in order to understand these relations I should sometimes have to consider them one by one, and sometimes only to bear them in mind, or embrace them in the aggregate, I thought that, in order the better to consider them individually, I should view them as subsisting between straight lines, than which I could find no objects more simple, or capable of being more distinctly represented to my imagination and senses; and on the other hand, that in order to retain them in the memory, or embrace an aggregate of many, I should express them by certain characters the briefest possible. In this way I believed that I could borrow all that was best both in Geometrical Analysis and in Algebra, and correct all the defects of the one by help of the other.

And, in point of fact, the accurate observance of these few precepts gave me, I take the liberty of saying, such ease in unravelling all the questions embraced in these two sciences, that in the two or three months I devoted to their examination, not only did I reach solutions of questions I had formerly deemed exceedingly difficult, but even as regards questions of the solution of which I continued ignorant, I was enabled, as it appeared to me, to determine the means whereby, and the extent to which, a solution was possible; results attributable to the circumstance that I commenced with the simplest and most general truths, and that thus each truth discovered was a rule available in the discovery of subsequent ones. Nor in this perhaps shall I appear too vain, if it be considered that, as the truth on any particular point is one, whoever apprehends the truth, knows all that on that point can be known. The child, for example, who has been instructed in the elements of Arithmetic, and has made a particular addition, according to rule, may be assured that he has found, with respect to the sum of the numbers before him, all that in this instance is within the reach of human genius. Now, in conclusion, the Method which teaches adherence to the true order, and an exact enumeration of all the conditions of the thing sought, includes all that gives certitude to the rules of Arithmetic.

But the chief ground of my satisfaction with this Method, was the assurance I had of thereby exercising my reason in all matters, if not with absolute perfection, at least with the greatest attainable by me: besides, I was conscious that by its use my mind was becoming gradually habituated to clearer and more distinct conceptions of its objects; and I hoped, also, from not having restricted this Method to any particular matter, to apply it to the difficulties of the other Sciences, with not less success than to those of Algebra. I should not, however, on this account have ventured at once on the examination of all the difficulties of the Sciences which presented themselves to me, for this would have been contrary to the order prescribed in the Method, but observing that the knowledge of such is dependent on principles borrowed from Philosophy, in which I found nothing certain, I thought it necessary first of all to endeavour to establish its principles. And because I observed, besides, that an inquiry of this kind was of all others of the greatest moment, and one in which precipitancy and anticipation in judgment were most to be dreaded, I thought that I ought not to approach it till I had reached a more mature age, (being at that time but twenty-three,) and had first of all employed much of my time in preparation for the work, as well by eradicating from my mind all the erroneous opinions I had up to that moment accepted, as by amassing variety of experience to afford materials for my reasonings, and by continually exercising myself in my chosen Method with a view to increased skill in its application. . . .

PART IV

I am in doubt as to the propriety of making my first meditations in the place above mentioned matter of discourse; for these are so metaphysical, and so uncommon, as not, perhaps, to be acceptable to every one. And yet, that it may be determined whether the foundations that I have laid are sufficiently secure, I find myself in a measure constrained to advert to them. I had long before remarked that, in relation to practice, it is sometimes necessary to adopt, as if above doubt, opinions which we discern to be highly uncertain, as has been already said; but as I then desired to give my attention solely to the search after truth, I thought that a procedure exactly the opposite was called for, and that I ought to reject as absolutely false all opinions in regard to which

I could suppose the least ground for doubt, in order to ascertain whether after that there remained aught in my belief that was wholly indubitable. Accordingly, seeing that our senses sometimes deceive us, I was willing to suppose that there existed nothing really such as they presented to us; and because some men err in reasoning, and fall into paralogisms, even on the simplest matters of Geometry, I, convinced that I was as open to error as any other, rejected as false all the reasonings I had hitherto taken for demonstrations; and finally, when I considered that the very same thoughts (presentations) which we experience when awake may also be experienced when we are asleep, while there is at that time not one of them true, I supposed that all the objects (presentations) that had ever entered into my mind when awake, had in them no more truth than the illusions of my dreams. But immediately upon this I observed that, whilst I thus wished to think that all was false, it was absolutely necessary that I, who thus thought, should be somewhat; and as I observed that this truth, *I think, hence I am,* was so certain and of such evidence, that no ground of doubt, however extravagant, could be alleged by the Sceptics capable of shaking it, I concluded that I might, without scruple, accept it as the first principle of the Philosophy of which I was in search.

In the next place, I attentively examined what I was, and as I observed that I could suppose that I had no body, and that there was no world nor any place in which I might be; but that I could not therefore suppose that I was not; and that, on the contrary, from the very circumstance that I thought to doubt of the truth of other things, it most clearly and certainly followed that I was; while, on the other hand, if I had only ceased to think, although all the other objects which I had ever imagined had been in reality existent, I would have had no reason to believe that I existed; I thence concluded that I was a substance whose whole essence or nature consists only in thinking, and which, that it may exist, has need of no place, nor is dependent on any material thing; so that "I," that is to say, the mind by which I am what I am, is wholly distinct from the body, and is even more easily known than the latter, and is such, that although the latter were not, it would still continue to be all that it is.

After this I inquired in general into what is essential to the truth and certainty of a proposition; for since I had discovered one which I knew to be true, I thought that I must likewise be able to discover the ground of this certitude. And as I observed that in the words *I think, hence I am,* there is nothing at all which gives me assurance of their truth beyond this, that I see very clearly that in order to think it is necessary to exist, I concluded that I might take, as a general rule, the principle, that all the things which we very clearly and distinctly conceive are true, only observing, however, that there is some difficulty in rightly determining the objects which we distinctly conceive.

In the next place, from reflecting on the circumstance that I doubted, and that consequently my being was not wholly perfect, (for I clearly saw that it was a greater perfection to know than to doubt,) I was led to inquire whence I had learned to think of something more perfect than myself; and I clearly recognised that I must hold this notion from some Nature which in reality was more perfect. As for the thoughts of many other objects external to me, as of the sky, the earth, light, heat, and a thousand more, I was less at a loss to know whence these came; for since I remarked in them nothing which seemed to render them superior to myself, I could believe that, if these were true, they were dependencies on my own nature, in so far as it possessed a certain perfection, and, if they were false, that I held them from nothing, that is to say, that they were in me because of a certain imperfection of my nature. But this could not be the case with the idea of a Nature more perfect than myself; for to receive it from nothing was a thing manifestly impossible; and, because it is not less repugnant that the more perfect should be an effect of, and dependence on the less perfect, than that something should proceed from nothing, it was equally impossible that I could hold it from myself: accordingly, it but remained that it had been placed in me by a Nature which was in reality more perfect than mine, and which even possessed within itself all the perfections of which I could form any idea; that is to say, in a single word, which was God. And to this I added that, since I knew some perfections which I did not possess, I was not the only being in existence, (I will here, with your permission, freely use the terms of the schools); but, on the contrary, that there was of necessity some other more perfect Being upon whom I was dependent, and from whom I had received all that I possessed; for if I had existed alone, and independently of every other being, so as to have had from myself all the perfection, however little, which I actually possessed, I should have been able, for the same reason, to have had from myself the whole remainder of perfection, of the want of which I was conscious, and thus could of myself have become infinite, eternal, immutable, omniscient, all-powerful, and, in fine, have possessed all the perfections which I could recognise in God. For in order to know the nature of God, (whose existence has been established by the preceding reasonings,) as far as my own nature permitted, I had only to consider in reference to all the properties of which I found in my mind some idea, whether their possession was a mark of perfection; and I was assured that no one which indicated any imperfection was in him, and that none of the rest was wanting. Thus I perceived that doubt, inconstancy, sadness, and such like, could not be found in God, since I myself would have been happy to be free from them. Besides, I had ideas of many sensible and corporeal things; for although I might suppose that I was dreaming, and that all which I saw or imagined was false, I could not, nevertheless, deny that the ideas were in reality in my thoughts. But, because I had already very clearly recognised in myself that the intelligent nature is distinct from the corporeal, and as I observed that all composition is an evidence of dependency, and that a state of dependency is manifestly a state of imperfection, I therefore determined that it could not be a perfection in God to be compounded of these two natures, and that consequently he was not so compounded; but that if there were any bodies in the world, or even any intelligences, or other natures that were not wholly perfect, their existence depended on his power in such a way that they could not subsist without him for a single moment.

I was disposed straightway to search for other truths; and when I had represented to myself the object of the geometers, which I conceived to be a continuous body, or a space indefinitely extended in length, breadth, and height or depth, divisible into divers parts which admit of different figures and sizes, and of being moved or transposed in all manner of ways, (for all this the geometers suppose to be in the object they contemplate,) I went over some of their simplest demonstrations. And, in the first place, I observed, that the great certitude which by common consent is accorded to these

demonstrations, is founded solely upon this, that they are clearly conceived in accordance with the rules I have already laid down. In the next place, I perceived that there
was nothing at all in these demonstrations which could assure me of the existence of
their object: thus, for example, supposing a triangle to be given, I distinctly perceived
that its three angles were necessarily equal to two right angles, but I did not on that
account perceive anything which could assure me that any triangle existed: while, on
the contrary, recurring to the examination of the idea of a Perfect Being, I found that
the existence of the Being was comprised in the idea in the same way that the equality
of its three angles to two right angles is comprised in the idea of a triangle, or as in
the idea of a sphere, the equidistance of all points on its surface from the centre, or
even still more clearly; and that consequently it is at least as certain that God, who
is this Perfect Being, is, or exists, as any demonstration of Geometry can be.

But the reason which leads many to persuade themselves that there is a difficulty in
knowing this truth, and even also in knowing what their mind really is, is that they
never raise their thoughts above sensible objects, and are so accustomed to consider
nothing except by way of imagination, which is a mode of thinking limited to material
objects, that all that is not imaginable seems to them not intelligible. The truth of
this is sufficiently manifest from the single circumstance, that the philosophers of the
Schools accept as a maxim that there is nothing in the Understanding which was not
previously in the Senses, in which however it is certain that the ideas of God and of
the soul have never been; and it appears to me that they who make use of their
imagination to comprehend these ideas do exactly the same thing as if, in order to
hear sounds or smell odours, they strove to avail themselves of their eyes; unless
indeed that there is this difference, that the sense of sight does not afford us an inferior
assurance to those of smell or hearing; in place of which, neither our imagination
nor our senses can give us assurance of anything unless our Understanding intervene.

Finally, if there be still persons who are not sufficiently persuaded of the existence
of God and of the soul, by the reasons I have adduced, I am desirous that they should
know that all the other propositions, of the truth of which they deem themselves
perhaps more assured, as that we have a body, and that there exist stars and an earth,
and such like, are less certain; for, although we have a moral assurance of these things,
which is so strong that there is an appearance of extravagance in doubting of their
existence, yet at the same time no one, unless his intellect is impaired, can deny,
when the question relates to a metaphysical certitude, that there is sufficient reason to
exclude entire assurance, in the observation that when asleep we can in the same way
imagine ourselves possessed of another body and that we see other stars and another
earth, when there is nothing of the kind. For how do we know that the thoughts which
occur in dreaming are false rather than those other which we experience when awake,
since the former are often not less vivid and distinct than the latter? And though men
of the highest genius study this question as long as they please, I do not believe that
they will be able to give any reason which can be sufficient to remove this doubt, unless
they presuppose the existence of God. For, in the first place, even the principle which
I have already taken as a rule, viz., that all the things which we clearly and distinctly
conceive are true, is certain only because God is or exists, and because he is a Perfect
Being, and because all that we possess is derived from him: whence it follows that our

ideas or notions, which to the extent of their clearness and distinctness are real, and proceed from God, must to that extent be true. Accordingly, whereas we not unfrequently have ideas or notions in which some falsity is contained, this can only be the case with such as are to some extent confused and obscure, and in this proceed from nothing, (participate of negation,) that is, exist in us thus confused because we are not wholly perfect. And it is evident that it is not less repugnant that falsity or imperfection, in so far as it is imperfection, should proceed from God, than that truth or perfection should proceed from nothing. But if we did not know that all which we possess of real and true proceeds from a Perfect and Infinite Being, however clear and distinct our ideas might be, we should have no ground on that account for the assurance that they possessed the perfection of being true.

But after the knowledge of God and of the soul has rendered us certain of this rule, we can easily understand that the truth of the thoughts we experience when awake, ought not in the slightest degree to be called in question on account of the illusions of our dreams. For if it happened that an individual, even when asleep, had some very distinct ideas, as, for example, if a geometer should discover some new demonstration, the circumstance of his being asleep would not militate against its truth; and as for the most ordinary error of our dreams, which consists in their representing various objects in the same way as our external senses, this is not prejudicial, since it leads us very properly to suspect the truth of the ideas of sense; for we are not unfrequently deceived in the same manner when awake; as when persons in the jaundice see all objects yellow, or when the stars or bodies at a great distance appear to us much smaller than they are. For, in fine, whether awake or asleep, we ought never to allow ourselves to be persuaded of the truth, of anything unless on the evidence of our Reason. And it must be noted that I say of our *Reason,* and not of our imagination or of our senses: thus, for example, although we very clearly see the sun, we ought not therefore to determine that it is only of the size which our sense of sight presents; and we may very distinctly imagine the head of a lion joined to the body of a goat, without being therefore shut up to the conclusion that a chimaera exists; for it is not a dictate of Reason that what we thus see or imagine is in reality existent; but it plainly tells us that all our ideas or notions contain in them some truth; for otherwise it could not be that God, who is wholly perfect and veracious, should have placed them in us. And because our reasonings are never so clear or so complete during sleep as when we are awake, although sometimes the acts of our imagination are then as lively and distinct, if not more so than in our waking moments, Reason further dictates that, since all our thoughts cannot be true because of our partial imperfection, those possessing truth must infallibly be found in the experience of our waking moments rather than in that of our dreams.

PART V

I would here willingly have proceeded to exhibit the whole chain of truths which I deduced from these primary; but as with a view to this it would have been necessary now to treat of many questions in dispute among the learned, with whom I do not wish to be embroiled, I believe that it will be better for me to refrain from this exposition, and only mention in general what these truths are, that the more judicious may be able to determine whether a more special account of them would conduce to the public advantage. I have ever remained firm in my original resolution to suppose no other principle than that of which I have recently availed myself in demonstrating the existence of God and of the soul, and to accept as true nothing that did not appear to me more clear and certain than the demonstrations of the geometers had formerly appeared; and yet I venture to state that not only have I found means to satisfy myself in a short time on all the principal difficulties which are usually treated of in Philosophy, but I have also observed certain laws established in nature by God in such a manner, and of which he has impressed on our minds such notions, that after we have reflected sufficiently upon these, we cannot doubt that they are accurately observed in all that exists or takes place in the world: and farther, by considering the concatention of these laws, it appears to me that I have discovered many truths more useful and more important than all I had before learned, or even had expected to learn.

But because I have essayed to expound the chief of these discoveries in a Treatise which certain considerations prevent me from publishing, I cannot make the results known more conveniently than by here giving a summary of the contents of this Treatise. It was my design to comprise in it all that, before I set myself to write it, I thought I knew of the nature of material objects. But like the painters who, finding themselves unable to represent equally well on a plain surface all the different faces of a solid body, select one of the chief, on which alone they make the light fall, and throwing the rest into the shade, allow them to appear only in so far as they can be seen while looking at the principal one; so, fearing lest I should not be able to comprise in my discourse all that was in my mind, I resolved to expound singly, though at considerable length, my opinions regarding light; then to take the opportunity of adding something on the sun and the fixed stars, since light almost wholly proceeds from them; on the heavens, since they transmit it; on the planets, comets, and earth, since they reflect it; and particularly on all the bodies that are upon the earth, since they are either coloured, or transparent, or luminous; and finally on man, since he is the spectator of these objects. Further, to enable me to cast this variety of subjects somewhat into the shade, and to express my judgment regarding them with greater freedom, without being necessitated to adopt or refute the opinions of the learned, I resolved to leave all the people here to their disputes, and to speak only of what would happen in a new world, if God were now to create somewhere in the imaginary spaces matter sufficient to compose one, and were to agitate variously and confusedly the different parts of this matter, so that there resulted a chaos as disordered as the poets ever feigned, and after that did nothing more than lend his ordinary concurrence to nature, and allow her to act in accordance with the laws which he had established. On this supposition, I, in the first place, described this matter, and essayed to represent it in such a manner that to my mind there can be nothing clearer and more intelligible, except what has been recently said regarding God and the soul; for I even expressly supposed that it possessed none of those forms or qualities which are so debated in the Schools, nor in general anything the knowledge of which is not so natural to our minds that no one can so much as imagine himself ignorant of it. Besides, I have pointed out what are the laws of nature; and, with no other principle upon which to found my reasonings except the infinite perfection of God, I endeavoured to demonstrate all those about which there could be any room for doubt, and to prove that they are such, that even if God had created more worlds, there could have been none in which these laws were not observed. Thereafter, I showed how the greatest part of the matter of this chaos must, in accordance with these laws, dispose and arrange itself in such a way as to present the appearance of heavens; how in the meantime some of its parts must compose an earth and some planets and comets, and others a sun and fixed stars. And, making a digression at this stage on the subject of light, I expounded at considerable length what the nature of that light must be which is found in the sun and the stars, and how thence in an instant of time it traverses the immense spaces of the heavens, and how from the planets and comets it is reflected towards the earth. To this I likewise added much respecting the substance, the situation, the motions, and all the different qualities of these heavens and stars; so that I thought I had said enough respecting them to show that there is nothing observable in the heavens or stars of our system that must not, or at least may not, appear precisely alike in those of the system which I described. I came next to speak of the earth in particular, and to show how, even though I had expressly supposed that God had given no weight to the matter of which it is composed, this should not prevent all its parts from tending exactly to its centre; how with water and air on its surface, the dispostion of the heavens and heavenly bodies, more especially of the moon, must cause a flow and ebb, like in all its circumstances to that observed in our seas, as also a certain current both of water and air from east to west, such as is likewise observed between the tropics; how the mountains, seas, fountains, and rivers might naturally be formed in it, and the metals produced in the mines, and the plants grow in the fields; and in general, how all the bodies which are commonly denominated mixed or composite might be generated: and, among other things in the discoveries alluded to, inasmuch as besides the stars, I knew nothing except fire which produces light, I spared no pains to set forth all that pertains to its nature,—the manner of its production and support, and to explain how heat is sometimes found without light, and light without heat; to show how it can induce various colours upon different bodies and other divers qualities; how it reduces some to a liquid state and hardens others; how it can consume almost all bodies, or convert them into ashes and smoke; and finally, how from these ashes, by the mere intensity of its action, it forms glass: for as this transmutation of ashes into glass appeared to me as wonderful as any other in nature, I took a special pleasure in describing it.

I was not, however, disposed, from these circumstances, to conclude that this world had been created in the manner I described; for it is much more likely that God made it at the first such as it was to be. But this is certain, and an opinion commonly received among theologians, that the action by which he now sustains it is the same with that by which he originally created it; so that even although he had from the beginning given it no other form than that of chaos, provided only he had established certain laws of nature, and had lent it his concurrence to enable it to act as it is wont to do, it may be believed, without discredit to the miracle of creation, that, in this way alone, things purely material might, in course of time, have become such as we observe them at present; and their nature is much more easily conceived when they are beheld coming in this manner gradually into existence, than when they are only considered as produced at once in a finished and perfect state.

From the description of inanimate bodies and plants, I passed to animals, and particularly to man. But since I had not as yet sufficient knowledge to enable me to treat of these in the same manner as of the rest, that is to say, by deducing effects from their causes, and by showing from what elements and in what manner Nature must produce them, I remained satisfied with the supposition that God formed the body of man wholly like to one of ours, as well in the external shape of the members as in the internal conformation of the organs, of the same matter with that I had described, and at first placed in it no Rational Soul, nor any other principle, in room of the Vegetative or Sensitive Soul, beyond kindling in the heart one of those fires without light, such as I had already described, and which I thought was not different from the heat in hay that has been heaped together before it is dry, or that which causes fermentation in new wines before they are run clear of the fruit. For, when I examined the kind of functions which might, as consequences of this supposition, exist in this body, I found precisely all those which may exist in us independently of all power of thinking, and consequently without being in any measure owing to the soul; in other words, to that part of us which is distinct from the body, and of which it has been said above that the nature distinctively consists in thinking,—functions in which the animals void of Reason may be said wholly to resemble us; but among which I could not discover any of those that, as dependent on thought alone, belong to us as men, while, on the other hand, I did afterwards discover these as soon as I supposed God to have created a Rational Soul, and to have annexed it to this body in a particualar manner which I described. . . .

I had expounded all these matters with sufficient minuteness in the Treatise which I formerly thought of publishing. And after these, I had shewn what must be the fabric of the nerves and muscles of the human body to give the animal spirits contained in it the power to move the members, as when we see heads shortly after they have been struck off still move and bite the earth, although no longer animated; what changes must take place in the brain to produce waking, sleep, and dreams, how light, sounds, odours, tastes, heat, and all the other qualities of external objects impress it with different ideas by means of the senses; how hunger, thirst, and the other internal affections can likewise impress upon it divers ideas; what must be understood by the common sense (*sensus communis*) in which these ideas are received, by the memory which retains them, by the fantasy which can change them in various ways, and out of them compose new ideas, and which, by the same means, distributing the animal spirits through the muscles, can cause the members of such a body to move in as many different ways, and in a manner as suited, whether to the objects that are presented to its senses or to its internal affections, as can take place in our own case apart from the guidance of the will. Nor will this appear at all strange to those who are acquainted with the variety of movements performed by the different automata, or moving machines fabricated by human industry, and that with help of but few pieces compared with the great multitude of bones, muscles, nerves, arteries, veins, and other parts that are found in the body of each animal. Such persons will look upon this body as a machine made by the hands of God, which is incomparably better arranged, and adequate to movements more admirable than is any machine of human invention. And here I specially stayed to show that, were there such machines exactly resembling in organs and outward form an ape or any other irrational animal, we could have no means of knowing that they were in any respect of a different nature from these animals; but if there were machines bearing the image of our bodies, and capable of imitating our actions as far as it is morally possible, there would still remain two most certain tests whereby to know that they were not therefore really men. Of these the first is that they could never use words or other signs arranged in such a manner as is competent to us in order to declare our thoughts to others: for we may easily conceive a machine to be so constructed that it emits vocables, and even that it emits some correspondent to the action upon it of external objects which cause a change in its organs; for example, if touched in a particular place it may demand what we wish to say to it; if in another it may cry out that it is hurt, and such like; but not that it should arrange them variously so as appositely to reply to what is said in its presence, as men of the lowest grade of intellect can do. The second test is, that although such machines might execute many things with equal or perhaps greater perfection than any of us, they would, without doubt, fail in certain others from which it could be discovered that they did not act from knowledge, but solely from the disposition of their organs: for while Reason is an universal instrument that is alike available on every occasion, these organs, on the contrary, need a particular arrangement for each particular action; whence it must be morally impossible that there should exist in any machine a diversity of organs sufficient to enable it to act in all the occurrences of life, in the way in which our reason enables us to act. Again, by means of these two tests we may likewise know the difference between men and brutes. For it is highly deserving of remark, that there are no men so dull and stupid, not even idiots, as to be incapable of joining together different words, and thereby constructing a declaration by which to make their thoughts understood; and that on the other hand, there is no other animal, however perfect or happily circumstanced, which can do the like. Nor does this inability arise from want of organs: for we observe that magpies and parrots can utter words like ourselves, and are yet unable to speak as we do, that is, so as to show that they understand what they say; in place of which men born deaf and dumb, and thus not less, but rather more than the brutes, destitute of the organs which others use in speaking, are in the habit of spontaneously inventing certain signs by which they discover their thoughts to those who, being usually in their company, have leisure to learn their language. And this proves not only that the brutes have less Reason than man, but that they have none at all: for we see that very little is required to enable a person to speak; and since a certain inequality of capacity is observable among animals of the same species, as well as among men, and since some are more capable of being instructed than others, it is incredible that the most perfect ape or parrot of its species, should not in this be equal to the most stupid infant of its kind, or at least to one that was crack-brained, unless the soul of brutes were of a nature wholly different from ours. And we ought not to confound speech with the natural movements which indicate the passions, and can be imitated by machines as well as manifested by animals; nor must it be thought with certain of the ancients, that the brutes speak, although we do not understand their language. For if such were the case, since they are endowed with many organs analogous to ours, they could as easily communicate their thoughts to us as to their fellows. It is also very worthy of remark, that, though there are many animals which manifest more industry than we in certain of their actions, the same animals are yet observed to show none at all in many others: so that the circumstance that they do better than we does not prove that they are endowed with mind, for it would thence follow that they possessed greater Reason than any of us, and could surpass us in all things; on the contrary, it rather proves that they are destitute of Reason, and that it is Nature which acts in them according to the disposition of their organs: thus it is seen, that a clock composed only of wheels and weights can number the hours and measure time more exactly than we with all our skill.

I had after this described the Reasonable Soul, and shewn that it could by no means be educed from the power of matter, as the other things of which I had spoken, but that it must be expressly created; and that it is not sufficient that it be lodged in the human body exactly like a pilot in a ship, unless perhaps to move its members, but that it is necessary for it to be joined and united more closely to the body, in order to have sensations and appetites similar to ours, and thus constitute a real man. I here entered, in conclusion, upon the subject of the soul at considerable length, because it is of the greatest moment: for after the error of those who deny the existence of God, an error which I think I have already sufficiently refuted, there is none that is more powerful in leading feeble minds astray from the straight path of virtue than the supposition that the soul of the brutes is of the same nature with our own; and consequently that after this life we have nothing to hope for or fear, more than flies and ants; in place of which, when we know how far they differ we much better comprehend the reasons which establish that the soul is of a nature wholly independent of the body, and that consequently it is not liable to die with the latter; and, finally, because no other causes are observed capable of destroying it, we are naturally led thence to judge that it is immortal.

PART VI

. . . I have never made much account of what has proceeded from my own mind; and so long as I gathered no other advantage from the Method I employ beyond satisfying myself on some difficulties belonging to the speculative sciences, or endeavouring to regulate my actions according to the principles it taught me, I never thought myself bound to publish anything respecting it. For in what regards manners, every one is so full of his own wisdom, that there might be found as many reformers as heads, if any were allowed to take upon themselves the task of mending them, except those whom God has constituted the supreme rulers of his people, or to whom he has given sufficient grace and zeal to be prophets; and although my speculations greatly pleased myself, I believed that others had theirs, which perhaps pleased them still more. But as soon as I had acquired some general notions respecting Physics, and beginning to make trial of them in various particular difficulties, had observed how far they can carry us, and how much they differ from the principles that have been employed up to the present time, I believed that I could not keep them concealed without sinning grievously against the law by which we are bound to promote, as far as in us lies, the general good of mankind. For by them I perceived it to be possible to arrive at knowledge highly useful in life, and in room of the Speculative Philosophy usually taught in the Schools, to discover a Practical, by means of which, knowing the force and action of fire, water, air, the stars, the heavens, and all the other bodies that surround us, as distinctly as we know the various crafts of our artizans, we might also apply them in the same way to all the uses to which they are adapted, and thus render ourselves the lords and possessors of nature. And this is a result to be desired, not only in order to the invention of an infinity of arts, by which we might be enabled to enjoy without any trouble the fruits of the earth, and all its comforts, but also and especially for the preservation of health, which is without doubt, of all the blessings of this life, the first and fundamental one; for the mind is so intimately dependent upon the condition and relation of the organs of the body, that if any means can ever be found to render men wiser and more ingenious than hitherto, I believe that it is in Medicine they must be sought for. It is true that the science of Medicine, as it now exists, contains few things whose utility is very remarkable: but without any wish to depreciate it, I am confident that there is no one, even among those whose profession it is, who does not admit that all at present known in it is almost nothing in comparison of what remains to be discovered; and that we could free ourselves from an infinity of maladies of body as well as of mind, and perhaps also even from the debility of age, if we had sufficiently ample knowledge of their causes, and of all the remedies provided for us by Nature. But since I designed to employ my whole life in the search after so necessary a Science, and since I had fallen in with a path which seems to me such, that if any one follow it he must inevitably reach the end desired, unless he be hindered either by the shortness of life or the want of experiments, I judged that there could be no more effectual provision against these two impediments than if I were faithfully to communicate to the public all the little I might myself have found, and incite men of superior genius to strive to proceed farther, by contributing, each according to his inclination and ability, to the experiments which it would be necessary to make, and also by informing the public of all they might discover, so that, by the last beginning where those before them had left off, and thus connecting the lives and labours of many, we might collectively proceed much farther than each by himself could do.

I remarked, moreover, with respect to experiments, that they become always more necessary the more one is advanced in knowledge; for, at the commencement it is better to make use only of what is spontaneously presented to our senses, and of which we cannot remain ignorant, provided we bestow on it any reflection, however slight, than to concern ourselves about more uncommon and recondite phaenomena: the reason of which is, that the more uncommon often only mislead us so long as the causes of the more ordinary are still unknown; and the circumstances upon which they depend are almost always so special and minute as to be highly difficult to detect. But in this I have adopted the following order: first, I have essayed to find in general the principles, or first causes, of all that is or can be in the world, without taking into consideration for this end anything but God himself who has created it, and without educing them from any other source than from certain germs of truths naturally existing in our minds. In the second place, I examined what were the first and most ordinary effects that could be deduced from these causes; and it appears to me that, in this way, I have found heavens, stars, an earth, and even on the earth, water, air, fire, minerals, and some other things of this kind, which of all others are the most common and simple, and hence the easiest to know. Afterwards, when I wished to descend to the more particular, so many diverse objects presented themselves to me, that I believed it to be impossible for the human mind to distinguish the forms or species of bodies that are upon the earth, from an infinity of others which might have been, if it had pleased God to place them there, or consequently to apply them to our use, unless we rise to causes through their effects, and avail ourselves of many particular experiments. Thereupon, turning over in my mind all the objects that had ever been presented to my sense, I freely venture to state that I have never observed any which I could not satisfactorily explain by the principles I had discovered. But it is necessary also to confess that the power of nature is so ample and vast, and these principles so simple and general, that I have hardly observed a single particular effect which I cannot at once recognise as capable of being deduced in many different modes from the principles, and that my greatest difficulty usually is to discover in which of these modes the effect is dependent upon them; for out of this difficulty I cannot otherwise extricate myself than by again seeking certain experiments, which may be such that their result is not the same, if it is in the one of these modes that we must explain it, as it would be if it were to be explained in the other. As to what remains, I am now in a position to discern, as I think, with sufficient clearness what course must be taken to make the majority of those experiments which may conduce to this end: but I perceive likewise that they are such and so numerous, that neither my hands nor my income, though it were a thousand times larger than it is, would be sufficient for them all; so that, according as henceforward I shall have the means of making more or fewer experiments, I shall in the same proportion make greater or less progress in the knowledge of nature. This was what I had hoped to make known by the Treatise I had written, and so clearly to exhibit the advantage that would thence accrue to the public, as to induce all who have the common good of man at heart, that is, all who are virtuous in truth, and not merely in appearance, or according to opinion, as well to communicate to me the experiments they had already made, as to assist me in those that remain to be made.

✍§ MAN A MACHINE

Julien Offray de Lamettrie

The revolution in the study of nature that we associate with the seventeenth century brought with it a new way of viewing human *nature as well. The full implications of this new perspective were not brought out immediately, however, partly because of their obvious bearings on reli-*

gion and morality. They also seemed to be contradicted by inner expe-
rience. Nevertheless, it was only a matter of time before someone would
maintain that man is simply a natural object like any other, no more
and no less, and attempt to develop this view consistently and com-
pletely. It was also predictable that when this happened, an outcry would
attend it.

The man who did it was Julien Offray de Lamettrie (1709–1751), a
student of the great Dutch physician Boerhave. Lamettrie had studied
theology with the Jansenists, but was completely converted to material-
ism and atheism by his observations of the effects of bodily ailments on
mental processes. After moving from Leyden to Paris, where he was
appointed surgeon to the guards, he published his ideas in The Natural
History of the Soul *(1745). The response was so violent that he had to*
return to Leyden, and three years later he was forced to leave there as
well. At this point King Frederick the Great of Prussia (see page 200)
invited him to practice medicine in Berlin and encouraged him to con-
tinue philosophizing; and in 1750, he published L'Homme machine,
spelling out his theory fully and provocatively. Upon his death a year
later at only forty-two, an address was read by Frederick himself to the
Berlin Academy praising the boldness and originality of Lamettrie's
thought.

. . . Experiments and observation alone ought to guide us here. These we find in
abundance, in the writings of such physicians as were philosophers, and not in those
philosophers, who were unacquainted with physic. The former have explored and un-
ravelled the labyrinth of Man. They alone have discovered to us those hidden springs
concealed under a cover, which hides from us so many wonders. They alone in a philosophical contemplation of the soul, have a thousand times surprized it in its misery and
grandeur; without despising it in one of these conditions, or idolizing it in the other.
Once more, I will be bold to say, these are the only authors that have a right to speak
on this subject. What would other lame philosophers say, and above all, the divines?
Is it not ridiculous to hear them determine without modesty, on a subject they have
never been qualified to examine thoroughly? a subject, from which they have been
always diverted by dark idle studies, that have tinctured them with a thousand, gross,
childish prejudices, and to say all in one word, have plunged them over head and ears
in fanaticism, which adds still to their ignorance in the mechanism of bodies.

But tho' we have chosen the best guides, yet we shall find many thorns, and obstacles
in our way.

Julien Offrey de Lamettrie, *Man a Machine,* **anon. trans. (London: for G. Smith, 1750),
pp. 5–11, 17–18, 23–24, 27–28, 32–36, 46–48, 54–55, 76–77, 81–87.**

Man is a machine so compound, that it is impossible to form at first a clear idea thereof, and consequently to define it. This is the reason, that all the enquiries the philosophers have made *a priori,* that is, by endeavouring to raise themselves on the wings of the understanding, have proved ineffectual. Thus it is only *a posteriori,* or as it were by disentangling the soul from the organs of the body, that we can, I do not say, discover with evidence the nature of man, but obtain the greatest degree of probability the subject will admit of.

Let us then follow the direction of experience, and not trouble our heads with the vain history of the opinions of philosophers. . . .

As many different constitutions as there are amongst men, so many different minds, characters, and manners. Even *Galen* * knew this truth, . . . that physic alone could change the minds and manners together with the body. It is true, that melancholy, bile, phlegm, blood, etc. according to the nature, quantity, and different mixture of these humours, not only produce differences in different men, but also render every individual different from what he was, before particular changes were induced in his fluids.

In diseases the soul is sometimes as it were eclipsed, and shews no sign of existence; sometimes one would say it was doubled, so far does passion transport it; sometimes its weakness vanishes, and a fool by the recovery of health, becomes a man of sense. Sometimes the noblest genius in the world sinks into stupidity, and never after recovers. Farewell, then to all those noble acquisitions of learning obtained with so much labour!

Here you may see a paralytic, who asks whether his leg be in bed; there a soldier who believes he still has the arm the surgeon has cut off. The memory of his former sensations, and of the part to which his soul referred them, causes his delusion and species of phrenzy. It suffices to speak to him of the amputated member, to make him recollect and renew, as it were, all its former sensations; which is done with a kind of displeasure of the imagination impossible to be expressed.

One man shall cry like a child at the approaches of death, which another perhaps will laugh at. What was it that could change the intrepidity of *Caius Julius, Seneca,* and *Petronius* † into pusillanimity and cowardice? An obstruction in the spleen, the liver, or some disorder in the *vena porta.* Why? Because the imagination is disorder'd at the same time, as the entrails, and hence arise all the different surprizing phaenomena of the hysteric, and hypochondriac affections.

What shall I say of those who believe they are transformed into wolves, cocks, pipkins, ‡ or believe that the dead suck, and live upon their blood? Or why should I take notice of those who think they see their noses, or some other member chang'd into glass, and who must be advised to lye on straw for fear of breaking them; to the end that they may find again the use of those parts, and their true flesh, when upon setting fire to the straw, they are afraid of being consumed, a fear which has sometimes cured a palsy? I ought to pass lightly over things that are well known by every body.

Nor shall I dwell upon the effects of sleep. Behold that wearied soldier! he snores in a trench, within the noise of a hundred cannon. His soul perceives nothing, his sleep

---

* [Galen: a Greek physician of the second century A.D., author of many treatises on medicine which were widely influential in the Middle Ages. (*Ed.*)]
† [Ancient Romans who were famous for their courage in the face of death. (*Ed.*)]
‡ [A small earthenware pot. (*Ed.*)]

is a perfect apoplexy. A bomb is ready to dash him in pieces; perhaps he will less feel this blow, than an insect that lies under his body.

On another side, a man, whom jealousy, hatred, avarice, or ambition devour, is incapable of finding the least repose. The stillest place, the most cooling and refreshing liquors, all become a subject of uneasiness to him, who has not freed his heart from the turbulency of the passions.

The body and soul seem to fall asleep together. In proportion as the motion of the blood grows calm, a soft soothing sense of peace and tranquility spreads itself over the whole machine; the soul finds itself sweetly weighed down with slumber, and sinks with the fibres of the brain: it becomes thus paralytic as it were, by degrees, together with all the muscles of the body. The latter are no longer able to support the head; the head itself can no longer bear the weight of thought; the soul is during sleep, as if it had no existence.

If the circulation goes on with too great rapidity; the soul cannot sleep. If the soul be thrown into too great an agitation, the blood loses its calm, and rushes thro' the veins with a noise that sometimes may be distinctly heard: such are the two reciprocal causes of insomnia. A frightful dream makes the heart beat double, and tears us from the sweet necessity of rest, as effectually as a lively pain, or pressing want. In a word, as the sole cessation of the functions of the soul produces sleep, man is subject even during some waking moments (when in reality the soul is no more than half awake) to certain sorts of revery or slumbers of the soul, which are very frequent, and sufficiently prove that the soul does not wait for the body to fall asleep. For if it does not entirely sleep, how little does it want of it? Since it is impossible for her to recollect one object, to which she gave attention, amidst that innumerable crowd of confused ideas, which as so many vanishing clouds had filled up, if I may so say, the atmosphere of the brain.

Opium has too great a relation with sleep, not to give it a place here. This drug intoxicates as well as wine, coffee, etc. every one according to its nature, and the quantity of the dose. It renders man happy in a state, which one would think to be the grave of all thoughts, as it is the image of death. What a pleasing lethargy! the soul would never be willing to quit it: she was torn as it were to pieces with the sharpest pains; but she has now no other sensation, than of the pleasure of suffering no longer, and of enjoying a charming tranquility. Opium seems even to change the will; it forces the soul that would fain wake and divert herself, to lie down with the body against her inclination. I waive mentioning here the history of poisons.

'Tis by lashing, as it were, the imagination, that coffee, that antidote of wine, dissipates our headaches and chagrins, without making us suffer, as the other liquor often does, the next day.

Let us consider the soul in its other wants. The human body is a machine that winds up its own springs: it is a living image of the perpetual motion. Food nourishes what a fever heats and excites. Without proper food the soul languishes, raves, and dies with faintness. It is like a taper, which revives in the moment it is going to be extinguished. Give but good nourishment to the body, pour into its tubes vigorous juices and strong liquors; then the soul, generous as these, arms itself with courage; and a soldier, whom water would have made run away, becoming undaunted, meets death with alacrity amidst the rattle of drums. Thus it is that hot water agitates the blood, which cold had calmed.

What a vast power there is in a repast! Joy revives in a disconsolate heart; it is transfused into the souls of all the guests, who express it by amiable conversation, or music. The hypochondriac mortal is overpowered with it; and the lumpish pedant is unfit for the entertainment. . . .

The different states of the soul are therefore always co-relative to the states of the body. But the better to shew all this dependency and its causes, let us make use of comparative anatomy, and open the entrails of men and brutes. What method can we have of knowing the human structure, but by being enlightened by a just comparison of the animal economy of both?

In general, the form and composition of the brains of quadrupeds are very near the same with those of man. There is the same figure, the same composition throughout: with this essential difference, that man of all animals has the most brains, and fullest of windings and folds in proportion to the bulk of his body; next to him are the ape, the beaver, the elephant, the dog, the fox, the Cat, etc. . . .

After quadrupeds, birds have the largest portion of brains. Fish have big heads indeed, but void of sense; as are the heads of a great part of mankind. They have not the callous body and have very little brains; but insects have none at all.

I shall not expatiate in a longer detail of all the varieties of nature, nor in conjectures; for both are infinite: as we may judge only by reading the treatises of *Willis de cerebro* and *de anima brutorum*.

I shall only conclude what evidently follows from these incontestable observations: first that the more savage animals are, the less brains they have: secondly, that this organ seems to be greater in some measure, in proportion to their docility: thirdly, that there is a constant and very surprizing law of nature, that the more is gained on the side of understanding and wit, the more is lost on the side of instinct. Now which overballances, the loss or the gain? . . .

The transition from animals to man is no way violent: to this all true philosophers will agree. What was man before the invention of words, and the knowledge of language? nothing but an animal of his kind, with much less natural instinct than others, of whom in such a state he could not imagine himself king; and distinguished from the ape and from other animals, only as the ape himself is distinguished; that is, by a more sensible physiognomy. Confined in this condition to the *intuitive knowlege* of the followers of *Leibnitz,** he saw nothing but figures and colours, without being able to distinguish any thing amongst them: old or young he was a child at every age, he stammered his sensations and wants, as a dog famished or tired with rest craves to eat, or to run about.

Words, languages, laws, sciences, and the liberal arts were introduced in time, and by them the rough diamond of our understanding was polished. Man has been broke and trained up, like any other animal; and he has learnt to be an author, as well as to be a porter. Geometricians have contrived to make the most difficult demonstrations

---

* [Leibniz (1646–1716): great German scientist and philosopher, whose spiritual "monadism" was one of the philosophies Lamettrie was trying to refute. (*Ed.*)]

and calculations, just as a monkey to put on, or take off his little hat, or jump upon his tractable dog. All was done by signs; each species comprehended what it could, and thus it was that men acquired *symbolical knowledge,* which still retains this name amongs the *German* philosophers.

Nothing, we see, is so simple as the mechanism of our education! All is reduced to sounds or words, that from the mouth of one pass thro' the ears of another, into the brain, which receives at the same time by the eyes the figure of bodies, of which these words are arbitrary signs. . . .

All this knowledge therefore, the vanity of which puffs up the giddy brain of our supercilious pedants, is nothing but a vast heap of words and figures, which form in the head the traces by which we distinguish and remember objects. All our ideas are revived, as a gardener that knows the plants, remembers their names as soon as he sees them. These words and figures are so connected in the brain, that we rarely happen to imagine a thing without the name, or the sign thereto annexed.

I always use the word *imagine,* because I am of opinion that every thing is imagined, and that all the parts of the soul may be justly reduced to the imagination only, which forms them all; and thus the judgment, reason, and memory are not absolute faculties of the soul, but real modifications of this kind of *medullary substance,* on which the objects painted in the eye are reflected, as from a magic lantern.

But if such be this wonderful and incomprehensible result of the organization of the brain, if all is conceived, all explained by the imagination, why should we divide the sensitive principle, which thinks in man? Is not this a manifest contradiction in the partizans for the simplicity of the mind? For whatever is divided, cannot without absurdity, be looked upon as indivisible. See to what the abuse of language reduces us; and the use of these pompous words *spirituality, immateriality,* often placed by chance, without being understood even by men of parts. . . .

According to the principles here laid down, and which I really look upon as true, he that has most imagination ought to be regarded as endowed with most wit, and genius; for all these words are synonimous; and once more I say it, 'tis a shameful abuse, to think as we often do, that we are speaking of different things, when we are only using different words or signs, to which we have annexed no idea, or real distinction.

The finest, the greatest, and the strongest imagination, is therefore the properest for the sciences as well as arts. I do not pretend to decide, whether more understanding be requisite to excell in the art of *Aristotle,* or *Descartes,* than in that of *Euripides,* or *Sophocles;* or whether nature put herself to greater expence to make a *Newton,* than to form a *Corneille* (a point I much doubt of) but certain it is, that the imagination alone differently applied, has formed their different triumphs, and rendered their memories immortal.

If a person is said to have but little judgment with a strong imagination, this is as much as to say, that the imagination being too much abandoned to itself, and almost constantly employed in looking at itself in the mirror of its sensations, has not sufficiently contracted the habit of examining them with attention: being more deeply moved with the traces and images, than with their truth or resemblance.

True it is, that such is vivacity of the springs of the imagination, that if attention, that key or mother of sciences, does not assist, it can only run slighty over the objects.

Like that bird on yonder spray, the imagination seems to be perpetually ready to take wing. Hurried with incessant rapidity by the vortex of the blood and animal spirits, one undulation makes an impression, which is immediately effaced by another; the soul pursues it, but often in vain: she must wait to bewail the loss of what she did not quickly lay hold of; and thus it is that the imagination, true image of time, is incessantly destroyed and renewed.

Such is the chaos, such the rapid and continual succession of our ideas; they drive one another successively, as one wave impels another; so that if the imagination does not employ a part of its muscles, poised as it were in an equilibrium upon the strings of the brain, so as to sustain itself some time on a fleeting object, and to avoid falling upon another, which it is not yet proper time to contemplate, it will never be worthy of the beautiful name of judgment. It will give a lively expression of what it has felt; it will form orators, musicians, painters, poets, but not one philosopher. On the contrary, if from our infancy the imagination be accustomed to bridle itself; not to give way to its own impetuosity, which forms nothing but splendid enthusiasts; to stop, to contain its ideas, and to revolve them in every sense, in order to view all the appearances of an object: then the imagination ready to judge, will embrace by reasoning the greatest sphere of objects, and its vivacity, which is always a good omen in children, and only needs the regulation of study and exercise, will become a clear-sighted penetration, without which we can make little progress in the sciences.

Such are the plain foundations upon which the structure of logic is erected. Nature designed them for the whole human species; but some have profited thereby, and others have only abused them.

In spite of all these prerogatives of man over brutes, 'tis an honour to him to be ranked in the same class. True it is, that 'till a certain age, he is more an animal than they, because he brought less instinct with him into the world.

What animal is there that would die with thirst in the midst of a river of milk? none but man. . . . He knows neither the food that is proper for him, nor the water that may drown him, nor the fire that may reduce him to ashes. Hold a blazing candle for the first time before a child, he will mechanically put his finger to it, to know what this new phaenomenon he sees is; at his own expence he will learn the danger, but he will not be catched again.

Put him with an animal upon the brink of a precipice; he alone will fall into it: he will be drowned, where the other will save himself by swimming. At fourteen or fifteen years of age, he scarce has a notion of the great pleasures that will attend him in the reproduction of his species; when a youth he knows not readily how to go about a sport which nature so quickly teaches all animals: He hides himself, as if he were ashamed to enjoy pleasure, and to be formed to be happy, whilst other animals seem to glory in being *Cynics*.* Without education they are without prejudice. Let us observe the boy and dog, that have both lost their masters in the high way; the child cries, he knows not whom to apply to. The dog better served by his scent, than the other by reason, will soon find his master out. . . .

---

* [Cynics: a Greek philosophic school founded by Antisthenes (*ca.* 444 B.C.–*ca.* 371 B.C.), which held all things in contempt except the simple, "natural" life of the animals. (*Ed.*)]

How shall we then at present define the law of nature? It is an inward principle, which instructs us in what we ought not to do to others, by putting us in mind of what we should not choose to be done to ourselves. May I be allow'd to adjoin to this general idea, that methinks this inward principle is nothing but a sort of fear or dread equally useful to the whole species and each individual; for perhaps we keep our hands from the purses and lives of other men, in order that we may the better secure our own life and property from violence. . . .

You see then that the law of nature is nothing but an inward principle which belongs to the imagination, as well as all others, amongst which we reckon thought. Consequently it supposes neither education, nor revelation, nor a law giver, at least it is not to be confounded with the civil laws, after the ridiculous manner of the divines.

Mad *Enthusiasts* with their arms may destroy the supporters of these truths; but the truths themselves can never be destroyed.

I do not here intend to call in question the existence of a supreme being; on the contrary I am of opinion that the greatest degree we can have of probability makes for this truth: but as this existence does not prove the necessity of one sort of worship more than another, we must therefore look upon it as a theoretical truth, which is but of little use in practice. As we may therefore say, after a deal of experience, that religion does not suppose strict probity, so the same reasons give us foundation to think that atheism does not exclude it.

Besides who knows but the cause of the existence of man, may be in the every existence itself? Perhaps he has been thrown by chance upon some spot of the surface of the earth, without a possibility of discovering why or whence he came; and with this knowledge only that he must live and die; like to those mushrooms which appear to day and are gone to morrow, or to those flowers which sprout up in ditches, or cover walls.

Let us not therefore lose ourselves in infinity, since we are incapable of having the least idea of it: it is impossible for us to trace the original of things; it is a matter really indifferent as to our happiness, whether matter has been from all eternity, or was created; whether there is or is not a supreme being. What folly then is it to torment oneself so much in searching after what is impossible to know, and which could not add any thing to our present felicity even if we were to gain our point. . . .

Such is the law of nature, and whoever observes it strictly, is a man of honesty, and deserves the esteem and confidence of mankind; but whoever swerves from it, and affects an outward shew of some other religion, is an impostor as well as a hypocrite, whom I entirely distrust.

After what has been said, let the giddy multitude think otherways: let them affirm that honesty itself must sooner be sacrific'd, than we should withdraw our belief of revelation: in a word, that we must have another religion than that of nature, let it be what it will. What misery! what pity! how high is the opinion of every one for that particular religion which he has embraced! We court not here the applause of the vulgar. He who rears up in his own mind altars to superstition, is born to worship idols, and was not design'd to feel the force and energy of true virtue.

But since all the faculties of the soul depend so much upon the proper organization of the brain, and of the whole body, that they appear evidently to be nothing but this organization itself; we may well call it an enlighten'd machine. For in short, tho' man alone had receiv'd the law of nature, would he, for this reason, be less a machine? Some more wheels, some more springs, than are found in other animals the most perfect; the brain in proportion seated more near the heart, and consequently receiving more blood; the same reason likewise given; in fine, some unknown cause or another might have produc'd this conscience which has such delicacy and exquisite feeling, that remorse as foreign to matter as thought; in a word, all that difference or distinction which is here suppos'd. Will organization serve all these purposes? yes, I say once more, it will: since thought evidently unfolds itself with the organs, why may we not allow that matter, of which they are compos'd, to be likewise susceptible of remorse, when once it has by time acquir'd the power of feeling?

The soul then, is nothing but an empty term, of which we have no idea, and which a man of a right understanding ought to make use of, only to express that part which thinks in us. The least principle of motion being granted, then animated bodies will have all that's requisite to make them move, feel, think, repent, in a word, enough to lead them into all the physical and moral consequences which depend thereon. . . .

To be a machine, to feel, to think, to be able to distinguish good and evil, as well as the eyes can different colours, in a word, to be born with an understanding and moral sense, yet at the same time, to be but an animal, or machine, in all this there is no more absurdity than in asserting that there is a Monkey, or Parrot, both which are capable of giving and receiving pleasure. Here I may take the opportunity to ask, who at first could have imagined, that one drop of the seminal liquor which is discharg'd in copulation, should be the occasion of such extatic pleasure, and afterwards spring up into a little creature, which in time, certain conditions being suppos'd, should itself feel the same transports? So far then am I from thinking that thought is inconsistent with organized matter, that I look upon it to be a property as much belonging thereto, as electricity, impenetrability, extension, etc. . . .

In reality, we ourselves are but as moles in the field of nature, and we make the same progression which that animal does; and 'tis our pride which pretends to set bounds to what is boundless. We are like a watch which should speak in this manner, (a writer of fables would make it a character of consequence in one of his performances.) "What is he but a blockhead, who takes upon himself to be my maker? am I to be call'd the creature of this silly mortal! I who divide the time! I who mark the course of the sun so exactly! I who repeat aloud the hours which I discover! No, no, this cannot be." In the same manner, we mortals, ungrateful wretches! look down with an air of contempt on the common parent of all kingdoms, as the chymists express it. We conceive, or rather we suppose, a cause superiour to that which we are all indebted to, and which has certainly made every thing in a manner that's wonderful and unconceivable. Matter has nothing contemptible in it, tho' it may appear so to coarse eyes, who despise it in the most shining works; and nature is free and unbounded in all her performances. She produces millions of men with more facility and pleasure, than a watch-maker frames a piece of clock-work. Her power is equally display'd in the production of the lowest insect, as it is in that of the more lofty creature, man. The animal kingdom costs her no more labour than the vegetable, and she can form the greatest genius with the same degree of ease, as she does an ear of corn. Let us not then be carried away by the strength of fancy alone, but let us examine those things which are presented to our eyes, and by this we may form a judgment of others which are beyond our sight, and hidden from our prying curiosity. Let us consider the Monkey, the Beaver, the Elephant, etc. in their actions and behaviour. Since it is evident, that they cannot act in the manner they do, without understanding, why should we refuse it to these animals? And if you grant them a soul, enthusiasts, then you are quite overthrown. You say, that you do not pretend to judge of the nature of this soul, whilst at the same time (O strange contradiction!) you openly affirm it to be deprived of immortality. Who does not at once perceive that it must be mortal, or immortal, according as ours is, and must undergo the same fate whatever it may be? 'Tis in this manner they run upon Scilla, whilst they are endeavouring to shun Charibdis with the utmost precaution.*

Dare to throw off those prejudices in which you are fetter'd: assert your liberty, and arm yourselves with the light of experience; then instead of being blinded by ignorance, and drawing inferences derogatory to the honour of nature, you will give her the praise and esteem she really deserves. Open your eyes only, and meddle not with what you are unable to comprehend. You will see that the husbandman whose light and understanding does not go beyond the furrow which he plows, does not essentially differ from the greatest genius, as has been prov'd by dissecting the heads of Descartes and Newton. Upon enquiry you'll be convinc'd that the fool and the idiot are only beasts in a human form, as a sensible monkey is a little man in a different shape; and in short, that all depends upon the different organization. An animal that's properly constructed, and has been taught astronomy, will be able to foretell an eclipse, as one which has been bred up in the school of Hippocrates, and spent some time in visiting the sick, will be able to prescribe a cure, or foretell when the distemper is incurable. 'Tis by this thread of truths and observations that we trace out matter, and affix to it that admirable property of thinking, tho' we cannot indeed, with our eyes, see this connexion, because the essential nature of this attribute is unknown to us.

Let us not pretend to say, that every machine, or animal, is entirely annihilated after death, nor that they put on another form, since we are quite in the dark as to this point. To affirm an immortal machine to be a chimera, or fiction of our brain appears to be as absurd as it would seem in Caterpillars, when they see the dead bodies of their kind, bitterly to lament the fate of their species, which would seem to them to be utterly destroy'd. The soul of these insects (for every animal has one peculiar to it) is too narrow, and confin'd to be able to comprehend the transformation of their Nature. Never did any one of the acutest amongst them, entertain the least notion that he would become a Butterfly. It is the very same case with us. What do we know of our future destiny, more than we do of our original? Let us then confess our total ignorance, since upon this our happiness is placed.

He who will think thus, shall be wise, just, pleased with his condition, and consequently happy; he will patiently expect death, without fearing, or desiring it; he will cherish life, thinking it unaccountable how disgust should corrupt the heart in a world abounding with so much joy; full of respect for nature; overflowing with gratitude,

---

* [Scylla and Charybdis: in Greek mythology, these were a many-armed monster and a whirlpool, which together made the Straits of Messina (between Italy and Sicily) almost impassable. (*Ed.*)]

affection, and love; all which rise in proportion to the bounty which he has received. Happy in short in the enjoyment of life, and pleas'd with being admitted a spectator of the universe, he will never think of attempting to destroy his own being, nor that of others; nay, so far from this, that he will have an universal benevolence to all mankind, and will be in love with this principle of humanity, even tho' in his enemies. He will not hate, but will be sorry for the vicious, they will appear to him as deform'd men. But in good nature, bearing with the infirmities of the mind and body, he will at the same time admire their beauty and vertue. Those who have been favoured by nature, will appear to him more worthy of esteem than others whom she has treated with the harshness of a step-mother. 'Tis thus, that the advocate for matter so often thinks and talks, and pays that respect, refus'd by others, to natural abilities, which are certainly the source of all acquired qualifications. In short the materialist, tho' his vanity may murmur against it, in reality is convinced, that he is only a machine, or animal, and he will not abuse any of his fellow creatures. Being instructed by nature how to regulate his actions, which are proportioned to that degree of analogy before-mentioned: In a word, following the law of nature given to all animals, he will not do to another, what he would not choose to be done to himself.

Let us conclude boldly then, that man is a machine; and that there is only one substance, differently modified in the whole universe. This is not an hypothesis raised upon the strength of things required, or suppos'd to be true; this is not the work of a man of prejudice, nor of my reason alone; I should have despised any other guide as unsure, had not my senses stepped forth, and if I may so say, holding up a lighted torch, induc'd me to pursue the road which shin'd with light. Experience has spoke to me in behalf of reason, and thus it is, that I have joyn'd them both together.

But it may be observed, that I have not made use of these proofs, or strong inferences, but as deductions immediately drawn from a number of physical observations, the truth of which no men of learning can dispute: and indeed it is them alone whom I acknowledge to be proper judges of the consequences which I have drawn, absolutely refusing to submit to the judgment of any prejudiced person, or of him who is unacquainted with anatomy; because in effect, he is ignorant of that philosophy which alone we make use of, that is, a knowledge in the structure of the human body. What will all the weak reeds of divinity, metaphysics and nonsense of the schools, avail against the firm and solid oak? Childish arms like to the foils made use of in fencing schools, which may give the pleasure of fencing, but will never enter the body of our antagonist. Need I here mention that I mean those fantastical, impertinent notions, those thread-bare pitiful reasonings, which as long as there is the least shadow of prejudice, or superstition upon earth, will be made upon the pretended incompatibility of two substances touching and moving each other without intermission? This is my system, or rather, this is the truth, if I am not much mistaken. It is short and plain: Let who will dispute it.

ᴥᵟ HISTORY OF THE ROYAL SOCIETY

Thomas Sprat

We sometimes forget that the remarkable progress of science in modern times depends not only on men of genius and their use of the experimental method, but on a host of social and political conditions. There must be an atmosphere receptive to free inquiry into the natural causes of things, and men must be free to publish and discuss the results of their inquiries. If some government were to close down all the laboratories, presses, and associations (including universities), that nation's scientific and technological progress would soon slow to a snail's pace, to be left far behind by its neighbors. When King Charles II granted a charter to the Royal Society of London in 1662, therefore, "for the Advancement of experimental Philosophy," it symbolized the opening of a new era.

Thomas Sprat's History *was published in 1667, apparently as a defense of the Society against charges of impiety, folly, or both. He himself was not a scientist, but the Bishop of Rochester; probably he was accepted as a member for the express purpose of writing a respectable apologia for the group. Its original members included many of the great English scientists of the day: Robert Boyle, Christopher Wren, Robert Hooke, and others.*

Bishop Sprat was anxious to stress the practical, utilitarian aspects of the researches carried on by the members of the Society, presumably in response to gibes such as that of King Charles himself that they "spend time only in weighing of ayre." Sprat therefore devoted some 160 pages of his History *to an account of some of the more useful researches, with such topics as these: "A Method for Making a History of the Weather," "A Proposal for Making Wine," "Experiments of the Recoiling of Guns," and "The History of the Generation and Ordering of Green-Oysters." But at the same time, Robert Boyle was distinguishing between elements and compounds and laying the theoretical foundations of modern chemistry by formulating the law ("Boyle's Law") that relates the temperature, pressure, and volume of a gas in a simple mathematical formula (that is, by "weighing ayre"!).*

(I)

I shall here present to the World, an Account of the *First Institution* of the *Royal Society;* and of the *Progress,* which they have already made: in hope, that this Learned and Inquisitive Age, will either think their Indeavours, worthy of its *Assistance;* or else will be thereby provok'd, to attempt some *greater Enterprise* (if any such can be found out) for the Benefit of humane life, by the Advancement of *Real Knowledge.* . . .

I shall therefore divide my Discourse into these three general Heads.

The *First* shall give a short view of the *Antient,* and *Modern* Philosophy; and of the most Famous Attempts, that have been made for its *Advancement:* that by observing wherein others have *excell'd,* and wherein they have been thought to *fail,* we may the better shew, what is to be expected, from these new Undertakers; and what mov'd them, to enter upon a way of Inquiry, different from that, on which the former have proceeded.

The *Second* shall consist of the *Narrative* it self: and out of their *Registers,* and *Journals,* which I have been permitted to peruse, shall relate the first Occasions of their Meetings, the Incouragement, and Patronage, which they have receiv'd; their *Patent,* their *Statutes,* the whole Order and Scheme of their *Design,* and the *Manner* of their Proceedings.

The *Third* shall try, to assert the *Advantage* and *Innocence* of this work, in respect of all *Professions,* and especially of *Religion;* and how proper, above others, it is, for the present temper of the *Age* wherein we live.

On the *First* and *Last* of these Particulars, it is not needful that I should long insist: because several *Great Men* have already so much prevented me about them; that there is hardly any thing can be spoken, in which I shall not almost tread in their very *Footsteps.* But yet it is requisite, that something be here said to that purpose, though it be only in *Repetition:* because I perceive, that there is still much prejudice remaining on many mens minds, towards any *now* Discoveries in *Natural* Things. This I shall try to remove, not that I imagine, that those Reasons can have any great effect in my *weak hands,* which were not able fully to prevail, when they were inforc'd by the Eloquence of those *Excellent Men,* who have gone before me in this Argument: But I rather trust to the inclination of the *Age* it self, wherein I write; which (if I mistake not) is farr more prepar'd to be perswaded to promote such Studies, then any other time that has gone before us. . . .

But my other instance * comes nearer home, and it is of the *Schole-men.* Whose works when I consider, it puts into my thoughts, how farre more importantly a good Method of thinking, and a right course of apprehending things, does contribute to-

Thomas Sprat, History of the Royal Society, J. I. Cope and H. W. Jones, eds. (St. Louis: Washington University Studies, 1959), pp. 1–2, 3–5, 15–18, 21–22, 52–53, 55–57, 61–63, 64–69, 73–74, 76, 81–83, 99–100, 124–125, 128–129 (1667 ed. of text).

* [He has been saying that science never flourishes when carried on primarily by priests. His first example was the Jews. (*Ed.*)]

wards the attaining of perfection in true knowledge, then the strongest, and most vigorous wit in the World, can do without them. It cannot without injustice be deny'd, that they were men of extraordinary strength of mind: they had a great quickness of imagination, and subtility of distinguishing: they very well understood the consequence of propositions: their natural endowments were excellent: their industry commendable: But they lighted on a wrong path at first, and wanted matter to contrive: and so, like the *Indians,* onely express'd a wonderful Artifice, in the ordering of the same Feathers into a thousand varities of Figures. I will not insist long on the Barbarousness of their style: though that too might justly be censur'd: for all the *antient Philosophers,* though they labor'd not to be full, and adorn'd in their Speech: yet they always strove to be easie, naturall, and unaffected. *Plato* was allow'd by all to be the chief Master of *Speaking,* as well as of *thinking.* And even *Aristotle* himself, whom alone these men ador'd, however he has been since us'd by his *Commentators,* was so careful about his words, that he was esteem'd one of the purest, and most polite Writers of his time. But the want of good Language, not being the *Schole-mens* worst defect, I shall pass it over: and rather stop a little, to examine the *matter* itself, and *order* in which they proceeded.

The *Subjects* about which they were most conversant, were either some of those *Arts,* which *Aristotle* had drawn into Method, or the more speculative parts of our *Divinity.* These they commonly handled after this fashion. They began with some generall Definitions of the things themselves, according to their universal Natures: Then divided them into their parts, and drew them out into severall propositions, which they layd down as Problems: these they controverted on both sides: and by many nicities of Arguments, and citations of Authorities, confuted their adversaries, and strengthened their own dictates. But though this Notional Warr had been carry'd on with farr more care, and calmness amongst them, then it was: yet it was never able to do any great good towards the enlargement of knowledge: Because it rely'd on *generall Terms,* which had not much foundation in *Nature;* and also because they took no other course, but that of *disputing.*

That this insisting altogether on establish'd *Axioms,* is not the most usefull way, is not only clear in such airy conceptions, which they manag'd: but also in those things, which lye before every mans observation, which belong to the life, and passions, and manners of men; which, one would think, might be sooner reduc'd into standing Rules. As for example: To make a prudent man in the affairs of State, It is not enough, to be well vers'd in all the conclusions, which all the *Politicians* in the World have devis'd, or to be expert in the Nature of Government, and Laws, Obedience, and Rebellion, Peace, and War: Nay rather a man that relyes altogether on such universal precepts, is almost certain to miscarry. But there must be a sagacity of judgement in particular things: a dexterity in discerning the advantages of occasions: a study of the humour, and interest of the people he is to govern: The same is to be found in *Philosophy;* a thousand fine Argumentations, and Fabricks in the mind, concerning the Nature of *Body, Quantity, Motion,* and the like, if they only hover a-loof, and are not squar'd to particular matters, they may give an empty satisfaction, but no benefit, and rather serve to *swell,* then *fill* the Soul.

But besides this, the very way of *disputing* itself, and inferring one thing from another alone, is not at all proper for the spreading of knowledge. It serves admirably well indeed, in those Arts, where the connexion between the propositions is necessary, as in the *Mathematicks,* in which a long train of *Demonstrations,* may be truly collected, from the certainty of the first foundation: But in things of probability onely, it seldom or never happens, that after some little progress, the main subject is not left, and the contenders fall not into other matters, that are nothing to the purpose: For if but one link in the whole chain be loose, they wander farr away, and seldom, or never recover their first ground again. In brief, *disputing* is a very good instrument, to sharpen mens wits, and to make them versatil, and wary defenders of the Principles, which they already know: but it can never much augment the *solid substance* of *Science* itself: And me thinks compar'd to *Experimenting,* it is like *Exercise* to the Body in comparison of *Meat:* For running, walking, wrestling, shooting, and other such active sports, will keep men in health, and breath, and a vigorous temper: but it must be a supply of new food that must make them grow: so it is in this case; much contention, and strife of argument, will serve well to explain obscure things, and strengthen the weak, and give a good, sound, masculine colour, to the whole masse of knowledge: But it must be a continued addition of observations, which must nourish, and increase, and give new Blood, and flesh, to the *Arts* themselves. . . .

*   *   *

But now it is time for me to dismiss this subtle generation of Writers: whom I would not have prosecuted so farr, but that they are still esteem'd by some men, the onely Masters of Reason. If they would be content, with any thing less then an Empire in Learning, we would grant them very much. We would permit them to be great, and profound Wits, as *Angelicall,* and *Seraphical,* as they pleas'd: We would commend them, as we are wont to do *Chaucer;* we would confess, that: they are admirable in comparison of the ignorance of their own Age: And, as Sir *Philip Sidney* of him, we would say of them; that it is to be wonder'd, how they could see so cleerly then, and we can see no cleerer now: But that they should still be set before us, as the great Oracles of all Wit, we can never allow. Suppose, that I should grant, that they are most usefull in the controversies of our *Church,* to defend us against the Heresies, and Schisms of our times: what will thence follow, but that they ought to be confin'd, within their own Bounds, and not be suffer'd to hinder the enlargement of the territories of other *Sciences?* Let them still prevail in the *Scholes,* and let them govern in disputations: But let them not over-spread all sorts of knowledge. That would be as ridiculous, as if, because we see, that Thorns, and Briers, by reason of their sharpness, are fit to stop a gap, and keep out wild Beasts; we should therefore think, they deserv'd to be planted all over every Field. And yet I should not doubt, (if it were not somewhat improper to the present discourse) to prove, that even in *Divinity* itself, they are not so necessary, as they are reputed to be: and that all, or most of our Religious controversies, may be as well decided, by plain reason, and by considerations, which may be fetch'd from the *Religion* of *mankind,* the Nature of *Government,* and *humane Society,* and *Scripture* itself, as by the multitudes of Authorities, and subtleties of disputes, which have been heretofore in use. . . .

(II)

Thus I am, at length, arriv'd at the second Part of my Method, the *Narration* it self. This I shall divide into three Periods of Time, according to the several Degrees of the *preparation, growth,* and *compleat Constitution* of the *Royal Society.* . . .

Their first purpose was no more, then onely the satisfaction of breathing a freer air, and of conversing in quiet one with another, without being ingag'd in the passions, and madness of that dismal Age. And from the Institution of that *Assembly,* it had been enough, if no other advantage had come, but this: That by this means there was a race of yong Men provided, against the next Age, whose minds receiving from them, their first Impressions of *sober* and *generous knowledge,* were invincibly arm'd against all the inchantments of *Enthusiasm.* . . .

For such a candid, and unpassionate company, as that was, and for such a gloomy season, what could have been a fitter Subject to pitch upon, then *Natural Philosophy?* To have been always tossing about some *Theological question,* would have been, to have made that their private diversion, the excess of which they themselves dislik'd in the publick: To have been eternally musing on *Civil business,* and the distresses of their Country, was too melancholy a reflexion: It was *Nature* alone, which could pleasantly entertain them, in that estate. The contemplation of that, draws our minds off from past, or present misfortunes, and makes them conquerers over things, in the greatest publick unhappiness: while the consideration of *Men,* and *humane affairs,* may affect us, with a thousand various disquiets; *that* never separates us into mortal Factions; *that* gives us room to differ, without animosity; and permits us, to raise contrary imaginations upon it, without any danger of a *Civil War.*

Their *meetings* were as frequent, as their affairs permitted: their proceedings rather by action, then discourse; chiefly attending some particular Trials, in *Chymistry,* or *Mechanicks:* they had no Rules nor Method fix'd: their intention was more, to communicate to each other, their discoveries, which they could make in so narrow a compass, than an united, constant, or regular inquisition. And me thinks, their constitution did bear some resemblance, to the *Academy* lately begun at *Paris:* where they have at last turn'd their thoughts, from *Words,* to experimental *Philosophy,* and perhaps in imitation of the *Royal Society.* Their manner likewise, is to assemble in a private house, to reason freely upon the works of Nature; to pass Conjectures, and propose Problems, on any Mathematical, or Philosophical Matter, which comes in their way. And this is an Omen, on which I will build some hope, that as they agree with us in what was done at *Oxford,* so they will go on farther, and come by the same degrees, to erect another *Royal Society* in *France.* I promise for these Gentlemen here (so well I know the generosity of their Design) that they will be most ready to accept their assistance. To them, and to all the Learned World besides, they call for aid. No difference of *Country, Interest,* or profession of *Religion,* will make them backward from taking, or affording help in this enterprize. And indeed all *Europe* at this time, have two general Wars, which they ought in honor to make: The one a *holy,* the other a *Philosophical:* The one against the common Enemy of *Christendom,* the other also against powerful, and barbarous Foes, that have not been fully subdu'd almost these six thousand years, *Ignorance,* and *False Opinions.* Against these, it becomes us, to go forth in one common expedition: All civil Nations joyning their *Armies* against the one, and their *Reason* against the other; without any petty contentions, about privileges, or precedence. . . .

I will here, in the first place, contract into few Words, the whole *summe* of their *Resolutions;* which I shall often have occasion, to touch upon in *parcels.* Their purpose is, in short, to make faithful *Records,* of all the Works of *Nature,* or *Art,* which can come within their reach: that so the present Age, and posterity, may be able to put a mark on the Errors, which have been strengthened by long prescription: to restore the Truths, that have lain neglected: to push on those, which are already known, to more various uses: and to make the way more passable, to what remains unreveal'd. This is the compass of their Design. And to accomplish this, they have indeavor'd, to separate the knowledge of *Nature,* from the colours of *Rhetorick,* the devices of *Fancy,* or the delightful deceit of *Fables.* They have labor'd to inlarge it, from being confin'd to the custody of a few; or from servitude to private interests. They have striven to preserve it from being over-press'd by a confus'd heap of vain, and useless particulars; or from being straitned and bounded too much up by General Doctrines. They have try'd, to put it into a condition of perpetual increasing; by settling an inviolable correspondence between the hand, and the brain. They have studi'd, to make it, not onely an Enterprise of one season, or of some lucky opportunity; but a business of time; a steddy, a lasting, a popular, an uninterrupted Work. They have attempted, to free it from the Artifice, and Humors, and Passions of Sects; to render it an Instrument, whereby Mankind may obtain a Dominion over *Things,* and not onely over one anothers *Judgements.* And lastly, they have begun to establish these Reformations in Philosophy, not so much, by any solemnity of Laws, or ostentation of Ceremonies; as by solid Practice, and examples: not, by a glorious pomp of Words; but by the silent, effectual, and unanswerable Arguments of real Productions.

This will more fully appear, by what I am to say on these four particulars, which shall make up this part of my Relation, the *Qualifications* of their *Members:* the *manner* of their *Inquiry:* their *weekly Assemblies:* and their *way* of *Registring.*

As for what belongs to the *Members* themselves, that are to constitute the *Society:* It is to be noted, that they have freely admitted Men of different Religions, Countries, and Professions of Life. This they were oblig'd to do, or else they would come far short of the largeness of their own Declarations. For they openly profess, not to lay the Foundation of an *English, Scotch, Irish, Popish,* or *Protestant* Philosophy; but a Philosophy of *Mankind.* . . .

By their *naturalizing* Men of all Countries, they have laid the beginnings of many great advantages for the future. For by this means, they will be able to settle a *constant Intelligence,* throughout all civil Nations; and make the *Royal Society* the general *Banck,* and Free-port of the World: A policy, which whether it would hold good, in the *Trade of England,* I know not: but sure it will in the *Philosophy.* We are to overcome the mysteries of all the Works of Nature; and not onely to prosecute such as are confin'd to one Kingdom, or beat upon one shore. We should not then refuse to list

all the aids, that will come in, how remote soever. If I could fetch my materials
whence I pleas'd, to fashion the *Idea* of a perfect Philosopher: he should not be all
of one *clime,* but have the different excellencies of several Countries. First, he should
have the *Industry, Activity,* and *Inquisitive humor* of the *Dutch, French, Scotch,* and
English, in laying the ground Work, the heap of Experiments: And then he should
have added the cold, and *circumspect,* and *wary* disposition of the *Italians,* and *Spaniards,* in meditating upon them, before he fully brings them into speculation. All this
is scarce ever to be found in one single Man: seldom in the same Countrymen: It must
then be supply'd, as well as it may, by a *Publick Council;* wherein the various dispositions of all these Nations, may be blended together. To this purpose, the *Royal
Society* has made no scruple, to receive all inquisitive strangers of all Countries, into
its number. And this they have constantly done, with such peculiar respect, that they
have not oblig'd them to the charge of contributions: they have always taken care,
that some of their Members, should assist them in interpreting all that pass'd, in
their publick Assemblies: and they have freely open'd their Registers to them; thereby
inviting them, to communicate forein Rarities, by imparting their own discoveries.
This has been often acknowledg'd, by many Learned Men, who have travell'd hither;
who have been introduc'd to their meetings, and have admir'd the decency, the gravity,
the plainess, and the calmness of their debates. This they have publish'd to the world:
and this has rous'd all our neighbors to fix their eies upon *England.* From hence they
expect the great improvements of knowledge will flow: and though, perhaps, they send
their *youth* into other parts, to learn *Fashion,* and *Breeding:* yet their *Men* come hither
for nobler ends; to be instructed, in the *masculine,* and the *Solid Arts of Life:* which
is a matter of as much greater Reputation, as it is more honorable, to teach Philosophers, than Children.

By their admission of Men of all *professions,* these *two* Benefits arise: The *one,*
that every *Art,* and every way of life already establish'd, may be secure of receiving no
damage by their Counsels. A thing which all new Inventions ought carefully to consult. It is in vain, to declare against the profit of the most, in any change that we would
make. We must not always deal with the violent current of popular passions; as they
do with the furious *Eager* in the *Severn:* Where the safest way is, to set the head of
the Boat directly against its force. But here Men must follow the shore; wind about
leisurably; and insinuate their useful alterations, by soft, and unperceivable degrees.
From the neglect of this Prudence, we often see men of great Wit, to have been over-
born by the multitude of their opposers; and to have found all their subtile projects too
weak, for custom, and interest: While being a little too much heated with a love of
their own fancies; they have rais'd to themselves more Enemies than they needed to
have done; by defying at once, too many things in use. But here, this danger is very
well prevented. For what suspicion can *Divinity, Law* or *Physick,* or any other course
of life have, that they shall be impair'd by these mens labours: when they themselves
are as capable of fitting amongst them as any others? Have they not the same security
that the whole Nation has for its lives and fortunes? of which this is esteem'd the
Establishment, that men of all forts, and qualities, give their voice in every law that
is made in *Parliament.* But the other benefit is, that by this equal Balance of all Pro-

fessions, there will no one particular of them overweigh the other, or make the *Oracle* onely speak their *private* sence: which else it were impossible to avoid. It is natural to all Ranks of men, to have some one Darling, upon which their care is chiefly fix'd. If *Mechanicks* alone were to make a Philosophy, they would bring it all into their Shops; and force it wholly to consist of Springs and Wheels, and Weights: if *Physicians,* they would not depart farr from their Art; scarce any thing would be consider'd, besides the *Body* of *Man,* the *Causes, Signs,* and *Cures* of Diseases. So much is to be found in Men of all conditions, of that which is call'd *Pedantry* in Scholars: which is nothing else but an obstinate addiction, to the forms of some private life, and not regarding general things enough. This freedom therefore, which they use, in embracing all assistance, is most advantageous to them: which is the more remarkable, in that they diligently search out, and join to them, all extraordinary men, though but of ordinary Trades. And that they are likely to continue this comprehensive temper hereafter, I will shew by one Instance: and it is the recommendation which the *King* himself was pleased to make, of the judicious Author of *the Observations on the Bills of Mortality:* In whose Election, it was so farr from being a prejudice, that he was a Shop-keeper of *London;* that His Majesty gave this particular charge to His Society, that if they found any more such Tradesmen, they should be sure to admit them all, without any more ado. From hence it may be concluded, what is their inclination towards the manual Arts; by the carefull regard which their *Founder,* and *Patron,* has engag'd them to have, for all sorts of *Mechanick Artists.*

But, though the *Society* entertains very many men of *particular Professions;* yet the farr greater Number are *Gentlemen,* free, and unconfin'd. By the help of this, there was hopefull Provision made against *two corruptions* of Learning, which have been long complain'd of, but never remov'd: The *one,* that *Knowledge* still degenerates, to consult *present profit* too soon; the *other,* that *Philosophers* have bin always *Masters, and Scholars;* some imposing, & all the other submitting; and not as equal observers without dependence.

The first of these may be call'd, the *marrying of Arts too soon;* and putting them to generation, before they come to be of Age; and has been the cause of much inconvenience. It weakens their strength; It makes an unhappy disproportion in their increase; while not the *best,* but the *most gainfull* of them flourish: But above all, it diminishes that very profit for which men strive. It busies them about possessing some petty prize; while Nature it self, with all its mighty Treasures, sips from them: and so they are serv'd like some foolish Guards; who, while they were earnest in picking up some small Money, that the Prisoner drop'd out of his Pocket, let the Prisoner himself escape, from whom they might have got a great randsom. This is easily declam'd against, but most difficult to be hindred. If any caution will serve, it must be this; to commit the Work to the care of such men, who, by the freedom of their education the plenty of their estates, and the usual generosity of Noble Bloud, may be well suppo'd to be most averse from such sordid considerations.

The second Error, wich is hereby endeavour'd to be remedied, is, that the Seats of Knowledg, have been for the most part heretofore, not *Laboratories,* as they ought to be; but onely *Scholes,* where some have taught, and all the rest *subscrib'd.* The consequences of this are very mischievous. For first, as many *Learners* as there are, so many hands, and brains may still be reckon'd upon, as useless. It being onely the *Master's* part, to examine, and observe; and the Disciples, to submit with silence, to what they conclude. But besides this, the very inequality of the Titles of *Teachers,* and *Scholars,* does very much suppress, and tame mens Spirits; which though it should be proper for Discipline and Education; yet is by no means consistent with a free Philosophical Con-sultation. It is undoubtedly true; that scarce any man's mind, is so capable of *thinking strongly,* in the presence of one, whom he *fears,* and *reverences;* as he is, when that restraint is taken off. And this is to be found not only in these weightier matters; but also (to give a lighter instance) in the Arts of *Discourse,* & *raillery* themselves. For we have often seen men of bold tempers, that have over-aw'd and govern'd the Wit of most Companies; to have been disturb'd, and dumb, & bashful as children, when some other man has been near, who us'd to out-talk them. Such a kind of natural soveraignty there is, in some mens minds over others: which must needs be farr greater, when it is advanc'd by long use & the venerable name of a *Master.* I shall only mention one prejudice more, & that is this; That from this onely teaching, and learning, there does not onely follow a continuance, but an increase of the yoak upon our Reasons. For those who take their opinions from others Rules, are commonly stricter Imposers upon their Scholars, than their own Authors were on them, or than the first Inventors of things themselves are upon others. Whatever the cause of this be; whether the first men are made meek, and gentle, by their long search, and by better understanding all the difficulties of Knowledg; while those that learn afterwards, onely hastily catching things in small *Systems,* are soon satisfy'd, before they have broken their pride, & so become more imperious: or, whether it arises from hence, that the same *meanness of Soul,* which made them bound their thoughts by others Precepts, makes them also *insolent* to their inferiors; as we always find *cowards* the most *cruel:* or whatever other cause may be alleg'd; the observation is certain, that the *Successors* are usually more positive, and Tyrannical, than the *beginners* of Sects. . . .

. . . It seems strange to me, that men should conspire, to believe all things more perplex'd, and difficult, than indeed they are. This may be shewn in most other matters; but in this particular in hand, it is most evident. Men did generally think, that no man was fit to meddle in matters of this consequence, but he that had bred himself up in a long course of Discipline for that purpose; that had the habit, the gesture, the look of a Philosopher. Whereas experience on the contrary tells us, that greater things are produc'd, by the *free* way, than the *formal.* This mistake may well be compar'd, to the conceit we had of *Souldiers,* in the beginning of the civil Warrs. None was thought worthy of that name, but he that could shew his wounds, and talk aloud of his exploits in the *Low-Countreys.* Whereas the whole business of fighting, was afterwards chiefly perform'd by *untravell'd Gentlemen, raw Citizens,* and *Generals,* that had scarce ever before seen a Battel. But to say no more, it is so farr from being a blemish; that it is rather the excellency of this Institution, that *men of various Studies* are introduc'd. For so there will be always many sincere witnesses standing by, whom self-love wil not persuade to report falsly, nor heat of invention carry to swallow a deceit too soon; as having themselves no hand in the making of the Experiment, but onely in the *Inspection.* So cautious ought men to be, in pronouncing even upon Matters of Fact.

The whole care is not to be trusted to *single* men: not to a *Company* all of *one mind;* not to *Philosophers;* not to *devout,* and religious men *alone:* By all these we have been already deluded; even by those whom I last nam'd, who ought most of all to abhorr falshood; of whom yet many have multiply'd upon us, infinite Stories, and false Miracles, without any regard to Conscience, or Truth. . . .

These therefore are the *Qualities,* which they have principally requir'd, in those, whom they admitted: still reserving to themselves a power of *increasing,* or keeping to their number, as they saw occasion. By this means, they have given assurance of an eternal quietness, and moderation, in their experimental progress; because they allow themselves to differ in the weightiest matter, even in the *way of Salvation* it self. By this they have taken care, that nothing shall be so remote, as to escape their reach: because some of their *Members* are still scattered abroad, in most of the habitable parts of the Earth. By this, they have provided, that no profitable thing shall seem too mean for their consideration, seeing they have some amongst them, whose life is employ'd about *little* things, as well as *great.* By this they have broken down the partition wall, and made a fair entrance, for *all conditions of men* to engage in these Studies; which were heretofore affrighted from them, by a groundless apprehension of their charge-ableness, and difficulty. Thus they have form'd that *Society,* which intends a *Philosophy,* for the use of *Cities,* and not for the retirements of *Schools,* to resemble the *Cities* themselves: which are compounded of all sorts of men, of the *Gown,* of the *Sword,* of the *Shop,* of the *Field,* of the *Court,* of the *Sea;* all mutually *assisting* each other. . . .

Of the *extent* of the *matter,* about which they have been already conversant, and intend to be hereafter; there can be no better measure taken, than by giving a *general prospect* of all the objects of mens thoughts: which can be nothing else, but either *God,* or *Men,* or *Nature.*

As for the First, they meddle no otherwise with *Divine things,* than onely as the *Power,* and *Wisdom,* and *Goodness* of the *Creator,* is display'd in the admirable order, and workman-ship of the Creatures. It cannot be deny'd, but it lies in the *Natural Philosophers* hands, best to advance that part of *Divinity:* which, though it fills not the mind, with such *tender,* and *powerful contemplations,* as that which shews us Man's *Redemption* by a *Mediator;* yet it is by no means to be pass'd by unregarded: but is an excellent ground to establish the other. This is *a Religion,* which is confirm'd, by the unanimous agreement of all sorts of Worships: and may serve in respect to *Christi-anity,* as *Solomon's* Porch to the *Temple;* into the one the *Heathens* themselves did also enter; but into the other, onely God's *peculiar People.*

In men, may be consider'd the *Faculties,* and operations of their *Souls;* The *constitu-tion of their Bodies,* and the *works of their Hands.* Of these, the *first* they omit: both because the knowledg and direction of them have been before undertaken, by some *Arts,* on which they have no mind to intrench, as the *Politicks, Morality,* and *Oratory:* and also because the *Reason,* the *Understanding,* the *Tempers,* the *Will,* the *Passions* of Men, are so hard to be reduc'd to any certain observation of the *Senses;* and afford so much room to the *observers* to falsifie or counterfeit: that if such discourses should be once entertain'd; they would be in danger of falling into *talking,* instead of *work-*

ing, which they carefully avoid. Such subjects therefore as these, they have hitherto
kept out. But yet, when they shall have made more progress, in *material* things, they
will be in a condition, of pronouncing more boldly on them too. For, though Man's
Soul, and *Body* are not onely one *natural Engine* (as some have thought) of whose
motions of all sorts, there may be as certain an accompt given, as of those of a Watch
or Clock: yet by long studying of the *Spirits,* of the *Bloud,* of the *Nourishment,* of
the parts, of the *Diseases,* of the *Advantages,* of the accidents which belong to *humane
bodies* (all which will come within their Province) there, without question, be very
neer ghesses made, even at the more *exalted,* and *immediate* Actions of the *Soul;* and
that too, without destroying its *Spiritual* and *Immortal* Being.

These two Subjects, *God,* and the *Soul,* being onely forborn: In all the rest, they
wander, at their pleasure: In the frame of *Mens bodies,* the ways for strong, healthful,
and long life: In the *Arts of Mens Hands,* those that either *necessity, convenience,* or
delight have produc'd: In the *works* of *Nature,* their helps, their varieties, redundan-
cies, and defects: and in bringing all these to the *uses* of *humane Society.* . . .

Those, to whom the conduct of the *Experiment* is committed, being dismiss'd with
these advantages, do (as it were) carry the eyes, and the imaginations of the whole
company into the *Laboratory* with them. And after they have perform'd the *Trial,* they
bring all the *History* of its *process* back again to the test. Then comes in the second
great Work of the Assembly; which is to *judg,* and *resolve* upon the matter of *Fact.*
In this part of their imployment, they us'd to take an exact view of the repetition of
the whole course of the *Experiment;* here they observ'd all the *chances,* and the
Regularities of the proceeding; what *Nature* does willingly, what constrain'd; what
with its own power, what by the succours of Art; what in a constant rode, and what
with some kind of sport and extravagance; industriously marking all the various shapes
into which it turns it self, when it is persued, and by how many secret passages it at
last obtains its end; never giving it over till the whole *Company* has been fully satisfi'd
of the certainty and constancy; or, on the otherside, of the absolute impossibility of the
effect. This *critical,* and *reiterated Scrutiny* of those things, which are the plain objects
of their eyes; must needs put out of all reasonable dispute, the reality of those operations, which the *Society* shall positively determine to have succeeded. If any shall still
think it a just *Philosophical liberty,* to be jealous of resting on their credit: they are
in the right; and their *dissentings* will be most thankfully receiv'd, if they be establish'd on solid works, and not onely on *prejudices,* or *suspicions.* To the *Royal Society*
it will be at any time almost as acceptable, to be *confuted,* as to *discover:* seeing, by
this means, they will accomplish their main *Design:* others will be inflam'd: many
more will labour; and so the *Truth* will be obtain'd between them: which may be as
much promoted by the *contentions* of hands, and eyes; as it is commonly injur'd by
those of Tongues. However, that men may not hence undervalue their *authority,*
because they themselves are not willing to impose, and to usurp a *dominion* over their
reason; I will tell them, that there is not any one thing, which is now approv'd and
practis'd in the World, that is confirm'd by stronger evidence, than this, which the
Society requires; except onely the *Holy Mysteries of our Religion.* In almost all
other matters of *Belief,* of *Opinion,* or of *Science;* the assurance, whereby men are

guided, is nothing near so firm, as this. And I dare appeal to all *sober men;* whether, feeling in all Countreys, that are govern'd by Laws, they expect no more, than the consent of two, or three witnesses, in matters of life, and estate; they will not think, they are fairly dealt withall, in what concerns their *Knowledg,* if they have the concurring Testimonies of *threescore or an hundred? . . .*

I have hitherto describ'd the first *Elements,* on which the *Royal Society* arose, and supported its beginnings: I have trac'd its progress from the first private indeavours of some of its *members,* till it became united into a *Regular constitution:* and from thence I have related their first *conceptions,* and *practices,* towards the setling of an universal, constant, and impartial survey of the whole *Creation.* There now remains to be added in this Third part of my *Narration,* an Account of the *Incouragements* they have receiv'd from abroad, and at home; and a Particular Enumeration of the *Principal Subjects,* about which they have been emploi'd since they obtain'd the *Royal Confirmation.*

I will first begin with the *esteem,* which all the Civil world abroad has conceiv'd of their *Enterprize.* And I mention this with the more willingness, because I believe, that our *Nation* ought justly to be reprov'd, for their excess of Natural *bashfulness,* and for their want of care, to have their most excellent things represented to Strangers with the best advantage. This silent, and reserv'd humour has no doubt been very prejudicial to us, in the judgment, that our Neighbours have often made, not only concerning the condition of our *Learning,* but also of our *Political affairs.* I will therefore trespass a little on this *disposition* of my *Countrymen,* and affirm, that as the *English* name does manifestly get ground, by the bravery of their *Arms,* the Glory of their *Naval Strength,* and the spreading of their *Commerce:* so there has been a remarkable addition to its renown, by the success, which all our *Neighbours* expect from this *Assembly.*

It is evident, that this *searching Spirit,* and this affection to *sensible Knowledge,* does prevail in most Countries round about us. 'Tis true, the conveniences for such labours, are not equal in all places. Some want the assistance of others *hands;* some the contribution of others *purses:* some the benefit of excellent *Instruments,* some the *Patronage* of the Civil *Magistrates:* But yet according to their several *powers,* they are every where intent on such *practical Studies.* And the most considerable effects of such attempts throughout *Europe,* have been still recommended to this *Society,* by their *Authors,* to be examin'd, approv'd, or corrected. . . .

But not to wander any farther in *particulars,* it may perhaps in *general* be safely computed, that there has been as large a communication of Forein *Arts,* and *Inventions,* to the *Royal Society,* within this small compass of time, as ever before did pass over the *English* Channel since the very first transportation of *Arts* into our *Island.* And that this benefit will still increase by the length of time is indubitable, from the *Reception,* which has been given to the *Scholars, Nobility, Embassadours,* and Forein *Princes,* who of late years have travell'd hither, to behold a *Country,* which had been the Stage of so famous a War, and so miraculous a Peace. All these have still visited the *Royal Society,* as one of the first, and Noblest *Fruits* of our *restoration.* From hence they have return'd home, with a free engagement of their assistance: the *men of learning* assuring it of a contribution of their *Labours,* and the *Statesmen,* and *Princes* of their *Authority,* and indeavours, in satisfying all *Philosophical Queries,* with which they have been plentifully furnish'd.

It would be a useless pomp to reckon up a *Catalogue* of their *Names:* especially seeing they are already recorded with gratitude, in a more lasting *Monument,* The *Register* of the *Society.* Only it will not, I think, be amiss, if I mention the visit of one *Prince,* because it may afford us a profitable observation. When the Duke of *Brunswyck and Lunenbourgh* was introduc'd into their weekly *Assembly,* and had subscrib'd his name to their *Statutes:* there was according to the Custom, one of the *Fellows* appointed, to interpret to him, what Experiments were produc'd, and examin'd at that meeting. But his *Highness* told them, that it was not necessary, they should put themselves to that trouble: for he well understood our Language, having been drawn to the study of it, out of a desire of reading our *Philosophical Books.* From whence there may this conclusion be made, that if ever our *Native Tongue* shall get any ground in *Europe,* it must be by augmenting its *Experimental Treasure.* Nor is it impossible, but as the *Feminine* Arts of *Pleasure,* and *Gallantry* have spread some of our Neighbouring Languages, to such a vast extent: so the *English Tongue* may also in time be more enlarg'd, by being the Instrument of conveying to the World, the *Masculine* Arts of *Knowledge.* . . .

♪ THEOLOGICO–POLITICAL TREATISE

Baruch Spinoza

Baruch Spinoza (1632–1677) was raised an Orthodox Jew in Amsterdam, Holland, one of the few places in seventeenth-century Europe where some religious diversity was tolerated (see page 68). In 1656 he was solemnly excommunicated from the Jewish community for holding false doctrines about God. The rest of his life was spent as a simple lens grinder, living in a rented room, composing and polishing in his spare time a few manuscripts that were to rock the learned world to its foundations. A student of Descartes as well as of medieval Jewish theology, his thought was in fact far more revolutionary in its implications—especially for religion and morality—than that of the more illustrious Frenchman.

His Theologico-Political Treatise, *published anonymously (even in Holland!) in 1670, was extraordinarily daring for its time. The work's*

*immediate purpose was to lend support to the efforts of the great
republican leader, Jan DeWitt (1625–1672), to have the Dutch Reformed
Church disestablished; but it went far beyond this to develop a new
attitude toward the Holy Scriptures and a new and compelling argument for individual liberty of thought and expression.*

PREFACE

Men would never be superstitious, if they could govern all their circumstances by set
rules, or if they were always favoured by fortune: but being frequently driven into
straits where rules are useless, and being often kept fluctuating pitiably between hope
and fear by the uncertainty of fortune's greedily coveted favours, they are consequently,
for the most part, very prone to credulity. The human mind is readily swayed this way
or that in times of doubt, especially when hope and fear are struggling for the mastery,
though usually it is boastful, over-confident, and vain. . . .

Superstition, then, is engendered, preserved, and fostered by fear. If anyone desire
an example, let him take Alexander, who only began superstitiously to seek guidance
from seers, when he first learnt to fear fortune in the passes of Sysis . . . ; whereas
after he had conquered Darius he consulted prophets no more, till a second time
frightened by reverses. When the Scythians were provoking a battle, the Bactrians had
deserted, and he himself was lying sick of his wounds, "he once more turned to superstition, the mockery of human wisdom, and bade Aristander, to whom he confided his
credulity, inquire the issue of affairs with sacrificed victims." Very numerous examples
of a like nature might be cited, clearly showing the fact, that only while under the
dominion of fear do men fall a prey to superstition; that all the portents ever invested
with the reverence of misguided religion are mere phantoms of dejected and fearful
minds; and lastly, that prophets have most power among the people, and are most
formidable to rulers, precisely at those times when the state is in most peril. I think
this is sufficiently plain to all, and will therefore say no more on the subject.

The origin of superstition above given affords us a clear reason for the fact, that
it comes to all men naturally, though some refer its rise to a dim notion of God,
universal to mankind, and also tends to show, that it is no less inconsistent and variable
than other mental hallucinations and emotional impulses, and further that it can only
be maintained by hope, hatred, anger, and deceit; since it springs, not from reason,
but solely from the more powerful phases of emotion. Furthermore, we may readily
understand how difficult it is, to maintain in the same course men prone to every form
of credulity. For, as the mass of mankind remains always at about the same pitch of
misery, it never assents long to any one remedy, but is always best pleased by a novelty
which has not yet proved illusive.

Baruch Spinoza, *Tractatus Theologico-Politicus*, trans. R. H. M. Elwes (2d ed.; London: George
Bell and Sons, 1889), I, 3, 4–11, 60–62, 76–79, 98–100, 101, 103, 175–176, 257, 258–265.

This element of inconsistency has been the cause of many terrible wars and revolutions; for, as Curtius well says . . . : "The mob has no ruler more potent than superstition," and is easily led, on the plea of religion, at one moment to adore its kings as gods, and anon to execrate and abjure them as humanity's common bane. Immense pains have therefore been taken to counteract this evil by investing religion, whether true or false, with such pomp and ceremony, that it may rise superior to every shock, and be always observed with studious reverence by the whole people—a system which has been brought to great perfection by the Turks, for they consider even controversy impious, and so clog men's minds with dogmatic formulas, that they leave no room for sound reason, not even enough to doubt with.

But if, in despotic statecraft, the supreme and essential mystery be to hoodwink the subjects, and to mask the fear, which keeps them down, with the specious garb of religion, so that men may fight as bravely for slavery as for safety, and count it not shame but highest honour to risk their blood and their lives for the vainglory of a tyrant; yet in a free state no more mischievous expedient could be planned or attempted. Wholly repugnant to the general freedom are such devices as enthralling men's minds with prejudices, forcing their judgment, or employing any of the weapons of quasi-religious sedition; indeed, such seditions only spring up, when law enters the domain of speculative thought, and opinions are put on trial and condemned on the same footing as crimes, while those who defend and follow them are sacrificed, not to public safety, but to their opponents' hatred and cruelty. If deeds only could be made the grounds of criminal charges, and words were always allowed to pass free, such seditions would be divested of every semblance of justification, and would be separated from mere controversies by a hard and fast line.

Now, seeing that we have the rare happiness of living in a republic, where everyone's judgment is free and unshackled, where each may worship God as his conscience dictates, and where freedom is esteemed before all things dear and precious, I have believed that I should be undertaking no ungrateful or unprofitable task, in demonstrating that not only can such freedom be granted without prejudice to the public peace, but also, that without such freedom, piety cannot flourish nor the public peace be secure.

Such is the chief conclusion I seek to establish in this treatise; but, in order to reach it, I must first point out the misconceptions which, like scars of our former bondage, still disfigure our notion of religion, and must expose the false views about the civil authority which many have most impudently advocated, endeavouring to turn the mind of the people, still prone to heathen superstition, away from its legitimate rulers, and so bring us again into slavery. As to the order of my treatise I will speak presently, but first I will recount the causes which led me to write.

I have often wondered, that persons who make a boast of professing the Christian religion, namely, love, joy, peace, temperance, and charity to all men, should quarrel with such rancorous animosity, and display daily towards one another such bitter hatred, that this, rather than the virtues they claim, is the readiest criterion of their faith. Matters have long since come to such a pass, that one can only pronounce a man Christian, Turk, Jew, or Heathen, by his general appearance and attire, by his frequenting this or that place of worship, or employing the phraseology of a particular sect—as for manner of life, it is in all cases the same. Inquiry into the cause of this anomaly leads me unhesitatingly to ascribe it to the fact, that the ministries of the Church are regarded by the masses merely as dignities, her offices as posts of emolument—in short, popular religion may be summed up as respect for ecclesiastics. The spread of this misconception inflamed every worthless fellow with an intense desire to enter holy orders, and thus the love of diffusing God's religion degenerated into sordid avarice and ambition. Every church became a theatre, where orators, instead of church teachers, harangued, caring not to instruct the people, but striving to attract admiration, to bring opponents to public scorn, and to preach only novelties and paradoxes, such as would tickle the ears of their congregation. This state of things necessarily stirred up an amount of controversy, envy, and hatred, which no lapse of time could appease; so that we can scarcely wonder that of the old religion nothing survives but its outward forms (even these, in the mouth of the multitude, seem rather adulation than adoration of the Deity), and that faith has become a mere compound of credulity and prejudices—aye, prejudices too, which degrade man from rational being to beast, which completely stifle the power of judgment between true and false, which seem, in fact, carefully fostered for the purpose of extinguishing the last spark of reason! Piety, great God! and religion are become a tissue of ridiculous mysteries; men, who flatly despise reason, who reject and turn away from understanding as naturally corrupt, these, I say, these of all men, are thought, O lie most horrible! to possess light from on High. Verily, if they had but one spark of light from on High, they would not insolently rave, but would learn to worship God more wisely, and would be as marked among their fellows for mercy as they now are for malice; if they were concerned for their opponents' souls, instead of for their own reputations, they would no longer fiercely persecute, but rather be filled with pity and compassion.

Furthermore, if any Divine light were in them, it would appear from their doctrine. I grant that they are never tired of professing their wonder at the profound mysteries of Holy Writ; still I cannot discover that they teach anything but speculations of Platonists and Aristotelians, to which (in order to save their credit for Christianity) they have made Holy Writ conform; not content to rave with the Greeks themselves, they want to make the prophets rave also; showing conclusively, that never even in sleep have they caught a glimpse of Scripture's Divine nature. The very vehemence of their admiration for the mysteries plainly attests, that their belief in the Bible is a formal assent rather than a living faith: and the fact is made still more apparent by their laying down beforehand, as a foundation for the study and true interpretation of Scripture, the principle that it is in every passage true and divine. Such a doctrine should be reached only after strict scrutiny and thorough comprehension of the Sacred Books (which would teach it much better, for they stand in need of no human fictions), and not be set up on the threshold, as it were, of inquiry.

As I pondered over the facts that the light of reason is not only despised, but by many even execrated as a source of impiety, that human commentaries are accepted as divine records, and that credulity is extolled as faith; as I marked the fierce controversies of philosophers raging in Church and State, the source of bitter hatred and dissension, the ready instruments of sedition and other ills innumerable, I determined to examine the Bible afresh in a careful, impartial, and unfettered spirit, making no assumptions concerning it, and attributing to it no doctrines, which I do not find clearly therein set down. With these precautions I constructed a method of Scriptural interpretation, and thus equipped proceeded to inquire—What is prophecy? in what sense did God reveal Himself to the prophets, and why were these particular men chosen by Him? Was it on account of the sublimity of their thoughts about the Deity and nature, or was it solely on account of their piety? These questions being answered, I was easily able to conclude, that the authority of the prophets has weight only in matters of morality, and that their speculative doctrines affect us little.

Next I inquired, why the Hebrews were called God's chosen people, and discovering that it was only because God had chosen for them a certain strip of territory, where they might live peaceably and at ease, I learnt that the Law revealed by God to Moses was merely the law of the individual Hebrew state, therefore that it was binding on none but Hebrews, and not even on Hebrews after the downfall of their nation. Further, in order to ascertain, whether it could be concluded from Scripture, that the human understanding is naturally corrupt, I inquired whether the Universal Religion, the Divine Law revealed through the Prophets and Apostles to the whole human race, differs from that which is taught by the light of natural reason, whether miracles can take place in violation of the laws of nature, and if so, whether they imply the existence of God more surely and clearly than events, which we understand plainly and distinctly through their immediate natural causes.

Now, as in the whole course of my investigation I found nothing taught expressly by Scripture, which does not agree with our understanding, or which is repugnant thereto, and as I saw that the prophets taught nothing, which is not very simple and easily to be grasped by all, and further, that they clothed their teaching in the style, and confirmed it with the reasons, which would most deeply move the mind of the masses to devotion towards God, I became thoroughly convinced, that the Bible leaves reason absolutely free, that it has nothing in common with philosophy, in fact, that Revelation and Philosophy stand on totally different footings. In order to set this forth categorically and exhaust the whole question, I point out the way in which the Bible should be interpreted, and show that all knowledge of spiritual questions should be sought from it alone, and not from the objects of ordinary knowledge. Thence I pass on to indicate the false notions, which have arisen from the fact that the multitude— ever prone to superstition, and caring more for the shreds of antiquity than for eternal truths—pays homage to the Books of the Bible, rather than to the Word of God. I show that the Word of God has not been revealed as a certain number of books, but was displayed to the prophets as a simple idea of the Divine mind, namely, obedience to God in singleness of heart, and in the practice of justice and charity; and I further point out, that this doctrine is set forth in Scripture in accordance with the opinions and understandings of those, among whom the Apostles and Prophets preached, to the end that men might receive it willingly, and with their whole heart.

Having thus laid bare the bases of belief, I draw the conclusion that Revelation has obedience for its sole object, and therefore, in purpose no less than in foundation and method, stands entirely aloof from ordinary knowledge; each has its separate province, neither can be called the handmaid of the other.

Furthermore, as men's habits of mind differ, so that some more readily embrace one form of faith, some another, for what moves one to pray may move another only to scoff, I conclude, in accordance with what has gone before, that everyone should be free to choose for himself the foundations of his creed, and that faith should be judged only by its fruits; each would then obey God freely with his whole heart, while nothing would be publicly honoured save justice and charity.

Having thus drawn attention to the liberty conceded to everyone by the revealed law of God, I pass on to another part of my subject, and prove that this same liberty can and should be accorded with safety to the state and the magisterial authority—in fact, that it cannot be withheld without great danger to peace and detriment to the community.

In order to establish my point, I start from the natural rights of the individual, which are co-extensive with his desires and power, and from the fact that no one is bound to live as another pleases, but is the guardian of his own liberty. I show that these rights can only be transferred to those whom we depute to defend us, who acquire with the duties of defence the power of ordering our lives, and I thence infer that rulers possess rights only limited by their power, that they are the sole guardians of justice and liberty, and that their subjects should act in all things as they dictate: nevertheless, since no one can so utterly abdicate his own power of self-defence as to cease to be a man, I conclude that no one can be deprived of his natural rights absolutely, but that subjects, either by tacit agreement, or by social contract, retain a certain number, which cannot be taken from them without great danger to the state.

From these considerations I pass on to the Hebrew State, which I describe at some length, in order to trace the manner in which Religion acquired the force of law, and to touch on other noteworthy points. I then prove, that the holders of sovereign power are the depositaries and interpreters of religious no less than of civil ordinances, and that they alone have the right to decide what is just or unjust, pious or impious; lastly, I conclude by showing, that they best retain this right and secure safety to their state by allowing every man to think what he likes, and say what he thinks. . . .

CHAPTER IV. OF THE DIVINE LAW

As the love of God is man's highest happiness and blessedness, and the ultimate end and aim of all human actions, it follows that he alone lives by the Divine law who loves God not from fear of punishment, or from love of any other object, such as sensual pleasure, fame, or the like: but solely because he has knowledge of God, or is convinced that the knowledge and love of God is the highest good. The sum and chief precept, then, of the Divine law is to love God as the highest good, namely, as we have said, not from fear of any pains and penalties, or from the love of any other object in which we desire to take pleasure. The idea of God lays down the rule that God is our highest good—in other words, that the knowledge and love of God is the ultimate aim to which all our actions should be directed. The worldling cannot understand these things, they appear foolishness to him, because he has too meagre a knowledge of

God, and also because in this highest good he can discover nothing which he can handle or eat, or which affects the fleshly appetites wherein he chiefly delights, for it consists solely in thought and the pure reason. They, on the other hand, who know that they possess no greater gift than intellect and sound reason, will doubtless accept what I have said without question.

We have now explained that wherein the Divine law chiefly consists, and what are human laws, namely, all those which have a different aim unless they have been ratified by revelation, for in this respect also things are referred to God (as we have shown above) and in this sense the law of Moses, although it was not universal, but entirely adapted to the disposition and particular preservation of a single people, may yet be called a law of God or Divine law, inasmuch as we believe that it was ratified by prophetic insight. If we consider the nature of natural Divine law as we have just explained it, we shall see

I That it is universal or common to all men, for we have deduced it from universal human nature.

II That it does not depend on the truth of any historical narrative whatsoever, for inasmuch as this natural Divine law is comprehended solely by the consideration of human nature, it is plain that we can conceive it as existing as well in Adam as in any other man, as well in a man living among his fellows, as in a man who lives by himself.

The truth of a historical narrative, however assured, cannot give us the knowledge nor consequently the love of God, for love of God springs from knowledge of Him, and knowledge of Him should be derived from general ideas, in themselves certain and known, so that the truth of a historical narrative is very far from being a necessary requisite for our attaining our highest good.

Still, though the truth of histories cannot give us the knowledge and love of God, I do not deny that reading them is very useful with a view to life in the world, for the more we have observed and known of men's customs and circumstances, which are best revealed by their actions, the more warily we shall be able to order our lives among them, and so far as reason dictates to adapt our actions to their dispositions.

III We see that this natural Divine law does not demand the performance of ceremonies—that is, actions in themselves indifferent, which are called good from the fact of their institution, or actions symbolizing something profitable for salvation, or (if one prefers this definition) actions of which the meaning surpasses human understanding. The natural light of reason does not demand anything which it is itself unable to supply, but only such as it can very clearly show to be good, or a means to our blessedness. Such things as are good simply because they have been commanded or instituted, or as being symbols of something good, are mere shadows which cannot be reckoned among actions that are the offspring, as it were, or fruit of a sound mind and of intellect. There is no need for me to go into this now in more detail.

IV Lastly, we see that the highest reward of the Divine law is the law itself, namely, to know God and to love Him of our free choice, and with an undivided and fruitful spirit; while its penalty is the absence of these things, and being in bondage to the flesh—that is, having an inconstant and wavering spirit. . . .

CHAPTER V. OF THE CEREMONIAL LAW

This, then, was the object of the ceremonial law, that men should do nothing of their own free will, but should always act under external authority, and should continually confess by their actions and thoughts that they were not their own masters, but were entirely under the control of others.

From all these considerations it is clearer than day that ceremonies have nothing to do with a state of blessedness, and that those mentioned in the Old Testament, *i.e.* the whole Mosaic Law, had reference merely to the government of the Jews, and merely temporal advantages.

As for the Christian rites, such as baptism, the Lord's Supper, festivals, public prayers, and any other observances which are, and always have been, common to all Christendom, if they were instituted by Christ or His Apostles (which is open to doubt), they were instituted as external signs of the universal church, and not as having anything to do with blessedness, or possessing any sanctity in themselves. Therefore, though such ceremonies were not ordained for the sake of upholding a government, they were ordained for the preservation of a society, and accordingly he who lives alone is not bound by them: nay, those who live in a country where the Christian religion is forbidden, are bound to abstain from such rites, and can none the less live in a state of blessedness. We have an example of this in Japan, where the Christian religion is forbidden, and the Dutch who live there are enjoined by their East India Company not to practise any outward rites of religion. I need not cite other examples, though it would be easy to prove my point from the fundamental principles of the New Testament, and to adduce many confirmatory instances; but I pass on the more willingly, as I am anxious to proceed to my next proposition. I will now, therefore, pass on to what I proposed to treat of in the second part of this chapter, namely, what persons are bound to believe in the narratives contained in Scripture, and how far they are so bound. Examining this question by the aid of natural reason, I will proceed as follows.

If anyone wishes to persuade his fellows for or against anything which is not self-evident, he must deduce his contention from their admissions, and convince them either by experience or by ratiocination; either by appealing to facts of natural experience, or to self-evident intellectual axioms. Now unless the experience be of such a kind as to be clearly and distinctly understood, though it may convince a man, it will not have the same effect on his mind and disperse the clouds of his doubt so completely as when the doctrine taught is deduced entirely from intellectual axioms—that is, by the mere power of the understanding and logical order, and this is especially the case in spiritual matters which have nothing to do with the senses.

But the deduction of conclusions from general truths *à priori,* usually requires a long chain of arguments, and, moreover, very great caution, acuteness, and self-restraint —qualities which are not often met with; therefore people prefer to be taught by experience rather than deduce their conclusion from a few axioms, and set them out in logical order. Whence it follows, that if anyone wishes to teach a doctrine to a whole nation (not to speak of the whole human race), and to be understood by all men in every particular, he will seek to support his teaching with experience, and will endeavour to suit his reasonings and the definitions of his doctrines as far as possible to the understanding of the common people, who form the majority of mankind, and he will not set them forth in logical sequence nor adduce the definitions which serve to establish them. Otherwise he writes only for the learned—that is, he will be understood by only a small proportion of the human race.

All Scripture was written primarily for an entire people, and secondarily for the whole human race; therefore its contents must necessarily be adapted as far as possible to the understanding of the masses, and proved only by examples drawn from experience. We will explain ourselves more clearly. The chief speculative doctrines taught in Scripture are the existence of God, or a Being Who made all things, and Who directs and sustains the world with consummate wisdom; furthermore, that God takes the greatest thought for men, or such of them as live piously and honourably, while He punishes, with various penalties, those who do evil, separating them from the good. All this is proved in Scripture entirely through experience—that is, through the narratives there related. No definitions of doctrine are given, but all the sayings and reasonings are adapted to the understanding of the masses. Although experience can give no clear knowledge of these things, nor explain the nature of God, nor how He directs and sustains all things, it can nevertheless teach and enlighten men sufficiently to impress obedience and devotion on their minds.

It is now, I think, sufficiently clear what persons are bound to believe in the Scripture narratives, and in what degree they are so bound, for it evidently follows from what has been said that the knowledge of and belief in them is particularly necessary to the masses whose intellect is not capable of perceiving things clearly and distinctly. Further, he who denies them because he does not believe that God exists or takes thought for men and the world, may be accounted impious; but a man who is ignorant of them, and nevertheless knows by natural reason that God exists, as we have said, and has a true plan of life, is altogether blessed—yes, more blessed than the common herd of believers, because besides true opinions he possesses also a true and distinct conception. Lastly, he who is ignorant of the Scriptures and knows nothing by the light of reason, though he may not be impious or rebellious, is yet less than human and almost brutal, having none of God's gifts.

We must here remark that when we say that the knowledge of the sacred narrative is particularly necessary to the masses, we do not mean the knowledge of absolutely all the narratives in the Bible, but only of the principal ones, those which, taken by themselves, plainly display the doctrine we have just stated, and have most effect over men's minds.

If all the narratives in Scripture were necessary for the proof of this doctrine, and if no conclusion could be drawn without the general consideration of every one of the histories contained in the sacred writings, truly the conclusion and demonstration of such doctrine would overtask the understanding and strength not only of the masses, but of humanity; who is there who could give attention to all the narratives at once, and to all the circumstances, and all the scraps of doctrine to be elicited from such a host of diverse histories? I cannot believe that the men who have left us the Bible as we have it were so abounding in talent that they attempted setting about such a method of demonstration, still less can I suppose that we cannot understand Scriptural doctrine till we have given heed to the quarrels of Isaac, the advice of Achitophel to Absalom, the civil war between Jews and Israelites, and other similar chronicles; nor can I think that it was more difficult to teach such doctrine by means of history to the Jews of early times, the contemporaries of Moses, than it was to the contemporaries of Esdras. But more will be said on this point hereafter, we may now only note that the masses are only bound to know those histories which can most powerfully dispose their mind to obedience and devotion. However, the masses are not sufficiently skilled to draw conclusions from what they read, they take more delight in the actual stories, and in the strange and unlooked-for issues of events than in the doctrines implied; therefore, besides reading these narratives, they are always in need of pastors or church ministers to explain them to their feeble intelligence.

But not to wander from our point, let us conclude with what has been our principal object—namely, that the truth of narratives, be they what they may, has nothing to do with the Divine law, and serves for nothing except in respect of doctrine, the sole element which makes one history better than another. The narratives in the Old and New Testaments surpass profane history, and differ among themselves in merit simply by reason of the salutary doctrines which they inculcate. Therefore, if a man were to read the Scripture narratives believing the whole of them, but were to give no heed to the doctrines they contain, and make no amendment in his life, he might employ himself just as profitably in reading the Koran or the poetic drama, or ordinary chronicles, with the attention usually given to such writings; on the other hand, if a man is absolutely ignorant of the Scriptures, and none the less has right opinions and a true plan of life, he is absolutely blessed and truly possesses in himself the spirit of Christ. . . .

CHAPTER VII. OF THE INTERPRETATION OF SCRIPTURE

. . . If we would separate ourselves from the crowd and escape from theological prejudices, instead of rashly accepting human commentaries for Divine documents, we must consider the true method of interpreting Scripture and dwell upon it at some length: for if we remain in ignorance of this we cannot know, certainly, what the Bible and the Holy Spirit wish to teach.

I may sum up the matter by saying that the method of interpreting Scripture does not widely differ from the method of interpreting nature—in fact, it is almost the same. For as the interpretation of nature consists in the examination of the history of nature, and therefrom deducing definitions of natural phenomena on certain fixed axioms, so Scriptural interpretation proceeds by the examination of Scripture, and inferring the intention of its authors as a legitimate conclusion from its fundamental principles. By working in this manner everyone will always advance without danger of error—that is, if they admit no principles for interpreting Scripture, and discussing its contents save such as they find in Scripture itself—and will be able with equal security to discuss what surpasses our understanding, and what is known by the natural light of reason. . . .

The universal rule, then, in interpreting Scripture is to accept nothing as an authoritative Scriptural statement which we do not perceive very clearly when we examine it in the light of its history. What I mean by its history, and what should be the chief points elucidated, I will now explain.

The history of a Scriptural statement comprises—

I The nature and properties of the language in which the books of the Bible were written, and in which their authors were accustomed to speak. We shall thus be able to investigate every expression by comparison with common conversational usages.

Now all the writers both of the Old Testament and the New were Hebrews: therefore, a knowledge of the Hebrew language is before all things necessary, not only for the comprehension of the Old Testament, which was written in that tongue, but also of the New: for although the latter was published in other languages, yet its characteristics are Hebrew.

II An analysis of each book and arrangement of its contents under heads; so that we may have at hand the various texts which treat of a given subject. Lastly, a note of all the passages which are ambiguous or obscure, or which seem mutually contradictory.

I call passages clear or obscure according as their meaning is inferred easily or with difficulty in relation to the context, not according as their truth is perceived easily or the reverse by reason. We are at work not on the truth of passages, but solely on their meaning. We must take especial care, when we are in search of the meaning of a text, not to be led away by our reason in so far as it is founded on principles of natural knowledge (to say nothing of prejudices): in order not to confound the meaning of a passage with its truth, we must examine it solely by means of the signification of the words, or by a reason acknowledging no foundation but Scripture. . . .

III Lastly, such a history should relate the environment of all the prophetic books extant; that is, the life, the conduct, and the studies of the author of each book, who he was, what was the occasion, and the epoch of his writing, whom did he write for, and in what language. Further, it should inquire into the fate of each book: how it was first received, into whose hands it fell, how many different versions there were of it, by whose advice was it received into the Bible, and, lastly, how all the books now universally accepted as sacred, were united into a single whole.

All such information should, as I have said, be contained in the "history" of Scripture. For, in order to know what statements are set forth as laws, and what as moral precepts, it is important to be acquainted with the life, the conduct, and the pursuits of their author: moreover, it becomes easier to explain a man's writings in proportion as we have more intimate knowledge of his genius and temperament.

Further, that we may not confound precepts which are eternal with those which served only a temporary purpose, or were only meant for a few, we should know what was the occasion, the time, the age, in which each book was written, and to what nation it was addressed.

Lastly, we should have knowledge on the other points I have mentioned, in order to be sure, in addition to the authenticity of the work, that it has not been tampered with by sacrilegious hands, or whether errors can have crept in, and, if so, whether they have been corrected by men sufficiently skilled and worthy of credence. All these things should be known, that we may not be led away by blind impulse to accept whatever is thrust on our notice, instead of only that which is sure and indisputable. . . .

CHAPTER XIII. IT IS SHOWN THAT SCRIPTURE TEACHES ONLY VERY SIMPLE DOCTRINES, SUCH AS SUFFICE FOR RIGHT CONDUCT

In the second chapter of this treatise we pointed out that the prophets were gifted with extraordinary powers of imagination, but not of understanding; also that God only revealed to them such things as are very simple—not philosophic mysteries,—and that He adapted His communications to their previous opinions. We further showed in Chap. V. that Scripture only transmits and teaches truths which can readily be comprehended by all; not deducing and concatenating its conclusions from definitions and axioms, but narrating quite simply, and confirming its statements, with a view to inspiring belief, by an appeal to experience as exemplified in miracles and history, and setting forth its truths in the style and phraseology which would most appeal to the popular mind (cf. Chap. VI., third division).

Lastly, we demonstrated in Chap. VII. that the difficulty of understanding Scripture lies in the language only, and not in the abstruseness of the argument.

To these considerations we may add that the Prophets did not preach only to the learned, but to all Jews, without exception, while the Apostles were wont to teach the gospel doctrine in churches where there were public meetings; whence it follows that Scriptural doctrine contains no lofty speculations nor philosophic reasoning, but only very simple matters, such as could be understood by the slowest intelligence.

I am consequently lost in wonder at the ingenuity of those whom I have already mentioned, who detect in the Bible mysteries so profound that they cannot be explained in human language, and who have introduced so many philosophic speculations into religion that the Church seems like an academy, and religion like a science, or rather a dispute.

It is not to be wondered at that men, who boast of possessing supernatural intelligence, should be unwilling to yield the palm of knowledge to philosophers who have only their ordinary faculties; still I should be surprised if I found them teaching any new speculative doctrine, which was not a commonplace to those Gentile philosophers whom, in spite of all, they stigmatize as blind; for, if one inquires what these mysteries lurking in Scripture may be, one is confronted with nothing but the reflections of Plato or Aristotle, or the like, which it would often be easier for an ignorant man to dream than for the most accomplished scholar to wrest out of the Bible. . . .

CHAPTER XX. THAT IN A FREE STATE EVERY MAN MAY THINK WHAT HE LIKES, AND SAY WHAT HE THINKS

If men's minds were as easily controlled as their tongues, every king would sit safely on his throne, and government by compulsion would cease; for every subject would shape his life according to the intentions of his rulers, and would esteem a thing true or false, good or evil, just or unjust, in obedience to their dictates. However, we have shown already (Chapter XVII.) that no man's mind can possibly lie wholly at the disposition of another, for no one can willingly transfer his natural right of free reason and judgment, or be compelled so to do. For this reason government which attempts to control minds is accounted tyrannical, and it is considered an abuse of sovereignty and a usurpation of the rights of subjects, to seek to prescribe what shall be accepted as true, or rejected as false, or what opinions should actuate men in their worship of God. All these questions fall within a man's natural right, which he cannot abdicate even with his own consent.

I admit that the judgment can be biassed in many ways, and to an almost incredible degree, so that while exempt from direct external control it may be so dependent on another man's words, that it may fitly be said to be ruled by him; but although this influence is carried to great lengths, it has never gone so far as to invalidate the statement, that every man's understanding is his own, and that brains are as diverse as palates. . . .

However unlimited, therefore, the power of a sovereign may be, however implicitly it is trusted as the exponent of law and religion, it can never prevent men from forming judgments according to their intellect, or being influenced by any given emotion. It is true that it has the right to treat as enemies all men whose opinions do not, on all subjects, entirely coincide with its own; but we are not discussing its strict rights, but its proper course of action. I grant that it has the right to rule in the most violent manner, and to put citizens to death for very trivial causes, but no one supposes it can do this with the approval of sound judgment. Nay, inasmuch as such things cannot be done without extreme peril to itself, we may even deny that it has the absolute power to do them, or, consequently, the absolute right; for the rights of the sovereign are limited by his power.

Since, therefore, no one can abdicate his freedom of judgment and feeling; since every man is by indefeasible natural right the master of his own thoughts, it follows that men thinking in diverse and contradictory fashions, cannot, without disastrous results, be compelled to speak only according to the dictates of the supreme power. Not even the most experienced, to say nothing of the multitude, know how to keep silence. Men's common failing is to confide their plans to others, though there be need for secrecy, so that a government would be most harsh which deprived the individual of his freedom of saying and teaching what he thought; and would be moderate if such freedom were granted. Still we cannot deny that authority may be as much injured by words as by actions; hence, although the freedom we are discussing cannot be entirely denied to subjects, its unlimited concession would be most baneful; we must, therefore, now inquire, how far such freedom can and ought to be conceded without danger to the peace of the state, or the power of the rulers; and this, as I said at the beginning of Chapter XVI., is my principal object.

It follows, plainly, from the explanation given above, of the foundations of a state, that the ultimate aim of government is not to rule, or restrain, by fear, nor to exact obedience, but contrariwise, to free every man from fear, that he may live in all possible security; in other words, to strengthen his natural right to exist and work without injury to himself or others.

No, the object of government is not to change men from rational beings into beasts or puppets, but to enable them to develop their minds and bodies in security, and to employ their reason unshackled; neither showing hatred, anger, or deceit, nor watched with the eyes of jealousy and injustice. In fact, the true aim of government is liberty.

Now we have seen that in forming a state the power of making laws must either be vested in the body of the citizens, or in a portion of them, or in one man. For, although men's free judgments are very diverse, each one thinking that he alone knows everything, and although complete unanimity of feeling and speech is out of the question, it is impossible to preserve peace, unless individuals abdicate their right of acting entirely on their own judgment. Therefore, the individual justly cedes the right of free action, though not of free reason and judgment; no one can act against the authorities without danger to the state, though his feelings and judgment may be at variance therewith; he may even speak against them, provided that he does so from rational conviction, not from fraud, anger, or hatred, and provided that he does not attempt to introduce any change on his private authority.

For instance, supposing a man shows that a law is repugnant to sound reason, and should therefore be repealed; if he submits his opinion to the judgment of the authorities (who, alone, have the right of making and repealing laws), and meanwhile acts in nowise contrary to that law, he has deserved well of the state, and has behaved as a good citizen should; but if he accuses the authorities of injustice, and stirs up the people against them, or if he seditiously strives to abrogate the law without their consent, he is a mere agitator and rebel.

Thus we see how an individual may declare and teach what he believes, without injury to the authority of his rulers, or to the public peace; namely, by leaving in their hands the entire power of legislation as it affects action, and by doing nothing against their laws, though he be compelled often to act in contradiction to what he believes, and openly feels, to be best.

Such a course can be taken without detriment to justice and dutifulness, nay, it is the one which a just and dutiful man would adopt. We have shown that justice is dependent on the laws of the authorities, so that no one who contravenes their accepted decrees can be just, while the highest regard for duty, as we have pointed out in the preceding chapter, is exercised in maintaining public peace and tranquillity; these could not be preserved if every man were to live as he pleased; therefore it is no less than undutiful for a man to act contrary to his country's laws, for if the practice became universal the ruin of states would necessarily follow.

Hence, so long as a man acts in obedience to the laws of his rulers, he in nowise contravenes his reason, for in obedience to reason he transferred the right of controlling his actions from his own hands to theirs. This doctrine we can confirm from actual custom, for in a conference of great and small powers, schemes are seldom carried unanimously, yet all unite in carrying out what is decided on, whether they voted for or against. But I return to my proposition.

From the fundamental notions of a state, we have discovered how a man may exercise free judgment without detriment to the supreme power: from the same premises we can no less easily determine what opinions would be seditious. Evidently those which by their very nature nullify the compact by which the right of free action was ceded. For instance, a man who holds that the supreme power has no rights over him, or that promises ought not to be kept, or that everyone should live as he pleases, or other doctrines of this nature in direct opposition to the above-mentioned contract, is seditious, not so much from his actual opinions and judgment, as from the deeds which they involve; for he who maintains such theories abrogates the contract which tacitly, or openly, he made with his rulers. Other opinions which do not involve acts violating the contract, such as revenge, anger, and the like, are not seditious, unless it be in some corrupt state, where superstitious and ambitious persons, unable to endure men of learning, are so popular with the multitude that their word is more valued than the law.

However, I do not deny that there are some doctrines which, while they are apparently only concerned with abstract truths and falsehoods, are yet propounded and published with unworthy motives. This question we have discussed in Chapter XV., and shown that reason should nevertheless remain unshackled. If we hold to the principle that a man's loyalty to the state should be judged, like his loyalty to God, from his actions only—namely, from his charity towards his neighbours; we cannot doubt that the best government will allow freedom of philosophical speculation no less than of religious belief. I confess that from such freedom inconveniences may sometimes arise, but what question was ever settled so wisely that no abuses could possibly spring therefrom? He who seeks to regulate everything by law, is more likely to arouse vices than to reform them. It is best to grant what cannot be abolished, even though it be in itself harmful. How many evils spring from luxury, envy, avarice, drunkenness, and the like, yet these are tolerated—vices as they are—because they cannot be prevented by legal enactments. How much more then should free thought be granted, seeing that it is in itself a virtue and that it cannot be crushed! Besides, the evil results can easily be checked, as I will show, by the secular authorities, not to mention that such freedom is absolutely necessary for progress in science and the liberal arts: for no man follows such pursuits to advantage unless his judgment be entirely free and unhampered.

But let it be granted that freedom may be crushed, and men be so bound down, that they do not dare to utter a whisper, save at the bidding of their rulers; nevertheless this can never be carried to the pitch of making them think according to authority, so that the necessary consequences would be that men would daily be thinking one thing and saying another, to the corruption of good faith, that mainstay of government, and to the fostering of hateful flattery and perfidy, whence spring stratagems, and the corruption of every good art.

It is far from possible to impose uniformity of speech, for the more rulers strive to curtail freedom of speech, the more obstinately are they resisted; not indeed by the avaricious, the flatterers, and other numskulls, who think supreme salvation consists in filling their stomachs and gloating over their money-bags, but by those whom good education, sound morality, and virtue have rendered more free. Men, as generally constituted, are most prone to resent the branding as criminal of opinions which they believe to be true, and the proscription as wicked of that which inspires them with piety towards God and man; hence they are ready to forswear the laws and conspire against the authorities, thinking it not shameful but honourable to stir up seditions and perpetuate any sort of crime with this end in view. Such being the constitution of human nature, we see that laws directed against opinions affect the generous-minded rather than the wicked, and are adapted less for coercing criminals than for irritating the upright; so that they cannot be maintained without great peril to the state.

Moreover, such laws are almost always useless, for those who hold that the opinions proscribed are sound, cannot possibly obey the law; whereas those who already reject them as false, accept the law as a kind of privilege, and make such boast of it, that authority is powerless to repeal it, even if such a course be subsequently desired.

To these considerations may be added what we said in Chapter XVIII. in treating of the history of the Hebrews. And, lastly, how many schisms have arisen in the Church from the attempt of the authorities to decide by law the intricacies of theological controversy! If men were not allured by the hope of getting the law and the authorities on their side, of triumphing over their adversaries in the sight of an applauding multitude, and of acquiring honourable distinctions, they would not strive so maliciously, nor would such fury sway their minds. This is taught not only by reason but by daily examples, for laws of this kind prescribing what every man shall believe and forbidding anyone to speak or write to the contrary, have often been passed, as sops or concessions to the anger of those who cannot tolerate men of enlightenment, and who, by such harsh and crooked enactments, can easily turn the devotion of the masses into fury and direct it against whom they will.

How much better would it be to restrain popular anger and fury, instead of passing useless laws, which can only be broken by those who love virtue and the liberal arts, thus paring down the state till it is too small to harbour men of talent. What greater misfortune for a state can be conceived than that honourable men should be sent like criminals into exile, because they hold diverse opinions which they cannot disguise? What, I say, can be more hurtful than that men who have committed no crime or wickedness should, simply because they are enlightened, be treated as enemies and put to death, and that the scaffold, the terror of evil-doers, should become the arena where the highest examples of tolerance and virtue are displayed to the people with all the marks of ignominy that authority can devise?

He that knows himself to be upright does not fear the death of a criminal, and shrinks from no punishment; his mind is not wrung with remorse for any disgraceful deed: he holds that death in a good cause is no punishment, but an honour, and that death for freedom is glory.

What purpose then is served by the death of such men, what example is proclaimed? the cause for which they die is unknown to the idle and the foolish, hateful to the turbulent, loved by the upright. The only lesson we can draw from such scenes is to flatter the persecutor, or else to imitate the victim.

If formal assent is not to be esteemed above conviction, and if governments are to retain a firm hold of authority and not be compelled to yield to agitators, it is imperative that freedom of judgment should be granted, so that men may live together in harmony, however diverse, or even openly contradictory their opinions may be. We cannot doubt that such is the best system of government and open to the fewest objections, since it is the one most in harmony with human nature. In a democracy (the most natural form of government, as we have shown in Chapter XVI.) everyone submits to the control of authority over his actions, but not over his judgment and reason; that is, seeing that all cannot think alike, the voice of the majority has the force of law, subject to repeal if circumstances bring about a change of opinion. In proportion as the power of free judgment is withheld we depart from the natural condition of mankind, and consequently the government becomes more tyrannical. . . .

I have thus shown:—I. That it is impossible to deprive men of the liberty of saying what they think. II. That such liberty can be conceded to every man without injury to the rights and authority of the sovereign power, and that every man may retain it without injury to such rights, provided that he does not presume upon it to the extent of introducing any new rights into the state, or acting in any way contrary to the existing laws. III. That every man may enjoy this liberty without detriment to the public peace, and that no inconveniences arise therefrom which cannot easily be checked. IV. That every man may enjoy it without injury to his allegiance. V. That laws dealing with speculative problems are entirely useless. VI. Lastly, that not only may such liberty be granted without prejudice to the public peace, to loyalty, and to the rights of rulers, but that it is even necessary for their preservation. For when people try to take it away, and bring to trial, not only the acts which alone are capable of offending, but also the opinions of mankind, they only succeed in surrounding their victims with an appearance of martyrdom, and raise feelings of pity and revenge rather than of terror. Uprightness and good faith are thus corrupted, flatterers and traitors are encouraged, and sectarians triumph, inasmuch as concessions have been made to their animosity, and they have gained the state sanction for the doctrines of which they are the interpreters. Hence they arrogate to themselves the state authority and rights, and do no scruple to assert that they have been directly chosen by God, and that their laws are Divine, whereas the laws of the state are human, and should therefore yield obedience to the laws of God—in other words, to their own laws. Everyone must see that this is not a state of affairs conducive to public welfare. Wherefore, as we have shown in Chapter XVIII., the safest way for a state is to lay down the rule that religion is comprised solely in the exercise of charity and justice, and that the rights of rulers in sacred, no less than in secular matters, should merely have to do with actions, but that every man should think what he likes and say what he thinks. . . .

⋙ PHILOSOPHICAL DICTIONARY

Voltaire

François-Marie Arouet (1694–1778), under the name of Voltaire, became the most celebrated man of letters of his age, first gaining an audience as dramatist and historian. A middle-class upstart in an aristocratic society, in intermittent trouble with the established authorities, Voltaire only gradually came to champion religious and political toleration against the power of the Catholic Church and the rigidities of an antiquated government. After being exposed to the more liberal climate of England and the more authoritarian one of Prussia, Voltaire emerged as the most famous of the philosophes, *the popularizers who sought to apply the methods and approaches of the physical sciences to the social problems of their own day.*

Voltaire's Philosophical Dictionary *caps his career as the propagator of the new ideas, particularly of religious toleration as against the authority of Catholic orthodoxy. He first began work on the book while living at the court of Frederick the Great of Prussia, who may have suggested the idea of a reference work in which the major prejudices of the times would be properly debunked. Soon after the first articles were composed in 1752, the work was interrupted for over a decade; the first of two volumes in pocket-size format did not appear in Geneva until 1764. Even though his polished ironical style was unmistakable, Voltaire loudly disclaimed having had any part in the production of the* Dictionary. *Indeed, the career of the book justified his caution. It was widely hailed (and bought) by people sympathetic to the ideals of the Enlightenment, but equally widely assailed (and suppressed) by the authorities of even such relatively open-minded countries as Holland. Voltaire, in the years after 1764, continued to revise and expand the articles of his* Dictionary, *which was republished in a number of varying editions. The selection below includes half a dozen characteristic articles.*

MASTER

How can one man become the master of another? And by what kind of incomprehensible magic has he been able to become the master of several other men? A great number of good volumes have been written on this subject, but I give the preference to an Indian fable, because it is short, and fables explain everything.

Adimo, the father of all the Indians, had two sons and two daughters by his wife Pocriti. The eldest was a vigorous giant, the youngest was a little hunchback, the two girls were pretty. As soon as the giant was strong enough, he lay with his two sisters, and caused the little hunchback to serve him. Of his two sisters, the one was his cook, the other his gardener. When the giant would sleep, he began by chaining his little brother to a tree; and when the latter fled from him, he caught him in four strides, and gave him twenty blows with the strength of an ox.

The dwarf submitted and became the best subject in the world. The giant, satisfied with seeing him fulfil the duties of a subject, permitted him to sleep with one of his sisters, with whom he was disgusted. The children who sprang from this marriage were not quite hunchbacks, but they were sufficiently deformed. They were brought up in the fear of God and of the giant. They received an excellent education; they were taught that their uncle was a giant by divine right, who could do what he pleased with all his family; that if he had some pretty niece or grand niece, he should have her without difficulty, and not one should marry her unless he permitted it.

The giant dying, his son, who was neither so strong or so great as he was, believed himself to be like his father, a giant by divine right. He pretended to make all the men work for him, and slept with all the girls. The family leagued against him: he was killed, and they became a republic.

The Siamese pretend, that on the contrary the family commenced by being republican; and that the giant existed not until after a great many years and dissensions: but all the authors of Benares and Siam agree that men lived an infinity of ages before they had the wit to make laws, and they prove it by an unanswerable argument, which is that even at present, when all the world piques itself upon having wit, we have not yet found the means of making a score of laws passably good.

It is still, for example, an insoluble question in India, whether republics were established before or after monarchies; if confusion has appeared more horrible to men than despotism! I am ignorant how it happened in order of time, but in that of nature we must agree that men are all born equal: violence and ability made the first masters; laws have made the present. . . .

SECT

Every sect, of whatever opinion it may be, is a rallying point for doubt and error. Scotists, Thomists, Realists, Nominalists, Papist, Calvinists, Molinists, and Jansenists, are only warlike appellations.

The Works of Voltaire, ed. John Morley (Paris: E. R. Dumont, 1901), XI, 238–240; XIII, 181–184; XIV, 30–33, 104–109, 193–200.

There is no sect in geometry; we never say: A Euclidian, an Archimedian. When truth is evident, it is impossible to divide people into parties and factions. Nobody disputes that it is broad day at noon.

That part of astronomy which determines the course of the stars, and the return of eclipses, being now known, there is no longer any dispute among astronomers.

It is similar with a small number of truths, which are similarly established; but if you are a Mahometan, as there are many men who are not Mahometans, you may possibly be in error.

What would be the true religion, if Christianity did not exist? That in which there would be no sects; that in which all minds necessarily agreed.

Now, in what doctrine are all minds agreed? In the adoration of one God, and in probity. All the philosophers who have professed a religion have said at all times: "There is a God, and He must be just." Behold then the universal religion, established throughout all time and among all men! The point then in which all agree is true; the systems in regard to which all differ are false.

My sect is the best, says a Brahmin. But, my good friend, if thy sect is the best, it is necessary; for if not absolutely necessary, thou must confess that it is useless. If, on the contrary, it is necessary, it must be so to all men; how then is it that all men possess not what is absolutely necessary to them? How is it that the rest of the world laughs at thee and thy Brahma?

When Zoroaster, Hermes, Orpheus, Minos, and all the great men say: Let us worship God, and be just, no one laughs; but all the world sneers at him who pretends, that to please God it is proper to die holding a cow by the tail; at him who cuts off a particle of foreskin for the same purpose; at him who consecrates crocodiles and onions; at him who attaches eternal salvation to the bones of dead men carried underneath the shirt, or to a plenary indulgence purchased at Rome for two sous and a half.

Whence this universal assemblage of laughing and hissing from one end of the universe to the other? It must be that the things which all the world derides are not evident truths. What shall we say to a secretary of Sejanus, who dedicates to Petronius a book, in a confused and involved style, entitled "The Truth of the Sibylline Oracles, Proved from Facts."

This secretary at first proves to you, that God sent upon earth many Sibyls, one after the other, having no other means of instructing men. It is demonstrated, that God communicated with these Sibyls, because the word "sibyl" signifies "Council of God." They ought to live a long time, for this privilege at least belongs to persons with whom God communicates. They amounted to twelve, because this number is sacred. They certainly predicted all the events in the world, because Tarquin the Proud bought their book from an old woman for a hundred crowns. What unbeliever, exclaims the secretary, can deny all these evident facts, which took place in one corner of the earth, in the face of all the world? Who can deny the accomplishment of their prophecies? Has not Virgil himself cited the predictions of the Sibyls? If we have not the first copies of the Sibylline books, written at a time when no one could read and write, we have authentic copies. Impiety must be silent before such proofs. Thus spoke Houteville to Sejanus, and hoped to obtain by it the place of chief augur, with a revenue of fifty thousand livres; but he obtained nothing.

That which my sect teaches me is obscure, I confess it, exclaims a fanatic; and it is in consequence of that obscurity that I must believe it; for it says itself that it abounds in obscurities. My sect is extravagant, therefore it is divine; for how, appearing so insane, would it otherwise have been embraced by so many people. It is precisely like the Koran, which the Sonnites say presents at once the face of an angel and that of a beast. Be not scandalized at the muzzle of the beast, but revere the face of the angel. Thus spoke this madman; but a fanatic of another sect replied to the first fanatic: It is thou who art the beast, and I who am the angel.

Now who will judge this process, and decide between these two inspired personages? The reasonable and impartial man who is learned in a science which is not that of words; the man divested of prejudice, and a lover of truth and of justice; the man, in fine, who is not a beast, and who pretends not to be an angel. . . .

SUPERSTITION

The superstitious man is to the knave, what the slave is to the tyrant; nay more—the superstitious man is governed by the fanatic, and becomes a fanatic himself. Superstition, born in Paganism, adopted by Judaism, infected the Church in the earliest ages. All the fathers of the Church, without exception, believed in the power of magic. The Church always condemned magic, but she always believed in it; she excommunicated sorcerers, not as madmen who were in delusion, but as men who really had intercourse with the devils.

At this day, one half of Europe believes that the other half has long been and still is superstitious. The Protestants regard relics, indulgences, macerations, prayers for the dead, holy water, and almost all the rites of the Roman church, as mad superstitions. According to them, superstition consists in mistaking useless practices for necessary ones. Among the Roman Catholics there are some, more enlightened than their forefathers, who have renounced many of these usages formerly sacred; and they defend their adherence to those which they have retained, by saying they are indifferent, and what is indifferent cannot be an evil.

It is difficult to mark the limits of superstition. A Frenchman travelling in India thinks almost everything superstitious; nor is he much mistaken. The archbishop of Canterbury asserts that the archbishop of Paris is superstitious; the Presbyterians cast the same reproach upon his grace of Canterbury, and are in their turn called superstitious by the Quakers, who in the eyes of the rest of Christians are the most superstitious of all.

It is then nowhere agreed among Christian societies what superstition is. The sect which appears to be the least violently attacked by this mental disease, is that which has the fewest rites. But if, with but few ceremonies, it is strongly attached to an absurd belief, that absurd belief is of itself equivalent to all the superstitious practices observed from the time of Simon the Magician, down to that of the curate Gaufredi. It is therefore evident that what is the foundation of the religion of one sect, is by another sect regarded as superstitious.

The Mussulmans accuse all Christian societies of it, and are accused of it by them. Who shall decide this great cause? Shall not reason? But each sect declares that reason is on its side. Force then will decide, until reason shall have penetrated into a sufficient number of heads to disarm force.

For instance: there was a time in Christian Europe when a newly married pair were not permitted to enjoy the nuptial rights, until they had bought that privilege of the bishop and the curate. Whosoever, in his will, did not leave a part of his property to the Church, was excommunicated, and deprived of burial. This was called dying unconfessed—i. e., not confessing the Christian religion. And when a Christian died intestate, the Church relieved the deceased from this excommunication, by making a will for him, stipulating for and enforcing the payment of the pious legacy which the defunct should have made.

Therefore it was, that Pope Gregory IX. and St. Louis ordained, after the Council of Nice, held in 1235, that every will to the making of which a priest had not been called, should be null; and the pope decreed that the testator and the notary should be excommunicated.

The tax on sins was, if possible, still more scandalous. It was force which supported all these laws, to which the superstition of nations submitted; and it was only in the course of time that reason caused these shameful vexations to be abolished, while it left so many others in existence.

How far does policy permit superstition to be undermined? This is a very knotty question; it is like asking how far a dropsical man may be punctured without his dying under the operation; this depends on the prudence of the physician.

Can there exist a people free from all superstitious prejudices? This is asking, Can there exist a people of philosophers? It is said that there is no superstition in the magistracy of China. It is likely that the magistracy of some towns in Europe will also be free from it. These magistrates will then prevent the superstition of the people from being dangerous. Their example will not enlighten the mob; but the principal citizens will restrain it. Formerly, there was not perhaps a single religious tumult, not a single violence, in which the townspeople did not take part, because these townspeople were then part of the mob; but reason and time have changed them. Their ameliorated manners will improve those of the lowest and most ferocious of the populace; of which, in more countries than one, we have striking examples. In short, the fewer superstitions, the less fanaticism; and the less fanaticism, the fewer calamities. . . .

TOLERATION

Of all religions, the Christian ought doubtless to inspire the most toleration, although hitherto the Christians have been the most intolerant of all men. Jesus, having deigned to be born in poverty and lowliness like his brethren, never condescended to practise the art of writing. The Jews had a law written with the greatest minuteness, and we have not a single line from the hand of Jesus. The apostles were divided on many points. St. Peter and St. Barnabas ate forbidden meats with the new stranger Christians, and abstained from them with the Jewish Christians. St. Paul reproached them with this conduct; and this same St. Paul, the Pharisee, the disciple of the Pharisee Gamaliel—this same St. Paul, who had persecuted the Christians with fury, and who after breaking with Gamaliel became a Christian himself—nevertheless, went afterwards to sacrifice in the temple of Jerusalem, during his apostolic vacation. For eight days he observed publicly all the ceremonies of the Jewish law which he had renounced; he even added devotions and purifications which were superabundant; he completely Judaized. The greatest apostle of the Christians did, for eight days, the very things for which men are condemned to the stake among a large portion of Christian nations.

Theudas and Judas were called Messiahs, before Jesus: Dositheus, Simon, Menander, called themselves Messiahs, after Jesus. From the first century of the Church, and before even the name of Christian was known, there were a score of sects in Judea.

The contemplative Gnostics, the Dositheans, the Cerintheins, existed before the disciples of Jesus had taken the name of Christians. There were soon thirty churches, each of which belonged to a different society; and by the close of the first century thirty sects of Christians might be reckoned in Asia Minor, in Syria, in Alexandria, and even in Rome.

All these sects, despised by the Roman government, and concealed in their obscurity, nevertheless persecuted each other in the hiding holes where they lurked; that is to say, they reproached one another. This is all they could do in their abject condition: they were almost wholly composed of the dregs of the people.

When at length some Christians had embraced the dogmas of Plato, and mingled a little philosophy with their religion, which they separated from the Jewish, they insensibly became more considerable, but were always divided into many sects, without there ever having been a time when the Christian church was reunited. It took its origin in the midst of the divisions of the Jews, the Samaritans, the Pharisees, the Sadducees, the Essenians, the Judaites, the disciples of John, and the Therapeutae. It was divided in its infancy; it was divided even amid the persecutions it sometimes endured under the first emperors. The martyr was often regarded by his brethren as an apostate; and the Carpocratian Christian expired under the sword of the Roman executioner, excommunicated by the Ebionite Christian, which Ebionite was anathematized by the Sabellian.

This horrible discord, lasting for so many centuries, is a very striking lesson that we ought mutually to forgive each other's errors: discord is the great evil of the human species, and toleration is its only remedy.

There is nobody who does not assent to this truth, whether meditating coolly in his closet, or examining the truth peaceably with his friends. Why, then, do the same men who in private admit charity, beneficence, and justice, oppose themselves in public so furiously against these virtues? Why!—it is because their interest is their god; because they sacrifice all to that monster whom they adore.

I possess dignity and power, which ignorance and credulity have founded. I trample on the heads of men prostrated at my feet; if they should rise and look me in the face, I am lost; they must, therefore, be kept bound down to the earth with chains of iron.

Thus have men reasoned, whom ages of fanaticism have rendered powerful. They have other persons in power under them, and these latter again have underlings, who enrich themselves with the spoils of the poor man, fatten themselves with his blood, and laugh at his imbecility. They detest all toleration, as contractors enriched at the expense of the public are afraid to render their accounts, and as tyrants dread the name of liberty. To crown all, in short, they encourage fanatics who cry aloud: Respect the absurdities of my master; tremble, pay, and be silent.

Such was the practice for a long time in a great part of the world; but now, when so many sects are balanced by their power, what side must we take among them? Every sect, we know, is a mere title of error; while there is no sect of geometricians, of algebraists, of arithmeticians; because all the propositions of geometry, algebra, and arithmetic, are true. In all the other sciences, one may be mistaken. What Thomist or Scotist theologian can venture to assert seriously that he goes on sure grounds?

If there is any sect which reminds one of the time of the first Christians, it is undeniably that of the Quakers. The apostles received the spirit. The Quakers receive the spirit. The apostles and disciples spoke three or four at once in the assembly in the third story; the Quakers do as much on the ground floor. Women were permitted to preach, according to St. Paul, and they were forbidden according to the same St. Paul: the Quakeresses preach by virtue of the first permission.

The apostles and disciples swore by yea and nay; the Quakers will not swear in any other form. There was no rank, no difference of dress, among apostles and disciples; the Quakers have sleeves without buttons, and are all clothed alike. Jesus Christ baptized none of his apostles; the Quakers are never baptized.

It would be easy to push the parallel farther; it would be still easier to demonstrate how much the Christian religion of our day differs from the religion which Jesus practised. Jesus was a Jew, and we are not Jews. Jesus abstained from pork, because it is uncleanly, and from rabbit, because it ruminates and its foot is not cloven; we fearlessly eat pork, because it is not uncleanly for us, and we eat rabbit which has the cloven foot and does not ruminate.

Jesus was circumcised, and we retain our foreskin. Jesus ate the Paschal lamb with lettuce, He celebrated the feast of the tabernacles; and we do nothing of this. He observed the Sabbath, and we have changed it; He sacrificed, and we never sacrifice.

Jesus always concealed the mystery of His incarnation and His dignity; He never said He was equal to God. St. Paul says expressly, in his Epistle to the Hebrews, that God created Jesus inferior to the angels; and in spite of St. Paul's words, Jesus was acknowledged as God at the Council of Nice.

Jesus has not given the pope either the march of Ancona or the duchy of Spoleto; and, notwithstanding, the pope possesses them by divine right. Jesus did not make a sacrament either of marriage or of deaconry; and, with us, marriage and deaconry are sacraments. If we would attend closely to the fact, the Catholic, apostolic, and Roman religion is, in all its ceremonies and in all its dogma, the reverse of the religion of Jesus!

But what! must we all Judaize, because Jesus Judaized all His life? If it were allowed to reason logically in matters of religion, it is clear that we ought all to become Jews, since Jesus Christ, our Saviour, was born a Jew, lived a Jew and died a Jew, and since He expressly said, that He accomplished and fulfilled the Jewish religion. But it is still more clear that we ought mutually to tolerate one another, because we are all weak, irrational, and subject to change and error. A reed prostrated by the wind in the mire—

ought it to say to a neighboring reed placed in a contrary direction: Creep after my fashion, wretch, or I will present a request for you to be seized and burned? . . .

WAR

All animals are perpetually at war; every species is born to devour another. There are none, even to sheep and doves, who do not swallow a prodigious number of imperceptible animals. Males of the same species make war for the females, like Menelaus and Paris. Air, earth, and the waters, are fields of destruction.

It seems that God having given reason to men, this reason should teach them not to debase themselves by imitating animals, particularly when nature has given them neither arms to kill their fellow-creatures, nor instinct which leads them to suck their blood.

Yet murderous war is so much the dreadful lot of man, that except two or three nations, there are none but what their ancient histories represent as armed against one another. Towards Canada, man and warrior are synonymous; and we have seen, in our hemisphere, that thief and soldier were the same thing. Manichaeans! behold your excuse.

The most determined of flatterers will easily agree, that war always brings pestilence and famine in its train, from the little that he may have seen in the hospitals of the armies of Germany, or the few villages he may have passed through in which some great exploit of war has been performed.

That is doubtless a very fine art which desolates countries, destroys habitations, and in a common year causes the death of from forty to a hundred thousand men. This invention was first cultivated by nations assembled for their common good; for instance, the diet of the Greeks declared to the diet of Phrygia and neighboring nations, that they intended to depart on a thousand fishers' barks, to exterminate them if they could.

The assembled Roman people judged that it was to their interest to go and fight, before harvest, against the people of Veii or the Volscians. And some years after, all the Romans, being exasperated against all the Carthaginians, fought them a long time on sea and land. It is not exactly the same at present.

A genealogist proves to a prince that he descends in a right line from a count, whose parents made a family compact, three or four hundred years ago, with a house the recollection of which does not even exist. This house had distant pretensions to a province, of which the last possessor died of apoplexy. The prince and his council see his right at once. This province, which is some hundred leagues distant from him, in vain protests that it knows him not; that it has no desire to be governed by him; that to give laws to its people, he must at least have their consent; these discourses only reach as far as the ears of the prince, whose right is incontestable. He immediately assembles a great number of men who have nothing to lose, dresses them in coarse blue cloth, borders their hats with broad white binding, makes them turn to the right and left, and marches to glory.

Other princes who hear of this equipment, take part in it, each according to his power, and cover a small extent of country with more mercenary murderers than Genghis Khan, Tamerlane, and Bajazet employed in their train. Distant people hear that they are going to fight, and that they may gain five or six sous a day, if they will be of the party; they divide themselves into two bands, like reapers, and offer their services to whoever will employ them.

These multitudes fall upon one another, not only without having any interest in the affair, but without knowing the reason of it. We see at once five or six belligerent powers, sometimes three against three, sometimes two against four, and sometimes one against five; all equally detesting one another, uniting with and attacking by turns; all agree in a single point, that of doing all the harm possible.

The most wonderful part of this infernal enterprise is that each chief of the murderers causes his colors to be blessed, and solemnly invokes God before he goes to exterminate his neighbors. If a chief has only the fortune to kill two or three thousand men, he does not thank God for it; but when he has exterminated about ten thousand by fire and sword, and, to complete the work, some town has been levelled with the ground, they then sing a long song in four parts, composed in a language unknown to all who have fought, and moreover replete with barbarism. The same song serves for marriages and births, as well as for murders; which is unpardonable, particularly in a nation the most famous for new songs.

Natural religion has a thousand times prevented citizens from committing crimes. A well-trained mind has not the inclination for it; a tender one is alarmed at it, representing to itself a just and avenging God; but artificial religion encourages all cruelties which are exercised by troops—conspiracies, seditions, pillages, ambuscades, surprises of towns, robberies, and murder. Each marches gaily to crime, under the banner of his saint.

A certain number of orators are everywhere paid to celebrate these murderous days; some are dressed in a long black close coat, with a short cloak; others have a shirt above a gown; some wear two variegated stuff streamers over their shirts. All of them speak for a long time, and quote that which was done of old in Palestine, as applicable to a combat in Veteravia.

The rest of the year these people declaim against vices. They prove, in three points and by antitheses, that ladies who lay a little carmine upon their cheeks, will be the eternal objects of the eternal vengeances of the Eternal; that Polyeuctus and Athalia are works of the demon; that a man who, for two hundred crowns a day, causes his table to be furnished with fresh sea-fish during Lent, infallibly works his salvation; and that a poor man who eats two sous and a half worth of mutton, will go forever to all the devils.

Of five or six thousand declamations of this kind, there are three or four at most, composed by a Gaul named Massillon, which an honest man may read without disgust; but in all these discourses, you will scarcely find two in which the orator dares to say a word against the scourge and crime of war, which contains all other scourges and crimes. The unfortunate orators speak incessantly against love, which is the only consolation of mankind, and the only mode of making amends for it; they say nothing of the abominable efforts which we make to destroy it.

You have made a very bad sermon on impurity—oh, Bourdaloue!—but none on these murders, varied in so many ways; on these rapines and robberies; on this universal rage which devours the world. All the united vices of all ages and places will never equal the evils produced by a single campaign.

Miserable physicians of souls! you exclaim, for five quarters of an hour, on some pricks of a pin, and say nothing on the malady which tears us into a thousand pieces! Philosophers! moralists! burn all your books. While the caprice of a few men makes that part of mankind consecrated to heroism, to murder loyally millions of our brethren, can there be anything more horrible throughout nature?

What becomes of, and what signifies to me, humanity, beneficence, modesty, temperance, mildness, wisdom, and piety, while half a pound of lead, sent from the distance of a hundred steps, pierces my body, and I die at twenty years of age, in inexpressible torments, in the midst of five or six thousand dying men, while my eyes which open for the last time, see the town in which I was born destroyed by fire and sword, and the last sounds which reach my ears are the cries of women and children expiring under the ruins, all for the pretended interests of a man whom I know not?

What is worse, war is an inevitable scourge. If we take notice, all men have worshipped Mars. Sabaoth, among the Jews, signifies the god of arms; but Minerva, in Homer, calls Mars a furious, mad, and infernal god.

The celebrated Montesquieu, who was called humane, has said, however, that it is just to bear fire and sword against our neighbors, when we fear that they are doing too well. If this is the spirit of laws, it is also that of Borgia and of Machiavelli. If unfortunately he says true, we must write against this truth, though it may be proved by facts.

This is what Montesquieu says: "Between societies, the right of natural defence sometimes induces the necessity of attacking, when one people sees that a longer peace puts another in a situation to destroy it, and that attack at the given moment is the only way of preventing this destruction."

How can attack in peace be the only means of preventing this destruction? You must be sure that this neighbor will destroy you, if he become powerful. To be sure of it, he must already have made preparations for your overthrow. In this case, it is he who commences the war; it is not you: your supposition is false and contradictory.

If ever war is evidently unjust, it is that which you propose: it is going to kill your neighbor, who does not attack you, lest he should ever be in a state to do so. To hazard the ruin of your country, in the hope of ruining without reason that of another, is assuredly neither honest nor useful; for we are never sure of success, as you well know.

If your neighbor becomes too powerful during peace, what prevents you from rendering yourself equally powerful? If he has made alliances, make them on your side. If, having fewer monks, he has more soldiers and manufacturers, imitate him in this wise economy. If he employs his sailors better, employ yours in the same manner: all that is very just. But to expose your people to the most horrible misery, in the so often false idea of overturning your dear brother, the most serene neighboring prince!
—it was not for the honorary president of a pacific society to give you such advice.

✑§ DISCOURSE ON INEQUALITY

Jean-Jacques Rousseau

Jean-Jacques Rousseau (1712–1778) was a paradoxical figure. A profoundly original and influential thinker whose writings marked an epoch in political theory, in educational theory, and in literature, he made lesser contributions to several other fields, notably music; yet he was never more than a gifted amateur in any field. Nor was he exactly a philosopher. He was not given that title by his contemporaries, and he seldom gets much attention in the histories of philosophy even today. He was capable of astounding lapses, and sometimes seems to be thinking with his heart rather than with his head. For much of his life he was ridden by neuroses, which toward the end probably amounted to insanity. Yet his impact on the modern world was second to none.

His mother died in childbirth, and he was given an eccentric education at home by his father, a Genevan watchmaker. After unsuccessful apprenticeships at various trades, he ran away and became a Catholic in exchange for free meals and lodging. A series of aristocratic ladies took a liking to him, and soon he was traveling in the highest Parisian society. He had no title, however, no income, and no profession; so, to make his position more secure, he made desultory forays into the study of the sciences and wrote a few articles and musical compositions of little consequence. But he obviously had great natural abilities, or he would not have been accepted in such exalted and competitive circles; and in 1750, when he won the first prize from the Academy of Dijon for his essay on the corrupting effect of the revival of the arts and sciences, these abilities began to find expression. He followed this in 1755 with another essay, called Discourse on the Origin and Foundation of Inequality among Men, *which failed to win the Dijon prize, but which was filled with brilliant insights.*

Rousseau was now a great success; but in accord with his celebration of the simple, natural life, he left Paris for a country retreat. Here he wrote his most influential books: a sentimental novel named La Nouvelle Héloïse *(1761), which started a wave of imitations;* Émile *(1762), a treatise in the form of a novel in which the doctrines of progressive education were first set forth; and* The Social Contract *(1762), an explosive essay in political theory.*

The Discourse on Inequality, *as it is usually called for short, sets forth the theory of human nature on which all his other writings rest. At its head he placed a quotation from Aristotle's* Politics: *"We should consider what is natural not in things depraved, but in those which are rightly ordered according to their nature." Rousseau finds that this doctrine leads to some surprising and revolutionary conclusions about man in eighteenth-century European society.*

'Tis of man I am to speak; and the very question, in answer to which I am to speak of him, sufficiently informs me that I am going to speak to men; for to those alone, who are not afraid of honouring truth, it belongs to propose discussions of this kind. I shall therefore maintain with confidence the cause of mankind before the sages, who invite me to stand up in its defence; and I shall think myself happy, if I can but behave in a manner not unworthy of my subject and of my judges.

I conceive two species of inequality among men; one which I call natural, or physical inequality, because it is established by nature, and consists in the difference of age, health, bodily strength, and the qualities of the mind, or of the soul; the other which may be termed moral, or political inequality, because it depends on a kind of convention, and is established, or at least authorized, by the common consent of mankind. This species of inequality consists in the different privileges, which some men enjoy, to the prejudice of others, such as that of being richer, more honoured, more powerful, and even that of exacting obedience from them.

It were absurd to ask, what is the cause of natural inequality, seeing the bare definition of natural inequality answers the question: it would be more absurd still to enquire, if there might not be some essential connection between the two species of inequality, as it would be asking, in other words, if those who command are necessarily better men than those who obey; and if strength of body or of mind, wisdom or virtue are always to be found in individuals, in the same proportion with power, or riches: a question, fit perhaps to be discussed by slaves in the hearing of their masters, but unbecoming free and reasonable beings in quest of truth.

What therefore is precisely the subject of this discourse? It is to point out, in the progress of things, that moment, when, right taking place of violence, nature became subject to law; to display that chain of surprising events, in consequence of which the strong submitted to serve the weak, and the people to purchase imaginary ease, at the expense of real happiness. . . .

FIRST PART

However important it may be, in order to form a proper judgment of the natural state of man, to consider him from his origin, and to examine him, as it were, in the first

French and English Philosophers, ed. Charles W. Eliot (New York: P. F. Collier and Son, The Harvard Classics, 1910), XXXIV, 167–168, 171–173, 175–180, 193–195, 198–200, 202, 207–210, 213–214, 227, 231–234.

embryo of the species; I shall not attempt to trace his organization through its successive approaches to perfection: I shall not stop to examine in the animal system what he might have been in the beginning, to become at last what he actually is; I shall not inquire whether, as Aristotle thinks, his neglected nails were no better at first than crooked talons; whether his whole body was not, bear-like, thick covered with rough hair; and whether, walking upon all-fours, his eyes, directed to the earth, and confined to a horizon of a few paces extent, did not at once point out the nature and limits of his ideas. I could only form vague, and almost imaginary, conjectures on this subject. Comparative anatomy has not as yet been sufficiently improved; neither have the observations of natural philosophy been sufficiently ascertained, to establish upon such foundations the basis of a solid system. For this reason, without having recourse to the supernatural informations with which we have been favoured on this head, or paying any attention to the changes, that must have happened in the conformation of the interior and exterior parts of man's body, in proportion as he applied his members to new purposes, and took to new aliments, I shall suppose his conformation to have always been, what we now behold it; that he always walked on two feet, made the same use of his hands that we do of ours, extended his looks over the whole face of nature, and measured with his eyes the vast extent of the heavens.

If I strip this being, thus constituted, of all the supernatural gifts which he may have received, and of all the artificial faculties, which we could not have acquired but by slow degrees; if I consider him, in a word, such as he must have issued from the hands of nature; I see an animal less strong than some, and less active than others, but, upon the whole, the most advantageously organized of any; I see him satisfying the calls of hunger under the first oak, and those of thirst at the first rivulet; I see him laying himself down to sleep at the foot of the same tree that afforded him his meal; and behold, this done, all his wants are completely supplied.

The earth left to its own natural fertility and covered with immense woods, that no hatchet ever disfigured, offers at every step food and shelter to every species of animals. Men, dispersed among them, observe and imitate their industry, and thus rise to the instinct of beasts; with this advantage, that, whereas every species of beasts is confined to one peculiar instinct, man, who perhaps has not any that particularly belongs to him, appropriates to himself those of all other animals, and lives equally upon most of the different aliments, which they only divide among themselves; a circumstance which qualifies him to find his subsistence, with more ease than any of them.

Men, accustomed from their infancy to the inclemency of the weather, and to the rigour of the different seasons; inured to fatigue, and obliged to defend, naked and without arms, their life and their prey against the other wild inhabitants of the forest, or at least to avoid their fury by flight, acquire a robust and almost unalterable habit of body; the children, bringing with them into the world the excellent constitution of their parents, and strengthening it by the same exercises that first produced it, attain by this means all the vigour that the human frame is capable of. Nature treats them exactly in the same manner that Sparta treated the children of her citizens; those who come well formed into the world she renders strong and robust, and destroys all the rest; differing in this respect from our societies, in which the state, by permitting children to become burdensome to their parents, murders them all without distinction, even in the wombs of their mothers.

The body being the only instrument that savage man is acquainted with, he employs it to different uses, of which ours, for want of practice, are incapable; and we may thank our industry for the loss of that strength and agility, which necessity obliges him to acquire. Had he a hatchet, would his hand so easily snap off from an oak so stout a branch? Had he a sling, would it dart a stone to so great a distance? Had he a ladder, would he run so nimbly up a tree? Had he a horse, would he with such swiftness shoot along the plain? Give civilized man but time to gather about him all his machines, and no doubt he will be an overmatch for the savage: but if you have a mind to see a contest still more unequal, place them naked and unarmed one opposite to the other; and you will soon discover the advantage there is in perpetually having all our forces at our disposal, in being constantly prepared against all events, and in always carrying ourselves, as it were, whole and entire about us. . . .

In regard to sickness, I shall not repeat the vain and false declamations made use of to discredit medicine by most men, while they enjoy their health; I shall only ask if there are any solid observations from which we may conclude that in those countries where the healing art is most neglected, the mean duration of man's life is shorter than in those where it is most cultivated? And how is it possible this should be the case, if we inflict more diseases upon ourselves than medicine can supply us with remedies! The extreme inequalities in the manner of living of the several classes of mankind, the excess of idleness in some, and of labour in others, the facility of irritating and satisfying our sensuality and our appetites, the too exquisite and out of the way ailments of the rich, which fill them with fiery juices, and bring on indigestions, the unwholesome food of the poor, of which even, bad as it is, they very often fall short, and the want of which tempts them, every opportunity that offers, to eat greedily and overload their stomachs; watchings, excesses of every kind, immoderate transports of all the passions, fatigues, waste of spirits, in a word, the numberless pains and anxieties annexed to every condition, and which the mind of man is constantly a prey to; these are the fatal proofs that most of our ills are of our own making, and that we might have avoided them all by adhering to the simple, uniform and solitary way of life prescribed to us by nature. Allowing that nature intended we should always enjoy good health, I dare almost affirm that a state of reflection is a state against nature, and that the man who meditates is a depraved animal. We need only call to mind the good constitution of savages, of those at least whom we have not destroyed by our strong liquors; we need only reflect, that they are strangers to almost every disease, except those occasioned by wounds and old age, to be in a manner convinced that the history of human diseases might be easily composed by pursuing that of civil societies. . . .

Let us therefore beware of confounding savage man with the men, whom we daily see and converse with. Nature behaves towards all animals left to her care with a predilection, that seems to prove how jealous she is of that prerogative. The horse, the cat, the bull, nay the ass itself, have generally a higher stature, and always a more robust constitution, more vigour, more strength and courage in their forests than in our houses; they lose half these advantages by becoming domestic animals; it looks as if all our attention to treat them kindly, and to feed them well, served only to bastardize them. It is thus with man himself. In proportion as he becomes sociable and a slave to others, he becomes weak, fearful, mean-spirited, and his soft and effeminate way of living at once completes the enervation of his strength and of his courage. We may add, that there must be still a wider difference between man and man in a savage and domestic condition, than between beast and beast; for as men and beasts have been treated alike by nature, all the conveniences with which men indulge themselves more than they do the beasts tamed by them, are so many particular causes which make them degenerate more sensibly. . . .

As yet I have considered man merely in his physical capacity; let us now endeavour to examine him in a metaphysical and moral light.

I can discover nothing in any mere animal but an ingenious machine, to which nature has given senses to wind itself up, and guard, to a certain degree, against everything that might destroy or disorder it. I perceive the very same things in the human machine, with this difference, that nature alone operates in all the operations of the beast, whereas man, as a free agent, has a share in his. One chooses by instinct; the other by an act of liberty; for which reason the beast cannot deviate from the rules that have been prescribed to it, even in cases where such deviation might be useful, and man often deviates from the rules laid down for him to his prejudice. Thus a pigeon would starve near a dish of the best flesh-meat, and a cat on a heap of fruit or corn, though both might very well support life with the food which they thus disdain, did they but bethink themselves to make a trial of it: it is in this manner dissolute men run into excesses, which bring on fevers and death itself; because the mind depraves the senses, and when nature ceases to speak, the will still continues to dictate.

All animals must be allowed to have ideas, since all animals have senses; they even combine their ideas to a certain degree, and, in this respect, it is only the difference of such degree, that constitutes the difference between man and beast: some philosophers have even advanced, that there is a greater difference between some men and some others, than between some men and some beasts; it is not therefore so much the understanding that constitutes, among animals, the specifical distinction of man, as his quality of a free agent. Nature speaks to all animals, and beasts obey her voice. Man feels the same impression, but he at the same time perceives that he is free to resist or to acquiesce; and it is in the consciousness of this liberty, that the spirituality of his soul chiefly appears: for natural philosophy explains, in some measure, the mechanism of the senses and the formation of ideas; but in the power of willing, or rather of choosing, and in the consciousness of this power, nothing can be discovered but acts, that are purely spiritual, and cannot be accounted for by the laws of mechanics.

But though the difficulties, in which all these questions are involved, should leave some room to dispute on this difference between man and beast, there is another very specific quality that distinguishes them, and a quality which will admit of no dispute; this is the faculty of improvement; a faculty which, as circumstances offer, successively unfolds all the other faculties, and resides among us not only in the species, but in the individuals that compose it; whereas a beast is, at the end of some months, all he ever will be during the rest of his life; and his species, at the end of a thousand years, precisely what it was the first year of that long period. Why is man alone subject to dotage? Is it not, because he thus returns to his primitive condition? And because, while the beast, which has acquired nothing and has likewise nothing to lose, continues always in possession of his instinct, man, losing by old age, or by accident, all the acquisitions he had made in consequence of his perfectability, thus falls back even lower than beasts themselves? It would be a melancholy necessity for us to be obliged to allow, that this distinctive and almost unlimited faculty is the source of all man's misfortunes; that it is this faculty, which, though by slow degrees, draws them out of their original condition, in which his days would slide away insensibly in peace and innocence; that it is this faculty, which, in a succession of ages, produces his discoveries and mistakes, his virtues and his vices, and, at long run, renders him both his own and nature's tyrant. . . .

Mandeville was very sensible that men, in spite of all their morality, would never have been better than monsters, if nature had not given them pity to assist reason: but he did not perceive that from this quality alone flow all the social virtues, which he would dispute mankind the possession of. In fact, what is generosity, what clemency, what humanity, but pity applied to the weak, to the guilty, or to the human species in general? Even benevolence and friendship, if we judge right, will appear the effects of a constant pity, fixed upon a particular object: for to wish that a person may not suffer, what is it but to wish that he may be happy? Though it were true that commiseration is no more than a sentiment, which puts us in the place of him who suffers, a sentiment obscure but active in the savage, developed but dormant in civilized man, how could this notion affect the truth of what I advance, but to make it more evident. In fact, commiseration must be so much the more energetic, the more intimately the animal, that beholds any kind of distress, identifies himself with the animal that labours under it. Now it is evident that this identification must have been infinitely more perfect in the state of nature than in the state of reason. It is reason that engenders self-love, and reflection that strengthens it; it is reason that makes man shrink into himself; it is reason that makes him keep aloof from everything that can trouble or afflict him: it is philosophy that destroys his connections with other men; it is in consequence of her dictates that he mutters to himself at the sight of another in distress, You may perish for aught I care, nothing can hurt me. Nothing less than those evils, which threaten the whole species, can disturb the calm sleep of the philosopher, and force him from his bed. One man may with impunity murder another under his windows; he has nothing to do but clap his hands to his ears, argue a little with himself to hinder nature, that startles within him, from identifying him with the unhappy sufferer. Savage man wants this admirable talent; and for want of wisdom and reason, is always ready foolishly to obey the first whispers of humanity. In riots and street-brawls the populace flock together, the prudent man sneaks off. They are the dregs of the people, the poor basket and barrow-women, that part the combatants, and hinder gentle folks from cutting one another's throats.

It is therefore certain that pity is a natural sentiment, which, by moderating in every individual the activity of self-love, contributes to the mutual preservation of the whole species. It is this pity which hurries us without reflection to the assistance of those we see in distress; it is this pity which, in a state of nature, stands for laws, for manners, for virtue, with this advantage, that no one is tempted to disobey her sweet and gentle voice: it is this pity which will always hinder a robust savage from plundering a feeble child, or infirm old man, of the subsistence they have acquired with pain and difficulty, if he has but the least prospect of providing for himself by any other means: it is this pity which, instead of that sublime maxim of argumentative justice, Do to others as you would have others do to you, inspires all men with that other maxim of natural goodness a great deal less perfect, but perhaps more useful, Consult your own happiness with as little prejudice as you can to that of others. It is in a word, in this natural sentiment, rather than in fine-spun arguments, that we must look for the cause of that reluctance which every man would experience to do evil, even independently of the maxims of education. Though it may be the peculiar happiness of Socrates and other geniuses of his stamp, to reason themselves into virtue, the human species would long ago have ceased to exist, had it depended entirely for its preservation on the reasonings of the individuals that compose it. . . .

Let us conclude that savage man, wandering about in the forests, without industry, without speech, without any fixed residence, an equal stranger to war and every social connection, without standing in any shape in need of his fellows, as well as without any desire of hurting them, and perhaps even without ever distinguishing them individually one from the other, subject to few passions, and finding in himself all he wants, let us, I say, conclude that savage man thus circumstanced had no knowledge or sentiment but such as are proper to that condition, that he was alone sensible of his real necessities, took notice of nothing but what it was his interest to see, and that his understanding made as little progress as his vanity. If he happened to make any discovery, he could the less communicate it as he did not even know his children. The art perished with the inventor; there was neither education nor improvement; generations succeeded generations to no purpose; and as all constantly set out from the same point, whole centuries rolled on in the rudeness and barbarity of the first age; the species was grown old, while the individual still remained in a state of childhood.

If I have enlarged so much upon the supposition of this primitive condition, it is because I thought it my duty, considering what ancient errors and inveterate prejudices I have to extirpate, to dig to the very roots, and show in a true picture of the state of nature, how much even natural inequality falls short in this state of that reality and influence which our writers ascribe to it.

In fact, we may easily perceive that among the differences, which distinguish men, several pass for natural, which are merely the work of habit and the different kinds of life adopted by men living in a social way. Thus a robust or delicate constitution, and the strength and weakness which depend on it, are oftener produced by the hardy or effeminate manner in which a man has been brought up, than by the primitive constitution of his body. It is the same thus in regard to the forces of the mind; and education not only produces a difference between those minds which are cultivated and those which are not, but even increases that which is found among the first in proportion to their culture; for let a giant and a dwarf set out in the same path, the giant at every step will acquire a new advantage over the dwarf. Now, if we compare the prodigious variety in the education and manner of living of the different orders of men in a civil state, with the simplicity and uniformity that prevails in the animal and savage life, where all the individuals make use of the same aliments, live in the same manner, and do exactly the same things, we shall easily conceive how much the difference between man and man in the state of nature must be less than in the state of society, and how much every inequality of institution must increase the natural inequalities of the human species.

But though nature in the distribution of her gifts should really affect all the preferences that are ascribed to her, what advantage could the most favoured derive from her partiality, to the prejudice of others, in a state of things, which scarce admitted any kind of relation between her pupils? Of what service can beauty be, where there is no love? What will wit avail people who don't speak, or craft those who have no affairs to transact? Authors are constantly crying out, that the strongest would oppress the weakest; but let them explain what they mean by the word oppression. One man will rule with violence, another will groan under a constant subjection to all his caprices: this is indeed precisely what I observe among us, but I don't see how it can be said of savage men, into whose heads it would be a harder matter to drive even the meaning of the words domination and servitude. One man might, indeed, seize on the fruits which another had gathered, on the game which another had killed, on the cavern which another had occupied for shelter; but how is it possible he should ever exact obedience from him, and what chains of dependence can there be among men who possess nothing? If I am driven from one tree, I have nothing to do but look out for another; if one place is made uneasy to me, what can hinder me from taking up my quarters elsewhere? But suppose I should meet a man so much superior to me in strength, and withal so wicked, so lazy and so barbarous as to oblige me to provide for his subsistence while he remains idle; he must resolve not to take his eyes from me a single moment, to bind me fast before he can take the least nap, lest I should kill him or give him the slip during his sleep: that is to say, he must expose himself voluntarily to much greater troubles than what he seeks to avoid, than any he gives me. And after all, let him abate ever so little of his vigilance; let him at some sudden noise but turn his head another way; I am already buried in the forest, my fetters are broke, and he never sees me again.

But without insisting any longer upon these details, every one must see that, as the bonds of servitude are formed merely by the mutual dependence of men one upon another and the reciprocal necessities which unite them, it is impossible for one man to enslave another, without having first reduced him to a condition in which he can not live without the enslaver's assistance; a condition which, as it does not exist in a state of nature, must leave every man his own master, and render the law of the strongest altogether vain and useless.

Having proved that the equality, which may subsist between man and man in a state of nature, is about imperceivable, and that it has very little influence, I must now proceed to show its origin, and trace its progress, in the successive developments of the human mind. . . .

SECOND PART

The first man, who, after enclosing a piece of ground, took it into his head to say, "This is mine," and found people simple enough to believe him, was the true founder of civil society. How many crimes, how many wars, how many murders, how many misfortunes and horrors, would that man have saved the human species, who pulling up the stakes or filling up the ditches should have cried to his fellows: Be sure not to listen to this imposter; you are lost, if you forget that the fruits of the earth belong equally to us all, and the earth itself to nobody! But it is highly probable that things were now come to such a pass, that they could not continue much longer in the same way; for as this idea of property depends on several prior ideas which could only spring up gradually one after another, it was not formed all at once in the human mind: men must have made great progress; they must have acquired a great stock of industry and knowledge, and transmitted and increased it from age to age before they could arrive at this last term of the state of nature. Let us therefore take up things a little higher, and collect into one point of view, and in their most natural order, this slow succession of events and mental improvements. . . .

Everything now begins to wear a new aspect. Those who heretofore wandered through the woods, by taking to a more settled way of life, gradually flock together, coalesce into several separate bodies, and at length form in every country distinct nations, united in character and manners, not by any laws or regulations, but by an uniform manner of life, a sameness of provisions, and the common influence of the climate. A permanent neighborhood must at last infallibly create some connection between different families. The transitory commerce required by nature soon produced, among the youth of both sexes living in contiguous cabins, another kind of commerce, which besides being equally agreeable is rendered more durable by mutual intercourse. Men begin to consider different objects, and to make comparisons; they insensibly acquire ideas of merit and beauty, and these soon produce sentiments of preference. By seeing each other often they contract a habit, which makes it painful not to see each other always. Tender and agreeable sentiments steal into the soul, and are by the smallest opposition wound up into the most impetuous fury: Jealousy kindles with love; discord triumphs; and the gentlest of passions requires sacrifices of human blood to appease it.

In proportion as ideas and sentiments succeed each other, and the head and the heart exercise themselves, men continue to shake off their original wildness, and their connections become more intimate and extensive. They now begin to assemble round a great tree: singing and dancing, the genuine offspring of love and leisure, become the amusement or rather the occupation of the men and women, free from care, thus gathered together. Every one begins to survey the rest, and wishes to be surveyed himself; and public esteem acquires a value. He who sings or dances best; the handsomest, the strongest, the most dexterous, the most eloquent, comes to be the most respected: this was the first step towards inequality, and at the same time towards vice. From these first preferences there proceeded on one side vanity and contempt, on the other envy and shame; and the fermentation raised by these new leavens at length produced combinations fatal to happiness and innocence.

Men no sooner began to set a value upon each other, and know what esteem was, than each laid claim to it, and it was no longer safe for any man to refuse it to another. Hence the first duties of civility and politeness, even among savages; and hence every voluntary injury became an affront, as besides the mischief, which resulted from it as an injury, the party offended was sure to find in it a contempt for his person more intolerable than the mischief itself. It was thus that every man, punishing the contempt expressed for him by others in proportion to the value he set upon himself, the effects of revenge became terrible, and men learned to be sanguinary and cruel. Such precisely was the degree attained by most of the savage nations with whom we are acquainted. And it is for want of sufficiently distinguishing ideas, and observing at how great a distance these people were from the first state of nature, that so many authors have hastily concluded that man is naturally cruel, and requires a regular system of police to be reclaimed; whereas nothing can be more gentle than he in his primitive state, when placed by nature at an equal distance from the stupidity of brutes, and the pernicious good sense of civilized man; and equally confined by instinct and reason to the care of providing against the mischief which threatens him, he is withheld by natural compassion from doing any injury to others, so far from being ever so little prone even to return that which he has received. For according to the axiom of the wise Locke, Where there is no property, there can be no injury.

But we must take notice, that the society now formed and the relations now established among men required in them qualities different from those, which they derived from their primitive constitution; that as a sense of morality began to insinuate itself into human actions, and every man, before the enacting of laws, was the only judge and avenger of the injuries he had received, that goodness of heart suitable to the pure state of nature by no means suited infant society; that it was necessary punishments should become severer in the same proportion that the opportunities of offending became more frequent, and the dread of vengeance add strength to the too weak curb of the law. Thus, though men were become less patient, and natural compassion had already suffered some alteration, this period of the development of the human faculties, holding a just mean between the indolence of the primitive state, and the petulant activity of self-love, must have been the happiest and most durable epoch. The more we reflect on this state, the more convinced we shall be, that it was the least subject of any to revolutions, the best for man, and that nothing could have drawn him out of it but some fatal accident, which, for the public good, should never have happened. The example of the savages, most of whom have been found in this condition, seems to confirm that mankind was formed ever to remain in it, that this condition is the real youth of the world, and that all ulterior improvements have been so many steps, in appearance towards the perfection of individuals, but in fact towards the decrepitness of the species.

As long as men remained satisfied with their rustic cabins; as long as they confined themselves to the use of clothes made of the skins of other animals, and the use of thorns and fish-bones, in putting these skins together; as long as they continued to consider feathers and shells as sufficient ornaments, and to paint their bodies of different colours, to improve or ornament their bows and arrows, to form and scoop out with sharp-edged stones some little fishing boats, or clumsy instruments of music; in a word, as long as they undertook such works only as a single person could finish, and stuck to such arts as did not require the joint endeavours of several hands, they lived free, healthy, honest and happy, as much as their nature would admit, and continued to enjoy with each other all the pleasures of an independent intercourse; but from the moment one man began to stand in need of another's assistance; from the moment it appeared an advantage for one man to possess the quantity of provisions requisite for two, all equality vanished; property started up; labour became necessary; and boundless forests became smiling fields, which it was found necessary to water with human sweat, and in which slavery and misery were soon seen to sprout out and grow with the fruits of the earth.

Metallurgy and agriculture were the two arts whose invention produced this great revolution. . . .

Things once arrived at this period, it is an easy matter to imagine the rest. I shall not stop to describe the successive inventions of other arts, the progress of language, the trial and employments of talents, the inequality of fortunes, the use or abuse of riches, nor all the details which follow these, and which every one may easily supply. I shall just give a glance at mankind placed in this new order of things.

Behold then all our faculties developed; our memory and imagination at work, self-love interested; reason rendered active; and the mind almost arrived at the utmost bounds of that perfection it is capable of. Behold all our natural qualities put in motion; the rank and condition of every man established, not only as the quantum of property and the power of serving or hurting others, but likewise as to genius, beauty, strength or address, merit or talents; and as these were the only qualities which could command respect, it was found necessary to have or at least to affect them. It was requisite for men to be thought what they really were not. To be and to appear became two very different things, and from this distinction sprang pomp and knavery, and all the vices which form their train. On the other hand, man, heretofore free and inde-pendent, was now in consequence of a multitude of new wants brought under subjec-tion, as it were, to all nature, and especially to his fellows, whose slave in some sense he became even by becoming their master; if rich, he stood in need of their services, if poor, of their assistance; even mediocrity itself could not enable him to do without them. He must therefore have been continually at work to interest them in his happi-ness, and make them, if not really, at least apparently find their advantage in labouring for his: this rendered him sly and artful in his dealings with some, imperious and cruel in his dealings with others, and laid him under the necessity of using ill all those whom he stood in need of, as often as he could not awe them into a compliance with his will, and did not find it his interest to purchase it at the expense of real services. In fine, an insatiable ambition, the rage of raising their relative fortunes, not so much through real necessity, as to over-top others, inspire all men with a wicked inclination to injure each other, and with a secret jealousy so much the more dangerous, as to carry its point with the greater security, it often puts on the face of benevolence. In a word, sometimes nothing was to be seen but a contention of endeavours on the one hand, and an opposition of interests on the other, while a secret desire of thriving at the expense of others constantly prevailed. Such were the first effects of property, and the inseparable attendants of infant inequality. . . .

By pursuing the progress of inequality in these different revolutions, we shall dis-cover that the establishment of laws and of the right of property was the first term of it; the institution of magistrates the second; and the third and last the changing of legal into arbitrary power; so that the different states of rich and poor were authorized by the first epoch: those of powerful and weak by the second; and by the third those of master and slave, which formed the last degree of inequality, and the term in which all the rest at last end, till new revolutions entirely dissolve the government, or bring it back nearer to its legal constitution. . . .

By thus discovering and following the lost and forgotten tracks, by which man from the natural must have arrived at the civil state; by restoring, with the intermediate positions which I have been just indicating, those which want of leisure obliges me to suppress, or which my imagination has not suggested, every attentive reader must unavoidably be struck at the immense space which separates these two states. 'Tis in this slow succession of things he may meet with the solution of an infinite number of problems in morality and politics, which philosophers are puzzled to solve. He will perceive that, the mankind of one age not being the mankind of another, the reason why Diogenes could not find a man was, that he sought among his contemporaries the man of an earlier period: Cato, he will then see, fell with Rome and with liberty, because he did not suit the age in which he lived; and the greatest of men served only to astonish that world, which would have cheerfully obeyed him, had he come into it five hundred years earlier. In a word, he will find himself in a condition to understand how the soul and the passions of men by insensible alterations change as it were their nature; how it comes to pass, that at the long run our wants and our pleasures change objects; that, original man vanishing by degrees, society no longer offers to our inspection but an assemblage of artificial men and factitious passions, which are the work of all these new relations, and have no foundation in nature. Reflection teaches us nothing on that head, but what experience perfectly confirms. Savage man and civilized man differ so much at bottom in point of inclinations and passions, that what constitutes the supreme happiness of the one would reduce the other to despair. The first sighs for nothing but repose and liberty; he desires only to live, and to be exempt from labour; nay, the ataraxy of the most confirmed Stoic falls short of his consummate indifference for every other object. On the contrary, the citizen always in motion, is perpetually sweating and toiling, and racking his brains to find out occupations still more laborious: He continues a drudge to his last minute; nay, he courts death to be able to live, or renounces life to acquire immortality. He cringes to men in power whom he hates, and to rich men whom he despises; he sticks at nothing to have the honour of serving them; he is not ashamed to value himself on his own weakness and the protection they afford him; and proud of his chains, he speaks with disdain of those who have not the honour of being the partner of his bondage. What a spectacle must the painful and envied labours of an European minister of state form in the eyes of a Caribbean! How many cruel deaths would not this indolent savage prefer to such a horrid life, which very often is not even sweetened by the pleasure of doing good? But to see the drift of so many cares, his mind should first have affixed some meaning to these words power and reputation; he should be apprised that there are men who consider as something the looks of the rest of mankind, who know how to be happy and satisfied with themselves on the testimony of others sooner than upon their own. In fact, the real source of all those differences, is that the savage lives within himself, whereas the citizen, constantly beside himself, knows only how to live in the opinion of others; insomuch that it is, if I may say so, merely from their judgment that he derives the consciousness of his own existence. It is foreign to my subject to show how this disposition engenders so much indifference for good and evil, notwithstanding so many and such fine discourses of morality; how everything, being reduced to appearances, becomes mere art and mummery; honour, friendship, virtue, and often vice itself, which we at last learn the secret to boast of; how, in short, ever inquiring of others what we are, and never daring to question ourselves on so delicate a point, in the midst of so much philosophy, humanity, and politeness, and so many sublime maxims, we have nothing to show for ourselves but a deceitful and frivolous exterior, honour without virtue, reason without wisdom, and pleasure without happiness. It is sufficient that I have proved that this is not the original condition of man, and that it is merely the spirit of society, and the inequality which society engenders, that thus change and transform all our natural inclinations.

I have endeavoured to exhibit the origin and progress of inequality, the institution and abuse of political societies, as far as these things are capable of being deduced from the nature of man by the mere light of reason, and independently of those sacred maxims which give to the sovereign authority the sanction of divine right. It follows from this picture, that as there is scarce any inequality among men in a state of nature, all that which we now behold owes its force and its growth to the development of our faculties and the improvement of our understanding, and at last becomes permanent and lawful by the establishment of property and of laws. It likewise follows that moral inequality, authorised by any right that is merely positive, clashes with natural right, as often as it does not combine in the same proportion with physical inequality: a distinction which sufficiently determines, what we are able to think in that respect of that kind of inequality which obtains in all civilized nations, since it is evidently against the law of nature that infancy should command old age, folly conduct wisdom, and a handful of men should be ready to choke with superfluities, while the famished multitude want the commonest necessaries of life.

ᵉᶾ THE SOCIAL CONTRACT

Jean-Jacques Rousseau

> *Rousseau's* Discourse on Inequality *(see pages 157–168) was preceded by a long and eloquent dedication to the Republic of Geneva, where he was born and spent his youth. The original home of Calvinism, with its emphasis on strict conformity to virtue within the community, Geneva might seem a strange place to eulogize at the start of so rebellious a work as the* Discourse. *But there is no inconsistency; and despite appearances, there is likewise no inconsistency between the* Discourse *and* The Social Contract.

For Rousseau's rebellion against eighteenth-century society is not on behalf of individualism, but on behalf of a kind of collectivism: a community in which individuals put the common good ahead of their own personal advantage and each member shares equally in both privileges and responsibilities. In the Discourse, *he speculated that man must at one time have lived in such cooperative communities, before his fatal tendency to self-love became dominant; in Calvin's Geneva, too, self-love was regarded as the cardinal sin, and the consensus of the "community of saints" replaced the traditional hierarchy as the source of authority in ecclesiastical matters, hence indirectly in politics as well.*

Thus when Rousseau came to write his major treatise on political theory, The Social Contract, or the Principles of Political Rights *(1762), his democratic collectivism was no longer new. The novelty was the logical rigor with which he nailed down doctrines that had earlier depended on eloquence and suggestion. This was a new Rousseau, meeting the philosophers on their own ground and vanquishing them—or at least daring to draw far more radical consequences than they for existing regimes: "Man is born free, and he is everywhere* [i.e., in eighteenth-century Europe] *in chains."*

These consequences were not lost on the regimes, either. Rousseau had to flee from France to Switzerland, and thence to England at the invitation of David Hume. But he quarreled with Hume, as he had quarreled with his benefactors all his life, and he returned to France in 1767 while still under sentence of exile. The embarrassed authorities left the illustrious and unbalanced old man alone, however, and in 1778 he suddenly died, possibly a suicide.

It was just eleven years later that the Bastille was stormed, and soon Robespierre and the Jacobins were quoting the Contrat Social *the way Christians had quoted the Bible. Its influence on Kant's doctrine of the autonomous human will, and on Hegel's theory of the state, was enormous. And when Karl Marx fulminated against the selfishness and corruption of the bourgeoisie, and foresaw "an association in which the free development of each is the condition for the free development of all," the spirit of Rousseau was abroad once again. It is still very much alive today.*

BOOK I

Chapter I. Subject of the First Book

Man is born free, and he is everywhere in chains. A man believes himself the master of others, but is for all that more a slave than they. How is this brought about? I do not know. What could make it legitimate? I think I can answer this question.

If I considered force alone and the effects derived from it, I should say: As long as a people is compelled to obey and obeys, it does well; as soon as it can shake off the yoke, and shakes it off, it does better: for, recovering its liberty by the same right by which it was taken away, either a people is justified in recovering its liberty, or there was no justification in taking it away.

Social order is a sacred right which serves as a basis for all others. But this right does not come from nature; it is founded upon conventions. We must know what these conventions are; but before reaching that point I must establish what I have just asserted. . . .

Chapter VI. The Social Compact

I suppose man arrived at a point where obstacles, which prejudice his preservation in the state of nature, outweigh, by their resistance, the force which each individual can employ to maintain himself in this condition. Then the primitive state can no longer exist; and mankind would perish did it not change its way of life.

Now, as men cannot engender new forces, but can only unite and direct those which exist, they have no other means of preservation than to form by aggregation a sum of forces which could prevail against resistance, and to put them in play by a single motive and make them act in concert.

This sum of forces can be established only by the concurrence of many; but the strength and liberty of each man being the primary instruments of his preservation, how can he pledge them without injury to himself and without neglecting the care which he owes to himself? This difficulty as related to my subject may be stated as follows:

"To find a form of association which shall defend and protect with the public force the person and property of each associate, and by means of which each, uniting with all, shall obey however only himself, and remain as free as before." Such is the fundamental problem of which the *Social Contract* gives the solution.

The clauses of this contract are so determined by the nature of the act, that the least modification would render them vain and of no effect; so that, although they may, perhaps, never have been formally enunciated, they are everywhere the same, everywhere tacitly admitted and recognized until, the social compact being violated, each enters again into his first rights and resumes his natural liberty,—thereby losing the conventional liberty for which he renounced it.

These clauses, clearly understood, may be reduced to one: that is, the total alienation

Jean-Jacques Rousseau, *The Social Contract*, trans. **Rose M. Harrington (New York: G. P. Putnam's Sons, 1898), pp. 2–3, 19–28, 34–38, 40–48, 158–162.**

of each associate with all his rights to the entire community,—for, first, each giving himself entirely, the condition is the same for all, and the conditions being the same for all, no one has an interest in making it onerous for the others.

Further, the alienation being without reserve, the union is as complete as it can be, and no associate has anything to claim: for, if some rights remained to individuals, as there would be no common superior who could decide between them and the public, each, being in some points his own judge, would soon profess to be so in everything; the state of nature would exist, and the association would necessarily become tyrannical and useless.

Finally, each giving himself to all, gives himself to none; and as there is not an associate over whom he does not acquire the same right as is ceded, an equivalent is gained for all that is lost, and more force to keep what he has.

If, then, we remove from the social contract all that is not of its essence, it will be reduced to the following terms: "Each of us gives in common his person and all his force under the supreme direction of the general will; and we receive each member as an indivisible part of the whole."

Immediately, instead of the individual person of each contracting party, this act of association produces a moral and collective body, composed of as many members as the assembly has votes, which receives from this same act its unity,—its common being, its life and its will. This public personage, thus formed by the union of all the others, formerly took the name of city, and now takes that of republic or body politic. This is called the *state* by its members when it is passive; the *sovereign* when it is active; and a *power* when comparing it to its equals. With regard to the associates, they take collectively the name *people*, and call themselves individually *citizens*, as participating in the sovereign authority, and *subjects*, as submitted to the laws of the state. But these terms are often confounded and are taken one for the other. It is enough to know how to distinguish them when they are employed with all precision.

Chapter VII. The Sovereign

We see by this formula that the act of association includes a reciprocal engagement between the public and individuals, and that each individual contracting, so to speak, with himself, finds himself engaged under a double relation: *i.e.,* as member of the sovereign to the individuals, and as member of the state to the sovereign. But the maxim of civil law, that no one is bound by engagements made with himself, cannot be applied here, for there is a great difference between an obligation to one's self and to a whole, of which the individual forms a part.

It should be observed, too, that public deliberation,—which may bind all subjects to the sovereign, on account of the two different relations under which each of them is considered,—cannot for the contrary reason bind the sovereign towards himself, and that consequently it is against the nature of the body politic that the sovereign impose upon himself a law which he cannot infringe. Being unable to consider himself except under the one relation, he is then in the position of an individual contracting with himself; whereby it is evident that there is not and cannot be any sort of obligatory fundamental law for the body of the people, not even the social contract. This does not mean that the body cannot engage itself perfectly towards others, in that which is not derogatory to this contract, for with regard to the foreigner, he becomes a simple being, an individual.

But the body politic or the sovereign, deriving its existence only from the sanctity of the contract, can never bind itself even towards others, to anything which is derogatory to this first act,—as to alienate some part of itself, or to submit to another sovereign. To violate the act by which it exists would be self-annihilation, and that which is nothing produces nothing.

As soon as this multitude is thus united into a body, one of the members cannot be injured without attacking the body, and still less can the body be injured without the members feeling its effects. Thus duty and interest alike oblige the two contracting parties to mutually aid each other; and the same men should seek to unite under this double relation, all the advantages which may be derived from it.

Now the sovereign, being formed only of the individuals comprising it, neither has nor could have interests contrary to theirs; consequently the sovereign power has no need of guaranty towards the subjects, for it is impossible for the body to seek to injure all its members and it will be seen hereafter that it can injure no one in particular.

The sovereign by the fact alone that it is, is always what it must be.

But this is not true of subjects towards a sovereign, to whom in spite of common interests, nothing binds them to their engagements unless means are taken to assure their fidelity. In fact each individual can, as man, have an individual will contrary to or different from the general will which he has as a citizen: his individual interest may speak quite differently from the common interest; his absolute and naturally independent existence may make him consider what he owes to the common cause as a gratuitous contribution, the loss of which would be less injurious to others than the payment of it would be onerous to him, and regarding the moral entity which constitutes the state as a legal fiction, because it is not a man, he would like to enjoy the rights of a citizen, without being willing to fulfil the duties of a subject; an injustice, the progress of which would cause the ruin of the body politic.

In order then that the social compact may not be an idle formula, it includes tacitly this engagement, which alone can give force to the others, that whoever shall refuse to obey the general will, shall be compelled to it by the whole body, which signifies nothing if not that he will be forced to be free; for it is this condition which, giving each citizen to the country, guarantees him from all personal dependence, a condition which forms the device and working of the political machine, and alone renders civil engagements legitimate, which without that would be absurd, tyrannical, and subject to great abuse.

Chapter VIII. The Civil State

The passage from the state of nature to the civil state produces in man a very remarkable change, by substituting in his conduct justice for interest, and giving to his actions a moral force which they lacked before. Then only does the voice of duty succeed to physical impulse, and law to appetite, and man who until then had thought only of himself, sees himself forced to act upon other principles, and to consult his reason before listening to his desires. Although he deprives himself in this state of several advantages which he holds from nature, he gains other advantages as great—his faculties exercise and develop, his ideas expand, his sentiments become ennobled, his whole spirit is elevated to such a point that, if the abuse of this new condition did not often degrade him below that from which he came, he ought to bless without ceasing the happy moment which took him from it forever, and which has made of a dull, stupid animal, an intelligent being—a man.

Let us reduce all this account to terms which may be easily compared: what man loses by the social contract is his natural liberty and an unlimited right to anything that tempts him, which he can obtain; what he gains is civil liberty and the ownership of all that he possesses. Not to be deceived in these compensations, we must distinguish the natural liberty, which has no limits but the strength of the individual, from civil liberty, which is limited by the general will; and possession, which is only the effect of the force or right of the first occupant, from the ownership which is founded only upon a positive title.

After what precedes, there ought to be added to the credit side of the civil state, that of moral liberty, which alone renders man master of himself; for the impulse of one appetite is slavery, and obedience to self-prescribed law is liberty. But I have already said too much about this. The philosophical meaning of the word liberty is not a part of my subject here. . . .

BOOK II

Chapter I. Sovereignty Is Inalienable

The first and most important consequence of the principles just established is, that only the general will can direct the forces of the state according to the object of its establishment, which is the common good; for if the opposition of individual interests has rendered the establishment of societies necessary, it is the accord of these same interests which has rendered it possible. It is what is common in these different interests which forms the social tie; and if there were not some point, upon which all interests were in accord, no society could exist. Now it is solely through this common interest that society should be governed.

I say then that sovereignty, being only the exercise of the general will, can never alienate itself, and that the sovereign, who is not a collective being, can be represented only by himself; power can transmit itself, but not will.

In fact, if it is not impossible that an individual will should accord in some points with the general will, it is at least impossible that this accord be unchangeable and permanent; for the individual will tends by its nature to preferences, and the general will to equality. It is still more impossible to have a guaranty of this accord; even should it always exist, it would be not the result of art but of chance. The sovereign may say: "I desire now what such a man desires, or at least what he says he desires"; but he cannot say: "What this man will desire to-morrow I shall still desire," for it is absurd to bind the will for the future, and no will can consent to anything contrary to the good of the person who wills. If then the people promises simply to obey, it dissolves by that act, it loses its quality as a people; the moment there is a master, there is no longer a sovereign, and from that time the body politic is destroyed.

This is not saying that the orders of chiefs may not pass for the general will, as long as the sovereign, free to oppose them, does not do so. In such a case, from universal silence, the consent of the people is presumed. This will be explained more at length.

Chapter II. Sovereignty Is Indivisible

For the same reason that sovereignty is inalienable, it is indivisible; for the will is general or it is not; it is the will of the body of the people, or of only a part of it. In the first case this declared will is an act of sovereignty and makes law; in the second it is only an individual will, or an act of magistracy; it is, at the most, a decree.

But our political writers, not being able to divide the sovereignty in its principle, divide it in its object; they divide it into force and will, into legislative power and executive power; into rights of impost, of justice and war; into interior administration and into power to treat with foreign countries; sometimes they confound all these parts and sometimes they separate them. They make of the sovereign a fantastic creature, formed of separate parts; it is as if they should compose a man with different bodies of which one would have the eyes, another the arms, another the feet, and nothing more. It is said that jugglers in Japan dismember a living child before the eyes of the spectators; then throwing all its members into the air, one after another, they make the child come down alive and whole again. This is very like the juggling of our political writers; after having dismembered the social body by an illusion worthy of a juggler, the scattered pieces are collected, nobody knows how.

This error arises from not having precise conceptions of the sovereign authority, and from having taken for parts of this authority what is only an emanation from it. Thus, for example, the acts declaring war and concluding peace are regarded as acts of sovereignty. This is not true, because each of the acts is not a law, but the application of a law, an individual act which determines the matter of the law, as will be seen when the idea attached to the word *law* becomes fixed.

In following in the same way the other divisions, it will be found that whenever the sovereignty is supposed to be divided, it is a mistake; that the rights which are taken as parts of this sovereignty are all subordinated to it, and always suppose a supreme will of which these rights give only the execution.

No one can tell how much obscurity this fault of inaccuracy has thrown over the decisions of authors on questions of political rights, when they have tried to judge the respective rights of kings and people upon principles which they had established. . . .

Chapter III. Whether the General Will Can Err

It follows from the preceding that the general will is always right, and always tends towards public utility; but it does not follow that the deliberations of the people always have the same rectitude. The people wishes its own good always, but it does not always see it; the people is never corrupted, but it is often deceived, and it is then only that it seems to desire what is evil.

There is often a great difference between the will of all and the general will: one regards the common interest only; the other regards private interests, and is only the sum of individual wills; but take from these same wills the plus and the minus, which destroy each other, and there will remain for the sum of the differences the general will.

If the people being sufficiently informed, deliberates, and citizens have no communication with each other,—from a great number of small differences will result the general will, and the conclusion will always be good. But when they divide into factions and partial associations at the expense of the whole, the will of each of these associations becomes general with regard to its members, and individual with regard to the state; it may then be said that there are not as many voters as men, but only as many as there are associations. The differences become less numerous and give a less general result. Finally, when one of these associations is so large as to surpass all the others, you no longer have the sum of small differences, but a single difference; then there is no longer a general will, and the opinion which prevails is only an individual opinion.

It is necessary, then, in order to have an expression of the general will that there be no partial society in the state, and that each citizen vote only in accordance with his own views; such was the one, sublime establishment of the great Lycurgus. If there are partial societies, their number must be increased and their inequality provided for, as did Solon, Numa, and Servius. These precautions are the only ones which insure that the general will will always be enlightened, and that the people will not be deceived.

Chapter IV. The Limits of Sovereign Power

If the state or city is but a moral entity, whose life consists in the union of its members, and if the most important of its cares is that of its own preservation, a universal and compulsory force is necessary to move and dispose each part in the manner most convenient for all. As nature gives to man absolute power over his members, the social compact gives to the body politic absolute power over its members; and it is this same power which, directed by the general will, bears, as I have said, the name of sovereignty.

But in addition to the public person, we have to consider the private persons comprising it, whose life and liberty are independent of it.

It is necessary then to distinguish the respective rights of the citizen and the sovereign, and the duties which the former is to fulfil in his quality of subject, from the natural rights which he ought to enjoy in his quality of man.

It is agreed that anything of power or property or liberty which is alienated by the social compact, is only a part of all the use of which is of importance to the community; but it must also be agreed that the sovereign alone is judge of its importance.

Any service that a citizen can render the state is due from him whenever the sovereign demands it; but the sovereign, for his part, cannot place any burden upon his subjects which will not be useful to the community; he cannot even desire to do so, for, under the law of reason as under the law of nature, there is nothing done without a purpose.

The engagements which link us to the social body are obligatory only because they are mutual, and their nature is such that in fulfilling them the individual cannot labor for others without working also for himself. Why is the general will always right, and why do all desire constantly the happiness of each, unless it is because there is no person who does not appropriate to himself the word each, and who does not think of himself while voting for all? Which proves that equality of rights, and the notion of justice produced by it, come from the preference which each gives to himself, and consequently from the nature of man; that the general will, to be really such, must be so in its object as well as in its essence; that it must start from all in order to apply to all; and that it loses its natural rectitude when it tends toward some individual and determined object, for then, judging of what is foreign to us, we have no true principle of equity to guide us.

In fact, as soon as there is question of a fact or of an individual right upon some point which has not been previously regulated by a general agreement, the affair becomes a subject of dispute; it is a suit in which the interested individuals are one of the parties and the public the other, but in which I see neither law to be followed nor judge to pronounce upon it. It would be ridiculous then to wish to rely upon an express decision of the general will, which can only be the conclusion of one of the parties, and which consequently is for the other only an individual foreign will, carried to injustice on this occasion and subject to error. So as an individual will cannot represent the general will, the general will in its turn changes its nature having an individual object, and cannot as a general will pronounce upon a man or a fact.

When the people of Athens, for example, elected their chiefs or reduced them to the ranks, awarding honors to one, and imposing punishments upon the other, and by a multitude of special decrees, exercised without distinction all the prerogatives of government, the people then had no longer a general will properly speaking; it acted no longer as sovereign, but as magistrate. This will appear contrary to the ordinary idea, but give me time before judging it to present my own.

It might be thought from this that what generalizes the will is not so much the number of votes, as it is the common interest which unites them; for in this establishment each submits necessarily to the conditions which he imposes upon others; admirable accord of interest and justice, which gives to common deliberations a character of equity. This vanishes in the discussion of any individual affair, for want of a common interest, which would unite and identify the ruling of the judge with that of the party.

By whatever path we return to the principle, we always reach the same conclusion; that the social compact establishes among citizens such an equality that they all engage under the same conditions, and should enjoy the same rights. Thus by the nature of the agreement, an act of sovereignty, that is, any authentic act of the general will, obliges or favors equally all citizens; so that the sovereign knows only the body of the nation and distinguishes no one of those composing it. What, then, is an act of sovereignty, properly speaking? It is not an agreement between a superior and an inferior, but an agreement of a body with each of its members,—a legitimate agreement, because it has the social contract for its basis; it is equitable because it is common to all; useful, because it can have no other object than the general good; and solid, because it has for guaranty the public force and the supreme power. As long as subjects submit only to such agreements, they obey nobody but their own wills: and to ask just how far the respective rights of sovereigns and citizens extend, is to ask to what point citizens can make engagements with themselves each with all, and all with each.

It will be seen from this that sovereign power, absolute, sacred, and inviolable as it is, does not overstep and cannot overstep the limits of general agreement, and that any man can dispose fully of what is left him of goods and liberty by these agreements; so that the sovereign never has the right to demand of one subject more than of another, because, then, the affair becoming individual, the sovereign power is no longer competent.

These distinctions once admitted, it is false that in the social contract there is any real renunciation on the part of the individual,—so false that, on the contrary, their situation is, from the effect of this contract, really preferable to what it was before, and that instead of an alienation, they have made an advantageous exchange of a mode of life which was uncertain and precarious for another, better and more sure,—of natural independence for liberty, of power to injure others for security, and of force which might be overcome by others, for a right which social union makes invincible. Even their lives which have been devoted to the state are continually protected by it; and when these are exposed for its defence, what do they more than return what they have received from it? What do they then more than they do frequently and with more danger in the state of nature? When engaging in inevitable combats, they would defend at the peril of life that which serves to preserve it for them.

All have to fight at the call of the nation, it is true; but no one needs to fight for himself.

Is it not a gain, to incur for that which makes our safety, a part of the risks which we would have to incur for ourselves were it taken from us? . . .

BOOK IV

Chapter I. The General Will Is Indestructible

As long as men united together look upon themselves as a single body, they have but one will relating to the common preservation and general welfare. Then all the energies of the state are vigorous and simple; its maxims are clear and luminous; there are no mixed, contradictory interests; the common prosperity shows itself everywhere, and requires only good sense to be appreciated. Peace, union, and equality are enemies of political subtleties. Upright, honest men are difficult to deceive, because of their simplicity; decoys and pretexts do not impose upon them, they are not cunning enough to be dupes. When we see among the happiest people in the world troops of peasants regulating the affairs of state under an oak, and conducting themselves wisely, can we help despising the refinements of other nations, who make themselves illustrious and miserable with so much art and mystery?

A state thus governed has need of few laws; and, in proportion as it becomes necessary to promulgate new ones this necessity will be universally recognized. The first to propose them will say only what all have already felt,—and it requires neither intrigues nor eloquence to cause to become laws what each has already resolved upon, as soon as he can be sure that others will do likewise.

What deceives reasoners is that, seeing only those states which are badly constituted from their origin, they are struck with the impossibility of maintaining such a policy: they smile to think of the foolish things which the people of London or Paris might be persuaded to do by an adroit, insinuating rogue. They do not know that Cromwell would have been put in irons by the people of Berne, and that the Duke of Beaufort would have been disciplined by the Genevese.

But when the social knot begins to relax, and the state to weaken, when individual interests commence to be felt, and small societies to influence the great, the common interest changes and finds opponents: unanimity no longer rules in the suffrages; the general will is no longer the will of all; contradictions and debates arise, and the best counsel does not prevail without dispute.

Finally, when the state, near its fall, exists only by a vain and illusory form; when the social tie is broken in all hearts; when the vilest interests flaunt boldly in the sacred name of the public welfare, then the general will becomes silent; all being guided by secret motives think no more like citizens than if the state had never existed. Iniquitous decrees are passed falsely under the name of law, which have for object individual interests only.

Does it follow that the general will is annihilated or corrupted? For it is always constant, inalterable, and pure; but it is subordinated to others which overbalance it. Each in detaching his interest from the common interest, sees that he cannot separate it entirely; but his part of the public misfortune seems nothing to him compared to the exclusive good which he thinks he has appropriated to himself. This particular good excepted, he desires the general well-being for his own interest as strongly as any other. Even in selling his vote for money he has not extinguished in himself the general will —he eludes it. The fault which he commits is in evading the question and answering something which has not been asked him; instead of saying by his vote, "It is advantageous to the state," he says, "It is advantageous to such a man or party that such or such counsel prevail." The law of public order in assemblies is not so much to maintain the general will there, as to see that it is always interrogated and always answers.

I should have here many reflections to make upon the simple right to vote upon each act of sovereignty, a right which nothing can take from citizens, and upon the right to think, to propose, to divide, to discuss, which the government has always taken great care to allow only to its members; but this important matter will require a separate treatise, and I cannot consider it fully here. . . .

ᴈᔕ CRITIQUE OF PURE REASON

Immanuel Kant

It is often said that the philosophers of the eighteenth-century Enlightenment had an exaggerated faith in the power of human reason, an uncritical belief in man's ability to solve all his problems simply by the application of the scientific method. This may have been true of literary figures like Pope or Voltaire, or of agitators like Tom Paine, but it simply was not true of the philosophers. Most of them, in fact, devoted

their efforts to defining the limits *of human reason and foresaw a slow
but steady advance in knowledge only if man could learn to restrain his
tendency to rush impetuously beyond these limits. Locke, Berkeley, Hume,
Condillac, Diderot, Rousseau, Kant—all these wrote of the need to
cease trying to storm the heavens and to content ourselves with knowledge
of the practical necessities of life. "Enlightenment" for them was primarily
a matter of self-knowledge; and self-knowledge, as for Socrates, was
in turn chiefly a matter of discovering how little we really know, or
can know.*

It is in this sense that the publication of the Critique of Pure Reason
*in 1781 by Immanuel Kant of Königsberg in East Prussia (1724–1804)
can be regarded as the climax of the Enlightenment. The way had been
prepared, notably by Locke and Hume, for a new philosophical outlook
to complement the science of Newton; but it was Kant who gave this
new outlook its characteristic form. In essence, it consisted of a new
theory of the human mind and its relation to nature. Instead of a receiving
apparatus, upon which objects imprint their properties as a signet ring
prints on wax, allowing us to form a more or less accurate representation
of the nature of things, Kant's analysis revealed a constructive, creative
power molding its objects according to its own laws of operation. One
implication of this is that we can never be sure how closely our ideas
"correspond to reality." Nor can we be sure of even exactly what this
phrase means, since reality for human beings is thus different from what it
would be for a being which perceives its environment differently—a
fish, say, or a god. But another implication is a glorious sense of freedom—
freedom to think, act, and feel spontaneously and creatively, and to build
a world of human values that transcends the bland uniformities of
Newtonian mechanics.*

*Both these themes are stressed in the following selection, which is from
the Preface to the second edition of the* Critique *(1787). Kant wrote
two more "critiques," of practical reason (1788) and of judgment
(1790), in which he further developed the second of these themes.
(The word "critique" as used here implies no negative evaluation;
it simply means a careful assessment of a claim, in this case the claim of
reason to yield knowledge.) Kant's works, sometimes known as "the
critical philosophy," constituted nothing less than a revolution in philosophy. Everything written in this field since his time must come to grips
with his arguments or risk being ignored as obsolete.*

Whether the treatment of such knowledge as lies within the province of reason does or does not follow the secure path of a science, is easily to be determined from the outcome. For if after elaborate preparations, frequently renewed, it is brought to a stop immediately it nears its goal; if often it is compelled to retrace its steps and strike into some new line of approach; or again, if the various participants are unable to agree in any common plan of procedure, then we may rest assured that it is very far from having entered upon the secure path of a science, and is indeed a merely random groping. In these circumstances, we shall be rendering a service to reason should we succeed in discovering the path upon which it can securely travel, even if, as a result of so doing, much that is comprised in our original aims, adopted without reflection, may have to be abandoned as fruitless.

That logic has already, from the earliest times, proceeded upon this sure path is evidenced by the fact that since Aristotle it has not required to retrace a single step, unless, indeed, we care to count as improvements the removal of certain needless subtleties or the clearer exposition of its recognised teaching, features which concern the elegance rather than the certainty of the science. It is remarkable also that to the present day this logic has not been able to advance a single step, and is thus to all appearance a closed and completed body of doctrine. If some of the moderns have thought to enlarge it by introducing *psychological* chapters on the different faculties of knowledge (imagination, wit, etc.), *metaphysical* chapters on the origin of knowledge or on the different kinds of certainty according to difference in the objects (idealism, scepticism, etc.), or *anthropological* chapters on prejudices, their causes and remedies, this could only arise from their ignorance of the peculiar nature of logical science. We do not enlarge but disfigure sciences, if we allow them to trespass upon one another's territory. The sphere of logic is quite precisely delimited; its sole concern is to give an exhaustive exposition and a strict proof of the formal rules of all thought, whether it be *a priori* or empirical, whatever be its origin or its object, and whatever hindrances, accidental or natural, it may encounter in our minds.

That logic should have been thus successful is an advantage which it owes entirely to its limitations, whereby it is justified in abstracting—indeed, it is under obligation to do so—from all objects of knowledge and their differences, leaving the understanding nothing to deal with save itself and its form. But for reason to enter on the sure path of science is, of course, much more difficult, since it has to deal not with itself alone but also with objects. Logic, therefore, as a propaedeutic, forms, as it were, only the vestibule of the sciences; and when we are concerned with specific modes of knowledge, while logic is indeed presupposed in any critical estimate of them, yet for the actual acquiring of them we have to look to the sciences properly and objectively so called.

Now if reason is to be a factor in these sciences, something in them must be known *a priori,* and this knowledge may be related to its object in one or other of two ways, either as merely *determining* it and its concept (which must be supplied from elsewhere) or as also *making it actual.* The former is *theoretical,* the latter *practical* knowledge of reason. In both, that part in which reason determines its object completely

Immanuel Kant's Critique of Pure Reason. Norman Kemp Smith, trans. and ed. (London: Macmillan & Co., Ltd., 1953), pp. 17–32.

a priori, namely, the *pure* part—however much or little this part may contain—must be first and separately dealt with, in case it be confounded with what comes from other sources. For it is bad management if we blindly pay out what comes in, and are not able, when the income falls into arrears, to distinguish which part of it can justify expenditure, and in which line we must make reductions.

Mathematics and physics, the two sciences in which reason yields theoretical knowledge, have to determine their objects *a priori,* the former doing so quite purely, the latter having to reckon, at least partially, with sources of knowledge other than reason.

In the earliest times to which the history of human reason extends, *mathematics,* among that wonderful people, the Greeks, had already entered upon the sure path of science. But it must not be supposed that it was as easy for mathematics as it was for logic—in which reason has to deal with itself alone—to light upon, or rather to construct for itself, that royal road. On the contrary, I believe that it long remained, especially among the Egyptians, in the groping stage, and that the transformation must have been due to a *revolution* brought about by the happy thought of a single man, the experiment which he devised marking out the path upon which the science must enter, and by following which, secure progress throughout all time and in endless expansion is infallibly secured. The history of this intellectual revolution—far more important than the discovery of the passage round the celebrated Cape of Good Hope—and of its fortunate author, has not been preserved. But the fact that Diogenes Laertius, in handing down an account of these matters, names the reputed author of even the least important among the geometrical demonstrations, even of those which, for ordinary consciousness, stand in need of no such proof, does at least show that the memory of the revolution, brought about by the first glimpse of this new path, must have seemed to mathematicians of such outstanding importance as to cause it to survive the tide of oblivion. A new light flashed upon the mind of the first man (be he Thales or some other) who demonstrated the properties of the isosceles triangle. The true method, so he found, was not to inspect what he discerned either in the figure, or in the bare concept of it, and from this, as it were, to read off its properties; but to bring out what was necessarily implied in the concepts that he had himself formed *a priori,* and had put into the figure in the construction by which he presented it to himself. If he is to know anything with *a priori* certainty he must not ascribe to the figure anything save what necessarily follows from what he has himself set into it in accordance with his concept.

Natural science was very much longer in entering upon the highway of science. It is, indeed, only about a century and a half since Bacon, by his ingenious proposals, partly initiated this discovery, partly inspired fresh vigour in those who were already on the way to it. In this case also the discovery can be explained as being the sudden outcome of an intellectual revolution. In my present remarks I am referring to natural science only in so far as it is founded on *empirical* principles.

When Galileo caused balls, the weights of which he had himself previously determined, to roll down an inclined plane; when Torricelli made the air carry a weight which he had calculated beforehand to be equal to that of a definite volume of water; or in more recent times, when Stahl changed metals into oxides, and oxides back into metal, by withdrawing something and then restoring it, a light broke upon all students of nature. They learned that reason has insight only into that which it produces after a plan of its own, and that it must not allow itself to be kept, as it were, in nature's leading-strings, but must itself show the way with principles of judgment based upon fixed laws, constraining nature to give answer to questions of reason's own determining. Accidental observations, made in obedience to no previously thought-out plan, can never be made to yield a necessary law, which alone reason is concerned to discover. Reason, holding in one hand its principles, according to which alone concordant appearances can be admitted as equivalent to laws, and in the other hand the experiment which it has devised in conformity with these principles, must approach nature in order to be taught by it. It must not, however, do so in the character of a pupil who listens to everything that the teacher chooses to say, but of an appointed judge who compels the witnesses to answer questions which he has himself formulated. Even physics, therefore, owes the beneficent revolution in its point of view entirely to the happy thought, that while reason must seek in nature, not fictitiously ascribe to it, whatever as not being knowable through reason's own resources has to be learnt, if learnt at all, only from nature, it must adopt as its guide, in so seeking, that which it has itself put into nature. It is thus that the study of nature has entered on the secure path of a science, after having for so many centuries been nothing but a process of merely random groping.

Metaphysics is a completely isolated speculative science of reason, which soars far above the teachings of experience, and in which reason is indeed meant to be its own pupil. Metaphysics rests on concepts alone—not, like mathematics, on their application to intuition. But though it is older than all other sciences, and would survive even if all the rest were swallowed up in the abyss of an all-destroying barbarism, it has not yet had the good fortune to enter upon the secure path of a science. For in it reason is perpetually being brought to a stand, even when the laws into which it is seeking to have, as it professes, an *a priori* insight are those that are confirmed by our most common experiences. Ever and again we have to retrace our steps, as not leading us in the direction in which we desire to go. So far, too, are the students of metaphysics from exhibiting any kind of unanimity in their contentions, that metaphysics has rather to be regarded as a battle-ground quite peculiarly suited for those who desire to exercise themselves in mock combats, and in which no participant has ever yet succeeded in gaining even so much as an inch of territory, not at least in such manner as to secure him in its permanent possession. This shows, beyond all questioning, that the procedure of metaphysics has hitherto been a merely random groping, and, what is worst of all, a groping among mere concepts.

What, then, is the reason why, in this field, the sure road to science has not hitherto been found? Is it, perhaps, impossible of discovery? Why, in that case, should nature have visited our reason with the restless endeavour whereby it is ever searching for such a path, as if this were one of its most important concerns? Nay, more, how little cause have we to place trust in our reason, if, in one of the most important domains of which we would fain have knowledge, it does not merely fail us, but lures us on by deceitful promises, and in the end betrays us! Or if it be only that we have thus far failed to find the true path, are there any indications to justify the hope that by renewed efforts we may have better fortune than has fallen to our predecessors?

The examples of mathematics and natural science, which by a single and sudden revolution have become what they now are, seem to me sufficiently remarkable to suggest our considering what may have been the essential features in the changed point of view by which they have so greatly benefited. Their success should incline us, at least by way of experiment, to imitate their procedure, so far as the analogy which, as species of rational knowledge, they bear to metaphysics may permit. Hitherto it has been assumed that all our knowledge must conform to objects. But all attempts to extend our knowledge of objects by establishing something in regard to them *a priori,* by means of concepts, have, on this assumption, ended in failure. We must therefore make trial whether we may not have more success in the tasks of metaphysics, if we suppose that objects must conform to our knowledge. This would agree better with what is desired, namely, that it should be possible to have knowledge of objects *a priori,* determining something in regard to them prior to their being given. We should then be proceeding precisely on the lines of Copernicus' initial hypothesis. Failing of satisfactory progress in explaining the movements of the heavenly bodies on the supposition that they all revolved round the spectator, he tried whether he might not have better success if he made the spectator to revolve and the stars to remain at rest. A similar experiment can be tried in metaphysics, as regards the *intuition* of objects. If intuition must conform to the constitution of the objects, I do not see how we could know anything of the latter *a priori;* but if the object (as object of the senses) must conform to the constitution of our faculty of intuition, I have no difficulty in conceiving such a possibility. Since I cannot rest in these intuitions if they are to become known, but must relate them as representations to something as their object, and determine this latter through them, either I must assume that the *concepts,* by means of which I obtain this determination, conform to the object, or else I assume that the objects, or what is the same thing, that the *experience* in which alone, as given objects, they can be known, conform to the concepts. In the former case, I am again in the same perplexity as to how I can know anything *a priori* in regard to the objects. In the latter case the outlook is more hopeful. For experience is itself a species of knowledge which involves understanding; and understanding has rules which I must presuppose as being in me prior to objects being given to me, and therefore as being *a priori.* They find expression in *a priori* concepts to which all objects of experience necessarily conform, and with which they must agree. As regards objects which are thought solely through reason, and indeed as necessary, but which can never—at least not in the manner in which reason thinks them—be given in experience, the attempts at thinking them (for they must admit of being thought) will furnish an excellent touchstone of what we are adopting as our new method of thought, namely, that we can know *a priori* of things only what we ourselves put into them.

This experiment succeeds as well as could be desired, and promises to metaphysics, in its first part—the part that is occupied with those concepts *a priori* to which the corresponding objects, commensurate with them, can be given in experience—the secure path of a science. For the new point of view enables us to explain how there can be knowledge *a priori;* and, in addition, to furnish satisfactory proofs of the laws which form the *a priori* basis of nature, regarded as the sum of the objects of experience—neither achievement being possible on the procedure hitherto followed. But this deduction of our power of knowing *a priori,* in the first part of metaphysics, has a consequence which is startling, and which has the appearance of being highly prejudicial to the whole purpose of metaphysics, as dealt with in the second part. For we are brought to the conclusion that we can never transcend the limits of possible experience, though that is precisely what this science is concerned, above all else, to achieve. This situation yields, however, just the very experiment by which, indirectly, we are enabled to prove the truth of this first estimate of our *a priori* knowledge of reason, namely, that such knowledge has to do only with appearances, and must leave the thing in itself as indeed real *per se,* but as not known by us. For what necessarily forces us to transcend the limits of experience and of all appearances is the *unconditioned,* which reason, by necessity and by right, demands in things in themselves, as required to complete the series of conditions. If, then, on the supposition that our empirical knowledge conforms to objects as things in themselves, we find that the unconditioned *cannot be thought without contradiction,* and that when, on the other hand, we suppose that our representation of things, as they are given to us, does not conform to these things as they are in themselves, but that these objects, as appearances, conform to our mode of representation, *the contradiction vanishes;* and if, therefore, we thus find that the unconditioned is not to be met with in things, so far as we know them, that is, so far as they are given to us, but only so far as we do not know them, that is, so far as they are things in themselves, we are justified in concluding that what we at first assumed for the purposes of experiment is now definitely confirmed. But when all progress in the field of the supersensible has thus been denied to speculative reason, it is still open to us to enquire whether, in the practical knowledge of reason, data may not be found sufficient to determine reason's transcendent concept of the unconditioned, and so to enable us, in accordance with the wish of metaphysics, and by means of knowledge that is possible *a priori,* though only from a practical point of view, to pass beyond the limits of all possible experience. Speculative reason has thus at least made room for such an extension; and if it must at the same time leave it empty, yet none the less we are at liberty, indeed we are summoned, to take occupation of it, if we can, by practical data of reason.

This attempt to alter the procedure which has hitherto prevailed in metaphysics, by completely revolutionising it in accordance with the example set by the geometers and physicists, forms indeed the main purpose of this critique of pure speculative reason. It is a treatise on the method, not a system of the science itself. But at the same time it marks out the whole plan of the science, both as regards its limits and as regards its entire internal structure. For pure speculative reason has this peculiarity, that it can measure its powers according to the different ways in which it chooses the objects of its thinking, and can also give an exhaustive enumeration of the various ways in which it propounds its problems, and so is able, nay bound, to trace the complete outline of a system of metaphysics. As regards the first point, nothing in *a priori* knowledge can be ascribed to objects save what the thinking subject derives from itself; as regards the second point, pure reason, so far as the principles of its knowledge are concerned, is a quite separate self-subsistent unity, in which, as in an organised body, every member exists for every other, and all for the sake of each, so that no principle can safely be taken in *any one* relation, unless it has been investigated in the *entirety* of its relations to the whole employment of pure reason. Consequently, metaphysics has also this singular advantage, such as falls to the lot of no other science which deals with objects (for *logic* is concerned only with the form of thought in general), that should it, through this critique, be set upon the secure path of a science, it is capable of acquiring exhaustive knowledge of its entire field. Metaphysics has to deal only with principles, and with the limits of their employment as determined by these principles themselves, and it can therefore finish its work and bequeath it to posterity as a capital to which no addition can be made. Since it is a fundamental science, it is under obligation to achieve this completeness. . . .

But, it will be asked, what sort of a treasure is this that we propose to bequeath to posterity? What is the value of the metaphysics that is alleged to be thus purified by criticism and established once for all? On a cursory view of the present work it may seem that its results are merely *negative,* warning us that we must never venture with speculative reason beyond the limits of experience. Such is in fact its primary use. But such teaching at once acquires a *positive* value when we recognise that the principles with which speculative reason ventures out beyond its proper limits do not in effect *extend* the employment of reason, but, as we find on closer scrutiny, inevitably *narrow* it. These principles properly belong [not to reason but] to sensibility, and when thus employed they threaten to make the bounds of sensibility coextensive with the real, and so to supplant reason in its pure (practical) employment. So far, therefore, as our Critique limits speculative reason, it is indeed *negative;* but since it thereby removes an obstacle which stands in the way of the employment of practical reason, nay threatens to destroy it, it has in reality a *positive* and very important use. At least this is so, immediately we are convinced that there is an absolutely necessary *practical* employment of pure reason—the *moral*—in which it inevitably goes beyond the limits of sensibility. Though [practical] reason, in thus proceeding, requires no assistance from speculative reason, it must yet be assured against its opposition, that reason may not be brought into conflict with itself. To deny that the service which the Critique renders is *positive* in character, would thus be like saying that the police are of no positive benefit, inasmuch as their main business is merely to prevent the violence of which citizens stand in mutual fear, in order that each may pursue his vocation in peace and security. That space and time are only forms of sensible intuition, and so only conditions of the existence of things as appearances; that, moreover, we have no concepts of understanding, and consequently no elements for the knowledge of things, save in so far as intuition can be given corresponding to these concepts; and that we can therefore have no knowledge of any object as thing in itself, but only in so far as it is an object of sensible intuition, that is, an appearance—all this is proved in the analytical part of the Critique. Thus it does indeed follow that all possible speculative knowledge of reason is limited to mere objects of *experience.* But our further contention must also be duly borne in mind, namely, that though we cannot *know* these objects as things in themselves, we must yet be in position at least to *think* them as things in themselves; otherwise we should be landed in the absurd conclusion that there can be appearance without anything that appears. Now let us suppose that the distinction, which our Critique has shown to be necessary, between things as objects of experience and those same things as things in themselves, had not been made. In that case all things in general, as far as they are efficient causes, would be determined by the principle of causality, and consequently by the mechanism of nature. I could not, therefore, without palpable contradiction, say of one and the same being, for instance the human soul, that its will is free and yet is subject to natural necessity, that is, is not free. For I have taken the soul in both propositions *in one and the same sense,* namely as a thing in general, that is, as a thing in itself; and save by means of a preceding critique, could not have done otherwise. But if our Critique is not in error in teaching that the object is to be taken *in a twofold sense,* namely as appearance and as thing in itself; if the deduction of the concepts of understanding is valid, and the principle of causality therefore applies only to things taken in the former sense, namely, in so far as they are objects of experience—these same objects, taken in the other sense, not being subject to the principle—then there is no contradiction in supposing that one and the same will is, in the appearance, that is, in its visible acts, necessarily subject to the law of nature, and so far *not free,* while yet, as belonging to a thing in itself, it is not subject to that law, and is therefore *free.* My soul, viewed from the latter standpoint, cannot indeed be known by means of speculative reason (and still less through empirical observation); and freedom as a property of a being to which I attribute effects in the sensible world, is therefore also not knowable in any such fashion. For I should then have to know such a being as determined in its existence, and yet as not determined in time—which is impossible, since I cannot support my concept by any intuition. But though I cannot *know,* I can yet *think* freedom; that is to say, the representation of it is at least not self-contradictory, provided due account be taken of our critical distinction between the two modes of representation, the sensible and the intellectual, and of the resulting limitation of the pure concepts of understanding and of the principles which flow from them.

If we grant that morality necessarily presupposes freedom (in the strictest sense) as a property of our will; if, that is to say, we grant that it yields practical principles—original principles, proper to our reason—as *a priori data* of reason, and that this would be absolutely impossible save on the assumption of freedom; and if at the same time we grant that speculative reason has proved that such freedom does not allow of being thought, then the former supposition—that made on behalf of morality—would have to give way to this other contention, the opposite of which involves a palpable contradiction. For since it is only on the assumption of freedom that the negation of morality contains any contradiction, freedom, and with it morality, would have to yield to the mechanism of nature.

Morality does not, indeed, require that freedom should be understood, but only that it should not contradict itself, and so should at least allow of being thought, and that as thus thought it should place no obstacle in the way of a free act (viewed in another relation) likewise conforming to the mechanism of nature. The doctrine of morality and the doctrine of nature may each, therefore, make good its position. This, however, is only possible in so far as criticism has previously established our unavoidable ignorance of things in themselves, and has limited all that we can theoretically *know* to mere appearances.

This discussion as to the positive advantage of critical principles of pure reason can be similarly developed in regard to the concept of *God* and of the *simple nature* of our *soul;* but for the sake of brevity such further discussion may be omitted. [From what has already been said, it is evident that] even the *assumption*—as made on behalf of the necessary practical employment of my reason—of *God, freedom,* and *immortality* is not permissible unless at the same time speculative reason be deprived of its pretensions to transcendent insight. For in order to arrive at such insight it must make use of principles which, in fact, extend only to objects of possible experience, and which, if also applied to what cannot be an object of experience, always really change this into an appearance, thus rendering all *practical extension* of pure reason impossible. I have therefore found it necessary to deny *knowledge,* in order to make room for *faith.* The dogmatism of metaphysics, that is, the preconception that it is possible to make headway in metaphysics without a previous criticism of pure reason, is the source of all that unbelief, always very dogmatic, which wars against morality.

Though it may not, then, be very difficult to leave to posterity the bequest of a systematic metaphysic, constructed in conformity with a critique of pure reason, yet such a gift is not to be valued lightly. For not only will reason be enabled to follow the secure path of a science, instead of, as hitherto, groping at random, without circumspection or self-criticism; our enquiring youth will also be in a position to spend their time more profitably than in the ordinary dogmatism by which they are so early and so greatly encouraged to indulge in easy speculation about things of which they understand nothing, and into which neither they nor anyone else will ever have any insight—encouraged, indeed, to invent new ideas and opinions, while neglecting the study of the better-established sciences. But, above all, there is the inestimable benefit, that all objections to morality and religion will be for ever silenced, and this in Socratic fashion, namely, by the clearest proof of the ignorance of the objectors. There has always existed in the world, and there will always continue to exist, some kind of metaphysics, and with it the dialectic that is natural to pure reason. It is therefore the first and most important task of philosophy to deprive metaphysics, once and for all, of its injurious influence, by attacking its errors at their very source.

Notwithstanding this important change in the field of the sciences, and the *loss* of its fancied possessions which speculative reason must suffer, general human interests remain in the same privileged position as hitherto, and the advantages which the world has hitherto derived from the teachings of pure reason are in no way diminished. The loss affects only the *monopoly of the schools,* in no respect the *interests of humanity.* I appeal to the most rigid dogmatist, whether the proof of the continued existence of our soul after death, derived from the simplicity of substance, or of the freedom of the will as opposed to a universal mechanism, arrived at through the subtle but ineffectual distinctions between subjective and objective practical necessity, or of the existence of God as deduced from the concept of an *ens realissimum* * (of the contingency of the changeable and of the necessity of a prime mover), have ever, upon passing out from the schools, succeeded in reaching the public mind or in exercising the slightest influence on it convictions? That has never been found to occur, and in view of the unfitness of the common human understanding for such subtle speculation, ought never to have been expected. Such widely held convictions, so far as they rest on rational grounds, are due to quite other considerations. The hope of a *future life* has its source

* ["A being supremely real." (*Ed.*)]

in that notable characteristic of our nature, never to be capable of being satisfied by what is temporal (as insufficient for the capacities of its whole destination); the consciousness of *freedom* rests exclusively on the clear exhibition of duties, in opposition to all claims of the inclinations; the belief in a wise and great *Author of the world* is generated solely by the glorious order, beauty, and providential care everywhere displayed in nature. When the Schools have been brought to recognise that they can lay no claim to higher and fuller insight in a matter of universal human concern than that which is equally within the reach of the great mass of men (ever to be held by us in the highest esteem), and that, as Schools of philosophy, they should limit themselves to the study of those universally comprehensible, and, for moral purposes, sufficient grounds of proof, then not only do these latter possessions remain undisturbed, but through this very fact they acquire yet greater authority. The change affects only the arrogant pretensions of the Schools, which would fain be counted the sole authors and possessors of such truths (as, indeed, they can justly claim to be in many other branches of knowledge), reserving the key to themselves, and communicating to the public their use only. . . . At the same time due regard is paid to the more moderate claims of the speculative philosopher. He still remains the sole authority in regard to a science which benefits the public without their knowing it, namely, the critique of reason. That critique can never become popular, and indeed there is no need that it should. For just as fine-spun arguments in favour of useful truths make no appeal to the general mind, so neither do the subtle objections that can be raised against them. On the other hand, both inevitably present themselves to everyone who rises to the height of speculation; and it is therefore the duty of the Schools, by means of a thorough investigation of the rights of speculative reason, once for all to prevent the scandal which, sooner or later, is sure to break out even among the masses, as the result of the disputes in which metaphysicians (and, as such, finally also the clergy) inevitably become involved to the consequent perversion of their teaching. Criticism alone can sever the root of *materialism, fatalism, atheism, free-thinking, fanaticism,* and *superstition,* which can be injurious universally; as well as of *idealism* and *scepticism,* which are dangerous chiefly to the Schools, and hardly allow of being handed on to the public. If governments think proper to interfere with the affairs of the learned, it would be more consistent with a wise regard for science as well as for mankind, to favour the freedom of such criticism, by which alone the labours of reason can be established on a firm basis, than to support the ridiculous despotism of the Schools, which raise a loud cry of public danger over the destruction of cobwebs to which the public has never paid any attention, and the loss of which it can therefore never feel. . . .

Part Three

Movements for Reform

✎§ NATIONAL ECONOMY

Johann Heinrich Gottlieb von Justi

*It is a curious paradox of the eighteenth century that in France and
England, where the Enlightenment was seemingly most influential,
government remained hidebound and traditionalist, although in countries
of northern, central and southern Europe that produced few major
philosophes, governmental administration became self-consciously rational
in its methods and aims. The answer to this puzzle is that the philosophes
—most of them men of letters with an occasional professor added for
ballast—represented only one strand, though by far the best known,
of enlightened reform. As the philosophes were men lacking practical
administrative experience (an administrator-philosophe like Turgot in
France was exceptional) who had, so to speak, "never met a payroll,"
their ideas were usually dismissed or ignored by princely policy makers
and their bureaucratic executives and administrators. In central Europe,
the foremost representatives of the Enlightenment were rather a group
of political theorists, usually called "cameralists." To the established
authorities, the credentials of the cameralists were far more impressive
than those of the philosophes: the cameralists were government officials
of extensive experience addressing themselves to the concrete problems
of rational administration. Since they appealed to the self-interest as
well as the sense of duty of the rulers, and to the budding professionalism
of the bureaucrats, their prescriptions were widely adopted, not only
in the German states, but also in Scandinavia, Italy, and Spain. Even an
atypically intellectual ruler like Frederick the Great of Prussia (see
page 200), in personal touch with many of the philosophes of his day,
relied on the cameralists for guidelines for his practical reforms.*

*The following selection is from the introduction to a two-volume
textbook on public administration written by the best known of the
eighteenth-century cameralists, Johann Heinrich Gottlieb von Justi
(1717–1771). The son of a judge and himself a trained lawyer, Justi
in the course of his career served the Austrian, Swedish, and Prussian
governments either as teacher of public administration or as government
official. Ironically, he died while imprisoned by Frederick the Great for
maladministration of the Prussian Bureau of Mines.*

ON THE NECESSITY OF THE ECONOMIC AND CAMERAL SCIENCES AND THE
WAYS AND MEANS BY WHICH THEY SHOULD BE TAUGHT AT UNIVERSITIES

The economic and cameral sciences have long been in existence, having been practiced
ever since private property was introduced among men and commonwealths instituted.
However feeble men's understanding may have been at that time, men did have to
abide by certain rules appropriate to their ends, if only to administer their wealth and
their households. The rulers of the commonwealths, seeking to run the state in an
orderly fashion, as well as to administer and manage their private and public fortunes,
had to draw up rules and regulations. These indeed are the heart of the economic
and cameral sciences. Even the teaching of these sciences and their exposition in writing is by no means novel. Already in the writings of Aristotle we find that he dealt
with certain aspects of these sciences. . . . Nonetheless, ancient though they be,
scholars have neglected these sciences above all the others that have found more than
enough laborers in their vineyard. . . . Had it not been for some people ensconced
in their offices and otherwise little given to learning, who shared their observations
and sketched some aspects of this field of science, we should encounter nothing but
desert and desolation. There has been equally little consideration given to the teaching
of these sciences at universities, even though other disciplines are overstaffed. Not
until several centuries after the founding of the universities was it deemed necessary
to endow a single professorial chair devoted to these sciences.

Less than thirty years ago, the late king of Prussia, himself a great administrator
who valued learning only according to its utility to the state, and who up to then had
had little use for the scholars of that time, was the first to have the idea of endowing
a university professorship for instruction in the economic sciences. This was in fact
carried out both at Frankfurt on the Oder and at Halle, though at Frankfurt the chair
was not maintained for very long, while that at Halle is still occupied. In the latter
case, the king was fortunate in finding in Privy-Councilor Gasser a man who did have
much skill in these sciences, although his thinking was not quite orderly and systematic
enough to develop them fully. Indeed, the king thought so much of his instruction
that a Prussian subject stood little chance of advancement unless he could show a
diploma from Gasser vouching for assiduous attendance at the economics lectures. The
Prussian king's example attracted the attention of other states to the advantage of such
professorships in economics. Hence similar chairs were founded at Upsala [Sweden],
at Göttingen and other German universities, as well as at such academic colleges as
Vienna and Brunswick. . . .

More often than not, the aim of such professors is to teach nothing but economic
and agricultural management, with only slight attention paid to general administration
and that of the royal prerogatives. The task, therefore, remains unfinished and the
course itself is generally so inadequately developed that it convinces no one of the
great advantages offered by these sciences. . . .

Johann H. G. von Justi, *Staatswirtschaft oder Systematische Abhandlung aller Oekonomischen
und Cameral-Wissenschaften die zur Regierung eines Landes erfodert* [*sic!*] *werden* (2d ed.;
Leipzig, 1758), I, xii–xvi, xix–xxiii, xxv–xxviii, xxx–xl, xlii–xliii. Translated by Peter Amann.

Another stumbling block to the acceptance and progress of the economic and cameral sciences at universities has been the very professors who have assumed these posts. This subject matter being formerly quite alien to the universities, the discipline has depended on government officials little given to learning; it has indeed been difficult to find skillful people capable of lecturing on these sciences. Almost all scholars are strangers to this field, while non-scholars, who through their service and experience have attained great practical knowledge in these sciences, are not up to giving academic lectures. They lack a structured outline, correct fundamental principles, clear-cut concepts; nor do they have the ability to lecture with sufficient clarity. . . .

In the meantime, even this imperfect presentation of fragmentary aspects of the economic and cameral sciences at the university level has already proven its utility to the world. There is no doubt but that the Prussian state administration enjoys a great superiority over that of other countries, a superiority that may be ascribed to the presence of a greater number of trained cameralists than anywhere else. I know several former students of Privy-Councilor Gasser's course in economics who in the course of time have developed great insight into the nature of cameralism. Ever since the incorporation of these sciences into the university curriculum, moreover, infinitely more numerous and thorough treatments of economic and administrative subjects have appeared than ever before. Indeed, most regions of Germany have witnessed a growing eagerness to deal with these uncommonly useful disciplines. Such success is not confined to ourselves: we observe that the Swedes, from the time that the economic sciences were introduced there, have shown a burning interest in this sort of investigation. To be quite fair, we must really confess that, humble as their antecedents are, they are now several steps ahead of us. Considering their great energy, they would have accomplished even more had they pursued their investigations more systematically and thoughtfully and in a less peasant-like manner. It is therefore easy to imagine the exceptional advantages that would accrue were the economic and cameral sciences to be taught at universities and colleges in a complete, coherent and thoroughgoing fashion. It was my intention in this introduction to demonstrate, first of all, the necessity of teaching these sciences at the universities. I now want to explore the ways and means by which this can be done on a sound basis. . . .

There are many different types of human knowledge and learning, . . . yet I will confine myself to establishing three classes that are founded on the goal as well as on the essence of the different sciences. Human knowledge may be necessary or it may be merely useful, or else it may be no more than enjoyable and pleasant. This classification rests on another to which it is intimately related. According to this second classification, there are also three sorts of human knowledge and learning: sciences may be indispensable to civic life and the performance of our essential duties; or they may enhance our natural condition and help us fulfill our duties more effectively; or, finally, they may bear no relationship to our duties, but serve only to enrich our stock of ideas and enlarge our understanding.

Without a doubt, the learning and the sciences which promote civic life and the exercise of our complete duties are essentials. We do not [after all] live simply in the state of nature, but rather in civil societies which we call commonwealths. . . . Among these essential branches of learning are natural and revealed religion, morals or ethics, the science of civil law. We require a knowledge of all these [sciences] in order to fulfill our duties according to our condition and the rank and position we occupy within the commonwealth.

Those disciplines which serve us well with respect to our natural condition and [lead] to the more complete fulfillment of our duties may be deemed merely useful. They are useful because they acquaint us with ourselves and with the things of this world around us, thus becoming means to mastering the essential sciences. . . . Among the former is natural science, as well as the majority of those sciences usually included in the domain of philosophy, provided, that is, that they are not weighed down with exaggerated subtleties and unproven theoretical constructs—as is often the case of metaphysics, astronomy and several other philosophic sciences. These latter should be classified as belonging to merely attractive and agreeable learning.

Those sciences, indeed, that have no bearing upon our duties, but only broaden our concepts and augment our understanding, must be considered to be strictly in the pleasurable and enjoyable class. We deal with them simply as thinking beings, and insofar as our minds gain new ideas these sciences delight us. . . . Ancient history, literature, fine arts and anything else that is usually included in the humanities make up this category. . . .

There is no doubt in my mind but that the economic and cameral sciences belong with essential learning, since they provide the very insight that is most needed in civil and social life. Without them, the government of commonwealths cannot exist. There is no institution or bureau in the administration of a state, no station or way of life that can dispense entirely with them. Statecraft fends off aggression from abroad and insures us against internal unrest and upheaval within society. Policecraft deals with health, with the security of private wealth and the good morals of the subjects, while attempting to insure adequate food supplies and [even] a surplus in the country. Commercial science may provide us with all the wealth and comforts which nature has allotted to our segment of the globe. Cameral science proper teaches us how to use the wealth of the state wisely and how to collect revenues adequate to maintaining the institutions and arrangements upon which the happiness of the state rests. How numerous, therefore, are the employments, how many the positions which require such knowledge! Can there be a single station in life, a single occupation, that can afford to do without at least household management, or the science of administering wealth and revenues wisely, and of increasing both?

It hardly seems necessary to observe that I have been making certain assumptions about the nature of universities and institutions of higher learning. Suffice it to make mention only of their purpose. To the extent that they are public institutions belonging to the state, they must have no other goal than to teach the youth trained in the lower schools the knowledge and learning required for useful service to the commonwealth and the complete fulfillment of their duties as servants of the state and as law-abiding citizens. That this is the intent of the government as far as universities and the higher schools are concerned . . . is undeniable. If the goal were merely to encourage learning, to improve the intelligence of the subjects or to broaden human knowledge with respect to its natural condition, no public, state-supported institutions would be needed. Without prejudice to the commonwealth, learning could simply be left to its own devices. . . .

Given this undeniable aim of universities and institutions of higher learning, it obviously follows, it seems to me, that the noblest object of such institutions must be to teach the economic and cameral sciences. I have demonstrated earlier that these sciences must be classified as necessary learning, indispensable to civic life, and of the greatest advantage in the constitution of the state. . . . Yet it is necessary that I should explain this somewhat further.

There are uncommonly few posts in the state service in which ability in the economic and cameral sciences is not the chief requirement. . . . The boards dealing exclusively with legal matters, the teachers in the institutes of higher education, the court and town physicians are exceptional in utilizing these sciences as an auxiliary rather than a principal means. Yet they must be outnumbered ten to one by other officials for whom expertise in these sciences is the chief prerequisite. To be convinced of this, one need only consider the legions of officials that are needed to staff cameral, police, and economic boards, the administration of the royal domain, that of the royal prerogatives and other revenues of the ruler, as well as the customs, postal, mining, salt, mint, forestry, tax and excise services. One should consider that the town councils, chiefly drawn from among the educated, are really police boards and that these judicial officials find the economic and cameral sciences as essential to them as jurisprudence. . . . Should competence be simply a matter of experience? Should an official be left to make innumerable blunders until he learns from his unfortunate mistakes, or should he even be allowed to remain a bungler all his life? . . .

I should not be accused of placing the burden of guilt for their failure to offer the economic and cameral sciences on the universities. They have no choice but to wait upon the orders of their superiors. The endowment for professorships, the creation of faculties, the sciences to be presented are dependent upon benefactors and patrons. For the time being, one cannot even blame the rulers, as perfection is reached by degrees rather than all at once. We have [after all] barely extricated ourselves from barbarism. The revival of Roman law and of institutions to teach it publicly was the first step which providence inspired in order to lead us out of the fog of ignorance which had surrounded us. Thus we owe much gratitude to Roman jurisprudence. It is scarcely miraculous, therefore, that for centuries the belief has persisted that all human wisdom was distilled into the corpus of Roman law. . . .

Today's effective state institutions, ordered according to the principles of economic and cameral science, are something new in the world. Two hundred years ago, no one in Germany knew anything of boards of finance. At that time it would have been difficult to imagine that some day consistent principles and rules would govern commercial policy, the encouragement of the food supply, and the administration of princely revenues. Nothing, of course, was known of cameralists. The ruler's outstanding judicial officials also administered his revenues, or else the matter was so casually regarded that the wife of the prince might be put in charge, just as the wife of any substantial private individual would manage her household. The effective organization of police and cameral administration which we observe in states nowadays grew only gradually, perhaps more in response to a good idea here, a bit of sound advice there, rather than according to coherent principles of the science of government. Perhaps the constitution of states has as yet to reach perfection. Perhaps it is only the happy fruit of our enlightened century finally to realize that the broad organization of the state in all its economic regulation and its financial aspects rests upon integrated principles that are truly scientific, derived as they are from the very nature of commonwealths. There are no grounds for reproach at a time when these affairs are rapidly progressing toward perfection. Given the nature of our temporal condition, things could not be other than what they are. . . .

Everywhere one hears intermittent complaints from educated men to the effect that it is the uneducated who are promoted to the most important positions in the state, while scholars, who have gone through bitter struggles to master their science, may thank God if they obtain some minor post that permits them to eke out a living. These complaints are indeed well founded. It is a fact that in the various countries today the most important appointments in the government are held by former lackeys, messengers, scribes, common gamekeepers, minor tax collectors, and the like; and many a scholar must find it strange indeed, and perhaps distressing, to have to bow humbly to people of this sort. Nevertheless—begging forgiveness—I find such complaints ill-founded. This former lackey, scribe or gamekeeper, by keeping his mind open, gradually acquired the practical grasp of the economic and cameral sciences which alone are useful in the running of the state. May one blame a ruler or the highest minister for promoting those who display abilities essential to the conduct of the state—the very abilities conspicuously absent among scholars? Good God, how could a ruler employ the most profound metaphysician, the greatest geometer, the most famous astronomer, the most meticulous antiquarian in the affairs of the state? True enough, once in a while, when their services are needed, they are consulted on some particular matter. This is why they draw a small salary. On the other hand, just because their advice is sought from time to time, is this reason enough to put them in charge of the financial, administrative, commercial, mining, and economic affairs of the state? . . .

On these grounds, it seems to me, it is quite important to prevail upon scholars to apply themselves more than ever before to the economic and cameral sciences. Yet the endowment of professorships and the administration of institutes of higher education are not within their power, but within that of rulers and ministers. As far as the latter are concerned, they are probably indifferent as to whether their future finance, administrative and economic experts are university-trained or self-educated through practice and experience in the lowest positions. I must therefore also attempt to persuade [the rulers] that it is essential to promote university instruction in the cameral sciences.

To allay any doubt that we are hereby dealing with true sciences whose teachings can be derived systematically from universal principles, we need only note prevailing conditions, which indicate that the merely practical cameralists, having gained their knowledge and insight by experience alone, are something short of heroes. They resemble those jurists and physicians who, having learned their science strictly by rote in the course of an apprenticeship, remain miserable blunderers all their lives. Although admittedly capable of applying what they have learned from their own experience, [the practical cameralists] will rarely have the capacity to invent new institutions or draw up new regulations. Even if they read books and look to the constitutions of other countries for guidance, they will get little comfort from it. What they miss is the overall structure of their science, the correct fundamental principles, the insight into the totality of things. Conditions differ greatly from country to country. They will therefore often run the danger of wanting to apply remedies unsuitable to their own land and out of harmony with the rest of their state's constitution. An institution that may have enjoyed a great success in this or that country may, in the process of being transplanted, turn out very badly and lead to great disadvantages. There are many examples in the world to convince us of this truth. Again and again this or that aspect of Prussian administration has been imitated, only to lead to bad results because the peculiar conditions of the country, its institutions and customs, had not been considered.

It has to be admitted, finally, that a merely practical cameralist, if endowed with a good fund of common sense, who works hard at familiarizing himself with the constitutions of other countries, may become a good specialist, able to master this or that aspect of state administration. Yet he will never make a good universal cameralist. Lacking coherent fundamental principles, he will never walk with confidence but will hesitate in the face of any incident and make dubious decisions. If he is convinced that he has made important improvements in certain aspects of government administration, in the end he will find out that he has caused some disruption in another part of the vast machinery of the state by failing to take adequate account of the interaction within this gigantic administration in which any one aspect impinges upon all others. . . .

Those cameralists, moreover, who have been trained solely in practical business, generally make the mistake of being overly solicitous of their master's interests. They know almost no other principle than this idol, before which they have been forced to bend the knee long before they ever became acquainted with administrative affairs. Whether these interests further the true and permanent advantage of the ruler, whether they are acceptable to the country and correspond to the veritable welfare of the state (not to speak of the happiness of the subjects), all this they ignore. The reason for this is easy to perceive: they have never drawn their knowledge of the rules of government administration from some idea of the nature of a commonwealth, from which general principles should be derived. . . .

The rulers and highest officials of the state should therefore consider the following: if they want to be served in the administration of the state in such a way that all its parts run smoothly; if they demand reliable regulations, institutions, and projects; if they have no other interest but that which is well founded, lasting, and corresponding to the true welfare of the state; then they will recognize the need to have the economic and cameral sciences taught at the universities, where these sciences will soon reach an [even] greater perfection. . . .

In my opinion, I have demonstrated adequately that it is necessary to teach the economic and cameral sciences at the universities. From this rule it follows that we ought also to prepare the youth in the lower schools for this. Indeed, there is no doubt that every upcoming, educated citizen ought to be familiar at least with the general teachings of the art of household management, which is the foundation for the sciences needed in the great administration of the state. Even the most elementary schools, where the children of the lowest mob are taught, should offer at least the basic rules that deal with the duties which will later be incumbent upon them as citizens, inhabitants of the state, and householders. In this instance, we seem to ignore the fact that it is no less necessary to train good and useful citizens than it is to train good Christians.

This leads me to the second point of our present discussion, namely the ways and means of teaching the cameral sciences at the university level. . . . It may be guessed that I would not consider one man adequate to teach the economic and cameral sciences at a university. At the very least, two teachers should be employed, one to deal chiefly with police and commercial science, the other with economics as such and financial science as his main subject. For if these disciplines are to be taught completely, thoroughly, and to full advantage, each of the professors must have enough time to develop fully this or that aspect of his field in a special course, in order that everyone may have the opportunity to perfect himself in what he deems to be his future specialty. One man wants to seek his fortune in the administration of manufactures, another in the tax and revenue service; a third devotes himself to forestry and its cameral management. All of them must have the opportunity to obtain intensive instruction in such specific aspects of public administration.

A university professorship of politics should be such that future ambassadors and ministers would profit by hearing the teacher lecture on statecraft, while his teaching should not seem ludicrous to real ministers and statesmen. A chemistry professor must be selected who is capable of lecturing on metal testing and smelting, and not merely on the preparation of medicines—something which every pharmacist's apprentice can master without trouble. Similarly, a teacher in mechanics should be able to lecture on machines used in mines and mining, while a professor of natural science should evince adequate knowledge of ores and fossils. Provided skillful, experienced and outstanding men are chosen, these six teachers (to whom a professor of civil and military engineering might be added) could constitute a separate faculty that would have an uncommonly wholesome effect on civic life. Many bureaus and state enterprises could consult them and find great use for their advice, instead of incurring the large costs of consulting experts abroad.

As to the actual presentation of the economic and cameral sciences, what is required is a basic course in which all these sciences are integrated into a single theoretical structure. This is needed so that young people may achieve an overall insight, a coherent concept of all the rules governing public administration so that they may be imbued with the correct principles derived from the nature of commonwealths. . . .

The first part of the present work may serve as a textbook for such an introductory course. In one single framework, it contains the noblest principles of all the economic sciences. One may find therein, first of all, the chief teachings of statecraft, then of police, which, taken in a broad sense, includes the commercial sciences. These two sciences make up the first book. The second book starts out by teaching about the most pressing duties of subjects, [duties] that form the basis for financial science, followed by general rules of household management and the loftiest doctrines of agriculture. . . .

After an adequate foundation for these sciences has been laid by means of this introductory course, the lectures should then proceed to each individual discipline. The first of these, economics, deals not merely with housekeeping rules, but embraces teachings about town management and, above all, agricultural administration. It is thus essential to begin with this science which underlies this whole field of knowledge. . . . Basically, the great housekeeping of the state rests upon the very rules which govern any other household. In both kinds of housekeeping the aim is to gain wealth, to conserve this gain and to utilize one's property wisely. Where the affairs of the state differ from those of private indivduals is in their infinitely greater scope. . . .

As this curriculum is organized, the specifically economic lectures are followed by police science. The latter deals in a sense with the first part of the great economy of the state, insofar as it comprises the chief rules for the preservation and the increase of the society's public wealth. To the extent that they depend upon governmental institutions, any means by which the wealth of the state can be augmented are within the province of police. Consequently it serves as the immediate preparation for the true cameral and financial science: indeed the police expert ought to sow in order that by and by the cameralist may reap. Since these sciences are very comprehensive, to do a really thorough and complete job the lectures on police should take up a whole year.

Finally, true cameral and financial science completes the curriculum, comprising as it does the second main part of the great economy of a commonwealth, namely the intelligent use of the state's wealth, as well as the entire internal administration. . . . While the first major objective of public administration must be the preservation and increase of the state's public fortune, the second aim is the wise use of this wealth for the internal preservation of the state. . . .

It would, undeniably, be very useful if this curriculum could begin with the history of police, commercial, economic and cameral administration. Yet aside from a modest beginning in Berlin, this sort of history remains to be written; we also lack a decent textbook for this purpose. . . .

In presenting my course of study for these sciences, I have hit upon a special way of teaching which I have found notably advantageous. I have made it a habit to confine my regular lecture to the first half hour. Thereupon I step down from my podium to spend the remainder of the hour standing, engaged in free and conversational discussion with my class on the material that has just been covered in lecture. I give them a chance to raise any questions about the matter at hand or to talk about what they have heard about cameral or police administration in this or that country. After they have freely offered their opinion, I consider it, raising objections, concurring, or adding information. Those who are too shy to take as active a role as the others, I encourage by asking them easy questions, by showing my satisfaction at their answers, and thus get them involved in the discussion. In this way, without attracting attention, I have helped them gain self-confidence. Nor am I narrowly tied to the specific day's assignment; rather, if one of the students brings up something related, I accept this, as I wish to avoid any semblance of compulsion. The good effects of such discussions have been so obvious that I have disregarded other people's strictures on my shortened lectures. . . . With a large university audience, this method is likely to encounter many inconveniences and fewer advantages; yet in small classes for eight to twelve students, the method can always be employed to great advantage. . . .

ESSAY ON THE FORMS OF GOVERNMENT AND ON THE DUTIES OF SOVEREIGNS

Frederick the Great

*Eighteenth-century observers as well as later historians have singled out the
activities of reforming monarchs among the characteristic features of the
age. Yet such rulers would have rejected indignantly the label "enlightened despots" which historians have affixed to them. A Frederick the
Great of Prussia, a Joseph II of Austria, a Leopold, Duke of Tuscany,
would have stressed the lawful, regular nature of their administrations
as their great contribution, in sharp contrast to the unpredictability
and whimsicality of despotism—though they would all have consented
to being called "enlightened."*

*To what extent did these rulers really break with the past in reforming
their states? What were their motives and what influences stirred them?
How far-reaching were their reforms and what set their limits? Twentieth-
century historians are by no means agreed on the answers to such questions, and it is certain that no one set of answers would fit the case of
every reform-minded ruler of the eighteenth century. Yet their differences
notwithstanding, their lack of reverence for the past, coupled to a rational
approach to problems, set these rulers apart from the "good kings" of
earlier ages.*

The Essay *below is the work of the most accomplished and most articulate of the new style eighteenth-century monarchs, Frederick the Great
(1712–1786), who owes his tag more to his conquest of Silesia from
Austria (and its retention through two grueling wars) than to the ambitious reorganization of his Prussian kingdom. Unlike most of the
enlightened rulers of his day, Frederick prided himself on being an intellectual as well as a competent king. Throughout his career he remained
on friendly terms with some of the French* philosophes. *The* Essay,
summarizing ideas that Frederick had developed more fully in his earlier
Political Testaments, *was originally written in French and privately
printed for the benefit of Voltaire (see page 146) and a few other kindred
souls.*

. . . As to monarchical government, of this there are various forms. The ancient feudal government, which some ages since was almost general in Europe, was established by the conquest of the Barbarians. The general of a horde rendered himself sovereign of the conquered country, and divided its provinces among his principal officers; who, it is true, were subject to the lord paramount, and who supplied him with troops when required; but, as some of these vassals became equally powerful with their chief, this formed state within state; and hence a series of civil wars, which were the misfortune of the whole. In Germany, these vassals are become independent; in France, England, and Spain, they are suppressed. The only example that remains, of that abominable form of government, is the republic of Poland.

In Turkey, the sovereign is despotic: he may with impunity commit the most atrocious cruelties; but it also often happens, by a vicissitude common to barbarous nations, or from a just retribution, that he in his turn is strangled.

With respect to the true monarchical government, it is the best or the worst of all others, accordingly as it is administered.

We have remarked that men granted preeminence to one of their equals, in expectation that he should do them certain services. These services consisted in the maintenance of the laws; a strict execution of justice; an employment of his whole powers to prevent any corruption of manners; and defending the state against its enemies. It is the duty of this magistrate to pay attention to agriculture; it should be his care that provisions for the nation should be in abundance, and that commerce and industry should be encouraged. He is a perpetual sentinel, who must watch the acts and the conduct of the enemies of the state. His foresight and prudence should form timely alliances, which should be made with those who might most conduce to the interest of the association.

By this short abstract, the various branches of knowledge, which each article in particular requires, will be perceived. To this must be added a profound study of the local situation of the country, which it is the magistrate's duty to govern, and a perfect knowledge of the genius of the nation; for the sovereign who sins through ignorance is as culpable as he who sins through malice: the first is the guilt of idleness, the latter of a vicious heart; but the evil that results to society is the same.

Princes and monarchs, therefore, are not invested with supreme authority that they may, with impunity, riot in debauchery and voluptuousness. They are not raised by their fellow citizens in order that their pride may pompously display itself, and contemptuously insult simplicity of manners, poverty and wretchedness. Government is not intrusted to them that they may be surrounded by a crowd of useless people, whose idleness engenders every vice.

The ill administration of monarchical government originates in various causes, the source of which is in the character of the sovereign. Thus a prince addicted to women suffers himself to be governed by his mistresses, and his favourites, who abuse the ascendancy they have over his mind, commit injustice, protect the most vicious, sell places, and are guilty of other similar acts of infamy. If the prince, through debility,

Posthumous Works of Frederick II, trans. T. Holcroft (London: 1789), V, *Political, Philosophical and Satyrical Miscellanies*, "An Essay on Forms of Government," 10–33.

should abandon the helm of the state to mercenary hands, I mean to ministers, in that case, each having different views, no one proceeds on general plans: the new minister fritters away what he finds already established, however excellent that may be, to acquire the character of novelty, and execute his own schemes, generally to the detriment of the public good. His successors do the like; they destroy and overturn with equal want of understanding, that they may be supposed to possess originality. Hence that succession of change and variation which allows no project time to take root; hence confusion, disorder, and every vice of a bad administration. Prevaricators have a ready excuse; they shelter their turpitude under these perpetual changes.

Men attach themselves to that which appertains to them, and the state does not appertain to these ministers, for which reason they have not its real good at heart; business is carelessly executed, and with a kind of stoic indifference; and hence results the decay of justice, and the ill administration of the finances and the military. From a monarchy, as it was, the government degenerates into a true aristocracy, in which ministers and generals conduct affairs according to their own fancies. There is no longer any comprehensive system; each pursues his own plans, and the central point, the point of unity, is lost. As all the wheels of a watch correspond to effect the same purpose, which is that of measuring time, so ought the springs of government to be regulated, that all the different branches of administration may equally concur to the greatest good of the state; an important object, of which we ought never to lose sight.

We may add, the personal interest of ministers and generals usually occasions them to counteract each other without ceasing, and sometimes to impede the execution of the best plans, because they had not been conceived by themselves. But the evil is at its utmost, when perverse minds are able to persuade the sovereign that his welfare and the public good are two things. The monarch then becomes the enemy of his people, without knowing why; is severe, rigorous, and inhuman, from mistake; for, the principle on which he acts being false, the consequences must necessarily be the same.

The sovereign is attached by indissoluble ties to the body of the state; hence it follows that he, by repercussion, is sensible of all the ills which afflict his subjects; and the people, in like manner, suffer from the misfortunes which affect their sovereign. There is but one general good, which is that of the state. If the monarch lose his provinces, he is no longer able as formerly to assist his subjects. If misfortune have obliged him to contract debts, they must be liquidated by the poor citizens; and, in return, if the people are not numerous, and if they are oppressed by poverty, the sovereign is destitute of all resource. These are truths so incontestable that there is no need to insist on them further.

I once more repeat, the sovereign represents the state; he and his people form but one body, which can only be happy as far as united by concord. The prince is to the nation he governs what the head is to the man; it is his duty to see, think, and act for the whole community, that he may procure it every advantage of which it is capable. If it be intended that a monarchical should excel a republican government, sentence is pronounced on the sovereign. He must be active, possess integrity, and collect his whole powers, that he may be able to run the career he has commenced. Here follow my ideas concerning his duties.

He ought to procure exact and circumstantial information of the strength and weakness of his country, as well relative to pecuniary resources as to population, finance, trade, laws, and the genius of the nation whom he is appointed to govern. If the laws are good they will be clear in their definitions; otherwise, chicanery will seek to elude their spirit to its advantage, and arbitrarily and irregularly determine on the fortunes of individuals. Law-suits ought to be as short as possible, to prevent the ruin of the appellants, who consume in useless expenses what is justly and duly their right. This branch of government cannot be too carefully watched, that every possible barrier may be opposed to the avidity of judges and counsellors. Every person is kept within the limits of their duty, by occasional visits into the provinces. Whoever imagines himself to be injured will venture to make his complaints to the commission; and those who are found to be prevaricators ought to be severely punished. It is perhaps superfluous to add that the penalty ought never to exceed the crime; that violence never ought to supersede law; and that it were better the sovereign should be too merciful than too severe.

As every person who does not proceed on principle is inconsistent in his conduct, it is still more necessary that the magistrate who watches over the public good should act from a determinate system of politics, war, finance, commerce, and law. Thus, for example, a people of mild manners ought not to have severe laws, but such as are adapted to their character. The basis of such systems ought always to be correspondent to the greatest good society can receive. Their principles ought to be conformable to the situation of the country, to its ancient customs, if they are good, and to the genius of the nation.

As an instance, it is a known truth, in politics, that the most natural allies, and consequently the best, are those whose interests concur, and who are not such near neighbours as to be engaged in any contest respecting frontiers. It sometimes happens that strange accidents give place to extraordinary alliances. We have seen, in the present times, nations that had always been rivals, and even enemies, united under the same banners. But these are events that rarely take birth, and which never can serve as examples. Such connections can be no more than momentary; whereas the other kind, which are contracted from a unity of interests, are alone capable of exertion. In the present situation of Europe, when all her princes are armed, and among whom preponderating powers rise up capable of crushing the feeble, prudence requires alliances should be formed with other powers, as well to secure aid, in case of attack, as to repress the dangerous projects of enemies, and to sustain all just pretensions, by the succour of such allies, in opposition to those by whom they are controverted.

Nor is this sufficient. It is necessary to have among our neighbours, especially among our enemies, eyes and ears which shall be open to receive, and report with fidelity, what they have seen and heard. Men are wicked. Care must especially be taken not to suffer surprise, because whatever surprises intimidates and terrifies, which never happens when preparations are made, however vexatious the event may be which there is reason to expect. European politics are so fallacious that the most sage may become dupes, if they are not always alert, and on their guard.

The military system ought, in like manner, to rest on good principles, which from experience are known to be certain. The genius of the nation ought to be understood; of what it is capable, and how far its safety may be risked by leading it against the enemy. The warlike customs of the Greeks and Romans are interdicted, in these ages. The discovery of gunpowder has entirely changed the mode of making war. A superiority of fire at present decides the day. Discipline, rules, and tactics have all been changed, in order that they may conform to this new custom; and the recent and enormous abuse of numerous trains of artillery, which incumber armies, obliges others, in like manner, to adopt this method; as well to maintain themselves in their posts as to attack the foe in those which they shall occupy, should reasons of importance so require. So many new refinements have, therefore, so much changed the art of war that it would, at present, be unpardonable temerity in a general who, in imitation of Turenne, Condé, or Luxembourg, should risk a battle according to the dispositions made by those great commanders, in the age in which they lived. Victory then was carried by valour and strength: it is at present decided by artillery; and the art of the general consists in his near approach to the army of the enemy, without suffering his own troops to be destroyed previous to the attack. To gain this advantage, it is necessary he should silence the fire of the enemy, by the superiority of that with which it is opposed.

The art of castrametation, or of deriving all possible advantage from the situation of the ground, will however remain eternally unchanged in the military system. Should new discoveries continue to be made, the generals who then shall live must of force comply with these novelties, and change whatever may need correction in tactics.

There are states which, from their situation and constitution, must be maritime powers: such are England, Holland, France, Spain, and Denmark. They are surrounded by the sea, and the distant colonies which they possess oblige them to keep a marine, to maintain communication and trade between the mother country and these detached members. There are other states, such as Austria, Poland, Prussia, and even Russia, some of which may well do without shipping; and others that would commit an unpardonable fault, in politics, were they to divide their forces by employing a part of their troops at sea, of the services of which they indispensably stand in need by land.

The number of troops which a state maintains ought to be in proportion to the troops maintained by its enemies. Their force should be equal, or the weakest is in danger of being oppressed. It perhaps may be objected that a king ought to depend on the aid of his allies. The reasoning would be good were allies what they ought to be; but their zeal is only lukewarm; and he who shall depend upon another as upon himself will most certainly be deceived. If frontiers permit them to be defended by fortresses, there must be no neglect in building, nor any expense spared to bring them to perfection. Of this France has given an example, and she has found the advantage of it on different occassions.

But neither politics nor the army can prosper if the finances are not kept in the greatest order, and if the prince himself be not a prudent economist. Money is like the wand of the necromancer, for by its aid miracles are performed. Grand political views, the maintenance of the military, and the best conceived plans for the ease of the people, will all remain in a lethargic state, if not animated by money. The economy of the sovereign is the more useful to the public good, because if he have not sufficient funds in reserve, either to supply the expenses of war, without loading his people with extraordinary taxes, or to succour citizens in times of public calamity, all these burthens will fall on the subject, who will be without the resource, in such unhappy times, of which they will then stand in the most need.

No government can exist without taxation, which is equally necessary to the republic and to the monarchy. The sovereign who labours in the public cause must be paid by the public; the judge the same, that he may have no need to prevaricate. The soldier must be supported that he may commit no violence, for want of having whereon to subsist. In like manner, it is necessary that those persons who are employed in collecting the finances should receive such salaries as may not lay them under any temptation to rob the public. These various expenses demand very considerable sums, and to these must still be added money that should only be laid apart to serve for extraordinary exigences. This money must all be necessarily levied on the people; and the grand art consists in levying so as not to oppress. That taxes may be equally and not arbitrarily laid on, surveys and registers should be made, by which, if the people are properly classed, the money will be proportionate to the income of the persons paying. This is a thing so necessary that it would be an unpardonable fault, in finance, if ill-imposed taxes should disgust the husbandman with his labours. Having performed his duties, it is afterward necessary he and his family should live in a certain degree of ease. Far from oppressing the nursing fathers of the state, they ought to be encouraged in the cultivation of the lands; for in this cultivation the true riches of a country consists.

The earth furnishes the most necessary part of subsistence, and those who till it are, as we have already said, the true nursing fathers of society. I shall perhaps be answered that Holland subsists, although the land does not yield a hundredth part of what the people consume. To this I reply, Holland is a small state, in which trade is the substitute for agriculture; but the more vast any government is the more ought rural economy to be encouraged.

Excise is another species of taxes, levied on cities, and this must be managed by able persons; otherwise, those provisions which are most necessary to life, such as bread, small beer, meat, etc. will be overloaded; and the weight will fall on the soldier, the labourer, and the artizan. The result will be, unhappily to the people, that the price of labour will be raised; consequently merchandize will become so dear as not to be saleable in foreign markets. Such is at present the case in Holland and in England. These two nations, having contracted immensely heavy debts in the last wars, have imposed new taxes to pay the interest; but, having very unadvisedly taxed labour, they have almost ruined their manufactures. Hence, all things having become dearer in Holland, the Dutch are obliged to purchase their cloths from Verviers and Liege; and England has lost a very considerable sale of her woollens in Germany. To obviate such inconveniences, the sovereign ought frequently to remember the condition of the poor, to imagine himself in the place of the peasant or the manufacturer, and then to say, "Were I born one among the class of citizens whose labours constitute the wealth of the state, what should I require from the king?" The answer which, on such a supposition, good sense would suggest it is his duty to put in practice.

In most of the kingdoms of Europe there are provinces in which the peasants are attached to the glebe, or are serfs to their lords. This, of all conditions, is the most unhappy, and that at which humanity most revolts. No man certainly was born to be the slave of his equal. We reasonably detest such an abuse; and it is supposed that nothing more than will is wanting to abolish so barbarous a custom. But this is not true; it is held on ancient tenures, and contracts made between the landholders and the colonists. Tillage is regulated according to the service performed by the peasantry; and whoever should suddenly desire to abolish this abominable administration would entirely overthrow the mode of managing estates, and must be obliged, in part, to indemnify the nobility for the losses which their rents must suffer.

The state of manufactures and of trade, an article no less important, next presents itself. For the country to be preserved in prosperity, it is indubitably necessary that the balance of trade should be in its favour. If it pay more for importation than it gains by exportation, the result will be that it will be annually impoverished. Let us suppose a purse in which there are a hundred ducats, from which let us daily take one, and put none in, and every body will allow that in a hundred days the purse will be empty. The means to avoid incurring any such loss are to work up all raw materials of which the country is in possession, and to manufacture foreign raw materials, that the price of labour may be gained, in order to procure a foreign market.

Three things are to be considered in respect to commerce: first the surplus of native products which are exported; next the products of foreign states, which enrich those by whom they are carried; and thirdly foreign merchandize, which home consumption obliges the state to import. The trade of any kingdom must be regulated according to these three articles, for of these only is it susceptible, according to the nature of things. England, Holland, France, Spain, and Portugal, have possessions in the two Indies, and more extensive resources for their merchant ships than other kingdoms. To profit by such advantages as we are in possession of, and to undertake nothing beyond our strength, is the advice of wisdom.

We have now to speak of what are the most proper means invariably to maintain those provinces in abundance, of which society stands in absolute need, that it may continue flourishing. The first is to be careful that the lands are well cultivated; to clear such grounds as are capable of tillage; to increase the breed of sheep and cattle, that the more may be gained by milk, butter, cheese and manure; afterward to obtain an exact statement of the quantity of the various species of corn, grown in good, indifferent, and bad seasons, and to subtract the quantity consumed, that from the result information may be gained of the surplus, and the point at which exportation ought to stop; or of the deficiency in consumption, and of the consequently necessary importation. Every sovereign, actuated by the public good, is obliged to keep storehouses abundantly furnished, that supplies may be ready, when the harvest is bad, and famine prevented. During the scarcity of the year 1771 and 1772, Germany beheld the miseries with which Saxony and the provinces of the empire were afflicted, because this very useful precaution had not been taken. The people pounded oak bark, on which they fed, and this wretched food did but accelerate death. Numerous families perished unsuccoured, and the desolation was universal. The survivors were pale, livid, and lean, and fled from their country to seek food elsewhere. The sight of them excited compassion: they would have been pitied by a heart of iron. What were the reproaches with which their governors ought to have loaded themselves, spectators as they were of such calamities, and unable to afford any relief!

We shall now speak of another article, which perhaps is equally interesting. There are few countries in which the people are all of one religious opinion; they often totally differ. There are some who are called sectaries. The question then is started— Is it requisite that the people should all think alike, or may each one be allowed to think as he pleases? Gloomy politicians will tell us every body ought to be of the same opinion, that there may be no division among the citizens. The priest will add whoever does not think like me is damned, and it is by no means proper that my king should be the king of the damned. The inevitable deduction is they must be destroyed in this world, that they may be the more prosperous in the next.

To this it is answered that all the members of one society never thought alike; that, among Christian nations, the majority are Anthropomorphites; that, among the Catholics, most of the people are idolaters, for I shall never be persuaded that a clown is capable of distinguishing between *Latria* and *Hyperdulia*. He simply and really adores the image he invokes. Therefore there are a number of heretics in all Christian sects. What is more, each man believes that which appears to him to be truth. A poor wretch may be constrained to pronounce a certain form of prayer, although he inwardly refuse his consent. His persecutor consequently has gained nothing. But, if we revert to the origin of all society, it will be found evident that the sovereign has no right to interfere in the belief of the subject. Would it not be madness to imagine men who have said to another man, their equal, "We raise you to be our superior, because we are in love with slavery; and we bestow on you the power of directing our thoughts, according to your will?" On the contrary, they have said, "We have need of you for the maintenance of those laws which we are willing to obey, and that we may be wisely governed and defended; but we also require that you should respect our freedom." This is the sentence pronounced, and it is without appeal. Nay, tolerance is itself so advantageous, to the people among whom it is established, that it constitutes the happiness of the state. As soon as there is that perfect freedom of opinion, the people are all at peace; whereas persecution has given birth to the most bloody civil wars, and such as have been the most inveterate and the most destructive. The least evil that results from persecution is to occasion the persecuted to emigrate. The population of France has suffered in certain provinces, and those provinces still are sensible of the revocation of the edict of Nantes.

Such are in general the duties imposed upon a prince, from which, in order that he may never depart, he ought often to recollect he himself is but a man, like the least of his subjects. If he be the first general, the first minister of the realm, it is not that he should remain the shadow of authority, but that he should fulfil the duties of such titles. He is only the first servant of the state, who is obliged to act with probity and prudence; and to remain as totally disinterested as if he were each moment liable to render an account of his administration to his fellow citizens.

Thus is he culpable, if he be prodigal of the money of the people, dispersing the produce of the taxes in luxury, pomp, or licentiousness. It is for him to watch over morals, which are the guardians of the laws, and to improve the national education, and not pervert it by ill examples. One of the most important objects is the preservation of good morals, in all their purity; to which the sovereign may greatly contribute, by distinguishing and rewarding those citizens who have performed virtuous actions, and testifying his contempt for such as are so depraved as not to blush at their own disorders. The prince ought highly to disapprove of every dishonest act, and refuse distinctions to men who are incorrigible.

There is another interesting object which ought not to be lost sight of, and which, if neglected, would be of irreparable prejudice to good morality; which is that princes are liable too highly to notice persons who are possessed of no other merit than that of great wealth. Honours, so undeservedly bestowed, confirm the people in the vulgar prejudice that wealth, only, is necessary to gain respect. Interest and cupidity will then break forth from the curb by which they are restrained. Each will wish to accumulate riches; and, to acquire these, the most iniquitous means will be employed. Corruption increases, takes root, and becomes general. Men of abilities and virtue are despised, and the public honour none but the bastards of Midas, who dazzle by their excessive dissipation and their pomp. To prevent national manners from being perverted to an excess so horrible, the prince ought to be incessantly attentive to distinguish nothing but personal merit, and to shew his contempt for that opulence which is destitute of morals and of virtue.

As the sovereign is properly the head of a family of citizens, the father of his people, he ought on all occasions to be the last refuge of the unfortunate; to be the parent of the orphan, and the husband of the widow; to have as much pity for the lowest wretch as for the greatest courtier; and to shed his benefactions over those who, deprived of all other aid, can only find succour in his benevolence.

Such, according to the principles which we established at the beginning of this Essay, is the most accurate conception we can form of the duties of a sovereign, and the only manner which can render monarchical government good and advantageous. Should the conduct of many princes be found different, it must be attributed to their having reflected but little on their institution, and its derivatory duties. They have borne a burthen with the weight and importance of which they were unacquainted, and have been misled from the want of knowledge; for in our times ignorance commits more faults than vice. Such a sketch of sovereignty will perhaps appear to the censorious the archetype of the Stoics; an ideal sage, who never existed except in imagination, and to whom the nearest approach was Marcus Aurelius. We wish this feeble Essay were capable of forming men like Aurelius; it would be the highest reward we could possibly expect, at the same time that it would conduce to the good of mankind.

We ought however to add that the prince who should pursue the laborious route which we have indicated would never attain absolute perfection; because, with all possible good will, he might be deceived in the choice of the persons whom he should employ in administration. Incidents might be depicted under false colours; his orders might not be punctually executed; iniquitous acts might be so concealed as never to arrive at his knowledge; and his ministers, rigorous and consequential, might be too severe, too haughty in their exactions. In fine, it is impossible a monarch should be every where, in an extensive kingdom. Such therefore is and must be the destiny of earthly affairs, that the degree of perfection which the happiness of the people requires, as far as it depends on government, never can be attained. Therefore, in this as in every thing else, we must of necessity remain satisfied, with that which is the least defective.

◄§ A GENERAL ESSAY ON TACTICS

Guibert

The philosophes of the eighteenth century are often caricatured as mere dilettantes dabbling in the arts and sciences while feeding the reading public's appetite for facile generalization. While many philosophes did range widely, performing a major function as popularizers of the methods, findings, and implications of contemporary science, their role was not confined to this: their ranks also included highly trained specialists applying empirical methods to their own specialty and at the same time seeking to relate their work to the broad aspirations of the Enlightenment.

Jacques-Antoine-Hippolyte, Count of Guibert (1743–1790) is a case in point. The son of an officer, Guibert was himself a professional military man who ended his career as a general in the French army. His General Essay on Tactics *(1772), a brilliant treatise drawing on the experience of the Seven Years' War (1756–1763), influenced two generations of military technicians and helped to contribute to French military superiority during the revolutionary and Napoleonic periods. Yet in his introduction to this highly technical book, Guibert attempted to integrate the tactical reforms that he advocated within a broad program of civil and political reform—even though the humanism of the Enlightenment might seem at odds with the enhanced destructive power for which Guibert spoke. The selection below, taken from the "Preliminary Discourse," also mirrors "the cult of antiquity" (and of ancient Rome in particular) that was widely influential in the second half of the eighteenth century.*

If we understand by Politics, the art of negotiating, or rather of intriguing; of fomenting revolutions in secret; of binding or breaking, in the obscurity of cabinets, treaties of alliance, of peace, of marriage, or of commerce; in that respect we are, without doubt, superior to the ancients, we have much more finesse and understanding than they. But if Politics be that sublime and vast science of governing a state internally and externally; of directing its private interests towards the general welfare; of rendering the subject happy, and of attaching him to its mode of government: then let us

M. Guibert, *A General Essay on Tactics with an Introductory Discourse upon the Present State of Politics and the Military Science in Europe,* anon. trans. (London, 1781), pp. 1–viii, xxi–xxv, xxvii–xxviii, xxxiv–xxxix, xliv–lviii.

agree to their being entirely unknown to our modern administrators, that our Richelieu, our Colbert, our d'Offat, our d'Estrades, cannot be put in competition with Licyrgus, Pericles, Numa, or other great statesmen of Greece, and of Rome. Let us likewise allow, that the Roman Senate, during the time of her splendor, presents to our mind the Atlas we read of in Fable, who bore on his shoulders the burthen of the world; while our government is but a brittle and complicated machine, which fortune and other circumstances actuate with motions irregular, uncertain, and volatile like themselves.

I am no blind admirer of the ancients, I know how a long succession of ages, the obscurity of ignorance, illusions of history, and the prepossessions of our own minds, give them the Colossal and marvellous. . . .

Thus it cannot be said I have an enthusiastic veneration for the government of ancient Rome. I do not pretend or conceive its being perfect, it certainly was not, since it had its shocks, its decay and its downfal. As it was the work of man it could not be so. But if that government, during the space of five hundred years, imprinted on the people who flourished under it, a character of vigour and majesty: if it engendered more heroes and better citizens, than the rest of the earth perhaps has produced since that era; if even in its most corrupt state, the vices of that people had a magnanimity and energy which fill us with wonder and surprize; in short, if that race of men became the masters of the world; I ought then to attribute such elevated effects to very powerful and constant causes. I can without being deceived, assure the world, that her state was more permanent and vigorous: that her Politics were more profound and extensive, in comparison to those which appear to me of other nations.

I admire Roman Policy in its successful days, when I see it founded on a settled plan: when that plan has for its basis virtue and patriotism; when I see Rome in her infancy but a weak colony without support, become in the most rapid manner a city, continually aggrandizing herself; overcome all her neighbours who were her enemies; making them either citizens or allies; in this manner growing formidable, as a river, which increaseth by the waters it receives in her course. I admire her Politics, when I see Rome engaged but in one war at a time, never granting a cessation of arms, but when the honour of the Roman name is fully satisfied; not elated by success; nor depressed by reverse of fortune; become a prey to the Gauls, and to flames, and regenerate out of her own ashes. In short, I admire Rome, when I examine her military and civil constitution; the laws of her militia; the education of her youth; her great men indifferently passing through each office of state, because they were qualified to fill them all; her citizens proud of their being Romans, and thinking themselves superior to crowned heads, whom they were accustomed to conquer. I say there very likely was, in some corner of the globe, an obscure and tranquil nation, whose members were more happy and peaceable, but certainly there never was a people who had so much grandeur, so much glory, or ever merited so much by their bravery and virtues.

Now, what a striking contrast do the Politics of Europe present to a philosophic mind, disposed to contemplate them? Tyrannical, ignorant, or weak administrations. The virtue and strength of nations, smothered under their vices; private interests prevalent over the general welfare; customs, that supplement to laws, oftentimes more efficacious than they, neglected, shunned, or corrupted; oppression of subjects reduced to a system; the expenses of administration exceeding by far the public revenues; taxes too great and heavy for the faculties and means of the contributors; population scanty and thinly scattered; the first rate necessary arts neglected for frivolous ones; luxury gradually undermining every state; in short, all governments indifferent about the fate of their subjects; and the subjects, by way of retaliation, equally indifferent about the success and welfare of governments.

If the philosopher, tired with such a numerous train of grievances, can repose or fix his mind on objects more consoling in their nature, it will be on some little state or states, which are but as mere points to the continent of Europe; on some moral and political truths, which, gradually filtrating through error, will by degrees unfolding themselves, at last one day or other reach the sovereign, place itself on the throne, and render posterity more happy.

Such is in particular the uneasy and anxious situation of subjects under the greatest part of governments, that they live with disgust and as machines; so, that if they had power to break their chains, they would provide themselves with new laws and new ministers. Was this the case, we should see half Germany extirpate the petty princes whom it groans under; Castile, Arragon, Ireland, would restore their Kings; Tuscany her Dukes; [1] Flanders her Counts, a number of other states, their ancient sovereigns, who lived amongst them without luxury, and on the revenue of their domains. We should see almost every province separate from its metropolis; all states nearly dissolve, or change their form. But what am I saying? At the same time, such is the weakness and infatuation of people, that, discontented, they murmur and remain in the same inactive state. They are enchained and fettered down to it by custom, and the vices of the age they live in.

This impotent fermentation is one of the most glaring proofs of the bad constitution of our governments. For, whilst on one side, the subjects suffer, and cry out, they on the other lose all spirit of redress. Each man lives for himself, seeking how to shelter himself from publick grievances, to profit by, or grow stupid and lethargick under them. In the midst of this general weakness and insanity, governments are weak themselves; yet, owing to that, they become fertile in petty resources; extend their authority and render it burthensome. They seem to be in secret war with their subjects. They corrupt one part of them in order to enslave the other. They are fearful, lest knowledge should be thrown into their affairs, knowing how much it discovers to the people their prerogatives, and the faults of those who govern the state. They foment luxury, perceiving that luxury enervates courage. As they have in their hands almost all the wealth of the state, (the cupidinous object of every citizen) they make riches the main spring of administration; from them they find means for the compensation and advancement of private persons; the reward of vice, which they increase; the recompence of virtue, which they debase. Then by a kind of fiscal operations, they again pump up the money

---

[1] *Since this was written, she has recognized them in the young Sovereign who reigns over her. He is busied in rendering her prosperous and happy. Let us then seize upon this welcome and rare opportunity to pay homage to a Prince, who feels the value and good effects of the love and happiness of man.* [The reference is to Leopold who later assumed the Habsburg crown. (*Ed.*)]

which their prodigality had lavished: a fatal circulation! and the effect of it is the utter ruin of one half of their nation, for the enslaving of the other. In short, it is this unfortunate art of division, of enfeebling, of degradation, calculated for the better ruling with more sway; and of oppressing without mutiny, which is called, in the generality of courts, the art of governing.

Would the philosophic mind be more satisfied, when it considers the military part of Europe? It would see each of its constitutions sketched one from the other, in the most pitiful manner; the countries in the South adopting the same mode of discipline as those in the North; the genius of a people directly opposite to the laws of their soldiery; the profession of a soldier abandoned to the most miserable and vile class of citizens; the veteran under arms, ever doomed to be wretched and despised. In proportion to the magnitude of states, armies are increased, burthensome to those states in times of peace; not calculated to insure them in time of war, because the remaining part of the subjects are a mere multitude of effeminate and pusilanimous wretches. It would, on its cursory inspection, find some progress made in the Tactics, and in other branches of the military science; it would admire some slight pieces in detail of our constitutions, the great genius of the King of Prussia, the momentaneous soar which he has given to his nation; but after all it will enquire, where is to be found a military establishment fixed on solid principles? Where is there a warlike people, enemies to luxury, friends to labour, and animated by their laws to a love of glory?

The impossibility of any kingdom's extending its domains by conquest, is not to be attributed entirely to its exact vigilance over the conduct of its neighbours, or to the intercourse and correspondence of courts, or to the ballance of power established throughout Europe. It rather proceeds from one country's not being superior to another, by their customs and their constitutions, that all of them are contained in their reciprocal spheres, by the debility and parity of their governments.

Nations which neither abound in treasures, nor population, whose peace establishment already exceeds their revenues, yet venture to declare war. They make a campaign or two with armies, they can neither recruit nor pay. Victory or defeat equally exhausts them. The mass of national debts increase; credit sinks; money fails; the fleet is unmanned, and the army wants soldiers. The ministry on both sides find it time to begin their negotiations: peace is made: some few colonies or provinces change their master: the source of quarrels is frequently left open; and each sets down amidst its ruins, occupied with paying its debts, and preparing for another war.

But let us suppose in Europe, there was to spring up a vigorous people, with genius, with power, and a happy form of government; a set of people that to strict virtue, and a national soldiery, joined a fixed plan of aggrandizement, who never lost sight of that system, who, knowing how to carry on a war with little expense, and to subsist by their conquests, was not reduced to the necessity of laying down their arms by the calculation of financiers. As the north wind bends the tender reed, those people would be seen to subjugate their neighbours, and overthrow our feeble constitutions.

That people will never spring up, because in Europe there is no nation new and powerful. All are assimilated and corrupted, as like each other as possible. They have all of them forms of government, foe to every sentiment of virtue and patriotism.

When corruption has made such progress; when she has attacked the principle of administration, ministers, the courts of kings, and the cradles of their children, it is then next to impossible to hope for a regeneration: for the spot from whence it would come, would be the very focus of that evil. . . .

What I conceive by Politics, is the art of governing a state in such a manner, that the subjects may be happy, the state powerful, and respected by her neighbours; when considered in that extensive point of light it becomes the most interesting science; from thence Politics are naturally divided into two parts, INTERIOR and EXTERIOR Politics.

The first is as a basis to the second. All which belongs to the happiness and strength of a people springs from their source, laws, manners, customs, prejudices, national spirit, justice, police, population, agriculture, trade, revenues of the nation, expenses of government, duties, application of their produce: they must view all these objects with a scope of genius and reflection: they must wing their flight above them to perceive those principal similarities, and that influence which links the one to the other; let them then draw near and hover round them, to observe and follow their details: let them not be lured by one more than the rest, because in Politics, that which sooner occasions one branch to fructify, very often drains a neighbouring one of its vegetating moisture, kills it, or even another branch at a greater distance. In short, they must be the precurse of every circumstance which pertains to administration; and to effect that, they must constitute one general system: with their eyes continually fixed upon it to determine the operation required; or the produce of those operations, to see if it concurs with the execution of the general plan.

While interior Politics thus prepare and bring to perfection every means within doors, exterior Politics examine what weight and consideration the result of those means can give to a state without; and on that she determines her system. They must be acquainted with every kind of relation, whose influence links their own country with others interests; to discover illusive and apparent interests from those that are real and permanent; those alliances which are but fugitive and ineffectual, from those useful and solid bonds that dictate the topographical position of countries, or the respective advantage of their contractors. They must afterwards calculate what military force a state requires to impose respect on their neighbours, to give weight to their negotiations. They should constitute their military force in respect to the genius and power of the country; especially in such a manner, that it might not be too great for its means, because it then drenches a state, and gives it a factitious and ruinous power. They should instil into it the best understanding, the greatest valour, the most consummate discipline, because then it would be less numerous, and this reduction of numbers less burthensome to the subjects. . . .

Interior Politics having thus prepared a state, with what facility external Politics can resolve upon the system of her own interests in opposition to her foreign ones, by the raising of a respectable military power! How easy it is to have armies invincible, in a state where its subjects are citizens, where they cherish and revere government, where they are fond of glory, where they are not intimidated at the idea of toiling for the general good! How a nation, once powerful by her interior resources, would be respected abroad! How her negotiations, by diminishing their complicated nature, would acquire weight! How her mode of conducting them might become free and and open! It is the folly of all our governments to practise in their negotiations so much obliquity and little faith. It is that which foments disorder in a state, which reciprocally endeavours to corrupt the members of administration. It is that which makes each nation, watchful of one another, and vie amongst themselves, bargaining for and purchasing peace; mutually rising out of troubles and distress. It is that which creates base and dangerous rivals of every kind; that perpetual encroachment of the trade of one nation on the trade of another; those laws of prohibition; those privileges which exclude the foreigner; those treaties which favour one country to the prejudice of the other; those chimerical calculations of the ballance of exports and imports, vile and complicated methods which never did, even by those who employed them with the greatest skill at the end of an age, add the least to the increase of government. In a word, it is the folly of our governments that make us jealous of the prosperity of other nations; desirous either to weaken or corrupt them; Politics like to those which they employ to make themselves impotent, and corrupt their own subjects; Politics quite opposite to those of a good government, who, without seeking to act contrary to the prosperity and strength of her neighbour, endeavours to rise above her, by her vigour and her virtues.

In like manner it is the weakness of our governments, which render our military constitutions so imperfect and so ruinous. It is that which, not being able to compose our armies with citizens, men who have a zeal for the service, or soldiers, not merely for the sake of gain, occasions them to be so numerous and burthensome. It is that which, not knowing how to make honour their reward, pays them with money alone. It is that which, not being able to rely on the courage and fidelity of the subject, because he lies enervated, and continually murmuring, takes into pay an auxiliary force. It is that which is always harrassing the frontiers of the country. In short, it is that which is continually occupied in extinguishing every military virtue in a state, not even so much as suffering it to develop itself amongst the troops, fearful lest from thence it should spread abroad amongst the civil, and arm that power one day or other against the abuses which oppress it. I shall soon return to the subject which concerns the military constitution; that part of Politics so important, and which is so universally neglected. . . .

Remark, that when Politics become more perfect, their difficulty is greatly diminished: the imperfection of a science almost always adds to its difficulty. The obscurity of ignorance, the sophisms of prejudice, throw their thick veil over its principles. By making it complicated, they multiply its difficulties. They think therefore by that means to make amends for its insufficiences. The basis of all their operations being faulty, erroneous consequences increase every day; they jar against each other. Soon there springs up a theory, a thousand times more interwoven and more perplexing to lay hold of, than the enchainment of those truths would be, which are regularly adopted by science. It is more especially in Politics, where the sequel of every deviation is so rapid and fatal. When that science shall be redressed and new modelled; when, like justice and virtue, it fixes its principles on a sure and immutable foundation, it will become simple, and enlighten that nation which is under its influence. It will cast off all those insignificant methods of detail, those supplements, those palliatives, whose imbecility has overcharged and corrupted every part of administration. . . .

In short, the state I have here painted will have an easy, simple, and solid administration. It will be similar to those amazing machines, whose works being little complicated, produce such great effects: the power of the state will be increased by its strength and prosperity; time which destroys all things will increase that power, it will confute a vulgar prejudice, which leads us to imagine, that empires are under the subjection of an imperious law of ruin and decay. If we cast our eyes over history that over-ruling law apparently exists, it is strongly engraven on the ruins of many thrones, on the tombs of such a multitude of people; but it is not irresistible, *it can be combated*. It is by no means comprehended in a part of that fatality, which, without end, occasions such a devastation and reproduction in the universe. Let a good government be the basis of an empire; let it know how to maintain the sanity of her principles, the state will be always rising until it has attained that point of ascendancy where its greatest force is deposited. If this government is skilful enough to find the point beyond which its elevation would but weaken, if it knows when to stop its movement, if it always is able to sustain it, the state fixed on that height of power, and on the stormy sea of fate, secured unshook, may see events on events, and ages without end, dash themselves to pieces at her well affirmed feet.

O my country! this picture may not always be a mere phantastick dream. Thou hast it in thy power to make it real: thou mayest be one time or other, that fortunate empire perhaps, one day escaping from the vices of the age, and under the happy influence of more favourable circumstances, a prince will be seated on thy throne, who will operate, and bring about this great revolution. From amongst the writings of my fellow citizens, perhaps in mine he may draw the laudable desire, and learn the method of carrying his schemes and wishes into execution. He soon would change our laws, our customs, infuse in our souls a happier doctrine, to government he would give a fresh and well-tempered spring; display to every part of administration the sacred light of truth, in lieu of our confined and complicated system of Politics, he would substitute that extensive and sublime science which I have endeavoured to draw the portrait of. Soon those false luminaries which led us astray would disappear, the dark cloud which kept us in ignorance would vanish from our sight, truths, uncontested truths, burst in upon us, and fill us with joy and admiration; those narrow minds which we honour with the name of genius; those prepossessions which we call well-grounded principles, would likewise fall to the ground and be no more. That amazing voluminous and complicate code of laws of our finances, of our army, would crumble away. The reputation of those sovereigns so highly flattered, and those ministers esteemed as able statesmen, before this great man would be reduced to nothing: he would give the nation that possible degree of perfection it could be capable of receiving. Finally, having compleated the finishing stroke of its prosperity, and not being farther capable of adding any thing more but the means of making it lasting and permanent, he then would change its form of government. Round his throne he would assemble his subjects, now become his children. He would say to them: "I am desirous of rendering you like myself, all happy and prosperous. I confer on you extensive privileges, which I have not injured myself, nor will I have my successors abuse. I have called you here to share with me in government. I conserve the honours of the crown, the right of giving you wise and wholesome laws." "The power of having them put in execution when you have ratified them amongst yourselves; absolute authority, the dictator in every crisis which threatens the state. Here are the statutes of this new form of government, look on her laws: I am not going to reign, but by them, to extend my sway beyond the irordinances. Let my family, who are going to take oath with me, succeed in their right, but by these conditions. Receive our oaths of allegiance in like manner as we receive yours. If infractions are made on either side, let the laws provide a proper sentence."

What a spirit of Politics would that be, that could inspire an all-powerful king with this magnanimous resolution! Could it be supposed, that a sovereign and his successors would be less happy, or have less authority in adopting it? . . .

It is a melancholy reflection, when we think that the first art which man invented, was that of destroying his fellow-creature, and it is a well attested truth in history, that ever since the beginning of ages, more schemes have been put in practice to prejudice the human specie, than to render it happy. The various passions of man originating with the world, engendered war, and from thence arose the desire to overcome and massacre with more success, what we in short call Military Science; weak at its first setting off, it was simply man against man, the art in taking advantage of each other's manual strength and activity. Amongst the first race of mankind it was confined, to wrestling, boxing, or the use of a few unwieldy weapons. When societies were raised and grew more enlightened, it soon began to spread itself, its power and means grew more combined, it assembled a greater concourse of men. It was then like what it is at this day amongst the Asiatics, an undigested, unformed, collection of knowledge, which scarce merits the appellation of science; when ambitious people rose in the world, this art, improved by them, became the instrument of their glory. Under their government it fixed the destiny of a people; it either ruined or supported empires; finally, by every country it was preferred to the arts and sciences, and by degrees, as they gained ground, so it became neglected.

Let us trace the military science through all its revolutions; we shall discover it successively running over various parts of the globe, carrying by turn glory and superiority over that people by whom it was cultivated, shunning rich and enlightened nations: as the soul possessed a greater portion of energy and courage amongst those who were rustic and poor, it therefore took up its residence amongst them. We shall remark particularly five or six great epochas, which are, properly speaking, the time and age wherein it flourished, and made such great and various alterations in its principles.

Amongst the Asiatics, yet more in particular with the Persians, the art of war first began to adopt a certain rule of consistency. The Egyptians, friends to science, therefore fond of peace, made less progress in it, and therefore were never victorious but under Sesostris. After the death of Cyrus, luxury drove it out of Persia, and it then reigned among the Grecians. That ingenious and brave people perfected and deduced it into regular principles. Alexander came, and by still making greater improvement, conquered Asia, the cradle it had been nursed in. At this epocha it appeared to be at its greatest summit of splendor, for the Phalanx was then esteemed the first ordinance in the universe. . . .

The discovery of gunpowder added nothing to the perfection of military science. It was only the means of furnishing fresh methods of destruction, and to give the last blow to chivalry: an institution that our present enlightened days ought to envy at those times of simplicity and ignorance! Fire-arms very apparently retarded the progress of the Tactics, for this reason, that armies then kept at a greater distance from each other, and chance and less combination was then comprised in the decision of battles. At last Gustavus and Nassau * appeared. The one fought for the liberty of his country, the other for the love of glory. Both studied antiquity. Each sought from among the ruins of ages, the scattered vestiges of discipline and the Tactics, being such outrés admirers of the ancients, they applied their principles in too servile a manner to the time they flourished in, and to the kind of arms then made use of. . . . But what is nevertheless an undoubted truth, is, that military science once more took its birth under them, and that Europe, astonished when she saw the troops, camps, and success of Gustavus, cried out, a miracle!

After his death . . . military art, in some few particulars, still made fresh progress. This was the time when great generals, commanders of little armies, effected great things, yet still the Tactics were in their infancy. It seemed as though they were apprehensive of losing sight of their first institutions. As if they were afraid of erring from their path in divitating from the ordinance of the ancients. . . . They cited the ancients on every occasion, never perceiving a space of two thousand years between us and them, and what necessity there was to have other principles, on account of arms, constitution, and more especially the temper of souls, being no longer what they were at that era.

The seventeenth century, and the beginning of this, by degrees, enlightened Europe in some particular branches of War: in respect to others, it either left it, or else plunged it in ignorance and darkness. Cohorn and Vauban brought to perfection the attack of places. We made great improvements in this art, and notwithstanding what the world is pleased to say, we certainly by far excelled the ancients; the same progress was not made in the art of defense, whether courage, being considered as the true bulwark of a place, had held down her head; or because they did not sufficiently conceive, that no good defense could be made but such as are in themselves offensive, and which spread innumerable difficulties in the way of the besiegers. . . .

Meanwhile various alterations were made in other respects, but poorly understood, very fatal to mankind, and to the perfecting of military science: as for example, armies became more numerous; their artillery increased daily. Louis XIV. who first set the example, was far from succeeding in it. The only thing he did was the engaging Europe to imitate his principles. When it is difficult to maintain and put armies in motion, the commanding of them must of course be likewise perplexing and difficult. Condé, Luxembourg, Eugene, Catinat, Vendome, Villars, by the ascendancy of their superior genius, knew how to move those unwieldy masses; but Villeroi, Marsin, Cumberland, and many others, were crushed under their ponderous burthens. Indeed

* [Military commanders during the Thirty Years' War, 1618–1648. (*Ed.*)]

how was it possible they could command them? These great men I have been speaking of, had nor organization, nor the Tactics in their armies. They left no rules or principles after them to work upon. Perhaps, and I dare even assert it, they were actuated more frequently by instinct, than by presentiment or reflection. From thence it ensues, that under them no great Generals could be formed: from thence, when at the head of their armies the genius of these eminent leaders failed them, they then fell into the obscurity of ignorance. They then accused fortune, nature, the degeneracy of the times, for the want of good Generals; necessity of course drove them to those chimerical causes. The qualifications of a Commander was at that time almost looked upon as an innate gift, a partial dispensation of nature. They scarce could believe that education and study were requisites. The art of war was not displayed in works of masters in a clear intelligent manner. . . . At that period a great division existed in the opinion of the military, whether the discovery of fire arms should change the general grounds of the Tactics? Whether the ordinance of the ancients should be rejected, on account of its depth, and the effect liable to be made on it by the artillery? All Europe was divided and floating between these opinions. They wrote and corresponded on every side, yet their discussions could throw light into nothing, nor clear up their doubts. . . .

Nevertheless the day approached, when this cloud of ignorance was ready to disappear. In the north was seen a second time the Phenomena of a warlike and well disciplined army. Charles XII. was fighting at the head of those brave Swedes, who were still animated with the daring spirit of Gustavus. His infantry was almost as indefatigable, and well disciplined as the Roman legions; they charged like them sword in hand, had excellent field officers, and not without some knowledge of modern manoeuvres. In short, if Charles XII. had improved the military science, with as much success and conduct as his grandfather established it, he very likely might have been the Frederick of his time. But his life was too short. Yet the query is, whether he had a proper store of knowledge, and a sufficient extent of capacity for the undertaking? His first successes were rapid, as those will ever be of a well disciplined army, over an ignorant multitude. He began like an Alexander, but afterwards conducted himself like a random adventurer, and at last finished like Gustavus. After his death the Swedes degenerated, and the Russians, who had conquered them without ever being their equals, became not the least more enlightened.

As the learned revolutions took their rise in the south, so it was ever the singular fate of the north to be the source of the military revolutions of Europe. A kingdom was just arising on the Oder, and on the Spry. These new sovereigns not being able to establish a maritime, nor a commercial power, went to work in raising an army, and in a very short time, by the means of their claims and their soldiers, they acquired weight in the general scale. Frederick II. came to the throne, and he completed that which had been traced out by his predecessors. A skilful prince, and replete with the study of the ancients, he displayed the most extensive genius. He doubled his troops in number, yet still more in discipline; produced a Tactic almost new; made expert generals, was himself the most skilful of them all; conquered a province that was more valuable than his own kingdom; with less resources and more glory he struggled with as many enemies as Louis XIV. and at last, with a small revenue, little population, little faculties in his subjects, he established the most formidable military power, and the most surprizing of any in Europe. As the age of Augustus and of Louis XIV. make such a principal figure in history, so this prince's reign will be considered as the most remarkable in the science of war.

Such is the reigning empire of custom and prejudice amongst a people, that, notwithstanding the king of Prussia was busied in levying troops and creating a Tactic, no other state ever dreamt of raising itself to its true point of perfection. In the year 1740 he frequently beat the Austrians. He took Silesia from them. These successes were the fruit and reward of his labour. During the peace which followed this war, he had encampments at Spandau and Magdeburg; that, which experience had taught was defective in his Tactic, he new modelled and brought to perfection; he introduced and practiced in his encampments those learned and advantageous manoeuvres; that inconceivable and decisive celerity become so useful, on account of our numerous armies, and the great extent of their front. Yet no other powers around him all this while were reflecting on his proceedings. . . .

In this war were seen great trains of artillery increasing to an immensity. The Russians dragged after them to the amount of six hundred pieces. The King of Prussia and the Austrians to three or four hundred: at the same time was seen falling to the ground that custom, which attached the same honour to the taking of a piece of cannon, as to that of a pair of colours. A great lesson then presented itself for the instruction of generals, the armies of the King of Prussia, not being overpowered by that kind of baggage, were ready to make forced marches: lose battles, with the greatest part of their cannon, and stop at two leagues distance from the ground where the battle was lost.

Light troops likewise were much increased in number. To armies so numerous, charged with such a quantity of equipage, ammunition and artillery, the most extensive positions, convoys so frequent, establishments so hazardous, a length of communications so apparently necessary, that it appeared as though, through envy of each side, they augmented those kind of troops that were merely destined to attack or cover them.

From both these changes, which all the belligerent powers have adopted in servily tracing the one upon the other, and which a General, a man of genius, might with advantage avoid the trouble occasioned by them, it occurs that in the first campaign, armies will be more expensive, more desolating, more incumbersome; that the light troops, baggage, etc. will be more numerous than the regular body, I mean by this last word, regular troops, those who gain the battles. From thence it follows, that though wars will be still less decisive; yet they will be more fatal to population and the state: every destructive invention, and all those mistaken calculations of Politics and the military, rebound on this unfortunate and languid idea of humanity. . . .

I say, that the science of modern war, compared with that of old times, is more tedious and embarrassing; however, I do not mean, that on all points it is more perfect and better known. In regard to some things it has made great progress: in others, at the expense of its perfection, it has spread and grown complicated. Our fire-arms are far superior to the missile weapons of the ancients. The science of our artillery far exceeds theirs of the Balista; our fortification is superior; such is the progress of the moderns; such is the effect of the knowledge of mathematics thrown on the science of war, that places now besieged, can defend themselves with much more art. But armies are become too multiplied; the artillery and the light troops have too much encreased; the frontiers of states on two and three lines are now in apropos covered with fortified towns; these places are unnecessarily decked with pieces of fortifications; the systems of engineers are for the most part too exclusive, too methodically, too little combined with the principles of the Tactic; armies become immense, as much on account of the augmentation of troops, as by the equipage and impediments they trail after them, therefore they are difficult to put in motion; the endless details of their subsistance constitutes a science, which the armies of the ancients, less numerous, more simple, and far better appointed, had not the least conception of: these are the errors and abuses which render this modern science so complicated, that multiply those instructions which compose it, that accounts for the scarcity of good generals. . . .

Thus the science of the present practice of war, in perfecting itself, in having a nearer proximity with its true principles, may then be more simple and less difficult. Armies being then better constituted and more manoeuvring, will have their numbers curtailed. Their divisions would be delineated, in a proportion happily combined, conformable to the nature of the country, and the kind of war they are engaged in. Their Tactics would be simple, analogical, susceptible to the turn their different movements may occasion. In such a case the officer of one division will know how to command the other. We should not then be witness to general officers, being ignorant of the details of those corps in which they never served, bely that title they are vested with; that title which, in giving them the power to command every branch, at the same time supposes them to have that universality of knowledge requisite for their own direction: armies thus formed, would be more easy to move and to conduct. That confined and routinous method, which fetters and diminishes every operation, would be abolished. Then the most daring expedition could be attempted. Forced marches could be made. They would then know how to engage and give battles by the effect of their manoeuvres. Be less on the defensive. Less nicety would be attended to about what they call the choice of positions. Topographical details would no longer have the same importance; military science would not then be so much overcharged; obstructions, being thus nearly removed, sobriety having taken place of luxury, the minute details of subsistance will then be less complicated, and less tiresome for the operations. The duty of an army-contractor would then consist in conveying the less equipage possible, and endeavour to find a subsistance on the produce of the country he is in. Artillery and fortification would improve daily. In every age they would follow the progress of mathematics, which, as their basis, they should work upon. But neither the one or the other would assume exclusive and absolute pretensions, systems which tend to multiply expense and trouble. In armies, and all military combinations, they would simply hold that rank their utility requires them to keep; under the direction of generals, they would be as useful aids employed to strengthen and support the troops. Finally, all the branches of military science would form as it were a compact bundle of rays; and this concourse of light, re-united in the mind of one man, would constitute him general, that is to say, capable to be the commander of an army.

It would be very interesting to see military science improve in simplifying herself in this manner, in becoming less difficult. I have already remarked, how the same revolution may be made in politics. This maxim would likewise take place in almost all the sciences, provided their theory was divested of all those errors which they are crowded with, of false methods, which make them so complicated and tiresome for those who study them. Then men, by attaining more rapidly to, and in greater numbers the extent of these sciences, might draw back the curtain, which stops them from seeing the bounds of their journey; then the shortness of their life would not hinder them any longer from embracing more than one at a time, and to extend the one in conformity with the others. Then the encyclopedia of human understanding, now become the repository of truth, would assume her reign, and affirm herself amidst the various alterations of ages: like a vigorous and flourishing tree, that has no unnecessary and pernicious branch, and by degrees as she encreases in age by spreading and strengthening the growth of her trunk, yields a shade, and her fruitful produce to her happy and diligent cultivators. . . .

❧ THE WEALTH OF NATIONS

Adam Smith

Adam Smith (1723–1790), the celebrated "father of political economy," lived the quiet and reasonable life so prized by philosophers of the Enlightenment. He resided at the Universities of Glasgow and Edinburgh (except for a sojourn in France), receiving visits from the great, corresponding with thinkers and statesmen everywhere. His fame results not so much from his discoveries of laws of economics, but because he mirrors so naturally and in such persuasively comprehensive prose a large number of his age's attitudes, presenting in the study of economics a universal image of man's life.

From philosophers he inherited the tradition of natural law that stemmed from Hobbes and was developed by Helvetius and Hume, basing his foundation on the self-interest supposedly inherent in man's makeup. He borrowed the belief in the self-regulating capacity of laissez faire, *though he significantly modified the Physiocrat theory by abandoning agriculture and mining as the sole sources of wealth, reaching back to the seventeenth century for the idea that labor of any kind creates wealth. Smith's advocacy, too, of economic freedom stems indirectly from ideas of religious toleration which had been current in Britain for over a hundred years. Just as the puritan merchants had once demanded freedom of individual choice in worship, they now came to see freedom of choice in economic activity as an extension of liberty generally. Mercantilism (see pages 71–84), once a prop designed to encourage business vigor, had come to mean either witless restriction of potential expansion or a downright appendage of tyranny. Smith joined political liberty with economics by condemning limitation of apprenticeship as "manifest encroachment upon the just liberty of the workman" and upheld free competition as "the obvious and simple system of natural liberty."*

The germinal quality of Smith's thought has spawned laudatory paeans, reflective amendment, retort, and creative departure. In his own day, he lived to see the gradual dismantling of mercantile regulation. The free traders of the mid-nineteenth-century "Manchester School" raised Smith's international division of labor from a theory to a revelation of world peace and unity. Great factory owners of a breed Smith could not have visualized excerpted Smithian slogans in justification of unrestricted industrialization and automation. On the other hand, his labor theory of value became one of the bases of Marx's criticism and socialism's discontents with the machine age. Though Smith hoped to extricate economics from political control, the issues he raised concerning governmental regulation have been of major controversy in modern political debate.

INTRODUCTION AND PLAN OF THE WORK

The annual labour of every nation is the fund which originally supplies it with all the necessaries and conveniences of life which it annually consumes, and which consist always either in the immediate produce of that labour, or in what is purchased with that produce from other nations.

According therefore, as this produce, or what is purchased with it, bears a greater or smaller proportion to the number of those who are to consume it, the nation will be better or worse supplied with all the necessaries and conveniences for which it has occasion.

But this proportion must in every nation be regulated by two different circumstances; first, by the skill, dexterity, and judgment with which its labour is generally applied; and, secondly, by the proportion between the number of those who are employed in useful labour, and that of those who are not so employed. Whatever be the soil, climate, or extent of territory of any particular nation, the abundance or scantiness of its annual supply must, in that particular situation, depend upon those two circumstances.

The abundance or scantiness of this supply too seems to depend more upon the former of those two circumstances than upon the latter. Among the savage nations of hunters and fishers, every individual who is able to work, is more or less employed in

Adam Smith, *An Inquiry into the Nature and Causes of the Wealth of Nations* (London: G. Routledge & Sons, 1892), I, 1–15, 16–17, 55–58, 427, 446–450, 452–453, 455–457, 472–473; II, 205–207.

useful labour, and endeavours to provide, as well as he can, the necessaries and conveniences of life, for himself, or such of his family or tribe as are either too old, or too young, or too infirm to go a hunting and fishing. Such nations, however, are so miserably poor, that from mere want, they are frequently reduced, or at least think themselves reduced, to the necessity sometimes of directly destroying, and sometimes of abandoning their infants, their old people, and those afflicted with lingering diseases, to perish with hunger, or to be devoured by wild beasts. Among civilized and thriving nations, on the contrary, though a great number of people do not labour at all, many of whom consume the produce of ten times, frequently of a hundred times more labour than the greater part of those who work; yet the produce of the whole labour of the society is so great, that all are often abundantly supplied, and a workman, even of the lowest and poorest order, if he is frugal and industrious, may enjoy a greater share of the necessaries and conveniences of life than it is possible for any savage to acquire.

The causes of this improvement, in the productive powers of labour, and the order, according to which its produce is naturally distributed among the different ranks and conditions of men in the society, make the subject of the First Book of this Inquiry.

Whatever be the actual state of the skill, dexterity, and judgment with which labour is applied in any nation, the abundance or scantiness of its annual supply must depend, during the continuance of that state, upon the proportion between the number of those who are annually employed in useful labour, and that of those who are not so employed. The number of useful and productive labourers, it will hereafter appear, is everywhere in proportion to the quantity of capital stock which is employed in setting them to work, and to the particular way in which it is so employed. The Second Book, therefore, treats of the nature of capital stock, of the manner in which it is gradually accumulated, and of the different quantities of labour which it puts into motion, according to the different ways in which it is employed.

Nations tolerably well advanced as to skill, dexterity, and judgment, in the application of labour, have followed very different plans in the general conduct or direction of it; and those plans have not all been equally favourable to the greatness of its produce. The policy of some nations has given extraordinary encouragement to the industry of the country; that of others to the industry of towns. Scarce any nation has dealt equally and impartially with every sort of industry. Since the downfall of the Roman empire, the policy of Europe has been more favourable to arts, manufactures, and commerce, the industry of towns; than to agriculture, the industry of the country. The circumstances which seem to have introduced and established this policy are explained in the Third Book.

Though those different plans were, perhaps, first introduced by the private interests and prejudices of particular orders of men, without any regard to, or foresight of, their consequences upon the general welfare of the society; yet they have given occasion to very different theories of political economy; of which some magnify the importance of that industry which is carried on in towns, others of that which is carried on in the country. Those theories have had a considerable influence, not only upon the opinions of men of learning, but upon the public conduct of princes and sovereign states. I have endeavoured in the Fourth Book, to explain, as fully and distinctly as I can, those different theories, and the principal effects which they have produced in different ages and nations.

To explain in what has consisted the revenue of the great body of the people, or what has been the nature of those funds, which, in different ages and nations, have supplied their annual consumption, is the object of these Four first Books. The Fifth and last Book treats of the revenue of the sovereign, or commonwealth. In this book I have endeavoured to show; first, what are the necessary expences of the sovereign, or commonwealth; which of those expences ought to be defrayed by the general contribution of the whole society; and which of them, by that of some particular part only, or of some particular members of it: secondly, what are the different methods in which the whole society may be made to contribute towards defraying the expences incumbent on the whole society, and what are the principal advantages and inconveniences of each of those methods: and, thirdly and lastly, what are the reasons and causes which have induced almost all modern governments to mortgage some part of this revenue, or to contract debts, and what have been the effects of those debts upon the real wealth, the annual produce of the land and labour of the society.

BOOK I. OF THE CAUSES OF IMPROVEMENT IN THE PRODUCTIVE POWERS OF LABOUR, AND OF THE ORDER ACCORDING TO WHICH ITS PRODUCE IS NATURALLY DISTRIBUTED AMONG THE DIFFERENT RANKS OF THE PEOPLE

Chapter I. Of the Division of Labour

The greatest improvement in the productive powers of labour, and the greater part of the skill, dexterity, and judgment with which it is anywhere directed, or applied, seem to have been the effects of the division of labour.

The effects of the division of labour, in the general business of society, will be more easily understood by considering in what manner it operates in some particular manufactures. It is commonly supposed to be carried furthest in some very trifling ones; not perhaps that it really is carried further in them than in others of more importance: but in those trifling manufactures which are destined to supply the small wants of but a small number of people, the whole number of workmen must necessarily be small; and those employed in every different branch of the work can often be collected into the same workhouse, and placed at once under the view of the spectator. In those great manufactures, on the contrary, which are destined to supply the great wants of the great body of the people, every different branch of the work employs so great a number of workmen, that it is impossible to collect them all into the same workhouse. We can seldom see more, at one time, than those employed in one single branch. Though in such manufactures, therefore, the work may really be divided into a much greater number of parts, than in those of a more trifling nature, the division is not near so obvious, and has accordingly been much less observed.

To take an example therefore, from a very trifling manufacture; but one in which the division of labour has been very often taken notice of, the trade of the pin-maker; a workman not educated to this business (which the division of labour has rendered a distinct trade), nor acquainted with the use of the machinery employed in it (to the invention of which the same division of labour has probably given occasion), could scarce, perhaps, with his utmost industry, make one pin in a day, and certainly could not make twenty. But in the way in which this business is now carried on, not only the whole work is a peculiar trade, but it is divided into a number of branches, of which the greater part are likewise peculiar trades. One man draws out the wire, another straights it, a third cuts it, a fourth points it, a fifth grinds it at the top for receiving the head; to make the head requires two or three distinct operations; to put it on, is a peculiar business, to whiten the pins is another; it is even a trade by itself to put them into the paper; and the important business of making a pin is, in this manner, divided into about eighteen distinct operations, which, in some manufactories, are all performed by distinct hands, though in others the same man will sometimes perform two or three of them. I have seen a small manufactory of this kind where ten men only were employed, and where some of them consequently performed two or three distinct operations. But though they were very poor, and therefore but indifferently accommodated with the necessary machinery, they could, when they exerted themselves, make among them about twelve pounds of pins in a day. There are in a pound upwards of four thousand pins of a middling size. Those ten persons, therefore, could make among them upwards of forty-eight thousand pins in a day. Each person, therefore, making a tenth part of forty-eight thousand pins, might be considered as making four thousand eight hundred pins in a day. But if they had all wrought separately and independently, and without any of them having been educated to this peculiar business, they certainly could not each of them have made twenty, perhaps not one pin in a day; that is, certainly not the two hundred and fortieth, perhaps not the four thousand eight hundredth part of what they are at present capable of performing, in consequence of a proper division and combination of their different operations.

In every other art and manufacture, the effects of the division of labour are similar to what they are in this very trifling one; though in many of them, the labour can neither be so much subdivided, nor reduced to so great a simplicity of operation. The division of labour, however, so far as it can be introduced, occasions, in every art, a proportionable increase of the productive powers of labour. The separation of different trades and employments from one another, seems to have taken place, in consequence of this advantage. This separation too is generally carried furthest in those countries which enjoy the highest degree of industry and improvement; what is the work of one man in a rude state of society, being generally that of several in an improved one. In every improved society, the farmer is generally nothing but a farmer; the manufacturer nothing but a manufacturer. The labour too which is necessary to produce any one complete manufacture, is almost always divided among a great number of hands. How many different trades are employed in each branch of the linen and woollen manufactures, from the growers of the flax and the wool, to the bleachers and smoothers of the linen, or to the dyers and dressers of the cloth! The nature of agriculture, indeed, does not admit of so many subdivisions of labour, nor of so complete a separation of one business from another, as manufactures. It is impossible to separate so entirely, the business of the grazier from that of the corn-farmer, as the trade of the carpenter is commonly separated from that of the smith. The spinner is almost always a distinct person from the weaver; but the ploughman, the harrower, the sower of the seed, and the reaper of the corn, are often the same. The occasions for those different sorts of labour returning with the different seasons of the year, it is impossible that one man should be constantly employed in any one of them. This impossibility of making so complete and entire a separation of all the different branches of labour employed in agriculture, is perhaps the reason why the improvement of the productive powers of labour in this art, does not always keep pace with their improvement in manufactures. The most opulent nations, indeed, generally excel all their neighbours in agriculture as well as in manufactures; but they are commonly more distinguished by their superiority in the latter than in the former. Their lands are in general better cultivated, and having more labour and expense bestowed upon them, produce more in proportion to the extent and natural fertility of the ground. But this superiority of produce is seldom much more than in proportion to the superiority of labour and expence. In agriculture, the labour of the rich country is not always much more productive than that of the poor; or, at least, it is never so much more productive, as it commonly is in manufactures. The corn of the rich country, therefore, will not always, in the same degree of goodness, come cheaper to market than that of the poor. The corn of Poland, in the same degree of goodness, is as cheap as that of France, notwithstanding the superior opulence and improvement of the latter country. The corn of France is, in the corn provinces, fully as good, and in most years nearly about the same price with the corn in England, though, in opulence and improvement, France is perhaps inferior to England. The corn-lands of England, however, are better cultivated than those of France, and the corn-lands of France are said to be much better cultivated than those of Poland. But though the poor country, notwithstanding the inferiority of its cultivation, can, in some measure, rival the rich in the cheapness and goodness of its corn, it can pretend to no such competition in its manufactures; at least if those manufactures suit the soil, climate and situation of the rich country. The silks of France are better and cheaper than those of England, because the silk manufacture, at least under the present high duties upon the importation of raw silk, does not so well suit the climate of England as that of France. But the hardware and the coarse woollens of England are beyond all comparison superior to those of France, and much cheaper too in the same degree of goodness. In Poland there are said to be scarce any manufactures of any kind, a few of those coarser household manufactures excepted, without which no country can well subsist.

This great increase in the quantity of work, which, in consequence of the division of labour, the same number of people are capable of performing, is owing to three different circumstances; first, to the increase of dexterity in every particular workman; secondly, to the saving of the time which is commonly lost in passing from one species of work to another; and lastly, to the invention of a great number of machines which facilitate and abridge labour, and enable one man to do the work of many.

First, the improvement of the dexterity of the workman necessarily increases the quantity of the work he can perform; and the division of labour, by reducing every man's business to some one simple operation, and by making this operation the sole employment of his life, necessarily increases very much the dexterity of the workman. A common smith, who, though accustomed to handle the hammer, has never been used to make nails, if upon some particular occasion he is obliged to attempt it, will scarce, I am assured, be able to make above two or three hundred nails in a day, and those too very bad ones. A smith who has been accustomed to make nails, but whose sole or principal business has not been that of a nailer, can seldom with his utmost diligence make more than eight hundred or a thousand nails in a day. I have seen several boys under twenty years of age who had never exercised any other trade but that of making nails, and who, when they exerted themselves, could make, each of them, upwards of two thousand three hundred nails in a day. The making of a nail, however, is by no means one of the simplest operations. The same person blows the bellows, stirs or mends the fire as there is occasion, heats the iron, and forges every part of the nail: In forging the head too he is obliged to change his tools. The different operations into which the making of a pin, or of a metal button, is subdivided, are all of them much more simple, and the dexterity of the person whose whole life it has been the sole business to perform them, is usually much greater. The rapidity with which some of the operations of those manufactures are performed, exceeds what the human hand could, by those who had never seen them, be supposed capable of acquiring.

Secondly, the advantage which is gained by saving the time commonly lost in passing from one sort of work to another, is much greater than we should at first view be apt to imagine it. It is impossible to pass very quickly from one kind of work to another, that is carried on in a different place, and with quite different tools. A country weaver, who cultivates a small farm, must lose a good deal of time in passing from his loom to the field, and from the field to his loom. When the two trades can be carried on in the same workhouse, the loss of time is no doubt much less. It is even in this case, however, very considerable. A man commonly saunters a little in turning his hand from one sort of employment to another. When he first begins the new work he is seldom very keen and hearty; his mind, as they say, does not go to it, and for some time he rather trifles than applies to good purpose. The habit of sauntering and of indolent careless application, which is naturally, or rather necessarily acquired by every country workman who is obliged to change his work and his tools every half hour, and to apply his hand in twenty different ways almost every day of his life; renders him almost always slothful and lazy, and incapable of any vigorous application even on the most pressing occasions. Independent, therefore, of his deficiency in point of dexterity, this cause alone must always reduce considerably the quantity of work which he is capable of performing.

Thirdly, and lastly, everybody must be sensible how much labour is facilitated and abridged by the application of proper machinery. It is unnecessary to give any example. I shall only observe, therefore, that the invention of all those machines by which labour is so much facilitated and abridged, seems to have been originally owing to the division of labour. Men are much more likely to discover easier and readier methods of attaining any object, when the whole attention of their minds is directed towards that single object, than when it is dissipated among a great variety of things. But in consequence of the division of labour, the whole of every man's attention comes naturally to be directed towards some one very simple object. It is naturally to be expected, therefore, that some one or other of those who are employed in each particular branch of labour should soon find out easier and readier methods of performing their own particular work, wherever the nature of it admits of such improvement. A great part of the machines made use of in those manufactures in which labour is most subdivided, were originally the inventions of common workmen, who, being each of them employed in some very simple operation, naturally turned their thoughts towards finding out easier and readier methods of performing it. Whoever has been much accustomed to visit such manufactures, must frequently have been shown very pretty machines, which were the inventions of such workmen, in order to facilitate and quicken their own particular part of the work. In the first fire-engines, a boy was constantly employed to open and shut alternately the communication between the boiler and the cylinder, according as the piston either ascended or descended. One of those boys, who loved to play with his companions, observed that, by tying a string from the handle of the valve which opened this communication to another part of the machine, the valve would open and shut without his assistance, and leave him at liberty to divert himself with his playfellows. One of the greatest improvements that has been made upon this machine, since it was first invented, was in this manner the discovery of a boy who wanted to save his own labour.

All the improvements in machinery, however, have by no means been the inventions of those who had occasion to use the machines. Many improvements have been made by the ingenuity of the makers of the machines, when to make them became the business of a peculiar trade; and some by that of those who are called philosophers or men of speculation, whose trade it is not to do anything, but to observe everything; and who, upon that account, are often capable of combining together the powers of the most distant and dissimilar objects. In the progress of society, philosophy or speculation becomes, like every other employment, the principal or sole trade and occupation of a particular class of citizens. Like every other employment too, it is subdivided into a great number of different branches, each of which affords occupation to a peculiar tribe or class of philosophers; and this subdivision of employment in philosophy, as well as in every other business, improves dexterity, and saves time. Each individual becomes more expert in his own peculiar branch, more work is done upon the whole, and the quantity of science is considerably increased by it.

It is the great multiplication of the productions of all the different arts, in consequence of the division of labour, which occasions, in a well-governed society, that universal opulence which extends itself to the lowest ranks of the people. Every workman has a great quantity of his own work to dispose of beyond what he himself has occasion for; and every other workman being exactly in the same situation, he is enabled to exchange a great quantity of his own goods for a great quantity, or, what comes to the same thing, for the price of a great quantity of theirs. He supplies them abundantly with what they have occasion for, and they accommodate him as amply with what he has occasion for, and a general plenty diffuses itself through all the different ranks of the society.

Observe the accommodation of the most common artificer or day-labourer in a civilized and thriving country, and you will perceive that the number of people of whose industry a part, though but a small part, has been employed in procuring him this accommodation, exceeds all computation. The woollen coat, for example, which covers the day-labourer, as coarse and rough as it may appear, is the produce of the joint labour of a great multitude of workmen. The shepherd, the sorter of the wool, the wool-comber or carder, the dyer, the scribbler, the spinner, the weaver, the fuller, the dresser, with many others, must all join their different arts in order to complete even this homely production. How many merchants and carriers, besides, must have been employed in transporting the materials from some of those workmen to others who often live in a very distant part of the country! how much commerce and navigation in particular, how many ship-builders, sailors, sail-makers, rope-makers, must have been employed in order to bring together the different drugs made use of by the dyer, which often come from the remotest corners of the world! What a variety of labour too is necessary in order to produce the tools of the meanest of those workmen! To say nothing of such complicated machines as the ship of the sailor, the mill of the fuller, or even the loom of the weaver, let us consider only what a variety of labour is requisite in order to form that very simple machine, the shears with which the shepherd clips the wool. The miner, the builder of the furnace for smelting the ore, the feller of the timber, the burner of the charcoal to be made use of in the smelting-house, the brickmaker, the bricklayer, the workmen who attend the furnace, the millwright, the forger, the smith, must all of them join their different arts in order to produce them. Were we to examine, in the same manner, all the different parts of his dress and household furniture, the coarse linen shirt which he wears next his skin, the shoes which cover his feet, the bed which he lies on, and all the different parts which compose it, the kitchen-grate at which he prepares his victuals, the coals which he makes use of for that purpose, dug from the bowels of the earth, and brought to him perhaps by a long sea and a long land carriage, all the other utensils of his kitchen, all the furniture of his table, the knives and forks, the earthen or pewter plates upon which he serves up and divides his victuals, the different hands employed in preparing his bread and his beer, the glass window which lets in the heat and the light, and keeps out the wind and the rain, with all the knowledge and art requisite for preparing that beautiful and happy invention, without which these northern parts of the world could scarce have afforded a very comfortable habitation, together with the tools of all the different workmen employed in producing those different conveniences; if we examine, I say, all these things, and consider what a variety of labour is employed about each of them, we shall be sensible that without the assistance and co-operation of many thousands, the very meanest person in a civilized country could not be provided, even according to, what we may falsely imagine, the easy and simple manner in which he is commonly accommodated. Compared, indeed, with the more extravagant luxury of the great, his accommodation must no doubt appear extremely simple and easy; and yet it may be true, perhaps, that the accommodation of an European prince does not always so much exceed that of an industrious and frugal peasant, as the accommodation of the latter exceeds that of many an African king, the absolute master of the lives and liberties of ten thousand naked savages.

Chapter II. Of the Principle Which Gives Occasion to the Division of Labour

. . . As it is by treaty, by barter, and by purchase, that we obtain from one another the greater part of those mutual good offices which we stand in need of, so it is this same trucking disposition which originally gives occasion to the division of labour.

In a tribe of hunters or shepherds a particular person makes bows and arrows, for example, with more readiness and dexterity than any other. He frequently exchanges them for cattle or for venison with his companions; and he finds at last that he can in this manner get more cattle and venison, than if he himself went to the field to catch them. From a regard to his own interest, therefore, the making of bows and arrows grows to be his chief business, and he becomes a sort of armourer. Another excels in making the frames and covers of their little huts or moveable houses. He is accustomed to be of use in this way to his neighbours, who reward him in the same manner with cattle and with venison, till at last he finds it his interest to dedicate himself entirely to this employment, and to become a sort of house carpenter. In the same manner a third becomes a smith or a brazier; a fourth a tanner or dresser of hides or skins, the principal part of the clothing of the savages. And thus the certainty of being able to exchange all that surplus part of the produce of his own labour, which is over and above his own consumption, for such parts of the produce of other men's labour as he may have occasion for, encourages every man to apply himself to a particular occupation, and to cultivate and bring to perfection whatever talent or genius he may possess for that particular species of business.

The difference of natural talents in different men is, in reality, much less than we are aware of; and the very different genius which appears to distinguish men of different professions, when grown up to maturity, is not upon many occasions so much the cause, as the effect of the division of labour. The difference between the most dissimilar characters, between a philosopher and a common street porter, for example, seems to arise not so much from nature, as from habit, custom, and education. When they came into the world, and for the first six or eight years of their existence, they were, perhaps, very much alike, and neither their parents nor playfellows could perceive any remarkable difference. About that age, or soon after, they come to be employed in very different occupations. The difference of talents comes then to be taken notice of, and widens by degrees, till at last the vanity of the philosopher is willing to acknowledge scarce any resemblance. But without the disposition to truck, barter, and exchange, every man must have procured to himself every necessary and conveniency of life which he wanted. All must have had the same duties to perform, and the same work to do, and there could have been no such difference of employment as could alone give occasion to any great difference of talents.

As it is this disposition which forms that difference of talents, so remarkable among men of different professions, so it is this same disposition which renders that difference useful. Many tribes of animals acknowledged to be all of the same species, derive from nature a much more remarkable distinction of genius, than what, antecedent to custom and education, appears to take place among men. By nature a philosopher is not in genius and disposition half so different from a street porter, as a mastiff is from a greyhound, or a greyhound from a spaniel, or this last from a shepherd's dog. Those different tribes of animals, however, though all of the same species, are of scarce any use to one another. The strength of the mastiff is not in the least supported either by the swiftness of the greyhound, or by the sagacity of the spaniel, or by the docility of the shepherd's dog. The effects of those different geniuses and talents, for want of the power or disposition to barter and exchange, cannot be brought into a common stock, and do not in the least contribute to the better accommodation and conveniency of the species. Each animal is still obliged to support and defend itself, separately and independently, and derives no sort of advantage from that variety of talents with which nature has distinguished its fellows. Among men, on the contrary, the most dissimilar geniuses are of use to one another; the different produces of their respective talents, by the general disposition to truck, barter, and exchange, being brought, as it were, into a common stock, where every man may purchase whatever part of the produce of other men's talents he has occasion for. . . .

Chapter VII. Of the Natural and Market Price of Commodities

There is in every society or neighbourhood an ordinary or average rate both of wages and profit in every different employment of labour and stock. This rate is naturally regulated, as I shall show hereafter, partly by the general circumstances of the society, their riches or poverty, their advancing, stationary, or declining condition; and partly by the particular nature of each employment.

There is likewise in every society or neighbourhood an ordinary or average rate of rent, which is regulated too, as I shall show hereafter, partly by the general circumstances of the society or neighbourhood in which the land is situated, and partly by the natural or improved fertility of the land.

These ordinary or average rates may be called the natural rates of wages, profit, and rent, at the time and place in which they commonly prevail.

When the price of any commodity is neither more nor less than what is sufficient to pay the rent of the land, the wages of the labour, and the profits of the stock employed in raising, preparing, and bringing it to market, according to their natural rates, the commodity is then sold for what may be called its natural price.

The commodity is then sold precisely for what it is worth, or for what it really costs the person who brings it to market; for though in common language what is called the prime cost of any commodity does not comprehend the profit of the person who is to sell it again, yet if he sells it at a price which does not allow him the ordinary rate of profit in his neighbourhood, he is evidently a loser by the trade; since by employing his stock in some other way he might have made that profit. His profit, besides, is his revenue, the proper fund of his subsistence. As, while he is preparing and bringing the goods to market, he advances to his workmen their wages, or their subsistence; so he advances to himself, in the same manner, his own subsistence, which is generally suitable to the profit which he may reasonably expect from the sale of his goods. Unless they yield him this profit, therefore, they do not repay him what they may very properly be said to have really cost him.

Though the price, therefore, which leaves him this profit, is not always the lowest at which a dealer may sometimes sell his goods, it is the lowest at which he is likely to sell them for any considerable time; at least where there is perfect liberty, or where he may change his trade as often as he pleases.

The actual price at which any commodity is commonly sold is called its market price. It may either be above, or below, or exactly the same with its natural price.

The market price of every particular commodity is regulated by the proportion between the quantity which is actually brought to market, and the demand of those who are willing to pay the natural price of the commodity, or the whole value of the rent, labour, and profit, which must be paid in order to bring it thither. Such people may be called the effectual demanders, and their demand the effectual demand: since it may be sufficient to effectuate the bringing of the commodity to market. It is different from the absolute demand. A very poor man may be said in some sense to have a demand for a coach and six; he might like to have it; but his demand is not an effectual demand, as the commodity can never be brought to market in order to satisfy it.

When the quantity of any commodity which is brought to market falls short of the effectual demand, all those who are willing to pay the whole value of the rent, wages, and profit, which must be paid in order to bring it thither, cannot be supplied with the quantity which they want. Rather than want it altogether, some of them will be willing to give more. A competition will immediately begin among them, and the market price will rise more or less above the natural price, according as either the greatness of the deficiency, or the wealth and wanton luxury of the competitors, happen to animate more or less the eagerness of the competition. Among competitors of equal wealth and luxury the same deficiency will generally occasion a more or less eager competition, according as the acquisition of the commodity happens to be of more or less importance to them. Hence the exorbitant price of the necessaries of life during the blockade of a town or in a famine.

When the quantity brought to market exceeds the effectual demand, it cannot be all sold to those who are willing to pay the whole value of the rent, wages, and profit, which must be paid in order to bring it thither. Some part must be sold to those who are willing to pay less, and the low price which they give for it must reduce the price of the whole. The market price will sink more or less below the natural price, according as the greatness of the excess increases more or less the competition of the sellers, or according as it happens to be more or less important to them to get immediately rid of the commodity. The same excess in the importation of perishables, will occasion a much greater competition than in that of durable commodities; in the importation of oranges, for example, than in that of old iron.

When the quantity brought to market is just sufficient to supply the effectual demand and no more, the market price naturally comes to be either exactly, or as nearly as can be judged of, the same with the natural price. The whole quantity upon hand can be disposed of for this price, and cannot be disposed of for more. The competition of the different dealers obliges them all to accept of this price, but does not oblige them to accept of less.

The quantity of every commodity brought to market naturally suits itself to the effectual demand. It is the interest of all those who employ their land, labour, or stock, in bringing any commodity to market, that the quantity never should exceed the effectual demand; and it is the interest of all other people that it never should fall short of that demand.

If at any time it exceeds the effectual demand, some of the component parts of its price must be paid below their natural rate. If it is rent, the interest of the landlords will immediately prompt them to withdraw a part of their land; and if it is wages or profit, the interest of the labourers in the one case, and of their employers in the other, will prompt them to withdraw a part of their labour or stock from this employment. The quantity brought to market will soon be no more than sufficient to supply the effectual demand. All the different parts of its price will rise to their natural rate, and the whole price to its natural price.

If, on the contrary, the quantity brought to market should at any time fall short of the effectual demand, some of the component parts of its price must rise above their natural rate. If it is rent, the interest of all other landlords will naturally prompt them to prepare more land for the arising of this commodity; if it is wages or profit, the interest of all other labourers and dealers will soon prompt them to employ more labour and stock in preparing and bringing it to market. The quantity brought thither will soon be sufficient to supply the effectual demand. All the different parts of its price will soon sink to their natural rate, and the whole price to its natural price.

The natural price, therefore, is, as it were, the central price, to which the prices of all commodities are continually gravitating. Different accidents may sometimes keep them suspended a good deal above it, and sometimes force them down even somewhat below it. But whatever may be the obstacles which hinder them from settling in this center of repose and continuance, they are constantly tending towards it. . . .

BOOK IV. OF SYSTEMS OF POLITICAL ECONOMY

Introduction

Political economy, considered as a branch of the science of a statesman or legislator, proposes two distinct objects: first, to provide a plentiful revenue or subsistence for the people, or more properly to enable them to provide such a revenue or subsistence for themselves; and secondly, to supply the state or commonwealth with a revenue sufficient for the public services. It proposes to enrich both the people and the sovereign.

The different progress of opulence in different ages and nations, has given occasion to two different systems of political economy, with regard to enriching the people. The one may be called the system of commerce, the other that of agriculture. I shall endeavour to explain both as fully and distinctly as I can, and shall begin with the system of commerce. It is the modern system, and is best understood in our own country and in our own times.

Chapter I. Of the Principle of the Commercial, or Mercantile System

. . . The importation of gold and silver is not the principal, much less the sole benefit which a nation derives from its foreign trade. Between whatever places foreign trade is carried on, they all of them derive two distinct benefits from it. It carries out that surplus part of the produce of their land and labour for which there is no demand among them, and brings back in return for it something else for which there is a demand. It gives a value to their superfluities, by exchanging them for something else, which may satisfy a part of their wants, and increase their enjoyments. By means of it, the narrowness of the home market does not hinder the division of labour in any particular branch of art or manufacture from being carried to the highest perfection. By opening a more extensive market for whatever part of the produce of their labour may exceed the home consumption, it encourages them to improve its productive powers, and to augment its annual produce to the utmost, and thereby to increase the real revenue and wealth of the society. These great and important services foreign trade is continually occupied in performing, to all the different countries between which it is carried on. They all derive great benefit from it, though that in which the merchant resides generally derives the greatest, as he is generally more employed in supplying the wants, and carrying out the superfluities of his own, than of any other particular country. To import the gold and silver which may be wanted, into the countries which have no mines, is, no doubt, a part of the business of foreign commerce. It is, however, a most insignificant part of it. A country which carried on foreign trade merely upon this account, could scarce have occasion to freight a ship in a century.

It is not by the importation of gold and silver, that the discovery of America has enriched Europe. By the abundance of the American mines, those metals have become cheaper. A service of plate can now be purchased for about a third part of the corn, or a third part of the labour, which it would have cost in the fifteenth century. With the same annual expense of labour and commodities, Europe can annually purchase about three times the quantity of plate which it could have purchased at that time. But when a commodity comes to be sold for a third part of what had been its usual price, not only those who purchased it before can purchase three times their former quantity, but it is brought down to the level of a much greater number of purchasers, perhaps no more than ten, perhaps no more than twenty times the former number. So that there may be in Europe at present not only more than three times, but more than twenty or thirty times the quantity of plate which would have been in it, even in its present state of improvement, had the discovery of the American mines never been made. So far Europe has, no doubt, gained a real conveniency, though surely a very trifling one. The cheapness of gold and silver renders those metals rather less fit for the purposes of money than they were before. In order to make the same purchases, we must load ourselves with a greater quantity of them, and carry about a shilling in our pocket where a groat would have done before. It is difficult to say which is most trifling, this inconveniency, or the opposite conveniency. Neither the one nor the other could have made any very essential change in the state of Europe. The discovery of America, however, certainly made a most essential one. By opening a new and inexhaustible market to all the commodities of Europe, it gave occasion to new divisions of labour and improvements of art, which, in the narrow circle of the ancient commerce, could never have taken place for want of a market to take off the greater part of their produce. The productive powers of labour were improved, and its produce increased in all the different countries of Europe, and together with it the real revenue and wealth of the inhabitants. The commodities of Europe were almost all new to America, and many of those of America were new to Europe. A new set of exchanges, therefore, began to take place which had never been thought of before, and which should naturally have proved as advantageous to the new, as it certainly did to the old continent. The savage injustice of the Europeans rendered an event, which ought to have been beneficial to all, ruinous and destructive to several of those unfortunate countries.

The discovery of a passage to the East Indies, by the Cape of Good Hope, which happened much about the same time, opened, perhaps, a still more extensive range to foreign commerce than even that of America, notwithstanding the greater distance. There were but two nations in America, in any respect superior to savages, and these were destroyed almost as soon as discovered. The rest were mere savages. But the empires of China, Indostan, Japan, as well as several others in the East Indies, without having richer mines of gold or silver, were in every other respect much richer, better cultivated, and more advanced in all arts and manufactures than either Mexico or Peru, even though we should credit, what plainly deserves no credit, the exaggerated accounts of the Spanish writers, concerning the ancient state of those empires. But rich and civilized nations can always exchange to a much greater value with one another, than with savages and barbarians. Europe, however, has hitherto derived much less advantage from its commerce with the East Indies, than from that with America. The Portuguese monopolized the East India trade to themselves for about a century, and it was only indirectly and through them, that the other nations of Europe could either send out or receive any goods from that country. When the Dutch, in the beginning of the last century, began to encroach upon them, they vested their whole East India commerce in an exclusive company. The English, French, Swedes, and Danes, have all followed their example, so that no great nation in Europe has ever yet had the benefit of a free commerce to the East Indies. No other reason need be assigned why it has never been so advantageous as the trade to America, which, between almost every nation of Europe and its own colonies, is free to all its subjects. The exclusive privileges of those East India companies, their great riches, the great favour and protection which these have procured them from their respective governments, have excited much envy against them. This envy has frequently represented their trade as altogether pernicious, on account of the great quantities of silver, which it every year exports from the countries from which it is carried on. The parties concerned have replied, that their trade, by this continual exportation of silver, might, indeed, tend to impoverish Europe in general, but not the particular country from which it was carried on; because, by the exportation of a part of the returns to other European countries, it annually brought home a much greater quantity of that metal than it carried out. Both the objection and the reply are founded in the popular notion which I have been just now examining. It is, therefore, unnecessary to say anything further about either. By the annual exportation of silver to the East Indies, plate is probably somewhat dearer in Europe than it otherwise might have been; and coined silver probably purchases a larger quantity both of labour and commodities. The former of these two effects is a very small loss, the latter a very small advantage; both too insignificant to deserve any part of the public attention. The trade to the East Indies, by opening a market to the commodities of Europe, or, what comes nearly to the same thing, to the gold and silver which is purchased with those commodities, must necessarily tend to increase the annual production of European commodities, and consequently the real wealth and revenue of Europe. That it has hitherto increased them so little, is probably owing to the restraints which it everywhere labours under. . . .

Chapter II. Of Restraints upon the Importation from Foreign Countries of Such Goods as Can Be Produced at Home

. . . The general industry of the society never can exceed what the capital of the society can employ. As the number of workmen that can be kept in employment by any particular person must bear a certain proportion to his capital, so the number of those that can be continually employed by all the members of a great society, must bear a certain proportion to the whole capital of that society, and never can exceed that proportion. No regulation of commerce can increase the quantity of industry in any society beyond what its capital can maintain. It can only divert a part of it into a direction into which it might not otherwise have gone; and it is by no means certain that this artificial direction is likely to be more advantageous to the society than that into which it would have gone of its own accord.

Every individual is continually exerting himself to find out the most advantageous employment for whatever capital he can command. It is his own advantage, indeed, and not that of the society, which he has in view. But the study of his own advantage naturally, or rather necessarily leads him to prefer that employment which is most advantageous to the society.

First, every individual endeavours to employ his capital as near home as he can, and consequently as much as he can in the support of domestic industry; provided always that he can thereby obtain the ordinary, or not a great deal less than the ordinary profits of stock. . . .

Secondly, every individual who employs his capital in the support of domestic industry, necessarily endeavours so to direct that industry, that its produce may be of the greatest possible value.

The produce of industry is what it adds to the subject or materials upon which it is employed. In proportion as the value of this produce is great or small, so will likewise be the profits of the employer. But it is only for the sake of profit that any man employs a capital in the support of industry; and he will always, therefore, endeavour to employ it in the support of that industry of which the produce is likely to be of the greatest value, or to exchange for the greatest quantity either of money or of other goods.

But the annual revenue of every society is always precisely equal to the exchangeable value of the whole annual produce of its industry, or rather is precisely the same thing with that exchangeable value. As every individual, therefore, endeavours as much as he can both to employ his capital in the support of domestic industry, and so to direct that industry that its produce may be of the greatest value; every individual necessarily labours to render the annual revenue of the society as great as he can. He generally, indeed, neither intends to promote the public interest, nor knows how much he is promoting it. By preferring the support of domestic to that of foreign industry, he intends only his own security; and by directing that industry in such a manner as its produce may be of the greatest value, he intends only his own gain, and he is in this, as in many other cases, led by an invisible hand to promote an end which was no part of his intention. Nor is it always the worse for the society that it was no part of it. By pursuing his own interest he frequently promotes that of the society more effectually than when he really intends to promote it. I have never known much good done by those who affected to trade for the public good. It is an affectation, indeed, not very common among merchants, and very few words need be employed in dissuading them from it.

What is the species of domestic industry which his capital can employ, and of which the produce is likely to be of the greatest value, every individual, it is evident, can, in his local situation, judge much better than any statesman or lawgiver can do for him. The statesman who should attempt to direct private people in what manner they ought to employ their capitals, would not only load himself with a most unnecessary attention, but assume an authority which could safely be trusted, not only to no single person, but to no council or senate whatever, and which would nowhere be so dangerous as in the hands of a man who had folly and presumption enough to fancy himself fit to exercise it.

To give the monopoly of the home-market to the produce of domestic industry, in any particular art or manufacture, is in some measure to direct private people in what manner they ought to employ their capitals, and must, in almost all cases, be either a useless or a hurtful regulation. If the produce of domestic can be brought there as cheap as that of foreign industry, the regulation is evidently useless. If it cannot, it must generally be hurtful. It is the maxim of every prudent master of a family, never to attempt to make at home what it will cost him more to make than to buy. The taylor does not attempt to make his own shoes, but buys them of the shoemaker. The shoemaker does not attempt to make his own clothes, but employs a taylor. The farmer attempts to make neither the one nor the other, but employs those different artificers. All of them find it for their interest to employ their whole industry in a way in which they have some advantage over their neighbours, and to purchase with a part of its produce, or what is the same thing, with the price of a part of it, whatever else they have occasion for.

What is prudence in the conduct of every private family, can scarce be folly in that of a great kingdom. If a foreign country can supply us with a commodity cheaper than we ourselves can make it, better buy it of them with some part of the produce of our own industry, employed in a way in which we have some advantage. The general industry of the country, being always in proportion to the capital which employs it, will not thereby be diminished, no more than that of the above-mentioned artificers; but only left to find out the way in which it can be employed with the greatest advantage. It is certainly not employed to the greatest advange, when it is thus directed towards an object which it can buy cheaper than it can make. The value of its annual produce is certainly more or less diminished, when it is thus turned away from producing commodities evidently of more value than the commodity which it is directed to produce. According to the supposition, that commodity could be purchased from foreign countries cheaper than it can be made at home. It could, therefore, have been purchased with a part only of the commodities, or, what is the same thing, with a part only of the price of the commodities, which the industry employed by an equal capital would have produced at home, had it been left to follow its natural course. The industry of the country, therefore, is thus turned away from a more to a less advantageous employment, and the exchangeable values of its annual produce, instead of being increased, according to the intention of the lawgiver, must necessarily be diminished by every such regulation. . . .

To expect, indeed, that the freedom of trade should ever be entirely restored in Great Britain, is as absurd as to expect that an Oceana or Utopia should ever be established in it. Not only the prejudices of the public, but what is much more unconquerable, the private interests of many individuals, irresistibly oppose it. Were the officers of the army to oppose with the same zeal and unanimity any reduction in the number of forces, with which master manufacturers set themselves against every law that is likely to increase the number of their rivals in the home market; were the former to animate their soldiers, in the same manner as the latter enflame their workmen, to attack with violence and outrage the proposers of any such regulation; to attempt to reduce the army would be as dangerous as it has now become to attempt to diminish in any respect the monopoly which our manufacturers have obtained against us. This monopoly has so much increased the number of some particular tribes of them, that, like an overgrown standing army, they have become formidable to the government, and upon many occasions intimidate the legislature. The member of parliament who supports every proposal for strengthening this monopoly, is sure to acquire not only the reputation of understanding trade, but great popularity and influence with an order of men whose numbers and wealth render them of great importance. If he opposes them, on the contrary, and still more if he has authority enough to be able to thwart them, neither the most acknowledged probity, nor the highest rank, nor the greatest public services, can protect him from the most infamous abuse and detraction, from personal insults, nor sometimes from real danger, arising from the insolent outrage of furious and disappointed monopolists.

The undertaker of a great manufacture, who, by the home markets being suddenly laid open to the competition of foreigners, should be obliged to abandon his trade, would no doubt suffer very considerably. That part of his capital which had usually been employed in purchasing materials and in paying his workmen, might, without much difficulty, perhaps, find another employment. But that part of it which was fixed in workhouses, and in the instruments of trade, could scarce be disposed of without considerable loss. The equitable regard, therefore, to his interest requires that changes of this kind should never be introduced suddenly, but slowly, gradually, and after a very long warning. The legislature, were it possible that its deliberations could be always directed, not by the clamorous importunity of partial interests, but by an extensive view of the general good, ought upon this very account, perhaps, to be particularly careful neither to establish any new monopolies of this kind, nor to extend further those which are already established. Every such regulation introduces some degree of real disorder into the constitution of the state, which it will be difficult afterwards to cure without occasioning another disorder. . . .

Chapter IX. Of Agricultural Systems

. . . The greatest and most important branch of the commerce of every nation, it has already been observed, is that which is carried on between the inhabitants of the town and those of the country. The inhabitants of the town draw from the country the rude produce which constitutes both the materials of their work and the fund of their subsistence; and they pay for this rude produce by sending back to the country a certain portion of it manufactured and prepared for immediate use. The trade which is carried on between these two different sets of people, consists ultimately in a certain quantity of rude produce exchanged for a certain quantity of manufactured produce. The dearer the latter, therefore, the cheaper the former; and whatever tends in any country to raise the price of manufactured produce, tends to lower that of the rude produce of the land, and thereby to discourage agriculture. The smaller the quantity of manufactured produce which any given quantity of rude produce, or, what comes to the same thing, which the price of any given quantity of rude produce is capable of purchasing, the smaller the exchangeable value of that given quantity of rude produce; the smaller the encouragement which either the landlord has to increase its quantity by improving, or the farmer by cultivating the land. Whatever, besides, tends to diminish in any country the number of artificers and manufacturers, tends to diminish the home market, the most important of all markets for the rude produce of the land, and thereby still further to discourage agriculture.

Those systems, therefore, which preferring agriculture to all other employments, in order to promote it, impose restraints upon manufacturers and foreign trade, act contrary to the very end which they propose, and indirectly discourage that very species of industry which they mean to promote. They are so far, perhaps, more inconsistent than even the mercantile system. That system, by encouraging manufactures and foreign trade more than agriculture, turns a certain portion of the capital of the society from supporting a more advantageous, to support a less advantageous species of industry. But still it really and in the end encourages that species of industry which it means to promote. Those agricultural systems, on the contrary, really and in the end discourage their own favourite species of industry.

It is thus that every system which endeavours, either, by extraordinary encouragements, to draw towards a particular species of industry a greater share of the capital of the society than what would naturally go to it; or, by extraordinary restraints, to force from a particular species of industry some share of the capital which would otherwise be employed in it; is in reality subversive of the great purpose which it means to promote. It retards, instead of accelerating, the progress of the society towards real wealth and greatness; and diminishes, instead of increasing, the real value of the annual produce of its land and labour.

All systems either of preference or of restraint, therefore, being thus completely taken away, the obvious and simple system of natural liberty establishes itself of its own accord. Every man, as long as he does not violate the laws of justice, is left perfectly free to pursue his own interest his own way, and to bring both his industry and capital into competition with those of any other man, or order of men. The sovereign is completely discharged from a duty, in the attempting to perform which he must always be exposed to innumerable delusions, and for the proper performance of which no human wisdom or knowledge could ever be sufficient; the duty of superintending the industry of private people, and of directing it towards the employments most suitable to the interest of the society. According to the system of natural liberty, the sovereign has only three duties to attend to; three duties of great importance, indeed, but plain and intelligible to common understandings: first, the duty of protecting the society from the violence and invasion of other independent societies; secondly, the duty of protecting, as far as possible, every member of the society from the injustice or oppression of every other member of it, or the duty of establishing an exact administration of justice; and, thirdly, the duty of erecting and maintaining certain public works and certain public institutions, which it can never be for the interest of any individual, or small number of individuals, to erect and maintain; because the profit could never repay the expence to any individual or small number of individuals, though it may frequently do much more than repay it to a great society.

The proper performance of those several duties of the sovereign necessarily supposes a certain expense; and this expense again necessarily requires a certain revenue to support it. In the following book, therefore, I shall endeavour to explain; first, what are the necessary expenses of the sovereign or commonwealth; and which of those expenses ought to be defrayed by the general contribution of the whole society; and which of them, by that of some particular part only, or of some particular members of the society: secondly, what are the different methods in which the whole society may be made to contribute towards defraying the expenses incumbent on the whole society, and what are the principal advantages and inconveniences of each of those methods: and thirdly, what are the reasons and causes which have induced almost all modern governments to mortgage some part of this revenue, or to contract debts, and what have been the effects of those debts upon the real wealth, the annual produce of the land and labour of the society. The following book, therefore, will naturally be divided into three chapters.

ON CRIMES AND PUNISHMENTS

Beccaria

It was inevitable that the philosophes *of the eighteenth century, in their attempt to bring all social institutions and ideas out of the shadow of obscurity into the sunlight of reason, would turn their attention to the subject of penology and criminology. In no area of life had there been a more haphazard history of semirational and irrational attempts to solve serious social problems; no area was more crucial in laying the foundations of a "rational society." In no area, we might add, did their studies have a wider-ranging or longer-lasting impact.*

The selection comes from the essay On Crimes and Punishments *by a young Italian nobleman. Cesare Bonesano, Marchese di Beccaria (1735–1794). Especially from the date of its French translation by the Abbé Morellet (1764), the essay immediately pointed out the illogic of current European practices and inspired a wave of reforms of great significance, such as the elimination of torture in ordinary criminal cases.*

Until the comparable revolution in the twentieth century emphasizing the sociological and psychological aspects of crime, Beccaria was the great pioneer of modern criminology.

The selection is mainly from the central sections of the work dealing with the philosophical foundations of law in general and the proper relationship between punishment and crime. The chapter on capital punishment quickly became a classic, as did the famous forty-first chapter on the prevention of crime.

TO THE READER

Some remnants of the laws of an ancient conquering people, which a prince who reigned in Constantinople some 1,200 years ago * caused to be compiled, mixed up afterwards with Lombard rites and packed in the miscellaneous volumes of private and obscure commentators—these are what form that set of traditional opinions which from a great part of Europe receive nevertheless the name of laws; and to this day it is a fact, as disastrous as it is common, that some opinion of Carpzovius some old custom pointed out by Clarus, or some form of torture suggested in terms of complacent ferocity by Farinaccius, constitute the laws, so carelessly followed by those, who in all trembling ought to exercise their government over the lives and fortunes of men. These laws, the dregs of the most barbarous ages, are examined in this book in so far as regards criminal jurisprudence, and I have dared to expose their faults to the directors of the public happiness in a style which may keep at a distance the unenlightened and intolerant multitude. The spirit of frank inquiry after truth, of freedom from commonplace opinions, in which this book is written, is a result of the mild and enlightened Government under which the Author lives. The great monarchs, the benefactors of humanity, who are now our rulers, love the truths expounded, with force but without fanaticism, by the obscure philosopher, who is only roused to indignation by the excesses of tyranny, but is restrained by reason; and existing abuses, for whosoever well studies all the circumstances, are the satire and reproach of past ages, and by no means of the present age or of its lawgivers. . . .

CHAPTER I. INTRODUCTION

Men for the most part leave the regulation of their chief concerns to the prudence of the moment, or to the discretion of those whose interest it is to oppose the wisest

Marchese di Beccaria, *On Crimes and Punishments,* **trans. James Anson Farrer (London: Chatto and Windus, 1880), pp. 111–112, 117–124, 132–134, 146–152, 165–180, 196–201, 242–246, 249–251.**

* [The reference is to the Code of Justinian. (*Ed.*)]

laws; such laws, namely, as naturally help to diffuse the benefits of life, and check that tendency they have to accumulate in the hands of a few, which ranges on one side of the extreme of power and happiness, and on the other all that is weak and wretched. It is only, therefore, after having passed through a thousand errors in matters that most nearly touch their lives and liberties, only after weariness of evils that have been suffered to reach a climax, that men are induced to seek a remedy for the abuses which oppress them, and to recognize the clearest truths, which, precisely on account of their simplicity, escape the notice of ordinary minds, unaccustomed as they are to analyse things, and apt to receive their impressions anyhow, from tradition rather than from inquiry.

We shall see, if we open histories, that laws, which are or ought to be covenants between free men, have generally been nothing but the instrument of the passions of some few men, or the result of some accidental and temporary necessity. They have never been dictated by an unimpassioned student of human nature, able to concentrate the actions of a multitude of men to a single point of view, and to consider them from that point alone—*the greatest happiness divided among the greatest number*. Happy are those few nations which have not waited for the slow movement of human combinations and changes to cause an approach to better things, after intolerable evils, but have hastened the intermediate steps by good laws; and deserving is that philosopher of the gratitude of mankind, who had the courage, from the obscurity of his despised study, to scatter abroad among the people the first seeds, so long fruitless, of useful truths.

The knowledge of the true relations between a sovereign and his subjects, and of those between different nations; the revival of commerce by the light of philosophical truths, diffused by printing; and the silent international war of industry, the most humane and the most worthy of rational men—these are the fruits which we owe to the enlightenment of this century. But how few have examined and combated the cruelty of punishments, and the irregularities of criminal procedures, a part of legislation so elementary and yet so neglected in almost the whole of Europe; and how few have sought, by a return to first principles, to dissipate the mistakes accumulated by many centuries, or to mitigate, with at least that force which belongs only to ascertained truths, the excessive caprice of ill-directed power, which has presented up to this time but one long example of lawful and cold-blooded atrocity! And yet the groans of the weak, sacrificed to the cruelty of the ignorant or to the indolence of the rich; the barbarous tortures, multiplied with a severity as useless as it is prodigal, for crimes either not proved or quite chimerical; the disgusting horrors of a prison, enhanced by that which is the cruellest executioner of the miserable—namely, uncertainty;—these ought to startle those rulers whose function it is to guide the opinion of men's minds. . . .

To examine and distinguish all the different sorts of crimes and the manner of punishing them would now be our natural task, were it not that their nature, which varies with the different circumstances of times and places, would compel us to enter upon too vast and wearisome a mass of detail. But it will suffice to indicate the most general principles and the most pernicious and common errors, in order to undeceive no less those who, from a mistaken love of liberty, would introduce anarchy, than those who would be glad to reduce their fellow-men to the uniform regularity of a convent.

What will be the penalty suitable for such and such crimes?

Is death a penalty really *useful and necessary* for the security and good order of society?

Are torture and torments *just,* and do they attain the *end* which the law aims at?

What is the best way of preventing crimes?

Are the same penalties equally useful in all times?

What influence have they on customs?

These problems deserve to be solved with such geometrical precision as shall suffice to prevail over the clouds of sophistication, over seductive eloquence, or timid doubt. Had I no other merit than that of having been the first to make clearer to Italy that which other nations have dared to write and are beginning to practise, I should deem myself fortunate; but if, in maintaining the rights of men and of invincible truth, I should contribute to rescue from the spasms and agonies of death any unfortunate victim of tyranny or ignorance, both so equally fatal, the blessings and tears of a single innocent man in the transports of his joy would console me for the contempt of mankind.

CHAPTER II. THE ORIGIN OF PUNISHMENTS—THE RIGHT OF PUNISHMENT

From Political morality, unless founded on the immutable sentiments of mankind, no lasting advantage can be hoped. Whatever law deviates from these sentiments will encounter a resistance which will ultimately prevail over it, just in the same way as a force, however slight, if constantly applied, will prevail over a violent motion applied to any physical body.

If we consult the human heart we shall therein discover the fundamental principles of the real right of the sovereign to punish crimes.

No man has gratuitously parted with a portion of his own liberty with a view to the public good; that is a chimera which only exists in romances. Each one of us would wish, if it were possible, that the covenants which bind others should not bind himself. There is no man but makes himself the central object of all the combinations of the globe.

The multiplication of the human race, slight in the abstract, but far in excess of the means afforded by nature, barren and deserted as it originally was, for the satisfaction of men's ever increasing wants, caused the first savages to associate together. The first unions necessarily led to others to oppose them, and so the state of war passed from individuals to nations.

Laws are the conditions under which men, leading independent and isolated lives, joined together in society, when tired of living in a perpetual state of war, and of enjoying a liberty which the uncertainty of its tenure rendered useless. Of this liberty they voluntarily sacrificed a part, in order to enjoy the remainder in security and quiet. The sum-total of all these portions of liberty, sacrificed for the good of each individually, constitutes the sovereignty of a nation, and the sovereign is the lawful trustee and administrator of these portions. But, besides forming this trust-fund, or deposit, it was necessary to protect it from the encroachments of individuals, whose aim it ever is not only to recover from the fund their own deposit, but to avail themselves of that contributed by others. "Sensible motives," were therefore wanted to divert the despotic will of the individual from re-plunging into their primitive chaos the laws of society. Such motives were found in punishments, established against transgressors of the laws; and I call them *sensible* motives, because experience has shown that the majority of men adopt no fixed rules of conduct, nor avoid that universal principle of dissolution, observable alike in the moral as in the physical world, save by reason of motives which directly strike the senses and constantly present themselves to the mind, counterbalancing the strong impressions of private passions, opposed as they are to the general welfare, not eloquence, nor declamations, nor the most sublime truths have ever sufficed to curb the passions for any length of time, when excited by the lively force of present objects.

As it, then, was necessity which constrained men to yield a part of their individual liberty, it is certain that each would only place in the general deposit the least possible portion—only so much, that is, as would suffice to induce others to defend it. The aggregate of these least possible portions constitutes the right of punishment; all that is beyond this is an abuse and not justice, a fact but not a right.[1] Punishments which exceed what is necesary to preserve the deposit of the public safety are in their nature unjust; and the more just punishments are, the more sacred and inviolable is personal security, and the greater the liberty that the sovereign preserves for his subjects. . . .

CHAPTER VI. IMPRISONMENT

An error, not less common than it is contrary to the object of society—that is, to the consciousness of personal security—is leaving a magistrate to be the arbitrary executor of the laws, free at his pleasure to imprison a citizen, to deprive a personal enemy of his liberty on frivolous pretexts, or to leave a friend unpunished in spite of the strongest proofs of his guilt. Imprisonment is a punishment which, unlike every other, must of necessity precede the declaration of guilt; but this distinctive character does not deprive it of the other essential of punishment, namely, that the law alone shall determine the cases under which it shall be merited. It is for the law, therefore, to point out the amount of evidence of a crime which shall justify the detention of the accused, and his subjection to examination and punishment. For such detention there may be sufficient proofs in common report, in a man's flight, in a non-judicial confession, or in the confession of an accomplice; in a man's threats against or constant

[1] *Note that the word Right is not opposed to the word Force; but the former is rather a modification of the latter; that is, the modification most advantageous to the greater number. And by justice I mean nothing else than the chain which is necessary for holding together private interests and preventing their breaking away into the original state of insociability.*

One must be careful not to attach to this word Justice the idea of anything real, as of a physical force or an independent entity; it is only a human mode of thinking, a mode that has unbounded influence over each one's happiness. Sill less do I mean that other kind of justice that has emanated from God, and has its immediate connection with the penalties and rewards of a future life.

enmity with the person injured; in all the facts of the crime, and similar indications. But these proofs should be determined by the laws, not by the judges, whose decisions, when they are not particular applications of a general maxim in a public code, are always adverse to political liberty. The more that punishments are mitigated, that misery and hunger are banished from prisons, that pity and mercy are admitted within their iron doors, and are set above the inexorable and hardened ministers of justice, the slighter will be the evidences of guilt requisite for the legal detention of the suspeceted.

A man accused of a crime, imprisoned and acquitted, ought to bear no mark of disgrace. How many Romans, accused of the gravest crimes and then found innocent, were reverenced by the people and honoured with magisterial positions! For what reason, then, is the lot of a man innocently accused so different in our own times? Because, in the criminal system now in vogue, the idea of force and might is stronger in men's minds than the idea of justice; because accused and convicted are thrown in confusion into the same dungeon; because imprisonment is rather a man's punishment than his mere custody; and because the two forces which should be united are separated from one another, namely, the internal force, which protects the laws, and the external force, which defends the throne and the nation. Were they united, the former, through the common sanction of the laws, would possess in addition a judicial capacity, although independent of that possessed by the supreme judicial power; and the glory that accompanies the pomp and ceremony of a military body would remove the infamy, which, like all popular sentiments, is more attached to the manner than the thing, as is proved by the fact that military prisons are not regarded in public estimation as so disgraceful as civil ones. There still remain among our people, in their customs and in their laws (always a hundred years, in point of merit, in arrear of the actual enlightenment of a nation), there still remain, I say, the savage impressions and fierce ideas of our ancestors of the North. . . .

CHAPTER XI. OATHS

A contradiction between the laws and the natural feelings of mankind arises from the oaths which are required of an accused, to the effect that he will be a truthful man when it is his greatest interest to be false; as if a man could really swear to contribute to his own destruction, or as if religion would not be silent with most men when their interest spoke on the other side. The experience of all ages has shown that men have abused religion more than any other of the precious gifts of heaven; and for what reason should criminals respect it, when men esteemed as the wisest have often violated it? Too weak, because too far removed from the senses, are for the mass of people the motives which religion opposes to the tumult of fear and the love of life. The affairs of heaven are conducted by laws absolutely different from those which govern human affairs; so why compromise those by these? Why place men in the terrible dilemma of either sinning against God or concurring in their own ruin? The law, in fact, which enforces such an oath commands a man either to be a bad Christian or to be a martyr. The oath becomes gradually a mere formality, thus destroying the force of religious feelings, which for the majority of men are the only pledge of their honesty. How useless oaths are has been shown by experience, for every judge will bear me out when I say that no oath has ever yet made any criminal speak the truth; and the same thing is shown by reason, which declares all laws to be useless, and consequently injurious, which are opposed to the natural sentiments of man. Such laws incur the same fate as dams placed directly in the main stream of a river: either they are immediately thrown down and overwhelmed, or a whirlpool formed by themselves corrodes and undermines them imperceptibly.

CHAPTER XII. TORTURE

A cruelty consecrated among most nations by custom is the torture of the accused during his trial, on the pretext of compelling him to confess his crime, of clearing up contradictions in his statements, of discovering his accomplices, of purging him in some metaphysical and incomprehensible way from infamy, or finally of finding out other crimes of which he may possibly be guilty, but of which he is not accused.

A man cannot be called *guilty* before sentence has been passed on him by a judge, nor can society deprive him of its protection till it has been decided that he has broken the condition on which it was granted. What, then, is that right but one of mere might by which a judge is empowered to inflict a punishment on a citizen whilst his guilt or innocence are still undetermined? The following dilemma is no new one: either the crime is certain or uncertain; if certain, no other punishment is suitable for it than that affixed to it by law; and torture is useless, for the same reason that the criminal's confession is useless. If it is uncertain, it is wrong to torture an innocent person, such as the law adjudges him to be, whose crimes are not yet proved.

What is the political object of punishments? The intimidation of other men. But what shall we say of the secret and private tortures which the tyranny of custom exercises alike upon the guilty and the innocent? It is important, indeed, that no open crime shall pass unpunished; but the public exposure of a criminal whose crime was hidden in darkness is utterly useless. An evil that has been done and cannot be undone can only be punished by civil society in so far as it may affect others with the hope of impunity. If it be true that there are a greater number of men who either from fear or virtue respect the laws than of those who transgress them, the risk of torturing an innocent man should be estimated according to the probabilty that any man will have been more likely, other things being equal, to have respected than to have despised the laws.

But I say in addition: it is to seek to confound all the relations of things to require a man to be at the same time accuser and accused, to make pain the crucible of truth, as if the test of it lay in the muscles and sinews of an unfortunate wretch. The law which ordains the use of torture is a law which says to men: "Resist pain; and if Nature has created in you an inextinguishable self-love, if she has given you an inalienable right of self-defence, I create in you a totally contrary affection, namely, an heroic self-hatred, and I command you to accuse yourselves, and to speak the truth between the laceration of your muscles and the dislocation of your bones."

This infamous crucible of truth is a still-existing monument of that primitive and savage legal system, which called trials by fire and boiling water, or the accidental decisions of combat, *judgments of God,* as if the rings of the eternal chain in the control of the First Cause must at every moment be disarranged and put out for the petty institutions of mankind. The only difference between torture and the trial by fire and water is, that the result of the former seems to depend on the will of the acccused, and that of the other two on a fact which is purely physical and extrinsic to the sufferer; but the difference is only apparent, not real. The avowal of truth under tortures and agonies is as little free as was in those times the prevention without fraud of the usual effects of fire and boiling water. Every act of our will is ever proportioned to the force of the sensible impression which causes it, and the sensibility of every man is limited. Hence the impression produced by pain may be so intense as to occupy a man's entire sensibility and leave him no other liberty than the choice of the shortest way of escape, for the present moment, from his penalty. Under such circumstances the answer of the accused is as inevitable as the impressions produced by fire and water; and the innocent man who is sensitive will declare himself guilty, when by so doing he hopes to bring his agonies to an end. All the difference between guilt and innocence is lost by virtue of the very means which they profess to employ for its discovery.

Torture is a certain method for the acquittal of robust villains and for the condemnation of inocent but feeble men. See the fatal drawbacks of this pretended test of truth —a test, indeed, that is worthy of cannibals; a test which the Romans, barbarous as they too were in many respects, reserved for slaves alone, the victims of their fierce and too highly lauded virtue. Of two men, equally innocent or equally guilty, the robust and courageous will be acquitted, the weak and the timid will be condemned, by virtue of the following exact train of reasoning on the part of the judge: "I as judge had to find you guilty of such and such a crime; you, AB, have by your physical strength been able to resist pain, and therefore I acquit you; you, CD, in your weakness have yielded to it; therefore I condemn you. I feel that a confession extorted amid torments can have no force, but I will torture you afresh unless you corroborate what you have now confessed."

The result, then, of torture is a matter of temperament, of calculation, which varies with each man according to his strength and sensibility; so that by this method a mathematician might solve better than a judge this problem: "Given the muscular force and the nervous sensibility of an innocent man, to find the degree of pain which will cause him to plead guilty to a given crime."

The object of examining an accused man is the ascertainment of truth. But if this truth is difficult to discover from a man's air, demeanour, or countenance, even when he is quiet, much more difficult will it be to discover from a man upon whose face all the signs, whereby most men, sometimes in spite of themselves, express the truth, are distorted by pain. Every violent action confuses and causes to disappear those trifling differences between objects, by which one may sometimes distinguish the true from the false.

A strange consequence that flows naturally from the use of torture is, that an innocent man is thereby placed in a worse condition than a guilty one, because if both are tortured the former has every alternative against him. For either he confesses the crime and is condemned, or he is declared innocent, having suffered an undeserved punishment. But the guilty man has one chance in his favour, since, if he resist the torture firmly, and is acquitted in consequence, he has exchanged a greater penalty for a smaller one. Therefore the innocent man can only lose, the guilty man gain, by torture. . . .

CHAPTER XV. THE MILDNESS OF PUNISHMENTS

From the simple consideration of the truths hitherto demonstrated it is evident that the object of punishment is neither to torment and inflict a sensitive creature nor to undo a crime already committed. Can he, whose function it is, so far from acting from passion, to tranquillise the private passions of his fellows, harbour in the body politic such useless cruelty, the instrument either of furious fanatics or of weak tyrants? Shall perchance the shrieks of an unhappy wretch call back from never-receding time actions already executed? The object, therefore, of punishment is simply to prevent the criminal from injuring anew his fellow-citizens, and to deter others from committing similar injuries; and those punishments and that method of inflicting them should be preferred which, duly proportioned to the offence, will produce a more efficacious and lasting impression on the minds of men and inflict the least torture on the body of a criminal.

Who can read history without being horror-struck at the barbarous and useless torments which men, who were called wise, in cold blood devised and executed? Who is there but must feel his blood boil, when he regards the thousands of wretches whom misery, either intended or tolerated by the laws (which have always favoured the few and outraged the many), has driven to a desperate return to the original state of nature; when he sees them either accused by men endowed with the same senses, and consequently with the same passions as themselves, of impossible crimes, the fiction of timid ignorance, or guilty of nothing but fidelity to their own principles; and when he sees them lacerated by slow tortures, subject to well-contrived formalities, an agreeable sight for a fanatical multitude?

In order that a punishment may attain its object, it is enough if the evil of the punishment exceeds the advantage of the crime, and in this excess of evil the certainty of punishment and the loss of the possible advantage from the crime ought to be considered as part; all beyond this is superfluous and consequently tyrannical. Men regulate their conduct by the reiterated impression of evils they know, not by reason of evils they ignore. Given two nations, in one of which, in the scale of punishments proportioned to the scale of crimes, the severest penalty is perpetual servitude, and in the other the wheel; I say that the former will have as great a dread of its severest punishment as the latter will have; and if there be any reason for transporting to the former country the greater penalties of the other, the same reasoning will serve for increasing still more the penalties of this latter country, passing imperceptibly from the wheel to the slowest and most elaborate tortures, nay, even to the last refinements of that science which tyrants understand only too well.

The more cruel punishments become, the more human minds harden, adjusting themselves, like fluids, to the level of objects around them; and the ever living force of the passions brings it about, that after a hundred years of cruel punishments, the wheel frightens men only just as much as at first did the punishment of prison.

The very severity of a punishment leads men to dare so much the more to escape it, according to the greatness of the evil in prospect; and many crimes are thus committed to avoid the penalty of a single one. Countries and times where punishments have been most severe have ever been those where the bloodiest and most inhuman deeds have been committed, the same spirit of ferocity that guided the hand of the legislator having guided also that of the parricide and assassin; on the throne dictating iron laws for the villainous souls of slaves to obey, and in the obscurity of private life urging to the slaughter of tyrants, only to create fresh ones in their stead.

Two other fatal consequences flow from the cruelty of punishments, and are contrary to their very purpose, the prevention of crimes. The first is, that it is not so easy to preserve the essential proportion between crime and punishment, because, however much a studied cruelty may diversify its forms, none of them can go beyond the extreme limit of endurance which is a condition of the human organisation and sensibility. When once this extreme limit is attained, it would be impossible to invent such a corresponding increase of punishment for still more injurious and atrocious crimes as would be necessary to prevent them. The other consequence is, that impunity itself arises from the severity of punishments. Men are restrained within limits both in good and evil; and a sight too atrocious for humanity can only be a passing rage, not a constant system, such as the laws ought to be; if the latter are really cruel, either they are changed, or themselves give rise to a fatal impunity.

I conclude with this reflection, that the scale of punishments should be relative to the condition of a nation. On the hardened minds of a people scarcely emerged from the savage state the impressions made should be stronger and more sensible. One needs a thunderbolt for the destruction of a fierce lion that faces round at the shot of a gun. But in proportion as men's minds become softened in the social state, their sensibility increases, and commensurate with that increase should be the diminution of the force of punishment, if it be desired to maintain any proportion between the object and the sensation that attends it.

CHAPTER XVI. CAPITAL PUNISHMENT

This useless prodigality of punishments, by which men have never been made any better, has driven me to examine whether the punishment of death be really useful and just in a well organised government. What kind of right can that be which men claim for the slaughter of their fellow-beings? Certainly not that right which is the source of sovereignty and of laws. For these are nothing but the sum-total of the smallest portions of individual liberty, and represent the general will, that is, the aggregate of individual wills. But who ever wished to leave to other men the option of killing him? How in the least possible sacrifice of each man's liberty can there be a sacrifice of the greatest of all goods, namely, of life? And if there could be that sacrifice, how would such a principle accord with the other, that a man is not the master of his own life?

Yet he must have been so, could he have given to himself or to society as a body this right of killing him.

The death penalty therefore is not a right; I have proved that it cannot be so; but it is a war of a nation against one of its members, because his annihilation is deemed necessary and expedient. But if I can show that his death is neither necessary nor expedient, I shall have won the cause of humanity.

The death of a citizen can only be deemed necessary for two reasons. The first is when, though deprived of his personal freedom, he has still such connections and power as threaten the national security; when his existence is capable of producing a dangerous revolution in the established form of government. The death of a citizen becomes then necessary when the nation is recovering or losing its liberty, or in a time of anarchy, when confusion takes the place of laws; but in times when the laws hold undisturbed sway, when the form of government correseponds with the wishes of a united nation, and is defended internally and externally by force, and by opinion which is perhaps even stronger than force, where the supreme power rests only with the real sovereign, and riches serve to purchase pleasures but not places, I see no necessity for destroying a citizen, except when his death might be the real and only restraint for diverting others from committing crimes; this latter case constituting the second reason for which one may believe capital punishment to be both just and necessary.

Since mankind generally suspicious always of the language of reason, but ready to bow to that of authority, remain unpersuaded by the experience of all ages, in which the supreme punishment has never diverted resolute men from committing offences against society; since also they are equally unmoved by the example of the Romans and by twenty years of the reign of the Empress Elizabeth of Russia, during which she presented this illustrious example to the fathers of their people, an example which is at least equivalent to many conquests bought by the blood of her country's sons, it is sufficient merely to consult human nature itself, to perceive the truth of the assertion I have made.

The greatest effect that any punishment has upon the human mind is not to be measured by its intensity but by its duration, for our sensibility is more easily and permanently affected by very slight but repeated impressions than by a strong but brief shock. Habit holds universal sway over every sentient being, and as we speak and walk and satisfy our needs by its aid, so moral ideas only stamp themselves on our mind by long and repeated impressions. It is not the terrible yet brief sight of a criminal's death, but the long and painful example of a man deprived of his liberty, who, having become as it were a beast of burthen, repays with his toil the society he has offended, which is the strongest restraint from crimes. Far more potent than the fear of death, which men ever have before their eyes in the remote distance, is the thought, so efficacious from its constant recurrence: "I myself shall be reduced to as long and miserable a condition if I commit similar misdeeds."

Capital punishment makes an impression in prospect which, with all its force, does not fully meet that ready spirit of forgetfulness, so natural to man even in his most important concerns, and so liable to be accelerated by his passions. As a general rule, men are startled by the sight of violent sufferings, but not for long, and therefore such impressions are wont so to transform them as to make of ordinary men whether Persians or Spartans; but in a free and settled government impressions should rather be frequent than strong.

Capital punishment becomes a spectacle for the majority of mankind, and a subject for compassion and abhorrence for others; the minds of the spectators are more filled with these feelings than with the wholesome terror the law pretends to inspire. But in moderate and continuing penalties the latter is the predominant feeling, because it is the only one. The limit, which the legislator should affix to the severity of penalties, appears to lie in the first signs of a feeling of compassion becoming uppermost in the minds of the spectators, when they look upon the punishment rather as their own than as that of the criminal.

In order that a punishment may be just, it must contain only such degrees of intensity as suffice to deter men from crimes. But as there is no one who on reflection would choose the total and perpetual loss of his liberty, however great the advantages offered him by a crime, the intensity of the punishment of servitude for life, substituted for capital punishment, has that in it which is sufficient to daunt the most determined courage. I will add that it is even more deterrent than death. Very many men face death calmly and firmly, some from fanaticism, some from vanity, which almost always attends a man to the tomb; others from a last desperate attempt either no longer to live or to escape from their misery; but neither fanaticism nor vanity have any place among fetters and chains, under the stick, under the yoke, in a cage of iron; the wretch thus punished is so far from terminating his miseries that with his punishment he only begins them.

The mind of man offers more resistance to violence and to extreme but brief pains than it does to time and to incessant weariness; for whilst it can, so to speak, gather itself together for a moment to repel the former, its vigorous elasticity is insufficient to resist the long and repeated action of the latter. In the case of capital punishment, each example presented of it is all that a single crime affords; in penal servitude for life, a single crime serves to present numerous and lasting warnings. And if it be important that the power of the laws should often be witnessed, there ought to be no long intervals between the examples of the death penalty; but this would presuppose the frequency of crimes, so that, to render the punishment effective, it must not make on men all the impression that it ought to make, in other words, it must be useful and not useful at the same time. And should it be objected that perpetual servitude is as painful as death, and therefore equally cruel, I will reply, that, taking into consideration all the unhappy moments of servitude, it will perhaps be even more painful than death; but whilst these moments are spread over the whole of a lifetime, death exercises all its force in a single moment. There is also this advantage in penal servitude, that it has more terrors for him who sees it than for him who suffers it, for the former thinks of the whole sum-total of unhappy moment, whilst the latter, by the unhappiness of the present moment, has his thoughts diverted from that which is to come. All evils are magnified in imagination, and every sufferer finds resources and consolations unknown to and unbelieved in by spectators, who substitute their own sensibility for the hardened soul of a criminal.

The following is the kind of reasoning adopted by the thief or the assassin, whose only motives for not breaking the laws are the gallows or the wheel. (I know that the analysis of one's own thoughts is an art only learnt by education, but a thief does not the less act according to certain principles because he is unable to express them.) "Of what sort," he argues, "are these laws that I am bound to observe, that leave so great an interval between myself and the rich man? He denies me the penny I ask of him, and excuses himself by ordering from me a work of which he himself knows nothing. Who has made these laws? Were they not made by rich and powerful men, who have never deigned to visit the wretched hovels of the poor, who have never divided a musty loaf of bread amid the innocent cries of famished children and the tears of a wife? Let us break these bonds, which are fatal to the greater number, and only useful to a few indolent tyrants; let us attack injustice in its source. I will return to my state of natural independence; I will live for some time happy and free on the fruits of my courage and address; and if the day should ever come when I have to suffer and repent for it, the time of suffering will be short, and I shall have one day of misery for many years of liberty and pleasure. As the king of a small band, I will correct the errors of fortune, and see these tyrants pale and tremble before one, whom in their insolent arrogance they rated lower than their horses or their dogs." Then religion hovers before the mind of the criminal, who turns everything to a bad use, and offering him a facile repentance and an almost certain eternity of bliss does much to diminish in his eyes the horror of that last tragedy of all.

But the man who sees in prospect a great number of years, or perhaps the whole of his life, to be passed in servitude and suffering before the eyes of fellow-citizens with whom he is living in freedom and friendship, the slave of those laws which had once protected him, makes a useful comparison of all these circumstances with the uncertain result of his crimes and with the shortness of the time for which he would enjoy their fruits. The ever present example of those whom he actually sees the victims of their own imprudence, impresses him much more strongly than the sight of a punishment which hardens rather than corrects him.

Capital punishment is injurious by the example of barbarity it presents. If human passions, or the necessities of war, have taught men to shed one another's blood, the laws, which are intended to moderate human conduct, ought not to extend the savage example, which in the case of a legal execution is all the more baneful in that it is carried out with studied formalities. To me it seems an absurdity, that the laws, which are the expression of the public will, which abhor and which punish murder, should themselves commit one; and that, to deter citizens from private assassination, they should themselves order a public murder. What are the true and the most useful laws? Are they not those covenants and conditions which all would wish observed and proposed, when the incessant voice of private interest is hushed or is united with the interest of the public? What are every man's feelings about capital punishment? Let us read them in the gestures of indignation and scorn with which everyone looks upon the executioner, who is, after all, an innocent administrator of the public will, a good citizen contributory to the public welfare, an instrument as necessary for the internal security of a State as brave soldiers are for its external. What, then, is the source of this contradiction; and why is this feeling, in spite of reason, ineradicable in mankind? Because men in their most secret hearts, that part of them which more than any other still preserves the original form of their first nature, have ever believed that their lives lie at no one's disposal, save in that of necessity alone, which, with its iron sceptre, rules the universe.

What should men think when they see wise magistrates and grave priests of justice with calm indifference causing a criminal to be dragged by their slow procedure to death; or when they see a judge, whilst a miserable wretch in the convulsions of his last agonies is awaiting the fatal blow, pass away coldly and unfeelingly, perhaps even with a secret satisfaction in his authority, to enjoy the comforts and pleasures of life? "Ah," they will say, "these laws are but the pretexts of force, and the studied cruel formalities of justice are but a conventional language, used for the purpose of immolating us with greater safety, like victims destined in sacrifice to the insatiable idol of tyranny. That assassination which they preach to us as so terrible a misdeed we see nevertheless employed by them without either scruple or passion. Let us profit by the example. A violent death seemed to us a terrible thing in the descriptions of it that were made to us, but we see it is a matter of a moment. How much less terrible will it be for a man who, not expecting it, is spared all that there is of painful in it."

Such are the fatal arguments employed, if not clearly, at least vaguely, by men disposed to crimes, among whom, as we have seen, the abuse of religion is more potent than religion itself.

If I am confronted with the example of almost all ages and almost all nations who have inflicted the punishment of death upon some crimes, I will reply, that the example avails nothing before truth, against which there is no prescription of time; and that the history of mankind conveys to us the idea of an immense sea of errors, among which a few truths, confusedly and at long intervals, float on the surface. Human sacrifices were once common to almost all nations, yet who for that reason will dare defend them? That some few states, and for a short time only, should have abstained from inflicting death, rather favours my argument than otherwise, because such a fact is in keeping with the lot of all great truths, whose duration is but as of a lightning flash in comparison with the long and darksome night that envelops mankind. That happy time has not yet arrived when truth, as error has hitherto done, shall belong to the majority of men; and from this universal law of the reign of error those truths alone have hitherto been exempt, which supreme wisdom has seen fit to distinguish from others, by making them the subject of a special revelation.

The voice of a philosopher is too feeble against the noise and cries of so many followers of blind custom, but the few wise men scattered over the face of the earth will respond to me from their inmost hearts; and, amid the many obstacles that keep it from a monarch, should truth perchance arrive in spite of him at his throne, let him know that it comes there attended by the secret wishes of all men; let him know that before his praises the bloody fame of conquerors will be silenced, and that posterity, which is just, will assign him the foremost place among the pacific triumphs of a Titus, an Antonine, or a Trajan.

Happy were humanity, if laws were now dictated to it for the first time, when we see on the thrones of Europe beneficent monarchs, men who encourage the virtues of peace, the sciences and the arts, who are fathers to their people, who are crowned citizens, and the increase of whose authority forms the happiness of their subjects, because it removes that intermediate despotism, more cruel because less secure, by which the people's wishes, always sincere, and always attended to when they can reach the throne, have been usually intercepted and suppressed. If they, I say, suffer the ancient laws to exist, it is owing to the infinite difficulties of removing from errors the revered rust of many ages; which is a reason for enlightened citizens to desire with all the greater ardour the continual increase of their authority. . . .

CHAPTER XXIII. PROPORTION BETWEEN CRIMES AND PUNISHMENTS

Not only is it the general interest that crimes should not be committed, but that they should be rare in proportion to the evils they cause to society. The more opposed therefore that crimes are to the public welfare, and the more numerous the incentives to them, the stronger should be the repellent obstacles. This principle accordingly establishes the necessity of a certain proportion between crimes and punishments.

If pleasure and pain are the motors of sensitive beings, if the invisible lawgiver of humanity has decreed rewards and punishments as one of the motives to impel men to even their noblest endeavours, the inexact distribution of these motives will give rise to that contradiction, as little noticed as it is of common occurrence, namely, that the laws punish crimes which are entirely of their own creation. If an equal penalty is attached to two crimes of unequal injury to society, the greater crime of the two, if it promise a greater advantage than the other, will have no stronger motive in restraint of its perpetration. Whoever, for example, sees the same punishment of death decreed for the man who kills a pheasant and the man who slays his fellow or falsifies an important document, will draw no distinction between such crimes; and thus moral sentiments, the product only of many ages and of much bloodshed, the slowest and most difficult attainment of the human mind, dependent, it has been thought, on the aid of the most sublime motives and on a parade of the gravest formalities, will be destroyed and lost.

It is impossible to prevent all the disorders that may arise in the universal conflict of human passions. Their increase depends on that of population and on the crossings of private interests, which cannot be directed with geometrical exactness to the public welfare. In political arithmetic the calculation of probabilities must be substituted for mathematical exactness. Glance at the history of the world, and you will see disorders increase with the increase of the bounds of empire; thus national feeling being to the same extent diminished, the general inducement to crime increases with the greater interest of each individual in such disorders, and on this account the necessity for aggravating penalties ever continues to increase.

That force, similar to the force of gravitation, which constrains us to seek our own well-being, only admits of counteraction in proportion to the obstacles opposed to it. The effects of this force make up the confused series of human actions; if these clash together and impede one another, punishments, which I would call *political obstacles,* prevent bad effects from resulting, without destroying the impelling cause, which lies in the sensibility inseparable from humanity; and the legislator, in enacting them, as the part of a clever architect, whose function it is to counteract the tendency of gravitation to cause a building to fall, and to bring to bear all the lines which contribute to its strength.

Given the necessity of the aggregation of mankind, and given the covenants which necessarily result from the very opposition of private interests, a scale of offences may be traced, beginning with those which tend directly to the destruction of society, and ending with acts of the smallest possible injustice committed against individual members of it. Between these extremes are comprised all the actions opposed to the public welfare which are called crimes, and which by imperceptible degrees decrease in enormity from the highest to the lowest. If the infinite and obscure combinations of human actions admitted of mathematical treatment, there ought to be a corresponding scale of punishments, varying from the severest to the slightest penalty. If there were an exact and universal scale of crimes and punishments, we should have an approximate and general test by which to gauge the degrees of tyranny and liberty in different governments, the relative state of the humanity or wickedness of different nations. But the wise legislator will rest satisfied with marking out the principal divisions in such a scale, so as not to invert their order, nor to affix to crimes of the first degree punishments due to those of the last.

CHAPTER XXIV. THE MEASURE OF PUNISHMENTS

We have seen that the true measure of crimes is the injury done to society. This is one of those palpable truths which, however little dependent on quadrants or telescopes for their discovery, and fully within the reach of any ordinary intelligence, are yet, by a marvellous combination of circumstances, only recognized clearly and firmly by some few thinkers, belonging to every nationality and to every age. But Asiatic ideas, and passions clothed with authority and power, have, generally by imperceptible movements, sometimes by violent assaults on the timid credulity of mankind, dissipated those simple notions, which perhaps formed the first philosophy of primitive communities, and to which the enlightenment of this age seems likely to reconduct us, but to do so with that greater sureness, which can be gained from an exact investigation into things, from a thousand unhappy experiences, and from the very obstacles that militate against it.

They who have thought that the criminal's intention was the true measure of crimes were in the wrong. For the intention depends on the actual impression of things upon a man, and on his precedent mental disposition, things which vary in all men and in each man, according to the very rapid succession of his ideas, his passions, and his circumstances. It would, therefore, be necessary to form not only a particular code for each citizen, but a fresh law for every crime. Sometimes with the best intentions men do the greatest evil to society; and sometimes with the very worst they do it the greatest good.

Others again measure crimes rather by the rank of the person injured than by their importance in regard to the public weal. Were this the true measure of crimes, any act of irreverence towards the Supreme Being should be punished more severely than the assassination of a monarch, whereas the superiority of His nature affords an infinite compensation for the difference of the offence.

Lastly, some have thought that the gravity of an act's sinfulness should be an element in the measure of crimes. But an impartial observer of the true relations between man and man, and between man and God, will easily perceive the fallacy of this opinion. For the former relationship is one of equality; necessity alone, from the clash of passions and opposing interests, having given rise to the idea of the *public utility*, the basis of human justice. But the other relationship is one of dependence on a perfect Being and Creator, who has reserved to Himself alone the right of being at the same time legislator and judge, and can alone unite the two functions without bad effects. If He has decreed eternal punishments to those who disobey His omnipotence, what insect shall dare to take the place of Divine justice, or shall wish to avenge that Being, who is all-sufficient to Himself, who can receive from things no impression of pleasure nor of pain, and who alone of all beings acts without reaction? The degree of sinfulness in an action depends on the unsearchable wickedness of the heart, which cannot be known by finite beings without a revelation. How, then, found thereon a standard for the punishment of crimes? In such a case men might punish when God pardons, and pardon when God punishes. If men can act contrary to the Almighty by offending Him, they may also do so in the punishments they inflict. . . .

CHAPTER XLI. THE PREVENTION OF CRIMES—OF KNOWLEDGE—MAGISTRATES —REWARDS—EDUCATION

It is better to prevent crimes than to punish them. This is the chief aim of every good system of legislation, which is the art of leading men to the greatest possible happiness or to the least possible misery, according to calculation of all the goods and evils of life. But the means hitherto employed for this end are for the most part false and contrary to the end proposed. It is impossible to reduce the turbulent activity of men to a geometrical harmony without any irregularity or confusion. As the constant and most simple laws of nature do not prevent aberrations in the movements of the planets, so, in the infinite and contradictory attractions of pleasure and pain, disturbances and disorder cannot be prevented by human laws. Yet this is the chimera that narrow-minded men pursue, when they have power in their hands. To prohibit a number of indifferent acts is not to prevent the crimes that may arise from them, but it is to create new ones from them; it is to give capricious definitions of virtue and vice which are proclaimed as eternal and immutable in their nature. To what should we be reduced if everything had to be forbidden us which might tempt us to a crime? It would be necessary to deprive a man of the use of his senses. For one motive that drives men to commit a real crime there are a thousand that drive them to the commission of those indifferent acts which are called crimes by bad laws; and if the likelihood of crimes is proportioned to the number of motives to commit them, an increase of the field of crimes is an increase of the likelihood of their commission. The majority of laws are nothing but privileges, or a tribute paid by all to the convenience of some few.

Would you prevent crimes, then cause the laws to be clear and simple, bring the whole force of a nation to bear on their defence, and suffer no part of it to be busied in overthrowing them. Make the laws to favour not so much classes of men as men themselves. Cause men to fear the laws and the laws alone. Salutary is the fear of the law, but fatal and fertile in crime is the fear of one man of another. Men as slaves are more sensual, more immoral, more cruel than free men; and, whilst the latter give their minds to the sciences or to the interests of their country, setting great objects before them as their model, the former, contented with the passing day, seek in the excitement of libertinage a distraction from the nothingness of their existence, and, accustomed to an uncertainty of result in everything, they look upon the result of their crimes as uncertain too, and so decide in favour of the passion that tempts them. If uncertainty of the laws affects a nation, rendered indolent by its climate, its indolence and stupidity is thereby maintained and increased; if it affects a nation, which though fond of pleasure is also full of energy, it wastes that energy in a number of petty cabals and intrigues, which spread distrust in every heart, and make treachery and dissimulation the foundation of prudence; if, again, it affects a courageous and brave nation, the uncertainty is ultimately destroyed, after many oscillations from liberty to servitude, and from servitude back again to liberty.

Would you prevent crimes, then see that enlightenment accompanies liberty. The evils that flow from knowledge are in inverse ratio to its diffusion; the benefits directly proportioned to it. A bold imposter, who is never a commonplace man, is adored by an ignorant people, despised by an enlightened one. Knowledge, by facilitating comparisons between objects and multiplying men's points of view, brings many different notions into contrast, causing them to modify one another, all the more easily as the same views and the same difficulties are observed in others. In the face of a widely diffused national enlightenment the calumnies of ignorance are silent, and authority, disarmed of pretexts for its manifestation, trembles; whilst the rigorous force of the laws remains unshaken, no one of education having any dislike to the clear and useful public compacts which secure the common safety, when he compares the trifling and useless liberty sacrificed by himself with the sum-total of all the liberties sacrificed by others, who without the laws might have been hostile to himself. Whoever has a sensitive soul, when he contemplates a code of well-made laws, and finds that he has only lost the pernicious liberty of injuring others, will feel himself constrained to bless the throne and the monarch that sits upon it. . . .

Another way of preventing crimes is to interest the magistrates who carry out the laws in seeking rather to preserve than to corrupt them. The greater the number of men who compose the magistracy, the less danger will there be of their exercising any undue power over the laws; for venality is more difficult among men who are under the close observation of one another, and their inducement to increase their individual authority diminishes in proportion to the smallness of the share of it that can fall to each of them, especially when they compare it with the risk of the attempt. If the sovereign accustoms his subjects, by formalities and pomp, by severe edicts, and by refusal to hear the grievances, whether just or unjust, of the man who thinks himself oppressed, to fear rather the magistrates than the laws, it will be more to the profit of the magistrates than to the gain of private and public security.

Another way to prevent crimes is to reward virtue. On this head I notice a general silence in the laws of all nations to this day. If prizes offered by academies to the discoverers of useful truths have caused the multiplication of knowledge and of good books, why should not virtuous actions also be multiplied, by prizes distributed from the munificence of the sovereign? The money of honour ever remains unexhausted and fruitful in the hands of the legislator who wisely distributes it.

Lastly, the surest but most difficult means of preventing crimes is to improve education—a subject too vast for present discussion, and lying beyond the limits of my treatise; a subject, I will also say, too intimately connected with the nature of government for it ever to be aught but a barren field, only cultivated here and there by a few philosophers, down to the remotest ages of public prosperity. A great man, who enlightens the humanity that persecutes him, has shown in detail the chief educational maxims of real utility to mankind; namely, that it consists less in a barren multiplicity of subjects than in their choice selection; in substituting originals for copies in the moral as in the physical phenomena presented by chance or intention to the fresh minds of youth; in inclining them to virtue by the easy path of feeling; and in deterring them from evil by the sure path of necessity and disadvantage, not by the uncertain method of command, which never obtains more than a simulated and transitory obedience.

CHAPTER XLII. CONCLUSION

From all that has gone before a general theorem may be deduced, of great utility, though little comformable to custom, that common lawgiver of nations. The theorem is this: "In order that every punishment may not be an act of violence, committed by one man or by many against a single individual, it ought to be above all things public, speedy, necessary, the least possible in the given circumstances, proportioned to its crime, dictated by the laws."

⤷ THE PROGRESS OF THE HUMAN MIND

Condorcet

Marie Jean Antoine Nicolas de Caritat, Marquis de Condorcet (1743–1794), was an important French mathematician, philosopher, and revolutionary. In 1785 he published an original treatise on the mathematical theory of probability, and he was an active member of the Academy of Sciences and of various other scientific organizations. But his importance rests chiefly on his role as a propagator of the religious and political theories of the Enlightenment.

*In 1786 Condorcet wrote a life of Turgot, the brilliant but controversial
statesman and economist. He followed this in 1789 with a life of Voltaire,
which was also widely read. In the same year he was elected to the
municipal government of Paris, then to the national legislative assembly;
and the remaining years of his life were filled with political activity of a
very high order. He was the chief author of the address to the European
powers in December, 1791 (see pages 375–376), of the new system of
state education, one of the permanent reforms of the Revolution, and
of the declaration for a republic (August, 1792) justifying the suspension
of the king and the calling of a National Convention. In the convention,
his draft of a constitution was rejected in favor of the more radical
proposal of the Jacobins.*

*Gradually his independence of mind became a political liability; and when
he spoke out (June, 1793) against the arrest of the Girondins, he was
forced to flee to escape the guillotine. His friends persuaded him to start
writing, before it was too late, the great work on the general history
of the human mind that he had been promising to write when he had
time. But it was too late. He got only as far as a "sketch" (Esquisse) of
the work in some two hundred pages, which he had planned to spell out
in much more detail; it is this from which our selections are taken.
In March, 1794, his political enemies discovered his hiding place,
and after a brief flight he was apprehended and imprisoned. The next
morning he was found dead in his cell, probably a suicide.*

*The Esquisse was published posthumously in 1795. Condorcet divides
the past history of man into nine stages or epochs. The first three precede
civilization: the hunting and fishing stage, the pastoral stage, and the
agricultural stage. The fourth and fifth stages correspond to ancient
Greece and Rome, and the sixth and seventh to the Middle Ages before
and after the Crusades. The eighth stage is ushered in by the invention of
printing, and the ninth by Descartes's formulation of the true method
of science (see pages 87–88). With the founding of the French Republic in
1792, Condorcet thought, man had entered upon a tenth and climactic
stage in his development, in which his rights would at last be recognized
and his potentialities developed. Our selections are drawn primarily
from the chapters dealing with the ninth and tenth stages, the most
original and influential parts of his book.*

INTRODUCTION

. . . Were we to confine our observations to an enquiry into the general facts and unvarying laws which the development of these faculties presents to us, in what is common to the different individuals of the human species, our enquiry would bear the name of metaphysics.

But if we consider this development in its results, relative to the mass of individuals co-existing at the same time on a given space and follow it from generation to generation, it then exhibits a picture of the progress of human intellect. This progress is subject to the same general laws, observable in the individual development of our faculties; being the result of that very development considered at once in a great number of individuals united in society. But the result which every instant presents, depends upon that of the preceding instants, and has an influence on the instants which follow.

This picture, therefore, is historical; since, subjected as it will be to perpetual variations, it is formed by the successive observation of human societies at the different eras through which they have passed. It will accordingly exhibit the order in which the changes have taken place, explain the influence of every past period upon that which follows it, and thus show, by the modifications which the human species has experienced, in its incessant renovation through the immensity of ages, the course which it has pursued, and the steps which it has advanced towards knowledge and happiness. From these observations on what man has heretofore been, and what he is at present, we shall be led to the means of securing and of accelerating the still further progress, of which, from his nature, we may indulge the hope.

Such is the object of the work I have undertaken; the result of which will be to show, from reasoning and from facts, that no bounds have been fixed to the improvement of the human faculties; that the perfectibility of man is absolutely indefinite; that the progress of this perfectibility, henceforth above the control of every power that would impede it, has no other limit than the duration of the globe upon which nature has placed us. The course of this progress may doubtless be more or less rapid, but it can never be retrograde; at least while the earth retains its situation in the system of the universe, and the laws of this system shall neither effect upon the globe a general overthrow, nor introduce such changes as would no longer permit the human race to preserve and exercise therein the same faculties, and find the same resources. . . .

It is between this degree of civilization and that in which we still find the savage tribes, that we must place every people whose history has been handed down to us, and who, sometimes making new advancements, sometimes plunging themselves again into ignorance, sometimes floating between the two alternatives or stopping at a certain limit, sometimes totally disappearing from the earth under the sword of conquerors, mixing with those conquerors, or living in slavery; lastly, sometimes receiving knowledge from a more enlightened people, to transmit it to other nations,—form an

Marquis de Condorcet, *Outlines of a Historical View of the Progress of the Human Mind*, anon. trans. from the 1795 ed. (Ann Arbor, Mich., n.d.), pp. iv–v, vii–x, 79–83, 85–90a, 103, 110–114, 116–125, 128–130.

unbroken chain of connection between the earliest periods of history and the age in which we live, between the first people known to us, and the present nations of Europe.

In the picture then which I mean to sketch, three distinct parts are perceptible.

In the first, in which the relations of travellers exhibit to us the condition of mankind in the least civilized nations, we are obliged to guess by what steps man in an isolated state, or rather confined to the society necessary for the propogation of the species, was able to acquire those first degrees of improvement, the last term of which is the use of an articulate language: an acquisition that presents the most striking feature, and indeed the only one, a few more extensive moral ideas and a slight commencement of social order excepted, which distinguishes him from animals living like himself in regular and permanent society. In this part of our picture, then, we can have no other guide than an investigation of the development of our faculties.

To this first guide, in order to follow man to the point in which he exercises arts, in which the rays of science begin to enlighten him, in which nations are united by commercial intercourse; in which, in fine, alphabetical writing is invented, we may add the history of the several societies that have been observed in almost every intermediate state: though we can follow no individual one through all the space which separates these two grand epochs of the human race.

Here the picture begins to take its colouring in great measure from the series of facts transmitted to us by history: but it is necessary to select these facts from that of different nations, and at the same time compare and combine them, to form the supposed history of a single people, and delineate its progress.

From the period that alphabetical writing was known in Greece, history is connected by an uninterrupted series of facts and observations, with the period in which we live, with the present state of mankind in the most enlightened countries of Europe; and the picture of the progress and advancement of the human mind becomes strictly historical. Philosophy has no longer any thing to guess, has no more suppositious combinations to form; all it has to do is to collect and arrange facts, and exhibit the useful truths which arise from them as a whole, and from the different bearings of their several parts.

There remains only a third picture to form,—that of our hopes, or the progress reserved for future generations, which the constancy of the laws of nature seems to secure to mankind. And here it will be necessary to shew by what steps this progress, which at present may appear chimerical, is gradually to be rendered possible, and even easy; how truth, in spite of the transient success of prejudices and the support they receive from the corruption of governments or of the people, must in the end obtain a durable triumph; by what ties nature has indissolubly united the advancement of knowledge with the progress of liberty, virtue, and respect for the natural rights of man; how these blessings, the only real ones, though so frequently seen apart as to be thought incompatible, must necessarily amalgamate and become inseparable, the moment knowledge shall have arrived at a certain pitch in a great number of nations at once, the moment it shall have penetrated the whole mass of a great people, whose language shall have become universal, and whose commercial intercourse shall embrace the whole extent of the globe. This union having once taken place in the whole enlightened class of men, this class will be considered as the friends of human kind, exerting themselves in concert to advance the improvement and happiness of the species. . . .

Every thing tells us that we are approaching the era of one of the grand revolutions of the human race. What can better enlighten us as to what we may expect, what can be a surer guide to us, amidst its commotions, than the picture of the revolutions that have preceded and prepared the way for it? The present state of knowledge assures us that it will be happy. But is it not upon condition that we know how to assist it with all our strength? And, that the happiness it promises may be less dearly bought, that it may spread with more rapidity over a greater space, that it may be more complete in its effects, is it not requisite to study, in the history of the human mind, what obstacles remain to be feared, and by what means those obstacles are to be surmounted? . . .

NINTH EPOCH: FROM DESCARTES TO THE FRENCH REPUBLIC

. . . And now we arrive at the period when philosophy, the most general and obvious effects of which we have before remarked, obtained an influence on the thinking class of men, and these on the people and their governments, that, ceasing any longer to be gradual, produced a revolution in the entire mass of certain nations, and gave thereby a secure pledge of the general revolution one day to follow that shall embrace the whole human species.

After ages of error, after wandering in all the mazes of vague and defective theories, writers upon politics and the law of nations at length arrived at the knowledge of the true rights of man, which they deduced from this simple principle: that *he is a being endowed with sensation, capable of reasoning upon and understanding his interests, and of acquiring moral ideas.*

They saw that the maintenance of his rights was the only object of political union, and that the perfection of the social art consisted in preserving them with the most entire equality, and in their fullest extent. They perceived that the means of securing the rights of the individual, consisting of general rules to be laid down in every community, the power of choosing these means, and determining these rules, could vest only in the majority of the community; and that for this reason, as it is impossible for any individual in this choice to follow the dictates of his own understanding, without subjecting that of others, the will of the majority is the only principle which can be followed by all, without infringing upon the common equality. . . .

It was now no longer practicable to divide mankind into two species, one destined to govern, the other to obey, one to deceive, the other to be dupes: the doctrine was obliged universally to be acknowledged, that all have an equal right to be enlightened respecting their interests, to share in the acquisition of truth, and that no political authorities appointed by the people for the benefit of the people, can be entitled to retain them in ignorance and darkness. . . .

There are certain operations, establishments, and institutions, beneficial to the community at large, which it is the office of the community to introduce, direct, and superintend, and which are calculated to supply the defects of personal inclination, and to parry the struggle of opposite interests, whether for the improvement of agriculture, industry, and commerce, or to prevent or diminish the evils entailed on our nature, or those which accident is continually accumulating upon us.

Till the commencement of the epoch we are now considering, and even for some time after, these objects had been abandoned to chance, to the rapacity of governments, to the artifices of pretenders, or to the prejudices and partial interests of the powerful classes of society; but a disciple of Descartes, the illustrious and unfortunate John de Witt, perceived how necessary it was that political economy, like every other science, should be governed by the principles of philosophy, and subjected to the rules of a rigid calculation.

It made however little progress, till the peace of Utrecht promised to Europe a durable tranquillity. From this period, neglected as it had hitherto been, it became a subject of almost general attention; and by Stuart, Smith, and particularly by the French economists, it was suddenly elevated, at least as to precision and purity of principles, to a degree of perfection, not to have been expected after the long and total indifference which had prevailed upon the subject.

The cause however of so unparalleled a progress is chiefly to be found in the advancement of that branch of philosophy comprehended in the term metaphysics, taking the word in its most extensive signification.

Descartes had restored this branch of philosophy to the dominion of reason. He perceived the propriety of deducing it from those simple and evident truths which are revealed to us by an investigation of the operations of the mind. But scarcely had he discovered this principle than his eager imagination led him to depart from it, and philosophy appeared for a time to have resumed its independence only to become the prey of new errors.

At length Locke made himself master of the proper clew. He shewed that a precise and accurate analysis of ideas, reducing them to ideas earlier in their origin or more simple in their structure, was the only means to avoid the being lost in a chaos of notions incomplete, incoherent, and undetermined, disorderly because suggested by accident, and afterwards entertained without reflecting on their nature.

He proved by this analysis, that the whole circle of our ideas results merely from the operations of our intellect upon the sensations we have received, or more accurately speaking, are compounded of sensations offering themselves simultaneously to the memory, and after such a manner, that the attention is fixed and the perception bounded to a particular branch or view of the sensations themselves.

He shewed that by taking one single word to represent one single idea, properly analyzed and defined, we are enabled to recall constantly the same idea, that is, the same simultaneous result of certain simple ideas, and of consequence can introduce this idea into a train of reasoning without risk of misleading ourselves.

On the contrary, if our words do not represent fixed and definite ideas, they will at different times suggest different ideas to the mind and become the most fruitful source of error.

In fine, Locke was the first who ventured to prescribe the limits of the human understanding, or rather to determine the nature of the truths it can ascertain and the objects it can embrace.

It was not long before this method was adopted by philosophers in general, in treating of morals and politics, by which a degree of certainty was given to those sciences little inferior to that which obtained in the natural sciences, admitting only of such conclusions as could be proved, separating these from doubtful notions, and content to remain ignorant of whatever is out of the reach of human comprehension. . . .

Hitherto we have exhibited the state of philosophy only among men by whom it has in a manner been studied, investigated, and perfected. It remains to mark its influence on the general opinion, and to show, that, while it arrived at the certain and infallible means of discovering and recognizing truth, reason at the same time detected the delusions into which it had so often been led by a respect for authority or a misguided imagination, and undermined those prejudices in the mass of individuals which had so long been the scourge, at once corrupting and inflicting calamity upon the human species.

The period at length arrived when men no longer feared openly to avow the right, so long withheld, and even unknown, of subjecting every opinion to the test of reason, or, in other words, of employing in their search after truth, the only means they possess for its discovery. Every man learned, with a degree of pride and exultation, that nature had not condemned him to see with the eyes and to conform his judgment to the caprice of another. The superstitions of antiquity accordingly disappeared; and the debasement of reason to the shrine of supernatural faith, was as rarely to be found in society as in the circles of metaphysics and philosophy.

A class of men speedily made their appearance in Europe, whose object was less to discover and investigate truth, than to disseminate it; who, pursuing prejudice through all the haunts and asylums in which the clergy, the schools, governments, and privileged corporations had placed and protected it, made it their glory rather to eradicate popular errors, than add to the stores of human knowledge; thus aiding indirectly the progress of mankind, but in a way neither less arduous, nor less beneficial.

In England, Collins and Bolingbroke, and in France, Bayle, Fontenelle, Montesquieu, and the respective disciples of these celebrated men, combated on the side of truth with all the weapons that learning, wit and genius were able to furnish; assuming every shape, employing every tone, from the sublime and pathetic to pleasantry and satire, from the most laboured investigation to an interesting romance or a fugitive essay: accommodating truth to those eyes that were too weak to bear its effulgence; artfully caressing prejudice, the more easily to strangle it; never aiming a direct blow at errors, never attacking more than one at a time, nor even that one in all its fortresses; sometimes soothing the enemies of reason, by pretending to require in religion but a partial toleration, in politics but a limited freedom; siding with despotism, when their hostilities were directed against the priesthood, and with priests, when their object was to unmask the despot; sapping the principle of both these pests of human happiness, striking at the root of both those baneful trees, while apparently wishing for the reform only of glaring abuses and seemingly confining themselves to lopping off the exuberant branches; sometimes representing to the partisans of liberty, that superstition, which covers despotism as with a coat of mail, is the first victim which ought to be sacrificed, the first chain that ought to be broken; and sometimes denouncing it to tyrants as the true enemy of their power, and alarming them with recitals of its hypocrtical conspiracies and its sanguinary vengeance. These writers, meanwhile, were uniform in their vindication of freedom of thinking and fredom of writing, as privileges upon which depended the salvation of mankind. They declaimed, without cessation or weariness, against the crimes both of fanatics and tyrants, exposing every feature of severity, of cruelty, of oppression, whether in religion, in administration, in manners, or in laws; commanding kings, soldiers, magistrates and priests, in the name of truth and of nature, to respect the blood of mankind; calling upon them, with energy to answer for the lives still profusely sacrificed in the field of battle or by the infliction of punishments, or else to correct this inhuman policy, this murderous insensibility; and lastly, in every place, and upon every occasion, rallying the friends of mankind with the cry of *reason, toleration, and humanity!*

Such was this new philosophy. Accordingly to those numerous classes that exist by prejudice, that live upon error, and that, but for the credulity of the people, would be powerless and extinct, it became a common object of detestation. It was every where received, and every where persecuted, having kings, priests, nobles and magistrates among the number of its friends as well as of its enemies. Its leaders, however, had almost always the art to elude the pursuits of vengeance, while they exposed themselves to hatred; and to screen themselves from persecution, while at the same time they sufficiently discovered themselves not to lose the laurels of their glory. . . .

But the new truths with which genius had enriched philosophy and the science of political economy, adopted in a greater or less degree by men of enlightened understandings, extended still farther their salutary influence.

The art of printing had been applied to so many subjects, books had so rapidly increased, they were so admirably adapted to every taste, every degree of information, and every situation of life, they afforded so easy and frequently so delightful an instruction, they had opened so many doors to truth, which it was impossible ever to close again, that there was no longer a class or profession of mankind from whom the light of knowledge could absolutely be excluded. Accordingly, though there still remained a multitude of individuals condemned to a forced or voluntary ignorance, yet was the barrier between the enlightened and unenlightened portion of mankind nearly effaced, and an insensible gradation occupied the space which separates the two extremes of genius and stupidity.

Thus there prevailed a general knowledge of the natural rights of man; the opinion even that these rights are inalienable and imprescriptible; a decided partiality for freedom of thinking and writing; for the enfranchisement of industry and commerce; for the melioration of the condition of the people; for the repeal of penal statutes against religious nonconformists; for the abolition of torture and barbarous punishments; the desire of a milder system of criminal legislation; of a jurisprudence that should give to innocence a complete security; of a civil code more simple, as well as more conformable to reason and justice; indifference as to systems of religion, considered at length as the offspring of superstition, or ranked in the number of political inventions; hatred of hypocrisy and fanaticism; contempt for prejudices; and lastly, a zeal for the propagation of truth. These principles, passing by degrees from the writings of philosophers into every class of society whose instruction was not confined to the catechism and the scriptures, became the common creed, the symbol and type of all men who were not idiots on the one hand, or, on the other, assertors of the policy of Machiavelism. In some countries these sentiments formed so nearly the general opinion, that the mass even of the people seemed ready to obey their dictates and act from their impulse.

The love of mankind, that is to say, that active compassion which interests itself in all the afflictions of the human race, and regards with horror whatever, in public institutions, in the acts of government, or the pursuits of individuals, adds to the inevitable misfortunes of nature, was the necessary result of these principles. It breathed in every work, it prevailed in every conversation, and its benign effects were already visible even in the laws and administration of countries subject to despotism.

The philosophers of different nations embracing, in their meditations, the entire interests of man, without distinction of country, of color, or of sect, formed, notwithstanding the difference of their speculative opinions, a firm and united phalanx against every description of error, every species of tyranny. Animated by the sentiment of universal philanthropy, they declaimed equally against injustice, whether existing in a foreign country, or exercised by their own country against a foreign nation. They impeached in Europe the avidity which stained the shores of America, Africa, and Asia with cruelty and crimes. The philosophers of France and England gloried in assuming the appellation, and fulfilling the duties, of *friends* to those very negroes whom their ignorant oppressors disdained to rank in the class of men. The French writers bestowed the tribute of their praise on the toleration granted in Russia and Sweden, while Beccaria refuted in Italy the barbarous maxims of Gallic jurisprudence. The French also endeavoured to open the eyes of England respecting her commercial prejudices, and her superstitious reverence for the errors of her constitution; while the virtuous Howard remonstrated at the same time with the French upon the cool barbarity which sacrificed so many human victims in their prisons and hospitals.

Neither the violence nor the corrupt arts of government, neither the intolerance of priests, nor even the prejudices of the people themselves, possessed any longer the fatal power of suppressing the voice of truth; and nothing remained to screen the enemies of reason, or the oppressors of liberty, from the sentence which was about to be pronounced upon them by the unanimous suffrage of Europe. . . .

By comparing the disposition of the public mind, which I have already sketched, with the prevailing systems of government, we shall perceive, without difficulty, that an important revolution was inevitable, and that there were two ways only in which it could take place: either the people themselves would establish a system of policy upon those principles of nature and reason, which philosophy had rendered so dear to their hearts; or government might hasten to supersede this event, by reforming its vices, and governing its conduct by the public opinion. One of these revolutions would be more speedy, more radical, but also more tempestuous; the other less rapid, less complete, but more tranquil: in the one, liberty and happiness would be purchased at the expense of transient evils; in the other, these evils would be avoided; but a part of the enjoyments necessary to a state of perfect freedom, would be retarded in its progress, perhaps, for a considerable period, though it would be impossible in the end that it should not arrive.

The corruption and ignorance of the rulers of nations have preferred, its seems, the former of these modes; and the sudden triumph of reason and liberty has avenged the human race. . . .

If we confine ourselves to exhibit the advantages deduced from the sciences in their immediate use or application to the arts, whether for the welfare of individuals or the prosperity of nations, we shall have shewn only a small part of the benefits they afford. The most important perhaps is, that prejudice has been destroyed, and the human understanding in some sort rectified; after having been forced into a wrong direction by absurd objects of belief transmitted from generation to generation, taught at the misjudging period of infancy, and enforced with the terrors of superstition and the dread of tyranny.

All the errors in politics and in morals are founded upon philosophical mistakes, which, themselves, are connected with physical errors. There does not exist any religious system, or supernatural extravagance, which is not founded on an ignorance of the laws of nature. The inventors and defenders of these absurdities could not foresee the successive progress of the human mind. Being persuaded that the men of their time knew every thing, they would ever know, and would always believe that in which they then had fixed their faith; they confidently built their reveries upon the general opinions of their own country and their own age.

The progress of natural knowledge is yet more destructive of these errors, because it frequently destroys them without seeming to attack them, by attaching to those who obstinately defend them the degrading ridicule of ignorance.

At the same time, the just habit of reasoning on the object of these sciences, the precise ideas which their methods afford, and the means of ascertaining or proving the truth, must naturally lead us to compare the sentiment which forces us to adhere to opinions founded on these real motives of credibility, and that which attaches us to our habitual prejudices, or forces us to yield to authority. This comparison is sufficient to teach us to mistrust these last opinions, to shew that they were not really believed, even when that belief was the most earnestly and the most sincerely professed. When this discovery is once made, their destruction becomes much more speedy and certain. . . .

TENTH EPOCH: FUTURE PROGRESS OF MANKIND

If man can predict, almost with certainty, those appearances of which he understands the laws; if, even when the laws are unknown to him, experience of the past enables him to foresee, with considerable probability, future appearances; why should we suppose it a chimerical undertaking to delineate, with some degree of truth, the picture of the future destiny of mankind from the results of its history? The only foundation of faith in the natural sciences is the principle, that the general laws, known or un-known, which regulate the phenomena of the universe, are regular and constant; and why should this principle, applicable to the other operations of nature, be less true when applied to the development of the intellectual and moral faculties of man? In short, as opinions formed from experience, relative to the same class of objects, are the only rule by which men of soundest understanding are governed in their conduct, why should the philosopher be proscribed from supporting his conjectures upon a similar basis, provided he attribute to them no greater certainty than the number, the consistency, and the accuracy of actual observations shall authorize?

Our hopes, as to the future condition of the human speices, may be reduced to three points: the destruction of inequality between different nations; the progress of equality in one and the same nation; and lastly, the real improvement of man.

Will not every nation one day arrive at the state of civilization attained by those people who are most enlightened, most free, most exempt from prejudices, as the French, for instance, and the Anglo-Americans? Will not the slavery of countries subjected to kings, the barbarity of African tribes, and the ignorance of savages gradually vanish? Is there upon the face of the globe a single spot the inhabitants of which are condemned by nature never to enjoy liberty, never to exercise their reason?

Does the difference of knowledge, of means, and of wealth, observable hitherto in all civilized nations, between the classes into which the people constituting those nations are divided; does that inequality, which the earliest progress of society has augmented, or, to speak more properly, produced, belong to civilization itself, or to the imperfections of the social order? Must it not continually weaken, in order to give place to that actual equality, the chief end of the social art, which, diminishing even the effects of the natural difference of the faculties, leaves no other inequality, subsisting but what is useful to the interest of all, because it will favour civilization, instruction, and industry, without drawing after it either dependence, humiliation or poverty? In a word, will not men be continually verging towards that state, in which all will possess the requisite knowledge for conducting themselves in the common affairs of life by their own reason, and of maintaining that reason uncontaminated by prejudices; in which they will understand their rights, and exercise them according to their opinion and their conscience; in which all will be able, by the develpment of their faculties, to procure the certain means of providing for their wants; lastly, in which folly and wretchedness will be accidents, happening only now and then, and not the habitual lot of a considerable portion of society?

In fine, may it not be expected that the human race will be meliorated by new discoveries in the sciences and the arts, and, as an unavoidable consequence, in the means of individual and general prosperity; by farther progress in the principles of conduct, and in moral practice; and lastly, by the real improvement of our faculties, moral, intellectual and physical, which may be the result either of the improvement of the instruments which increase the power and direct the exercise of those faculties, or of the improvement of our natural organization itself?

In examining the three questions we have enumerated, we shall find the strongest reasons to believe, from past experience, from observation of the progress which the sciences and civilization have hitherto made, and from the analysis of the march of the human understanding, and the development of its faculties, that nature has fixed no limits to our hopes.

If we take a survey of the existing state of the globe, we shall perceive, in the first place, that in Europe the principles of the French constitution are those of every enlightened mind. We shall perceive that they are too widely disseminated, and too openly professed, for the efforts of tyrants and priests to prevent them from penetrating by degrees into the miserable cottages of their slaves, where they will soon revive those embers of good sense, and rouse that silent indignation which the habit of suffering and terror have failed totally to extinguish in the minds of the oppressed.

If we next look at the different nations, we shall observe in each, particular obstacles opposing, or certain dispositions favouring this revolution. We shall distinguish some in which it will be effected, perhaps slowly, by the wisdom of the respective governments; and others in which, rendered violent by resistance, the governments themselves will necessarily be involved in its terrible and rapid motions.

Can it be supposed that either the wisdom or the senseless feuds of European nations, co-operating with the slow but certain effects of the progress of their colonies, will not shortly produce the independence of the entire new world; and that then, European population, lending its aid, will fail to civilize or cause to disappear, even without conquest, those savage nations still occupying there immense tracts of country?

Run through the history of our projects and establishments in Africa or in Asia, and you will see our monopolies, our treachery, our sanguinary contempt for men of a different complexion or a different creed, and the proselyting fury or the intrigues of our priests, destroying that sentiment of respect and benevolence which the superiority of our information and the advantages of our commerce had at first obtained.

But the period is doubtless approaching, when, no longer exhibiting to the view of these people corruptors only or tyrants, we shall become to them instruments of benefit, and the generous champions of their redemption from bondage. . . .

The march of these people will be less slow and more sure than ours has been, because they will derive from us that light which we have been obliged to discover, and because for them to acquire the simple truths and infallible methods which we have obtained after long wandering in the mazes of error, it will be sufficient to seize upon their developments and proofs in our discourses and publications. If the progress of the Greeks was lost upon other nations, it was for want of a communication between the people; and to the tyrannical domination of the Romans must the whole blame be ascribed. But, when mutual wants shall have drawn closer the intercourse and ties of all mankind; when the most powerful nations shall have established into political principles equality between societies as between individuals, and respect for the independence of feeble states, as well as compassion for ignorance and wretchedness; when to the maxims which bear heavily upon the spring of the human faculties, those shall succeed which favour their action and energy, will there still be reason to fear that the globe will contain spaces inaccessible to knowledge, or that the pride of despotism will be able to oppose barriers to truth that will long be insurmountable?

Then will arrive the moment in which the sun will observe in its course free nations only, acknowledging no other master than their reason; in which tyrants and slaves, priests and their stupid or hypocritical instruments, will no longer exist but in history and upon the stage; in which our only concern will be to lament their past victims and dupes, and, by the recollection of their horrid enormities, to exercise a vigilant circumspection, that we may be able instantly to recognize and effectually to stifle by the force of reason, the seeds of superstition and tyranny, should they ever presume again to make their appearance upon the earth.

In tracing the history of societies we have had occasion to remark, that there frequently exists a considerable distinction between the rights which the law acknowledges in the citizens of a state, and those which they really enjoy; between the equality established by political institutions, and that which takes place between the individual members: and that to this disproportion was chiefly owing the destruction of liberty in the ancient republics, the storms which they had to encounter, and the weakness that surrendered them into the power of foreign tyrants.

Three principal causes may be assigned for these distinctions: inequality of wealth, inequality of condition between him whose resources of subsistence are secured to himself and descendable to his family, and him whose resources are annihilated with the termination of his life, or rather of that part of his life in which he is capable of labour; and lastly, inequality of instruction.

It will therefore behove us to shew, that these three kinds of real inequality must continually diminish; but without becoming absolutely extinct, since they have natural and necessary causes, which it would be absurd as well as dangerous to think of destroying; nor can we attempt even to destroy entirely their effects, without opening at the same time more fruitful sources of inequality, and giving to the rights of man a more direct and more fatal blow. . . .

The equality of instruction we can hope to attain, and with which we ought to be satisfied, is that which excludes every species of dependence, whether forced or voluntary. We may exhibit, in the actual state of human knowledge, the easy means by which this end may be attained even for those who can devote to study but a few years of infancy, and, in subsequent life, only some occasional hours of leisure. We might shew, that by a happy choice of the subjects to be taught, and of the mode of inculcating them, the entire mass of a people may be instructed in every thing necessary for the purposes of domestic economy; for the transaction of their affairs; for the free development of their industry and their faculties; for the knowledge, exercise and protection of their rights; for a sense of their duties, and the power of discharging them; for the capacity of judging both their own actions, and the actions of others, by their own understanding; for the acquisition of all the delicate or dignified sentiments that are an honour to humanity; for freeing themselves from a blind confidence in those to whom they may entrust the care of their interests, and the security of their rights; for choosing and watching over them, so as no longer to be the dupes of those popular errors that torment and way-lay the life of man with superstitious fears and chimerical hopes; for defending themselves against prejudices by the sole energy of reason; in fine, for escaping from the delusions of imposture, which would spread snares for their fortune, their health, their freedom of opinion and of conscience, under the pretext of enriching, of healing, and of saving them. . . .

The advantages that must result from the state of improvement, of which I have proved we may almost entertain the certain hope, can have no limit but the absolute perfection of the human species, since, in proportion as different kinds of equality shall be established as to the various means of providing for our wants, as to a more universal instruction, and a more entire liberty, the more real will be this equality, and the nearer will it approach towards embracing every thing truly important to the happiness of mankind.

It is then by examining the progression and the laws of this perfection, that we can alone arrive at the knowledge of the extent or boundary of our hopes.

It has never yet been supposed, that all the facts of nature, and all the means of acquiring precision in the computation and analysis of those facts, and all the connections of objects with each other, and all the possible combinations of ideas, can be exhausted by the human mind. The mere relations of magnitude, the combinations, quantity and extent of this idea alone, form already a system too immense for the mind of man ever to grasp the whole of it; a portion, more vast than that which he may have penetrated, will always remain unknown to him. It has, however, been imagined, that, as man can know a part only of the objects which the nature of his intelligence permits him to investigate, he must at length reach the point at which, the number and complication of those he already knows having absorbed all his powers, farther progress will become absolutely impossible.

But, in proportion as facts are multiplied, man learns to class them, and reduce them to more general facts, at the same time that the instruments and methods for observing them, and registering them with exactness, acquire a new precision: in proportion as relations more multifarious between a greater number of objects are discovered, man continues to reduce them to relations of a wider denomination, to express them with greater simplicity, and to present them in a way which may enable a given strength of mind, with a given quantity of attention, to take in a greater number than before: in proportion as the understanding embraces more complicated combinations, a simple mode of announcing these combinations renders them more easy to be treated. Hence it follows that truths, the discovery of which was accompanied with the most laborious efforts, and which at first could not be comprehended but by men of the severest attention, will after a time be unfolded and proved in methods that are not above the efforts of an ordinary capacity. And thus should the methods that led to new combinations be exhausted, should their applications to questions, still unresolved, demand exertions greater than the time or the powers of the learned can bestow, more general methods, means more simple would soon come to their aid, and open a farther career to genius. The energy, the real extent of the human intellect may remain the same; but the instruments which it can employ will be multiplied and improved; but the language which fixes and determines the ideas will acquire more precision and compass; and it will not be here, as in the science of mechanics where, to increase the force, we must diminish the velocity; on the contrary the methods by which genius will arrive at the discovery of new truths, augment at once both the force and the rapidity of its operations.

In a word, these changes being themselves the necessary consequences of additional progress in the knowledge of truths of detail, and the cause which produces a demand for new resources, producing at the same time the means of supplying them, it follows that the actual mass of truths appertaining to the sciences of observation, calculation and experiment, may be perpetually augmented, and that without supposing the faculties of man to possess a force and activity, and a scope of action greater than before. . . .

If we pass to the progress of the arts, those arts particularly the theory of which depends on these very same sciences, we shall find that it can have no inferior limits;

that their processes are susceptible of the same improvement, the same simplifications, as the scientific methods; that instruments, machines, looms, will add every day to the capabilities and skill of man—will augment at once the excellence and precision of his works, while they will diminish the time and labour necessary for executing them; and that then will disappear the obstacles that still oppose themselves to the progress in question, accidents which will be foreseen and prevented; and, lastly, the unhealthiness at present attendant upon certain operations, habits and climates.

A smaller portion of ground will then be made to produce a portion of provisions of higher value or greater utility; a greater quantity of enjoyment will be procured at a smaller expense of consumption; the same manufactured or artificial commodity will be produced at a smaller expense of raw materials, or will be stronger and more durable; every soil will be appropriated to productions which will satisfy a greater number of wants with the least labour, and taken in the smallest quantities. Thus the means of health and frugality will be encreased, together with the instruments in the arts of production, of curing commodities and manufacturing their produce, without demanding the sacrifice of one enjoyment by the consumer.

Thus, not only the same species of ground will nourish a greater number of individuals, but each individual, with a less quantity of labour, will labour more successfully, and be surrounded with greater conveniences.

It may, however, be demanded, whether, amidst this improvement in industry and happiness, where the wants and faculties of men will continually become better proportioned, each successive generation possess more various stores, and of consequence in each generation the number of individuals be greatly increased; it may, I say, be demanded, whether these principles of improvement and increase may not, by their continual operation, ultimately lead to degeneracy and destruction? Whether the number of inhabitants in the universe at length exceeding the means of existence, there will not result a continual decay of happiness and population, and a progress towards barbarism, or at least a sort of oscillation between good and evil? Will not this oscillation, in societies arrived at this epoch, be a perennial source of periodical calamity and distress? In a word, do not these considerations point out the limit at which all farther improvement will become impossible, and consequently the perfectibility of man arrive at a period which in the immensity of ages it may attain, but which it can never pass?

There is, doubtless, no individual that does not perceive how very remote from us will be this period: but must it one day arrive? It is equally impossible to pronounce on either side respecting an event, which can only be realized at an epoch when the human species will necessarily have acquired a degree of knowledge, of which our short-sighted understandings can scarcely form an idea. And who shall presume to foretell to what perfection the art of converting the elements of life into substances fitted for our use, may, in a progression of ages, be brought?

But supposing the affirmative, supposing it actually to take place, there would result from it nothing alarming, either to the happiness of the human race, or its indefinite perfectibility; if we consider, that prior to this period the progress of reason will have walked hand in hand with that of the sciences; that the absurd prejudices of superstition will have ceased to infuse into morality a harshness that corrupts and degrades, instead of purifying and exalting it; that men will then know, that the duties they may be under relative to propagation will consist not in the question of giving *existence* to a greater number of beings, but *happiness;* will have for their object, the general welfare of the human species; of the society in which they live; of the family to which they are attached; and not the puerile idea of encumbering the earth with useless and wretched mortals. Accordingly, there might then be a limit to the possible mass of provision, and of consequence to the greatest possible population, without that premature destruction, so contrary to nature and to social prosperity, of a portion of the beings who may have received life, being the result of those limits. . . .

It will be impossible for men to become enlightened upon the nature and development of their moral sentiments, upon the principles of morality, upon the motives for conforming their conduct to those principles, and upon their interests, whether relative to their individual or social capacity, without making, at the same time, an advancement in moral practice, not less real than that of the science itself. Is not a mistaken interest the most frequent cause of actions contrary to the general welfare? Is not the impetuosity of our passions the continual result, either of habits to which we addict ourselves from a false calculation, or of ignorance of the means by which to resist their first impulse, to divert, govern, and direct their action?

Is not the practice of reflecting upon our conduct; of trying it by the touchstone of reason and conscience; of exercising those humane sentiments which blend our happiness with that of others, the necessary consequence of the well-directed study of morality, and of a greater equality in the conditions of the social compact? Will not that consciousness of his own dignity, appertaining to the man who is free, that system of education built upon a more profound knowledge of our moral constitution, render common to almost every man those principles of a strict and unsullied justice, those habitual propensities of an active and enlightened benevolence, of a delicate and generous sensibility, of which nature has planted the seeds in our hearts, and which wait only for the genial influence of knowledge and liberty to expand and to fructify? In like manner as the mathematical and physical sciences tend to improve the arts that are employed for our most simple wants, so is it not equally in the necessary order of nature that the moral and political sciences should exercise a similar influence upon the motives that direct our sentiments and our actions?

What is the object of the improvement of laws and public institutions, consequent upon the progress of these sciences, but to reconcile, to approximate, to blend and unite into one mass the common interest of each individual with the common interest of all? What is the end of the social art, but to destroy the opposition between these two apparently jarring sentiments? And will not the constitution and laws of that country best accord with the intentions of reason and nature where the practice of virtue shall be least difficult, and the temptations to deviate from her paths least numerous and least powerful.

What vicious habit can be mentioned, what practice contrary to good faith, what crime even, the origin and first cause of which may not be traced in the legislation, institutions and prejudices of the country in which we observe such habit, such practice, or such crime to be committed?

In short, does not the well-being, the prosperity, resulting from the progress that will be made by the useful arts, in consequence of their being founded upon a sound theory, resulting, also, from an improved legislation, built upon the truths of the political sciences, naturally dispose men to humanity, to benevolence, and to justice? Do not all the observations, fine, which we proposed to develop in this work prove, that the moral goodness of man, the necessary consequence of his organization, is, like all his other faculties, susceptible of an indefinite improvement? and that nature has connected, by a chain which cannot be broken, truth, happiness, and virtue?

Among those causes of human improvement that are of most importance to the general welfare, must be included, the total annihilation of the prejudices which have established between the sexes an inequality of rights, fatal even to the party which it favours. In vain might we search for motives by which to justify this principle, in difference of physical organization, of intellect, or of moral sensibility. It had at first no other origin but abuse of strength, and all the attempts which have since been made to support it are idle sophisms.

And here we may observe, how much the abolition of the usages authorized by this prejudice, and of the laws which it has dictated, would tend to augment the happiness of families; to render common the virtues of domestic life, the fountain-head of all the others; to favour instruction, and, especially, to make it truly general, either because it would be extended to both sexes with greater equality, or because it cannot become general, even to men, without the concurrence of the mothers of families. Would not this homage, so long in paying, to the divinities of equity and good sense, put an end to a too fertile principle of injustice, cruelty, and crime, by superseding the opposition hitherto maintained between that natural propensity, which is, of all others, the most imperious, and the most difficult to subdue, and the interests of man, or the duties of society? Would it not produce, what has hitherto been a mere chimera, national manners of a nature mild and pure, formed, not by imperious privations, by hypocritical appearances, by reserves imposed by the fear of shame or religious terrors, but by habits freely contracted, inspired by nature and avowed by reason?

The people being more enlightened, and having resumed the right of disposing for themselves of their blood and their treasure, will learn by degrees to regard war as the most dreadful of all calamities, the most terrible of all crimes. The first wars that will be superseded, will be those into which the usurpers of sovereignty have hitherto drawn their subjects for the maintenance of rights pretendedly hereditary.

Nations will know, that they cannot become conquerors without losing their freedom; that perpetual confederations are the only means of maintaining their independence; that their object should be security, and not power. By degrees commercial prejudices will die away; a false mercantile interest will lose the terrible power of imbuing the earth with blood, and of ruining nations under the idea of enriching them. As the people of different countries will at last be drawn into closer intimacy, by the principles of politics and morality, as each, for its own advantage, will invite foreigners to an equal participation of the benefits which it may have derived either from nature or its own industry, all the causes which produce, envenom, and perpetuate national animosities, will one by one disappear, and will no more furnish to warlike insanity either fuel or pretext.

Institutions, better combined than those projects of perpetual peace which have occupied the leisure and consoled the heart of certain philosophers, will accelerate the progress of this fraternity of nations; and wars, like assassinations, will be ranked in the number of those daring atrocities, humiliating and loathsome to nature; and which fix upon the country or the age whose annals are stained with them, an indelible opprobrium. . . .

All the causes which contribute to the improvement of the human species, all the means we have enumerated that insure its progress, must, from their very nature, exercise an influence always active, and acquire an extent for every increasing. The proofs of this have been exhibited, and from their development in the work itself they will derive additional force: accordingly we may already conclude, that the perfectibility of man is indefinite. Meanwhile we have hitherto considered him as possessing only the same natural faculties, as endowed with the same organization. How much greater would be the certainty, how much wider the compass of our hopes, could we prove that these natural faculties themselves, that this very organization, are also susceptible of melioration? And this is the last question we shall examine.

The organic perfectibility or deterioration of the classes of the vegetable, or species of the animal kingdom, may be regarded as one of the general laws of nature.

This law extends itself to the human race; and it cannot be doubted that the progress of the sanative art, that the use of more wholesome food and more comfortable habitations, that a mode of life which shall develop the physical powers by exercise, without at the same time impairing them by excess; in fine, that the destruction of the two most active causes of deterioration, penury and wretchedness on the one hand, and enormous wealth on the other, must necessarily tend to prolong the common duration of man's existence, and secure him a more constant health and a more robust constitution. It is manifest that the improvement of the practice of medicine, become more efficacious in consequence of the progress of reason and the social order, must in the end put a period to transmissible or contagious disorders, as well to those general maladies resulting from climate, ailments, and the nature of certain occupations. Nor would it be difficult to prove that this hope might be extended to almost every other malady, of which it is probable we shall hereafter discover the most remote causes. Would it even be absurd to suppose this quality of melioration in the human species as susceptible of an indefinite advancement; to suppose that a period must one day arrive when death will be nothing more than the effect either of extraordinary accidents, or of the slow and gradual decay of the vital powers; and that the duration of the middle space, of the interval between the birth of man and this decay, will itself have no assignable limit? Certainly man will not become immortal; but may not the distance between the moment in which he draws his first breath, and the common term when, in the course of nature, without malady, without accident, he finds it impossible any longer to exist, be necessarily protracted? As we are now speaking of a progress that is capable of being represented with precision, by numerical quantities or by lines, we shall embrace the opportunity of explaining the two meanings that may be affixed to the word *indefinite*.

In reality, this middle term of life, which in proportion as men advance upon the ocean of futurity, we have supposed incessantly to increase, may receive additions either in conformity to a law by which, though approaching continually an illimitable extent, it could never possibly arrive at it; or a law by which, in the immensity of ages, it may acquire a greater extent than any determinate quantity whatever that may be assigned as its limit. In the latter case, this duration of life is indefinite in the strictest sense of the word, since there exist no bounds on this side of which it must necessarily stop. And in the former, it is equally indefinite to us; if we cannot fix the term, it may for ever approach, but can never surpass; particularly if, knowing only that it can never stop, we are ignorant in which of the two senses the term indefinite is applicable to it: and this is precisely the state of the knowledge we have as yet acquired relative to the perfectibility of the species.

Thus, in the instance we are considering, we are bound to believe that the mean duration of human life will for ever increase, unless its increase be prevented by the physical revolutions of the system: but we cannot tell what is the bound which the duration of human life can never exceed; we cannot even tell, whether there be any circumstance in the laws of nature which has determined and laid down its limit.

But may not our physical faculties, the force, the sagacity, the acuteness of the senses, be numbered among the qualities, the individual improvement of which it will be practicable to transmit? At attention to the different breeds of domestic animals must lead us to adopt the affirmative of this question, and a direct observation of the human species itself will be found to strengthen the opinion.

Lastly, may we not include in the same circle the intellectual and moral faculties? May not our parents, who transmit to us the advantages or defects of their conformation, and from whom we receive our features and shape, as well as our propensities to certain physical affections, transmit to us also that part of organization upon which intellect, strength of understanding, energy of soul or moral sensibility depend? Is it not probable that education, by improving these qualities, will at the same time have an influence upon, will modify and improve this organization itself? Analogy, an investigation of the human faculties, and even some facts, appear to authorize these conjectures, and thereby to enlarge the boundary of our hopes.

Such are the questions with which we shall terminate the last division of our work. And how admirably calculated is the view of the human race, emancipated from its chains, released alike from the dominion of chance, as well as from that of the enemies of its progress, and advancing with a firm and indeviate step in the paths of truth, to console the philosopher lamenting the errors, the flagrant acts of injustice, the crimes with which the earth is still polluted? It is the contemplation of this prospect that rewards him for all his efforts to assist the progress of reason and the establishment of liberty. He dares to regard these efforts as a part of the eternal chain of the destiny of mankind; and in this persuasion he finds the true delight of virtue, the pleasure of having performed a durable service, which no vicissitude will ever destroy in a fatal operation calculated to restore the reign of prejudice and slavery. This sentiment is the asylum into which he retires, and to which the memory of his persecutors cannot follow him: he unites himself in imagination with man restored to his rights, delivered from oppression, and proceeding with rapid strides in the path of happiness: he forgets his own misfortunes while his thoughts are thus employed; he lives no longer to adversity, calumny and malice, but becomes the associate of these wiser and more fortunate beings whose enviable condition he so earnestly contributed to produce.

✺ POPULATION

Thomas Robert Malthus

*Since the eighteenth century, supporters of the ideals of liberal and demo-
cratic social progress have had to contend with opponents who have
asserted the undesirability of this movement. A different kind of opposition has come from those who, although asserting their sympathy with
its aims, declare that these aims are impossible to achieve. Such a writer
was Thomas Robert Malthus (1766–1834), widely read English clergyman, economist, and man of letters. In his famous* Essay on the Principle
of Population *(1798), from which the following selections are taken,
his principal opponent is the equally well-known English anarchist
and social philosopher William Godwin (1756–1836), whose book*
Political Justice *(1793), was, for a long time, the great radical classic.
Godwin, like Condorcet (see pages 258–259), had argued for the perfectibility of individuals and society by a clearing away of those coercive social
institutions which stood in the way of the operation of man's natural
goodness.*

*Although Malthus' book on population did not deter the progressive
movement, it did provide a convenient rationale for those whose interest
demanded that the movement be slowed down, and from time to time
there have been echoes of its pessimistic message. His influence has also
been considerable in the development of social science generally, and
by Darwin's own admission, in the development of the theory of biological
evolution.*

CHAPTER I

The great and unlooked for discoveries that have taken place of late years in natural
philosophy, the increasing diffusion of general knowledge from the extension of the
art of printing, the ardent and unshackled spirit of inquiry that prevails throughout
the lettered and even unlettered world, the new and extraordinary lights that have been
thrown on political subjects which dazzle and astonish the understanding, and particularly that tremendous phenomenon in the political horizon, the French revolution,
which, like a blazing comet, seems destined either to inspire with fresh life and vigour,
or to scorch up and destroy the shrinking inhabitants of the earth, have all concurred

Thomas Robert Malthus, *Population: The First Essay* (Ann Arbor, Mich.: University of
Michigan Press, 1959), pp. 1–13, 61–72.

to lead many able men into the opinion that we were touching on a period big with the most important changes, changes that would in some measure be decisive of the future fate of mankind.

It has been said that the great question is now at issue, whether man shall henceforth start forwards with accelerated velocity towards illimitable, and hitherto unconceived improvement, or be condemned to a perpetual oscillation between happiness and misery, and after every effort remain still at an immeasurable distance from the wished-for goal.

Yet, anxiously as every friend of mankind must look forwards to the termination of this painful suspense, and eagerly as the inquiring mind would hail every ray of light that might assist its view into futurity, it is much to be lamented that the writers on each side of this momentous question still keep far aloof from each other. Their mutual arguments do not meet with a candid examination. The question is not brought to rest on fewer points, and even in theory scarcely seems to be approaching to a decision.

The advocate for the present order of things is apt to treat the sect of speculative philosophers either as a set of artful and designing knaves who preach up ardent benevolence and draw captivating pictures of a happier state of society only the better to enable them to destroy the present establishments and to forward their own deep-laid schemes of ambition, or as wild and mad-headed enthusiasts whose silly speculations and absurd paradoxes are not worthy the attention of any reasonable man.

The advocate for the perfectibility of man, and of society, retorts on the defender of establishments a more than equal contempt. He brands him as the slave of the most miserable and narrow prejudices; or, as the defender of the abuses of civil society, only because he profits by them. He paints him either as a character who prostitutes his understanding to his interest, or as one whose powers of mind are not of a size to grasp any thing great and noble, who cannot see above five yards before him, and who must therefore be utterly unable to take in the views of the enlightened benefactor of mankind.

In this unamicable contest the cause of truth cannot but suffer. The really good arguments on each side of the question are not allowed to have their proper weight. Each pursues his own theory, little solicitous to correct or improve it by an attention to what is advanced by his opponents.

The friend of the present order of things condemns all political speculations in the gross. He will not even condescend to examine the grounds from which the perfectibility of society is inferred. Much less will he give himself the trouble in a fair and candid manner to attempt an exposition of their fallacy.

The speculative philosopher equally offends against the cause of truth. With eyes fixed on a happier state of society, the blessings of which he paints in the most captivating colours, he allows himself to indulge in the most bitter invectives against every present establishment, without applying his talents to consider the best and safest means of removing abuses and without seeming to be aware of the tremendous obstacles that threaten, even in theory, to oppose the progress of man towards perfection.

It is an acknowledged truth in philosophy that a just theory will always be confirmed by experiment. Yet so much friction, and so many minute circumstances occur in practice, which it is next to impossible for the most enlarged and penetrating mind to foresee, that on few subjects can any theory be pronounced just, that has not stood the test of experience. But an untried theory cannot fairly be advanced as probable, much less as just, till all the arguments against it have been maturely weighed and clearly and consistently refuted.

I have read some of the speculations on the perfectibility of man and of society with great pleasure. I have been warmed and delighted with the enchanting picture which they hold forth. I ardently wish for such happy improvements. But I see great, and, to my understanding, unconquerable difficulties in the way to them. These difficulties it is my present purpose to state, declaring, at the same time, that so far from exulting in them, as a cause of triumph over the friends of innovation, nothing would give me greater pleasure than to see them completely removed.

The most important argument that I shall adduce is certainly not new. . . . I should certainly therefore not think of advancing it again, though I mean to place it in a point of view in some degree different from any that I have hitherto seen, if it had ever been fairly and satisfactorily answered.

The cause of this neglect on the part of the advocates for the perfectibility of mankind is not easily accounted for. I cannot doubt the talents of such men as Godwin and Condorcet. I am unwilling to doubt their candour. To my understanding, and probably to that of most others, the difficulty appears insurmountable. Yet these men of acknowledged ability and penetration, scarcely deign to notice it, and hold on their course in such speculations, with unabated ardour and undiminished confidence. I have certainly no right to say that they purposely shut their eyes to such arguments. I ought rather to doubt the validity of them, when neglected by such men, however forcibly their truth may strike my own mind. Yet in this respect it must be acknowledged that we are all of us too prone to err. If I saw a glass of wine repeatedly presented to a man, and he took no notice of it, I should be apt to think that he was blind or uncivil. A juster philosophy might teach me rather to think that my eyes deceived me and that the offer was not really what I conceived it to be.

In entering upon the argument I must premise that I put out of the question, at present, all mere conjectures, that is, all suppositions, the probable realization of which cannot be inferred upon any just philosophical grounds. A writer may tell me that he thinks man will ultimately become an ostrich. I cannot properly contradict him. But before he can expect to bring any reasonable person over to his opinion, he ought to shew, that the necks of mankind have been gradually elongating, that the lips have grown harder and more prominent, that the legs and feet are daily altering their shape, and that the hair is beginning to change into stubs of feathers. And till the probability of so wonderful a conversion can be shewn, it is surely lost time and lost eloquence to expatiate on the happiness of man in such a state; to describe his powers, both of running and flying, to paint him in a condition where all narrow luxuries would be contemned, where he would be employed only in collecting the necessaries of life, and where, consequently, each man's share of labour would be light, and his portion of leisure ample.

I think I may fairly make two postulata.

First, That food is necessary to the existence of man.

Secondly, That the passion between the sexes is necessary and will remain nearly in its present state.

These two laws, ever since we have had any knowledge of mankind, appear to have been fixed laws of our nature, and, as we have not hitherto seen any alteration in them, we have no right to conclude that they will ever cease to be what they now are, without an immediate act of power in that Being who first arranged the system of the universe, and for the advantage of his creatures, still executes, according to fixed laws, all its various operations.

I do not know that any writer has supposed that on this earth man will ultimately be able to live without food. But Mr. Goodwin has conjectured that the passion between the sexes may in time be extinguished. As, however, he calls this part of his work a deviation into the land of conjecture, I will not dwell longer upon it at present than to say that the best arguments for the perfectibility of man are drawn from a contemplation of the great progress that he has already made from the savage state and the difficulty of saying where he is to stop. But towards the extinction of the passion between the sexes, no progress whatever has hitherto been made. It appears to exist in as much force at present as it did two thousand or four thousand years ago. There are individual exceptions now as there always have been. But, as these exceptions do not appear to increase in number, it would surely be a very unphilosophical mode of arguing, to infer merely from the existence of an exception, that the exception would, in time, become the rule, and the rule the exception.

Assuming then, my postulata as granted, I say, that the power of population is indefinitely greater than the power in the earth to produce subsistence for man.

Population, when unchecked, increases in a geometrical ratio. Subsistence increases only in an arithmetical ratio. A slight acquaintance with numbers will shew the immensity of the first power in comparison of the second.

By that law of our nature which makes food necessary to the life of man, the effects of these two unequal powers must be kept equal.

This implies a strong and constantly operating check on population from the difficulty of subsistence. This difficulty must fall some where and must necessarily be severely felt by a large portion of mankind.

Through the animal and vegetable kingdom, nature has scattered the seeds of life abroad with the most profuse and liberal hand. She has been comparatively sparing in the room and the nourishment necessary to rear them. The germs of existence contained in this spot of earth, with ample food, and ample room to expand in, would fill millions of worlds in the course of a few thousand years. Necessity, that imperious all pervading law of nature, restrains them within the prescribed bounds. The race of plants, and the race of animals shrink under this great restrictive law. And the race of man cannot, by any efforts of reason, escape from it. Among plants and animals its effects are waste of seed, sickness, and premature death. Among mankind, misery and vice. The former, misery, is an absolutely necessary consequence of it. Vice is a highly probable consequence, and we therefore see it abundantly prevail, but it ought not, perhaps, to be called an absolutely necessary consequence. The ordeal of virtue is to resist all temptation to evil.

This natural inequality of the two powers of population and of production in the earth and that great law of our nature which must constantly keep their effects equal form the great difficulty that to me appears insurmountable in the way to the perfectibility of society. All other arguments are of slight and subordinate consideration in comparison of this. I see no way by which man can escape from the weight of this law which pervades all animated nature. No fancied equality, no agrarian regulations in their utmost extent, could remove the pressure of it even for a single century. And it appears, therefore, to be decisive against the possible existence of a society, all the members of which should live in ease, happiness, and comparative leisure; and feel no anxiety about providing the means of subsistence for themselves and families.

Consequently, if the premises are just, the argument is conclusive against the perfectibility of the mass of mankind.

I have thus sketched the general outline of the argument, but I will examine it more particularly, and I think it will be found that experience, the true source and foundation of all knowledge, invariably confirms its truth.

CHAPTER II

I said that population, when unchecked, increased in a geometrical ratio, and subsistence for man in an arithmetical ratio.

Let us examine whether this position be just.

I think it will be allowed, that no state has hitherto existed (at least that we have any account of) where the manners were so pure and simple, and the means of subsistence so abundant, that no check whatever has existed to early marriages, among the lower classes, from a fear of not providing well for their families, or among the higher classes, from a fear of lowering their condition in life. Consequently in no state that we have yet known has the power of population been left to exert itself with perfect freedom.

Whether the law of marriage be instituted or not, the dictate of nature and virtue seems to be an early attachment to one woman. Supposing a liberty of changing in the case of an unfortunate choice, this liberty would not affect population till it arose to a height greatly vicious; and we are now supposing the existence of a society where vice is scarcely known.

In a state therefore of great equality and virtue, where pure and simple manners prevailed, and where the means of subsistence were so abundant that no part of the society could have any fears about providing amply for a family, the power of population being left to exert itself unchecked, the increase of the human species would evidently be much greater than any increase that has been hitherto known.

In the United States of America, where the means of subsistence have been more ample, the manners of the people more pure, and consequently the checks to early marriages fewer than in any of the modern states of Europe, the population has been found to double itself in twenty-five years.

This ratio of increase, though short of the utmost power of population, yet as the result of actual experience, we will take as our rule, and say, that population, when unchecked, goes on doubling itself every twenty-five years or increases in a geometrical ratio.

Let us now take any spot of earth, this Island for instance, and see in what ratio the subsistence it affords can be supposed to increase. We will begin with it under its present state of cultivation.

If I allow that by the best possible policy, by breaking up more land and by great encouragements to agriculture, the produce of this Island may be doubled in the first twenty-five years, I think it will be allowing as much as any person can well demand.

In the next twenty-five years, it is impossible to suppose that the produce could be quadrupled. It would be contrary to all our knowledge of the qualities of land. The very utmost that we can conceive, is, that the increase in the second twenty-five years might equal the present produce. Let us then take this for our rule, though certainly far beyond the truth, and allow that by great exertion, the whole produce of the Island might be increased every twenty-five years, by a quantity of subsistence equal to what it at present produces. The most enthusiastic speculator cannot suppose a greater increase than this. In a few centuries it would make every acre of land in the Island like a garden.

Yet this ratio of increase is evidently arithmetical.

It may be fairly said, therefore, that the means of subsistence increase in an arithmetical ratio. Let us now bring the effects of these two ratios together.

The population of the Island is computed to be about seven millions, and we will suppose the present produce equal to the support of such a number. In the first twenty-five years the population would be fourteen millions, and the food being also doubled, the means of subsistence would be equal to this increase. In the next twenty-five years the population would be twenty-eight millions, and the means of subsistence only equal to the support of twenty-one millions. In the next period, the population would be fifty-six millions, and the means of subsistence just sufficient for half that number. And at the conclusion of the first century the population would be one hundred and twelve millions and the means of subsistence only equal to the support of thirty-five millions, which would leave a population of seventy-seven millions totally unprovided for.

A great emigration necessarily implies unhappiness of some kind or other in the country that is deserted. For few persons will leave their families, connections, friends, and native land, to seek a settlement in untried foreign climes, without some strong subsisting causes of uneasiness where they are, or the hope of some great advantages in the place to which they are going.

But to make the argument more general and less interrupted by the partial views of emigration, let us take the whole earth, instead of one spot, and suppose that the restraints to population were universally removed. If the subsistence for man that the earth affords was to be increased every twenty-five years by a quantity equal to what the whole world at present produces, this would allow the power of production in the earth to be absolutely unlimited, and its ratio of increase much greater than we can conceive that any possible exertions of mankind could make it.

Taking the population of the world at any number, a thousand millions, for instance, the human species would increase in the ratio of—1, 2, 4, 8, 16, 32, 64, 128, 256, 512, etc. and subsistence as—1, 2, 3, 4, 5, 6, 7, 8, 9, 10, etc. In two centuries and a quarter, the population would be to the means of subsistence as 512 to 10: in three centuries as 4096 to 13, and in two thousand years the difference would be almost incalculable, though the produce in that time would have increased to an immense extent.

No limits whatever are placed to the productions of the earth; they may increase for ever and be greater than any assignable quantity; yet still the power of population being a power of a superior order, the increase of the human species can only be kept commensurate to the increase of the means of subsistence, by the constant operation of the strong law of necessity acting as a check upon the greater power.

The effects of this check remain now to be considered.

Among plants and animals the view of the subject is simple. They are all impelled by a powerful instinct to the increase of their species, and this instinct is interrupted by no reasoning or doubts about providing for their offspring. Wherever therefore there is liberty, the power of increase is exerted, and the super-abundant effects are repressed afterwards by want of room and nourishment, which is common to animals and plants, and among animals, by becoming the prey of others.

The effects of this check on man are more complicated. Impelled to the increase of his species by an equally powerful instinct, reason interrupts his career and asks him whether he may not bring beings into the world, for whom he cannot provide the means of subsistence. In a state of equality, this would be the simple question. In the present state of society, other considerations occur. Will he not lower his rank in life? Will he not subject himself to greater difficulties than he at present feels? Will he not be obliged to labour harder? and if he has a large family, will his utmost exertions enable him to support them? May he not see his offspring in rags and misery, and clamouring for bread that he cannot give them? And may he not be reduced to the grating necessity of forfeiting his independence, and of being obliged to the sparing hand of charity for support?

These considerations are calculated to prevent, and certainly do prevent, a very great number in all civilized nations from pursuing the dictate of nature in an early attachment to one woman. And this restraint almost necessarily, though not absolutely so, produces vice. Yet in all societies, even those that are most vicious, the tendency to a virtuous attachment is so strong that there is a constant effort towards an increase of population. This constant effort as constantly tends to subject the lower classes of the society to distress and to prevent any great permanent amelioration of their condition.

The way in which these effects are produced seems to be this.

We will suppose the means of subsistence in any country just equal to the easy support of its inhabitants. The constant effort towards population, which is found to act even in the most vicious societies, increases the number of people before the means of subsistence are increased. The food therefore which before supported seven millions must now be divided among seven millions and a half or eight millions. The poor consequently must live much worse, and many of them be reduced to severe distress. The number of labourers also being above the proportion of the work in the market, the price of labour must tend toward a decrease, while the price of provisions would at the same time tend to rise. The labourer therefore must work harder to earn the same as he did before. During this season of distress, the discouragements to marriage, and the difficulty of rearing a family are so great that population is at a stand. In the mean time the cheapness of labour, the plenty of labourers, and the necessity of an increased industry amongst them, encourage cultivators to employ more labour upon their land, to turn up fresh soil, and to manure and improve more completely what is already in tillage, till ultimately the means of subsistence become in the same proportion to the population as at the period from which we set out. The situation of the labourer being then again tolerably comfortable, the restraints to population are in some degree loosened, and the same retrograde and progressive movements with respect to happiness are repeated.

This sort of oscillation will not be remarked by superficial observers, and it may be difficult even for the most penetrating mind to calculate its periods. Yet that in all old states some such vibration does exist, though from various transverse causes, in a much less marked, and in a much more irregular manner than I have described it, no reflecting man who considers the subject deeply can well doubt.

Many reasons occur why this oscillation has been less obvious, and less decidedly confirmed by experience, than might naturally be expected.

One principal reason is that the histories of mankind that we possess are histories only of the higher classes. We have but few accounts that can be depended upon of the manners and customs of that part of mankind, where these retrograde and progressive movements chiefly take place. A satisfactory history of this kind, of one people, and of one period, would require the constant and minute attention of an observing mind during a long life. Some of the objects of enquiry would be, in what proportion to the number of adults was the number of marriages, to what extent vicious customs prevailed in consequence of the restraints upon matrimony, what was the comparative mortality among the children of the most distressed part of the community and those who lived rather more at their ease, what were the variations in the real price of labour, and what were the observable differences in the state of the lower classes of society with respect to ease and happiness, at different times during a certain period.

Such a history would tend greatly to elucidate the manner in which the constant check upon population acts and would probably prove the existence of the retrograde and progressive movements that have been mentioned, though the times of their vibration must necessarily be rendered irregular, from the operation of many interrupting causes, such as the introduction or failure of certain manufactures, a greater or less prevalent spirit of agricultural enterprize, years of plenty, or years of scarcity, wars and pestilence, poor laws, the invention of processes for shortening labour without the proportional extension of the market for the commodity, and, particularly, the difference between the nominal and real price of labour, a circumstance which has perhaps more than any other contributed to conceal this oscillation from common view.

It very rarely happens that the nominal price of labour universally falls, but we well know that it frequently remains the same, while the nominal price of provisions has been gradually increasing. This is, in effect, a real fall in the price of labour, and during this period the condition of the lower orders of the community must gradually grow worse and worse. But the farmers and capitalists are growing rich from the real cheapness of labour. Their increased capitals enable them to employ a greater number of men. Work therefore may be plentiful, and the price of labour would consequently rise. But the want of freedom in the market of labour, which occurs more or less in all communities, either from parish laws, or the more general cause of the facility of combination among the rich, and its difficulty among the poor, operates to prevent the price of labour from rising at the natural period, and keeps it down some time longer; perhaps, till a year of scarcity, when the clamor is too loud, and the necessity too apparent to be resisted.

The true cause of the advance in the price of labour is thus concealed, and the rich affect to grant it as an act of compassion and favour to the poor, in consideration of a year of scarcity, and, when plenty returns, indulge themselves in the most unreasonable of all complaints, that the price does not again fall, when a little reflection would shew them that it must have risen long before but from an unjust conspiracy of their own.

But though the rich by unfair combinations contribute frequently to prolong a season of distress among the poor, yet no possible form of society could prevent the almost constant action of misery upon a great part of mankind, if in a state of inequality, and upon all, if all were equal.

The theory on which the truth of this position depends appears to me so extremely clear that I feel at a loss to conjecture what part of it can be denied.

That population cannot increase without the means of subsistence is a proposition so evident that it needs no illustration.

That population does invariably increase where there are the means of subsistence, the history of every people that have ever existed will abundantly prove.

And that the superior power of population cannot be checked without producing misery or vice, the ample portion of these too bitter ingredients in the cup of human life and the continuance of the physical causes that seem to have produced them bear too convincing a testimony.

But in order more fully to ascertain the validity of these three propositions, let us examine the different states in which mankind have been known to exist. Even a cursory review will, I think, be sufficient to convince us that these propositions are incontrovertible truths. . . .

CHAPTER X

In reading Mr. Godwin's ingenious and able work on political justice, it is impossible not to be struck with the spirit and energy of his style, the force and precision of some of his reasonings, the ardent tone of his thoughts, and particularly with that impressive earnestness of manner which gives an air of truth to the whole. At the same time, it must be confessed that he has not proceeded in his enquiries with the caution that sound philosophy seems to require. His conclusions are often unwarranted by his premises. He fails sometimes in removing the objections which he himself brings forward. He relies too much on general and abstract propositions which will not admit of application. And his conjectures certainly far outstrip the modesty of nature.

The system of equality which Mr. Godwin proposes is, without doubt, by far the most beautiful and engaging of any that has yet appeared. An amelioration of society to be produced merely by reason and conviction wears much more the promise of permanence, than any change effected and maintained by force. The unlimited exercise of private judgment is a doctrine inexpressibly grand and captivating and has a vast superiority over those systems where every individual is in a manner the slave of the public. The substitution of benevolence as the master-spring and moving principle of society, instead of self-love, is a consummation devoutly to be wished. In short, it is impossible to contemplate the whole of this fair structure, without emotions of delight and admiration, accompanied with ardent longing for the period of its accomplishment. But, alas! that moment can never arrive. The whole is little better than a dream, a beautiful phantom of the imagination. These "gorgeous palaces" of happiness and immortality, these "solemn temples" of truth and virtue will dissolve, "like the baseless fabric of a vision," when we awaken to real life and contemplate the true and genuine situation of man on earth.

Mr. Godwin, at the conclusion of the third chapter of his eighth book, speaking of population, says, "There is a principle in human society, by which population is perpetually kept down to the level of the means of subsistence. Thus among the wandering tribes of America and Asia, we never find through the lapse of ages that population has so increased as to render necessary the cultivation of the earth." This principle, which Mr. Godwin thus mentions as some mysterious and occult cause and which he does not attempt to investigate, will be found to be the grinding law of necessity, misery, and the fear of misery.

The great error under which Mr. Godwin labours throughout his whole work is the attributing almost all the vices and misery that are seen in civil society to human institutions. Political regulations and the established administration of property are with him the fruitful sources of all evil, the hotbeds of all the crimes that degrade mankind. Were this really a true state of the case it would not seem a hopeless task to remove evil completely from the world, and reason seems to be the proper and adequate instrument for effecting so great a purpose. But the truth is, that though human institutions appear to be the obvious and obtrusive causes of much mischief to mankind, yet, in reality they are light and superficial, they are mere feathers that float on the surface, in comparison with those deeper seated causes of impurity that corrupt the springs and render turbid the whole stream of human life.

Mr. Godwin, in his chapter on the benefits attendant on a system of equality, says, "The spirit of oppression, the spirit of servility, and the spirit of fraud, these are the immediate growth of the established administration of property. They are alike hostile to intellectual improvement. The other vices of envy, malice, and revenge are their inseparable companions. In a state of society where men lived in the midst of plenty and where all shared alike the bounties of nature, these sentiments would inevitably expire. The narrow principle of selfishness would vanish. No man being obliged to guard his little store or provide with anxiety and pain for his restless wants, each would lose his individual existence in the thought of the general good. No man would be an enemy to his neighbour, for they would have no subject of contention, and, of consequence, philanthropy would resume the empire which reason assigns her. Mind would be delivered from her perpetual anxiety about corporal support, and free to expatiate in the field of thought, which is congenial to her. Each would assist the enquiries of all."

This would, indeed, be a happy state. But that it is merely an imaginary picture, with scarcely a feature near the truth, the reader, I am afraid, is already too well convinced.

Man cannot live in the midst of plenty. All cannot share alike the bounties of nature. Were there no established administration of property, every man would be obliged to guard with force his little store. Selfishness would be triumphant. The subjects of contention would be perpetual. Every individual mind would be under a constant anxiety about corporal support, and not a single intellect would be left free to expatiate in the field of thought.

How little Mr. Godwin has turned the attention of his penetrating mind to the real state of man on earth will sufficiently appear from the manner in which he endeavours to remove the difficulty of an overcharged population. He says, "The obvious answer to this objection, is, that to reason thus is to foresee difficulties at a great distance. Three fourths of the habitable globe is now uncultivated. The parts already cultivated are capable of immeasureable improvement. Myriads of centuries of still increasing population may pass away, and the earth be still found sufficient for the subsistence of its inhabitants."

I have already pointed out the error of supposing that no distress and difficulty would arise from an overcharged population before the earth absolutely refused to produce any more. But let us imagine for a moment Mr. Godwin's beautiful system of equality realized in its utmost purity, and see how soon this difficulty might be expected to press under so perfect a form of society. A theory that will not admit of application cannot possibly be just.

Let us suppose all the causes of misery and vice in this island removed. War and contention cease. Unwholesome trades and manufactories do not exist. Crowds no longer collect together in great and pestilent cities for purposes of court intrigue, of commerce, and vicious gratifications. Simple, healthy, and rational amusements take place of drinking, gaming, and debauchery. There are no towns sufficiently large to have any prejudicial effects on the human constitution. The greater part of the happy inhabitants of this terrestrial paradise live in hamlets and farm-houses scattered over the face of the country. Every house is clean, airy, sufficiently roomy, and in a healthy situation. All men are equal. The labours of luxury are at end. And the necessary labours of agriculture are shared amicably among all. The number of persons, and the produce of the island, we suppose to be the same as at present. The spirit of benevolence, guided by impartial justice, will divide this produce among all the members of the society according to their wants. Though it would be impossible that they should all have animal food every day, yet vegetable food, with meat occasionally, would satisfy the desires of a frugal people and would be sufficient to preserve them in health, strength, and spirits.

Mr. Godwin considers marriage as a fraud and a monopoly. Let us suppose the commerce of the sexes established upon principles of the most perfect freedom. Mr. Godwin does not think himself that this freedom would lead to a promiscuous intercourse, and in this I perfectly agree with him. The love of variety is a vicious, corrupt, and unnatural taste and could not prevail in any great degree in a simple and virtuous state of society. Each man would probably select himself a partner, to whom he would adhere as long as that adherence continued to be the choice of both parties. It would be of little consequence, according to Mr. Godwin, how many children a woman had or to whom they belonged. Provisions and assistance would spontaneously flow from the quarter in which they abounded, to the quarter that was deficient. And every man would be ready to furnish instruction to the rising generation according to his capacity.

I cannot conceive a form of society so favourable upon the whole to population. The irremediableness of marriage, as it is at present constituted, undoubtedly deters many from entering into that state. An unshackled intercourse on the contrary would be a most powerful incitement to early attachments, and as we are supposing no anxiety about the future support of children to exist, I do not conceive that there would be one woman in a hundred, of twenty three, without a family.

With these extraordinary encouragements to population, and every cause of depopulation, as we have supposed, removed, the numbers would necessarily increase faster than in any society that has ever yet been known. I have mentioned, on the authority of a pamphlet published by a Dr. Styles and referred to by Dr. Price, that the inhabitants of the back settlements of America doubled their numbers in fifteen years. England is certainly a more healthy country than the back settlements of America, and as we have supposed every house in the island to be airy and wholesome, and the encouragements to have a family greater even than with the back settlers, no probable reason can be assigned why the population should not double itself in less, if possible, than fifteen years. But to be quite sure that we do not go beyond the truth, we will only suppose the period of doubling to be twenty-five years, a ratio of increase, which is well known to have taken place throughout all the Northern States of America.

There can be little doubt that the equalization of property which we have supposed, added to the circumstance of the labour of the whole community being directed chiefly to agriculture, would tend greatly to augment the produce of the country. But to answer the demands of a population increasing so rapidly, Mr. Godwin's calculation of half an hour a day for each man, would certainly not be sufficient. It is probable that the half of every man's time must be employed for this purpose. Yet with such, or much greater exertions, a person who is acquainted with the nature of the soil in this country, and who reflects on the fertility of the lands already in cultivation, and the barrenness of those that are not cultivated, will be very much disposed to doubt whether the whole average produce could possibly be doubled in twenty-five years from the present period. The only chance of success would be the ploughing up all the grazing countries and putting an end almost entirely to the use of animal food. Yet a part of this scheme might defeat itself. The soil of England will not produce much without dressing, and cattle seem to be necessary to make that species of manure which best suits the land. In China it is said that the soil in some of the provinces is so fertile as to produce two crops of rice in the year without dressing. None of the lands in England will answer to this description.

Difficult, however, as it might be to double the average produce of the island in

twenty-five years, let us suppose it effected. At the expiration of the first period therefore, the food, though almost entirely vegetable, would be sufficient to support in
health, the doubled population of fourteen millions.

During the next period of doubling, where will the food be found to satisfy the
importunate demands of the increasing numbers. Where is the fresh land to turn up?
where is the dressing necessary to improve that which is already in cultivation? There
is no person with the smallest knowledge of land, but would say that it was impossible that the average produce of the country could be increased during the second
twenty-five years by a quantity equal to what it at present yields. Yet we will suppose
this increase, however improbable, to take place. The exuberant strength of the argument allows of almost any concession. Even with this concession, however, there
would be seven millions at the expiration of the second term, unprovided for. A
quantity of food equal to the frugal support of twenty-one millions, would be to be
divided among twenty-eight millions.

Alas! what becomes of the picture where men lived in the midst of plenty, where
no man was obliged to provide with anxiety and pain for his restless wants, where
the narrow principle of selfishness did not exist, where Mind was delivered from her
perpetual anxiety about corporal support and free to expatiate in the field of thought
which is congenial to her. This beautiful fabric of imagination vanishes at the severe
touch of truth. The spirit of benevolence, cherished and invigorated by plenty, is
repressed by the chilling breath of want. The hateful passions that had vanished,
reappear. The mighty law of self-preservation, expels all the softer and more exalted
emotions of the soul. The temptations to evil are too strong for human nature to
resist. The corn is plucked before it is ripe, or secreted in unfair proportions, and the
whole black train of vices that belong to falsehood are immediately generated. Provisions no longer flow in for the support of the mother with a large family. The children
are sickly from insufficient food. The rosy flush of health gives place to the pallid
cheek and hollow eye of misery. Benevolence yet lingering in a few bosoms, makes
some faint expiring struggles, till at length self-love resumes his wonted empire and
lords it triumphant over the world.

No human institutions here existed, to the perverseness of which Mr. Godwin
ascribes the original sin of the worst men. No opposition had been produced by them
between public and private good. No monopoly had been created of those advantages
which reason directs to be left in common. No man had been goaded to the breach of
order by unjust laws. Benevolence had established her reign in all hearts: and yet in
so short a period as within fifty years, violence, oppression, falsehood, misery, every
hateful vice, and every form of distress, which degrade and sadden the present state
of society, seem to have been generated by the most imperious circumstances, by laws inherent in the nature of man, and absolutely independent of all human regulations. . . .

It may be curious to observe, in the case that we have been supposing, how some
of the laws which at present govern civilized society, would be successively dictated
by the most imperious necessity. As man, according to Mr. Godwin, is the creature of
the impressions to which he is subject, the goadings of want could not continue long,
before some violations of public or private stock would necessarily take place. As these
violations increased in number and extent, the more active and comprehensive intel-

lects of the society would soon perceive, that while population was fast increasing, the yearly produce of the country would shortly begin to diminish. The urgency of the case would suggest the necessity of some immediate measures to be taken for the general safety. Some kind of convention would then be called, and the dangerous situation of the country stated in the strongest terms. It would be observed, that while they lived in the midst of plenty, it was of little consequence who laboured the least, or who possessed the least, as every man was perfectly willing and ready to supply the wants of his neighbour. But that the question was no longer, whether one man should give to another, that which he did not use himself; but whether he should give to his neighbour the food which was absolutely necessary to his own existence. It would be represented, that the number of those that were in want very greatly exceeded the number and means of those who should supply them: that these pressing wants, which from the state of the produce of the country could not all be gratified, had occasioned some flagrant violations of justice: that these violations had already checked the increase of food, and would, if they were not by some means or other prevented, throw the whole community in confusion: that imperious necessity seemed to dictate that a yearly increase of produce should, if possible, be obtained at all events: that in order to effect this first, great, and indispensible purpose, it would be adviseable to make a more complete division of land, and to secure every man's stock against violation by the most powerful sanctions, even by death itself.

It might be urged perhaps by some objectors, that, as the fertility of the land increased, and various accidents occurred, the share of some men might be much more than sufficient for their support, and that when the reign of self-love was once established, they would not distribute their surplus produce without some compensation in return. It would be observed, in answer, that this was an inconvenience greatly to be lamented; but that it was an evil which bore no comparison to the black train of distresses, that would inevitably be occasioned by the insecurity of property: that the quantity of food which one man could consume, was necessarily limited by the narrow capacity of the human stomach: that it was not certainly probable that he should throw away the rest; but that even if he exchanged his surplus food for the labour of others, and made them in some degree dependent on him, this would still be better than that these others should absolutely starve.

It seems highly probable, therefore, that an administration of property, not very different from that which prevails in civilized states at present, would be established, as the best, though inadequate, remedy, for the evils which were pressing on the society.

The next subject that would come under discussion, intimately connected with the preceding, is, the commerce between the sexes. It would be urged by those who had turned their attention to the true cause of the difficulties under which the community laboured, that while every man felt secure that all his children would be well provided for by general benevolence, the powers of the earth would be absolutely inadequate to produce food for the population which would inevitably ensue: that even, if the whole attention and labour of the society were directed to this sole point, and if, by the most perfect security of property, and every other encouragement that could be thought of, the greatest possible increase of produce were yearly obtained; yet still, that the increase of food would by no means keep pace with the much more rapid increase of population: that some check to population therefore was imperiously called for: that the most natural and obvious check seemed to be, to make every man provide for his own children, that this would operate in some respect, as a measure and guide in the increase of population; as it might be expected that no man would bring beings into the world, for whom he could not find the means of support: that where this notwithstanding was the case, it seemed necessary, for the example of others, that the disgrace and inconvenience attending such a conduct, should fall upon the individual, who had thus inconsiderately plunged himself and innocent children in misery and want.

The institution of marriage, or at least, of some express or implied obligation on every man to support his own children, seems to be the natural result of these reasonings in a community under the difficulties that we have supposed.

The view of these difficulties, presents us with a very natural origin of the superior disgrace which attends a breach of chastity in the woman, than in the man. It could not be expected that women should have resources sufficient to support their own children. When therefore a woman was connected with a man, who had entered into no compact to maintain her children; and aware of the inconveniences that he might bring upon himself, had deserted her, these children must necessarily fall for support upon the society, or starve. And to prevent the frequent recurrence of such an inconvenience, as it would be highly unjust to punish so natural a fault by personal restraint or infliction, the men might agree to punish it with disgrace. The offence is besides more obvious and conspicuous in the woman, and less liable to any mistake. The father of a child may not always be known, but the same uncertainty cannot easily exist with regard to the mother. Where the evidence of the offence was most complete, and the inconvenience to the society at the same time the greatest, there, it was agreed, that the largest share of blame should fall. The obligation on every man to maintain his children, the society would enforce, if there were occasion; and the greater degree of inconvenience or labour, to which a family would necessarily subject him, added to some portion of disgrace which every human being must incur, who leads another into unhappiness, might be considered as a sufficient punishment for the man.

That a woman should at present be almost driven from society, for an offence, which men commit nearly with impunity, seems to be undoubtedly a breach of natural justice. But the origin of the custom, as the most obvious and effectual method of preventing the frequent recurrence of a serious inconvenience to a community, appears to be natural, though not perhaps perfectly justifiable. This origin, however, is now lost in the new train of ideas which the custom has since generated. What at first might be dictated by state necessity, is now supported by female delicacy; and operates with the greatest force on that part of society, where, if the original intention of the custom were preserved, there is the least real occasion for it.

When these two fundamental laws of society, the security of property, and the institution of marriage, were once established, inequality of conditions must necessarily follow. Those who were born after the division of property, would come into a world already possessed. If their parents, from having too large a family, could not give them sufficient for their support, what are they to do in a world where every thing is appropriated? We have seen the fatal effects that would result to a society, if every man had a valid claim to an equal share of the produce of the earth. The members of a family which was grown too large for the original division of land appropriated to it, could not then demand a part of the surplus produce of others, as a debt of justice. It has appeared, that from the inevitable laws of our nature, some human beings must suffer from want. These are the unhappy persons who, in the great lottery of life, have drawn a blank. The number of these claimants would soon exceed the ability of the surplus produce to supply. Moral merit is a very difficult distinguishing criterion, except in extreme cases. The owners of surplus produce would in general seek some more obvious mark of distinction. And it seems both natural and just, that except upon particular occasions, their choice should fall upon those, who were able, and professed themselves willing, to exert their strength in procuring a further surplus produce; and thus at once benefitting the community, and enabling these proprietors to afford assistance to greater numbers. All who were in want of food would be urged by imperious necessity to offer their labour in exchange for this article so absolutely essential to existence. The fund appropriate to the maintenance of labour, would be, the aggregate quantity of food possessed by the owners of land beyond their own consumption. When the demands upon this fund were great and numerous, it would naturally be divided in very small shares. Labour would be ill paid. Men would offer to work for a bare subsistence, and the rearing of families would be checked by sickness and misery. On the contrary, when this fund was increasing fast; when it was great in proportion to the number of claimants, it would be divided in much larger shares. No man would exchange his labour without receiving an ample quantity of food in return. Labourers would live in ease and comfort; and would consequently be able to rear a numerous and vigorous offspring.

On the state of this fund, the happiness, or the degree of misery prevailing among the lower classes of people in every known State at present chiefly depends. And on this happiness, or degree of misery, depends the increase, stationariness, or decrease of population.

And thus it appears, that a society constituted according to the most beautiful form that imagination can conceive, with benevolence for its moving principle, instead of self-love, and with every evil disposition in all its members corrected by reason and not force, would, from the inevitable laws of nature, and not from any original depravity of man, in a very short period, degenerate into a society, constructed upon a plan not essentially different from that which prevails in every known State at present; I meant a society divided into a class of proprietors, and a class of labourers and with self-love the main-spring of the great machine. . . .

~§ *Part Four*

Impressions of the Age

Courtiers, Gentlemen, and Laboring Poor

The 200 years (1650–1850) spanned by this volume witnessed such diverse movements as divine-right monarchy and working-class democracy. It is difficult to find truly representative social types in an age of rapidly changing manners and styles of life and of ideas. The vignettes presented here depict the world of the court and the courtier at the turn of the eighteenth century, that of the eighteenth-century gentleman and of the nineteenth-century urban poor.

The Duke of Saint-Simon (1675–1755) was a long-term resident and observer of the court of Louis XIV of France at a time when French style was imitated throughout Europe in everything ranging from the width of cuff lace to the design of military fortifications. Yet Saint-Simon, a haughty old-line aristocrat, noticed only dazzling mediocrity, which he chronicled in pitiless if garrulous detail in his Memoirs. *No one would guess from his portrayal of the Great Monarch that Louis, pomp and circumstance notwithstanding, was one of the hardest-working kings on record.*

By the eighteenth century the English middle class had come a long way since the days of Chaucer. No longer did the merchant take pride in his humble roots: he looked instead to the court for his ideals. If he could not purchase a title—and many kings sold them for pin money—he bought a military commission and entitled himself "captain," or went into the church, thus becoming "doctor" or even "dean." At the very least he could put "esquire" or "gent." after his name. It is for this audience that Joseph Addison (1672–1719) and Richard Steele (1672–1729) addressed themselves with their newspaper, The Spectator, *from which this selection is taken. It was to polite and urbane essays such as these that London gentlemen looked for models of the accepted attitudes and fashions of the day.*

Neither court memoirs nor genteel newspapers bothered to depict the world of the majority, which, until the end of the nineteenth century, was matter-of-factly referred to as "the poor." It is to the credit of Henry Mayhew (1812–1887), English journalist and man of letters, that in the London of the 1840s and 1850s he made, to cite his own words, "the first attempt to publish the history of a people, from the lips of the people themselves—giving a literal description of their labour, their earnings, their trials, and their sufferings; and in their own 'unvarnished' language; and to portray the condition of their homes and their families by personal observation of the places, and direct communion with the individuals."

For years Mayhew and several collaborators roamed the streets of the British capital, questioning, observing, checking, and recording myriads of facts and thousands of life histories. The end result is a poignant encyclopedia of London street life as variegated and pathetic as the fictional world created by Mayhew's contemporary, Charles Dickens.

✍§ MEMOIRS

Saint-Simon

I will not speak much of the King's manner of living when with the army. His hours were determined by what was to be done, though he held his councils regularly; I will simply say, that morning and evening he ate with people privileged to have that honor. When anyone wished to claim it, the first gentleman of the chamber on duty was appealed to. He gave the answer, and if favorable you presented yourself the next day to the King, who said to you, "Monsieur, seat yourself at table." That being done, all was done. Ever afterward you were at liberty to take a place at the King's table, but with discretion. The number of the persons from whom a choice was made was, however, very limited. Even very high military rank did not suffice. M. de Vauban, at the siege of Namur, was overwhelmed by the distinction. The King did the same honor at Namur to the Abbé de Grancey, who exposed himself everywhere to confess the wounded and encourage the troops. No other Abbé was ever so distinguished. All the clergy were excluded save the cardinals, and the bishops, peers, or the ecclesiastics who held the rank of foreign princes.

At these repasts everybody was covered; it would have been a want of respect, of which you would have been immediately informed, if you had not kept your hat on your head. The King alone was uncovered. When the King wished to speak to you, or you had occasion to speak to him, you uncovered. You uncovered, also, when Monseigneur or Monsieur spoke to you, or you to them. For princes of the blood you merely put your hand to your hat. The King alone had an armchair. All the rest of the company, Monseigneur included, had seats, with backs of black morocco leather, which could be folded up to be carried, and which were called "Parrots." Except at the army, the King never ate with any man, under whatever circumstances; not even with the Princes of the blood, save sometimes at their wedding feasts.

Let us return now to the Court.

At eight o'clock the chief *valet de chambre* on duty, who alone had slept in the royal chamber, and who had dressed himself, awoke the King. The chief physician, the chief surgeon, and the nurse (as long as she lived), entered at the same time. The

The Duke of Saint-Simon, *Memoirs*, trans. Bayle St. John (New York: M. W. Dunne, 1901), I, 30–41.

latter kissed the King; the others rubbed and often changed his shirt, because he was in the habit of sweating a great deal. At the quarter, the grand chamberlain was called (or, in his absence, the first gentleman of the chamber), and those who had, what was called the *grandes entrées.* The chamberlain (or chief gentleman) drew back the curtains which had been closed again, and presented the holy water from the vase, at the head of the bed. These gentlemen stayed but a moment, and that was the time to speak to the King, if anyone had anything to ask of him; in which case the rest stood aside. When, contrary to custom, nobody had aught to say, they were there but for a few moments. He had opened the curtains and presented the holy water, presented also a prayer book. Then all passed into the cabinet of the council. A very short religious service being over, the King called, they re-entered. The same officer gave him his dressing gown; immediately after, other privileged courtiers entered, and then everybody, in time to find the King putting on his shoes and stockings, for he did almost everything himself and with address and grace. Every other day we saw the King shave himself; and he had a little short wig in which he always appeared, even in bed, and on medicine days. He often spoke of the chase, and sometimes said a word to somebody. No toilet table was near him; he had simply a mirror held before him.

As soon as he was dressed, he prayed to God, at the side of his bed, where all the clergy present knelt, the cardinals without cushions, all the laity remaining standing; and the captain of the guards came to the balustrade during the prayer, after which the King passed into his cabinet.

He found there, or was followed by all who had the *entrée,* a very numerous company, for it included everybody in any office. He gave orders to each for the day; thus within a half a quarter of an hour it was known what he meant to do; and then all this crowd left directly. The bastards, a few favorites, and the valets alone were left. It was then a good opportunity for talking with the King; for example, about plans of gardens and buildings; and conversation lasted more or less according to the person engaged in it.

All the Court meantime waited for the King in the gallery, the captain of the guard being alone in the chamber seated at the door of the cabinet. At morning the court waited in the saloon; at Trianon in the front rooms as at Meudon; at Fontainebleau in the chamber and antechamber. During this pause the King gave audiences when he wished to accord any, spoke with whoever he might wish to speak secretly to, and gave secret interviews to foreign ministers in presence of Torcy. They were called "secret" simply to distinguish them from the uncommon ones by the bedsides.

The King went to mass, where his musicians always sang an anthem. He did not go below except on grand *fêtes* or at ceremonies. While he was going to and returning from mass, everybody spoke to him who wished, after apprising the captain of the guard, if they were not distinguished; and he came and went by the door of the cabinets into the gallery. During the mass the ministers assembled in the King's chamber where distinguished people could go and speak or chat with them. The King amused himself a little upon returning from mass and asked almost immediately for the Council. Then the morning was finished.

On Sunday, and often on Monday, there was a council of state; on Tuesday a finance council; on Wednesday council of state; on Saturday finance council. Rarely were two held in one day or any on Thursday or Friday. Once or twice a month there was a council of dispatches on Monday morning; but the order that the Secretaries of State took every morning between the King's rising and his mass, much abridged this kind of business. All the ministers were seated according to rank, except at the council of dispatches, where all stood except the sons of France, the chancellor, and the Duc de Beauvilliers.

Thursday morning was almost always blank. It was the day for audience that the King wished to give—often unknown to any—backstair audiences. It was also the grand day taken advantage of by the bastards, the valets, etc., because the King had nothing to do. On Friday after the mass the King was with his confessor, and the length of their audiences was limited by nothing, and might last until dinner. At Fontainebleau on the mornings when there was no Council, the King usually passed from mass to Madame de Maintenon's and so at Trianon and Marly. It was the time of their *tête-à-tête* without interruption. Often on the days when there was no Council the dinner hour was advanced, more or less for the chase or the promenade. The ordinary hour was one o'clock; if the Council still lasted, then the dinner waited and nothing was said to the King.

The dinner was always *au petit couvert,* that is, the King ate by himself in his chamber upon a square table in front of the middle window. It was more or less abundant, for he ordered in the morning whether it was to be "a little," or "very little" service. But even at this last, there were always many dishes, and three courses without counting the fruit. The dinner being ready, the principal courtiers entered; then all who were known; and the first gentlemen of the chamber on duty, informed the King.

I have seen, but very rarely, Monseigneur and his sons standing at their dinners, the King not offering them a seat. I have continually seen there the Princes of the blood and the cardinals. I have often seen there also Monsieur, either on arriving from St. Cloud to see the King, or arriving from the council of dispatches (the only one he entered) give the King his napkin and remain standing. A little while afterward, the King, seeing that he did not go away, asked him if he would not sit down; he bowed, and the King ordered a seat to be brought for him. A stool was put behind him. Some moments after the King said, "Nay then, sit down, my brother." Monsieur bowed and seated himself until the end of the dinner, when he presented the napkin.

At other times when he came from St. Cloud, the King, on arriving at the table, asked for a plate for Monsieur, or asked him if he would dine. If he refused, he went away a moment after, and there was no mention of a seat; if he accepted, the King asked for a plate for him. The table was square, he placed himself at one end, his back to the cabinet. Then the grand chamberlain (or the first gentleman of the chamber) gave him drink and plates, taking them from him as he finished with them, exactly as he served the King; but Monsieur received all this attention with strongly marked politeness. When he dined thus with the King he much enlivened the conversation. The King ordinarily spoke little at table unless some familiar favorite was near. It was the same at his rising. Ladies scarcely ever were seen at these little dinners.

I have, however, seen the Maréchale de la Mothe, who came in because she had been used to do so as governess to the children of France, and who received a seat, because she was a duchess. Grand dinners were very rare, and only took place on grand occasions, and then ladies were present.

Upon leaving the table the King immediately entered his cabinet. That was the time for distinguished people to speak to him. He stopped at the door a moment to listen, then entered; very rarely did anyone follow him, never without asking him for permission to do so; and for this few had the courage. If followed he placed himself in the embrasure of the window nearest to the door of the cabinet, which immediately closed of itself, and which you were obliged to open yourself on quitting the King. This also was the time for the bastards and the valets.

The King amused himself by feeding his dogs, and remained with them more or less time, then asked for his wardrobe, changed before the very few distinguished people it pleased the first gentleman of the chamber to admit there, and immediately went out by the back stairs into the court of marble to get into his coach. From the bottom of that staircase to the coach, anyone spoke to him who wished.

The King was fond of air, and when deprived of it his health suffered; he had headaches and vapors caused by the undue use he had formerly made of perfumes, so that for many years he could not endure any, except the odor of orange flowers; therefore if you had to approach anywhere near him you did well not to carry them.

As he was but little sensitive to heat or cold, or even rain, the weather was seldom sufficiently bad to prevent his going abroad. He went out for three objects: stag hunting, once or more each week; shooting in his parks (and no man handled a gun with more grace and skill), once or twice each week; and walking in his gardens for exercise, and to see his workmen. Sometimes he made picnics with ladies, in the forest at Marly or at Fontainebleau, and in this last place, promenades with all the Court around the canal, which was a magnificent spectacle. Nobody followed him in his other promenades but those who held principal offices, except at Versailles or in the gardens of Trianon. Marly had a privilege unknown to the other places. On going out from the *château*, the King said aloud, "Your hats, gentlemen," and immediately courtiers, officers of the guard, everybody, in fact, covered their heads, as he would have been much displeased had they not done so; and this lasted all the promenade, that is, four or five hours in summer, or in other seasons, when he dined early at Versailles to go and walk at Marly, and not sleep there.

The stag hunting parties were on an extensive scale. At Fontainebleau everyone went who wished; elsewhere only those were allowed to go who had obtained the permission once for all, and those who had obtained leave to wear the *justaucorps,* which was a blue uniform with silver and gold lace, lined with red. The King did not like too many people at these parties. He did not care for you to go if you were not fond of the chase. He thought that ridiculous, and never bore ill will to those who stopped away altogether.

It was the same with the play table, which he liked to see always well frequented —with high stakes—in the saloon at Marly, for lansquenet and other games. He amused himself at Fontainebleau during bad weather by seeing good players at tennis, in which he had formerly excelled; and at Marly by seeing mall played, in which he had also been skillful. Sometimes when there was no Council, he would make presents of stuff, or of silverware, or jewels, to the ladies, by means of a lottery, for the tickets of which they paid nothing. Madame de Maintenon drew lots with the others, and almost always gave at once what she gained. The King took no ticket.

Upon returning home from walks or drives, anybody, as I have said, might speak to the King from the moment he left his coach till he reached the foot of his staircase. He changed his dress again, and rested in his cabinet an hour or more, then went to Madame de Maintenon's and on the way anyone who wished might speak to him.

At ten o'clock his supper was served. The captain of the guard announced this to him. A quarter of an hour after the King came to supper, and from the antechamber of Madame de Maintenon to the table again, anyone spoke to him who wished. This supper was always on a grand scale, the royal household (that is, the sons and daughters of France), at table, and a large number of courtiers and ladies present, sitting or standing, and on the evening before the journey to Marly all those ladies who wished to take part in it. That was called presenting yourself for Marly. Men asked in the morning, simply saying to the King, "Sire, Marly." In later years the King grew tired of this, and a valet wrote up in the gallery the names of those who asked. The ladies continued to present themselves.

After supper the King stood some moments, his back to the balustrade of the foot of his bed, encircled by all his Court; then, with bows to the ladies, passed into his cabinet, where on arriving, he gave his orders. He passed a little less than an hour there, seated in an armchair, with his legitimate children and bastards, his grandchildren, legitimate and otherwise, and their husbands or wives. Monsieur in another armchair; the princesses upon stools, Monseigneur and all the other princes standing.

The King, wishing to retire, went and fed his dogs; then said good night, passed into his chamber to the ruelle of his bed, where he said his prayers, as in the morning, then undressed. He said good night with an inclination of the head, and while everybody was leaving the room stood at the corner of the mantlepiece, where he gave the order to the colonel of the guards alone. Then commenced what was called the *petit coucher,* at which only the specially privileged remained. That was short. They did not leave until he got into bed. It was a moment to speak to him. Then all left if they saw anyone buckled to the King. For ten or twelve years before he died the *petit coucher* ceased, in consequence of a long attack of gout he had had; so that the Court was finished at the rising from supper.

On medicine days, which occurred about once a month, the King remained in bed, then heard mass. The royal household came to see him for a moment, and Madame de Maintenon seated herself in the armchair at the head of his bed. The King dined in bed about three o'clock, everybody being allowed to enter the room, then rose, and the privileged alone remained. He passed afterward into his cabinet, where he held a council, and afterward went, as usual, to Madame de Maintenon's and supped at ten o'clock, according to custom.

During all his life, the King failed only once in his attendance at mass. It was with the army, during a forced march; he missed no fast day, unless really indisposed. Some days before Lent, he publicly declared that he should be very much displeased if anyone ate meat or gave it to others, under any pretext. He ordered the grand *prevôt* to look to this, and report all cases of disobedience. But no one dared to disobey his commands, for they would soon have found out the cost. They extended even to Paris, where the lieutenant of police kept watch and reported. For twelve or fifteen years he had himself not observed Lent, however. At church he was very respectful. During his mass everybody was obliged to kneel at the *Sanctus,* and to remain so until after the communion of the priest; and if he heard the least noise, or saw anybody talking during the mass, he was much displeased. He took the communion five times a year, in the collar of the Order, band, and cloak. On Holy Thursday he served the poor at dinner; at the mass he said his chaplet (he knew no more), always kneeling, except at the Gospel.

He was always clad in dresses more or less brown, lightly embroidered, but never at the edges, sometimes with nothing but a gold button, sometimes black velvet. He wore always a vest of cloth, or of red, blue, or green satin, much embroidered. He used no ring; and no jewels, except in the buckles of his shoes, garters, and hat, the latter always trimmed with Spanish point, with a white feather. He had always the *cordon bleu* outside, except on *fêtes,* when he wore it inside, with eight or ten millions of precious stones attached.

Rarely a fortnight passed that the King did not go to Saint Germains, even after the death of King James II. The Court of Saint Germains came also to Versailles, but oftener to Marly, and frequently to sup there; and no *fête* or ceremony took place to which they were not invited, and at which they were not received with all honors. Nothing could compare with the politeness of the King for this Court, or with the air of gallantry and of majesty with which he received it at any time. Birthdays, or the *fête* days of the King and his family, so observed in the courts of Europe, were always unknown in that of the King; so that there never was the slightest mention of them, or any difference made on their account.

The King was but little regretted. His valets and a few other people felt his loss, scarcely anybody else. His successor was not yet old enough to feel anything. Madame entertained for him only fear and considerate respect. Madame la Duchess de Berry did not like him, and counted now upon reigning undisturbed. M. le Duc d'Orléans could scarcely be expected to feel much grief for him. And those who may have been expected did not consider it necessary to do their duty. Madame de Maintenon was wearied with him ever since the death of the Dauphine; she knew not what to do, or with what to amuse him; her constraint was tripled because he was much more with her than before. She had often, too, experienced much ill humor from him. She had attained all she wished, so whatever she might lose in losing him, she felt herself relieved, and was capable of no other sentiment at first. The *ennui* and emptiness of her life afterward made her feel regret. As for M. du Maine, the barbarous indecency of his joy need not be dwelt upon. The icy tranquillity of his brother, the Comte de Toulouse, neither increased nor diminished. Madame la Duchess d'Orléans, surprised me. I had expected some grief, I perceived only a few tears, which upon all occasions flowed very readily from her eyes, and which were soon dried up. Her bed, which she was very fond of, supplied what was wanting during several days, amid obscurity which she by no means disliked. But the window curtains were soon withdrawn and grief disappeared.

As for the Court it was divided into two grand parties, the men hoping to figure, to obtain employ, to introduce themselves; and they were ravished to see the end of a reign under which they had nothing to hope for; the others, fatigued with a heavy yoke, always overwhelmingly, and of the ministers much more than of the King, were charmed to find themselves at liberty. Thus all, generally speaking, were glad to be delivered from continual restraint, and were eager for change.

Paris, tired of a dependence which had enslaved everything, breathed again in the hope of liberty, and with joy at seeing at an end the authority of so many people who abused it. The provinces in despair at their ruin and their annihilation breathed again and leaped for joy; and the Parliament and the robe destroyed by edicts and by revolutions, flattered themselves the first that they should figure, the other that they should find themselves free. The people ruined, overwhelmed, desperate, gave thanks to God, with a scandalous *éclat,* for a deliverance, their most ardent desires had not anticipated.

Foreigners delighted to be at last, after so many years, quit of a monarch who had so long imposed his law upon them, and who had escaped from them by a species of miracle at the very moment in which they counted upon having subjugated him, contained themselves with much more decency than the French. The marvels of the first three quarters of this reign of more than seventy years, and the personal magnanimity of this King until then so successful, and so abandoned afterward by fortune during the last quarter of his reign—had justly dazzled them. They made it a point of honor to render to him after his death what they had constantly refused him during life. No foreign Court exulted: all plumed themselves upon praising and honoring his memory. The Emperor wore mourning as for a father, and although four or five months elapsed between the death of the King and the Carnival, all kinds of amusements were prohibited at Vienna during the Carnival, and the prohibition was strictly observed. A monstrous fact was, that toward the end of this period there was a single ball and a kind of *fête* that the Comte du Luc, our own ambassador, was not ashamed to give to the ladies, who seduced him by the *ennui* of so dull a Carnival. This complaisance did not raise him in estimation at Vienna or elsewhere. In France people were contented with ignoring it.

As for our ministry and the intendants of the Provinces, the financiers and what may be called the *canaille,* they felt all the extent of their loss. We shall see if the realm was right or wrong in the sentiments it held, and whether it found soon after that it had gained or lost.

To finish at once all that regards the King, let me here say, that his entrails were taken to Notre Dame, on the 4th of September, without any ceremony, by two almoners of the King, without accompaniment. On Friday, the 6th of September, the Cardinal de Rohan, carried the heart to the Grand Jesuits, with very little accompaniment or pomp. Except the persons necessary for the ceremony, not half a dozen courtiers were present. It is not for me to comment upon this prompt ingratitude, I, who for fifty-two years, have never once missed going to St. Denis on the anniversary of the death of Louis XIII., and have never seen a single person there on the same errand. On the 9th of September, the body of the late King, was buried at St. Denis. The Bishop of Aleth pronounced the oration. Very little expense was gone to; and nobody was found who cared sufficiently for the late King to murmur at the economy. On Friday, the 25th of October, his solemn obsequies took place at St. Denis in a confusion, as to rank and precedence, without example. On Thursday, the 28th of November, the solemn obsequies were again performed, this time at Notre Dame, and with the usual ceremonies.

ᴇᷟ THE SPECTATOR

Joseph Addison and *Richard Steele*

NO. 1

I have observed, that a Reader seldom peruses a Book with Pleasure, 'till he knows whether the Writer of it be a black or a fair Man, of a mild or cholerick Disposition, Married or a Batchelor, with other Particulars of the like nature, that conduce very much to the right understanding of an Author. To gratifie this Curiosity, which is so natural to a Reader, I design this Paper, and my next, as Prefatory Discourses to my following Writings, and shall give some Account in them of the several Persons that are engaged in this Work. As the chief Trouble of Compiling, Digesting, and Correcting will fall to my Share, I must do my self the Justice to open the Work with my own History.

I was born to a small Hereditary Estate, which, according to the Tradition of the Village where it lies, was bounded by the same Hedges and Ditches in *William* the Conquerer's Time that it is at present, and has been delivered down from Father to Son whole and entire, without the Loss or Acquisition of a single Field or Meadow, during the Space of six hundred Years. There runs a Story in the Family, that when my Mother was gone with Child of me about three Months, she dreamt that she was brought to Bed of a Judge: Whether this might proceed from a Law-Suit which was then depending in the Family, or my Father's being a Justice of the Peace, I cannot determine; for I am not so vain as to think it presaged any Dignity that I should arrive at in my future Life, though that was the Interpretation which the Neighbourhood put upon it. The Gravity of my Behaviour at my very first Appearance in the World, and all the Time that I sucked, seemed to favour my Mother's Dream: For, as she has often told me, I threw away my Rattle before I was two Months old, and would not make use of my Coral 'till they had taken away the Bells from it.

As for the rest of my Infancy, there being nothing in it remarkable, I shall pass it over in Silence. I find, that, during my Nonage, I had the Reputation of a very sullen Youth, but was always a Favourite of my School-master, who used to say, *that my Parts were solid and would wear well.* I had not been long at the University, before I distinguished my self by a most profound Silence: For during the Space of eight Years, excepting in the publick Exercises of the College, I scarce uttered the Quantity

Joseph Addison and Richard Steele, *The Spectator*, Vol. I (1711), nos. 1, 2; Vol. II (1711), no. 81.

of an hundred Words; and indeed do not remember that I ever spoke three Sentences together in my whole Life. Whilst I was in this Learned Body I applied my self with so much Diligence to my Studies, that there are very few celebrated Books, either in the Learned or the Modern Tongues, which I am not acquainted with.

Upon the Death of my Father I was resolved to travel into Foreign Countries, and therefore left the University, with the Character of an odd unaccountable Fellow, that had a great deal of Learning, if I would but show it. An insatiable Thirst after Knowledge carried me into all the Countries of *Europe,* in which there was any thing new or strange to be seen; nay, to such a Degree was my Curiosity raised, that having read the Controversies of some great Men concerning the Antiquities of *Egypt,* I made a Voyage to *Grand Cairo,* on purpose to take the Measure of a Pyramid; and as soon as I had set my self right in that Particular, returned to my Native Country with great Satisfaction.

I have passed my latter Years in this City, where I am frequently seen in most Publick Places, tho' there are not above half a dozen of my select Friends that know me; of whom my next Paper shall give a more particular Account. There is no place of general Resort, wherein I do not often make my appearance; sometimes I am seen thrusting my Head into a Round of Politicians at *Will's,* and listning with great Attention to the Narratives that are made in those little Circular Audiences. Sometimes I smoak a Pipe at *Child's;* and whilst I seem attentive to nothing but the *Post-Man,* over-hear the Conversation of every Table in the Room. I appear on *Sunday* nights at St. *James's* Coffee-House, and sometimes join the little Committee of Politicks in the Inner Room, as one who comes there to hear and improve. My face is likewise very well known at the *Grecian,* the *Cocoa-Tree,* and in the Theatres both of *Drury-Lane* and the *Hay-Market.* I have been taken for a Merchant upon the *Exchange* for above these ten Years, and sometimes pass for a *Jew* in the Assembly of Stock-Jobbers at *Jonathan's.* In short, where-ever I see a Cluster of People I always mix with them, though I never open my Lips but in my own Club.

Thus I live in the World, rather as a Spectator of Mankind, than as one of the Species; by which means I have made myself a Speculative Statesman, Soldier, Merchant, and Artizan, without ever medling with any Practical Part in Life. I am very well versed in the Theory of an Husband, or a Father, and can discern the Errors in the Oeconomy, Busines and Diversion of others, better than those who are engaged in them; as standers-by discover Blots, which are apt to escape those who are in the Game. I never espoused any Party with Violence, and am resolved to observe an exact Neutrality between the Whigs and Tories, unless I shall be forced to declare myself by the Hostilities of either Side. In short, I have acted in all the Parts of my Life as a Looker-on, which is the Character I intend to preserve in this Paper. . . .

NO. 2

The first of our Society is a Gentleman of *Worcestershire,* of antient Descent, a Baronet, his Name Sir ROGER DE COVERLY. His great Grandfather was Inventor of that famous Country-Dance which is call'd after him. All who know that Shire are very well acquainted with the Parts and Merits of Sir ROGER. He is a Gentleman that is very singular in his Behaviour, but his Singularities proceed from his good Sense, and are Contradictions to the Manners of the World, only as he thinks the World is in the wrong. However, this Humour creates him no Enemies, for he does nothing with Sourness or Obstinacy; and his being unconfined to Modes and Forms, makes him but the readier and more capable to please and oblige all who know him. When he is in town he lives in *Soho-Square:* It is said, he keeps himself a Batchelor by reason he was crossed in Love, by a perverse beautiful Widow of the next County to him. Before this Disappointment, Sir ROGER was what you call a fine Gentleman, had often supped with my Lord *Rochester* and Sir *George Etherege,* fought a Duel upon his first coming to Town, and kick'd Bully *Dawson* in a publick Coffee-house for calling him Youngster. But being ill used by the above-mentioned Widow, he was very serious for a Year and a half; and though, his Temper being naturally jovial, he at last got over it, he grew careless of himself, and never dressed afterwards; he continues to wear a Coat and Doublet of the same Cut that were in Fashion at the Time of his Repulse, which, in his merry Humours, he tells us, has been in and out twelve Times since he first wore it. 'Tis said Sir ROGER grew humble in his Desires after he had forgot this cruel Beauty, insomuch that it is reported he has frequently offended in Point of Chastity with Beggars and Gypsies: But this is look'd upon by his Friends rather as Matter of Raillery than Truth. He is now in his Fifty sixth Year, cheerful, gay, and hearty, keeps a good House both in Town and Country; a great Lover of Mankind; but there is such a mirthful Cast in his Behaviour, that he is rather beloved than esteemed: His Tenants grow rich, his Servants look satisfied, all the young Women profess Love to him, and the young Men are glad of his Company: When he comes into a House he calls the Servants by their Names, and talks all the way up Stairs to a Visit. I must not omit that Sir ROGER is a Justice of the *Quorum;* that he fills the chair at a Quarter-Session with great Abilities, and three Months ago gain'd universal Applause by explaining a Passage in the Game-Act.

The Gentleman next in Esteem and Authority among us, is another Batchelor, who is a Member of the *Inner Temple;* a Man of great Probity, Wit, and Understanding; but he has chosen his Place of Residence rather to obey the Direction of an old humoursom Father, than in pursuit of his own Inclinations. He was placed there to study the Laws of the Land, and is the most learned of any of the House in those of the Stage. *Aristotle* and *Longinus* are much better understood by him than *Littleton* or *Cooke.* The Father sends up every Post Questions relating to Marriage-Articles, Leases, and Tenures, in the Neighbourhood; all which Questions he agrees with an Attorney to answer and take care of in the Lump: He is studying the Passions themselves, when he should be inquiring into the Debates among Men which arise from them. He knows the Argument of each of the Orations of *Demosthenes* and *Tully,* but not one Case in the Reports of our own Courts. No one ever took him for a Fool, but none, except his intimate Friends, know he has a great deal of Wit. This Turn makes him at once both disinterested and agreeable: As few of his Thoughts are drawn from Business, they are most of them fit for Conversation. His Taste of Books is a little too just for the Age he lives in; he has read all, but approves of very few. His Familiarity with the Customs, Manners, Actions, and Writings of the Antients, makes him a very delicate

Observer of what occurs to him in the present World. He is an excellent Critick, and the Time of the Play is his Hour of Business; exactly at five he passes thro' *New-Inn,* crosses thro' *Russel-Court,* and takes a turn at *Will's* 'till the play begins; he has his Shooes rubbed and his Perriwig powder'd at the Barber's as you go into the *Rose.* It is for the Good of the Audience when he is at a Play, for the Actors have an Ambition to please him.

The Person of next Consideration is Sir ANDREW FREEPORT, a Merchant of great Eminence in the City of *London.* A Person of indefatigable Industry, strong Reason, and great Experience. His Notions of Trade are noble and generous, and (as every rich Man has usually some sly Way of Jesting, which would make no great Figure were he not a rich Man) he calls the Sea the *British Common.* He is acquainted with Commerce in all its Parts, and will tell you that it is a stupid and barbarous Way to extend Dominion by Arms; for true Power is to be got by Arts and Industry. He will often argue, that if this Part of our Trade were well cultivated, we should gain from one Nation; and if another, from another. I have heard him prove, that Diligence makes more lasting Acquisitions than Valour, and that Sloth has ruined more Nations than the Sword. He abounds in several frugal Maxims, among which the greatest Favourite is, "A Penny saved is a Penny got." A General Trader of good Sense, is pleasanter company than a general Scholar; and Sir ANDREW having a natural unaffected Eloquence, the Perspicuity of his Discourse gives the same Pleasure that Wit would in another Man. He has made his Fortunes himself; and says that *England* may be richer than other Kingdoms, by as plain Methods as he himself is richer than other Men; tho' at the same Time I can say this of him, that there is not a point in the Compass but blows home a Ship in which he is an Owner.

Next to Sir ANDREW in the Club-room sits Captain SENTRY, a Gentleman of great Courage, good Understanding, but invincible Modesty. He is one of those that deserve very well, but are very awkward at putting their Talents within the Observation of such as should take Notice of them. He was some Years a Captain, and behaved himself with great Gallantry in several Engagements, and at several Sieges; but having a small Estate of his own, and being next Heir to Sir ROGER, he has quitted a Way of Life in which no Man can rise suitably to his Merit, who is not something of a Courtier as well as a Soldier. I have heard him often lament, that in a Profession where Merit is placed in so conspicuous a View, Impudence should get the better of Modesty. When he has talked to this Purpose I never heard him make a sour Expression, but frankly confess that he left the World, because he was not fit for it. A strict Honesty and an even regular Behaviour, are in themselves Obstacles to him that must press through Crowds, who endeavour at the same End with himself, the Favour of a Commander. He will however in his Way of Talk excuse Generals, for not disposing according to Men's Desert, or enquiring into it: For, says he, that great Man who has a Mind to help me, has as many to break through to come at me, as I have to come at him: Therefore he will conclude, that the Man who would make a Figure, especially in a military Way, must get over all false Modesty, and assist his Patron against the Importunity of other Pretenders, by a proper Assurance in his own Vindication. He says it is a civil Cowardice to be backward in asserting what you ought to expect, as it is a military Fear to be slow in attacking when it is your Duty. With this Candour does the Gentleman speak of himself and others. The same Frankness runs through all his Conversation. The military Part of his Life has furnish'd him with many Adventures, in the Relation of which he is very agreeable to the Company; for he is never over-bearing, though accustomed to command Men in the utmost Degree below him; nor ever too obsequious, from an Habit of obeying Men highly above him.

But that our Society may not appear a Set of Humourists unacquainted with the Gallantries and Pleasures of the Age, we have among us the gallant WILL. HONEY-COMB, a Gentleman who according to his Years should be in the Decline of his Life, but having ever been very careful of his Person, and always had a very easie Fortune, Time has made but very little Impression, either by Wrinkles on his Forehead, or Traces in his Brain. His Person is well turn'd, of a good Height. He is very ready at that sort of Discourse with which Men usually entertain Women. He has all his Life dressed very well, and remembers Habits as others do men. He can smile when one speaks to him, and laughs easily. He knows the History of every Mode, and can inform you from which of the *French* King's Wenches our Wives and Daughters had this Manner of curling their Hair, that Way of placing their Hoods; whose Frailty was covered by such a Sort of Petticoat, and whose Vanity to shew her Foot made that Part of the Dress so short in such a Year. In a Word, all his Conversation and Knowledge has been in the female World: As other Men of his Age will take Notice to you what such a Minister said upon such and such an Occasion, he will tell you when the Duke of *Monmouth* danced at Court such a Woman was then smitten, another was taken with him at the Head of his Troop in the *Park*. In all these important Relations, he has ever about the same Time received a kind Glance or a Blow of a Fan from some celebrated Beauty, Mother of the Present Lord such-a-one. If you speak of a young Commoner that said a lively thing in the House, he starts up, "He has good Blood in his Veins, *Tom Mirabell* begot him, the Rogue cheated me in that affair; that young Fellow's Mother used me more like a Dog than any Woman I ever made Advances to." This way of Talking of his very much enlivens the Conversation among us of a more sedate Turn; and I find there is not one of the Company, but my self, who rarely speak at all, but speaks of him as of that Sort of Man, who is usually called a well-bred fine Gentleman. To conclude his Character, where Women are not concern'd, he is an honest worthy Man.

I cannot tell whether I am to account him whom I am next to speak of, as one of our Company; for he visits us but seldom, but when he does it adds to every Man else a new Enjoyment of himself. He is a Clergyman, a very philosophick Man, of general Learning, great Sanctity of Life, and the most exact good Breeding. He has the Misfortune to be of a very weak Constitution, and consequently cannot accept of such Cares and Business as Preferments in his Function would oblige him to: He is there-fore among Divines what a Chamber-Counsellor is among Lawyers. The Probity of his Mind, and the Integrity of his Life, create him Followers, as being eloquent or loud advances others. He seldom introduces the Subject he speaks upon; but we are so far gone in Years, that he observes, when he is among us, an Earnestness to have him fall on some divine Topick, which he always treats with much Authority, as one who has no Interests in this World, as one who is hastening to the Object of all his Wishes, and conceives Hope from his Decays and Infirmities. These are my ordinary Companions. . . .

NO. 81

About the middle of last Winter I went to see an *Opera* at the Theatre in the *Hay-Market,* where I could not but take notice of two Parties of very Fine Women, that had placed themselves in the opposite Side-Boxes, and seemed drawn up in a kind of Battle-Array one against another. After a short Survey of them, I found they were *Patched* differently; the Faces, on one Hand, being Spotted on the Right Side of the Forehead, and those upon the other on the Left. I quickly perceived that they cast Hostile Glances upon one another; and that their Patches were placed in those different Situations, as Party-Signals to distinguish Friends from Foes. In the Middle-Boxes, between these two opposite Bodies, were several Ladies who Patched indifferently on both sides of their Faces, and seemed to sit there with no other Intention but to see the *Opera.* Upon Enquiry I found, that the Body of *Amazons* on my Right Hand, were Whigs; and those on my Left, Tories; and that those who had placed themselves in the Middle-Boxes were a Neutral Party, whose Faces had not yet declared themselves. These last, however, as I afterwards found, diminished daily, and took their Party with one Side or the other; insomuch that I observed in several of them, the Patches which were before dispersed equally, are now all gone over to the Whig, or Tory Side of the Face. The Censorious say, That the Men whose Hearts are aimed at are very often the Occasions that one part of the Face is thus Dishonoured, and lyes under a kind of Disgrace, while the other is so much Set off and Adorned by the Owner; and that the Patches turn to the Right or to the Left, according to the Principles of the Man who is most in Favour. But whatever may be the Motives of a few Fantastical Coquets, who do not Patch for the Publick Good, so much as for their own Private Advantage; it is certain, that there are several Women of Honour who Patch out of Principle, and with an Eye to the Interest of their Country. Nay, I am informed, that some of them adhere so steadfastly to their Party, and are so far from Sacrificing their Zeal for the Publick to their Passion for any particular Person, that in a late Draught of Marriage-Articles a Lady has stipulated with her Husband, That, whatever his Opinions are, she shall be at Liberty to Patch on which side she pleases.

I must here take notice, that *Rosalinda,* a Famous Whig Partizan, has most unfortunately a very beautiful Mole on the Tory part of her Forehead; which, being very conspicuous, has occasioned many Mistakes, and given an Handle to her Enemies to misrepresent her Face, as tho' it had Revolted from the Whig Interest. But whatever this natural Patch may seem to intimate, it is well known that her Notions of Government are still the same. This unlucky Mole however has mis-led several Coxcombs; and, like the hanging out of false Colours, made some of them converse with *Rosalinda* in what they thought the Spirit of her Party, when on a sudden she has given them an unexpected Fire, that has sunk them all at once. If *Rosalinda* is unfortunate in her

Mole, *Nigranilla* is as unhappy in a Pimple, which forces her, against her Inclinations, to Patch on the Whig side.

I am told that many virtuous Matrons, who formerly have been taught to believe that this Artificial Spotting of the Face was unlawful, are now reconciled by a Zeal for their Cause, to what they could not be prompted by a Concern for their Beauty. This way of declaring War upon one another, puts me in mind of what is reported of the Tigress, that several Spots rise in her Skin when she is angry; or as Mr. *Cowley* has imitated the Verses that stand as the Motto of this Paper,

> . . . *She Swells with angry Pride,*
> *And calls forth all her Spots on ev'ry side.*

When I was in the Theatre the time above-mentioned, I had the Curiosity to count the Patches on both Sides, and found the Tory patches to be about twenty Stronger than the Whig; but to make amends for this small Inequality, I the next Morning found the whole Puppet-show filled with the Faces spotted after the Whiggish manner. Whether or no the Ladies had retreated hither in order to rally their Forces I cannot tell: but the next Night they came in so great a Body to the Opera, that they outnumbered the Enemy.

This Account of Party-Patches will, I am afraid, appear improbable to those who live at a distance from the fashionable World; but as it is a Distinction of a very singular Nature and what perhaps may never meet with a Parallel, I think I should not have discharged the Office of a faithful Spectator had I not recorded it.

I have, in former Papers, endeavoured to expose this Party-Rage in Women, as it only serves to aggravate the Hatreds and Animosities that reign among Men, and in a great measure deprives the Fair Sex of those peculiar Charms with which Nature has endowed them.

When the *Romans* and *Sabines* were at War, and just upon the point of giving Battle, the Women, who were allied to both of them, interposed with so many Tears and Intreaties, that they prevented the mutual Slaughter which threatened both Parties, and united them together in a firm and lasting Peace.

I would recommend this noble Example to our *British* Ladies, at a time when their Country is torn with so many unnatural Divisions, that if they continue, it will be a Misfortune to be born in it. The *Greeks* thought it so improper for Women to interest themselves in Competitions and Contentions, that for this Reason, among others, they forbad them, under Pain of Death, to be present at the *Olympick* Games, notwithstanding these were the publick Diversions of all *Greece*.

As our *English* women excel those of all Nations in Beauty, they should endeavour to outshine them in all other Accomplishments proper to the Sex, and to distinguish themselves as tender Mothers and faithful Wives, rather than as furious Partizans. Female Virtues are of a Domestick turn. The Family is the proper Province for Private Women to Shine in. If they must be showing their Zeal for the Publick, let it not be against those who are perhaps of the same Family, or at least of the same Religion or Nation, but against those who are the open, professed, undoubted Enemies of their Faith, Liberty, and Country. When the *Romans* were pressed with a Foreign Enemy, the Ladies voluntarily contributed all their Rings and Jewels to assist the Government under a publick Exigence; which appeared so laudable an Action in the Eyes of their Countrymen, that from thenceforth it was permitted by a Law to pronounce publick Orations at the Funeral of a Woman in Praise of the deceased Person, which till that time was peculiar to Men. Would our *English* Ladies, instead of sticking on a Patch against those of their own Country, shew themselves so truly Publick-spirited as to Sacrifice every one her Necklace against the Common Enemy, what Decrees ought not to be made in favour of them?

Since I am recollecting upon this Subject such Passages as occur to my Memory out of ancient Authors, I cannot omit a Sentence in the Celebrated Funeral Oration of *Pericles,* which he made in Honour of those Brave *Athenians* that were Slain in a Fight with the *Lacedemonians.* After having addressed himself to the several Ranks and Orders of his Countrymen, and shewn them how they should behave themselves in the Publick Cause, he turns to the Female part of his Audience; "And as for you (says he) I shall advise you in very few Words: Aspire only to those Virtues that are peculiar to your Sex: follow your natural Modesty, and think it your greatest Commendation not to be talked of one way or other.". . .

⊷§ LONDON LABOUR AND THE LONDON POOR

Henry Mayhew

OF THE NUMBER OF COSTERMONGERS AND OTHER STREET-FOLK

The number of costermongers,—that it is to say, of those street-sellers attending the London "green" and "fish markets,"—appears to be, from the best data at my command, now 30,000 men, women, and children. The census of 1841 gives only 2,045 "hawkers, hucksters, and pedlars," in the metropolis, and no costermongers or street-sellers, or street-performers at all. This number is absurdly small, and its absurdity is accounted for by the fact that not one in twenty of the costermongers, or of the people with whom they lodged, troubled themselves to fill up the census returns—the majority of them being unable to read and write, and others distrustful of the purpose for which the returns were wanted.

The costermongering class extends itself yearly; and it is computed that for the last five years it has increased considerably faster than the general metropolitan population. This increase is derived partly from *all* the children of costermongers following the father's trade, but chiefly from working men, such as the servants of greengrocers or of innkeepers, when out of employ, "taking to a coster's barrow" for a livelihood; and the same being done by mechanics and labourers out of work. At the time of the famine

Henry Mayhew, *London Labour and the London Poor* (London: Griffin, Bohn & Co., 1861), I, 4–6, 43–45, 418–423; III, 233–239.

in Ireland, it is calculated, that the number of Irish obtaining a living in the London streets must have been at least doubled. . . .

But, great as is this number, still the costermongers are only a portion of the street-folk. Besides these, there are, as we have seen, many other large classes obtaining their livelihood in the streets. The street musicians, for instance, are said to number 1,000, and the old clothesmen the same. There are supposed to be at the best 500 sellers of water-cresses; 200 coffee-stalls; 300 cats-meat men; 250 ballad-singers; 200 play-bill sellers; from 800 to 1,000 bone-grubbers and mud-larks; 1,000 crossing-sweepers; another thousand chimney-sweeps, and the same number of turncocks and lamp-lighters; all of whom, together with the street-performers and showmen, tinkers, chair, umbrella, and clock-menders, sellers of bonnet-boxes, toys, stationery, songs, last dying-speeches, tubs, pails, mats, crockery, blacking, lucifers, corn-salves, clothes-pegs, brooms, sweetmeats, razors, dog-collars, dogs, birds, coals, sand—scavengers, dustmen, and others, make up, it may be fairly assumed, full thirty thousand adults, so that, reckoning men, women, and children, we may truly say that there are upwards of fifty thousand individuals, or about a fortieth-part of the entire population of the metropolis getting their living in the streets.

Now of all modes of obtaining subsistence, that of street-selling is the most precarious. Continued wet weather deprives those who depend for their bread upon the number of people frequenting the public thoroughfares of all means of living; and it is painful to think of the hundreds belonging to this class in the metropolis who are reduced to starvation by three or four days successive rain. Moreover, in the winter, the street-sellers of fruit and vegetables are cut off from the ordinary means of gaining their livelihood, and, consequently, they have to suffer the greatest privations at a time when the severity of the season demands the greatest amount of physical comforts. To expect that the increased earnings of the summer should be put aside as a provision against the deficiencies of the winter, is to expect that a precarious occupation should beget provident habits, which is against the nature of things, for it is always in those callings which are the most uncertain, that the greatest amount of improvidence and intemperance are found to exist. It is not the well-fed man, be it observed, but the starving one that is in danger of surfeiting himself.

Moreover, when the religious, moral, and intellectual degradation of the great majority of these fifty thousand people is impressed upon us, it becomes positively appalling to contemplate the vast amount of vice, ignorance and want, existing in these days in the very heart of our land. The public have but to read the following plain unvarnished account of the habits, amusements, dealings, education, politics, and religion of the London costermongers in the nineteenth century, and then to say whether they think it safe—even if it be thought fit—to allow men, women, and children to continue in such a state. . . .

OF THE COSTER-GIRLS

. . . The story of one coster-girl's life may be taken as a type of the many. When quite young she is placed out to nurse with some neighbour, the mother—if a fond one—visiting the child at certain periods of the day, for the purpose of feeding it, or sometimes, knowing the round she has to make, having the infant brought to her at certain places, to be "suckled." As soon as it is old enough to go alone, the court is its play-ground, the gutter its school-room, and under the care of an elder sister the little one passes the day, among children whose mothers like her own are too busy out in the streets helping to get the food, to be able to mind the family at home. When the girl is strong enough, she in her turn is made to assist the mother by keeping guard over the younger children, or, if there be none, she is lent out to carry about a baby, and so made to add to the family income by gaining her sixpence weekly. Her time is from the earliest years fully occupied; indeed, her parents cannot afford to keep her without doing and getting *something*. Very few of the children receive the least education. "The parents," I am told, "never give their minds to learning, for they say, 'What's the use of it? *that* won't yarn a gal a living.' " Everything is sacrificed—as, indeed, under the circumstances it must be—in the struggle to live—aye! and to live *merely*. Mind, heart, soul, are all absorbed in the belly. The rudest form of animal life, physiologists tell us, is simply a locomotive stomach. Verily, it would appear as if our social state had a tendency to make the highest animal sink into the lowest.

At about seven years of age the girls first go into the streets to sell. A shallow-basket is given to them, with about two shillings for stock-money, and they hawk, according to the time of year, either oranges, apples, or violets; some begin their street education with the sale of water-cresses. The money earned by this means is strictly given to the parents. Sometimes—though rarely—a girl who has been unfortunate during the day will not dare to return home at night, and then she will sleep under some dry arch or about some market, until the morrow's gains shall ensure her a safe reception and shelter in her father's room.

The life of the coster-girls is as severe as that of the boys. Between four and five in the morning they have to leave home for the markets, and sell in the streets until about nine. Those that have more kindly parents, return then to breakfast, but many are obliged to earn the morning's meal for themselves. After breakfast, they generally remain in the streets until about ten o'clock at night; many having nothing during all that time but one meal of bread and butter and coffee, to enable them to support the fatigue of walking from street to street with the heavy basket on their heads. In the course of a day, some girls eat as much as a pound of bread, and very seldom get any meat, unless it be on a Sunday.

There are many poor families that, without the aid of these girls, would be forced into the workhouse. They are generally of an affectionate disposition, and some will perform acts of marvellous heroism to keep together the little home. It is not at all unusual for mere children of fifteen to walk their eight or ten miles a day, carrying a basket of nearly two hundred weight on their heads. A journey to Woolwich and back, or to the towns near London, is often undertaken to earn the 1*s*. 6*d*. their parents are anxiously waiting for at home.

Very few of these girls are married to the men they afterwards live with. Their courtship is usually a very short one; for, as one told me, "the life is such a hard one, that a girl is ready to get rid of a *little* of the labour at any price.". . .

THE LIFE OF A COSTER-GIRL

. . . The one I fixed upon was a fine-grown young woman of eighteen. She had a habit of curtsying to every question that was put to her. Her plaid shawl was tied over the breast, and her cotton-velvet bonnet was crushed in with her carrying her basket. She seemed dreadfully puzzled where to put her hands, at one time tucking them under her shawl, warming them at the fire, or measuring the length of her apron, and when she answered a question she invariably addressed the fireplace. Her voice was husky from shouting apples.

"My mother has been in the streets selling all her lifetime. He uncle learnt her the markets and she learnt me. When business grew bad she said to me, 'Now you shall take care on the stall, and I'll go and work out charing.' The way she learnt me the markets was to judge of the weight of the baskets of apples, and then said she, 'Always bate 'em down, a'most a half.' I always liked the street-life very well, that was if I was selling. I have mostly kept a stall myself, but I've known gals as walk about with apples, as have told me that the weight of the baskets is sich that the neck cricks, and when the load is took off, it's just as if you'd a stiff neck, and the head feels as light as a feather. The gals begins working very early at our work; the parents makes them go out when a'most babies. There's a little gal, I'm sure she an't more than half-past seven, that stands selling water-cresses next my stall, and mother was saying, 'Only look there, how that little one has to get her living afore she a'most knows what a penn'orth means.'

"There's six on us in family, and father and mother makes eight. Father used to do odd jobs with the gas-pipes in the streets, and when work was slack we have very hard times of it. Mother always liked being with us at home, and used to manage to keep us employed out of mischief—she'd give us an old gown to make into pinafores for the children and such like! She's been very good to us, has mother, and so's father. She always liked to hear us read to her whilst she was washing or such like! and then we big ones had to learn the little ones. But when father's work got slack, if she had no employment charing, she'd say, 'Now I'll go and buy a bushel of apples,' and then she'd turn out and get a penny that way. I suppose by sitting at the stall from nine in the morning till the shops shuts up—say ten o'clock at night, I can earn about 1*s.* 6*d.* a day. It's all according to the apples—whether they're good or not—what we makes. If I'm unlucky, mother will say, 'Well, I'll go out to-morrow and see what *I* can do;' and if I've done well, she'll say 'Come you're a good hand at it; you've done famous.' Yes, mother's very fair that way. Ah! there's many a gal I knows whose back has to suffer if she don't sell her stock well; but, thank God! I never get more than a blowing up. My parents is very fair to me.

"I dare say there ain't ten out of a hundred gals what's living with men, what's been married Church of England fashion. I know plenty myself, but I don't, indeed, think it right. It seems to me that the gals is fools to be 'ticed away, but, in coorse, they needn't go without they likes. This is why I don't think it's right. Perhaps a man will have a few words with his gal, and he'll say, 'Oh! I ain't obliged to keep her!' and he'll turn her out: and then where's that poor gal to go? Now, there's a gal I knows as came to me no later than this here week, and she had a dreadful swole face and a awful black eye; and I says, 'Who's done that?' and she says, says she, 'Why, Jack'—just in that way; and then she says, says she, 'I'm going to take a warrant out to-morrow.' Well, he gets the warrant that same night, but she never appears again him, for fear of getting more beating. That don't seem to me to be like married people ought to be. Besides, if parties is married, they ought to bend to each other; and they won't, for sartain, if they're only living together. A man as is married is obligated to keep his wife if they quarrels or not; and he says to himself, says he, 'Well, I may as well live happy, like.' But if he can turn a poor gal off, as soon as he tires of her, he begins to have noises with her, and then gets quit of her altogether. Again, the men takes the money of the gals, and in coorse ought to treat 'em well—which they don't. This is another reason: when the gal is in the family way, the lads mostly sends them to the workhouse to lay in, and only goes sometimes to take them a bit of tea and shuggar; but, in coorse, married men wouldn't behave in such likes to their poor wives. . . ."

THE COAL-HEAVERS

The transition from the artisan to the labourer is curious in many respects. In passing from the skilled operative of the west-end to the unskilled workman of the eastern quarter of London, the moral and intellectual change is so great, that it seems as if we were in a new land, and among another race. The artisans are almost to a man red-hot politicians. They are sufficiently educated and thoughtful to have a sense of their importance in the State. It is true they may entertain exaggerated notions of their natural rank and position in the social scale, but at least they have read, and reflected, and argued upon the subject, and their opinions are entitled to consideration. The political character and sentiments of the working classes appear to me to be a distinctive feature of the age, and they are a necessary consequence of the dawning intelligence of the mass. As their minds expand, they are naturally led to take a more enlarged view of their calling, and to contemplate their labours in relation to the whole frame-work of society. They begin to view their class, not as a mere isolated body of workmen, but as an integral portion of the nation, contributing their quota to the general welfare. If property has its duties as well as its rights; labour, on the other hand, they say, has its rights as well as its duties. The artisans of London seem to be generally well-informed upon these subjects. That they express their opinions violently, and often savagely, it is my duty to acknowledge; but that they are the unenlightened and un-thinking body of people that they are generally considered by those who never go among them, and who see them only as "the dangerous classes," it is my duty also to deny. So far as my experience has gone, I am bound to confess, that I have found the skilled labourers of the metropolis the very reverse, both morally and intellectually, of what the popular prejudice imagines them.

The unskilled labourers are a different class of people. As yet they are as unpolitical as footmen, and instead of entertaining violent democratic opinions, they appear to have no political opinions whatever; or, if they do possess any, they rather lead towards the maintenance of "things as they are," than towards the ascendancy of the working people. I have lately been investigating the state of the coalwhippers, and these reflections are forced upon me by the marked difference in the character and sentiments of these people from those of the operative tailors. . . .

The labourers, in point of numbers, rank second on the occupation-list of the metropolis. The domestic servants, as a body of people, have the first numerical position, being as many 168,000, while the labourers are less than one-third that number, or 50,000 strong. They, however, are nearly twice as many as the boot and shoemakers, who stand next upon the list, and muster 28,000 individuals among them; and they are more than twice as many as the tailors and breeches-makers, who are fourth in regard to their number, and count 23,500 persons. After these come the milliners and dressmakers, who are 20,000 in number. . . .

Before visiting the district of Wapping, where the greater part of the coal labour is carried on, I applied to the Clerk and Registrar of the Coal Exchange for the statistics connected with the body of which he is an officer. Such statistics—as to the extent of their great traffic, the weekly returns of sales, in short, the ramifications of an inquiry embracing maritime, mercantile, mining, and labouring interests, are surely the weekly routine of the business of the Registrar's office. I was promised a series of returns by the gentleman in question, but I did not receive and could not obtain them. Another officer, the Secretary of the Meters' Office, when applied to, with the sanction of his co-officer, the Clerk and Registrar, required a written application which should be attended to! I do not allude to these gentlemen with the slightest inclination unduly to censure them. The truth is, with questions affecting labour and the poor they have little sympathy. The labourer, in their eyes, is but a machine; so many labourers are as so many horse-power. To deny, or withhold, or delay information required for the purposes of the present inquiry is, however, unavailing. The matter I have given in fulness and in precision, without any aid from the gentlemen referred to shows that it was more through courtesy than through necessity that I applied to them in the first instance. . . .

The coalwhippers, previous to the passing of the Act of Parliament in 1843, were employed and paid by the publicans in the neighbourhood of the river, from Tower-hill to Limehouse. Under this system, none but the most dissolute and intemperate obtained employment; in fact, the more intemperate they were the more readily they found work. The publicans were the relatives of the northern shipowners; they mostly had come to London penniless, and being placed in a tavern by their relatives, soon became shipowners themselves. There were at that time seventy taverns on the north side of the Thames, below bridge, employing coalwhippers, and all of the landlords making fortunes out of the earnings of the people. When a ship came to be "made up," that is, for the hands to be hired, the men assembled round the bar in crowds and began calling for drink, and outbidding each other in the extent of their orders, so as to induce the landlord to give them employment. If one called for beer, the next would be sure to give an order for rum; for he who spent most at the public-house had the greatest chance of employment. After being "taken on," their first care was to put up a score at the public-house, so as to please their employer, the publican. In the morning before going to their work, they would invariably call at the house for a quartern of gin or rum; and they were obliged to take off with them to the ship "a bottle," holding nine pots of beer, and that of the worst description, for it was the invariable practice among the publicans to supply the coalwhippers with the very worst articles at the highest prices. When the men returned from their work they went back to the public-house, and there remained drinking the greater part of the night. He must have been a very steady man indeed, I am told, who could manage to return home sober to his wife and family. The consequence of this was, the men used to pass their days and chief part of their nights, drinking in the public-house; and I am credibly informed that frequently, on the publican settling with them after leaving the ship, instead of having anything to receive they were brought in several shillings in debt; this remained as a score for the next ship: in fact, it was only those who were in debt to the publican who were sure of employment on the next occasion. . . .

Since the passing of the Act, establishing the Coalwhippers' Office, and thus taking the employment and pay of the men out of the hands of the publicans, so visible has been the improvement in the whole character of the labourers, that they have raised themselves in the respect of all who know them.

Within the last few years they have established a Benefit Society, and they expended in the year 1847, according to the last account, 646*l.* odd, in the relief of the sick and the burial of the dead. They have also established a superannuation fund, out of which they allow 5*s.* per week to each member who is incapacitated from old age or accident. They are, at the present time, paying such pensions to twenty members. . . .

Further than this they have established a school, with accommodation for six hundred scholars, out of their small earnings. On one occasion as much as 80*l.* was collected among the men for the erection of this institution.

The men are liable to many accidents; some fall off the plank into the hold of the vessel, and are killed; others are injured by large lumps of coal falling on them; and, indeed, so frequent are these disasters, that the Commissioners have directed that the indivisible fraction which remains, after dividing the earnings of the men into nine equal parts, should be applied to the relief of the injured; and although the fund raised by these insignificant means amounts in the course of the year to 30*l.* or 40*l.*, the whole is absorbed by the calamities.

Furnished with this information as to the general character and regulations of the calling, I then proceeded to visit one of the vessels in the river, so that I might see the nature of the labour performed. No one on board the vessel (the—, of Newcastle) was previously aware of my visit or its object. I need not describe the vessel, as my business is with the London labourers in the coal trade. It is necessary, however, in order to show the nature of the labour of coal-whipping, that I should state that the average depth of coal in the hold of a collier, from ceiling to combing, is sixteen feet, while there is an additional seven feet to be reckoned for the basketman's "boom," which makes the height that the coals have to be raised by the whippers from twenty-three to thirty feet. The complement of a gang of coalwhippers is about nine. In the hold are four men, who relieve each other in filling a basket—only one basket being in use with coal. The labour of these four men is arduous: so exhausting is it in hot weather that their usual attire is found to be cumbrous, and they have often to work merely in their trousers or drawers. As fast as these four men in the hold fill the basket, which holds 1¼cwt., four whippers draw it up. This is effected in a peculiar and, to a person unused to the contemplation of the process, really an impressive manner. The four whippers stand on the deck, at the foot of what is called "a way." This way resembles a short rude ladder: it is formed of four-broken oars lashed lengthways, from four to five feet in height (giving a step from oar to oar of more than a foot), while the upright spars to which they are attached are called "a derrick." At the top of this "derrick" is a "gin," which is a revolving wheel, to which the ropes holding the basket, "filled" and "whipped," are attached. The process is thus one of manual labour with mechanical aid. The basket having been filled in the hold, the whippers correctly guessing the time for the filling—for they never look down into the hold—skip up the "way," holding the ropes attached to the basket and the gin, and pulling the ropes at two skips, simultaneously, as they ascend. They thus hoist the loaded basket some height out of the hold, and, when hoisted so far, jump down, keeping exact time in their jump, from the topmost beam of the way on to the deck, so giving the momentum of their bodily weight to the motion communicated to the basket. While the basket is influenced by this motion and momentum, the basket-man, who is stationed on a plank flung across the hold, seizes the basket, runs on with it (the gin revolving) to "the boom," and shoots the contents into the weighing-machine. The boom is formed of two upright poles, with a cross-pole attached by way of step, on to which the basket-man vaults, and rapidly reversing the basket, empties it. This process is very quickly effected, for if the basket-man did not avail himself of the swing of the basket, the feat would be almost beyond a man's strength, or, at least, he would soon be exhausted by it. . . .

This process is not only remarkable for its celerity but for another characteristic. Sailors, when they have to "pull away" together, generally time their pulling to some rude chant; their "Yo, heave, yo," is thought not only to regulate but to mitigate the weight of their labour. The coalwhippers do their work in perfect silence: they do it indeed like work, and hard work, too. The basket-man and the meter are equally silent, so that nothing is heard but the friction of the ropes, the discharge of the coal from the basket into the machine, and from the machine into the barge. The usual amount of work done by the whippers in a day (but not as an average, one day with another) is to unload, or whip, ninety-eight tons! To whip one ton, sixteen basketfuls are required; so that to whip a single ton these men jump up and down 144 feet: for a day's work of ninety-eight tons, they jump up and down 13,088 feet. . . .

The following statement was given to me by a coalwhipper on board this vessel:—

"We should like better wages, but then we have enemies. Now suppose you, sir, are a coal-merchant, and this gentleman here freights a ship of the captain—you understand me? The man who freights the ships that way is paid, by the captain, ninepence a ton, for a gang of nine men, such as you've seen—nine coalwhippers—but these nine men, you understand me, are paid by the merchant (or buyer) only eightpence a ton; so that by every ton he clear a penny, without any labour or trouble whatsoever. I and my fellows is dissatisfied, but can't help ourselves. . . ."

The coalwhippers all present the same aspect—they are all black. In summer, when the men strip more to their work, perspiration causes the coal-dust to adhere to the skin, and blackness is more than ever the rule. All about the ship partakes of the grimness of the prevailing hue. The sails are black; the gilding on the figure-head of the vessel becomes blackened, and the very visitor feels his complexion soon grow sable. The dress of the whippers is of every description; some have fustian jackets, some have sailors' jackets, some loose great coats, some Guernsey frocks. Many of them work in strong shirts, which once were white with a blue stripe: loose cotton necker-chiefs are generally worn by the whippers. All have black hair and black whiskers—no matter what the original hue; to the more stubbly beards and moustachios the coal-dust adheres freely between the bristles, and may even be seen, now and then, to glitter in the light amidst the hair. The barber, one of these men told me, charged nothing extra for shaving him, although the coal-dust must be a formidable thing to the best-tempered razor. In approaching a coal-ship in the river, the side has to be gained over barges lying alongside—the coal crackling under the visitor's feet. He must cross them to reach a ladder of very primitive construction, up which the deck is to be reached. It is a jest among the Yorkshire seamen that every thing is black in a collier, especially the soup. When the men are at work in whipping or filling, the only spot of white discernible on their hands is a portion of the nails.

There are no specific hours for the payment of these men: they are entitled to their money as soon as their work is reported to be completed. Nothing can be better than the way in which the whippers are now paid. The basket-man enters the office of the pay-clerk of the coal commission at one door, and hands over an adjoining counter an amount of money he has received from the captain. The pay-clerk ascertains that the amount is correct. He then divides the sum into nine portions, and, touching a spring to open a door, he cries out for "Gang such a number." The nine men, who, with many others, are in attendance in rooms provided for them adjacent to the pay-office, appear immediately, and are paid off. I was present when nine whippers were paid for the discharge of 363½ tons. . . .

These 363½ tons, at 8*d*. per ton, realized to each man, for five days' work, 1*l*. 6*s*. 4¼*d*.; 10*s*. of which had been paid to each as subsistence money during the progress of the work. . . .

MEETING OF THIEVES

As a further proof, however, of the demoralizing influences of the low lodging-houses, I will now conclude my investigations into the subject with a report of the meeting of vagrants, which I convened for the express purpose of consulting them generally upon several points which had come under my notice in the course of my inquiries. The Chronicle reporter's account of this meeting was as follows:—

A meeting of an unprecedented character was held at the British Union School-room, Shakespeare-walk, Shadwell, on Monday evening last. The use of the school-room was kindly granted by Mr. Fletcher, the proprietor, to whose liberality we stand indebted for many similar favours. It was convened by our Metropolitan Correspondent, for the purpose of assembling together some of the lowest class of male juvenile thieves and vagabonds who infest the metropolis and the country at large; and although privately called, at only two days' notice, by the distribution of tickets of admission among the class in question at the various haunts and dens of infamy to which they resort, no fewer than 150 of them attended on the occasion. The only condition to entitle the parties to admission was that they should be vagrants, and under twenty years of age. They had all assembled some time before the hour for commencing the proceedings arrived, and never was witnessed a more distressing spectacle of squalor, rags, and wretchedness. Some were young men, and some mere children; one, who styled himself a "cadger," was six years of age, and several who confessed themselves "prigs" were only ten. The countenances of the boys were of various characters. Many were not only good-looking, but had a frank, ingenuous expression that seemed in no way connected with innate roguery. Many, on the other hand, had the deep-sunk and half-averted eye which are so characteristic of natural dishonesty and cunning. Some had the regular features of lads born of parents in easy circumstances. The hair of most of the lads was cut very close to the head, showing their recent liberation from prison; indeed, one might tell by the comparative length of the crop, the time that each boy had been out of gaol. All but a few of the elder boys were remarkable, amidst the rags, filth, and wretchedness of their external appearance, for the mirth and carelessness impressed upon their countenances. At first their behaviour was very noisy and disorderly: coarse and ribald jokes were freely cracked, exciting general bursts of laughter; while howls, cat-calls, and all manner of unearthly and indescribable yells threatened for some time to render the object of the meeting utterly abortive. At one moment a lad would imitate the bray of a jack-ass, and immediately the whole hundred and fifty would fall to braying. Then some ragged urchin would crow like a cock, whereupon the place would echo again with a hundred and fifty cock-crows. Then, as a black boy entered the room, one of the young vagabonds would shout out "swe-ee-op." This would be received with peals of laughter, and followed by a general repetition of the same cry. Next, a hundred and fifty cat-calls of the shrillest possible description would almost split the ears. These would be succeeded by cries of "Strike up, you catgut scrapers," "Go on with your barrow," "Flare up, my never-sweats," and a variety of other street sayings. Indeed, the uproar which went on before the meeting began will be best understood if we compare it to the scene presented by a public menagerie at feeding time. The greatest difficulty, as might be expected, was experienced in collecting the subjoined statistics of their character and condition. By a well-contrived and persevering mode of inquiry, however, the following facts were elicited:—

With respect to their *ages,* the youngest boy present was 6 years old. He styled himself a "cadger," and said that his mother, who is a widow, and suffering from ill-health, sends him into the streets to beg. There were seven of 10 years of age, three of 12, three of 13, ten of 14, ten of 15, eleven of 16, twenty of 17, twenty-six of 18, and forty-five of 19.

Nineteen had *fathers and mothers* still living; thirty-nine had only one parent, and eighty were orphans in the fullest sense of the word, having neither father nor mother alive.

Of *professed beggars* there were fifty, and sixty-six who acknowledged themselves to be *habitual thieves*. The announcement that the greater number present were thieves pleased them exceedingly, and was received with three rounds of applause.

Twelve of the youths assembled had been *in prison* once (two of these were but 10 years of age) ; 5 had been in prison twice; 3, thrice; 4, four times; 7, five times; 8, six times; 5, seven times; 4, eight times; 2, nine times (1 of them 13 years of age) ; 5, ten times; 5, twelve times; 2, thirteen times; 3, fourteen times; 2, sixteen times; 3, seventeen times; 2, eighteen times; 5, twenty times; 6, twenty-four times; 1, twenty-five times; 1, twenty-six times; and 1, twenty-nine times. The announcements in reply to the questions as to the number of times that any of them had been in prison were received with great applause, which became more and more boisterous as the number of imprisonments increased. When it was announced that one, though only 19 years of age, had been in prison as many as twenty-nine times, the clapping of hands, the cat-calls, and shouts of "brayvo!" lasted for several minutes, and the whole of the boys rose to look at the distinguished individual. Some chalked on their hats the figures which designated the sum of the several times that they had been in gaol.

As to the *causes of their vagabondism,* it was found that 22 had run away from their homes, owing to the ill-treatment of their parents; 18 confessed to having been ruined through their parents allowing them to run wild in the streets, and to be led astray by bad companions; and 15 acknowledged that they had been first taught thieving in a lodging-house.

Concerning the vagrant habits of the youths, the following facts were elicited: 78 regularly roam through the country every year, 65 sleep regularly in the casual wards of the unions, and 52 occasionally slept in tramper's lodging-houses throughout the country.

Respecting their *education,* according to the popular meaning of the term, 63 of the 150 were able to read and write, and they were principally thieves. . . .

The process of interrogating them in the mass having been concluded, the next step was to call several of them separately to the platform, to narrate, in their peculiar style and phraseology, the history of their own career, together with the causes which had led them to take up a life of dishonesty. The novelty of their position as speech-makers seemed peculiarly exciting to the speakers themselves, and provoked much merriment and interest amongst the lads. Their antics and buffoonery in commencing their addresses were certainly of the most ludicrous character. The first speaker, a lad of 17 years of age, ascended the platform, dressed in a torn "wide-a-wake" hat, and a dirty smock-frock. He began:—Gentlemen [immense applause and laughter], I am a Brummagem lad [laughter]. My father has been dead three years, and my mother seven. When my father died I had to go and live along with my aunt. I fell out of employment, and went round about the town, and fell into the company of a lot of chaps, and went picking ladies' pockets. Then I was in prison once or twice, and I came to London, and have been in several prisons here. I have been in London three years; but I have been out of it several times in that time. I can't get anything honest to do; and I wish I could get something at sea, or in any foreign land. I don't care what or where it is [cheers and yells].

Another lad about 16, clad in a ragged coat, with a dirty face and matted hair, next came forward and said—My father was a soldier, and when I growed up to about ten years I joined the regiment as a drummer in the Grenadier Guards. I went on and got myself into trouble, till at last I got turned away, and my father left the regiment. I then went out with some more chaps and went thieving, and have been thieving about two years now. [Several voices—"Very good;" "that's beautiful;" "I hope you do it well."]

The third boy, who stated that he had been twenty-four times in prison, said he belonged to Hendon, in Middlesex, and that his father left his mother seventeen years ago, and he did not know whether he was dead or alive. He went to Christ-church school for some time, but afterwards picked up with bad companions, and went a thieving. He went to school again, but again left it to go a thieving and cadging with bad companions. He had been doing that for the last five years; and if he could get out of it he would be very glad to leave it [cheers].

The fourth lad (who was received with loud cheering, evidently indicating that he was a well-known character) said, he came from the city of York, and was a farrier. His father died a few years ago, and then he took to work; but "the play" led him on to be a thief, and from that time to the present he had done nothing but beg or thieve. If he could go to Australia he would be very glad; as if he stopped in England he feared he should do nothing but thieve to the end [laughter, with cries of "well done," "very well spoken"].

The next speaker was about 18 years of age, and appeared a very sharp intelligent lad. After making a very grave but irresistibly comical prefatory bow, by placing his hand at the back of his head, and so (as it were) forcing it to give a nod, he proceeded: My father is an engineer's labourer, and the first cause of my thieving was that he kept me without grub, and wallopped me [laughter]. Well, I was at work at the same time that he was, and I kept pilfering, and at last they bowled me out [loud cheers]. I got a showing up, and at last they turned me away; and, not liking to go home to my father, I ran away. I went to Margate, where I had some friends, with a shilling in my pocket. I never stopped till I got to Ramsgate, and I had no lodging except under the trees, and had only the bits of bread I could pick up. When I got there my grandfather took me in and kept me for a twelvemonth. My mother's brother's wife had a spite against me, and tried to get me turned away. I did not know what thieving was then; and I used to pray that her heart might be turned, because I did not know what would become of me if my grandfather turned me away. But she got other people to complain of me, and say I was a nuisance to the town; but I knowed there was no fault in me; but, however, my grandfather said he could put up with me no longer, and turned me away. So after that I came back to London, and goes to the union. The first night I went there I got tore up [cheers and laughter]. Everything was torn off my back, and the bread was taken away from me, and because I said a word I got well wallopped [renewed laughter]. They "small-ganged" me; and afterwards I went seven days to prison because others tore my clothes. When I went in there—this was the first time—a man said to me, "What are you here for?" I said, "For tearing up." The man said to another, "What are you here for?" and the other made answer, "For a handkerchief." The man then said, "Ah, that's something like;" and he said to me, "Why are you not a thief—you will only get to prison for that." I said, "I will." Well, after that I went pilfering small things, worth a penny or two-pence at first; but I soon saw better things were as easy to be got as them, so I took them [laughter]. I picked up with one that knowed more than me. He fairly kept me for some time, and I learnt as well as him. I picked him up in a London work-house. After that I thought I would try my friends again, and I went to my uncle at Dover, but he could do nothing for me, so I got a place at a butcher's, where I fancied myself fairly blessed, for I had 2s. a week and my board and washing. I kept a twelve-month there honest, without thieving. At last my master and I fell out and I left again, so I was forced to come up to London, and there I found my old companions in the Smithfield pens—they were not living anywhere. I used to go to the workhouse and used to tear up and refuse to work, and used to get sent to "quod," and I used to curse the day when it was my turn to go out. The governor of the prison used to say he hoped he wouldn't see my face there again; but I used to answer, "I shall be here again to night, because it's the only place I've got." That's all I've got to say.

The next lad, who said he had been fourteen times in prison, was a taller, cleaner, and more intelligent-looking youth than any that had preceded him. After making a low affected bow, over the railing, to the company below, and uttering a preliminary a-hem or two with the most ludicrous mock gravity, he began by saying:—"I am a native of London. My father is a poor labouring man, with 15s. a week—little enough, I think, to keep a home for four, and find candlelight [laughter]. I was at work look-ing after a boiler at a paper-stainer's in Old-street-road at 6s. a week, when one night they bowled me out. I got the sack, and a bag to take it home in [laughter]. I got my wages, and ran away from home, but in four days, being hungry, and having no money, I went back again. I got a towelling, but it did not do me much good. My father did not like to turn me out of doors, so he tied me to the leg of the bedstead [laughter]. He tied my hands and feet so that I could hardly move, but I managed somehow to turn my gob (mouth) round and gnawed it away. I run down stairs and got out at the back door and over a neighbour's wall, and never went home for nine months. I never bolted with anything. I never took anything that was too hot for me. The cap-tain of a man-of-war about this time took me into his service, where I remained five weeks till I took a fever, and was obliged to go to the hospital. When I recovered, the captain was gone to Africa; and not liking to go home, I stepped away, and have been from home ever since. I was in Brummagem, and was seven days in the new 'stir' (prison), and nearly broke my neck. When I came out, I fell into bad company, and went cadging, and have been cadging ever since; but if I could leave off, and go to the Isle of Dogs, the Isle of Man, or the Isle of Woman [laughter], or any other foreign place, I would embrace the opportunity as soon as I could. And if so be that any gentleman would take me in hand, and send me out, I would be very thankful to him, indeed. And so good night" [cheers].

A dirty little boy, fourteen years of age, dressed in a big jacket, next stood forward. He said his father was a man-of-war's man, and when he came home from sea once his father, his mother, and all of them got drunk. The lad then stole 4d. from his father's pocket. After this, when he was sent for sixpenny rum he used to fetch fourpenny, and for fourpenny gin threepenny; and for fourpenny beer he used to fetch threepenny, and keep the difference to himself. His mother used to sell fruit, and when she left him at the stall he used to eat what he could not sell, and used to sell some to get marbles and buttons. Once he stole a loaf from a baker's shop. The man let him off, but his father beat him for it. The beating did him no good. After that he used to go "smugging" [running away with] other people's things. Then one day his father caught him, and tied his leg to the bedstead, and left him there till he was pretty near dead. He ran away afterwards, and has been thieving ever since. . . .

Mr. Mayhew then addressed them on another point. He said he had seen many notorious thieves in the course of his investigations. Since then he had received them at all hours into his house—men of the most desperate and women of the most abandoned characters—but he had never lost a *6d.* worth of his property by them. One thief he had entrusted with a sovereign to get changed, and the lad returned and gave him back the full amount in silver. He had since gone out to America. Now he would ask all those present whether, if he were to give them a sovereign, they would do the same? [Several voices here called out that they would, and others that they would not. Others, again, said that they would to him, but to no one else.]

Here one of the most desperate characters present, a boy who had been twenty-six times in prison, was singled out from the rest, and a sovereign given to him to get changed, in order to make the experiment whether he would have the honesty to return the change or abscond with it in his possession. He was informed, on receiving it, that if he chose to decamp with it, no proceedings should be taken against him. He left the room amid the cheers of his companions, and when he had been absent a few moments all eyes were turned towards the door each time it opened, anxiously expecting his arrival, to prove his trustworthiness. Never was such interest displayed by any body of individuals. They mounted the forms in their eagerness to obtain the first glimpse of his return. It was clear that their honour was at stake; and several said they would kill the lad in the morning if he made off with the money. Many minutes elapsed in almost painful suspense, and some of his companions began to fear that so large a sum of money had proved too great a temptation for the boy. At last, however, a tremendous burst of cheering announced the lad's return. The delight of his companions broke forth again and again, in long and loud peals of applause, and the youth advanced amidst triumphant shouts to the platform, and gave up the money in full.

The assemblage was then interrogated as to the effect of flogging as a punishment; and the general feeling appeared to be that it hardened the criminal instead of checking his depravity, and excited the deadliest enmity in his bosom at the time towards the person inflicting it. When asked whether they had seen any public executions, they almost all cried out that they had seen Manning and his wife hung; others said that they had seen Rush and Sarah Thomas executed. They stated that they liked to go a "death-hunting," after seeing one or two executed. It hardened them to it, and at last they all got to thieve under the gallows. They felt rather shocked at the sight of an execution at first; but, after a few repetitions, it soon wore off.

Before the meeting broke up several other lads expressed a strong desire to make statements. . . .

The proceedings then terminated. The assemblage, which had become more rational and manageable towards the close, dispersed, quite peaceably it should be added, and the boys were evidently sincerely grateful for the efforts being made to bring their misfortunes before the notice of those in whose power it may be to alleviate them.

Before they were dismissed, as much money was dispensed to each as would defray his night's lodging.

~§ *Part Five*

The Revolutionary Epoch

✒ THE DECLARATION OF INDEPENDENCE

Second Continental Congress

> *As early as September, 1773, Benjamin Franklin's satire on British imperial policy had charted the widening gulf between the Thirteen Colonies and the mother country, yet not until the measures of retaliation following the Boston Tea Party did the crisis become acute. Even so, throughout 1774 and 1775, Lexington and Concord notwithstanding, there was no serious demand for a final break with Great Britain.*
>
> *Public opinion gradually changed when in the fall of 1775 it became obvious that the moderate approach of petitioning for the redress of American grievances was proving futile, the English government having committed itself to a policy of force. By late spring of 1776, aided by Tom Paine's propaganda and hostile British legislation, the definitive separation became a fact.*
>
> *On June 7, 1776, the Continental Congress began discussion of a resolution for independence introduced by the Virginia delegation. To save time, a five-man committee to draw up a draft resolution was appointed four days later. One of the five, Thomas Jefferson, came to be the chief author of the Declaration, although his version, which originally included a strong condemnation of slavery, was first amended by John Adams and Benjamin Franklin before being debated by the Congress. On July 4, a Declaration of Independence was adopted unanimously after the Pennsylvania and South Carolina delegations had consented to change their vote for the sake of unity.*

THE UNANIMOUS DECLARATION OF THE THIRTEEN UNITED STATES OF AMERICA

When in the Course of human events, it becomes necessary for one people to dissolve the political bands which have connected them with another, and to assume among the Powers of the earth, the separate and equal station to which the Laws of Nature and of Nature's God entitle them, a decent respect to the opinions of mankind requires that they should declare the causes which impel them to the separation.

We hold these truths to be self-evident, that all men are created equal, that they are endowed by their Creator with certain unalienable Rights, that among these are Life,

"The Declaration of Independence," in *Documents of American History*, ed. H. S. Commager (7th ed.; New York: Appleton-Century-Crofts, Inc., 1962), pp. 100–102.

Liberty and the pursuit of Happiness. That to secure these rights, Governments are instituted among Men, deriving their just powers from the consent of the governed. That whenever any Form of Government becomes destructive of these ends, it is the Right of the People to alter or to abolish it, and to institute new Government, laying its foundation on such principles and organizing its powers in such form, as to them shall seem most likely to effect their Safety and Happiness. Prudence, indeed, will dictate that Governments long established should not be changed for light and transient causes; and accordingly all experience hath shown, that mankind are more disposed to suffer, while evils are sufferable, than to right themselves by abolishing the forms to which they are accustomed. But when a long train of abuses and usurpations, pursuing invariably the same Object evinces a design to reduce them under absolute Despotism, it is their right, it is their duty, to throw off such Government, and to provide new Guards for their future security.—Such has been the patient sufferance of these Colonies; and such is now the necessity which constrains them to alter their former Systems of Government. The history of the present King of Great Britain is a history of repeated injuries and usurpations, all having in direct object the establishment of an absolute Tyranny over these States. To prove this, let Facts be submitted to a candid world.

He has refused his Assent to Laws, the most wholesome and necessary for the public good.

He has forbidden his Governors to pass Laws of immediate and pressing importance, unless suspended in their operation till his Assent should be obtained; and when so suspended, he has utterly neglected to attend to them.

He has refused to pass other Laws for the accommodation of large districts of people, unless those people would relinquish the right of Representation in the Legislature, a right inestimable to them and formidable to tyrants only.

He has called together legislative bodies at places unusual, uncomfortable, and distant from the depository of their Public Records, for the sole purpose of fatiguing them into compliance with his measures.

He has dissolved Representative Houses repeatedly, for opposing with manly firmness his invasions on the rights of the people.

He has refused for a long time, after such dissolutions, to cause others to be elected; whereby the Legislative Powers, incapable of Annihilation, have returned to the People at large for their exercise; the State remaining in the mean time exposed to all the dangers of invasion from without, and convulsions within.

He has endeavoured to prevent the population of these States; for that purpose obstructing the Laws of Naturalization of Foreigners; refusing to pass others to encourage their migration hither, and raising the conditions of new Appropriations of Lands.

He has obstructed the Administration of Justice, by refusing his Assent to Laws for establishing Judiciary Powers.

He has made Judges dependent on his Will alone, for the tenure of their offices, and the amount and payment of their salaries.

He has erected a multitude of New Offices, and sent hither swarms of Officers to harass our People, and eat out their substance.

He has kept among us, in times of peace, Standing Armies without the Consent of our legislature.

He has affected to render the Military independent of and superior to the Civil Power.

He has combined with others to subject us to a jurisdiction foreign to our constitution, and unacknowledged by our laws; giving his Assent to their acts of pretended legislation:

For quartering large bodies of armed troops among us:

For protecting them, by a mock Trial, from Punishment for any Murders which they should commit on the Inhabitants of these States:

For cutting off our Trade with all parts of the world:

For imposing taxes on us without our Consent:

For depriving us in many cases, of the benefits of Trial by Jury:

For transporting us beyond Seas to be tried for pretended offences:

For abolishing the free System of English Laws in a neighbouring Province, establishing therein an Arbitrary government, and enlarging its Boundaries so as to render it at once an example and fit instrument for introducing the same absolute rule into these Colonies:

For taking away our Charters, abolishing our most valuable Laws, and altering fundamentally the Forms of our Governments:

For suspending our own Legislature, and declaring themselves invested with Power to legislate for us in all cases whatsoever.

He has abdicated Government here, by declaring us out of his Protection and waging War against us.

He has plundered our seas, ravaged our Coasts, burnt our towns, and destroyed the lives of our people.

He is at this time transporting large armies of foreign mercenaries to compleat the works of death, desolation and tyranny, already begun with circumstances of Cruelty & perfidy scarcely paralleled in the most barbarous ages, and totally unworthy the Head of a civilized nation.

He has constrained our fellow Citizens taken Captive on the high Seas to bear Arms against their Country, to become the executioners of their friends and Brethren, or to fall themselves by their Hands.

He has excited domestic insurrections amongst us, and has endeavoured to bring on the inhabitants of our frontiers, the merciless Indian Savages, whose known rule of warfare, is an undistinguished destruction of all ages, sexes and conditions.

In every stage of these Oppressions We have Petitioned for Redress in the most humble terms: Our repeated Petitions have been answered only by repeated injury. A Prince, whose character is thus marked by every act which may define a Tyrant, is unfit to be the ruler of a free People.

Nor have We been wanting in attention to our British brethren. We have warned them from time to time of attempts by their legislature to extend an unwarrantable jurisdiction over us. We have reminded them of the circumstances of our emigration and settlement here. We have appealed to their native justice and magnanimity, and we have conjured them by the ties of our common kindred to disavow these usurpations, which, would inevitably interrupt our connections and correspondence. They too have been deaf to the voice of justice and of consanguinity. We must, therefore, acquiesce in the necessity, which denounces our Separation, and hold them, as we hold the rest of mankind, Enemies in War, in Peace Friends.

We, therefore, the Representatives of the united States of America, in General Congress, Assembled, appealing to the Supreme Judge of the world for the rectitude of our intentions, do, in the Name, and by Authority of the good People of these Colonies, solemnly publish and declare, That these United Colonies are, and of Right ought to be Free and Independent States; that they are Absolved from all Allegiance to the British Crown, and that all political connection between them and the State of Great Britain, is and ought to be totally dissolved; and that as Free and Independent States, they have full Power to levy War, conclude Peace, contract Alliances, establish Commerce, and to do all other Acts and Things which Independent States may of right do. And for the support of this Declaration, with a firm reliance on the Protection of Divine Providence, we mutually pledge to each other our Lives, our Fortunes and our sacred Honor.

✍ THE FEDERALIST, NUMBERS 10 AND 51

James Madison

What was to be the first and most durable of modern written constitutions was born in the midst of heated controversy. The Constitutional Convention that adjourned in Philadelphia on September 17, 1787, had gone far beyond its instructions in drawing up an entirely new instrument of national government instead of confining itself to amending the existing Articles of Confederation. It had been agreed that the new Constitution would have to be ratified by at least nine states before it could go into effect. Powerful opposition to what the Philadelphia Convention had accomplished was rooted in the state of New York. Of the three delegates that New York had sent to Philadelphia, only one, Alexander Hamilton, had endorsed the Constitution. No sooner had the Convention adjourned than the state's Governor Clinton launched a bitter attack upon its work in a series of published letters signed "Cato."

The most effective defense of the Constitution was organized by Alexander Hamilton, who enlisted the talents of John Jay and James Madison for a series of what came to be eighty-five letters signed "Publius" that appeared in New York newspapers between late October, 1787, and early April,

1788. Shortly afterward, the essays were published in book-form under the title The Federalist.

Federalist Numbers 10 and 51 are generally agreed to be the work of James Madison (1751–1836), the future fourth President of the United States and the man who had played the single greatest role at the Philadelphia Convention. To his defense of the Constitution, Madison brought not only many years of experience in Virginian and national politics, but also his wide reading in political theory. He owed his heaviest intellectual debt to the French philosophe *Montesquieu, whose* Spirit of the Laws, *published earlier in the century, had popularized the doctrine of the separation of powers.*

NUMBER 10

Among the numerous advantages promised by a well constructed union, none deserves to be more accurately developed, than its tendency to break and control the violence of faction. The friend of popular governments, never finds himself so much alarmed for their character and fate, as when he contemplates their propensity to this danger-ous vice. He will not fail, therefore, to set a due value on any plan which, without violating the principles to which he is attached, provides a proper cure for it. The instability, injustice, and confusion introduced into the public councils, have, in truth, been the mortal diseases under which popular governments have every where perished; as they continue to be the favourite and fruitful topics from which the adversaries to liberty derive their most specious declamations. The valuable improvements made by the American constitutions on the popular models, both ancient and modern, cannot certainly be too much admired; but it would be an unwarrantable partiality, to con-tend that they have as effectually obviated the danger on this side, as was wished and expected. Complaints are every where heard from our most considerate and virtuous citizens, equally the friends of public and private faith, and of public and personal liberty, that our governments are too unstable; that the public good is disregarded in the conflicts of rival parties; and that measures are too often decided, not according to the rules of justice, and the rights of the minor party, but by the superior force of an interested and overbearing majority. However anxiously we may wish that these com-plaints had no foundation, the evidence of known facts will not permit us to deny that they are in some degree true. It will be found, indeed, on a candid review of our situation, that some of the distresses under which we labour, have been erroneously charged on the operation of our governments; but it will be found, at the same time, that other causes will not alone account for many of our heaviest misfortunes; and, particularly, for that prevailing and increasing distrust of public engagements, and alarm for private rights, which are echoed from one end of the continent to the other.

Alexander Hamilton, James Madison, and John Jay, in *The Federalist*, ed. B. F. Wright (Cambridge: Harvard University Press, 1961), pp. 60–70, 355–359.

These must be chiefly, if not wholly, effects of the unsteadiness and injustice, with which a factious spirit has tainted our public administration.

By a faction, I understand a number of citizens, whether amounting to a majority or minority of the whole, who are united and actuated by some common impulse of passion, or of interest, adverse to the rights of other citizens, or to the permanent and aggregate interests of the community.

There are two methods of curing the mischiefs of faction: The one, by removing its causes; the other, by controlling its effects.

There are again two methods of removing the causes of faction: The one, by destroying the liberty which is essential to its existence; the other, by giving to every citizen the same opinions, the same passions, and the same interests.

It could never be more truly said, than of the first remedy, that it is worse than the disease. Liberty is to faction, what air is to fire, an aliment, without which it instantly expires. But it could not be a less folly to abolish liberty, which is essential to political life, because it nourishes faction, than it would be to wish the annihilation of air, which is essential to animal life, because it imparts to fire its destructive agency.

The second expedient is as impracticable, as the first would be unwise. As long as the reason of man continues fallible, and he is at liberty to exercise it, different opinions will be formed. As long as the connexion subsists between his reason and his self-love, his opinions and his passions will have a reciprocal influence on each other; and the former will be objects to which the latter will attach themselves. The diversity in the faculties of men, from which the rights of property originate, is not less an insuperable obstacle to an uniformity of interests. The protection of these faculties, is the first object of government. From the protection of different and unequal faculties of acquiring property, the possession of different degrees and kinds of property immediately results: and from the influence of these on the sentiments and views of the respective proprietors, ensues a division of the society into different interests and parties.

The latent causes of faction are thus sown in the nature of man; and we see them every where brought into different degrees of activity, according to the different circumstances of civil society. A zeal for different opinions concerning religion, concerning government, and many other points, as well of speculation as of practice; an attachment to different leaders, ambitiously contending for pre-eminence and power; or to persons of other descriptions, whose fortunes have been interesting to the human passions, have, in turn, divided mankind into parties, inflamed them with mutual animosity, and rendered them much more disposed to vex and oppress each other, than to co-operate for their common good. So strong is this propensity of mankind, to fall into mutual animosities, that where no substantial occasion presents itself, the most frivolous and fanciful distinctions have been sufficient to kindle their unfriendly passions, and excite their most violent conflicts. But the most common and durable source of factions, has been the various and unequal distribution of property.—Those who hold, and those who are without property, have ever formed distinct interests in society. Those who are creditors, and those who are debtors, fall under a like discrimination. A landed interest, a manufacturing interest, a mercantile interest, a monied interest, with many lesser interests, grow up of necessity in civilized nations, and divide them into different classes, actuated by different sentiments and views. The regulation of these various and interfering interests, forms the principal task of modern legislation, and involves the spirit of party and faction in the necessary and ordinary operations of government.

No man is allowed to be a judge in his own cause; because his interest would certainly bias his judgment, and, not improbably, corrupt his integrity. With equal, nay, with greater reason, a body of men, are unfit to be both judges and parties, at the same time; yet, what are many of the most important acts of legislation, but so many judicial determinations, not indeed concerning the rights of single persons, but concerning the rights of large bodies of citizens? and what are the different classes of legislators, but advocates and parties to the causes which they determine? Is a law proposed concerning private debts? It is a question to which the creditors are parties on one side, and the debtors on the other. Justice ought to hold the balance between them. Yet the parties are, and must be, themselves the judges; and the most numerous party, or, in other words, the most powerful faction, must be expected to prevail. Shall domestic manufactures be encouraged, and in what degree, by restrictions on foreign manufactures? are questions which would be differently decided by the landed and the manufacturing classes; and probably by neither with a sole regard to justice and the public good. The apportionment of taxes, on the various descriptions of property, is an act which seems to require the most exact impartiality; yet there is, perhaps, no legislative act in which greater opportunity and temptation are given to a predominant party, to trample on the rules of justice. Every shilling with which they over-burden the inferior number, is a shilling saved to their own pockets.

It is in vain to say, that enlightened statesmen will be able to adjust these clashing interests, and render them all subservient to the public good. Enlightened statesmen will not always be at the helm: nor, in many cases, can such an adjustment be made at all, without taking into view indirect and remote considerations, which will rarely prevail over the immediate interest which one party may find in disregarding the rights of another, or the good of the whole.

The inference to which we are brought is, that the *causes* of faction cannot be removed; and that relief is only to be sought in the means of controlling its *effects*.

If a faction consists of less than a majority, relief is supplied by the republican principle, which enables the majority to defeat its sinister views, by regular vote. It may clog the administration, it may convulse the society; but it will be unable to execute and mask its violence under the forms of the constitution. When a majority is included in a faction, the form of popular government, on the other hand, enables it to sacrifice to its ruling passion or interest, both the public good, and the rights of other citizens. To secure the public good and private rights against the danger of such a faction, and at the same time to preserve the spirit and the form of popular government, is then the great object to which our inquiries are directed. Let me add, that it is the great desideratum, by which alone this form of government can be rescued from the opprobrium under which it has so long laboured, and be recommended to the esteem and adoption of mankind.

By what means is this object attainable? Evidently by one of two only. Either the existence of the same passion or interest in a majority, at the same time, must be prevented; or the majority, having such co-existent passion or interest, must be rendered, by their number and local situation, unable to concert and carry into effect schemes of oppression. If the impulse and the opportunity be suffered to coincide, we well know, that neither moral nor religious motives can be relied on as an adequate control. They are not found to be such on the injustice and violence of individuals, and lose their efficacy in proportion to the number combined together; that is, in proportion as their efficacy becomes needful.

From this view of the subject, it may be concluded that a pure democracy, by which I mean a society consisting of a small number of citizens, who assemble and administer the government in person, can admit of no cure for the mischiefs of faction. A common passion or interest will, in almost every case, be felt by a majority of the whole; a communication and concert, results from the form of government itself; and there is nothing to check the inducements to sacrifice the weaker party, or an obnoxious individual. Hence it is, that such democracies have ever been spectacles of turbulence and contention; have ever been found incompatible with personal security, or the rights of property; and have in general, been as short in their lives, as they have been violent in their deaths. Theoretic politicians, who have patronised this species of government, have erroneously supposed, that by reducing mankind to a perfect equality in their political rights, they would, at the same time, be perfectly equalised and assimilated in their possessions, their opinions, and their passions.

A republic, by which I mean a government in which the scheme of representation takes place, opens a different prospect, and promises the cure for which we are seeking. Let us examine the points in which it varies from pure democracy, and we shall comprehend both the nature of the cure, and the efficacy which it must derive from the union.

The two great points of difference, between a democracy and a republic, are, first, the delegation of the government, in the latter, to a small number of citizens elected by the rest; secondly, the greater number of citizens, and greater sphere of country, over which the latter may be extended.

The effect of the first difference is, on the one hand, to refine and enlarge the public views, by passing them through the medium of a chosen body of citizens, whose wisdom may best discern the true interest of their country, and whose patriotism and love of justice, will be least likely to sacrifice it to temporary or partial considerations. Under such a regulation, it may well happen, that the public voice, pronounced by the representatives of the people, will be more consonant to the public good, than if pronounced by the people themselves, convened for the purpose. On the other hand, the effect may be inverted. Men of factious tempers, of local prejudices, or of sinister designs, may by intrigue, by corruption, or by other means, first obtain the suffrages, and then betray the interest of the people. The question resulting is, whether small or extensive republics are most favourable to the election of proper guardians of the public weal; and it is clearly decided in favour of the latter by two obvious considerations.

In the first place, it is to be remarked, that however small the republic may be, the representatives must be raised to a certain number, in order to guard against the cabals of a few; and that, however large it may be, they must be limited to a certain number, in order to guard against the confusion of a multitude. Hence the number of representatives in the two cases not being in proportion to that of the constituents, and being proportionably greatest in the small republic, it follows, that if the proportion of fit characters be not less in the large than in the small republic, the former will present a greater option, and consequently a greater probability of a fit choice.

In the next place, as each representative will be chosen by a greater number of citizens in the large than in the small republic, it will be more difficult for unworthy candidates to practise with success the vicious arts, by which elections are too often carried; and the suffrages of the people being more free, will be more likely to center in men who possess the most attractive merit, and the most diffusive and established characters.

It must be confessed, that in this, as in most other cases, there is a mean, on both sides of which inconveniences will be found to lie. By enlarging too much the number of electors, you render the representative too little acquainted with all their local circumstances and lesser interests; as by reducing it too much, you render him unduly attached to these, and too little fit to comprehend and pursue great and national objects. The federal constitution forms, in this respect, a happy combination; the great and aggregate interest being referred to the national—the local and particular, to the state legislatures.

The other point of difference is, the greater number of citizens, and extent of territory, which may be brought within the compass of republican, than of democratic government; and it is this circumstance principally which renders factious combinations less to be dreaded in the former, than in the latter. The smaller the society, the fewer probably will be the distinct parties and interests composing it; the fewer the distinct parties and interests, the more frequently will a majority be found of the same party; and the smaller the number of individuals composing a majority, and the smaller the compass within which they are placed, the more easily will they concert and execute their plans of oppression. Extend the sphere, and you take in a greater variety of parties and interest; you make it less probable that a majority of the whole will have a common motive to invade the rights of other citizens; or if such a common motive exists, it will be more difficult for all who feel it to discover their own strength, and to act in unison with each other. Besides other impediments, it may be remarked, that where there is a consciousness of unjust or dishonourable purpose, communication is always checked by distrust, in proportion to the number whose concurrence is necessary.

Hence it clearly appears, that the same advantage, which a republic has over a democracy, in controlling the effects of faction, is enjoyed by a large over a small republic—is enjoyed by the union over the states composing it. Does this advantage consist in the substitution of representatives, whose enlightened views and virtuous sentiments render them superior to local prejudices, and to schemes of injustice? It will not be denied, that the representation of the union will be most likely to possess these requisite endowments. Does it consist in the greater security afforded by a greater variety of parties, against the event of any one party being able to outnumber and oppress the rest? In an equal degree does the increased variety of parties, comprised within the union, increase this security. Does it, in fine, consist in the greater obstacles opposed to the concert and accomplishment of the secret wishes of an unjust and interested majority? Here, again, the extent of the union gives it the most palpable advantage.

The influence of factious leaders may kindle a flame within their particular states, but will be unable to spread a general conflagration through the other states: A religious sect may degenerate into a political faction in a part of the confederacy; but the variety of sects dispersed over the entire face of it, must secure the national councils against any danger from that source: A rage for paper money, for an abolition of debts, for an equal division of property, or for any other improper or wicked project, will be less apt to pervade the whole body of the union, than a particular member of it; in the same proportion as such a malady is more likely to taint a particular county or district, than an entire state.

In the extent and proper structure of the union, therefore, we behold a republican remedy for the diseases most incident to a republican government. And according to the degree of pleasure and pride we feel in being republicans, ought to be our zeal in cherishing the spirit, and supporting the character of federalists.

NUMBER 51

To the People of the State of New York:

To what expedient, then, shall we finally resort, for maintaining in practice the necessary partition of power among the several departments, as laid down in the Constitution? The only answer that can be given is, that as all these exterior provisions are found to be inadequate, the defect must be supplied, by so contriving the interior structure of the government as that its several constituent parts may, by their mutual relations, be the means of keeping each other in their proper places. Without presuming to undertake a full development of this important idea, I will hazard a few general observations, which may perhaps place it in a clearer light, and enable us to form a more correct judgment of the principles and structure of the government planned by the convention.

In order to lay a due foundation for that separate and distinct exercise of the different powers of government, which to a certain extent is admitted on all hands to be essential to the preservation of liberty, it is evident that each department should have a will of its own; and consequently should be so constituted that the members of each should have as little agency as possible in the appointment of the members of the others. Were this principle rigorously adhered to, it would require that all the appointments for the supreme executive, legislative, and judiciary magistracies should be drawn from the same fountain of authority, the people, through channels having no communication whatever with one another. Perhaps such a plan of constructing the several departments would be less difficult in practice than it may in contemplation appear. Some difficulties, however, and some additional expense would attend the execution of it. Some deviations, therefore, from the principle must be admitted. In the constitution of the judiciary department in particular, it might be inexpedient to insist rigorously on the principle: first, because peculiar qualifications being essential in the members, the primary consideration ought to be to select that mode of choice which best secures these qualifications; secondly, because the permanent tenure by which the appointments are held in that department, must soon destroy all sense of dependence on the authority conferring them.

It is equally evident, that the members of each department should be as little dependent as possible on those of the others, for the emoluments annexed to their offices. Were the executive magistrate, or the judges, not independent of the legislature in this particular, their independence in every other would be merely nominal.

But the great security against a gradual concentration of the several powers in the same department, consists in giving to those who administer each department the necessary constitutional means and personal motives to resist encroachments of the others. The provision for defence must in this, as in all other cases, be made commensurate to the danger of attack. Ambition must be made to counteract ambition. The interest of the man must be connected with the constitutional rights of the place. It may be a reflection on human nature, that such devices should be necessary to control the abuses of government. But what is government itself, but the greatest of all reflections on human nature? If men were angels, no government would be necessary. If angels were to govern men, neither external nor internal controls on government would be necessary. In framing a government which is to be administered by men over men, the great difficulty lies in this: you must first enable the government to control the governed; and in the next place oblige it to control itself. A dependence on the people is, no doubt, the primary control on the government; but experience has taught mankind the necessity of auxiliary precautions.

This policy of supplying, by opposite and rival interests, the defect of better motives, might be traced through the whole system of human affairs, private as well as public. We see it particularly displayed in all the subordinate distributions of power, where the constant aim is to divide and arrange the several offices in such a manner as that each may be a check on the other—that the private interest of every individual may be a sentinel over the public rights. These inventions of prudence cannot be less requisite in the distribution of the supreme powers of the State.

But it is not possible to give to each department an equal power of self-defence. In republican government, the legislative authority necessarily predominates. The remedy for this inconveniency is to divide the legislature into different branches; and to render them, by different modes of election and different principles of action, as little connected with each other as the nature of their common functions and their common dependence on the society will admit. It may even be necessary to guard against dangerous encroachments by still further precautions. As the weight of the legislative authority requires that it should be thus divided, the weakness of the executive may require, on the other hand, that it should be fortified. An absolute negative on the legislature appears, at first view, to be the natural defence with which the executive magistrate should be armed. But perhaps it would be neither altogether safe nor alone sufficient. On ordinary occasions it might not be exerted with the requisite firmness, and on extraordinary occasions it might be perfidiously abused. May not this defect of an absolute negative be supplied by some qualified connection between this weaker department and the weaker branch of the stronger department, by which the latter may be led to support the constitutional rights of the former, without being too much detached from the rights of its own department?

If the principles on which these observations are founded be just, as I persuade myself they are, and they be applied as a criterion to the several State constitutions, and to the federal Constitution, it will be found that if the latter does not perfectly correspond with them, the former are infinitely less able to bear such a test.

There are, moreover, two considerations particularly applicable to the federal system of America, which place that system in a very interesting point of view.

First. In a single republic, all the power surrendered by the people is submitted to the administration of a single government; and the usurpations are guarded against by a division of the government into distinct and separate departments. In the compound republic of America, the power surrendered by the people is first divided between two distinct governments, and then the portion allotted to each subdivided among distinct and separate departments. Hence a double security arises to the rights of the people. The different governments will control each other, at the same time that each will be controlled by itself.

Second. It is of great importance in a republic not only to guard the society against the oppression of its rulers, but to guard one part of the society against the injustice of the other part. Different interests necessarily exist in different classes of citizens. If a majority be united by a common interest, the rights of the minority will be insecure. There are but two methods of providing against this evil: the one by creating a will in the community independent of the majority—that is, of the society itself; the other, by comprehending in the society so many separate descriptions of citizens as will render an unjust combination of a majority of the whole very improbable, if not impracticable. The first method prevails in all governments possessing an hereditary or self-appointed authority. This, at best, is but a precarious security; because a power independent of the society may as well espouse the unjust views of the major, as the rightful interests of the minor party, and may possibly be turned against both parties. The second method will be exemplified in the federal republic of the United States. Whilst all authority in it will be derived from and dependent on the society, the society itself will be broken into so many parts, interests and classes of citizens, that the rights of individuals, or of the minority, will be in little danger from interested combinations of the majority. In a free government the security for civil rights must be the same as that for religious rights. It consists in the one case in the multiplicity of interests, and in the other in the multiplicity of sects. The degree of security in both cases will depend on the number of interests and sects; and this may be presumed to depend on the extent of country and number of people comprehended under the same government. This view of the subject must particularly recommend a proper federal system to all the sincere and considerate friends of republican government, since it shows that in exact proportion as the territory of the Union may be formed into more circumscribed Confederacies, or States, oppressive combinations of a majority will be facilitated; the best security, under the republican forms, for the rights of every class of citizens, will be diminished; and consequently the stability and independence of some member of the government, the only other security, must be proportionally increased. Justice is the end of government. It is the end of civil society. It ever has been and ever will be pursued until it be obtained, or until liberty be lost in the pursuit. In a society under the forms of which the stronger faction can readily unite and oppress the weaker, anarchy may as truly be said to reign as in a state of nature, where the weaker individual is not secured against the violence of the stronger; and as, in the latter state, even the stronger individuals are prompted, by the uncertainty of their condition, to submit to a government which may protect the weak as well as themselves; so, in the former state, will the more powerful factions or parties be gradually induced, by a like motive, to wish for a government which will protect all parties, the weaker as well as the more powerful. It can be little doubted that if the State of Rhode Island was separated from the Confederacy and left to itself, the insecurity of rights under the popular form of government within such narrow limits would be displayed by such reiterated oppressions of factious majorities that some power altogether independent of the people would soon be called for by the voice of the very factions whose misrule had proved the necessity of it. In the extended republic of the United States, and among the great variety of interests, parties, and sects which it embraces, a coalition of a majority of the whole society could seldom take place on any other principles than those of justice and the general good; whilst there being thus less danger to a minor from the will of a major party, there must be less pretext, also, to provide for the security of the former, by introducing into the government a will not dependent on the latter, or, in other words, a will independent of the society itself. It is no less certain than it is important, notwithstanding the contrary opinions which have been entertained, that the larger the society, provided it lie within a practical sphere, the more duly capable it will be of self-government. And happily for the *republican cause,* the practicable sphere may be carried to a very great extent, by a judicious modification and mixture of the *federal principle.*

ON THE RELIGION OF THE WHITE MAN

Sogoyewapha

> *"Red Jacket" was the name given to Sogoyewapha (ca. 1752–1830),
> a chief of the Seneca Indian tribe living in central New York State. The
> name came from an embroidered scarlet jacket presented to him by a British
> officer during the Revolution; in the War of 1812, he fought on the
> American side.*
>
> *The following speech was delivered at a council of chiefs of the Six Nations
> in the summer of 1805, after a Mr. Cram, a missionary, had spoken of
> the work he proposed to do among them. It requires little comment,
> except perhaps the suggestion that this speech be placed alongside the*

picture of the Indians that we get from the early colonists and that has become embedded in the American mind by hundreds of Hollywood westerns. From the unaccustomed perspective of this speech (and there are dozens of such speeches on record), the march of "civilization" across the continent takes on a somewhat different significance.

Friend and brother: It was the will of the Great Spirit that we should meet together this day. He orders all things and has given us a fine day for our council. He has taken His garment from before the sun and caused it to shine with brightness upon us. Our eyes are opened that we see clearly; our ears are unstopped that we have been able to hear distinctly the words you have spoken. For all these favors we thank the Great Spirit, and Him only.

Brother, this council fire was kindled by you. It was at your request that we came together at this time. We have listened with attention to what you have said. You requested us to speak our minds freely. This gives us great joy; for we now consider that we stand upright before you and can speak what we think. All have heard your voice and all speak to you now as one man. Our minds are agreed.

Brother, you say you want an answer to your talk before you leave this place. It is right you should have one, as you are a great distance from home and we do not wish to detain you. But first we will look back a little and tell you what our fathers have told us and what we have heard from the white people.

Brother, listen to what we say. There was a time when our forefathers owned this great island. Their seats extended from the rising to the setting sun. The Great Spirit had made it for the use of Indians. He had created the buffalo, the deer, and other animals for food. He had made the bear and the beaver. Their skins served us for clothing. He had scattered them over the country and taught us how to take them. He had caused the earth to produce corn for bread. All this He had done for His red children because He loved them. If we had some disputes about our hunting-ground they were generally settled without the shedding of much blood.

But an evil day came upon us. Your forefathers crossed the great water and landed on this island. Their numbers were small. They found friends and not enemies. They told us they had fled from their own country for fear of wicked men and had come here to enjoy their religion. They asked for a small seat. We took pity on them, granted their request, and they sat down among us. We gave them corn and meat; they gave us poison in return.

The white people, brother, had now found our country. Tidings were carried back and more came among us. Yet we did not fear them. We took them to be friends. They called us brothers. We believed them and gave them a larger seat. At length their numbers had greatly increased. They wanted more land; they wanted our country. Our eyes were opened and our minds became uneasy. Wars took place. Indians were hired

The World's Famous Orations, ed. William Jennings Bryan (10 vols.; New York: Funk and Wagnalls Company, 1906), VIII, 9–13.

to fight against Indians, and many of our people were destroyed. They also brought strong liquor among us. It was strong and powerful, and has slain thousands.

Brother, our seats were once large and yours were small. You have now become a great people, and we have scarcely a place left to spread our blankets. You have got our country, but are not satisfied; you want to force your religion upon us.

Brother, continue to listen. You say that you are sent to instruct us how to worship the Great Spirit agreeably to His mind; and, if we do not take hold of the religion which you white people teach we shall be unhappy hereafter. You say that you are right and we are lost. How do we know this to be true? We understand that your religion is written in a Book. If it was intended for us, as well as you, why has not the Great Spirit given to us, and not only to us, but why did He not give to our forefathers the knowledge of that book, with the means of understanding it rightly. We only know what you tell us about it. How shall we know when to believe, being so often deceived by the white people?

Brother, you say there is but one way to worship and serve the Great Spirit. If there is but one religion, why do you white people differ so much about it? Why not all agreed, as you can all read the Book?

Brother, we do not understand these things. We are told that your religion was given to your forefathers and has been handed down from father to son. We also have a religion which was given to our forefathers and has been handed down to us, their children. We worship in that way. It teaches us to be thankful for all the favors we receive, to love each other, and to be united. We never quarrel about religion.

Brother, the Great Spirit has made us all, but He has made a great difference between His white and His red children. He has given us different complexions and different customs. To you He has given the arts. To these He has not opened our eyes. We know these things to be true. Since He has made so great a difference between us in other things, why may we not conclude that He has given us a different religion according to our understanding? The Great Spirit does right. He knows what is best for His children; we are satisfied.

Brother, we do not wish to destroy your religion or take it from you. We only want to enjoy our own.

Brother, you say you have not come to get our land or our money, but to enlighten our minds. I will now tell you that I have been at your meetings and saw you collect money from the meeting. I can not tell what this money was intended for, but suppose that it was for your minister; and, if we should conform to your way of thinking, perhaps you may want some from us.

Brother, we are told that you have been preaching to the white people in this place. These people are our neighbors. We are acquainted with them. We will wait a little while and see what effect your preaching has upon them. If we find it does them good, makes them honest, and less disposed to cheat Indians, we will then consider again of what you have said.

Brother, you have now heard our answer to your talk, and this is all we have to say at present. As we are going to part, we will come and take you by the hand, and hope the Great Spirit will protect you on your journey and return you safe to your friends.

✑ TWO LOCAL FRENCH REVOLUTIONARY CAHIERS

In most of the records of history, the masses of the people, inarticulate and hence unheard, are marked absent. Even during great social and political upheavals, the claims of revolutionary leaders to speak for "the people" can rarely be verified. In this respect, 1789 in France is a signal exception. According to late medieval procedure, whenever the French king called a meeting of the Estates-General, he began by requesting his subjects, segregated according to their estate—clergy, nobility, and commoners— to draw up cahiers de doléances, *or "booklets of grievances." In March of 1789, therefore, villagers and townsmen (as well as nobles and clergymen) met locally throughout France to voice complaints and formulate the grievances which they wanted redressed by the Estates-General. For the Third Estate, these local* cahiers *were then combined into more inclusive (but historically less revealing) district and general* cahiers, *which were meant as instructions for the deputies elected to the Estates-General.*

The two cahiers *below are the work of the commoners of a little country town, Saint-Denis-de-Duclair, and a small village, Saint-Germain-sous-Cailly, both near the city of Rouen in the province of Normandy. In the case of the former* cahier, *the first thirty provisions seem to have been drafted largely by two local lawyers of prominence, whose presence may be explained by the proximity of Rouen, seat of a* parlement *or sovereign appeals court. The last provisions seem to have been added at random in the course of the town meeting, which was attended by about one-third of the male heads of households. The original manuscript bears about sixty signatures, indicating that about three-quarters of those attending could at least sign their names. In the case of the latter* cahier *(that of Saint-Germain-sous-Cailly), the meeting that drafted the grievances was attended by almost two-thirds of the local householders. This village list of complaints obviously lacks the lawyer's touch. As Normandy was the traditional home of peasant textile industry, the fear of competition from England or from English machines expressed in both* cahiers *is a characteristic regional grievance. The two* cahiers *give an idea of the range of sophistication among rural and semirural localities in 1789.*

SAINT-DENIS-DE-DUCLAIR

[Rouen district, on March 25, 1789] Population: 300 households (1500). Lord and protector: The Abbot of Jumièges. Meeting held "in the church and the choir," J. L. Neufville, attorney-at-law, member of the bar of the sovereign court of Rouen, dean of the lawyers of the court of high justice of Duclair, presiding. Present: Adr. Lefebvre (harness-maker, 9 *livres*),* Letanneur, Pasquier (day laborer, 2 1.), Damane Sr. (10 1.), Alex. Damane (3 1.), Cl. Corvée (tax collector, 16 1.), Den. Lecouteux (independent farmer, 236 1.), Cavoret, Guil. Rueville (servant, 10 1.), Lemettais, Coignet (mason, 7 1.), Poisson (clock-maker, 5 1.), Capon, Jac. [N.] Neufville (mayor, 70 1.), Tribout, Jac. Campigny (shoemaker, 2 1.), Ruault, Jac. Morel (royal soldier, 1 1.), J. Cusson Jr. (9 1.), Gaudré (tavernkeeper, 14 1.), Lefebvre (harness maker, 5 1.), Lebret (grocer, 17 1.), J. Cusson (mason, 5 1.), J. B. Hamelin (tailor, 2 1.), Durdent (independent farmer, 233 1.), J. Lemonnier (baker, 5 1.), Lo. Leriche (tailor, 5 1.), Ferré, Lo. Rivière (wood-turner, 1 1.), Lo. Gruchy (butcher, 1 1.), Lo. Corduron (shoemaker, 8 1.), Lo. Tuvache (court clerk, 9 1.), Crevel (tanner, 15 1.), Capon Jr. (tavernkeeper, 4 1.), Samson (mason, 15 1.), Leger Jr., Cordier, Guéroult, Jac. Langreney (merchant, 8 1.), Mic Delaunay (tailor, 5 1.), Salet, Imbert, Baudet, Cottard, Lanneau, N. Collot (confection baker, 4 1.), N. Lemarchand (2 1.), N. Boeville (9 1.), P. Gaudré (shoemaker, 2 1.), Dumesnil, P. Géhanne (confection baker, 9 1.), P. Viel (confection baker, 12 1.), P. Burdent (court clerk, 9 1.), P. Marescot (day laborer, 1 1.), P. Persil (barrelmaker, 13 1.), Nic. Lamant (merchant, 13 1.), J. B. Poullain, called Grandchamp [merchant], (86 1.), Guil. Caillouel, (lawyer, 25 1.), Lo. Violette (roofer, 3 1.), Rob. Amant (day laborer, 1 1.), Lalouette, Sicard, Leclerc, Leroy, Guil. Quevilly, Geo. Blard (teamster, 11 1.), Morel, Aumont, Thorel Jr., Lambert (called Little John, 2 1.), J. Lemarchand (day laborer, 5 1.), Thuillier, Levallois (miller, 420 1.), Chesnel, Bullet, P. Hamelin (tailor, 6 1.), Sénéchal (independent farmer, 55 1.), P. Lecouteux (independent farmer, 40 1.), Gaudouville, J. Lacoste, Den. Le Cley. Delegates [to the district meeting]: Guil. David, Math. Caillouel (attorney-at-law, member of the bar of the sovereign court of Paris), Jac. Lo. Neufville (member of the bar of the sovereign court of Rouen), Jac. N. Neufville (mayor), J. B. Poullain, (called Grandchamp, merchant).

CAHIER

Each order, each community, each private citizen having been invited by the king's letter of January 24 of this year to propose, remonstrate and advise concerning anything

Cahiers de doléances du tiers état du baillage de Rouen pour les Etats généraux de 1789, **II,** **Le baillage principal,** "Collection de documents inédits sur l'histoire économique de la révolution française," ed. **Marc Bouloiseau** (Rouen: Imprimerie administrative de la Seine-Maritime, 1960), 71–81. Translated by Peter Amann.

* [Accompanying figures refer to tax assessments. (*Ed.*)]

that might further the regeneration and salvation of our dear fatherland, we would be guilty of ingratitude and treason were we to fail in cooperating in this long sought for and long awaited task with all the power and understanding that we command.

As the [existing] abuses are innumerable, it is morally impossible to set all things right at the first meeting of the Estates-General. While the voice of truth, ever eloquent and persuasive, has been heard to the far ends of the kingdom, individual self-interest, so difficult to still, continues to murmur softly. Let us therefore confine ourselves to requesting what may be accomplished at this time, though giving a glimpse of something better that may not be difficult of ultimate attainment.

[1] The municipality of Duclair desires that, at least in matters of taxation, the votes of its deputies to the Estates-General be counted by head, regardless of the order [to which they belong], since all citizens ought to contribute in proportion to their wealth. Should the first two orders oppose this, however, and should it prove impossible to bring them to reason, it would be prudent to accept their pretensions for the time being, in order to avoid a schism that would be the greatest of misfortunes. Yet this should be done only after they have formally agreed that all taxes are to be borne by all orders without distinction.

Constitution

[2] Want the Estates-General to deal, before anything else, with the Constitution of the state, which should be defined by a few clear laws. They ought to lay down the limits of legislative and executive power in accordance with the laws of the kingdom and, above all, with justice and universal reason that are far more ancient and more sacred than any written legislation.

The laws that may be drawn from the nature of man and from his relations with his peers are simple, and the members that will make up the Estates-General will discover them easily. One of the constitutional provisions of the state should set down at what intervals the Estates-General are to be called in the future and should determine their composition and powers.

[3] With regard to their convocation: every three years; as to their composition: the Third Estate should account for at least half [of the membership], with at least one representative for every twenty thousand citizens. If voting by head were to encounter opposition, or if this manner of deliberation were to entail excessive drawbacks, especially where legislation is involved, we would desire in that case to have no more than two orders of [legislative] chambers.

[4] With regard to their powers: they alone would have the right to levy taxes, determine their duration and, together with the king, establish general laws. *Lex fit consensu populi et authorisati regis* [Law is to be enacted by popular consent and with the authorization of the king]. They will receive and check the accounts of the ministers of different departments and decide upon their budgets.

Once the constitution has been carefully thought through and freely decided upon, two important questions will draw the attention of the deputies: the administration of finances and that of justice.

Finances

[5]   Before anything else, the state indebtedness should be examined and [the amount involved] determined. As to remedies, while a multitude of schemes, some of them specious, have been proposed, it is not up to a simple country town to calculate and weigh their [respective] merits and demerits as far as a vast kingdom is concerned. The deputies, therefore, ought to concentrate upon solving this problem, however difficult it may appear in [such] a vast administration.

[6]   To see to the needs of the state in such a way that, while real and personal property are to be constrained as little as possible, each citizen contributes proportionately to the advantages which he enjoys. If, after the reports of the worthy and virtuous minister who by his labors supports the beneficent views of the good king who governs us, the Assembly could manage to solve [this problem], France would enjoy a prosperity beyond our power of imagination.

[7]   The simpler taxes are to be, and the closer to their source they are to be collected, the nearer will we come to our goal. According to this principle, all taxes the collection of which is difficult and expensive, all those which hinder national industry or [restrict] the personal liberty of the citizen, must be suppressed. We demand therefore the suppression of the salt tax, *aides* [indirect taxes], tobacco taxes and the excise on leathers and meat, the lowering of inspection dues and the removal of internal customs barriers.

[8]   As to what should take the place of such taxes, this seems simple to us as far as the countryside is concerned. The *taille* [chief direct property tax], head tax, excise on wine, twentieth tax, the tax dispensing from the payment of the salt tax, the tax exempting from payment of the *aides* [indirect tax], etc., could be combined into a single tax. Each province will have to raise its determined quota. The provincial assemblies would allocate the sum decided upon for each district among the municipalities and these, in turn, among the property owners of the parish. Every three months the mayor or revenue collector would deposit his funds in the district treasury, which would then forward them to the provincial treasury or directly to the royal treasury. Transportation charges could be avoided by the use of letters of credit drawn upon the provincial treasuries in order to defray governmental expenditures.

[9]   A royal tithe could take the place of all these [other] taxes. This type of levy, despite all its faults (for what tax has none?) seems so simple to us and so far removed from the arbitrary, that we authorize our deputies to propose it, requesting, and indeed instructing them to adopt a better one if they can discover it. As to taxes in the cities, they could be [levied] either on real estate or on personal property. We shall leave it to their prudence to decide which might seem more advantageous.

[10]   To lighten the burden of taxation, pensions should be granted only to those who have rendered special service to the state, nor should any individual receive more than one [pension].

Administration of Justice. Civil Legislation

[11] There are great abuses in the administration of justice. It would take one volume to list them in detail and several [more] to indicate remedies. Let us confine ourselves to a few observations.

[12] We want a greater number of sovereign courts in the kingdom, in such a way that they be forty or fifty miles apart, so that no plaintiff should have to travel more than twenty-five miles to obtain justice. There should be no more than two degrees of jurisdiction.

[13] The abolition of seignorial courts with jurisdiction over capital crimes, of all special tribunals and of the privilege of initiating a suit in a superior court.

[14] We want a royal bailiff's court in the chief town of each district, to be composed of three judges and the king's attorney, *who are to reside there,* and whose jurisdiction would extend to twenty-five or thirty parishes. This court of the first instance would have final jurisdiction in any case involving up to one hundred *livres* and would accept all types of cases. [For suits involving sums of] above one hundred *livres* and up to four thousand *livres,* appeals would be directed to the district court, while [for sums] above four thousand appeals would go directly to the king's council.

[15] At least half the members of each court should be drawn from the Third Estate.

[16] Stays of proceedings which are so unfavorable to commerce as well as decrees by which the king intervenes on his own initiative should be disallowed.

[17] The sale of offices should henceforth be suppressed. In the future no office should carry noble status which is to be granted to merit alone.

[18] Different local customary law codes should be brought closer together and even integrated into a single code.

In order to cut down as much as possible on the expenses involved in legal proceedings that weigh so heavily on the poor, we want justices of the peace [whose jurisdiction] might be called rural courts. [In a sense] they are already in place, for they would be made up of the village officials, freely elected by their fellow citizens. They would meet every Sunday after evening services to judge those cases that have to do with workers' or servants' wages and the seizures of domestic animals; as far as misdemeanors are concerned, slander not involving battery and all summary proceedings entailing less than one hundred *livres* [can be brought up] upon a simple summons on unstamped paper from the village clerk. In appealing, cases could be carried to the district court as the only appellate jurisdiction, there to be judged without cost as requiring no further preliminary investigation. If such a worthy project were to be adopted for the bailiwick of Rouen, we could add fuller instructions.

Criminal Laws

[19] That our criminal laws have great flaws has been a general complaint for a long time. We have suffered from these flaws and they are known. Zealous and learned citizens have pointed out remedies. The deputies should therefore choose and sanction that scheme of legislation which they will deem nearest to perfection.

We want the severity of punishments lessened, as horrible tortures have never made citizens virtuous. [Punishments] should be proportionate to the crime in accordance with the eternally true principle. Crimes and punishments should be classified in an accurate manner in order to avoid arbitrary [decisions].

[20]   The preliminary hearing should take place in the presence of at least two judges. Once the identity of the accused has been verified and he has been confronted with the witnesses, he should be granted a defense attorney *of his choice.* Sentence should be pronounced in public, after the charges have been read and after the accused has been heard in person and through his lawyer.

[21]   At least six judges, of whom no less than four are to concur, should be required before an order for an arrest be decreed. Unless taken in the act, no man should be arrested and imprisoned without a court order. From this [rule] would follow the abolition of *lettres de cachet* [imprisonment by special order of the king] and all other arbitrary procedures.

[22]   No sentence imposing degrading or corporal punishment should be pronounced in a district or appeal court by less than seven judges, five of whom should concur in the judgment. The highest court of appeals should require fifteen judges, of whom at least twelve must confirm the sentence. If on questions of fact, trial by jury could be instituted, the personal freedom of citizens would take a great step forward.

Other Matters

[23]   After dealing with these major problems [the Estates-General] might consider the disposal of the royal domain lands. In small states, where such domains may defray the expenses of government, [this institution] seems advantageous to us. In a large state, where they constitute no more than an almost imperceptible fraction of the revenues of which the greater part is absorbed in the costs of collection, we believe that these possessions are disadvantageous. Were it not for the limitations of this *cahier,* these ideas could be developed much more fully. The domain should be disposed of not by sale but by enfeoffment. [The terms of] the lease should be stipulated in measures or pounds of grain, in order that the terms reflect any rise in staple prices. In this way obvious drawbacks could be avoided. While the direct domain would remain in the king's hands, its revenues would at all times reflect the [market] value of the properties.

Concerning the Militia

[24]   It is necessary that the state be defended. Every citizen is pledged to his fatherland: these are two demonstrable truths. The way in which the militia is raised is nonetheless defective. The more property one owns, the more binding the obligation to defend the state in person. In the present order [of things], the opposite is true. To defend one's country, one must love it, serve it with joy, even with enthusiasm. Look at the peoples of the ancient world, where the soldier was required to be a citizen. With us, the contrary is true. *Esprit de corps,* so dangerous in all states, is essential in armies as a spur to glory. Only despotism can [afford to] be satisfied with mercenary armies made up of people of no account, having neither property nor fatherland. The lofty prince who governs us and his present minister are far from wishing to extend the absolute sway of what is the greatest of evils for both monarch and people.

To remedy this abuse, a truly national militia should be established. Every unmarried citizen from the age of eighteen to that of forty should be considered a potential soldier, though if such a contingent were to be too large, it could be limited. Each community would furnish its contingent of recruits. The districts would make up companies, the departments battalions, and the provinces regiments bearing the provincial name. Officers would be chosen form the same province. Every individual would, in competing for honors, perform prodigious feats of valor for the sake of his countrymen, his relatives and his friends. On such and such a day, it would be said: Normandy [or] Guyenne decided the victorious outcome of the battle.

Let us stop. We are carried away by the desire for what is best. Merely to suggest is our task, yet who can be concerned with the happiness of his fatherland without being carried away by this noble sentiment?

The Tithes

[25] Tithes did not come into being by divine ordinance among Christians. This truth may be demonstrated by examining the first eight centuries of the church's history; yet it is also true that clergymen must be supported. If the Estates-General failed to find other means of dealing with this [need], it seems just to retain the tithe [for their sake]. In that case, however, it should revert to what it had been originally.

So that no one may accuse the community of Duclair of being lost in pipe dreams, let us cite laws on the books: *Ut decimae populi in quatuor partes dividantur: prima pars episcopis, alia clericis, tertia pauperibus, quarta in fabricia ipsius ecclesiae* [that the tithes of the people be divided into four parts: the first part for the bishops, the second for the clerics, the third for the poor, the fourth for the establishments of the church itself]. (Capitularies of Charlemagne, year 801, and second capitulary, year 805.)

As the bishops and the cathedrals have their own private revenues and domains, they no longer have a claim to a tithe. In any case, it seems that this was granted to them only to insure that all church pulpits were to be filled. It would therefore be just to turn over the first two parts in their entirety to the local priests and their vicars.

[26] *Tertia pauperibus* [a third for the poor]. For a long time people have been concerned with the suppression of begging in France. Of the multitude of means that have been tried, none has succeeded. No one has dared to hit upon the simplest way and the only one which will cut the root of the evil. By funneling one quarter of the tithe to the poor, the latter can regain their veritable patrimony without violating [private] property.

[27] *Quarta in fabricia ipsius ecclesiae* [the fourth for the establishment of the church itself]. The use of this fourth part is also literally spelled out. The maintenance, the decoration of the churches and parsonages should no longer be left to the charge of the parish that is already burdened with a tax as heavy as the tithe.

According to these principles, then, it seems obvious that the totality of the tithe should be restored to the parishes, in case this tax is to be retained. In those circumstances, regulations will be needed to apportion the tax throughout the kingdom.

[28] Occasionally there are [two] small, adjoining parishes. It would be desirable [in those instances] to combine them in such a way that masses would be said at two different hours, much to the convenience of the parishioners.

Freedom of the Press

[29] Whatever its drawbacks, this is no longer thought of as a problem. It is true that [freedom of the press] may be abused; yet censorship, unable to prevent the circulation of wicked works, has prevented excellent ones from seeing the light of day.

Division of the Common Lands

[30] While common lands are advantageous to private individuals, they constitute an evil in a great society. It therefore seems desirable to divide them, yet the question is how to do it. If they are distributed in proportion to [existing] private [property] holdings belonging to individuals, the poor are ruined. If they should be divided by household and by family, the rich will object. Nonetheless, dividing them by families seems preferable to us: it is inequitable to give much to those who already have a great deal.

[31] Sound provisions for forest conservation are needed. This question is of the greatest consequence for the welfare of the state and the citizens.

[32] We seek the removal of impediments retarding the progress of agriculture and commerce, among which are the guilds of the towns. Whoever has a skill should have the liberty to exercise it; besides, competition encourages industry. The abolition of all exclusive privileges in manufacturing, etc., . . . are contrary to the spirit of trade, the life of which is freedom.

[33] It will be important to examine carefully the influence exercised by the recent commercial treaty with England [1786], and, after calculating its advantages and drawbacks, reach whatever decision that reason, justice and the public interest dictate.

[34] We want all leases of church-owned lands to remain in force, notwithstanding the death of the [clerical] incumbents. The nullification of such contracts upon their decease is extremely harmful to agriculture. The tenant farmer, uncertain of possession when the incumbent is of advanced age, cannot cultivate the land as effectively as if he were sure of the usufruct. When an incumbent dies in November or December, [the tenant] is sometimes summoned on the thirtieth or thirty-first of the month to quit the farm on the following day. If he dares to complain against such flagrant injustice, he is called to appear before a commission in Paris which will always rule against him; consequently, the unhappy man finds himself with his family, his belongings, his domestic animals, bereft of resources and shelter during the bitterest season. "But," the new incumbent will say, "my predecessor received a large bribe which came right out of the revenues that I am entitled to!" The answer to this objection is easy: in the future, church lands should be leased only after public announcement and auction, while all bribes should be prohibited.

[35] All simple [church] benefices [clerical positions that are endowed with land or other income-producing property] which the king is entitled to fill, could, when a vacancy occurs, be made into stewardships and their revenues used to liquidate the debts of the clergy.

[36] If, after the needs of the state have been satisfied and income and outlay brought into balance, a sinking fund could be set up, this would be very worthwhile.

Whoever would be in charge of this operation would each year redeem notes and certificates of indebtedness drawn on the state up to an agreed upon amount. By this means the debt, and consequently the interest payments, would progressively diminish each year and we would have the hope of seeing [the debt] liquidated within a certain number of years.

[37]   Abolition of the right of *franc-fief* [a special property-transfer tax applying to noble landed estates from which nobles, but *not* commoners were exempt]. This right is an indirect tax imposed on the Third Estate. If the first two orders renounced their fiscal privileges as reason and justice dictate, this privilege should be among them. Besides, this right is the source of a great evil. No merchant or rich farmer, who by dint of perseverance and industry has succeeded in amassing something of a fortune by devoting many years to labors that are useful to his fellow citizens and to the state, can purchase a fief without paying this tax. If, in order to circumvent it, he also buys an office which carries noble status, he and his descendants are precluded from pursuing their useful occupation.

[38]   The redemption of seignorial privileges, such as the monopoly on milling, wine pressing, etc. The suppression of forced appraisements and sales as burdensome.

[39]   The suppression of seignorial dues, the reform of road and bridge [maintenance]. Equality of weights and measures. Destruction of wild beasts, of the overabundance of game and of the dovecotes—[all of which are] opposed to [the interests of] agriculture. Gamekeepers should be forbidden to use offensive weapons and to kill, as is their wont, domestic animals.

[40]   One year's grain supply should be stored within the kingdom, in order to avoid shortages and times of high prices, the baleful effects of which we are witnessing at this very moment.

[41]   We will not speak at all of subsidies to agriculture, manufacturing and commerce. Let the disastrous taxes be suppressed and the impediments hindering industry removed, and the French genius, supported by a most fertile soil, shall take flight and only want for direction. At such a time, this truly industrious and hardworking nation shall, through its own efforts, take its place where it belongs—in the first rank of agricultural and commercial peoples.

[42]   Yet several of these questions could be discussed in the assemblies of the provincial estates that will be requested by the deputies for all French provinces, and especially for Normandy who has a legal claim [to provincial estates].

SAINT-GERMAIN-SOUS-CAILLY

(Rouen district; population, 57 households; Lord and protector, Madame de Joyeuse. Meeting, March 29 [1789], in church; 34 present, Cl. Dubuc, Mayor, Presiding.)

CAHIER

[1]   We demand the suppression of taxes and excises on goods entering towns and their replacement by a single tax.

[2]   We request that salt be free [of taxes].

[3]   The suppression of begging, with each parish making up the losses of these poor by assessing itself in such a way that the poor will not suffer.

[4]   We ask the suppression of seignorial monopolies on flour milling.

[5]   The discontinuance of the exemption from the *taille* [basic real property tax] and the head tax, [presently] enjoyed by noble persons, postmasters, and bourgeois who own country estates.

[6]   The closing of taverns in the countryside.

[7]   We demand the regulation of irregular tithes.

[8]   We demand new provisions for the maintenance of the highways. It is indeed unfortunate that the poor, and others not owning carts, should have to contribute to the maintenance of highways which they never use. It would be much juster if these gentlemen of the clergy and the nobility paid their share, together with the post and stagecoach masters, who use them a great deal without paying anything.

[9]   Let us draw attention to the [lottery] drawings [to choose] soldiers in the provinces and let us request their abolition. This often deprives farmers and the old and infirm of a son on whom they rely. Bachelors between the ages of eighteen and forty could be asked to pay a modest sum which would be used to hire volunteers.

[10]   [We want] the freedom to destroy crow rookeries.

[12]   We demand that the practice of buying offices be stopped.

[13]   We demand that the rabbits be destroyed.

[14]   We ask that the pigeons be confined to their dovecotes from the beginning of July to the first of November.

[15]   We demand that bread price-fixing be extended to rural bakeries.

[16]   The prohibition of the English cotton-working machines that undermine trade and reduce the poor to indigence.

[17]   We demand the prohibition of grain exports.

Burke-Priestley Debate
on the French Revolution

From its beginnings, the French Revolution aroused lively interest in the Western world. Within a few years enthusiastic partisans and determined opponents of the French Revolution could be found throughout Europe and the United States. The reason for this passionate response was the widely held belief—which the revolutionaries themselves did nothing to dispel— that France had become the laboratory for political and social experimentation from which other countries would draw lessons for their own renovation. Conservatives and radicals tacitly agreed that the problems of irresponsible power and inherited privilege which the French Revolution sought to solve could be found in some form or other in all European countries and even in the republican United States. In this sense the French Revolution clearly had universal significance.

In Great Britain the initial reaction to the events in France was hesitant. It was the publication of Edmund Burke's Reflections on the Revolution in France *in the fall of 1790 which helped to swing the sentiment of the British ruling class strongly against the revolution—long before the French drift to republicanism and the wholesale use of terror. The* Reflections *went through ten editions in one year and in translation had a similar impact in German-speaking areas. In form, Burke's diatribe was a letter to a young French friend, which grew to book length in the course of the year that Burke devoted to its composition. More directly, the work also sought to answer a dissenting English clergyman, Dr. Price, who had equated the French movement with the Glorious Revolution of 1688–1689 in England.*

The son of an Irish lawyer, Edmund Burke (1729–1797) gave up a legal career to become a man of letters. His obvious intellectual gifts attracted the attention of Whig political leaders, and through the patronage of one of the great Whig aristocrats, Burke entered parliament in 1766. He soon gained a reputation as the most brilliant orator in Whig ranks. At the onset of the American Revolution, he championed the cause of the colonists, not only on the grounds that British tradition was on their side, but also because, regardless of the legal issues, conciliation was the only sensible policy for all concerned. Unlike Burke's stand on the American Revolution in which he acted as chief spokesman for his party, his condemnation of the French Revolution led, despite general public acclaim, to the disintegration of the Whigs, who split into sympathizers and opponents of the revolution.

Burke's attack evoked a number of answering pamphlets. One of the more effective was Joseph Priestley's Letters to Edmund Burke, *which first appeared in January, 1791, and went through three editions within a few months. Priestley (1733–1804), unlike Burke, was not a politician, nor, except incidentally, a political theorist. He is best known to us as the discoverer of oxygen, but his fame in his own day rested as much on his writings as a rather unorthodox theologian and his activities as a dissenting (i.e., a Protestant outside the official Anglican church) minister. In July, 1791, as a result of his defense of the French Revolution, Priestley's house was sacked by a Birmingham mob, an incident which led to his emigration to the United States in 1794.*

❧ REFLECTIONS ON THE REVOLUTION IN FRANCE

Edmund Burke

You will observe that from Magna Charta to the Declaration of Right it has been the uniform policy of our constitution to claim and assert our liberties as an *entailed inheritance* derived to us from our forefathers, and to be transmitted to our posterity—as an estate specially belonging to the people of this kingdom, without any reference whatever to any other more general or prior right. By this means our constitution preserves a unity in so great a diversity of its parts. We have an inheritable crown, an inheritable peerage, and a House of Commons and a people inheriting privileges, franchises, and liberties from a long line of ancestors.

This policy appears to me to be the result of profound reflection, or rather the happy effect of following nature, which is wisdom without reflection, and above it. A spirit of innovation is generally the result of a selfish temper and confined views. People will not look forward to posterity, who never look backward to their ancestors. Besides, the people of England well know that the idea of inheritance furnishes a sure principle of conservation and a sure principle of transmission, without at all excluding a principle of improvement. It leaves acquisition free, but it secures what it acquires. Whatever advantages are obtained by a state proceeding on these maxims are locked fast as in a sort of family settlement, grasped as in a kind of mortmain * forever. By a constitutional policy, working after the pattern of nature, we receive, we hold, we transmit our government and our privileges in the same manner in which we enjoy and transmit our property and our lives. The institutions of policy, the goods of fortune, the gifts of providence are handed down to us, and from us, in the same course and order. Our political system is placed in a just correspondence and symmetry with the order of the world and with the mode of existence decreed to a permanent body composed of transitory parts, wherein, by the disposition of a stupendous wisdom, molding together the great mysterious incorporation of the human race, the whole, at one time, is never old or middle-aged or young, but, in a condition of unchangeable constancy, moves on through the varied tenor of perpetual decay, fall, renovation, and progression. Thus, by preserving the method of nature in the conduct of the state, in what we improve we are never wholly new; in what we retain we are never wholly obsolete. By adhering in this manner and on those principles to our forefathers, we are guided not by the superstition of antiquarians, but by the spirit of philosophic analogy. In this choice of inheritance we have given to our frame of polity the image of a relation in blood, binding up the constitution of our country with our dearest domestic ties, adopting our fundamental laws into the bosom of our family affections, keeping inseparable and cherishing with the warmth of all their combined and mutually reflected charities our state, our hearths, our sepulchres, and our altars.

Through the same plan of a conformity to nature in our artificial institutions, and

Edmund Burke, *Reflections on the Revolution in France* (New York: The Liberal Arts Press, 1955), pp. 37–44, 46–51, 54–60, 66–72, 98–100, 290–291.

* [Perpetual tenure. (*Ed.*)]

by calling in the aid of her unerring and powerful instincts to fortify the fallible and feeble contrivances of our reason, we have derived several other, and those no small, benefits from considering our liberties in the light of an inheritance. Always acting as if in the presence of canonized forefathers, the spirit of freedom, leading in itself to misrule and excess, is tempered with an awful gravity. This idea of a liberal descent inspires us with a sense of habitual native dignity which prevents that upstart insolence almost inevitably adhering to and disgracing those who are the first acquirers of any distinction. By this means our liberty becomes a noble freedom. It carries an imposing and majestic aspect. It has a pedigree and illustrating ancestors. It has its bearings and its ensigns armorial. It has its gallery of portraits, its monumental inscriptions, its records, evidences, and titles. We procure reverence to our civil institutions on the principle upon which nature teaches us to revere individual men: on account of their age and on account of those from whom they are descended. All your sophisters cannot produce anything better adapted to preserve a rational and manly freedom than the course that we have pursued, who have chosen our nature rather than our speculations, our breasts rather than our inventions, for the great conservatories and magazines of our rights and privileges.

You might, if you pleased, have profited of our example and have given to your recovered freedom a correspondent dignity. Your privileges, though discontinued, were not lost to memory. Your constitution, it is true, whilst you were out of possession, suffered waste and dilapidation; but you possessed in some parts the walls and, in all, the foundations of a noble and venerable castle. You might have repaired those walls; you might have built on those old foundations. Your constitution was suspended before it was perfected, but you had the elements of a constitution very nearly as good as could be wished. In your old states * you possessed that variety of parts corresponding with the various descriptions of which your community was happily composed; you had all that combination and all that opposition of interests; you had that action and counteraction which, in the natural and in the political world, from the reciprocal struggle of discordant powers, draws out the harmony of the universe. These opposed and conflicting interests which you considered as so great a blemish in your old and in our present constitution interpose a salutary check to all precipitate resolutions. They render deliberation a matter, not of choice, but of necessity; they make all change a subject of *compromise,* which naturally begets moderation; they produce *temperaments* preventing the sore evil of harsh, crude, unqualified reformations and rendering all the headlong exertions of arbitrary power, in the few or in the many, forever impracticable. Through that diversity of members and interests, general liberty had as many securities as there were separate views in the several orders, whilst, by pressing down the whole by the weight of a real monarchy, the separate parts would have been prevented from warping, and starting from their allotted places.

You had all these advantages in your ancient states, but you chose to act as if you had never been molded into civil society and had everything to begin anew. You began ill, because you began by despising everything that belonged to you. You set up your trade without a capital. If the last generations of your country appeared without much luster in your eyes, you might have passed them by and derived your claims

* [Estates-General. (*Ed.*)]

from a more early race of ancestors. Under a pious predilection for those ancestors, your imaginations would have realized in them a standard of virtue and wisdom beyond the vulgar practice of the hour; and you would have risen with the example to whose imitation you aspired. Respecting your forefathers, you would have been taught to respect yourselves. You would not have chosen to consider the French as a people of yesterday, as a nation of low-born servile wretches until the emancipating year of 1789. In order to furnish, at the expense of your honor, an excuse to your apologists here for several enormities of yours, you would not have been content to be represented as a gang of Maroon * slaves suddenly broke loose from the house of bondage, and therefore to be pardoned for your abuse of the liberty to which you were not accustomed and ill fitted. Would it not, my worthy friend, have been wiser to have you thought, what I, for one, always thought you, a generous and gallant nation, long misled to your disadvantage by your high and romantic sentiments of fidelity, honor, and loyalty; that events had been unfavorable to you, but that you were not enslaved through any illiberal or servile disposition; that in your most devoted submission you were actuated by a principle of public spirit, and that it was your country you worshiped in the person of your king? Had you made it to be understood that in the delusion of this amiable error you had gone further than your wise ancestors, that you were resolved to resume your ancient privileges, whilst you preserved the spirit of your ancient and your recent loyalty and honor; or if, diffident of yourselves and not clearly discerning the almost obliterated constitution of your ancestors, you had looked to your neighbors in this land who had kept alive the ancient principles and models of the old common law of Europe meliorated and adapted to its present state—by following wise examples you would have given new examples of wisdom to the world. You would have rendered the cause of liberty venerable in the eyes of every worthy mind in every nation. You would have shamed despotism from the earth by showing that freedom was not only reconcilable, but, as when well disciplined it is, auxiliary to law. You would have had an unoppressive but a productive revenue. You would have had a flourishing commerce to feed it. You would have had a free constitution, a potent monarchy, a disciplined army, a reformed and venerated clergy, a mitigated but spirited nobility to lead your virtue, not to overlay it; you would have had a liberal order of commons to emulate and to recruit that nobility; you would have had a protected, satisfied, laborious, and obedient people, taught to seek and to recognize the happiness that is to be found by virtue in all conditions. . . .

Compute your gains: see what is got by those extravagant and presumptuous speculations which have taught your leaders to despise all their predecessors, and all their contemporaries, and even to despise themselves until the moment in which they become truly despicable. By following those false lights, France has bought undisguised calamities at a higher price than any nation has purchased the most unequivocal blessings! France has bought poverty by crime! France has not sacrificed her virtue to her interest, but she has abandoned her interest, that she might prostitute her virtue. All other nations have begun the fabric of a new government, or the reformation of an old, by establishing originally or by enforcing with greater exactness some rites or other of religion. All other people have laid the foundations of civil freedom in severer

* [West Indian. (*Ed.*)]

manners and a system of a more austere and masculine morality. France, when she let loose the reins of regal authority, doubled the license of a ferocious dissoluteness in manners and of an insolent irreligion in opinions and practice, and has extended through all ranks of life, as if she were communicating some privilege or laying open some secluded benefit, all the unhappy corruptions that usually were the disease of wealth and power. This is one of the new principles of equality in France. . . .

They have seen the French rebel against a mild and lawful monarch with more fury, outrage, and insult than ever any people has been known to rise against the most illegal usurper or the most sanguinary tyrant. Their resistance was made to concession, their revolt was from protection, their blow was aimed at a hand holding out graces, favors, and immunities.

This was unnatural. The rest is in order. They have found their punishment in their success: laws overturned; tribunals subverted; industry without vigor; commerce expiring; the revenue unpaid, yet the people impoverished; a church pillaged, and a state not relieved; civil and military anarchy made the constitution of the kingdom; everything human and divine sacrificed to the idol of public credit, and national bankruptcy the consequence; and, to crown all, the paper securities of new, precarious, tottering power, the discredited paper securities of impoverished fraud and beggared rapine, held out as a currency for the support of an empire in lieu of the two great recognized species [i.e. gold and silver] that represent the lasting, conventional credit of mankind, which disappeared and hid themselves in the earth from whence they came, when the principle of property, whose creatures and representatives they are, was systematically subverted. . . .

After I had read over the list of the persons and descriptions elected into the *Tiers Etat* [i.e. the commoners], nothing which they afterwards did could appear astonishing. Among them, indeed, I saw some of known rank, some of shining talents; but of any practical experience in the state, not one man was to be found. The best were only men of theory. But whatever the distinguished few may have been, it is the substance and mass of the body which constitutes its character and must finally determine its direction. In all bodies, those who will lead must also, in a considerable degree, follow. They must conform their propositions to the taste, talent, and disposition of those whom they wish to conduct; therefore, if an assembly is viciously or feebly composed in a very great part of it, nothing but such a supreme degree of virtue as very rarely appears in the world, and for that reason cannot enter into calculation, will prevent the men of talent disseminated through it from becoming only the expert instruments of absurd projects! If, what is the more likely event, instead of that unusual degree of virtue, they should be actuated by sinister ambition and a lust of meretricious glory, then the feeble part of the assembly, to whom at first they conform, becomes in its turn the dupe and instrument of their designs. In this political traffic, the leaders will be obliged to bow to the ignorance of their followers, and the followers to become subservient to the worst designs of their leaders. . . .

Judge, Sir, of my surprise when I found that a very great proportion of the assembly (a majority, I believe, of the members who attended) was composed of practitioners in the law. It was composed, not of distinguished magistrates, who had given pledges to their country of their science, prudence, and integrity; not of leading advocates, the glory of the bar; not of renowned professors in universities, but for the far greater part, as it must in such a number, of the inferior, unlearned, mechanical, merely instrumental members of the profession. There were distinguished exceptions, but the general composition was of obscure provincial advocates, of stewards of petty local jurisdictions, country attornies, notaries, and the whole train of the ministers of municipal litigation, the fomenters and conductors of the petty war of village vexation. From the moment I read the list, I saw distinctly, and very nearly as it has happened, all that was to follow. . . .

Whenever the supreme authority is vested in a body so composed, it must evidently produce the consequences of supreme authority placed in the hands of men not taught habitually to respect themselves, who had no previous fortune in character at stake, who could not be expected to bear with moderation, or to conduct with discretion, a power which they themselves, more than any others, must be surprised to find in their hands. Who could flatter himself that these men, suddenly and, as it were, by enchantment snatched from the humblest rank of subordination, would not be intoxicated with their unprepared greatness? Who could conceive that men who are habitually meddling, daring, subtle, active, of litigious dispositions and unquiet minds would easily fall back into their old condition of obscure contention and laborious, low, and unprofitable chicane? Who could doubt but that, at any expense to the state, of which they understood nothing, they must pursue their private interests, which they understand but too well? It was not an event depending on chance or contingency. It was inevitable; it was necessary; it was planted in the nature of things. They must *join* (if their capacity did not permit them to *lead*) in any project which could procure to them a *litigious constitution* which could lay open to them those innumerable lucrative jobs which follow in the train of all great convulsions and revolutions in the state, and particularly in all great and violent permutations of property. Was it to be expected that they would attend to the stability of property, whose existence had always depended upon whatever rendered property questionable, ambiguous, and insecure? Their objects would be enlarged with their elevation, but their disposition and habits, and mode of accomplishing their designs, must remain the same.

Well! but these men were to be tempered and restrained by other descriptions, of more sober and more enlarged understandings. Were they then to be awed by the supereminent authority and awful dignity of a handful of country clowns who have seats in that assembly, some of whom are said not to be able to read and write, and by not a greater number of traders who, though somewhat more instructed and more conspicuous in the order of society, had never known anything beyond their counting house. No! Both these descriptions were more formed to be overborne and swayed by the intrigues and artifices of lawyers than to become their counterpoise. With such a dangerous disproportion, the whole must needs be governed by them. To the faculty of law was joined a pretty considerable proportion of the faculty of medicine. This faculty had not, any more than of the law, possessed in France its just estimation. Its professors, therefore, must have the qualities of men not habituated to sentiments of dignity. But supposing they had ranked as they ought to do, and as with us they do actually, the sides of sickbeds are not the academies for forming statesmen and legislators. Then came the dealers in stocks and funds, who must be eager, at any expense, to change their ideal paper wealth for the more solid substance of land. To these were joined men of other descriptions, from whom as little knowledge of, or attention to, the interests of a great state was to be expected, and as little regard to the stability of any institution; men formed to be instruments, not controls. Such in general was the composition of the *Tiers Etat* in the National Assembly, in which was scarcely to be perceived the slightest traces of what we call the natural landed interest of the country.

We know that the British House of Commons, without shutting its doors to any merit in any class, is, by the sure operation of adequate causes, filled with everything illustrious in rank, in descent, in hereditary and in acquired opulence, in cultivated talents, in military, civil, naval, and politic distincton that the country can afford. But supposing, what hardly can be supposed as a case, that the House of Commons should be composed in the same manner with the *Tiers Etat* in France, would this dominion of chicane be borne with patience or even conceived without horror? God forbid I should insinuate anything derogatory to that profession which is another priesthood, administrating the rights of sacred justice. But whilst I revere men in the functions which belong to them, and would do as much as one man can do to prevent their exclusion from any, I cannot, to flatter them, give the lie to nature. They are good and useful in the composition; they must be mischievous if they preponderate so as virtually to become the whole. Their very excellence in their peculiar functions may be far from a qualification for others. It cannot escape observation that when men are too much confined to professional and faculty habits and, as it were, inveterate in the recurrent employment of that narrow circle, they are rather disabled than qualified for whatever depends on the knowledge of mankind, on experience in mixed affairs, on a comprehensive, connected view of the various, complicated, external and internal interests which go to the formation of that multifarious thing called a state. . . .

When men of rank sacrifice all ideas of dignity to an ambition without a distinct object and work with low instruments and for low ends, the whole composition becomes low and base. Does not something like this now appear in France? Does it not produce something ignoble and inglorious—a kind of meanness in all the prevalent policy, a tendency in all that is done to lower along with individuals all the dignity and importance of the state? Other revolutions have been conducted by persons who, whilst they attempted or affected changes in the commonwealth, sanctified their ambition by advancing the dignity of the people whose peace they troubled. They had long views. They aimed at the rule, not at the destruction, of their country. They were men of great civil and great military talents, and if the terror, the ornament of their age. They were not like Jew brokers, contending with each other who could best remedy with fraudulent circulation and depreciated paper the wretchedness and ruin brought on their country by their degenerate councils. . . .

Believe me, Sir, those who attempt to level, never equalize. In all societies, consisting of various descriptions of citizens, some description must be uppermost. The levelers, therefore, only change and pervert the natural order of things; they load the edifice of society by setting up in the air what the solidity of the structure requires to be on the ground. The association of tailors and carpenters, of which the republic (of Paris, for instance) is composed, cannot be equal to the situation into which by the worst of usurpations—an usurpation on the prerogatives of nature—you attempt to force them. . . .

You do not imagine that I wish to confine power, authority, and distinction to blood and names and titles. No, Sir. There is no qualification for government but virtue and wisdom, actual or presumptive. Wherever they are actually found, they have, in whatever state, condition, profession, or trade, the passport of Heaven to human place and honor. Woe to the country which would madly and impiously reject the service of the talents and virtues, civil, military, or religious, that are given to grace and to serve it, and would condemn to obscurity everything formed to diffuse luster and glory around a state! Woe to that country, too, that, passing into the opposite extreme, considers a low education, a mean contracted view of things, a sordid, mercenary occupation as a preferable title to command! Everything ought to be open, but not indifferently, to every man. No rotation; no appointment by lot; no mode of election operating in the spirit of sortition or rotation can be generally good in a government conversant in extensive objects. Because they have no tendency, direct or indirect, to select the man with a view to the duty or to accommodate the one to the other. I do not hesitate to say that the road to eminence and power, from obscure condition, ought not to be made too easy, nor a thing too much of course. If rare merit be the rarest of all rare things, it ought to pass through some sort of probation. The temple of honor ought to be seated on an eminence. If it be opened through virtue, let it be remembered, too, that virtue is never tried but by some difficulty and some struggle.

Nothing is a due and adequate representation of a state that does not represent its ability as well as its property. But as ability is a vigorous and active principle, and as property is sluggish, inert, and timid, it never can be safe from the invasion of ability unless it be, out of all proportion, predominant in the representation. It must be represented, too, in great masses of accumulation, or it is not rightly protected. The characteristic essence of property, formed out of the combined principles of its acquisition and conservation, is to be *unequal*. The great masses, therefore, which excite envy and tempt rapacity must be put out of the possibility of danger. Then they form a natural rampart about the lesser properties in all their gradations. The same quantity of property, which is by the natural course of things divided among many, has not the same operation. Its defensive power is weakened as it is diffused. In this diffusion each man's portion is less than what, in the eagerness of his desires, he may flatter himself to obtain by dissipating the accumulations of others. The plunder of the few would indeed give but a share inconceivably small in the distribution to the many. But the many are not capable of making this calculation; and those who lead them to rapine never intend this distribution.

The power of perpetuating our property in our families is one of the most valuable and interesting circumstances belonging to it, and that which tends the most to the perpetuation of society itself. It makes our weakness subservient to our virtue, it grafts benevolence even upon avarice. The possessors of family wealth, and of the distinction which attends hereditary possession (as most concerned in it), are the natural securities for this transmission. With us the House of Peers is formed upon this principle. It is wholly composed of hereditary property and hereditary distinction, and made, therefore, the third of the legislature and, in the last event, the sole judge of all property in all its subdivisions. The House of Commons, too, though not necessarily, yet in fact, is always so composed, in the far greater part. Let those large proprietors be what they will—and they have their chance of being amongst the best—they are, at the very worst, the ballast in the vessel of the commonwealth. For though hereditary wealth and the rank which goes with it are too much idolized by creeping sycophants and the blind, abject admirers of power, they are too rashly slighted in shallow speculations of the petulant, assuming, short-sighted coxcombs of philosophy. Some decent, regulated pre-eminence, some preference (not exclusive appropriation) given to birth is neither unnatural, nor unjust, nor impolitic.

It is said that twenty-four millions ought to prevail over two hundred thousand. True; if the constitution of a kingdom be a problem of arithmetic. . . . To men who *may* reason calmly, it is ridiculous. The will of the many and their interest must very often differ, and great will be the difference when they make an evil choice. A government of five hundred country attornies and obscure curates is not good for twenty-four millions of men, though it were chosen by forty-eight millions, nor is it the better for being guided by a dozen of persons of quality who have betrayed their trust in order to obtain that power. At present, you seem in everything to have strayed out of the high road of nature. The property of France does not govern it. Of course, property is destroyed and rational liberty has no existence. All you have got for the present is a paper circulation and a stock-jobbing constitution; and as to the future, do you seriously think that the territory of France, upon the republican system of eighty-three independent municipalities (to say nothing of the parts that compose them), can ever be governed as one body or can ever be set in motion by the impulse of one mind? When the National Assembly has completed its work, it will have accomplished its ruin. These commonwealths will not long bear a state of subjection to the republic of Paris. They will not bear that this body should monopolize the captivity of the king and the dominion over the assembly calling itself national. Each will keep its own portion of the spoil of the church to itself; and it will not suffer either that spoil, or the more just fruits of their industry, or the natural produce of their soil to be sent to swell the insolence or pamper the luxury of the mechanics of Paris. In this they will see none of the equality, under the pretense of which they have been tempted to throw off their allegiance to their sovereign as well as the ancient constitution of their country. There can be no capital city in such a constitution as they have lately made. They have forgot that, when they framed democratic governments, they had virtually dismembered their country. The person whom they persevere in calling king has not power left to him by the hundredth part sufficient to hold together this collection of republics. The republic of Paris will endeavor, indeed, to complete the debauchery of the army, and illegally to perpetuate the assembly, without resort to its constituents, as the means of continuing its despotism. It will make efforts, by becoming the heart of a boundless paper circulation, to draw everything to itself; but in vain. All this policy in the end will appear as feeble as it is now violent. . . .

It is no wonder, therefore, that with these ideas of everything in their constitution and government at home, either in church or state, as illegitimate and usurped, or at best as a vain mockery, they look abroad with an eager and passionate enthusiasm. Whilst they are possessed by these notions, it is vain to talk to them of the practice of their ancestors, the fundamental laws of their country, the fixed form of a constitution whose merits are confirmed by the solid test of long experience and an increasing public strength and national prosperity. They despise experience as the wisdom of unlettered men; and as for the rest, they have wrought underground a mine that will blow up, at one grand explosion, all examples of antiquity, all precedents, charters, and acts of parliament. They have "the rights of men." Against these there can be prescription, against these no agreement is binding; these admit no temperament and no compromise; anything withheld from their full demand is so much of fraud and injustice. Against these their rights of men let no government look for security in the length of its continuance, or in the justice and lenity of its administration. . . .

Far am I from denying in theory, full as far is my heart from withholding in practice (if I were of power to give or to withhold) the *real* rights of men. In denying their false claims of right, I do not mean to injure those which are real, and are such as their pretended rights would totally destroy. If civil society be made for the advantage of man, all the advantages for which it is made become his right. It is an institution of beneficence; and law itself is only beneficence acting by a rule. Men have a right to live by that rule; they have a right to do justice, as between their fellows, whether their fellows are in public function or in ordinary occupation. They have a right to the fruits of their industry and to the means of making their industry fruitful. They have a right to the acquisitions of their parents, to the nourishment and improvement of their offspring, to instruction in life, and to consolation in death. Whatever each man can separately do, without trespassing upon others, he has a right to do for himself; and he has a right to a fair portion of all which society, with all its combinations of skill and force, can do in his favor. In this partnership all men have equal rights, but not to equal things. He that has but five shillings in the partnership has as good a right to it as he that has five hundred pounds has to his larger proportion. But he has not a right to an equal dividend in the product of the joint stock; and as to the share of power, authority, and direction which each individual ought to have in the management of the state, that I must deny to be amongst the direct original rights of man in civil society, for I have in my contemplation the civil social man, and no other. It is a thing to be settled by convention.

If civil society be the offspring of convention, that convention must be its law. That convention must limit and modify all the descriptions of constitution which are formed under it. Every sort of legislative, judicial, or executory power are its creatures. They can have no being in any other state of things; and how can any man claim under the conventions of civil society rights which do not so much as suppose its existence —rights which are absolutely repugnant to it? One of the first motives to civil society, and which becomes one of its fundamental rules, is *that no man should be judge in his own cause.* By this each person has at once divested himself of the first fundamental right of uncovenanted man, that is, to judge for himself and to assert his own cause. He abdicates all right to be his own governor. He inclusively, in a great measure, abandons the right of self-defense, the first law of nature. Men cannot enjoy the rights of an uncivil and of a civil state together. That he may obtain justice, he gives up his right of determining what it is in points the most essential to him. That he may secure some liberty, he makes a surrender in trust of the whole of it.

Government is not made in virtue of natural rights, which may and do exist in total independence of it, and exist in much greater clearness and in a much greater degree of abstract perfection; but their abstract perfection is their practical defect. By having a right to everything they want everything. Government is a contrivance of human wisdom to provide for human *wants.* Men have a right that these wants should be provided for by this wisdom. Among these wants is to be reckoned the want, out of civil society, of a sufficient restraint upon their passions. Society requires not only that the passions of individuals should be subjected, but that even in the mass and body, as well as in the individuals, the inclinations of men should frequently be thwarted, their will controlled, and their passions brought into subjection. This can only be done *by a power out of themselves,* and not, in the exercise of its function, subject to that will and to those passions which it is its office to bridle and subdue. In this sense the restraints on men, as well as their liberties, are to be reckoned among their rights. But as the liberties and the restrictions vary with times and circumstances and admit to infinite modifications, they cannot be settled upon any abstract rule; and nothing is so foolish as to discuss them upon that principle.

The moment you abate anything from the full rights of men, each to govern himself, and suffer any artificial, positive limitation upon those rights, from that moment the whole organization of government becomes a consideration of convenience. This it is which makes the constitution of a state and the due distribution of its powers a matter of the most delicate and complicated skill. It requires a deep knowledge of human nature and human necessities, and of the things which facilitate or obstruct the various ends which are to be pursued by the mechanism of civil institutions. The state is to have recruits to its strength, and remedies to its distempers. What is the use of discussing a man's abstract right to food or medicine? The question is upon the method of procuring and administering them. In that deliberation I shall always advise to call in the aid of the farmer and the physician rather than the professor of metaphysics.

The science of constructing a commonwealth, or renovating it, or reforming it, is, like every other experimental science, not to be taught *a priori.* Nor is it a short experience that can instruct us in that practical science, because the real effects of moral causes are not always immediate; but that which in the first instance is prejudicial may be excellent in its remoter operation, and its excellence may arise even from the ill effects it produces in the beginning. The reverse also happens: and very plausible schemes, with very pleasing commencements, have often shameful and lamentable conclusions. In states there are often some obscure and almost latent causes, things which appear at first view of little moment, on which a very great part of its prosperity or adversity may most essentially depend. The science of government being therefore so practical in itself and intended for such practical purposes—a matter which requires experience, and even more experience than any person can gain in his whole life, however sagacious and observing he may be—it is with infinite caution that any man ought to venture upon pulling down an edifice which has answered in any tolerable degree for ages the common purposes of society, or on building it up again without having models and patterns of approved utility before his eyes.

These metaphysic rights entering into common life, like rays of light which pierce into a dense medium, are by the laws of nature refracted from their straight line. Indeed, in the gross and complicated mass of human passions and concerns the primitive rights of men undergo such a variety of refractions and reflections that it becomes absurd to talk of them as if they continued in the simplicity of their original direction. The nature of man is intricate; the objects of society are of the greatest possible complexity; and, therefore, no simple disposition or direction of power can be suitable either to man's nature or to the quality of his affairs. When I hear the simplicity of contrivance aimed at and boasted of in any new political constitutions, I am at no loss to decide that the artificers are grossly ignorant of their trade or totally negligent of their duty. The simple governments are fundamentally defective, to say no worse of them. If you were to contemplate society in but one point of view, all these simple modes of polity are infinitely captivating. In effect each would answer its single end much more perfectly than the more complex is able to attain all its complex purposes. But it is better that the whole should be imperfectly and anomalously answered than that, while some parts are provided for with great exactness, others might be totally neglected or perhaps materially injured by the overcare of a favorite member.

The pretended rights of these theorists are all extremes; and in proportion as they are metaphysically true, they are morally and politically false. The rights of men are in a sort of *middle,* incapable of definition, but not impossible to be discerned. The rights of men in governments are their advantages; and these are often in balances between differences of good, in compromises sometimes between good and evil, and sometimes between evil and evil. Political reason is a computing principle: adding, subtracting, multiplying, and dividing, morally and not metaphysically, or mathematically, true moral denominations.

By these theorists the right of the people is almost always sophistically confounded with their power. The body of the community, whenever it can come to act, can meet with no effectual resistance; but till power and right are the same, the whole body of them has no right inconsistent with virtue, and the first of all virtues, prudence. Men have no right to what is not reasonable and to what is not for their benefit. . . .

I confess to you, Sir, I never liked this continual talk of resistance and revolution, or the practice of making the extreme medicine of the constitution its daily bread. . . .

You see, Sir, that in this enlightened age I am bold enough to confess that we are generally men of untaught feelings, that, instead of casting away all our old prejudices, we cherish them to a very considerable degree, and, to take more shame to ourselves, we cherish them because they are prejudices; and the longer they have lasted and the more generally they have prevailed, the more we cherish them. We are afraid to put men to live and trade each on his own private stock of reason, because we suspect that this stock in each man is small, and that the individuals would do better to avail themselves of the general bank and capital of nations and of ages. Many of our men of speculation, instead of exploding general prejudices, employ their sagacity to discover the latent wisdom which prevails in them. If they find what they seek, and they seldom fail, they think it more wise to continue the prejudice, with the reason involved, than to cast away the coat of prejudice and to leave nothing but the naked reason; because prejudice, with its reason, has a motive to give action to that reason, and an affection which will give it permanence. Prejudice is of ready application in the emergency; it previously engages the mind in a steady course of wisdom and virtue and does not leave the man hesitating in the moment of decision skeptical, puzzled, and unresolved. Prejudice renders a man's virtue his habit, and not a series of unconnected acts. Through just prejudice, his duty becomes a part of his nature.

Your literary men and your politicians, and so do the whole clan of the enlightened among us, essentially differ in these points. They have no respect for the wisdom of others, but they pay it off by a very full measure of confidence in their own. With them it is a sufficient motive to destroy an old scheme of things because it is an old one. As to the new, they are in no sort of fear with regard to the duration of a building run up in haste, because duration is no object to those who think little or nothing has been done before their time, and who place all their hopes in discovery. They conceive, very systematically, that all things which give perpetuity are mischievous, and therefore they are at inexpiable war with all establishments. They think that government may vary like modes of dress, and with as little ill effect; that there needs no principle of attachment, except a sense of present convenience, to any constitution of the state. They always speak as if they were of opinion that there is a singular species of compact between them and their magistrates which binds the magistrate, but which has nothing reciprocal in it, but that the majesty of the people has a right to dissolve it without any reason but its will. Their attachment to their country itself is only so far as it agrees with some of their fleeting projects; it begins and ends with that scheme of polity which falls in with their momentary opinion.

These doctrines, or rather sentiments, seem prevalent with your new statesmen. But they are wholly different from those on which we have always acted in this country.

I hear it is sometimes given out in France that what is doing among you is after the example of England. I beg leave to affirm that scarcely anything done with you has originated from the practice or the prevalent opinions of this people, either in the act or in the spirit of the proceeding. Let me add that we are as unwilling to learn these lessons from France as we are sure that we never taught them to that nation. The cabals here who take a sort of share of your transactions as yet consist of but a handful of people. If, unfortunately, by their intrigues, their sermons, their publications, and by a confidence derived from an expected union with the counsels and forces of the French nation, they should draw considerable numbers into their faction, and in consequence should seriously attempt anything here in imitation of what has been done with you, the event, I dare venture to prophesy, will be that, with some trouble to their country, they will soon accomplish their own destruction. This people refused to change their law in remote ages from respect to the infallibility of popes, and they will not now alter it from a pious implicit faith in the dogmatism of philosophers, though the former was armed with the anathema and crusade, and though the latter should act with the libel and the lamp-iron. . . .

Whatever they are, I wish my countrymen rather to recommend to our neighbors the example of the British constitution than to take models from them for the improvement of our own. In the former, they have got an invaluable treasure. They are not, I think, without some causes of apprehension and complaint, but these they do not owe to their constitution but to their own conduct. I think our happy situation owing to our constitution, but owing to the whole of it, and not to any part singly, owing in a great measure to what we have left standing in our several reviews and reformations as well as to what we have altered or superadded. Our people will find employment enough for a truly patriotic, free, and independent spirit in guarding what they possess from violation. I would not exclude alteration neither, but even when I changed, it should be to preserve. I should be led to my remedy by a great grievance. In what I did, I should follow the example of our ancestors. I would make the reparation as nearly as possible in the style of the building. A politic caution, a guarded circumspection, a moral rather than a complexional timidity were among the ruling principles of our forefathers in their most decided conduct. Not being illuminated with the light of which the gentlemen of France tell us they have got so abundant a share, they acted under a strong impression of the ignorance and fallibility of mankind. He that had made them thus fallible rewarded them for having in their conduct attended to their nature. Let us imitate their caution if we wish to deserve their fortune or to retain their bequests. Let us add, if we please, but let us preserve what they have left; and, standing on the firm ground of the British constitution, let us be satisfied to admire rather than attempt to follow in their desperate flights the aeronauts of France. . . .

↤⸱§ LETTERS TO THE RIGHT HONOURABLE EDMUND BURKE
Joseph Priestley

LETTER I. OF THE GENERAL PRINCIPLES OF THE FRENCH REVOLUTION

Dear Sir,

I do not wonder that the late revolution in the French government has excited *your* attention, and that of a great part of the nation. "It is," as you justly say, p. 11, "all circumstances taken together, the most astonishing that has hitherto happened in the world." It is, therefore, a most interesting object both to philosophical and practical politicians. It behoves them particularly to consider the principles on which it has been made, that if the conduct of the leaders in the business has been right, and if the scheme promises to be beneficial to the country, it may, as far as their situations are similar, be imitated in other countries; and that, if their conduct has been wrong, and

Joseph Priestley, *Letters to the Right Honourable Edmund Burke* (3rd ed.; Birmingham, 1791), pp. 1–9, 22–33, 143–147, 149–152, 154–155.

the result of it unpromising, the example may serve to deter others from any attempt of the like kind. . . .

Notwithstanding "the sacredness," as you call it, p. 29, "of an hereditary principle of succession," in our government, you allow of "a power of change in its application in cases of extreme emergency," adding, however, that "the change should be confined to the *peccant part* only." Nor do you deny that the great end and object of all government, that which makes it preferable to a state of anarchy, is *the good of the people.* It is *better* for them, and they are *happier* in a state of society and government. For the same reason, you must allow that that particular form of government, which is best adapted to promote the happiness of any people, is the best for that people.

If you admit thus much, you must also allow that, since every private person is justified in bettering his condition, and indeed commended for it; a nation is not to be condemned for endeavouring to better theirs. Consequently, if they find their form of government to be a bad one, whether it was so originally, or became so through abuse or accident, they will do very well to change it for a better. A partial change, no doubt, will be preferable to a total one, if a partial change will be sufficient for the purpose. But if it appear that all attempts to mend an old constitution would be in vain, and the people prefer a new one, their neighbours have no more business to find fault with them, than with any individual, who should think it more advisable to pull down an old and inconvenient house, and build another from the foundation, rather than lay out his money in repairs. Nations, no doubt, as well as individuals, may judge wrong. They may act precipitately, and they may suffer in consequence of it: but this is only a reason for caution, and does not preclude a right of judging and acting for themselves, in the best manner that they can.

"The very idea," you say, p. 44, "of the fabrication of a new government is enough to fill us with disgust and horror." It is, no doubt, far from being a thing desirable in itself; but it may nevertheless be necessary; and for all the evils arising from the change, you should blame not the framers of the new government, but the wretched state of the old one, and those who brought it into that state. That some very material change was wanting in the old government of France, you cannot deny, after allowing, p. 195, that "in that country the unlimited power of the sovereign over the persons of his subjects, was inconsistent with law and liberty." On other occasions, I believe you have expressed yourself in a stronger manner than this. If *law* and *liberty* were wanting in the old constitution, the peccant part must have been the very foundation of it, so that nothing effectual could have been done short of taking down the whole.

If these incontrovertible *principles* and *facts* be admitted, I can see no reason for your exclaiming so violently as you do against the late revolution in France. Besides, whatever has been done, and in whatever manner it has been done, if the nation itself, whom alone it concerns, do not complain, we have no business to complain for them, any farther than the interest we take in the welfare of others, may lead us to feel for the distresses which we apprehend their folly and precipitancy may bring upon them. I shall, however, briefly consider the principal of your objections to this revolution.

You consider the present National Assembly of France as usurpers, assuming a power that does not belong to them. . . .

Now, Sir, even allowing this to be true; admitting this National Assembly to have had no regular summons to meet, or to do any business at all; supposing them to have been men who rose out of the earth, or who dropped down from the clouds, or that no body could tell whence they came, and that, without any authority whatever, they took upon themselves to frame a new constitution of government for the French nation; if the nation really approve of it, acquiesce in it, and actually adopt it, it becomes from that time their own act, and the Assembly can only be considered as the proposers and advisers. It is the acquiescence of the people that gives any form of government its proper sanction, and that legalizes it. Changes of government cannot be brought about by established forms and rules, because there is no superior power to prescribe those rules. There are no supreme courts comprehending these great objects. Also, the cases occur so rarely, and they are so unlike to one another, that it would be to no purpose to look for precedents.

Now, that the French revolution is justifiable on this plain principle, is evident from the single circumstance of the National Assembly having continued their sittings without molestation, and from their decrees having been actually obeyed, for something more than a year at least. This Assembly does not consist, I believe, of more than about one thousand persons, and at first they had no army at their command; whereas at present the whole force of the state is in their hands. This force could not have been transferred from the king to them, without the consent both of the army, and of the nation which supports that army. As the nation does not complain of this translation of power, it is evident they do not think themselves aggrieved, and that the change has been made with their approbation. Here, then, we see all the marks of a *legal government,* or a government that is really the *choice of the people.* I do not say what difficulties may hereafter arise (which if they do, they will probably be the effect of their former government) to induce them to change their opinion. For neither that nation, nor any other, is omniscient and infallible.

Without examining into the former system of government, or the administration of it, we may take for granted, that it must have become extremely odious to the country in general, from the almost universal, and the very hearty, concurrence with which the revolution was brought about. A whole people is not apt to revolt, till oppression has become extreme, and been long continued, so that they despair of any other remedy than that desperate one. The strength of an established government, especially when it is in few hands, and has a large standing army at its command, is almost infinite; so that many nations quietly suffer every evil, and the country becomes in a manner desolate, without their making any attempt to relieve themselves. This is the case in all the Turkish dominions, and is said to be very nearly so in Spain and other countries. Whenever, therefore, we see a whole nation, or a great majority of it, rising as one man against an old government, and overturning it, we may safely conclude that their provocation was great, and their cause good.

An oppressed people do not, however, in general *see* any thing more than what they immediately *feel.* All they think of is to shake off the load which they can no longer bear; and having thought of nothing but the particular evil that galled them, they are very apt, in their future settlement, to guard against *that* only, without attending to the whole of their new situation, and the greater evils that may possibly arise from it. Whether the French have done so or not, time must discover. But if the people in general be well informed, and well disposed, they may make many experiments of new forms of government without much inconvenience; and though beginning with a very imperfect one, they adopt a very good one at the last.

Was it not predicted that the Americans, on their breaking off from this country, would run into universal confusion, and immediately fall to cutting one another's throats? But though that disruption was a violent one, and was effected by a war, which drained all their resources, they never suffered for want of government. When the war was over, they bore very contentedly several imperfect and disjointed forms; and now, having taken much time to deliberate on the subject, they have adopted a more comprehensive one. But of *this* they only propose to make trial, and if it should not answer, they will, no doubt, endeavour to improve upon it.

Now, why may not this be the case with the French, especially as they have no enemies to contend with, and interrupt their proceedings? I am not able to demonstrate the wisdom of several parts of the frame of government at present adopted by the National Assembly, owing, probably, to my not being master of the whole system; and many of the remarks that you have made upon it, may, for any thing that I know, be very just; but not being a judge of their circumstances, and consequently of all their reasons, I presume that they could not at the time have done better. In future however, whatever it be that is now deficient may be supplied. And considering the apparent strength of the ancient French government, and the great numbers that depend upon it (far more, I should imagine, than upon the court and the ministry in this country) I wonder that the revolution was brought about with so much ease, and so little bloodshed.

LETTER III. OF THE NATURE OF GOVERNMENT, AND THE RIGHTS OF MEN AND OF KINGS

Dear Sir,

Considering how much has been written on the subject of *government* since the Revolution in this country, an event which more than any thing else contributed to open the eyes of Englishmen, with respect to the true principles of it, it is not a little extraordinary that any man of reading and reflexion, as you are, should depart from them so much as you have done.

To vindicate this Revolution, Lord Somers, Bishop Hoadley, Mr. Locke, and many others, have laid it down as a maxim, that all power in any state is derived from the people, and that the great object of all government, is the public good. As a consequence from these fundamental principles, they maintain that all magistrates, being originally appointed by the people, are answerable to them for their conduct in office, and removeable at their pleasure. The right of resisting an oppressive government, that is, such as the people shall deem to be oppressive, they hold most sacred. . . .

To make the *public good* the standard of right or wrong, in whatever relates to society and government, besides being the most natural and rational of all rules, has the farther recommendation of being the easiest of application. Either what *God has ordained,* or what *antiquity* authorises, may be very difficult to ascertain; but what regulation is most conducive to the *public good,* though not always without its difficulties, yet in general it is much more easy to determine. But suppose a nation should never have had a free government, or could not prove that they ever had one, are they for that reason always to continue slaves? Would it be unlawful, or wrong, in the Turks to do what the French nation has now done?

You treat with ridicule the idea of the *rights of men,* and suppose that mankind, when once they have entered into a state of society, necessarily abandon all their proper *natural rights;* and thenceforth have only such as they derive from society. "As to the share of power," you say, p. 87, "authority and direction, which each individual ought to have in the management of the state, that I must deny to be among the direct original rights of man in civil society; for I have in my contemplation the civil, social man, and no other. It is a thing to be settled by convention."

But what does this *convention* respect, beside the secure enjoyment of such *advantages,* or *rights,* as have been usually termed *natural,* as life, liberty, and property, which men had *from nature,* without societies or artificial combinations of men? Men cannot, surely, be said to *give up* their natural rights by entering into a compact for the better securing of them. And if they make a wise compact, they will never wholly exclude themselves from all share in the administration of their government, or some controul over it. For without *this* their stipulated rights would be very insecure.

However, should any people be so unwise as to leave the whole administration of their government, without any express right of controul, in the hands of their magistrates, if those magistrates do not give the people what they deem to be an equivalent for what they gave up for the accommodation of others, they are certainly at liberty to consider the original compact as broken. They then revert to a state of nature, and may enter into a new state of society, and adopt a new form of government, in which they may make better terms for themselves.

It is one of the most curious paradoxes in this work of yours, which abounds with them, that the rights of men above-mentioned (called by you, p. 91, "the pretended rights of the French theorists) are all extremes, and in proportion as they are metaphysically true, they are morally and politically false." Now by *metaphysically* true can only be meant *strictly* and *properly* true, and how this can be in any sense *false,* is to me incomprehensible. If the above-mentioned rights be the *true,* that is the *just,* and *reasonable* rights of men, they ought to be provided for in all states, and all forms of government; and if they be not, the people have just cause to complain, and to look out for some mode of redress.

You strongly reprobate the doctrine of *kings being the choice of the people.* . . .

You equally reprobate the doctrine of the king being the *servant of the people,* whereas the law, as you say, p. 41, calls him *our sovereign lord the king.* . . .

If, as you expressly acknowledge, the only rational end of the power of a king is the *general advantage,* that is, the *good of the people,* must not the people be of course the judges, whether they derive advantage from him, and his government, or not, that is, whether they be well or ill *served* by him? Though there is no express, there is, you must acknowledge, a virtual, *compact between the king and the people.* This, indeed, is particularly mentioned in the Act which implies the abdication of king James, though you say, p. 38, it is *too guarded and too circumstantial;* and what can this compact be, but a stipulation for protection, etc. on the part of the king, and allegiance on the part of the people? If, therefore instead of *protection,* they find *oppression,* certainly allegiance is no longer due. Hence, according to common sense, and the principles of the Revolution, the right of a subject to resist a tyrant, and dethrone him; and what is this, but, in other words, shocking as they may sound to your ears, dismissing, or *cashiering a bad servant,* as a person who had abused his trust.

So fascinating is the situation in which our kings are placed, that it is of great importance to remind them of the true relation they bear to *the people,* or, as they are fond of calling them *their people.* They are too apt to imagine that their rights are independent of the will of the people, and consequently that they are not accountable to them for any use they may make of their power; and their numerous dependents, and especially the clergy, are too apt to administer this pleasing intoxicating poison. This was the ruin of the Stuarts, and it is a danger that threatens every prince, and every country, from the same quarter. Your whole book, Sir, is little else than a vehicle for the same poison, inculcating, but inconsistently enough, a *respect for princes,* independent of their being originally the choice of the people, as if they had some natural and indefeasible right to reign over us, they being born to command, and we to obey; and then, whether the origin of this power be *divine,* or have any other source independent of the people, it makes no difference to us.

With the superstitious respect for kings, and the spirit of chivalry, which nothing but an age of extreme barbarism recommended, and which civilization has banished, you seem to think that every thing great and dignified has left us, "Never, never more," you say, p. 113, "shall we behold that generous loyalty to rank and sex, that proud submission, that dignified obedience, that subordination of the heart, that kept alive even in servitude itself the spirit of an exalted freedom. The unbought grace of life, the cheap defence of nations, the nurse of manly sentiment and heroic enterprize, is gone. It is gone; that sensibility of principle, that chastity of honour, which felt a stain like a wound, which inspired courage whilst it mitigated ferocity, which enobled whatever it touched, and under which vice itself lost half its evil, by losing all its grossness."

This is perhaps the most admired passage in your whole performance; but it appears to me, that in a great pomp of *words,* it contains but few *ideas,* and some of them inconsistent and absurd. So different also are men's feelings, from the difference, no doubt of our educations, and the different sentiments we voluntarily cherish through life, that a situation which gives you the idea of *pride,* gives me that of *meanness.* You are proud of what, in my opinion, you ought to be ashamed, the idolatry of a fellow creature, and the abasement of yourself. It discovers a disposition from which no "manly sentiment, or heroic enterprize" can be expected. I submit to a king, or to any other civil magistrate, because the good order of society requires it, but I feel no *pride* in that *submission;* and the "subordination of my heart." I reserve for *character* only, not for *station.* As a citizen, the object of my respect is *the nation* and *the laws.* The *magistrates,* by whatever name they are called, I respect only as the confidential servants of the nation, and the administrators of the laws.

These sentiments, just in themselves, and favouring of no superstition, appear to me to become men, whom nature has made equal, and whose great object, when formed into societies, it should be to promote their common happiness. I am proud of feeling myself *a man among men,* and I leave it to you, Sir, to be "proud of your *obedience,* and to keep alive," as well as you can, "in servitude itself the spirit of an exalted freedom." I think it much easier, at least, to be preserved *out* of a state of servitude than *in* it. You take much pains to gild your chains, but they are chains still. . . .

Though we do not chuse any particular king, the nation originally chose to be *governed by kings,* with such limitations, with respect to their duty and prerogatives, as they then chose to prescribe. And whether the departure from the original and proper duty of a king be made at once, or by degrees, which has generally been the case; and though the people may have been restrained by their circumstances from checking the incroachments of their kings, the *right* of doing it must ever remain inherent in them. They must always have a power of resuming what themselves gave, when the condition on which it was given is not performed. They can surely recall a trust that has been abused, and reinstate themselves in their former situation, or in a better, if they can find one.

If there be, what you allow, a *compact of sovereignty,* who are the *parties,* but the *people* and the *king;* and if the compact be broken on his side, are not the rank and the privileges, which he held upon the condition of observing the terms of the compact, forfeited? "The rule of succession," you say, "is according to the laws of his country." But what, according to yourself, is the origin of both our common and statute law?

"Both these descriptions of law," you say, p. 28, "are of the same force, and are derived from an equal authority, emanating from the common agreement, and original compact of the state (*communi sponsione reipublicae*) and as such are equally binding on king and people too, as long as the terms are observed, and they continue the same body politic." Laws, then, not coming down from heaven, but being *made* by men, may also be *changed* by them; and what is a *constitution of government,* but the *greater laws* of the state? Kings, therefore, as well as the people, may violate these laws by which they are equally bound; and if other violaters of law be punishable, by degradation or otherwise, why should kings be excepted? Are *their* violations of the law, or the constitution, less injurious to the commonwealth than those of other transgressors? Let the punishment of kings be as *grave* and *decorous,* p. 23, as you please, but let justice, substantial justice, be done.

LETTER XIV. OF THE PROSPECT OF THE GENERAL ENLARGEMENT OF LIBERTY, CIVIL AND RELIGIOUS, OPENED BY THE REVOLUTION IN FRANCE

Dear Sir,

I cannot conclude these *Letters,* without congratulating, not *you,* Sir, or the many admirers of your performance, who have no feeling of *joy* on the occasion, but the French nation, and the world; I mean the liberal, the rational, and the virtuous part of the world, on the great revolution that has taken place in France, as well as on that which some time ago took place in America. Such events as these teach the doctrine of *liberty, civil* and *religious,* with infinitely greater clearness and force, than a thousand treatises on the subject. They speak a language intelligible to all the world, and preach a doctrine congenial to every human heart.

These great events, in many respects unparalleled in all history, make a totally new, a most wonderful, and important, aera in the history of mankind. It is, to adopt your own rhetorical style, a change from darkness to light, from superstition to sound knowledge, and from a most debasing servitude to a state of the most exalted freedom. It is a liberating of all the powers of man from that variety of fetters, by which they have hitherto been held. So that, in comparison with what has been, now only can we expect to see what men really are, and what they can do.

The generality of governments have hitherto been little else than a combination of *the few,* against *the many;* and to the mean passions and low cunning of these few, have the great interests of mankind been too long sacrificed. Whole nations have been deluged with blood, and every source of future prosperity has ben drained, to gratify the caprices of some of the most despicable, or the most execrable, of the human species. For what else have been the generality of kings, their ministers of state, or their mistresses, to whose wills whole kingdoms have been subject? What can we say of those who have hitherto taken the lead in conducting the affairs of nations, but that they have commonly been either *weak* or *wicked,* and sometimes both? Hence the common reproach of all histories, that they exhibit little more than a view of the vices and miseries of mankind. From this time, therefore, we may expect that it will wear a different, and more pleasing aspect.

Hitherto, also, infinite have been the mischiefs in which all nations have been involved on account of *religion,* with which, as it concerns only God and men's own consciences, civil government, as such, has nothing to do. Statesmen, misled by ignorant or interested priests, have taken upon them to prescribe what men should believe and practice, in order to get to heaven, when they themselves have often neither believed, nor practised, any thing under that description. They have set up idols, to which all men, under the severest penalties, have been compelled to bow; and the wealth and power of populous nations, which might have been employed in great and useful undertakings, have been diverted from their proper channels, to enforce their un-righteous decrees. By this means have mankind been kept for ages in a state of bondage worse than Egyptian, the bondage of the mind.

How glorious, then, is the prospect, the reverse of all the past, which is now opening upon us, and upon the world. Government, we may now expect to see, not only in theory, and in books, but in actual practice, calculated for the general good, and taking no more upon it than the general good requires; leaving all men the enjoyment of as many of their *natural rights* as possible, and no more interfering with matters of religion, with men's notions concerning God, and a future state, than with philosophy, or medicine.

After the noble example of America, we may expect, in due time, to see the govern-ing powers of all nations confining their attention to the *civil* concerns of them, and consulting their welfare in the present state only; in consequence of which they may all be flourishing and happy. *Truth* of all kinds, and especially *religious truth,* meeting with no obstruction, and standing in no need of heterogeneous supports, will then establish itself by its own evidence; and whatever is *false* and delusive, all the forms of superstition, every corruption of true religion, and all usurpation over the rights of conscience, which have been supported by power or prejudice, will be universally exploded, as they ought to be.

Together with the general prevalence of the true principles of civil government, we may expect to see the extinction of all *national prejudice* and enmity, and the establishment of *universal peace* and good will among all nations. When the affairs of the various societies of mankind shall be conducted by those who shall truly represent them, who shall feel as they feel, and think as they think, who shall really understand, and consult their interests, they will no more engage in those mutually offensive *wars,* which the experience of many centuries has shown to be constantly expensive and ruinous. They will no longer covet what belongs to others, and which they have found to be of no real service to them, but will content themselves with making the most of their own.

The very idea of *distant possessions* will be even ridiculed. The East and the West Indies, and every thing *without ourselves* will be disregarded, and wholly excluded from all European systems; and only those divisions of men, and of territory, will take place, which the common convenience requires, and not such as the mad and insatiable ambition of princes demands. No part of America, Africa, or Asia, will be held in subjection to any part of Europe, and all the intercourse that will be kept up among them, will be for their mutual advantage.

The causes of *civil wars,* the most distressing of all others, will likewise cease, as well as those of foreign ones. They are chiefly contentions for *offices,* on account of the power and emoluments annexed to them. But when the *nature* and *uses* of all civil offices shall be well understood, the power and emoluments annexed to them, will not be an object sufficient to produce a war. Is it at all probable, that there will ever be a civil war in America about the presidentship of the *United States?* And when the chief magistracies in other countries shall be reduced to their proper standard, they will be no more worth contending for, than they are in America. . . .

Other remaining causes of civil war are different opinions about modes of government, and differences of interests betwen provinces. But when mankind shall be a little more accustomed to reflection, and consider the miseries of civil war, they will have recourse to any other method of deciding their differences, in preference to that of the sword. It was taken for granted, that the moment America had thrown off the yoke of Great Britain, the different states would go to war among themselves, on some of these accounts. But the event has not verified the prediction, nor is it at all probable that it ever will. The people of that country are wiser than such prophets in this.

If *time* be allowed for the discussion of differences, so great a majority will form one opinion, that the minority will see the necessity of giving way. Thus will *reason* be the umpire in all disputes, and extinguish civil wars as well as foreign ones. The empire of reason will ever be the reign of peace. . . .

In this new condition of the world, there may still be *kings,* but they will be no longer *sovereigns,* or *supreme lords,* no human beings to whom will be ascribed such titles as those of *most sacred,* or *most excellent majesty.* There will be no more such a profanation of epithets, belonging to God only, by the application of them to mortals like ourselves. There will be *magistrates,* appointed and paid for the conservation of order, but they will only be considered as the first *servants of the people,* and accountable to them. Standing armies, those instruments of tyranny, will be unknown, though the people may be trained to the use of arms, for the purpose of repelling the invasion of *Barbarians.* For no other description of men will have recourse to war, or think of disturbing the repose of others; and till they become civilized, as in the natural progress of things they necessarily must, they will be sufficiently overawed by the superior power of nations that are so.

There will still be *religion,* and of course *ministers* of it; as there will be teachers of philosophy, and practitioners in medicine; but it will no longer be the concern of the state. There will be no more *Lord Bishops,* or *Archbishops,* with the titles, and powers, of temporal princes. Every man will provide religion for himself; and therefore it will be such as, after due enquiry, and examination, he shall think to be founded on truth, and best calculated to make men good citizens, good friends, and good neighbours in this world, as well as to fit them for another.

Government, being thus simple in its objects, will be unspeakably less *expensive* than it is at present, as well as far more *effectual* in answering its proper purpose. There will then be little to provide for besides the administration of justice, or the preservation of the peace, which it will be the interest of every man to attend to, in aid of government.

They are chiefly our vices and follies that lay us under contribution, in the form of the *taxes* we now pay; and they will, of course, become superfluous, as the world grows wiser and better. It is a most unreasonable sum that we now pay for the single article of *government.* We give, perhaps, the amount of one half of our property, for the secure enjoyment of the rest, which, after all, for want of a good police, is very insecure. . . .

If you, Sir, together with your old or your new friends, can steer the ship of the state through the storm, which we all see to be approaching, you will have more wisdom and steadiness than has yet been found in any who have hitherto been at the head of our affairs. And if, in these circumstances, you can save the *church,* as well as the *state,* you will deserve no less than *canonization,* and St. Edmund will be the greatest name in the calendar. But, great occasions call forth, and in a manner create, great and unknown ability, as we have lately seen in the history of the American revolution. A good providence also governs the world, and therefore we need not despair.

If the condition of other nations be as much bettered as that of France will probably be, by her improved system of government, this great crisis, dreadful as it appears in prospect, will be *a consummation devoutly to be wished for,* and though calamitous to many, perhaps to many innocent persons, will be eventually most glorious and happy. . . .

I am, Dear Sir,

Your very humble servant,

J. Priestley

Birmingham, Jan. 1, 1791

Debate on Revolutionary War

Throughout the winter of 1791–1792, Paris was stirred by a public debate over war or peace in the press, the Legislative Assembly, and the political clubs. The two speeches below were delivered before the Society of the Friends of the Constitution, better known as the Jacobin Club, composed of middle-class enthusiasts for the revolution who had come to distrust the monarchy, even if all of them were not yet openly republican. The speeches reproduced here date, respectively, from December 30, 1791, and from January 2, 1792. They constituted neither the opening nor the closing round in the Brissot-Robespierre debate, for each speaker had already given one prior address on foreign policy and each was to expound upon the issue on later occasions.

Jacques Pierre Brissot de Warville (1754–1793) had made a name for himself as pamphleteer and publisher of a leading radical newspaper, The French Patriot. *In 1791 he had been elected deputy from Paris to the Legislative Assembly, where he exercised considerable influence over the committee in charge of foreign policy. Later, he was to become a leading spokesman of a loosely organized parliamentary faction, the Girondins, who, long on oratory but short on administrative ability, dominated the revolutionary government throughout most of 1792 and into 1793. Brissot was executed by his political enemies, led by Robespierre, in 1793.*

Maximilien de Robespierre (1758–1794), a provincial lawyer turned politician, had been noted as a thoroughgoing democrat while a deputy to the Constituent Assembly from 1789 to 1791. At the time of the debate, he was prosecuting attorney for the Paris municipality, but was also active, as was Brissot, in the deliberations of the Jacobin Club. Ironically, within less than two years Robespierre was to head the dictatorial Committee of Public Safety, created to deal with the emergency stemming from a war that he had sought so hard to prevent. In late 1791, however, Brissot and Robespierre shared a concern for greater democracy and a distrust of the monarchy and its supporters.

On one level the Brissot-Robespierre debate can be understood only in its unique historical background. To men like Brissot and Robespierre, the constitution that had been completed in 1791 was suspect because its executive, Louis XVI, was unreliable as a constitutional monarch. It was rightly believed that both Louis and his Austrian queen, Marie-Antoinette, had tried to gain support from among Europen princes, particularly

*from the queen's brother, Leopold of Austria. In June, 1791, the French
royal family had tried to flee, only to be captured. Although the king was
ultimately reinstated because moderates could not find an acceptable
substitute for him, his immediate use of his veto power to block legislation
against the émigrés, the aristocratic refugees who talked of a counter-
revolutionary crusade against France, thickened the atmosphere of distrust.
As early as 1790, various French revolutionary reforms had also raised
howls from affected foreign princes, the Pope included. Shortly after the
recapture of the French royal family, the so-called Declaration of Pillnitz,
by which the rulers of Austria and Prussia threatened intervention in
behalf of the monarchy, encouraged French revolutionary warhawks.
By November a French ultimatum demanded the expulsion of the émigrés
from the principality of the Prince-Bishop of Trier (who controlled the
oft-mentioned Coblentz), which was in turn followed by an ultimatum
to Austria demanding that it publicly abandon its claim to intervene
in French affairs. By April, 1792, France was at war; Brissot had won the
debate.*

*On another level it would be a mistake to stress only the uniqueness of
this problem of war and revolution. Most major social revolutions
have been accompanied by war, either because the revolutionaries have
had to face foreign intervention (or have opted for preventive war in the
belief that such intervention was inevitable) or because the revolutionaries
sought to spread their gospel by force of arms. Any list of significant
twentieth-century social revolutions—Mexico, Russia, Spain, China,
Cuba, Vietnam—suggests that the link of war to revolution is more than
a matter of historical accident. In this broader sense the Brissot-Robespierre
debate raises issues that our age shares with the closing years of the
eighteenth century.*

⤚§ THE CASE FOR WAR

Jacques Pierre Brissot

Gentlemen   I have promised to respond to the objections that have been raised against
going over to the attack. I am going to fulfill my promise, though I cannot answer all
objections, for this would fill volumes. I have picked the most striking ones and, while
ignoring both phrase-mongering and parody as proving nothing, I shall abide only

Société des Amis de la Constitution, *Second Discours de J. P. Brissot, député*, 30 decembre
1791 (Paris, January, 1792), pp. 1–11, 13–27. Translated by Peter Amann.

by the arguments. I shall also ignore the insinuations against my patriotism printed and spread on this occasion. A patriot of twenty years' standing does not change overnight. Only yesterday did I elaborate my ideas before the National Assembly. Did anyone notice a change in my love for liberty, my hatred toward the enemies of equality, my watchfulness toward the ministers, or even in my language? Some ardent patriots are too quick to suspect all those whose thinking does not always coincide with theirs. Brothers, you have assigned a post to me [as member of the National Assembly]. I shall not desert it for one moment, yet three months of experience have deepened my insight. You are patriots like myself, but I know the arena and the arms by which the people may conquer better than you.

Before disposing of the objections raised against me, I must recall in a few words what I believe having proved in my first speech. I showed [then] that nothing but the decision to [wage] war was consonant in every respect with the dignity of the French nation, its safety, the preservation of the revolution and the return of public prosperity.

It has been demonstrated that France must consent to everlasting dishonor if, after conquering her [own] liberty, she permits a few thousand highwaymen [the armed French *émigré* nobles gathered at Coblentz and other German principalities along the Franco-German frontier] to insult twenty-five million people with impunity.

It has been demonstrated that the security of the French domain is compromised far more by calmly awaiting the enemy at home than by forestalling him.

It has been demonstrated that the constitution shall be stabilized more rapidly if we can master the discontented who are constantly stirring within, that these dissidents will vanish much more easily if we deprive them of their single support abroad, namely this army of refugees that encourages their intrigues, and with whose chiefs they never stop hatching plots that are ever discovered and ever re-formed.

It has been demonstrated that public credit will be re-established more promptly if the nation, at last adopting the attitude that befits it, addresses the governments secretly fomenting revolt and openly protecting the rebels in a language worthy of liberty.

It has been demonstrated to anyone carefully observing the current state of Europe, that there is no major power seriously willing or effectively able to arrest the French nation in its march toward freedom; that all of them, though detesting our new regime, are, and shall be, forced to respect it; that their little alliances, their small impractical schemes, are no more than veritable toys with which they seek to reassure and deceive each other.

Finally, it has been demonstrated that if there are betrayals to fear, they are far more dangerous within the kingdom than without.

How do our opponents counter so many arguments proving that France must take the offensive both against the rebels who defy her and foreigners protecting them? Dodging the arguments, they concentrate on awakening suspicions and fears. "You should suspect," they say, "the ministers' eagerness to go to war after they have opposed it all this time."

I confess that this sudden ardor should make patriots uneasy; more than once did I myself believe that I perceived a germ of treason. If, nonetheless, one can manage to explain, to prove that this about-face is only a matter of appearance, then it seems to me that the strongest objection to the war in people's minds will be removed.

People tend to confuse the present cabinet with the one it replaced. What did the former ministers want? [They were] brought up in the *ancien régime,* detesting the new, burning to restore the king to his ancient authority, secretly despising the National Assembly. . . .

Another aim animates the present ministry: as the men have changed, so has their course altered. Most of these ministers owe their unexpected rise to the revolution, while the counter-revolution would indubitably entail their fall. These obscure plebeians would never be forgiven for having sullied the steps of the throne. Convinced as they must be of this [possible] catastrophe, how could they be stupid enough to favor a rebel party that views their authority with horror and which, if it ever triumphed, would thrust them from the seats of power? The present ministry, allies of the moderates when it is a question of fighting patriots, will thus fight the aristocrats at the side of the patriots, having common interests with the latter. It must seek to destroy Coblentz, for Coblentz shelters its enemies, and that is why you see all its hired hacks preaching war.

Here, then, is the reasonable explanation of the eagerness with which our ministers clamor for war against the German princes. In a successful war they see a sure guarantee of retaining their offices. . . .

I do not contend that all the secret committees with which the Tuileries Palace [Paris residence of the king] is honeycombed share the views of the present ministry. I do not contend that there no longer is a party seeking the reestablishment of a patriciate or its resuscitation by means of a two-chamber legislature. I do not claim that there is no correspondence with Coblentz, nor that there may not be a few individuals secretly hoping for the success of the Coblentz refugees and therefore little inclined to launch an attack against them; that they feign bellicosity in order to make us stand for peace; I shall not deny that other individuals, who are almost as important, seek war because they see therein the possibility of forcing the hand of the Emperor [Leopold II of Austria who also held the elective title of Emperor of the Holy Roman Empire] and of Prussia. Yet I say that all these small, fragmentary cabals working at cross-purposes should not deflect from its course a great people that must act according to its principles and power.

I say, that in order to outwit those who oppose war but pretend to seek it, war must be declared. I say, that to outwit those who rely on the Emperor and the refugees, we must once more forestall either the invasion or the [calling of a European] conference with which we are threatened. . . .

I say, that these diverse factions' hope of enlisting the powers in their cause by compromising them in this war is unfounded. My arguments concerning the two Houses of Austria and Berlin are, I contend, still valid, namely that neither really wants war and that both would run heavy risks in opting for it. I say, that should France have to deal with them—something which seems almost inconceivable to me—she should nonetheless go on the offensive in order to rid herself, whatever the cost, of this fear of foreign nations, or else renounce freedom altogether: no one is free with the knife of terror suspended over his head. I say, that the patriots, that France herself, must at last scorn these petty intrigues, these obscure machinations of various committees which animate the court and throw it into perpetual turmoil. . . .

"But by violating their territory, you will antagonize the German peoples, whom," it has been added, "you imagine imbued with libertarian principles, when [on the contrary] they have not forgotten the cruelties wrought in the Palatinate" [during the French invasion of 1688–1689].

What! Do you suppose that by attacking the highwaymen at Coblentz, we ourselves shall wage war like highwaymen? A free people has too much self-respect to stoop to such horrors. A free man goes straight up to his enemy, meets him face to face, overcomes him or dies. But as to the children, the women, the farmers' and artisans' property—all this is sacred to [the free men] and he respects them religiously. Tyrants can transform the most beautiful landscape into desert; a free man would rather people the deserts with men free and happy like himself. For a free man, the thatched peasant hut commands more respect than the palace. [The former] is the asylum of innocence which the free man reveres, dreading to shed innocent tears. These are the principles that will guide the French army. . . . They will wipe clean the ghastly scenes of the Palatinate that have sullied, not the nation, but ministerial despotism. Then the Germans shall see the difference between a people fighting for its freedom and an army upholding the whims of a few crowned brigands. All right! Don't shout yet that this is impossible, a mirage! Let me cite the conduct of the French army in America: not one complaint was heard against it, even though it was as yet unenlightened by liberty. By fighting shoulder to shoulder with free men, their sacred example inspired the French to virtue.

Yes, when the Germans, groaning under the yoke of the Electors [the prince-bishops ruling the German states adjoining France] shall see the French army unfurl the tricolor banner in their midst; when they shall see how it protects, rather than devastates, their possessions, how supplies are bought and paid for instead of being pillaged, how it threatens only those who seek to defend the rebels; when they shall see in the French camp, not an enemy camp, but a peaceful mobile city where law and order reign; when they shall see the French striving only for [German] happiness and freedom; then shall the Germans shower them with blessings, instead of rising up against them. Then shall the two be bound by a gentle yet solid fraternity, resting not on fleeting expediency but on eternal principles held in common.

My appraisal of the situation of the foreign powers has been challenged. I have proved to you that, far from being formidable, they neither want nor can wage war. . . . Because of his warlike impetuosity, victory has almost always favored the Frenchman when he has been on the offensive, even though he fought for some measly point of honor or for some miserable ribbon. What then will be his stature when he fights for his liberty, his rights, his fatherland—for at last he shall have one. Either I am mistaken about the profound influence which liberty exercises over the human spirit, or else I must believe that every patriot will be a hero.

In this frame of mind, what indeed do you have to fear from these armed automatons, henceforth more dangerous to the tyrants dragging them to battle than to their enemies; these automatons suddenly brought to life by the sight of your banners on which liberty shines, by the cap [the Phrygian cap, symbol of the Revolution] on your pikes, by the magic sounds of your chant: "Ah, Ça ira!" [famous French revolutionary song] which, gentlemen, henceforth be your battle hymn. . . .

Even if the possibility of this miracle be contested, can you deny the influence of secret contacts between two armies? Formerly the French were well liked. Today they will be blessed. It is impossible that Germans, seeing in Frenchmen nothing but friends to all men, liberators of mankind, should wish to keep on fighting for the honor of their tyrants.

Well, gentlemen, I must reiterate that my prediction has already been fulfilled. Ask that merchant of human flesh, the Prince of Hesse, how many of his soldiers came back from the American campaigns. The Germans, finding brothers in the Americans, laid down their arms and traded them for plows. [Now] they live happy and free, electing their representatives, making their own laws, instead of being cudgeled, chained and starved at the pleasure of his Electoral Highness.

The German princes, having been taught [a lesson] by this experience, are far from wishing to repeat it. Like my opponents, I realize what hold pride has upon their soul. Aware of the immense loathing of kings for liberty, for equality, I myself harbor an eternal, irreconcilable hatred for them. Yet I am also aware that sometimes these princes calculate their interests, to which they subordinate even their most violent passions. . . .

I have counted and shall always continue to count on the predisposition of peoples toward freedom, whereas our opponents question that [these nations] are on the verge of liberty. "Despotism has crushed them," they [our opponents] cry out. Who has given you the measure of their thralldom? Are their bonds really stronger than those which enslaved the French nation? Was there ever a people that seemed farther removed from freedom than did the French people? Was there no talk of its frivolity, its fickleness, its terror of the *bastilles* [prison fortresses], its mad thirst for pleasure, the twelve centuries of its enslavement? Indeed! All this vanished on July 14, 1789 [the date of the storming of the Bastille in Paris], and that day punctured the claims of all those who had calculated the probabilities of a people's resurrection according to the scale of their own ignorance and their own corruption. . . .

Let us stop, gentlemen, let us stop slandering whole peoples by claiming that they are farther away from liberty than we ourselves were. Even had this been true originally, our example has helped them make prodigious headway. Our constitution, which is becoming known throughout the world, day by day makes them increasingly mature. And why should the German, being serious, thoughtful, generally well-off, not be close to reaching freedom? He reads, he is well-to-do; hence he is learning to prefer the language of liberty. . . .

Descartes said: "Give me a fulcrum and I shall raise the world." This idea is even truer in politics than in mechanics. Find a fulcrum to raise the universe against the tyrants and the universe shall be free. This fulcrum has in fact been discovered. What am I saying? There is one in each hemisphere: one in the United States, the other in France. Here are the two everlasting workshops of universal liberty, the two asylums for those who fall by the wayside.

"Do you know of any people," some cry out, "who succeeded in gaining their freedom while waging foreign, civil and religious war under the leadership of a treacherous despotism?"

Of what importance is it to us whether or not such a thing has ever occurred? Is there in all of ancient history a revolution like ours? Show me a people who, after twelve centuries' servitude, reconquered its liberty! We will create something the like of which has never existed.

Yes, we will vanquish the nobles, priests and electors and thereby establish our public credit and our prosperity, or else we shall be beaten and betrayed. And the traitors shall at last be discovered and punished, as we pluck out everything that stands in the way of the French nation's greatness. I confess to you, gentlemen, I have but one fear: that we shall not be betrayed. We need vast treacheries! Therein lies our salvation; for within France's bosom still stir strong doses of poison that must burst out. The body is sound; there is nothing to fear. The great treasons, fatal to the traitors themselves, shall render service to the peoples.

The men who constantly quote ancient history in order to frighten us about such betrayals start from false analogies. Their starting point is the past, whereas the present bears no resemblance whatsoever to what occurred in the past. We are creating new centuries, new revolutions. The invention of printing traced a line of demarcation as between the ancient centuries and the centuries of the future. The ancient peoples' ignorance, the impossibility of bringing them sudden enlightenment, inevitably made them puppets in the hands of intrigue. The press has and shall continue to make tyranny more difficult, while reason, gradually illuminating all men, will preserve them from demagogy.

It is easy to point to Caesar and Pompey and to indulge in glittering oratory about their usurpations in order to frighten us about the war. Yet for the man who plunges into the depth of centuries, undeterred by a few superficial resemblances, what have Caesar and Pompey in common with our generals, Rome in common with France? Rome was founded on a system of conquest abhorrent to France. Rome had numerous professional armies. Ours, on the other hand, shall not be maintained on a permanent footing, for among the services which the French Revolution will render to Europe will rank the destruction of the whole system of standing armies [to be achieved] by demonstrating their superfluity at the very time when the taxes required to support them are becoming increasingly burdensome.

Always on the move, the Roman armies speculated on pillage and conquered lands, whereas our constitution proscribes this spirit of bellicose rapacity. The Roman armies were composed of brigands, adventurers, foreigners without property or any other profession than the sword. The French army will comprise citizen-soldiers, joined to their fatherland by family links, by their possessions, their industry, their rights as citizens. These citizen-soldiers, save in war time ever mingling with the citizen class, would never be tempted to turn against it, to tear it apart as the Roman soldiers did who constituted a caste apart. The Roman soldier had no tie to Rome; he saw no one, he loved no one but the general who could grant him land and money. Quite literally, he was the soldier of Pompey rather than the soldier of the Republic. Yet where in France are the conquered lands and piles of gold with which a Caesar could sway his soldiery and the masses to his will?

Rome had no clubs, no patriotic societies, no printing presses, no newspapers; tyranny becomes impossible wherever such patriotic clubs, wherever printing presses exist. They constitute the many tocsins quickly sounding the alarm whenever the enemy appears.

The Roman regime carried the seeds of its own destruction within its bosom. In order to keep in power, the Senate, a [legally] irremovable and aristocratic body, had to embroil the [Roman] people in frequent wars. The wars created clever and ambitious generals, who then used their soldiers to enslave both Senate and people. Thus the Senate destroyed itself.

France is not in this position at all. Her Senate, named by the people, is drawn from the very bosom of that people. Being renewed at frequent intervals, this revocable Senate can only be the friend of the people who elect it. It must seek peace, because in peacetime everyone pays lower taxes, people's commerce and industry flourish and their enjoyment is increased. Thus war is the enemy of the representative system and, as wars will be rare, there is no ground to fear serfdom at the hands of Caesars and Pompeys.

How indeed can the National Assembly decreeing war against rebels be compared with the Roman Senate declaring war to deflect the assaults of the Roman people? Does the National Assembly crush the French people under its yoke? Does it need butchery to retain power? False and absurd comparisons!

Well! What has become of these terrors of a dictatorship that war will thrust into the hands of our generals, our ministers?

Let us analyze this fear-ridden word *dictatorship* and we shall see how alien it is to us. What was a dictator? A man chosen by the Senate during some dangerous crisis to govern the commonwealth on his own, a man whose supreme will took the place of the law and whose inviolability opened the floodgate for every crime. Yet by declaring war on the small German princes, are we suspending the operation of the laws and the reign of the constitution? Are we elevating both our generals and our ministers above [the constitution]? Must the law bow its head before their despotic axes? [The *fasces*, an axe surrounded by a bundle of rods, was the Roman symbol of public authority.] Are they covered by unlimited inviolability? No, nothing of the sort exists. The courts remain; the law remains; the constitution alone is mistress; the [constituted] powers still yield to it, their agents checked by being held responsible. The National Assembly continues to see to it that this responsibility is exercised.

Once more, what is there to fear from this mythical dictatorship? "It shall spring up [in the future]," some people clamor. "Ambitious men are only awaiting the right moment to seize the *fasces*." Yes, but the axe of the law also hangs suspended above the heads of the ambitious.

I ask again: Where is the army, where the people to support this ambitious man? Where are the treasures with which to seduce both? The army is composed in part of national guards, in part of regulars to whom no general could offer advantages that surpass those which the revolution has granted them. All the French people are not in Paris, any more than all the people of the Roman Empire were in Rome. The people of Paris are not alone in having the rights of French citizenship, any more than were the people who lived in Rome. The people of Paris do not hold plebiscites as the people of Rome did. Let us suppose . . . a Caesar sufficiently skillful, rich, and mad to attempt the seduction of Parisians. This does not mean that he thereby subjects the other great cities to his sway, [cities] whose citizens would check his ambitious plans. Caesar could still bend an irremovable Senate to his will. But what of a Senate that changes every other year? What man can be rich or stupid enough to try to bribe it? Observe, finally, the immense accumulation of wealth that Caesar lavished, squandered, to chain the Roman people to his chariot: the gold of the whole universe piled up in Rome by centuries of conquest! Now the only national wealth presently at the disposal of a French Caesar, the national *assignats* [paper money backed by church lands confiscated by the revolutionary government] would be destroyed in the hands of the usurper by the effect of the very violence that would have raised him to power.

In this way, gentlemen, by analyzing all these great examples drawn from ancient history, we find how inapplicable they are to our current situation. . . .

National guards, universal freedom of the press, equality of rights, a large population: these are the four great features that insure French liberty forever, that distinguish [France's] revolution from all other revolutions.

The people made [the revolution]; the people reap the benefits. As in the course of centuries reason will progress, the people will reap ever greater benefits and hence will be ever more inclined to maintain [the revolution]. And that is why I told you so confidently that you have nothing more to fear, neither traitors nor demagogues. The people are here, the people of twenty-five million souls, that is, and not merely the people of a capital city—that is to say, the entire people whose views are daily maturing through public discussion. This people, experiencing daily the sweetness of having been relieved of so many burdens under which despotism had crushed them, within two years has shot ahead by almost a century in terms of reasoning powers, pride, enthusiasm for everything great and beautiful. No, this people will not stand for chains again; rather than that, they would fight, they would perish. . . .

By speaking as I do, I do not mean to bank on the armed insurrection of the people. I refer to the peaceful insurrection of public opinion against great outrages. There lies our strength, constituting the remedy against the constitution's flaws: it is to be found in the infallible instinct, the prompt and sure judgment, the people's incorruptibility and inalterable attachment to liberty. All these virtues cannot help but grow, offering us ever more certain guarantees for our freedom.

This is the people that some fear to lead in combat against disciplined automatons. As though [that people] were not brave enough, I do not say to vanquish (even mercenaries can do that), but to sustain defeat without being cast down, to return to the battlefield with even greater eagerness, even greater pride, until the crown of victory be won.

We are warned about defeats. Well, what difference does it make if through such defeats we succeed in maintaining liberty? For one Saratoga or one Yorktown, how many failures did the Americans not experience? This is the distinction between an army of free men and one of slaves: the latter is often ruined by victory, while not even defeats can destroy the former.

"But you will lack patriotic generals," [they say]. They will appear, let there be no doubt about it! Within a few months, did not America see a bookseller, Knox, and a doctor, Warren, shine among the most skillful warriors, though neither had ever handled a gun? Well? What was Washington himself when the war of independence broke out? An almost unknown colonel who had seen little service. . . .

They tell me that America was in a far more favorable position than ourselves in having a powerful ally in France. They forget that the Americans had won at Saratoga even before the alliance with the French. . . .

They tell me that the Americans were helped by Cornwallis' mistakes. Your adversaries will have more than their share of Cornwallises. These conceited tacticians are strangers to the tactics of a free people.

They tell us, furthermore, in order to discourage us—and they look upon this objection as unanswerable—that the blaze is burning in our own home. To carry it to the enemy's house will not extinguish it. Yet they do not tell you that this very enemy supplies the torches with which it is ever rekindled. Thus, to make straight for the fire abroad is the real way of extinguishing the domestic conflagration.

They tell us that to start a war is to underwrite the continued devaluation of our paper currency. And I tell you that failure to declare war would destroy confidence in our *assignats* to the extent that it can be destroyed. For they always forget that these *assignats* are the world's soundest money, that this money represents excellent land that cannot run away. They forget that, come what may, the *assignat* cannot be discredited even in the event of a counter-revolution, as it would be to the counter-revolutionaries' interest to avoid turmoil and to win over the people. By hurling anathemas against the *assignat,* which is in everyone's hands and in everyone's possession, they would alienate [the people] and invite trouble. The *assignats* thus cannot be discredited, provided people use reason instead of letting that absurd thermometer, the rate of exchange, prejudice them. Yet to the extent that this rate of exchange does influence the value of the *assignats,* and since its decline is due to the opinion that France is powerless to defeat the rebels, we must at last pulverize them in order to unmask those who seek to discredit our paper money.

They have also told you that we should reorganize our finances instead of waging war. Yet financial prosperity hinges on the annihilation of the rebels. Their obstinacy entails prodigious expenses while making tax collection more difficult. Going on the offensive is therefore essential to the improvement of the financial situation. . . .

They forget that this war should not extend more than twenty-five or thirty miles beyond the frontiers and that, consequently, most of the supplies may be carted from France. They forget, finally, that whenever the cooperation of the two powers [legislative and executive] becomes evident, whenever this war will have revived the concept of French power, it will be easy then to devise financial procedures to render the purchase of war materiel less costly. . . .

Gentlemen, patriots cannot long remain divided when it comes to the glory of liberty, of the dearest interests of our fatherland.

All these reasons combine [to justify] going on the offensive. I am therefore happy to believe that this same sentiment will bring us together and that, putting aside divisive subtleties that are metaphysical rather than real, we shall grasp the necessity of taking up arms against the foreigners who defy us. Not only does our honor call for [war], but all nations secretly invite it. This attack will sound the tocsin of their awakening, shaking all the foreign *bastilles.* You will rapidly spread upheaval in the countries you invade, and you will electrify all spirits. Scarcely had it become known that you were threatening Coblentz, when the hearts of the Belgian patriots were stirred. Thinking their moment had arrived, they raised once again the sacred symbol of liberty, while many of them sought asylum within your walls to prepare their arms against the tyrants. Dutchmen, Flemings, Liégeois await but your explosion to set off their own and cast off their yoke. With what speed this movement will spread everywhere! Heaven seems to destine the globe to periodic political revolutions. Remember the crusades, when Europe, arming itself for the sake of a few superstitions, rose up to crush the Hydra in response to the voice of a single man.

The moment for another crusade has arrived, one with a much nobler, a much holier purpose. This is a crusade for universal freedom. Here each soldier will be a Peter the Hermit, a Bernard, and will be even more eloquent than they. He will not preach mystical dogmas, but what everyone knows and wants—liberty. Let the kings stop conjuring up the chimera of propaganda, or, rather, let them discover at last where it really exists and threatens them—in the soul of every soldier who will say to his enemy: "Brother, I have come not to slaughter you but to lift the yoke under which you groan. I have come to show you the road to happiness. Like yourself, I was a slave. I took to arms and the tyrant vanished. Here I am, free; you too can become free; here is my arm."

No, it is not within the power of any man to arrest this revolution. It is the effect of reason, and reason speaks to every man and in every language. The French Revolution is on every tongue. Everyone has come to know its sublime maxim: a people need only will to be free. . . .

⨳ THE CASE AGAINST WAR

Maximilien de Robespierre

The greatest controversies that divide mankind often rest on a misunderstanding. Unless I am mistaken, such is even the present case. It should suffice to clear up [this misunderstanding] and all good citizens will rally to principles and to truth.

Of the two opinions that have clashed at this gathering, one draws upon all the ideas flattering the imagination, upon all the brilliant hopes inspired by enthusiasm and generous sentiments, and is supported by all the means which the most active and powerful of governments can muster to influence public opinion. The other relies only on cold reason and the melancholy truth. In order to please, one must defend the first [opinion]. In order to be useful, one must champion the second, even in the certain knowledge of displeasing all those who wield the power of punishing. I myself opt for the latter [opinion].

Shall we wage war or shall we make peace? Shall we attack our enemies or await them in our homes? Such a formulation fails, I believe, to pose the question in all its

Discours et rapports de Robespierre, ed. C. Vellay (Paris: E. Fasquelle, 1908), pp. 110–137. Translated by Peter Amann.

complexity and scope. What should be the decision of the nation and its representatives with regard to our internal and external enemies? This is the real vantage point from which the question should be considered if one wants to be all-inclusive and discuss it with the precision it demands. Whatever the fruits of our efforts, what matters above all is to enlighten the nation as to its true interests and those of its foes, rather than to deprive liberty of its last bastion by deluding public opinion. This is my objective in taking issue chiefly with Monsieur Brissot's views.

If skillful strokes, if a brilliant and prophetic portrait depicting the results of a war ending in the fraternal embrace of all the European peoples are adequate reasons for deciding so weighty a question, then I shall agree that Monsieur Brissot has reached a complete solution. Yet his speech seemed to me marred by something of no significance in an academic oration, but of some import in the greatest of all political debates; namely, he consistently avoids the fundamental point of the question so as to erect his whole system on an absolutely ruinous base.

Certainly a war undertaken to extend the reign of liberty appeals to me as much as it does to Monsieur Brissot. I too could succumb to the pleasure of foretelling all its marvels. If only I were master of France's destiny, if only my inclination controlled her forces and resources, I should have sent an army into Belgium long ago; I should have gone to the aid of the Liégeois [the episcopal principality of Liège in what today would be Belgium] and smashed the chains of the Dutch. Nothing would please me more than such expeditions. True, rather than declaring war on rebel subjects at all, I would even have deprived them of their [initial] will to draw together. I should not have permitted enemies who are more formidable and closer to us to protect them, thus raising more serious internal threats.

Yet given the circumstances in which I find this country, looking with concern about me, I ask myself whether the war that we would wage would be one resembling what is being promised to us with such enthusiasm. I ask myself: Who proposes it, how, in what circumstances, and why?

The crux of the matter is the totally extraordinary situation in which we find ourselves. No doubt you have consistently ignored it. Yet I have proved what has been obvious to everyone, namely, that the current proposal of war is the outcome of a long-held plan by the internal foes of our freedom. I have pointed out their aim to you, as well as their means of execution. . . .

You yourself agreed that war suited the *émigrés,* that it suited the ministry and the court schemers—a large faction whose all too well-known leaders have long been behind every move of the executive power. All the mouthpieces of the aristocracy and the government have joined the chorus [for war]. Lastly, whoever can believe in good faith that, ever since the start of this revolution, the conduct of the court has not been consistently opposed to the principles of equality and respect for the rights of the people would be regarded as bereft of his senses. Anyone claiming that the court would propose so fateful a measure as war without tying it into its schemes would show little better judgment. Now, can you contend that it is inconsequential to the state's welfare whether warfare is guided by love of liberty or by the spirit of despotism, by fidelity or by perfidy? Yet how have you countered all these irrefutable facts? What have you said that would dissipate these many justified suspicions? Your reaction to the very basic assumptions of this debate shows up your whole approach [for what it is].

"Mistrust," you said in your first speech, *"mistrust is a horrible state. It prevents the two powers* [executive and legislative] *from acting in concert; it deters the people from accepting the executive power's action by cooling* [the people's] *affection and loosening their obedience."*

Mistrust—a horrible state? Is this the language of a free man who thinks no price is too high to pay for liberty? . . .

There is no doubt today that a powerful and dangerous league against equality and the principles of our freedom has come into being. It is known that this alliance, after sacrilegiously undermining the basis of the constitution [after the flight of the king in June 1791 and his recapture, the constitution was amended to make it more acceptable to him], is busy completing its task, and that [this alliance] dominates the court and rules the ministers. . . . You were content to assert that the intriguers are incapable of jeopardizing freedom. Are you aware that it is such schemers who are the cause of people's misfortunes? Are you unaware that schemers abetted by the force and treasure of the government cannot be neglected? Are you unaware that, ever since the king's departure (the mystery of which is beginning to clear up), they have caused the revolution to retrogress and have carried out the most culpable attacks on liberty with impunity? Whence suddenly so much indulgence or such [a sense of] security?

"Don't be alarmed," the same speaker has told us, "if this faction wants war. Don't be alarmed if its lead is followed by the court and the ministers, if the newspapers, *which the ministry subsidizes,* preach war. While the ministers will indeed always join the moderates against the patriots, they will combine with both patriots and moderates against the *émigrés.*" What a reassuring and luminous theory! You agree that the ministers are the patriots' enemies. The moderates, whom they favor, want to make our constitution aristocratic and you want us to go along with their plans? The ministers subsidize—you are the one who said this—newspapers, with the aim of snuffing out all public spirit, erasing the principles of freedom, praising the most dangerous of its foes, libeling all the good citizens—and you want me to trust the ministers' views and principles?

You think that the executive's agents are more likely to adopt the maxims of equality and to defend the people's rights in all their purity, rather than to make a deal with the members of the dynasty [the *émigré* brothers of the king] and the court's friends at the expense of both people and patriots, the latter of whom are already openly being called sedition-mongers? Aren't aristocrats of every shade demanding war and aren't all their echoes taking up the war cry as well? No doubt we should not distrust their intentions either. I myself admire your bliss unenviously. You were destined to defend liberty without harboring suspicions, without alienating its enemies, without finding yourself in opposition to the court, the ministers, or the moderates. How easy and smiling the paths of patriotism have become!

As for myself, the further I have progressed along this course [of patriotism] the more numerous the obstacles and enemies that I have encountered, the more abandoned I have found myself by those who had started out with me; and, I confess, were I to find myself surrounded by courtiers, aristocrats, and moderates, I might at least be tempted to think I had fallen into bad company. . . .

Far from broaching the true state of the question, you have always run away from it. All that you have said misses the point. . . .

What matter to us, for instance, your long and pompous dissertations on the American war? What does open war waged by a people against its tyrants have to do with a system of conspiracy managed by the government itself against burgeoning liberty? Had the Americans triumphed over English tyranny by fighting under English banners and under English generals against their own allies, the American example would have been cited with profit. One could even add that of the Dutch and the Swiss, had the former relied on the Duke of Alba [the most ruthless Spanish opponent of Dutch independence], the latter on the princes of Austria and Burgundy [from whom the independence of the Swiss cantons was actually exacted] to avenge their wrongs and to insure their freedom. What matter, moreover, the lightning victories over universal despotism and aristocracy that you win from the speaker's platform? As though the nature of things yielded so neatly to oratorical [flights of the] imagination! Is it the people or the genius of liberty that is to head the plan being proposed to us? For the court is [made up of] its officers and its ministers. You keep forgetting that this fact throws off every calculation. . . .

From what I have said earlier, it follows that it might turn out that those who demand war and who would be in charge of it intend something other than to deal a fatal blow to the revolution's foes and to royal absolutism's friends. Yet no matter; you yourself will start off by taking care of the conquest of Germany singlehandedly. Your triumphant army will promenade among all the neighboring peoples. You will set up municipalities, directories, and national assemblies everywhere (a sublime thought, as you yourself exclaim), as though the destiny of empires were controlled by figures of speech. Our generals, as led by yourself, will have become the constitution's missionaries, our camp a school for public law. The foreign monarch's satellites, far from obstructing the execution of this project, will even anticipate our aims, not in order to repel us, but in order to lend us their ear.

It is too bad that truth and common sense give the lie to these magnificent predictions; in the nature of things the march of reason makes but slow progress. The most vicious of governments can count on powerful support from a people's prejudices, habits, and training. Despotism, depraving the soul of man, even exacts adoration; whereas initially liberty has a suspicious and frightening appearance. No politician can dream up a more extravagant idea than to believe that all it takes to make a foreign people adopt one's laws and one's constitution is for a people to appear with arms in hand. No one loves armed missionaries; the first counsel suggested by nature and prudence is to repulse them as enemies. I have said that such an invasion would be more likely to reawaken memories of the conflagration of the Palatinate * and of the last wars than to make our constitutional ideas germinate. The mass of the people in these regions is more familiar with the former events than with our constitution. The reports of enlightened men familiar with them contradict everything that we have been told

* [The reference is to the systematic "scorched earth" policy carried out in the German Rhineland by the armies of Louis XIV in 1689. (*Ed.*)]

concerning the fervor with which they [supposedly] sigh for our constitution and our armies. Before the effects of our revolution can be felt abroad, [the latter] must be consolidated [at home]. Wishing to carry freedom to them before we ourselves have gained it is to insure our own enslavement and that of the whole world.

To think that, from the moment one people gives itself a constitution, all others will respond instantly to this signal, is to nourish an absurd and exaggerated idea of things. Would the example of America that you have cited have been sufficient to break our chains had it not been [for the fact] that time and favorable circumstances had gradually brought on this revolution? The Declaration of [the] Rights [of Man] is no [sudden] sun ray illuminating all men instantaneously. Lightning does not strike all thrones at the same moment. It is easier to write [the Declaration of Rights] out on paper or to etch it on copper than to restore to the hearts of men its sacred letters, erased by ignorance, passion, and despotism. What am I saying? Even among you who have promulgated it, is it not daily repudiated, trampled underfoot and ignored? Does equality of rights really extend beyond the letter of our constitutional charge? Is not despotism, is not aristocracy reviving under different forms, again raising its hideous head? Are not weakness, virtue, and innocence still oppressed in the very name of the laws and of liberty? Does the constitution which, it is claimed, is the offspring of the Declaration of Rights really resemble its mother? What am I saying? Does this virgin, once a radiant celestial beauty, still resemble her [former] self? Was she not bruised and soiled at the impure hands of this conspiracy that disturbs and tyrannizes France today and that, awaiting only the adoption of the perfidious measures that I have been opposing, [seeks] to consummate its fatal plans? How can you then believe that at the very moment chosen by our internal enemies for war, the constitution can work the miracles it has not succeeded in producing at home?

I am far from claiming that, given time, our revolution will not influence the fate of the globe even sooner than present appearances seem to portend. God forbid that I should renounce such sweet hope. Yet I maintain that this will not happen today. I maintain that, at the very least, we have no proof and that in case of doubt we should not stake our liberty on this. I maintain that in order to carry such a venture to a successful conclusion at any time, the will [to prevail] is essential, whereas the government and its chief agents lack such a will, as they have openly admitted.

Lastly, do you want a sure antidote to all the illusions which you have been fed? Simply consider the natural course of revolutions. In constituted states, as is the case with almost all European countries, there are three powers: the monarch, the aristocrats, and the people. The people, however, are impotent. A revolution occurring in such a country can only be gradual. It is initiated by the nobles, the clergy, the rich, with the support of the people, to the extent that the latter's interest corresponds with the former's in resisting the dominant power—the monarch's. Thus in your case [in France], it was the *parlements* [sovereign courts], the nobles, the clergy, and the rich who set the revolution in motion, with the people making a belated appearance. When [those who began the revolution] became aware that the people could recover their sovereignty, they regretted [their action], or at least sought to arrest [the course of] the revolution. Nonetheless, they had been the initiators; without their resistance and miscalculations, the nation would still be under the yoke of despotism. According to this historical and moral verity, you may judge to what extent you may rely on the nations of Europe in general.

There the aristocrats, warned by our very example, are far from giving the signal for insurrection. In order to keep the people in irons and in ignorance, in order to escape the Declaration of Rights, these aristocrats, as hostile to the people and to equality as our own, have, also like our own, allied themselves to their governments. Do not point to the movements that are conspicuous in a few parts of Leopold's domains, and particularly in Belgium, for these movements are absolutely independent of our revolution and our present principles. The Belgian revolution took shape before our own did, [until] it was arrested by the intrigues of the court of Vienna, seconded by the French court's agents. Although today it may be ready to start up again, the influence, power and wealth of the aristocrats, and particularly of the clergy, that began [that revolution] is such that a century separates the Austrian Lowlands from yourselves, just as a century divides the people of your northern frontier provinces from those of your capital. To introduce abruptly into Belgium your secular organization of the clergy and the rest of your constitution would be enough to reconsolidate Leopold's power. By the force of superstition and habit, these people are condemned to attain liberty only by way of an aristocratic [stage].

On the basis of calculations as uncertain as these, how can one compromise the destiny of France and of all [other] peoples? . . .

Leave off, therefore, leave off all this deceptive rhetoric! Do not offer us this touching picture of happiness in order to draw us into real misfortunes. Give us fewer agreeable descriptions and more wise counsel.

You are even dispensed from talking at such great length about the resources, the interests and passions of the present princes and governments of Europe. You reproach me for not having discussed them fully enough. No! I shall do nothing of the sort: 1) because I do not want to stake the salvation of my country on conjectures which by their very nature are uncertain; 2) because no one is worth refuting who claims that all of the European powers banded together, allied to our internal enemies, are incapable of putting a common army into the field to back up the system of intrigue which I have described; 3) finally, this is not the heart of the question, for I maintain and shall prove that, whether the court or its supporting coalition wage war in earnest, or whether they do no more than prepare and threaten, in either case will they have furthered the success of their veritable plans.

At least spare yourself the contradictions which your system constantly displays. Do not tell us, first, that it is merely a question of chasing *the knights of Coblentz* twenty or thirty miles and returning in triumph, then that it is a matter of smashing the nations' chains. Don't tell us at one time that the European rulers will be the indifferent spectators of our conflict with the *émigrés* and of our incursions on German territory, while telling us at another time that we shall overthrow the governments of all these princes.

Yet even were I to adopt your favorite hypothesis, I would deduce from it an argument which I defy all your system's adherents to rebut convincingly. I offer them the following dilemma: either we must fear the foreign powers' intervention, in which case all your calculations are off; or the foreign powers will not become involved in your expedition at all, in which latter case France would confront no enemy other than that handful of *émigré* aristocrats, whom we barely noticed a little while ago. Do you claim that suddenly their power should alarm us? Supposing that [their power] is threatening, would it not evidently derive from their support by our internal foes whom you regard without mistrust? Everything proves that this ridiculous war is a scheme of the court and of the factions that tear us apart. To declare war on the basis of the court's good faith, to violate foreign territory—is this anything other than to support its views? . . .

Are the state's most vital interests to be dealt with in so cavalier a fashion?

Before you lose your way in international politics and among the countries of the European princes, look back at your internal position. Reestablish order at home before carrying liberty elsewhere. But you act as though this should not even be your concern, as though the ordinary rules of common sense did not apply to great politicoes. To put our finances back in order and put a stop to peculation, to arm the people and the national guards, to accomplish all that the government up to this point has tried to prevent, to be unafraid of our foes' attacks and the ministers' intrigues, to re-kindle public morale and the aversion to tyranny by means of good laws sustained by the energy, dignity and wisdom that alone can render us invincible in the face of our enemies—are all these just ridiculous ideas? War, war, from the very instant that the court demanded it! This decision is to supersede any other concern [as though] making war wiped out any other debt owed to the people. War against those who should be judged by a national tribunal, or war against the German princes? Confidence, adoration to our internal enemies! But what am I saying? Have we indeed any internal foes? No, you don't know of any. All you know is Coblentz. Have you not claimed that Coblentz is the focus of the infection? It is therefore not Paris? Is there no tie between Coblentz and another place not far from ourselves? You dare claim that the retrogression of the revolution has been caused by the fright that the long-despised fugitive aristocrats inspire? And from this very same nation you expect all kinds of miracles!

Hear then, that according to the opinion of all enlightened Frenchmen, the real Coblentz and its leaders are centered in France. The Coblentz of the Archbishop of Trier is but one cog in the far-reaching conspiracy against liberty. If you don't know all that, you are ignorant of everything going on in this country. If you are aware of it, why deny it? Why distract public attention from our most dangerous enemies to other things, if not in order to lead us into an ambush?

Evidently there are other people who, while fully alive to the gravity of our disease and its real cause, err as to the remedy. In a sort of despair, they want to embrace the idea of a foreign war, as though hoping that the very action of war would restore us to life, and that from the general confusion order and freedom would emerge. They commit the most fatal of errors in failing to grasp our circumstances and by confounding absolutely separate concepts. In the course of revolutions movements occur that are favorable to and others that are noxious to liberty, just as in illnesses there are salutary and mortal crises.

Favorable movements are those squarely directed against the tyrants, such as the American insurrection or that of July 14 [1789]. In our present circumstances, on the other hand, a foreign war, provoked and directed by the government, is a reactionary movement, a crisis that could lead to the death of the body politic. Such a war can only fool public opinion, lull the nation's justifiable anxiety, and forestall the salutary crisis that might have been brought on by the attacks of the enemies of freedom. It is from this point of view that I first drew attention to the disadvantages of this war. During a foreign war the people, as I have already mentioned, distracted by military events from the political deliberations concerning the essential foundations of liberty, pay less serious attention to the [hidden] maneuvers of the schemers who undermine [freedom], to the executive power that unsettles it, or to the corruption of the representatives who fail to defend it. This policy has always been known and, Monsieur Brissot notwithstanding, the example of the Roman aristocracy is applicable and striking. Whenever the people clamored for their rights against the usurpations of Senate and patricians, the Senate declared war. Then the people, forgetting their rights and their injuries, became so preoccupied with the war that they spared the Senate's powers, thus allowing the patricians to triumph once more.

War is good for military officers, for ambitious men, for speculators gambling on events of this sort. It is good for ministers whose activities war covers with a heavy and almost sacred veil. It is good for the court, good for the executive power whose authority, popularity, and preponderance is enhanced by virtue of war. It is good for the coalition of nobles, schemers, and moderates governing France, since they will be able to put their heroes and adherents at the head of the army. The court can deliver the powers of the state into the hands of men willing to serve it when the occasion arises, particularly when the latter have had a sort of patriotic reputation manufactured for them. They will gain the soldiers' hearts and confidence in order to enlist them more strongly in the cause of royalism and moderation. This is the only kind of seduction I dread for our soldiers: I don't need reassurance about their openly and willingly deserting the common weal. . . .

Can one get around all these facts by a dissertation on Roman dictatorship and by comparing Caesar to our generals? It has been said that through war the aristocrats within would be controlled by cutting them off from the inspiration for their scheming. Not at all, for they guess all all too well their secret confederates' intention to be fearful of the consequence. Sowing division and fanaticism, depraving public opinion, they will become even more active in the secret war which they have been waging against us with impunity. The moderate party in particular, whose leaders are the instigators of this conspiracy, will come to display all its sinister influence, all the while wearing the livery of patriotism. Then it will be in the name of the public weal, that anyone daring to voice his suspicion of the conduct or intentions of the executive power's agents. . . . namely, the generals, who will have become the hope and idols of the nation, will be reduced to silence. If one of these generals were destined to achieve some apparent success (which, I believe, would be neither very injurious to the *émigrés* nor fatal to their protectors), what ascendancy would not this provide for his party? What services could he not render the court? We would then seee a more determined war waged against the friends of freedom. We would then see the triumph of the perfidious system of egotism and intrigue. Once public opinion will have been corrupted, to what lengths will not the executive power and the subversives in its service go in their usurpations? . . .

"Our generals," you say, "will not betray us. And if we are betrayed, so much the better." I shall not tell you that I find this taste for treason singular, for in this respect

I agree with you. Yes, our foes are too clever to betray us openly in the way you mean. The kind of treason we have to fear, as I have just explained to you, does not alert public vigilance. It prolongs the people's sleep until the moment has come to enchain them. This kind of treason leaves us helpless. All those who lull the people into somnolence work in behalf of treason. And, note well, in order to succeed at this it is not even necessary to wage war seriously. All that it takes is to put us on a wartime footing. Talking of the idea of foreign war suffices. Even if nothing more is garnered than the millions collected in advance [preparation], all labor would not be lost. These twenty millions, especially at the present moment, are worth at least as much as the patriotic speeches preaching confidence and war to the people. . . .

You have been astonished, you have said, to hear the people's advocate slander and vilify the people. Surely I did not expect such a reproach. First of all, know that I am not the people's advocate, that I never claimed such an ostentatious title. I belong to the people; this is all I have ever been and want to be. . . .

What, then, should I say to the reproach of having vilified and slandered the people? No, one does not vilify what one loves; one does not slander oneself.

I to have vilified the people! It is true that I am ignorant of [the art of] flattering the people in order to bring about their destruction, that I am ignorant of the trick of leading them on flower-strewn paths to the edge of the abyss. On the contrary, it is I who have learned to displease those not of the people by defending almost singlehandedly the rights of the poorest and most miserable citizens against a majority of the legislators. It was I who upheld the Declaration of Rights against all [those who by setting up] discrimination based on tax assessment opened a chasm between one set of citizens and another. It was I who defended, not only the people's rights but their character and their virtue, who maintained in the face of pride and prejudice that the vices detrimental to humanity and the social order (as well as the artificial needs and egotism which they bred) steadily decreased as one moved from the throne to the peasant's hut. It was I who was willing to seem an extremist, [to appear] stubborn, even conceited, in order to be just.

It is scarcely the true way of showing one's respect for the people to lull them to sleep by praising their strength and liberty. It consists rather in defending the people by forearming them against their own faults—for faults they have. The phrase "The people never sleep" is, in this sense, very dangerous. No one has given us a truer idea [of the people] than did Rousseau, because no one loved them more than he. "The people always desire what is good, but do not always perceive it." To complete the theory of governmental principles, it would be enough to add that the people's mandatories often perceive what is good but do not always desire it. The people want what is good because the commonwealth is their interest, because good laws are their safeguard. Their mandatories do not always want it, because they acquire their own special interests and want to wield the authority confided to them to enhance their own pride. Read what Rousseau has written about representative government and judge for yourself whether the people may sleep with impunity. The people, nevertheless, feel more keenly and see more sharply all that has to do with the first principles of justice and humanity than most of their so-called superiors. Their common sense in this respect is often superior to the wit of clever men. Yet the people lack a similar aptitude for uncovering the ramifications of the artful politics designed to deceive and enslave them. Their natural goodness makes them the dupes of political charlatans, [a fact] which the latter know and use to their profit.

When the people awaken in all their power and majesty (something which happens but once in the course of centuries), everything bows before them. Before them, despotism grovels in the dust, feigning death like a cowardly and vicious animal confronting a lion. Yet [despotism] soon rises again, flattering the people in order to substitute trickery for force. As soon as the despot utters the word "liberty," the people, assuming his conversion, show joy and enthusiasm. Immense treasures—the public wealth—are handed over to the despot, thus offering him colossal power. Though despotism can now dangle irresistible lures before the ambition and cupidity of its supporters, the people can offer only their esteem to those who serve them. Soon all those combining vice and talent side with despotism in carrying out its organized plan of intrigue and seduction. Above all, despotism tries to corrupt public opinion by reawakening ancient prejudices and habits as yet not eliminated and to encourage a moral depravity as yet not regenerated. Despotism nips new virtues in the bud, while the unnumbered horde of its ambitious slaves spreads false maxims everywhere. Nothing but quiet and confidence is preached to the citizens. The word "liberty" becomes almost a seditious cry as its most zealous defenders are persecuted and slandered. Attempts are made to lead astray, to seduce, or to overcome the people's delegates. [Henceforth] the men who betray the people's confidence and sell their rights enjoy the fruits of their misdeeds in peace. They shall confront imitators who, while opposing them, only aspire to replace them. . . . In time, disunity will prevail everywhere; all the tyrants' snares will be sprung; the enemies of equality will be fully assembled, led by the very men entrusted with public authority, by which time the class of citizens most influential by education and wealth will be ready to join the [despot's] faction.

Here [then] lies the nation, facing the choice of servitude or civil war. Insurrection is the remedy suggested to the people; yet is even this remedy of last resort possible? In such a vast state, torn by disunity, for all areas to rise at once is impossible, yet any partial insurrection is regarded as an act of rebellion punishable by law, a law wielded by conspirators' hands. Though the people are sovereign, they cannot exercise their sovereignty. While the people as a whole cannot meet, the law forbids any fraction of the people [to assemble and] to deliberate. What am I saying? Neither opinion nor thought would then remain free. Writers would be in the government's pay. Defenders of liberty still daring to raise a voice would be looked upon as sedition-mongers, for sedition is any sign of life displeasing to the stronger. [Defenders of liberty] would drink the hemlock like Socrates, expire under the sword of tyranny like Sidney, or disembowel themselves like Cato.

Is this terrifying picture actually applicable to our own situation? No, we have not yet reached the last stage of opprobrium and misfortune to which the people's credulity and the tyrants' perfidy point. They are attempting to lead you there. Though we have perhaps already taken sizeable steps in that direction, we still have a long way to go. I hope, I do not even doubt, but that freedom will triumph, provided only that we adopt sooner or later, indeed as soon as possible, the principles and characters of free men, that we close our ears to the siren song attracting us to the shoals of despotism, that we stop marching like a dumb flock along the road by which we are being led to slavery or to death. . . .

৶ SPEECH ON REVOLUTIONARY POLICY

Maximilien de Robespierre

During one crucial year, from July, 1793, to July, 1794, revolutionary France was governed by a dictatorial government of national emergency. This temporary dictatorship had been improvised when the French National Assembly (which, for the period 1792–1795, went by the name of "National Convention") extended the powers of one of its already-existing committees, staffing it with a group of extraordinarily able and determined revolutionaries. This Committee of Public Safety assumed most executive and many administrative governmental functions—conducting war and foreign policy, ordering arrests, directing the country's economic life, proposing new legislation—although remaining ultimately accountable to the Convention. Every month the dozen members of the committee were regularly reelected to their posts by the legislature. In this sense the Committee of Public Safety always remained a revocable dictatorship.

In the summer of 1793, when the committee assumed power, the French Republic was in desperate straits. Except for the districts around Paris, much of France was in open rebellion against the central government. "Federalist" insurrections in Normandy, at Bordeaux, Marseille, and Lyon, had been sparked by a purge of republican moderates from the Convention in June, 1793. In the west, in Brittany and the Vendée, Catholicism and aversion to the draft had rallied the peasants to counter-revolution. At the same time, French armies, disorganized by the mass desertion of aristocratic officers, were caving in before Spanish, Piedmontese, Austrian, and Prussian assaults, while the British fleet controlled the French coastline. By February, 1794, by sheer organizing ability complemented by appeals to patriotism as well as by ruthless repression, the Committee of Public Safety had succeeded in mastering both the internal and external threat. By a combination of persuasion and violence, the central government's authority had been reestablished throughout France, and the war, though by no means won, was gradually moving from French to foreign soil.

The speech of Maximilien de Robespierre (see page 375) of February 5, 1794, defending the policy of the Committee of Public Safety before the National Convention, should be considered against this background of a desperate but successful revolutionary effort. Although at this time Robespierre was only one of eleven members of the committee (one member had been purged earlier), he usually appeared as the committee's public spokesman before the legislature and before the Paris Jacobin Club. In the public mind he therefore came to be identified with the whole committee to the point where he was widely believed to wield dictatorial powers. In point of fact, in July, 1794, when, for a variety of contradictory reasons, his policies lost the support of the majority of of his colleagues on the Committee of Public Safety and of the National Convention as well, Robespierre and his closest collaborators were promptly removed, outlawed, and executed.

After having long proceeded at random, and hurried on, as it were, by the impulse of contrary factions, the Representatives of the French People have at length shown a character and a government.—A sudden change in the fortune of the nation announced to Europe the regeneration which was effected in the National Representation: But it must be allowed, that till that moment to which I allude, we were guided, in circumstances so tempestuous, rather by the love of Public Good and a sense of the wants of our Country, than by an exact theory, and the precise rules of conduct which we had not leisure to trace out. It is time to define clearly the object of the Revolution, and the boundary at which we wish to arrive. It is time to give an account to ourselves both of the obstacles which still keep us at a distance from it, and of the means which we ought to adopt in order to reach it—a simple and important idea which seems never to have been perceived. How could a vile and corrupted Government dare to realize it? a King, a haughty Senate, a Caesar, a Cromwell, must first cover their projects with the veil of religion, intrigue with every vice, caress all parties, crush that composed of men of worth, oppress or deceive the People, to attain the end of their perfidious ambition. Had we not had a greater task to perform; had nothing been in agitation here, but the interests of a faction, or of a new aristocracy, we might have believed, with certain writers still more ignorant than wicked, that the plan of the French Revolution was written in every respect in the works of TACITUS and MACHIAVEL, and might have sought for the duties of the Representatives of the People in the History of AUGUSTUS, TIBERIUS or VESPASIAN, or even in that of certain French Legislators, as all Tyrants are worthy of serving each other as models; for, some shades of cruelty or perfidy excepted, all Tyrants resemble each other.

Robespierre's Speech to the National Convention of France on the Seventh [sic!] of February 1794 on the Principles of Moral Policy Which Ought to Actuate the Convention in the Internal Administration of the Republic (London, 1794), pp. 3–27.

As for me, I shall entrust the whole world with your political secrets, in order that all the Friends of their Country may rally at the call of Reason and Public Interest; in order that the French Nation may be respected in all countries of the universe to which a knowledge of their real principles may be conveyed; and in order that intriguers, who always endeavour to fill the places of other intriguers, may be judged by public opinion according to sure and easy rules. We must at a distance take precautions to commit the destiny of Liberty into the hands of Truth, which is eternal, rather than into those of men, who pass away; and in such a manner, that if Government forgets the interests of the People, or if it fall into the hands of corrupted men, according to the natural course of things, the light of known principles may discover their treacheries, and that every new faction may find its destruction in the perfidy of its crimes. Happy the people who can attain this point! For whatever new insults may be prepared for them, an order of things, where Public Reason is the guaranty of their Liberty, presents innumerable resources. What is the object to which we look forward? The peaceable enjoyment of Liberty and Equality, the reign of that Eternal Justice, the laws of which have been engraven, not on marble or stone, but in the hearts of all men, even in that of the Slave, who forgets them, or that of the Tyrant, who denies them. We wish for an order of things in which all the mean and cruel passions may be unknown; in which all the beneficent and generous passions may be called forth by the laws; in which ambition may be the desire of meriting glory, and of serving the Country; in which distinctions shall arise only from that Equality by which the Citizen is subjected to the Magistrate, the Magistrate to the People, and the People to Justice: in which the Country shall insure the happiness of each individual, and in which each individual shall with pride enjoy the glory and prosperity of his Country; in which the mind shall be enlarged by the continual communication of Republican sentiments, and by the necessity of meriting the esteem of a great people; in which the arts shall be the decorations of Liberty which enobles them, Commerce the source of Public Riches, and not of the overgrown opulence of some families.

We wish to substitute in our Country morality for self-interest, probity for honour, principles for custom, duties for ceremony, the empire of reason for the tyranny of fashion, the contempt of vice for that of misfortune, dignity for insolence, greatness of mind for vanity, love of glory for love of money, good men for good companions, merit for intrigue, genius for wit, truth for splendour, the charms of happiness for the languor of voluptuousness, the greatness of man for the littleness of the great, a magnanimous people, powerful and happy, for a people polite, frivolous, and wretched; that is to say, all the virtues and all the wonderful effects of a Republic, for all the vices and ridiculous pageantry of a Monarchy. In a word, we wish to comply with the will of nature, to accomplish the destiny of mankind, to keep the promises of philosophy, and to acquit Providence for the long reign of vice and tyranny.

Let France, formerly illustrious among slavish countries, eclipsing the glory of all free states who have existed, become a model to nations, the terror of oppressors, the ornament of the Universe, and in sealing our courage with our blood, may we at last see dawn around us the Aurora of universal felicity. This is our ambition—this is our object. What kind of Government can realize these wonders? A Democratic or Republican Government alone. These two words are synonimous, notwithstanding the abuse of vulgar language; for an Aristocracy is no more a Republic than Monarchy. Democracy is not a state in which the people, continually assembled, regulate by themselves all public affairs; still less that, where an hundred thousand factions of the people, by separate measures rash and contradictory, decide the fate of a whole society. Such a government never existed, and it could never exist without bringing back the people to despotism. Democracy is a state in which the people are the Sovereign guided by laws of their own framing, and in which they do every thing by themselves that can be done properly, and by Delegates what they cannot do of themselves.

It is then in the principles of the Democratic Government that you must search for the rules of your political conduct. But to found and consolidate Democracy amongst us—to arrive at the peaceful reign of constitutional laws, we must terminate the war of Liberty against Tyranny, and happily steer through the storms of the Revolution: such is the object of the Revolutionary system which you have organized. You ought still to regulate your conduct according to the tempestuous circumstances under which the Republic is, and the plan of your administration ought to be the result of the spirit of the Revolutionary Government, combined with the general principles of Democracy: but what is the fundamental principle of a Democratical or Popular Government; that is to say, the essential spring which supports it and puts it in motion? It is virtue; I speak of public virtue, which effected so many wonders in Greece and Rome, and which ought to produce much more astonishing wonders in the French Republican, of that virtue which is nothing else than the love of one's country and of its laws. But as the essence of a Republic or Democracy, is equality, it follows, that love of one's country necessarily comprehends the love of equality. It is true that this sublime sentiment supposes a preference of Public Interest to all Private Interest; from which it results, that the love of one's country supposes also, or produces all the virtues; for what else are they but that strength of soul which renders it capable of making these sacrifices? And how can the slave of avarice or ambition, for example, sacrifice his idol to his country?

Virtue is not only the soul of Democracy, but it cannot exist but in that government. In a Monarchy I know only one individual who can love his country, and who to do that has not even occasion for virtue. It is the Monarch; the reason is, that of all the inhabitants of his states, the Monarch is the only one who has a country.—Is he not the Sovereign? Is he not in the place of the people? And what is one's country if it is not the country where one is a Citizen, and a member of the Sovereign? By a consequence of the same principle in Aristocratical states, the word country signifies nothing but for families who have seized on the Sovereignty. It is only a Democracy where the State is really the Country of all the individuals who compose it, and which may reckon as many defenders interested in its cause as it contains Citizens. This is the superiority of free People over others. If Athens and Sparta triumphed over the tyrants of Asia, and the Swiss over the tyrants of Spain and Austria, it was owing entirely to this cause—but the French are the first People in the World who have established a real Democracy, by inviting all men to Equality and the Rights of Citizens in the utmost extent; and this, in my opinion, is the real cause why all the tyrants leagued against the Republic have been defeated.

Great consequences must, from this moment, be drawn from the principles I have laid down. Since Virtue and Equality are the soul of the Republic, and since your object is to found and consolidate this form of Government, it follows, that the first rule of your political conduct ought to be to direct all your operations towards the support of Equality, and to the promoting of Virtue; for the first care of the Legislator ought to be to strengthen the principle of Government. Every thing, therefore, which tends to excite the love of one's Country, to reform manners, to elevate the mind, to direct the passions of the heart towards the Public Interest, ought to be adopted or established by you; every thing that tends to concentrate them in the meanness of self, to awaken their desire for little things, and their contempt for great, ought to be rejected or repressed by you.

In the system of the French Revolution, what is immoral is impolitic, what tends to corrupt is Counter-revolutionary. Weakness, vices, prejudices, are the way to Royalty. Hurried away perhaps too often by the force of our ancient habitudes, as much as by the insensible bent of human weakness, towards false ideas and pusillanimous sentiments—we have much more to guard against excess of weakness than excess of energy. The greatest quicksand, perhaps, which we have to avoid, is not fervour of zeal, but rather lassitude of the Public Good, and dissidence of our own courage. Wind up, therefore, continually the spring of Republican Government instead of suffering it to be relaxed.

I have no occasion to say that I will not here justify any excess. The most sacred principles are abused. It belongs to the wisdom of Government to consult circumstances, to seize favourable opportunities, and to choose means, respecting the manner of paving the way for great events. It is an eseential part of talents to accomplish them, as wisdom is itself a part of virtue. We do not pretend to cast the French Republic in the mould of that of Sparta—we wish to give it neither the austerity nor the corruption of cloisters. I have presented to you in its full purity the moral and political principles of Popular Government. You have then a compass to direct you amidst the storms of jarring passions, and that hurricane of intrigue, which surrounds you. You have the touchstone, by which you may prove all the laws and all the propositions made to you; and continually comparing them with this principle, you may hereafter avoid the usual quicksand of all great assemblies, the danger of surprises, and precipitate, incoherent, and contradictory measures; and may give to all your operations that unity, wisdom and dignity, which ought to announce you as the first People of the World. It is not the easy consequences of the principle of Democracy that we ought to detail—it is the simple and easy principle itself which ought to be displayed.

Republican virtue may be considered as it relates to the People, and as it relates to the Government.—It is necessary in both. When the Government alone is destitute of it, a resource remains in that of the people; but when the people themselves are corrupted, Liberty is lost. Virtue, fortunately, is natural to the people, in spite of Aristocratical prejudices. A nation is truly corrupted, when, after having lost by degrees its character and its liberty, it passes from Democracy to Aristocracy or Monarchy: this is the death of the political body through decrepitude. When after four hundred years of glory, avarice, at length, banished from Sparta morals, together with the laws of LYCURGUS; in vain did AGIS lay down his life in attempting to recall them.

In vain did DEMOSTHENES thunder forth against PHILIP: PHILIP found at Athens degenerate advocates more eloquent than DEMOSTHENES. There is still at Athens a population as numerous as in the time of MILTIADES and ARISTIDES; but there are no longer Athenians, Of what avail is it that BRUTUS killed the tyrant? Tyranny still lives in hearts; and Rome exists no longer but in BRUTUS. But, when, by prodigious efforts of courage and reason, a people break the chains of despotism to convert them into trophies to Liberty; when by the force of their moral temperament they escape, in some measure, from the arms of death to resume all the vigour of youth; when, in terms, feeling and haughty, intrepid and tractable, they can be checked neither by ramparts almost impregnable, nor by the numerous armies of tyrants marshalled against them, while they stop of themselves before the image of the Law, if they do not soar with rapidity to the height of their destiny, it can only be through the fault of those who govern them. Besides, it may be said, in one sense, that the people, to love justice and equality, have no need of great virtue: it will be sufficient for them to love themselves. But the Magistrate is obliged to sacrifice his interest to the interest of the people, and the pride of power to equality.

Above all, the law must speak with authority to him who is the organ of it: Government must feel its own weight, to keep all its parts in harmony with it. If there exists a representative body, a first authority constituted by the people, it belongs to it to continually watch over, and repress all public functionaries: but how will it be repressed if not by its own virtue? The more elevated this source of public order is, the purer it ought to be. The representative body then must begin by subjecting, in its own bosom, all private passions to a general passion for the public good. Happy are representatives when their glory and interest, as much as their duty, attach them to the cause of liberty! From this let us deduce a great truth: It is, that the characteristic of popular government is to have a confidence in the people, and to be severe to one's self. To this all the exposition of our theory would be confined, had you to guide the vessel of the Republic only during a calm. But the tempest howls, and the present state of the Revolution imposes on you another task.

The great purity of the basis of the French Revolution, the sublimity even of its object, is precisely what constitutes our strength and our weakness—our strength, because it gives us the ascendancy of truth over imposture; and the rights of public over private interest: our weakness, because it rallies against us all vicious men; all those who, in their hearts, were plotting to plunder the people; all those who wished to plunder them with impunity; all those who opposed liberty as a personal misfortune; and those who embraced the Revolution as a trade, and the Republic as their prey. Hence the defection of so many ambitious and avaricious men who, since the time when we started, abandoned us on the road, because they did not undertake the journey with a view of arriving at the same point.

It may be said, that two contrary Genii, who have been represented as contending for the empire of nature, combat, in this grand epoch of the history of mankind, to fix unalterably the destiny of the world; and that France is the theatre of this formidable contest: without all the tyrants surround you; within all the friends of tyranny conspire against you, and they will continue to conspire until vice be deprived of its hopes. We must destroy the internal and external enemies of the Republic, or perish along with it; but in this situation, the first maxim of your policy ought to be to rule the people by reason, and your enemies by terror. If the spring of popular government, during peace, be virtue, the spring of popular government, during a revolution, is both *virtue* and *terror:* virtue, without which, terror is fatal: terror, without which, virtue is ineffectual. Terror is nothing else than speedy, severe, and inflexible justice. It is, therefore, an emanation of virtue. It is not so much a distinct principle, as a consequence of the general principle of democracy applied to the most urgent wants of the country.

It has been said that terror is the main spring of a despotic government—Shall ours then resemble despotism? Yes, as the sword which glances in the hand of the hero of liberty resembles that with which the satellites of Tyranny are armed. Let the Despot by terror govern his debased subjects: as a despot, he is in the right. Subdue by terror the enemies of Liberty, and you will be right, as the founders of the Republic. The government of a Revolution is the despotism of Liberty against Tyranny. Is force made only to protect vice? and is it not to strike the haughty head that thunder is destined? Nature imposes upon every moral and physical being the law of providing for its own preservation. Vice destroys innocence, in order to reign; and innocence struggles with all its force in the hands of vice.

Let tyranny reign one day, and next morning there will not remain a single patriot. How long will the fury of despots be called justice, and the justice of the people barbarity and rebellion? How tender one is towards oppressors, and inexorable towards the oppressed! Nothing is more natural than that whoever does not hate vice cannot love virtue; one or the other, however, must fall. Indulgence towards the Royalists, exclaim some; pardon for villains! No—pardon for innocence; pardon for the weak; pardon for the unfortunate; pardon for humanity! Protection is due from society only to peaceable Citizens: there are no Citizens in a Republic but Republicans: Royalists and Aliens are rather enemies. Is not this terrible war excited by Liberty against Tyranny indivisible? Are not our internal in alliance with our external enemies? Are the assassins, who tear the country within, the intriguers and traitors who fell themselves, the libelists paid to discredit the cause of the people, to destroy public virtue, to kindle up the flames of civil discord, and to pave the way for a political by a moral counter-revolution, are these people less criminal, or less dangerous than the tyrants whom they serve? All those who interpose their patricide lenity between these villains and the avenging sword of National Justice, resemble those who should throw themselves between the satellites of tyrants and the bayonets of our soldiers; all the transports of their false sensibility appear to me only as sighs, emitted towards England and Austria.

For whom then should their hearts melt with pity? For those 20,000 heroes, the flower of the nation, destroyed by the swords of the enemies of Liberty, or by the poignards of royal and federalist assassins! No—these were only plebeians, patriots. To be entitled to tender feelings, one must at least be the widow of a General, who has twenty times betrayed his country. One must almost prove, that one has caused ten thousand Frenchmen to be sacrificed, as a Roman General, to obtain a triumph, must have killed, I believe, ten thousand of the enemy.—People hear with cool indifference a recital of the horrors committed by the tyrants against the defenders of Liberty; our women dreadfully mutilated; our children massacred in the arms of their mothers; our prisoners suffering exquisite torments on account of their sublime and affecting heroism; and yet the too slow punishment of a few monsters, who have fattened on the pure blood of their country, is called horrid butchery. The misery of generous citizens, who have sacrificed to the noblest of causes their brethren, children and wives, is beheld with little emotion: but the most generous consolations are lavished on the wives of conspirators. It is admitted that they pervert justice and plead against Liberty, the cause of their relations and accomplices: they are made almost a privileged corporation. Ye creditors and pensioners of the People, with what mildness are we still the dupes of words? How much aristocracy and moderatism still govern us by the destructive maxims they have given us! Aristocracy defends itself better by its intrigues, than patriotism by its services. Revolutions are governed by the chicane of Palaces; conspiracies against the Republic are treated like the trials of individuals. Tyranny kills— Liberty pleads—and the code made by the conspirators themselves, is the law by which they are tried.

When the safety of the Country is concerned, the testimony of the Universe cannot be substituted for evidence, nor evidence for literal proof. Slowness in passing sentence is equivalent to impunity. The uncertainty of punishment encourages all criminals, and yet complaints are made of the severity of Justice! Complaints are made that the enemies of the Republic are kept in confinement! Examples are fought for in the history of tyrants, because they will not select them from that of the People, nor draw them from the genius of threatened Liberty. At Rome, when the Consul discovered a conspiracy, and stifled it at the same time by the death of the accomplices of Cataline, he was accused of having violated the established forms. By whom was this done? by the ambitious Caesar, who wished to encrease his party of conspirators; by the Pisos; by Clodius; and all the bad citizens who dreaded the virtue of a true Roman, and the severity of the laws. To punish the oppressors of mankind is clemency; to pardon them barbarity. The severity of tyrants, has no other principle than severity: that of the Republican government arises from beneficence. Woe to him, therefore, who shall dare to direct towards the People that terror which ought to approach only its enemies. Woe to him who, confounding the unavoidable terrors of patriotism with the devised errors of perfidy, or with the crimes of conspirators, shall abandon the dangerous intriguer to pursue the peaceable citizen! Perish the villain, who dares to abuse the sacred name of Liberty, or the arms which have been entrusted to him, to convey mourning or death into the hearts of the patriots! There can be no doubt that this abuse has existed. It has, doubtless, been exaggerated by aristocracy; but if there existed in the Republic only one virtuous man, persecuted by the enemies of Liberty, it would be the duty of Government to use the utmost diligence to discover him, and avenge him in an exemplary manner.

But must it be concluded from these persecutions, excited against the patriots, by the hypocritical zeal of the Counter-revolutionists, that we ought to set at liberty the Counter-revolutionists, and to renounce severity? These new crimes of aristocracy only prove the necessity of it. What does the audacity of our enemies prove, if not the remissness with which they have been pursued? It is owing, in a great measure, to the doctrine which has been preached up to give them confidence. If you reject this advice, your enemies will accomplish their end, and will receive from your own hands the reward of the last of their crimes. How weak would it be to consider some victories, gained by patriotism, as the end of all our dangers?

Take a view of our real situation, and you will find that vigilance and energy will be more necessary for you than ever. A secret malevolence every where thwarts the operations of Government. The fatal influence of foreigners, though more concealed, is neither less active, nor less fatal. It is perceived that undaunted vice only uses more address to conceal its progress. The internal enemies of the French People are divided into two sections, as an army into two corps. They march under banners of different colours, and by different routes; but they both march towards the same object. This òbject is the disorganization of the Popular Government, the ruin of the Convention; that is to say, the triumph of tyranny—one of these two factions drives us towards weakness, the other to excess. The one wishes to convert Liberty into a bacchanalian, the other into a prostitute. Subaltern intriguers, and even good citizens misled, avenge themselves sometimes on both parties; but the chiefs belong to the cause of Kings and Aristocracy, and always unite against the Patriots. These villains, even when they make war against each other, do not hate one another so much as they detest honest men. The country is their prey: the quarrel respecting the partition of it; but they league together against those who defend it. The name of *Moderates* has been given to the one: there is, perhaps, more ingenuity than justness in the denomination of *ultra-revolutionists,* by which the other has been distinguished. This denomination, which cannot in any case be applied to honest men, who by zeal may be led beyond the sound policy of the Revolution, does not exactly characterize those perfidious men, whom tyranny keeps in pay, in order to endanger, by false or destructive applications, the sacred principles of our Revolution.

The false Revolutionist is, perhaps, still oftener on this side than beyond the Revolution. He is moderate, he is mad with patriotism, according to circumstances. What he will think to morrow is resolved in the Prussian, English, Austrian, and even Russian Committees. He opposes measures of energy; and exaggerates them when he cannot prevent them. Severe towards innocence, but indulgent towards vice, accusing even the guilty who are not rich enough to purchase his silence, nor of importance enough to be the objects of his zeal, but taking good care never to expose himself so far as to defend virtue calumniated; discovering sometimes open plots; tearing the mask from traitors unmasked, and even decapitated, but extolling traitors alive and possessed of influence; eager always to embrace the opinion of the moment, and no less attentive never to enlighten it, and above all never to oppose it; always ready to adopt bold measures, provided they are attended with many inconveniencies; calumniating those which present only advantages, or adding to them those amendments which may render them hurtful; oeconomical in speaking truth, and speaking it only with a view of acquiring a right to lie with impunity; distributing good, drop by drop, and pouring out mischief by torrents; filled with ardour for grand Revolutions, which are of no avail; more than indifferent for those which may honour the cause of the People, and save the Country; setting great value on forms of patriotism; strongly attached, like devotees, of whom he declares himself the enemy, to recluse practices, he would rather use one hundred red caps than do one good action.

What difference do you find between these people and your moderates? They are servants employed by the same master; or, if you choose, accomplices, who pretend to quarrel that they may the better conceal their crimes. Judge them not by the difference of language, but by the identity of results. Is not he who attacks the National Convention by foolish speeches, and he who deceives, to expose it to danger, in concert with him who by unjust severity obliges patriotism to tremble for itself, and to invoke humanity in favour of aristocracy and treason? One would invite France to the conquest of the world, who had no other design than to invite tyrants to conquer France. The foreign hypocrite, who, five years ago, declared Paris to be the capital of the world, transcribed only in another jargon the anathemas of the vile federalists * who devoted Paris to destruction. To preach up atheism is only a method of absolving superstition, and of accusing philosophy; and the war declared against the Deity is only a diversion in favour of royalty. What other method remains of combating liberty? Will they, after the example of the first champions of aristocracy, go and extol the mildness of slavery, the advantages of monarchy, the supernatural genius and incomparable virtue of kings? will they proclaim the vanity of the rights of man, and of the principles of Eternal Justice? will they go and raise from the grave the Nobility and Clergy, or claim the imprescriptible rights of the higher citizens, to their double succession? No—it is much more convenient to assume the mask of patriotism, to disfigure by insolent parodies the sublime drama of the Revolution, and to endanger the cause of liberty by hypocrtical moderation, and by studied acts of folly.

Thus Aristocracy constitutes itself into popular assemblies: Counter-revolutionary pride conceals, under rags, its plots and its poignards; fanaticism destroys its own altars; royalty celebrates, in songs, the victories of the Republic; the Nobility, galled by recollection, tenderly embrace equality, in order to stifle it; and tyranny, stained with the blood of the defenders of liberty, bestrews their grave with flowers. If the hearts of all are not changed, how many visages are masked!—How many traitors intermeddle in our affairs only to ruin us!—Do you wish to put them to the proof?— Ask from them the bond of an oath and declarations, that they will perform real services. Is it necessary to act? they harangue. Is deliberation required? they wish to begin by acting. Are the times peaceable? they oppose every useful change. Are they tempestuous? they speak of reforming every thing to overturn every thing. Do you wish to repress the seditious? they remind you of the clemency of CAESAR. Do you wish to snatch the patriots from persecution? they propose to you as a model the firmness of BRUTUS. They discover that such a one acted nobly when he served the Republic; but they are silent when he betrays it. Is peace useful? they display to you the palms of victory. Is war necessary? they extol to you the sweets of peace. Is it requisite to defend our territories? they wish to go and drive the tyrants beyond the seas and the mountains. Are we desirous of recovering fortresses? they wish to take

* [Refers to various provincial rebellions against the Paris government, like those in Lyon and Marseille in 1793. (*Ed.*)]

churches by assault, and to scale Heaven. They forget the Austrians in order to make war on devotees. Is it necessary to support our cause by the fidelity of our Allies? they declaim against all Governments, and propose to you to put even the great MOGUL in a state of accusation. Do the people go to the capitol to thank GOD for their victories? they give vent to lamentations for our past misfortunes. Are we preparing to gain new ones? they disseminate among us, hatred, division, persecution, and discouragement. Is it requisite to realize the sovereignty of the people, and concentrate their strength by a firm and respectable Government? they find that the principles of the Government violate the sovereignty of the people. Is it necessary to assert the rights of the people oppressed by the Government? they speak only of respect for the laws, and the constituted authorities.

They have found out an admirable expedient to second the efforts of the Republican Government, which is to disorganize and degrade it completely; to make war on the patriots who have contributed to our success. Do you seek for the means of supplying your armies with provisions? Are you employed in tearing from avarice and timidity those provisions which they hoard? they emit patriotic groans for the public misery, and announce famine. The desire of preventing the evil is to them always a motive for increasing it. In the North, they have killed the poultry, and deprived us of eggs, under the pretence that the poultry consumed grain. In the South it was in agitation to destroy the mulberry and orange trees, under pretence that silk is an object of luxury, and oranges a superfluity. You can never imagine what excesses hypocritical counter-revolutionists have committed in order to tarnish the cause of the Revolution.

Can you believe that, in countries where superstition has exercised the greatest power, not satisfied with overloading the operations respecting worship with all those forms which would render them odious, they have spread terror among the people, by propagating a report, that all the children below ten years of age, and all the old people above seventy, were to be put to death! This report has been propagated above all in the *ci-devant* * Britanny, and in the departments of the Rhine and Mozelle. This is one of the crimes ascribed to the *ci-devant* Public Accuser of the criminal tribunal of Strasburgh. The tyrannical follies of this man render probable every thing related of CALIGULA and HELIOGABALUS; but one can scarcely give credit to them, even when proofs are exhibited. He carried his madness so far as to put women in a state of requisition for his own use. We are assured that he employed this method to get married. Whence issued all of a sudden, that swarm of foreigners, priests, nobility and intriguers of every kind, who, at the same moment dispersed themselves throughout the Republic, to execute, in the name of philosophy, the plan of a counter-revolution, which could not be defeated but by the force of public reason? Execrable conception, worthy of the genius of foreign courts leagued against liberty, and of the corruption of all the internal enemies of the Republic! It is thus that with the continual miracles operated by the virtue of a great people, intrigue always intermixes the baseness of its criminal plots—a baseness commanded by tyrants, and which they afterwards make the basis of their ridiculous manifestoes, to keep the ignorant people sunk in the mire of opprobrium, and in the paths of slavery.

* [Former; often referring to a position or status prior to the revolution. (*Ed.*)]

But what does liberty suffer from the crimes of its enemies? Is the sun, when obscured by a passing cloud, less that luminary, which animates all nature? Does the impure scum, with which the ocean covers its shores, render it less awful? In perfidious hands all the remedies of our evils become poisons. Whatever you may do, whatever you may say, they will turn against you even the truths which you have unfolded. Thus, for example, after having every where scattered the seeds of civil war by a violent attack on religious prejudices, they will endeavour to arm fanaticism and aristocracy with those measures, even, which, you have prescribed in favour of liberty of worship. Had you left a free course to the conspiracy, it would have produced, a little later, a terrible and universal re-action. If you check it, they will endeavour to profit by it, by persuading the people that you afford protection to priests and the moderates. You must not even be astonished if the authors of this system are those priests who have been the most forward to acknowledge their quackery. If patriots, hurried away by a pure, but inconsiderate zeal, have, in some parts become the dupes of their intrigues, they will throw the whole blame on the patriots; for the first point of their Machiavelian doctrine is to ruin the Republic, by ruining the Republicans, as one subdues a people by destroying the army which defends them. From this we may appreciate one of their favourite doctrines, which is, that men ought to be accounted as nothing: a maxim of regal origin, and which implies that all the friends of liberty must be abandoned to them.

It is to be remarked, that the destiny of men who seek only to promote the public good, is to become the victims of those whose sole wish is to promote their own. This arises from two causes; the first is, that intriguers carry on their attack with the vices of the ancient government; the second, that the patriots defend themselves only with the virtues of the new. Such an internal situation ought to appear to you worthy of your whole attention; if you reflect that you have to combat, at the same time, the tyrants of Europe, to maintain 1,200,000 men in arms; and that government is obliged to repair, continually, by energy and vigilance, all those evils which the innummerable multitude of our enemies have been creating to us during the course of five years.

What is the remedy of all those evils? I know no other than the expansion of that general spring of the Republic, virtue. Democracy perishes by two kinds of excess—the aristocracy of those who govern, or the contempt of the people for those authorities which they themselves have established—a contempt which causes every club, and every individual, to assume the public power, and which, by excess of disorder, conducts the people to annihilation, or the government of One. The double talk of the moderates, and counter-revolutionists, is to keep us continually tossed between these two quicksands. The Representatives of the people may avoid them both; for government has it always in its power to be just or wise; and when it possesses this character, it is sure of the confidence of the people.

It is very true, that the object of all our enemies is to dissolve the Convention.— It is true, that the Allies flatter themselves that they shall be able to destroy your energy, and to deprive you of the public confidence which you have merited; this is the first instruction given to their emissaries. But it is a truth which ought to be considered as trivial in politics, that a great body, invested with the confidence of a great people, cannot be ruined, but by themselves. Of this your enemies are not ignorant. You need not doubt, therefore, that they exert themselves, above all, to rouse amongst you all those passions which can second their insidious designs. What can they do against the National Representation, if they do not extort from it by surprise, impolitic acts which may furnish pretences for their criminal declamations? They must necessarily wish, therefore, to have agents of two kinds—some who endeavour to degrade it by their speeches, and others, even among its own body, who strive to deceive it, in order to endanger its glory, and the interests of the Republic.

To carry on their attack with success, it was necessary to begin by making war in the departments, on the Representatives who had shewn themselves worthy of your confidence, and against the Committee of Public Safety. They were attacked, therefore, by party-men who seemed to combat against each other. What could they do better than to enfeeble the government of the Convention, and to break all the springs of it in a moment which ought to have decided the fate of the Republic and of tyrants? Far be it from me to imagine that there still remains amongst you a single man base enough to wish to serve the cause of tyrants! But still farther from me be the crime, which would not be pardoned, of deceiving the National Convention, and of betraying the French people by a criminal silence! For a free people have this happiness, that truth, which is the scourge of despots, forms always their strength, and ensures their safety. But it is true, that there still exists a danger for our liberty, the only serious danger, perhaps, which it has to encounter.

This danger is a plan which has been formed of rallying all the enemies of the Republic, by reviving the spirit of party; of persecuting the patriots; of discouraging and ruining the faithful agents of the Republican government; and of destroying those parts which are most essential for the public service. They have endeavoured to deceive the Convention respecting men and things; they have wished to deceive it, in regard to the causes of abuses which they exaggerate, in order to render it impossible to remedy them; they have endeavoured to fill it with false terror, in order to mislead or enfeeble it; they have attempted to divide it; they have, above all, attempted to divide the Representatives of the People, sent into the department, and the Committee of Public Safety; they wished to obliged the former to thwart the measures of the central authority, to bring back disorder and confusion; they wished to sour them on their return, to render them, without their knowledge, the instruments of a cabal.

Foreigners take advantage of all these private passions, and even of patriotism abused. They, at first, adopted the plan of proceeding straight to their object, by calumniating the Committee of Public Safety; they then openly flattered themselves that it would sink under the weight of its laborious functions. Victory, and the fortune of the French people saved it. Since that period, they have adopted the plan of praising it, enfeebling it, and destroying the fruits of all its labours. All these vague declamations against the necessary agents of the Committee, all the plans of disorganization disguised under the name of reforms, already rejected by the Convention, and revived at present with strange affectation; that eagerness to applaud intriguers whom the Committee of Public Safety ought to have removed; that terror struck into good citizens; that indulgence with which conspirators are encouraged; all that system of imposture and intrigue, the principal author of which is a man whom you expelled from among you, is directed against the National Convention, and tends to realize the wishes of all the enemies of France. It is since the epocha when that system was announced, in libels, and realized by public acts, that Aristocracy and Royalty have begun to raise their insolent heads; that patriotism has been again persecuted throughout the whole Republic; and that the national authority has experienced a resistance, the habit of which intriguers had begun to lose.

In short, these indirect attacks, were they attended with no other inconvenience than that of dividing the energy and attention of those who have to support the immense burthen, with which you are loaded, and distract them too often from the grand measures of public safety, to employ them in defeating dangerous intrigues, might still be considered as a diversion useful to our enemies; but let us take courage; here is the sanctuary of truth; here reside the founders of the Republic, the avengers of mankind, and the destroyers of tyrants. Here to destroy an abuse, it will be sufficient to point it out. It is sufficient for us to call, in name of our country, councils of the self-love or weakness of individuals to the love of virtue, and the glory of the National Convention.

I call for a solemn discussion on all the causes of these disturbances, and on every thing that can have an influence on the progress of the Revolution. I conjure it not to suffer any private or secret interest to usurp an ascendancy over the general will of the Assembly, and the indestructable power of reason. I shall, at present confine myself to propose to you to consecrate, by your formal approbation, the moral and political truths, on which ought to be founded your internal Administration, and the stability of the Republic, as you have already consecrated the principles of your conduct towards foreign nations; by this you will give confidence to all good citizens, and deprive conspirators of their hopes; will secure your own progress; confound the intrigues and calumnies of Kings; and will honour your cause and character in the eyes of all nations.

Give to the French People a pledge of your zeal for protecting patriotism, of your inflexible justice on crimnals, and of your attachment to the cause of the People. Order the principles of morality and politics, which I have unfolded, to be proclaimed in your name, both within and without the Republic!

ON THE STATE OF EUROPE BEFORE AND AFTER THE FRENCH REVOLUTION

Friedrich von Gentz

> *Friedrich von Gentz (1764–1832) was the Edmund Burke (see page 352)*
> *of the German-speaking world. As a Prussian official already noted for*
> *his brilliant intellectual gifts, Gentz began his literary career by translating*
> *and writing a commentary on the Englishman's* Reflections on the
> Revolution in France, *which came to exercise as great an influence in*

Germany as it had in England. Though an Anglophile throughout much of his career, Gentz, unlike Burke, did not reject the whole philosophy of the Enlightenment, and was strongly influenced by Kant's thought (see pages 178–179). In the middle 1790s Gentz found his real vocation as political pamphleteer and journalist opposing not so much the French Revolution —he was considerably more reform-minded than Burke—as the expansion of French power which the revolution had triggered. Although Gentz accepted subsidies from various like-minded governments, his influence was derived from the very independence of his views. During the Napoleonic era Gentz switched to Austrian government service, and growing increasingly conservative, ended up as confidant and right-hand man of the architect of the postrevolutionary reaction, Prince Metternich (see page 445).

Gentz's State of Europe *was written in the fall of 1801 in reply to the tract* L'Etat de la France à la Fin de l'An VIII *["The State of France at the End of the Year VIII" (i.e., 1800)], written by Hauterive, a Napoleonic propagandist. In 1801 the Peace of Lunéville between France and Austria had shattered the second European coalition and left France not only extended to its "natural" frontiers (thus incorporating the German Rhineland and what today would be Belgium), but with a string of satellite states from Holland to southern Italy. England, though still at war with Napoleon, was to conclude a short-lived peace in the year following the publication of* On the State of Europe Before and After the French Revolution.

Whoever takes upon him to assert, that, at a certain period, the political system was utterly corrupted, and the federal constitution either eminently defective or totally annihilated, must be able to show, that at that period there existed no guaranty of public security; that the balance of power was entirely destroyed; that the weaker states could no longer find refuge or protection against the usurpations of the stronger; that one or a few of the powerful endangered the peace and security of the rest, and rendered their existence precarious; that the disputes of nations were no longer determinable by negotiations or treaties; and that war and force were the only resource, the only policy, the umpire in all their differences.

Was this the state of the federative system of Europe at the commencement of the French revolution? I should contradict my own opinion were I to hesitate a moment to confess, that at that time the political system laboured under great defects, and was pervaded by many errors; that it was far, very far, removed from that perfect

Friedrich von Gentz, *On the State of Europe Before and After the French Revolution*, trans. J. C. Herries (London, 1802), pp. 90–93, 179–180, 209–215, 246–265.

federal constitution, which we contemplate in idea; that the balance between the principal powers was by no means secured; and that the situation of the smaller states was in many respects dangerous and precarious. A great part of these errors and defects was the immediate consequence of the rapid civilization of Europe, by which the former proportions between the leading states were altered, and the disproportion between four or five preponderant nations on the one hand, and a great number of small, dispersed, and insignificant states on the other, was considerably augmented. This disproportion excited and encouraged many and various plans of ambition and usurpation; and at length added to the numberless combinations of modern politics, the celebrated system of partition, which inflicted so deep and dangerous a wound on the federal constitution.

But I can never be persuaded to believe that "at the time of the French revolution, the political system of Europe had reached the last stage of decay and disorganization; that its every prop and foundation was destroyed;" and that "it presented nothing but imbecility, anarchy, and confusion." * The history of the twenty-five years which elapsed between the peace of Hubertsburg and Fontainebleau, and the beginning of the disturbances in France, contradicts this assertion in every respect; the most indisputable facts stand in opposition to it; the slightest glance at the situation of Europe, during that period, confirms the very reverse. The federal constitution was at least as perfect as it ever had been since the thirty years war; nay, it was even more efficient and entire. The changes which Europe had experienced in the last 150 years had been as happily and wisely grafted on the former political relations, as, from the joint operation of accident and prudence (such is the nature of every federative system), could ever have been desired or expected; the balance of power was adjusted as effectually and as favourably as a liberal and reasonable policy could desire; and if there were some events which infringed the sacred principles of the federal constitution, they were at least avenged by the unanimous indignation, and the marked disapprobation of all contemporaries. Europe possessed, in every reasonable sense of the word, a federative constitution, a political balance, and a law of nations.

To explain these truths, it will not be necessary to descend to a minute and particular analysis of the political relations existing at that period. It is sufficient if we dwell upon the leading features of the picture. The fate of Europe depends upon the fortunes and political relations of the powers which preponderate in the general system. If the balance be preserved among these; if their political existence and internal organization be safely established; if, by their mutual action and reaction, they protect and secure the independence of the smaller states (so much, at least, as the weak can be secure in a community with the strong); if there is no dangerous preponderance to be perceived, which threatens to oppress the rest, or to involve them in endless war; we may rest satisfied with the federal constitution which fulfils these most essential points, notwithstanding many errors and defects. And such was the federal constitution of Europe before the French revolution. . . .

The federal system of Europe, and the law of nations, were yet capable of much improvement; left many reasonable desires, many just demands, unsatisfied. There was more than one important point relating both to peace and war, which had never

* [All quotes are from Hauterive, *The State of France.* (*Ed.*)]

been sufficiently discussed, and remained to be regulated by general convention. The irregular distribution of the territories of several powerful empires; the uncertainty of their limits, the remote situation of their provinces (often entirely surrounded by those of other powers); the great number of small defenceless states, whose very independence was sometimes a burden to them; the numerous and various pretensions of the different sovereigns; and the want, so often felt, of a more comprehensive code of public law: all these were evils of which no enlightened European could remain insensible. Perpetual peace, the ever cherished, ever disappointed hope of mankind, seemed still beyond the reach of political wisdom; the world continued to be vexed with disputes concerning the limits, the right of succession, the privileges of commerce and navigation of the several powers, and still oftener by the ambition of princes, and the unruly passions of their subjects.

But all these defects would never have induced an impartial judge to condemn the whole edifice as ruinous and unserviceable. We might have expected from time, and the improved condition of society, the remedies for these evils; our consolatory hopes of the future were founded upon the successful efforts of the past. It became more and more manifest during the last twenty years before the revolution, that the principles of government, and the law of nations, were advancing towards perfection; and that a period of peace, concord, and universal amelioration, was fast approaching. . . .

. . . The revolution, and that alone, overturned the political system by an unfortunate attempt to support it; dissolved every federal obligation, subverted and demolished every pillar of the balance of power, and converted the federal constitution of Europe into a scene of anarchy and confusion, whence no human skill or wisdom will speedily deliver it without the miraculous interference of Providence.

That Europe, in its present unnatural and helpless condition—the dreadful result of ten successive years of convulsions and misfortune—that Europe now possesses no federal constitution, now scarce retains any public law, is a melancholy truth, in which all parties seem to agree. . . .

I shall not minutely examine the causes that have rendered the present war so destructive in its character, and so unfortunate to most of the nations concerned in it; of which the dangerous preponderance of France has been the last, most important, and permanent effect. I shall confine myself to a few observations, of which the truth is too evident to expose me to contradiction. That series of misfortunes was not a simple phenomenon; it was the result of circumstances extremely complex and intricate. On the one hand genius and depravity, and on the other inevitable inferiority, with deplorable, perhaps condemnable weakness, assisted each other to produce it. It is difficult to say which was the principal of these co-operating causes; but each must be taken into the account; each was at once cause and effect, each at once an original principle and complementary condition of the other.

Future ages will do ample justice to the extraordinary energy and steady perseverance, the unshaken intrepidity and military talents, the daring enterprises and inexhaustible resources of war displayed by France amidst the storms of the revolution, to the wondering nations of Europe in arms. But history will remind us, too, that this extraordinary vigour grew from the same root with a no less extraordinary depravity; and that the means of such unheard-of efforts, such gigantic enterprises, could only be afforded by a revolution that trampled on all rights, tore down every barrier of civil polity, and gave a loose to every irregular passion. Moreover, this enormous military greatness is less a subject of wonder, when we reflect that every social and civil consideration, the interest of justice, and even of humanity, the welfare, and in a certain degree the existence of a great nation, the rich harvest of the past, and the seeds of the future, were sacrificed to that splendid but unprofitable greatness.

On the other hand it is evident that the powers leagued against the revolution could not imitate the proceedings, adopt the measures, and use the means of the common enemy, without risking all they were contending for, and introducing to their own countries the very evils they were combating: the difference always existing between the resources of a coalition and those of a revolutionary government, produced the necessary inferiority of the enemies of France. But it is equally evident that this unavoidable disproportion, this necessary inferiority, are far from being sufficient to explain all the events of our times. Some evil genius seems to have perplexed the councils of every cabinet, and paralyzed their political and military energies; for it has been their fate to meet the most trying difficulties with pitiful projects, half-measures, weak and incapable instruments, and a deplorable deficiency of every thing the magnitude of the occasion required. They too late, if ever, learned the character of their enemy, and how to combat revolutionary weapons and resources. There was no plan, coherence, or uniformity in their proceedings; no two of them were of one opinion. Their unfortunate dissensions, the fatal influence of their private interests, their want of unanimity and concert, the tardiness and indecision of their measures, redoubled the strength and courage of their enemy. Capable at most of a weak and partial defence, unequal to a vigorous and uniform attack, they formed no effective coalition, but were merely a reluctant assemblage of ill-according parts. They were, in short, unfortunately for the interests of Europe, any thing imaginable, except what the subtle declamations of the enemy, and the easy credulity of the age, have represented and believed.

The issue of a war so conducted between such parties, could not be doubtful, and, in fact, was exactly such as had been predicted by all men of judgment and penetration. The first of its unfortunate results was the entire failure of the original and only object of the coalesced powers. While they were all wasting their strength, and many of them hastening to ruin, the revolution was triumphant; the most scandalous enormities remained unpunished; the perpetrators of the most atrocious crimes that ever disgraced the earth, ascended the throne of Lewis XIV. assumed a plenitude of authority to which the power of that mighty despot bears no comparison, and drowned the monarchy of France in the blood of its last defenders. But this was not all; they overran the neighbouring states; they devoured the substance of the richest countries in Europe; they carried the symbol of their tyranny under the name of the Tree of Liberty, through an hundred provinces; they extended their territory on all sides by conquest, by forced alliances, or by compulsatory treaties; and when all this was accomplished, resistance no longer possible, the dominion of the revolutionary rulers established, and the balance of Europe irrecoverably lost; the single hope that yet remained—that of seeing the monstrous edifice fall to pieces of itself—suddenly vanished; the scene changed, and this colossal fabric, these new resources, these territorial acquistions, these forced connexions, this military power and terrible preponderance, were all consolidated in the hands of a regular, skilful, and comparatively popular government. The old revolutionary system was demolished as a useless pile. No principle of rule was now acknowledged but the will and ambition of the reigning party, and the genius of its chief; and this government, thus strengthened and consolidated, gave laws to a great part of Europe.

Such is the state of things at the present moment.* The political system which resisted the violence of so many storms until the French revolution, and whose strong foundations had defied the vicissitudes of fortune, and the lapse of time, has been converted into a heap of ruins by the revolution, and its necessary companion the war. Europe, say the friends as well as enemies of the preponderant power; Europe has entirely lost its balance. Let us now proceed to inquire if there be any hope of seeing it re-established. . . .

I will here briefly recapitulate the foregoing observations, and present the following results of this view of the present relations between France and Europe; which, though indeed only my individual opinion, is founded throughout upon facts.

1st   France has extended her limits on all sides by military or revolutionary operations. She has destroyed the independence of the neighbouring states, either by regular conquest, as in the case of Flanders, Savoy, the Rhine lands, etc. or under colour of alliance, as with Holland, Spain, Switzerland, and the Italian republics; or finally, by the right of power only, as in the subjection of all Italy as far as the Adige. The ancient constitutions of all these countries have been demolished, and France has established an empire upon their ruins, which has no parallel in Europe.

2dly   This total obliteration of her former limits, this destruction of every safeguard of her neighbours; this military force, alike extraordinary in extent and efficacy, and far exceeding even her territorial aggrandizement in proportion; these have given a preponderance to France, against which no continental power, not even the greatest, can contend with any chance of success.

3dly   Were France to abuse this prodigious preponderance, and, not content with her present acquisitions, were she to prescribe too hard conditions to the rest of Europe, a general league would be the only means of resisting the danger.

4thly   Such is the geographical, military, and political situation of France, that no league against her could be in the least effectual, in which Austria or Prussia, or both, are not engaged. . . .

6thly   Austria and Prussia must therefore act in concert, to afford a hope of effectual protection to Germany in any future war.

7thly   But an intimate alliance between those two powers, is the most improbable, the most difficult of all political combinations. Thus vanishes the basis of every federative guarantee against France, as soon as we have discovered it.

8thly   In the whole sphere of federal relations there is no alliance (in the common acceptation of the word) that can form a counterpoise to France. This can only be accomplished by the means always dangerous and uncertain, of a coalition, whenever the necessity of an active resistance shall arise: and as every coalition against France must

* [The autumn of 1801. (*Ed.*)]

be general (because the whole of Germany, and consequently all the allies of the leading powers of the Empire must necessarily be engaged in it); so the only refuge that remains to Europe against France, is the most dangerous, the most uncertain, the most intricate and difficult of all political measures.

I am aware of some objections likely to be made to this reasoning in general (whose intrinsic consistency, I think, will hardly be impeached), and will answer them beforehand.

On the one hand, it will be said (such are the topics of consolation most frequently held forth), "To what purpose are all these melancholy calculations? What is the use of thus reckoning and balancing remote dangers against hypothetical remedies? The speculations of politics are as hills of sand, whose shape and figure vary every instant with the winds of heaven. What assurance have we that a few years, nay, a few months, may not put an end to this preponderance of France, so frightfully described to us? The genius of a few enterprising minds, the genius of one man, raised that nation from the depth of ruin to its present greatness and stability. That which depends upon an uncertain life, must be itself uncertain. . . ."

To this I answer: Politics, speculative as well as practicable, have to do with no elements but such as actually exist; and when they look forward to the future, their calculations must always rest upon present realities, and not upon accidental or personal circumstances, upon empty hypotheses or mere possibilities. The probability of the long or short duration of the present state of France, her military and political ascendant, is a subject of speculation and reflection for the politician. But whatever the result (merely hypothetical and conditional) of his researches, it cannot affect the indisputable truth, that at present there is no prospect but of *power* to France and *danger* to the rest of Europe. Should France suddenly fall, or gradually decline, we would draw new conclusions from new premises. . . .

But so long as the present relations endure, all systems, principles, doctrines, and measures must be built upon these; and as long as Europe on the one hand, and France on the other, continue as they now stand, in this first year of the nineteenth century, it must be permitted to assert, that there exists no federal constitution, no balance of power, no solid and durable peace.

On the other hand, I shall meet with objections of a different, and perhaps more specious nature. "A revolution has been accomplished in the political system. This might have been prevented, and the former system preserved with all its defects, if the strength of Europe, more firmly united, had been more efficaciously directed. But the past cannot be undone; the present and the future only should occupy the science of politics. Why are they both represented so comfortless? There never existed a balance of power in the strict sense of the word; there always have been preponderating states: the weak have always been obnoxious to danger; there always have been pretexts for oppression, occasions for injustice, and subjects of war in Europe. Supposing the ascendancy acquired by France to be as you describe it, does it follow that all security, liberty, independence, and stability must be annihilated for ever in the rest of Europe? Will not France cease to be dangerous to other nations from the very circumstance of her having nothing more to wish for, nothing more to undertake? What is there now to call forth her exertions? Every new conquest would be a burden to the republic; every new conquest would diminish her strength. Will she go forth upon unprofitable adventures beyond the Alps, the Rhine, and the Pyrennees? Or, will she exterminate kingdoms which she cannot govern? . . .

"Let us forget the past; let every state conform with prudent resignation to its present circumstances; let each improve its present advantages, and renounce all destructive ambition, all unnatural and extravagant systems, all false and turbulent politics. The great powers of Europe, whose broad and solid foundations resisted the torrent of the revolution, are still powerful enough to defy every wanton attack, to cultivate and improve their states by peaceful economy, to make their subjects happy, and to maintain their political dignity. The rest is all error and illusion; whether a certain number of little sovereigns, or one great republican power, give laws beyond the Rhine, the Meuse, and the Adige, must be matter of indifference to the rest of Europe, since the ancient posessors are expelled, and the former constitutions abolished. . . ."

The following observations will answer these arguments; the strongest which any advocate for the present state of Europe, any defender of the ascendancy of France, can oppose to the just apprehensions of the world, and reasonable warnings of political speculation.

1st Whether the present government of France deserve the unlimited confidence required by its partisans, is not within the sphere of my present inquiry. . . . We will consider it as only desirous of concord and peace, of security and justice; as hitherto guiltless of any proceeding calculated to justify our former apprehensions, or to excite new ones, to inspire mistrust, or to suppress reviving hopes: to grant this is surely the extreme of moderation.

2dly But the character of the present French government is no security for the future. It is a leading maxim in every rational system of practicable politics, that every power is dangerous to the rest, which possesses the means of disturbing the general peace, and wants nothing but the will to use them. . . .

3dly As the personal character of the present government of France, or indeed of any government whatever, cannot ensure the dispositions of its successors; as even the present wishes, acts, and declarations of a sovereign, are no security for his intentions and proceedings at a future period; even so do the obvious interests of a power afford no perfect assurance of its views and conduct. This observation must, however, only be taken in a limited sense. In the ordinary course of things the true interests of a nation are no inadequate criterion of the conduct which in all reasonable probability we are to expect from it, while there is a due balance of power, or a constitution in which it is nearly balanced; when there is no danger of an immediate revolution, and no state sufficiently preponderant to effect a sudden subversion of the whole system. For it may always be supposed, that in any given period, as of fifty or an hundred years, the wise and imprudent counsels by which it is directed, will at least counterbalance each other; that the principles of its real welfare, though for a time forgotten, will always be recurred to; and that, on the whole, its true interest will be the leading object of the government. The politician will therefore generally be right in his conclusions, who makes the interest of each state a principal ground of every speculation concerning its future conduct. But this maxim ceases to be useful in times when the state of Europe may be altered in a moment by a single resolution. When any power attains so great a

degree of influence and preponderance in the political system, that the slightest deviations of its politics may endanger all existing relations, and threaten a general subversion; it would be madness to dismiss every apprehension, and continue in perfect
security, because war and conquest may be opposite to the permanent interests of that
nation. For who will venture to assure us, that the men intrusted with this extraordinary
power, will never give way to the impulse of ambition, avarice, or resentment, and
gratify the passions of the moment, regardless of those permanent interests? This
would be sufficient, in the present state of Europe, to produce the most extensive
desolation.

4thly When we consider the present state of France, and what she has experienced during the last ten years, we shall find it difficult, perhaps impossible, to determine what maxims and conduct her interests will constantly prescribe to her. Self-
preservation is naturally the first object of every government. Where that is best
secured by pacific measures, and an adherence to the principles of moderation and
justice, there justice and moderation will prevail. But when circumstances require a
contrary conduct, and a government feels itself obliged to assume a lofty and decided
tone, and engage in great and splendid undertakings, to support its sinking popularity,
to counteract an aspiring faction, or to awe the turbulence of a seditious people; then
moderation is sacrificed to the interests of the moment; and who will be found bold
enough to deny that the French government may possibly be thus circumstanced? Does
not every thing about that government indicate the probability of critical situations,
frequent changes, and a long state of uncertainty?

But should the present and every future government of France invariably renounce
all views of usurpation, and make moderation the leading principle of its politics; . . .
yet the relations between France and the rest of Europe would not therefore be less
unequal, constrained, and dangerous. For, besides the disputes arising from ambition,
avarice, or wanton provocations among nations; there are differences of another nature, which originate in the doubtfulness of their rights, the insufficiency of their
treaties, and the often unavoidable concurrence of their several interests. These disputes, and the wars, which, in extreme cases, are the only means of deciding them, will
never cease to occur, while there are separate states, without a perfect system of public
law among them. But these unavoidable wars must, in the present situation of Europe,
be productive of the most dreadful misfortunes. The slightest misunderstanding about
an undefined boundary, a doubtful right of sovereignty or navigation (not to mention
the greater ones, that might in time arise by the decease of princes about the right of
succession), the slightest difference between France and any neighbouring state, would,
on account of the immense preponderance of the French power, raise such a storm as
to threaten all Europe with destruction. The dictates of sound policy prescribe the
necessity of a natural or artificial balance of power; not only to prevent the wanton and
dangerous abuse of it on the part of a preponderating state; but even to maintain a
due proportion of strength in those ordinary wars, which human wisdom is often unable
to avert, and to preserve the political system from shocks that might prove fatal to its
existence. Whenever this balance is destroyed, the security of the whole is immediately
annihilated, whether the maxims that govern each particular state be just or unjust,
warlike or pacific.

5thly In the present state of things, there is a constant source of political disturbance, a perpetual cause of war, in the necessary disposition of the humbled and oppressed nations, in their unextinguishable resentment towards their haughty and oppressive conqueror. . . . Until the power of France shall again be reduced to its just proportion in the system of Europe, the prevailing sentiment in all other countries, or at least in the principal European states, will be a secret desire of thwarting her preponderance; a secret and insurmountable hatred of that monopoly of influence and dominion which France has so victoriously asserted. . . . An unnatural and oppressive constitution, incompatible with the safety and dignity of Europe in general, can have no prospect of duration. The indestructible elasticity of springs too forcibly compressed, will always tend to restore their natural state. All the treaties in the world cannot confirm and preserve a state of things repugnant to every principle of freedom, to all equality of power, to the fundamental laws of the social and federal constitution, to the wishes, propensities, and views of the great majority of nations and individuals.

6thly Should any man deny the force of truth of all these arguments, and assert, in contradiction to experience, to the evidence of the past and present, and to the true principles of politics, that neither the mutability of the views and characters of the rulers of France, nor the uncertainty of their future dispositions, nor the chance of their private interests being incompatible with the general interest and peace of Europe, nor the danger with which even an ordinary war would threaten all Europe when there is no balance of power, nor the natural and insurmountable propensity to dissolve unnatural obligations—should he assert, that none of these causes of dissension, enmity, and war, are sufficiently active and important to justify the apprehensions here entertained; and that, notwithstanding all these obvious sources of perpetual internal discord, the constitution established by the French revolution, and the events of its unhappy war, may endure in peace and harmony, as well as the former or any other political combination; he must at least allow, that such a constitution does not deserve the appellation of a federative system, either in the former, or any other proper acceptation of the words. He must be prepared to assert, that the balance of power, as hitherto conceived, is only an empty term; that Europe can exist and prosper under circumstances different from those formerly held necessary and essential to it; and that federative policy is in future to proceed upon new and unheard-of principles, in utter contradiction to all which prevailed before, and hitherto unconfirmed by any experience. According to all former grounds of judgment, all ancient rule of conduct in politics, the present situation of Europe is a state of political anarchy, of constant and unextinguishable war. Those who maintain the contrary, must either renounce all consistency, or disclaim every principle hitherto received.

These remarks on the present relations between France and Europe, are totally uninfluenced by hatred or prejudice against the French republic. They flow from a free and impartial consideration of the subject, from the real state and natural course of things, and from an unconstrained application of the simplest rules of the science of politics. Every enlightened friend of the French nation must as readily subscribe to them, as the bitterest enemy of France, or the most determined adversary of her present constitution. It is a characteristic property of all great disorders in the political system, that they do as much injury to the states apparently benefited by the destruction of the balance, as to the immediate losers by the disproportion introduced. It is the true and permanent interest of every nation without exception, to preserve a due proportion between its own strength, and that of its neighbours; and to maintain a just distribution of power among all the members of the federative system. The advantages of a dangerous ascendancy are always deceitful; for the public welfare of a nation cannot be secure, without the satisfaction of its neighbours, and the confidence of the world. An enlightened policy requires a due attention to these important requisites of peace, on the part of the greatest as well as the smallest states. Were France to distinguish her true interests; were the voice of reason to prevail above the dictates of ambition and avarice; her statesmen would easily be convinced, that what now is called, by a shameless abuse of words, the federative system of Europe, is nothing but a compound of inordinate power on the one hand, and impotence on the other; in which no real independence, no stability or security, and no permanent peace can exist; and which is consequently incompatible with the general welfare.

◄§ LETTERS

Napoleon Bonaparte

One hundred and fifty years after the fall of Napoleon Bonaparte (1769–1821), during any one year more books on Napoleon and his era are published in France than on any other historical topic or period. This fascination has not been confined to France. There is something irresistible in the drama of an obscure Corsican nobleman rising to be Emperor of the French and conqueror of Europe, only to die a prisoner on a remote island in the south Atlantic.

Napoleon Bonaparte unquestionably owed his rise to the French Revolution. This outsider, with his thick Italian accent and his mediocre record as a scholarship student in a French military academy, would probably not have gone very far in the hierarchical, caste-conscious society of the Old Regime. The revolution, by depleting the old aristocratic officer corps, stressing ability over seniority, and fomenting the wars that are bread and butter to an ambitious young officer, gave dozens of able noncommissioned officers and second lieutenants the chance to show what they could do. Indeed, as a protégé of the Robespierre brothers, Bonaparte also came close to becoming the revolution's victim when his patrons and their followers were purged in 1794. Yet by 1795 he had proved himself to his superiors in putting down a Paris insurrection; by 1796, entrusted with the Italian command, he was clearly on his way.

*Only after his accession to power in 1799 does his relationship to the
revolution and its ideology become increasingly ambiguous and complex.
The same adjectives come to mind in appraising his foreign policy. Historians know very well what he did, but divide sharply in assessing his
motives and in identifying the mainspring of his dynamism. This dis-
agreement cannot be ascribed to lack of information: aside from the full
range of official documents, Napoleon's course can be traced in the
literally tens of thousands of letters he dictated to teams of secretaries,
writing on every conceivable subject to a variety of individuals under
all sorts of circumstances. Such was the range and complexity—and
perhaps, inconsistency—of this remarkable man that almost any interpretation of his life can find some support in the records that he left
behind. The letters included here, though chronologically arranged, are
meant not to provide a continuous commentary on Napoleon's career,
but to illustrate the range and variety of his activities and interests.*

TO H.M. THE KING OF GREAT BRITAIN AND IRELAND

Paris, December 25, 1799

Called by the will of the French people to hold the highest office in the Republic, I
think it proper, upon assuming my functions, to inform Your Majesty of the fact by
my own hand.

Is there to be no end to the war which, for the past eight years, has desolated every
quarter of the globe? Is there no means by which we can come to an understanding?
How is it that the two most enlightened nations in Europe, both stronger and more
powerful than their safety and independence require, consent to sacrifice their commercial success, their internal prosperity, and the happiness of their homes, to dreams
of imaginary greatness? How is it that they do not envisage peace as their greatest
glory as well as their greatest need?

Such sentiments cannot be strange to Your Majesty's heart, for you rule a free nation
for the sole end of making it happy.

I beg Your Majesty to believe that, in broaching this subject, it is my sincere desire
to make a practical contribution, for the second time, towards the establishment of a
general peace. I do so by a *démarche* that is prompt, confidential, and freed from
those formalities which may be necessary to save the face of a weak state, but which
between great powers become a mask of mutual trickery.

If France and England abuse their power, they can, for a long time yet, stave off

Napoleon Self-Revealed, ed. and trans. J. M. Thompson (Boston: Houghton Mifflin Company,
1934), pp. 69–70, 81, 111–112, 134–137, 171–172, 178–181, 207–208, 209, 210–212, 231–
232, 318–319, 324–325, 359–362.

exhaustion; but it would be an international disaster; and I make bold to say that the fate of every civilised nation depends upon the ending of a war which is embroiling the whole world.

TO CITIZEN D'ANDIGNÉ [1]

Paris, December 30, 1799

I have been pleased at reading the letter from the most remarkable citizens of the western Departments. They show a disposition which does them honour, and which will, I am confident, be useful to the country.

Only too much French blood has flowed during the last ten years; yet there are enlightened men, in whom the sentiment of honour still burns, who fail to use all their influence on behalf of a government solely concerned to re-establish order, justice, and true freedom—a government which will soon be surrounded by the trust and respect of all Europe, and which will soon have the glory of proclaiming, for a second time, that peace for which the whole world is crying out.

Be sure, then, to tell your fellow-citizens that never again shall revolutionary laws devastate the fair soil of France, that the Revolution is over, that consciences will be utterly and absolutely free, that protection will be given equally to all citizens, and relieved from any taint of prejudice, and that, for myself, I shall appreciate and know how to reward any services rendered on behalf of peace and quietness. . . .

TO CITIZEN RIPAULT [2]

Paris, July 23, 1801

Citizen Ripault is to see that he is supplied every day with all the papers that come out, except the 11 political papers. He will read them carefully, make an abstract of everything they contain likely to affect the public point of view, especially with regard to religion, philosophy, and political opinion. He will send me this abstract between 5 and 6 o'clock every day.

Once every ten days he will send me an analysis of all the books or pamphlets which have appeared during that period, calling attention to any passages that might bear on moral questions, or interest me in a political or moral connexion.

He will take pains to procure copies of all the plays which are produced, and to analyse them for me, with observations of the same character as those above mentioned. This analysis must be made, at latest, within 48 hours of the production of the plays.

He is to send me every 1st and 6th day, between 5 and 6 o'clock, a list of all the bills, posters, advertisements, etc. which deserve attention, as well as anything that has

[1] [. . . *On December 27, following an armistice of November 24, d'Andigné, the Chouan leader, came to Paris, and discussed terms of pacification with Napoleon. On December 28 an amnesty was offered to all rebels who would lay down arms.*]

[2] [. . . *Ripault was Napoleon's librarian till 1807.*]

come to his knowledge, and anything that has been done or said in the various Institutes, literary meetings, sermons, new educational establishments, or fashionable trials, that might be of interest from a political and moral point of view.

In consideration of these new duties imposed upon citizen Ripault, I am instructing the Minister for Home Affairs to pay him 500 francs a month, and I am ordering Pfister to give him a like amount.

NOTE

Paris, March 1, 1805

His Majesty has abolished the Imperial School of Agriculture, which could only have occasioned idle talk, and useless expenditure. He would like to give some real encouragement to agriculture. In o.der to do so, one must know the state of agriculture in the different Departments.

It is prosperous in the Upper and Lower Rhine Department, in the North, Belgium, Pas-de-Calais, Somme, Aisne, Oise, Seine and Marne, Seine and Oise, and in most of Eure and Loire, in Lower Seine, Calvados, the Channel, and the Departments that were once Languedoc, in Lot, Vaucluse, the Rhône estuary, Saône and Loire, Upper Saône, part of Côte d'Or, and the six Departments of Piedmont. It will be prosperous, too, in the four new Departments of the Rhine, as soon as the sale of national property puts the land under the control of those who really cultivate it.

It is to the other Departments, then, that we must convey our encouragements. In most of these Departments cultivation is in the hands of labourers or *métayers*,* who care for nothing beyond making their living, and who never improve their holdings. These are not the people to be encouraged. It is the rich land-owners, who do something to increase the value of their property, and who are the only class to think about their interests, and to be concerned for the future of themselves and of their children.

People of this kind are not encouraged by grants or money, but by medals, and decorations, and eulogies addressed to them by or on behalf of the sovereign. Every Prefect must therefore get to know which land-owners and agriculturalists in his Department distinguish themselves either by the extent and skill of their farming, or by their superior breeding and rearing of live-stock. Every year the Minister for Home Affairs will distribute, to those who deserve them, either a medal, or the badge of the Legion of Honour (as the case may be), or a letter of congratulation and encouragement from the Emperor.

A certain number of foreign rams, and of specially fine bulls, will be distributed, as has been done already. In the Departments suitable for horse-breeding, prizes will be given to encourage the owners of good stallions. Agriculture, like every other art, owes its improvement to comparison, and to good models.

In those Departments which are still isolated from educational centres, good landlords should be encouraged to send their sons to study the methods in use in Departments where agriculture is flourishing; and they should be stimulated by eulogies and marks of distinction.

* [Sharecroppers. (*Ed.*)]

Money is no use in a matter of this kind. The greedy class will be coming to apply for grants, and will plead their useless journeys as a ground for fresh subsidies.

TO PRINCE EUGENE [3]

Munich, December 31, 1805

Here I am at Munich. I have arranged your marriage with Princess Augusta, and it has been announced in the papers. The princess came to see me this morning, and I had a long talk with her. She is very pretty. I am enclosing a portrait of her on a cup; but it doesn't do her justice. . . .

(I) DIRECT. TO HIS HOLINESS THE POPE

Munich, January 7, 1806

Most Holy Father; I am in receipt of a letter from Your Holiness under date November 13. I cannot but be keenly affected by the fact that, when all the powers in English pay banded together to wage an unjust war against me, Your Holiness should lend your ear to ill advice, and write to me in such immoderate terms. Your Holiness is perfectly free either to keep my minister at Rome, or to dismiss him. The occupation of Ancona [4] is an immediate and necessary consequence of the military incompetence of the Holy See. It was better for Your Holiness to see that fortress in my hands than in those of the Turks or English. Your Holiness complains that, since your return from Paris, you have had nothing but disappointments. The reason is that all those who used to call themselves my friends, only because they feared my power, have since then taken heart from the strength of the coalition, and changed their tune: thus, since Your Holiness returned to Rome, I have met with nothing but refusal on your part, whatever the occasion; and this even in matters of the first importance for religion, as, for instance, the question of preventing a revival of Protestantism in France. I have always considered myself the protector of the Holy See; and it was in this capacity that I occupied Ancona. I have always considered myself, like my Valois and Bourbon predecessors, as the eldest son of the Church, and as the sole bearer of the sword with which to protect it, and to put it beyond danger of defilement by Greeks and Moslems. I shall continue to protect it, whatever the mistakes, ingratitude, and ill-will of the men whom these last three months have unmasked. They thought I was done for; but, by the success with which he favoured my arms, God has signally demonstrated his protection of my cause. So long as Your Holiness consults the true friends of religion, and your own heart, I shall be your friend. I repeat; if Your Holiness wishes to dismiss my minister, you are free to do so; and free to summon, if you prefer them, the English,

[3] [. . . *Eugene* [*Napoleon's adoptive son*] *was in Italy, and had not been consulted. He married Princess Augusta Amelia of Bavaria on January 13, 1806.*]

[4] [. . . *Ancona was occupied by French troops before the Austrian campaign of 1805. The Pope's protest reached Napoleon just before Austerlitz. This is his answer. Cardinal Consalvi was the Papal Secretary of State.*]

and the Caliph of Constantinople. Only, as I do not wish to expose Cardinal Fesch to such affronts, I shall send a layman in his place. Besides, Cardinal Consalvi shows him so much dislike, that he has never met with anything but rebuffs, whilst every favour has gone to my enemies. Yet, God knows, I have done more for religion than any other prince alive.

Hereby I pray God, Most Holy Father, to preserve you for many years in the rule and government of our Holy Mother Church.

Your devoted son, Emperor of the French and King of Italy.

(II) INDIRECT. TO CARDINAL FESCH

Munich, January 7, 1806

The Pope has written to me, under date November 13th, a quite ridiculous and lunatic letter: these people thought I was dead. I occupied Ancona because, in spite of your representations, nothing had been done to defend it; besides, things are so badly organised that, whatever had been done, it could never have been held against anyone. Make it clearly understood that I won't stand any more of this nonsense, and that I won't tolerate the presence of a Russian or Sardinian minister at Rome. It is my intention to recall you, and to replace you by a layman. As these imbeciles see no harm in a Protestant occupying the French throne, I shall send them a Protestant ambassador. Tell Consalvi that, if he has any care for his country, he must either do what I required of him, or resign his post. Tell him that I'm religious, but that I'm no bigot. Remind him that Constantine distinguished the civilian sphere from the military, and that I too can nominate a senator to command in my name in Rome. It is a nice idea, all this talk of religion, by those who have admitted the Russians, and rejected Malta, and are now trying to get rid of my minister! These are the people who prostitute religion. Is there any such thing as an apostolic nuncio in Russia? Tell Consalvi, tell the Pope himself if you like, that he may want to turn my minister out of Rome, but that I can equally well come and put him back there. Can nothing be done with these fellows except by force? They are letting religion go to ruin in Germany by refusing to finish the business of the Concordat: it is the same in Bavaria, the same in Italy. They are becoming the laughing-stock of courts and peoples. I have given them good advice, but they would never listen to it. I suppose they thought that the Russians and English and Neapolitans would have respected the Pope's neutrality! For the Pope's purposes, I am Charlemagne. Like Charlemagne, I join the crown of France with the crown of the Lombards. My empire, like Charlemagne's, marches with the East. I therefore expect the Pope to accommodate his conduct to my requirements. If he behaves well, I shall make no outward changes: if not, I shall reduce him to the status of bishop of Rome. They complain of my arranging Italian affairs without consulting them. Do they want things to be as they are in Germany, where there are no services left, no sacraments, and no religion? Tell them that, unless they make an end of their present behaviour, I shall hold them up to all Europe as mere egoists, and shall settle the affairs of the church in Germany with the Arch-chancellor, and without them. Really, there is nothing in the world so utterly unreasonable as the Court of Rome.

TO LOUIS NAPOLÉON, KING OF HOLLAND *

Osterode, March 30, 1807

The news I hear is so extraordinary that I cannot believe it is true. They tell me that you have restored to the nobles in your states their titles and privileges. Is it possible that you are so short-sighted as not to see how fatal such a step would be to you, to your people, to France, and to myself? How could you, a French prince, have violated your simplest vow—to maintain equality among your subjects? I refuse to believe it can be true.

You are as good as renouncing the French throne: for a man who has broken his oath, a man who has robbed a nation of the fruit of fifteen years' fighting, toil, and endeavour, would be unworthy of such a position. I have, too, my own just grounds of complaint. For a long time past you have consistently acted against my advice. This cannot go on. My ambassador has instructions to inform you in so many words that, unless you revoke this measure, he is under orders to leave Holland, and I have done with you. You are an ungrateful brother, and the advisers under whose influence you have fallen are a pack of criminals. Further, I tell you this plainly, since you care nothing for good advice, that I will not have Frenchmen wearing your Order: so you can save yourself the trouble of conferring it on anyone. I have asked my ambassador for a copy of the act re-establishing nobility: if this measure is not rescinded, I shall look upon you as an inveterate foe. But perhaps I am making mountains out of mole-hills. The simple truth is, you have lost your head. Unless you retract this measure, look out for the consequences. You shall no longer be a French citizen, nor a prince of my blood. Haven't you sense enough to see that if your claim to the Dutch throne were to rest on noble birth, you would be at the bottom of the list? Is this all I am to expect of you? At the present rate, the next claim to a title will be to have fought against France, and to have sold ships to the English. Every local grandee will take up old claims to a title. Could nobody make you realise that you were alienating the people of Amsterdam —indeed, every Dutchman? An Order of nobility is bearable in a military country: in a commercial one it is intolerable. I think better of the humblest shop-keeper in Amsterdam than of the highest noble in Holland.

REMARKS ON A SCHEME FOR ESTABLISHING A FACULTY OF LITERATURE AND HISTORY AT THE COLLÈGE DE FRANCE

Finkenstein, April 19, 1807

. . . Education in the true sense of the word has a number of objects. One must learn to speak and write correctly—what is generally called grammar and *belles-lettres*. This need is met in every *lycée*,† and every educated man has been through a course in rhetoric.

* [Napoleon's brother. (*Ed.*)]
† [State-run, selective secondary school with a classical curriculum. (*Ed.*)]

After the need of correct speech and writing comes that of counting and measuring; and this the *lycées* have met by their mathematical classes, covering the various branches of arithmetic and mechanics. There follow the outlines of several other studies, such as chronology and geography; and some ideas of history are also included in the curriculum of the *lycées*.

Thus the institution of three stages of education enables every well-to-do citizen to have been through his courses of rhetoric and mathematics, and to have acquired some ideas about history, geography, and chronology. A youth who leaves his *lycée* at 16 knows not only the rules of French, the classical writers, the construction of a speech, the forms of rhetoric, the methods of calming and exciting the feelings of an audience, and in fact all that is taught in a course of *belles-lettres;* he knows also the chief eras of history, and the geographical divisions of the world; he can measure and calculate; and he has a general idea of the most striking phenomena of nature, and of the principles of balance and movement in solid and fluid bodies.

If he wishes to go to the Bar, to enter the Army or the Church, or to take up literature; if he intends to join one of the expert departments, and become a geographer, an engineer, or a surveyor—in all these events he has had the general education necessary as a ground-work for the advanced study that his profession requires; and it is at the moment of choosing a profession that an opportunity is given for specialization.

Does he want to devote himself to the art of war, engineering, or artillery? If so, he enters the specialised school of mathematics, i.e., the Polytechnic. What he learns there is the corollary of what he learnt in his elementary studies of mathematics; but the knowledge so acquired has to be developed and applied, and he proceeds to the various branches of Higher Mathematics. It is no longer merely a matter of general education, as in the *lycées,* but of a science to be mastered. The Observatory is another specialised school of mathematics.

The Natural History Museum, up to a certain point, may be counted in the same class, for there is a real analogy between the way in which different branches of knowledge are acquired and compared in botany and the other natural sciences, and it is in virtue of this that they have been classed among the exact and positive sciences. If it were possible to teach a smattering of botany, natural history, chemistry, and astronomy in the *lycées,* it could only be on the educational (as distinct from the scientific) level; for such elementary ideas would never make anyone a botanist, an astronomer, or a chemist.

Are there enough specialised schools for the exact sciences nowadays? Has this department been treated on a broad scale, like the rest of the éducational programme? These are questions that the Home Secretary should be investigating, if it has not been done already.

After the specialised schools of mathematics come those of law and medicine. These have been organised with special care, and need no extension. Law and medicine cannot avoid specialisation; for they are studied only by those who are going to practise the professions for which they are indispensable.

Generally speaking it is not the business of the specialised schools to give the preliminary instruction, which, to be adequate, must include the elements of most branches of knowledge, and which, as given in the *lycées,* fits young people, when they reach the age of discretion, to adopt one or other of the professions. On the contrary, it is their special business to teach some particular branch of knowledge from A to Z, so as to make a well-educated young man useful to society in some particular profession.

It follows that a school for advanced study is not an educational establishment, in the ordinary sense, but an establishment devoted to the instruction of men destined for some particular science or learned profession.

Mathematics, physics, natural history, medicine, and jurisprudence are all sciences, because they involve facts, observation, and comparison; because the discoveries which they make one by one accumulate, and form a series, linking age with age, and extending every day the scientific domain; and because the facts and their relationship, the art of classifying them, and the method of observing and comparing them, can be taught and understood.

The Minister wishes to have schools for the advanced study of literature: yet if the above considerations are sound, it is difficult to attach any meaning to the term. It is intended to teach eloquence, to teach poetry. But what remains to be taught in these subjects, beyond what every young man has learnt in his rhetoric class at school? It only takes a month or two to understand the structure of poetry, or to learn how to analyse a speech. To write well in verse and prose constitutes eloquence; but there is nothing in this art which can be taught in a more advanced way than in the *lycées.* There one is taught to write correctly, and to know and appreciate the best models; one is introduced to the canonical literature of good taste, and set to study the rules of composition, whether for tragedies or comedies, songs or epics: but one is never taught actually to compose any of these things. The creative talent in literature, as in music and painting, is an individual gift: it belongs to those personal faculties whose development is perhaps fostered by special circumstances, or by the customs of a particular age. In these creations of mind and genius, the mind or genius arrives at its finest achievements suddenly, and by means known only to itself. In tragedy, comedy, and epic poetry we have never surpassed the Greeks; they are still our models: whereas in the exact sciences, which rest upon the observation and comparison of facts, every enlightened age has made fresh advances. All this is so well understood, that a teacher of eloquence will not waste his time explaining the principles of the various *genres* of intellectual expression: he might just as well teach grammar and rhetoric, a knowledge of which has already been acquired at the *lycées.* Instead, he lectures, comments, quotes examples, and criticises model compositions; and whether it be done in an Athenaeum, a club, or a drawing-room, the result is no more than glorified table-talk. Is that a time for criticising the classics? What can be said that hasn't been said before? For criticising modern books, then?—the last thing anyone would do. There is therefore no meaning to be attached to a 'school for the advanced study of literature,' as there is to a club, a *salon,* or even an academy for teaching or lecturing. The whole business belongs, not to education in the proper sense, or to any specialised profession, but to the social amenities. . . .

TO JÉRÔME NAPOLÉON,* KING OF WESTPHALIA

Fontainebleau, November 15, 1807

I enclose the Constitution for your Kingdom. It embodies the conditions on which I renounce all my rights of conquest, and all the claims I have acquired over your state. You must faithfully observe it. I am concerned for the happiness of your subjects, not only as it affects your reputation, and my own, but also for its influence on the whole European situation. Don't listen to those who say that your subjects are so accustomed to slavery that they will feel no gratitude for the benefits you give them. There is more intelligence in the Kingdom of Westphalia than they would have you believe; and your throne will never be firmly established except upon the trust and affection of the common people. What German opinion impatiently demands is that men of no rank, but of marked ability, shall have an equal claim upon your favour and your employment, and that every trace of serfdom, or of a feudal hierarchy between the sovereign and the lowest class of his subjects, shall be done away. The benefits of the Code Napoléon, public trial, and the introduction of juries, will be the leading features of your government. And to tell you the truth, I count more upon their effects, for the extension and consolidation of your rule, than upon the most resounding victories. I want your subjects to enjoy a degree of liberty, equality, and prosperity hitherto unknown to the German people. I want this liberal regime to produce, one way or another, changes which will be of the utmost benefit to the system of the Confederation, and to the strength of your monarchy. Such a method of government will be a stronger barrier between you and Prussia than the Elbe, the fortresses, and the protection of France. What people will want to return under the arbitrary Prussian rule, once it has tasted the benefits of a wise and liberal administration? In Germany, as in France, Italy, and Spain, people long for equality and liberalism. I have been managing the affairs of Europe long enough now to know that the burden of the privileged classes was resented everywhere. Rule constitutionally. Even if reason, and the enlightenment of the age, were not sufficient cause, it would be good policy for one in your position; and you will find that the backing of public opinion gives you a great natural advantage over the absolute Kings who are your neighbours.

TO MARSHAL VICTOR, GOVERNOR OF BERLIN

Venice, December 6, 1807

I have received your letter informing me that Prince Augustus of Prussia is misbehaving himself at Berlin. I am not surprised to hear it. He is a good-for-nothing. He has been wasting his time at Coppet, making love to Mme de Staël,† and can have picked

* [Napoleon's youngest brother. (*Ed.*)]

† [French writer and liberal opposed to Napoleon. (*Ed.*)]

up nothing but bad principles there. We can't let it go on. Tell him that the first time he opens his mouth you will arrest him, and shut him up in a castle, and send Mme de Staël there too, to console him! A Prussian prince is the greatest bore in the world!

TO ALEXANDER I, EMPEROR OF RUSSIA

Paris, February 2, 1808

General Savary has just arrived, and I have spent two whole hours with him talking about Your Majesty. Everything he said touched my heart; I cannot lose a moment in thanking you for all the kindness that you have shown him, and that you are extending to my ambassador.

Your Majesty will have seen the latest speeches in the English Parliament, and its decision to carry on the war to the bitter end. This being so, I am writing direct to Caulaincourt. If Your Majesty will condescend to have a talk with him, he will explain my views. Nothing but measures on a really large scale will now enable us to secure peace, and to carry out our common designs. Your Majesty ought to enlarge and strengthen your army. All the help and assistance at my disposal will be freely given you; I have no feeling of jealousy towards Russia; my only desire is for her prosperity, her glory, and the further extension of her frontiers. Will Your Majesty graciously listen to the advice of one who claims to be honestly and affectionately attached to you? Your need is to remove the Swedes further from your capital. Extend your frontiers as far as you like in their direction. I am ready to help you in this with all the means in my power.

A Russo-French army of 50,000 men, including perhaps a few Austrians, marching viâ Constantinople into Asia, would no sooner appear on the Euphrates, than it would put England into a panic, and make her beg for mercy from the Continental powers. I am within striking distance in Dalmatia, Your Majesty on the Danube. Within a month of our plans being made this army could be at the Bosphorus. The blow would be felt in India, and England would collapse. I should refuse no preliminary stipulations that would enable me to achieve so great a result. But the reciprocal interests of our States must be balanced and combined. This can only be done in an interview with Your Majesty, especially if it is preceded by frank discussions between Romanzof and Caulaincourt, and by the despatch to Paris of someone who is really in our confidence. M. de Tolstoi is a fine fellow, but he is full of prejudices and distrust where France is concerned, and he is far from understanding the full significance of what happened at Tilsit, or the new orientation given to the world by the close friendship between Your Majesty and myself. The whole thing could be decided, and the agreement signed, before March 15. By May 1 our army could be in Asia, and Your Majesty's troops at Stockholm. Then the English, threatened in India, and expelled from the Levant, will be crushed under the weight of the events with which the atmosphere would be charged. Your Majesty and I should, no doubt, have preferred the pleasures of peace, and a life spent in the midst of our vast empires, regenerating them and making them happy by the arts and blessings of good government. This the enemies of the world will not allow: they must aggrandise themselves at our expense. Prudence and policy therefore dictate that we should do as destiny demands, and go whither we are led by the irresistible march of events. If we do so, this cloud of pygmy powers, whose only interests is to see whether the events of to-day can be parallelled in the newspaper accounts of the eighteenth century, will accommodate themselves to the movement imposed by Your Majesty and myself; whilst the Russian people will be grateful for the glory, the wealth, and the fortunes flowing from these great events.

Thus, in a few lines, I tell Your Majesty my inmost thoughts. What was done at Tilsit will rule the destiny of the world. Perhaps a touch of cowardice on Your Majesty's part, as well as on my own, led us to prefer a certain and immediate benefit to a better and more perfect setlement: but, since England will not have it so, let us recognise that the moment has come for great changes and great events.

TO COUNT FOUCHÉ, MINISTER OF POLICE

Valladolid, January 13, 1809

Now that we are in 1809, I think it would be useful to have some articles written, in good style, contrasting the misfortunes from which France was suffering in 1709 with the prosperous state of the Empire in 1809. The comparison should be worked out under several heads—territory and population, internal welfare, international prestige, finance, etc. You have got men competent to write 5 or 6 good articles on this very important subject, and to give public opinion a lead in the right direction. Louis XIV spent his time building Versailles, and a number of hunting-lodges. We spend our time improving Paris, from its water-supply to its palaces, from its markets to the Temple of Victory, and the Stock Exchange. Everything wanted doing, and everything is being done.

Starting from that point, one could go to speak of the perfection and simplicity that we have given to our institutions, and the tranquil flow of ideas that characterises 1809. In 1709 the edict of Nantes had been revoked, and the Protestants were being persecuted; Marshal Villars was wasting his generalship on civil war in the Cévennes, and Père Lachaise tyrannised over the conscience of the old King.[5] In 1809 the altars have been set up again, and we tolerate differences in religion. Under the head of morals, it could be pointed out that bishops no longer frequent houses of ill repute, or the ante-chambers of the rich, but stay at home in their dioceses. There is material for some splendid articles here. But we don't want to undertake a long work that would never be finished. We might have an article once a month, and all of them under the same title, "1709 and 1809."

[5] [. . . *The Edict of Nantes was revoked by Louis XIV in 1685. In 1703, Marshal Villars was recalled from a successful campaign in Germany to put down a rising of the* Camisards [*Calvinists*] *in the Cévennes* [*in southern France*]. *The Jesuit Père La Chaise was Louis XIV's confessor from 1674 to 1709.*]

TO M. MARET, DUKE OF BASSANO, MINISTER FOR FOREIGN AFFAIRS

Zanivki, right bank of the Beresina, near Zembine [6]

November 29, 1812

I have received your letter of November 25. You say nothing about France, and give me no news from Spain, though it is a fortnight since I received any information, or any messages, and I am completely in the dark.

I am marching on Vilekïa. It would be as well for Wrede and others to concentrate there, in order to make sure of the old bridges, and to construct a new one: have the necessary tools and materials ready.

We had a very hot action yesterday with Admiral Tchitchakof and Wittgenstein. We beat the former, who attacked us along the right bank on the Borisof road, and checked the latter, who was trying to seize the bridges over the Beresina. We took 6,000 prisoners: but we are much distressed at the loss of a brigade 3,000 strong under General Partouneaux, which took the wrong road, lost its way, and has apparently been captured. We have had no news of it for two days. The Duke of Reggio and a number of generals have been wounded.

The army is strong in numbers, but terribly disorganised. It would take a fortnight to reconstitute the regiments, and where is a fortnight to come from? The disorganisation is due to cold and privations. We shall soon be at Vilna: shall we be able to to hold out there? Yes, if we can do so for a week; but if we are attacked during the first week, it is doubtful whether we could stay there. Food, food, food! Without it, there is no limit to the horrors this undisciplined mass of men may bring upon the town. Perhaps the army will not rally until it is behind the Niemen. Things being in this pass, I may think it necessary for France, the Empire, and even the army, that I should be in Paris. Give me your advice.

There must have been a number of messengers captured. If you haven't had news of me since the 11th, write to Paris.

I am particularly anxious that there should be no foreign agents at Vilna. The army is not for exhibition purposes at the moment. Get rid of any who are there: for instance, you might tell them that you are going, and that I am going, to Warsaw, and direct them to follow us there, naming a day for their departure.

TO THE PRINCE OF NEUCHÂTEL, MAJOR-GENERAL OF THE GRAND ARMY

Waldheim, May 7, 1813

. . . The Prince of Eckmühl must move at once on Hamburg, occupy the town, and order General Vandamme into Mecklenburg. Here are his instructions.

He is to arrest summarily all citizens of Hamburg who have served as "Senators of

[6] [. . . *On November 26–9, Napoleon crossed the Beresina by extemporized bridges (the bridge on the Borisof road having been destroyed), but at the cost of some 30,000 men, largely wounded and stragglers. On December 5 he left the remnant of his army behind, and returned post-haste to Paris, which he reached on the 18th.*]

Hamburg." He is to court-martial the five chief culprits among them, and have them shot. The rest he will send to France, under strong escort, in order that they may be incarcerated in a state prison. He must sequestrate their property, and declare it confiscated: their houses, landed property, and so forth will fall into the crown domains. He is to disarm the whole town, shoot the officers of the Hanseatic Legion, and dispatch to France all who have enlisted in that regiment, in order that they may be sent to the galleys. As soon as the troops arrive at Schwerin, and without any warning, he must try to seize the Prince and his family, and send them to France for state imprisonment; for these dukes have been traitors to the Confederation. Their ministers will be treated in the same way. . . .

He is to draw up a list of 500 persons for proscription out of the 32nd military division, choosing the richest and worst-behaved. He will arrest them, and sequestrate their property, which will pass into the crown domains. This step is particularly necessary at Oldenburg.

He is to impose an indemnity of 50 millions on the towns of Hamburg and Lübeck, and to take steps for the assessment and prompt payment of this sum.

Everywhere he must disarm the countryside, arrest the gendarmes, artillerymen, coastguards, officers, soldiers, and officials: all have served against us, and therefore all are traitors. Their property is to be confiscated. Above all, he must not forget the Hamburg families who have behaved badly, and who are ill-disposed. The properties must be alienated; otherwise one can never be sure of the country.

Hamburg must be put in a state of defence, the gates be provided with draw-bridges, cannon placed on the ramparts, the parapets heightened, and a citadel established on the Hamburg side, so that 4–5,000 men may be safe there from any attack by the people within or the enemy without. . . . All these measures are obligatory. The Governor may not modify them in any particular. He is to declare that they are enforced by my express order, and to carry them out with such prudence as time and place require. Every individual known to have taken a leading part in the revolt must be shot or sent to the galleys. . . .

TO THE SOVEREIGNS OF EUROPE

Paris, April 4, 1815

Monsieur, my Brother,

You will have learnt, during the course of the last month, of my landing again in France, of my entry into Paris, and of the departure of the Bourbon family. Your Majesty must by now be aware of the real nature of these events. They are the work of an irresistible power, of the unanimous will of a great nation conscious of its duties and of its rights. A dynasty forcibly reimposed upon the French people was no longer suitable for it: the Bourbons refused to associate themselves with the national feelings or the national customs; and France was forced to abandon them. The popular voice called for a liberator. The expectation which had decided me to make the supreme sacrifice was in vain. I returned; and from the place where my foot first touched the shore I was carried by the affection of my subjects into the bosom of my capital.

My first and heartfelt anxiety is to repay so much affection by the maintenance of an honourable peace. The re-establishment of the Imperial throne was necessary for the happiness of Frenchmen: my dearest hope is that it may also secure repose for the whole of Europe. Each national flag in turn has had its gleam of glory: often enough, by some turn of fortune, great victories have been followed by great defeats. To-day a finer arena offers itself to the sovereigns of Europe, and I am the first to descend into it. I have provided the world in the past with a programme of great contests: it will please me better in future to acknowledge no rivalry but that of the advocates of peace, and no combat but a crusade for the felicity of mankind. It is France's pleasure to make a frank avowal of this noble ideal. Jealous of her independence, she will always base her policy upon an unqualified respect for the independence of other peoples. . . .

TO KING JOSEPH

Philippeville, June 19, 1815

. . . All is not lost. I suppose that, when I reassemble my forces, I shall have 150,000 men. The *fédérés* and national guards (such as are fit to fight) will provide 100,000 men, and the regimental depots another 50,000. I shall thus have 300,000 soldiers ready at once to bring against the enemy. I will use carriage-horses to drag the guns; raise 100,000 men by conscription; arm them with muskets taken from royalists, and from national guards unfit for service; organise a mass levy in Dauphiné, the Lyon district, Burgundy, Lorraine, Champagne; and overwhelm the foe. But people must help me, and not deafen me with advice. I am just off to Laon. I am sure to find somebody there. I have heard nothing of Grouchy. If he has not been captured, as I rather fear, that will give me 50,000 men within 3 days—plenty to keep the enemy occupied, and to give Paris and France time to do their duty. The Austrians are slow marchers: the Prussians are afraid of the peasantry, and dare not advance too far. There is still time to retrieve the situation. Write and tell me how the Chamber has been affected by this disastrous skirmish. I trust the deputies will realise that it is their duty at this crisis to stand by me, and to help me to save France. Prepare them to give me worthy support. Above all, steadfastness and courage!

TO THE PRINCE REGENT OF ENGLAND

Ile d'Aix, July 14, 1815

Your Royal Highness: victimised by the factions which divide my country, and by the hostility of the European powers, I have ended my political career; and I come, as Themistocles [7] did, to claim a seat by the hearth of the British people. I put myself

[7] [. . . *Themistocles, ostracised from Athens in 472 B.C., and pursued from Corcyra to Epirus, obtained the protection of Admetus, King of the Molossians.*]

under the protection of British law—a protection which I claim from Your Royal Highness, as the strongest, the stubbornest, and the most generous of my foes.

⤷ SPEECH ON THE NAPOLEONIC REGIME
Abbé de Montesquiou

Toward the end of Napoleon's imperial career, not only were his close civilian and military collaborators reexamining their personal commitment, but the emperor's mass support as well was clearly waning. Under these circumstances, a calm and judicious verdict on the Napoleonic regime could not be reached. Not only did the authoritarian state wield persuasive weapons against criticism, but fifteen years of official propaganda had obscured the failures and, in a sense, even the successes of the government by rendering all its claims suspect. The simple lack of information about the outcome of Napoleonic policies made an intelligent assessment impossible.

In 1814, in the face of crushing defeat at the hands of a European coalition and of general apathy in France, Napoleon resigned and was banished to the island of Elba in the Mediterranean. The Bourbon dynasty, almost forgotten in the generation since its overthrow in 1792, was restored, because there was no clear support for any alternative acceptable to the victors. It was obvious that Louis XVIII—an old man in 1814— could succeed only by conciliating the new vested interests created by the revolutionary and Napoleonic regimes—which included the peasantry, the middle classes, and the army.

The retrospective "state of the nation" speech delivered by the Abbé de Montesquiou, the moderate Minister of the Interior, before the French parliament, reflected the restored monarchy's wish to rally all men of good sense to the new government by a down-to-earth, sensible approach to the problems of the day. The actual author of the speech was a young history professor turned secretary-general of the Ministry of the Interior, François Guizot (1787–1874). Guizot's background made him an ideal exponent of the new moderate royalism, constitutional in fact if not in name. As a Protestant of middle-class background, Guizot was not likely to favor a return to the restrictive aristocratic society of the eighteenth century, nor, as the son of a victim of the revolutionary terror, did he endorse the open democratization of government and society. Although the speech was clearly a partisan indictment of the regime that had just fallen, it was exacting in its factual detail and balanced in tone. Its good intentions notwithstanding, the restored monarchy was unable to mobilize public support. Napoleon's brief return in 1815 is usually regarded as a resounding popular vote of no confidence in the Bourbons rather than as an unconditional endorsement of Bonapartism.

Guizot's own career was only beginning. He was first to achieve eminence as an outstanding historian; later, in the 1840s, he would become the conservative prime minister of the constitutional monarchy of Louis-Philippe.

Gentlemen   His Majesty, assuming once again the reins of government, has wished to acquaint his peoples with the state in which he has found France. While the cause of the misfortunes which afflicted our country has disappeared, its effects still linger. For a long time to come, even under a government that will only seek to restore, France will suffer from the blows dealt by a government that sought only to destroy. It is necessary, therefore, to inform the nation about the extent and the cause of its sufferings, so that it may be able to appreciate and to second the efforts designed to allay them. Thus enlightened as to the scope and nature of the evil, the nation will want to share her king's labors and efforts in reestablishing what he did not destroy, in healing wounds that he did not inflict, and in righting wrongs not of his doing.

Unquestionably, the war has been the main reason for France's misfortunes. Hitherto history has never offered the example of a great nation incessantly embroiled against its wishes in more and more hazardous enterprises. The spectacle of a civilized people condemned to trade its happiness and peace for the migrant life of barbarians has evoked astonishment mixed with terror. Family ties were broken, children were doomed to die four hundred miles from their parents. No hope of being reunited softened this horrible separation which people grew accustomed to consider inevitable and final. Breton peasants, having conducted their sons to the place of departure, were seen returning to their parish church to recite premature prayers for the dead.

It is impossible to evaluate the frightful number of men whom the former government consumed. Fatigue and disease carried off as many as did warfare. Enterprises were so vast and carried out with such speed that everything was sacrificed to assure their success. There was no reliable hospital service, nor were ambulances regularly supplied. These worthy soldiers, whose courage was France's glory, who gave ever new proofs of energy and endurance, who upheld so brilliantly the national honor, were neglected in their suffering and helplessly exposed to misfortunes which they could no longer bear. French charity was insufficient to make up for this cruel negligence,

Abbé de Montesquiou, "Speech on the Napoleonic Régime before the French Chamber of Deputies, July 12, 1814," *Le Moniteur universel*, July 13, 1814, pp. 771–774. Translated by Peter Amann.

and contingents of men who would once have made up great armies were thus wiped out without seeing combat. Hence arose the necessity of multiplying the number of levies, of continually replacing almost worn-out armies with newly raised ones. The statistics of the draft calls from the end of the Russian campaign are terrifying:

11 January 1813	350,000
3 April, Honor Guards	10,000
First levy of the National Guards	80,000
National Guards for the coasts	90,000
24 August, Army of Spain	30,000
9 October, Class of 1814 and earlier	120,000
Class of 1815	160,000
15 November, recall [to the colors of all classes] from the Year II [1793] to 1814	300,000
January 1814, engagement of equipped cavalry	17,000
1814, organized mass levies	143,000
	1,300,000

Fortunately these last levies could not be fully raised, nor did the war last long enough to mow down all those who had joined the colors. Yet by itself this account of the demands imposed upon the population within a space of fourteen to fifteen months underlines the losses which the nation must have sustained during twenty-two years.

There were, nevertheless, several factors that helped to compensate for these losses: improvements in the life of the rural inhabitants as a result of the breakup of large estates, of the equal division of inheritances, and of the spread of vaccination have no doubt been among the most significant. By relying on these and by overstating their effects, attempts were made to minimize the nation's sacrifices. The greater the number of men lost by France, the more determined the attempts to prove that the country could amply sustain this frightful destruction. Yet even had the publicized accounts been accurate, they would merely have demonstrated that the number of births justified a feeling of indifference in the face of the number of deaths.

Things were carried even further. It was claimed that conscription itself was a source of population increase, an impure source introducing disorder and immorality in marriages imprudently and precipitately contracted. Single men alone were subject to the draft; hence there were numerous unhappy households, many ridiculous or unsuitable unions. Some common folk, soon wearied by a condition they had chosen only to escape the draft, came to court the very dangers they had sought to avoid, by volunteering as substitutes in order to extricate themselves from a poverty they had not foreseen or to cast off ill-suited ties.

How could one fail to conclude, moreover, that though the draft, by multiplying these deplorable marriages, might increase the number of births, France each year was being drained of a large part of its already grown men who constitute the real strength of a nation? Indeed the figures bear out what naturally followed: while the population of less than twenty years of age increased, that above [that age sustained] a prodigious and incontestable decline.

Thus at the very time the government was sapping the sources of national prosperity, it proudly displayed the remnants of that prosperity that had continued to resist [the government's] fatal measures. It sought to cover up the harm it inflicted [by hiding] behind the well-being that still persisted and for which it could take no credit. Master of a country where prolonged labor had piled up great riches, where civilization had made the happiest progress, where industry and commerce had expanded prodigiously over the last sixty years, [the government] seized all these fruits of so many generations' work, of so many centuries' experience in order to enlist them now in behalf of its fatal plans, now to cloak the woeful effects of its own influence. The simple account of the kingdom's present state will show the continual struggle of national prosperity against a destructive principle, with the former incessantly under attack, often laid low by terrible blows, and ever left to its own inadequate resources.

MINISTRY OF THE INTERIOR

Agriculture has undergone real progress in France, progress that had begun long before the Revolution. Since that time new factors have accelerated its course, which would have had far more significant effects were it not for the fatal events that have nullified or circumscribed their influence.

Learned societies propagated advanced methods of agriculture, as did rich landed proprietors with their experimentation and instruction by example. Schools of veterinary medicine were founded to check the disaster of livestock epidemics. [All these] had the most positive results on the diverse branches of the rural economy, yet the government's errors and faults constantly raised obstacles to progress.

The Continental System inflicted enormous losses on vineyard owners. In the south of France many vineyards were rooted out when the low prices for wine and spirits generally discouraged this type of cultivation.

The experimental farm at Rambouillet, founded in 1786 by Louis XVI, had begun the introduction of Merino sheep into France. A great number of landowners had started similar undertakings. In 1799 the Perpignan farm was founded, followed by seven similar establishments within the next few years. The number of Merino sheep was growing, while our own breeds improved day by day. Yet the chief of the government, who sought to subject the march of nature to his restless ambition, became convinced that this improvement was neither sufficiently widespread nor rapid. A decree of 8 March 1811 ordered the creation of five hundred stations for Merino rams, each with two hundred rams, and also subjected the owners of private flocks to intolerable inspection. Discouraged by the many injunctions and prohibitions, offended by this continual surveillance that impeded them in their business and in managing their interests, the landowners soon gave up their sheepfolds. The breed, instead of improving rapidly, began to deteriorate. As war expenditures prevented the government from devoting adequate resources to its own sheep-stations, this imprudent measure cost France twenty millions that had previously been fruitfully used to propagate Merino sheep as well as to improve native breeds.

The creation of horse-breeding establishments met with greater success. First founded by the old government, they had been destroyed by the Revolution and were not completely reestablished until 1806. At that time six stud farms, thirty stud stations, and some experimental breeding establishments were organized. At the end of 1813 these farms held a total of 1,364 stallions, yet in the course of the same year 80,000 horses were requisitioned without consideration or choice. Approximate statistics figure the loss of horses since 1 January 1812 at 230,000. Cavalry mounts generally cost the government 400 to 600 francs per horse, which in terms of money puts the loss at about 105,200,000 francs.

Mining has increased substantially in France. Our territory now has 478 mines of all sorts in operation, employing 17,000 workers, and yielding a gross product for France of 26,800,000 francs and taxes to the state of 251,000 francs. The tax was allocated to the Bureau of Mines, but this special fund, amounting to 700,000 francs last January 1, has been used up for war expenditures, so that the staff [of the Bureau] has been going without salaries.

It is in the midst of such continual vexations, of such fickle and tyrannical legislation, of general impoverishment, that our fields have been cultivated, our mines operated, even our flocks at least in part preserved and improved! The fact that agriculture has progressed even under an oppressive government demonstrates better than anything else our nation's industriousness and its aptitude for this most basic human art. Is it a small thing to have worn down the farmer by that active tyranny that reached into the last thatch-covered hut? To have deprived him of his [field] hands, his capital, to have condemned him to ransom his sons only to have them carried off again? [The practice of] requisitioning, that most cunning invention of despotism, siphoning off all at once the entire fruits of his labor? Will posterity believe that we have seen one man set himself up as the absolute master over our properties and our sustenance, forcing us to bring [our goods] to a specific gathering place where they would be confiscated? A whole population leaving its homes with its cattle, its horses, its grain stores, to deliver up its wealth and its resources to this new overlord! Fortunate indeed if his agents did not add their infamous graft to our miseries! Yet let us throw a veil over these indignities and let us forget the excesses of tyranny to admire the gifts which nature's creator has granted to us. What other land could have resisted so many calamities? Yet such is the superiority of our soil and the industry of our farmers that agriculture will shine forth more brightly than ever [under the paternal regime that has come to end its miseries].

Manufacturing industry needs to find the same freedom once more. Mechanical engineering and chemistry, bolstered by numerous discoveries skillfully applied to technology, had made for rapid progress. The Continental System, by forcing manufacturers to rely on hitherto unexploited resources within our own territory, has had some useful consequences. Yet the obstacles raised against the importation of many raw materials and the lack of competition stemming from this, raised the prices of most commodities of French manufacture immeasurably, thus striking a fateful blow at the rights and interests of consumers. Some of these obstacles have already been eliminated. Reasonable laws dealing with imports and exports will henceforth harmonize the interests of consumers and manufacturers, interests that are only at odds when the claims of one or the other side are exaggerated.

If the reports of the factory owners may be believed, cotton manufactures now employ 400,000 workers and a capital of one hundred million. The manufactures of Rouen [textile center in Normandy] have already regained a brisk activity.

The linen manufactures of Laval and Brittany suffered greatly from the war with Spain, which [country] had been their chief outlet.

Silk manufactures met the same fate. It was through Spain that their products were shipped to America and the colonies. Though the manufacturers shifted their activity to northern Europe, the Italian market was soon the only one still retained. It is true that our internal consumption of silks increased, but how much would we not gain by free access to all of Europe, when our superiority in this type of manufacture is so patent?

In 1787 the Lyons silk manufactures had up to fifteen thousand looms in operation. During the last war this number fell to eight thousand. Already manufacturing is picking up again, for the city of Lyons has received very substantial orders.

The manufacture of cloth, leathers, etc., also suffered from the interruption of communications with foreign countries. In general, industry never stopped resisting the fatal influence of the Continental System and the laws associated with it. Though industry's attempts did not always remain fruitless, this merely pointed up the absurdity of the system. If industry could have fully utilized its forces, instead of wasting them in continual efforts at attenuating the effects of bad laws, what might not have been accomplished? And for how much may one not hope, now that the laws will support industry instead of weighting it down with chains.

COMMERCE

The prohibitive laws did even greater damage to commerce than to industry. If the difficulty of access to world markets restricted our manufacturers, at least within the market they did retain, their commodities were protected from foreign competition. If this deflection of manufacturing hurt the interests of consumers, at least a certain class of citizens realized some profit from it.

Yet commerce needs a broader and freer field of activity. Reduced to petty and unprofitable speculations, whenever it raised its sights, commerce fell victim to the indecision of a government that sought to subject it to governmental whims and schemes. The system of licenses ruined or demoralized a great number of traders by deluding them with [false] hopes, which would only be dashed by the same will which had raised them. Ventures that are necessarily risky require stable laws to support human foresight. This sudden and continual shifting between a system of [import] licenses and the complete prohibition [of imports] has been the cause of immense commercial losses. What peace of mind, moreover, could the merchants enjoy when they saw in the government a rival as rapacious as it was powerful, always careful to exploit the very area from which they were excluded? Only prolonged peace and stable, liberal laws will restore sufficient confidence among the merchants so that they may devote themselves without fear to their useful labors.

Such, in short, is the current situation as to the agricultural, industrial and commercial activity of the nation. . . . This activity, that required only freedom and encouragement, was constantly hindered and slowed down by the influence of a government which, seeking to master or to direct everything, undermined the very welfare it claimed to further. . . .

ADMINISTRATION OF TOWNSHIPS AND CHARITABLE INSTITUTIONS

The wish to take stock of and to watch over all French revenues, preliminary to seizing them one day, has been the chief motive for the methods used to administer communal property. By a decree of 4 Thermidor, Year X [1802], townships were divided into two classes: those with incomes above 20,000 francs constituted the first class, while the second comprised those with revenues below that sum. Budgets, including all [anticipated] incomes and [proposed] expenditures, had to be submitted in advance to the Minister of the Interior by townships of the first class; those of the second class submitted theirs to the prefects [official appointees of the Ministry of the Interior heading each French *département*].

A new decree forced all townships with incomes above 10,000 francs to have their budgets audited by the government; hence often harmful delays arose in the conduct of municipal administration. Ever new taxes with which the townships were saddled multiplied the transactions. Simple maintenance repairs amounting to more than 300 francs required special estimates that had to be checked and approved by the minister. This manner of administration which, adopted with moderation and restricted within reasonable limits, would have had the advantage of introducing greater regularity and exactness in municipal administration, resulted [instead] in an interminable dilatoriness of administration that frequently paralyzed all its activity. . . .

The administration of charitable institutions is in an even worse condition. This department had nonetheless undergone very important improvements since 1789, both as to allocation of funds and to its internal administration. Yet as early as 1811 the state of the finances prevented the government from assigning to this service the funds that were to have been allotted to it. A decree of 19 January 1811 granted no more than four million for the expenditures of foundling homes throughout the kingdom [to cover] expenses annually totalling nine million. By the beginning of 1813, charitable institutions in Paris already had an estimated deficit of 210,000 francs, a deficit that has risen fantastically since then due to the placing of military patients into civilian hospitals without contributing to the cost of these beds. On this account alone the Ministry of War owes Paris hospitals the sum of 1,395,365 francs 60 centimes. Supplies, drugs, etc., are exhausted; reserves of furniture, linens, etc., are either exhausted or lost. While the value of this loss cannot yet be calculated, it amounts to several millions.

PUBLIC WORKS

After this report on general administration, let us turn our attention to public works. Great works have been undertaken, some for truly useful purposes, many others from ostentation or for reasons having nothing to do with the happiness of France. While magnificent roads fanned out beyond our frontiers, internal roads were neglected, while local cart tracks, left to [the care of] townships no longer financially able to keep them in good repair, deteriorated badly. Special funds voted by the *départements* for road work were diverted from this use, as well as 15,500,000 francs deposited for this purpose in the sinking fund. The bureau of roads and bridges has a deficit of more than twenty-eight millions, yet this department will have to take care of all the extraordinary repairs occasioned by the disasters of the last campaign. Thirty main bridges have been cut or burned, and provisional reconstruction, using only wood, will cost 1,800,000 francs. So far, damage sustained by the roads and the sums required to recondition them cannot be estimated, but one may predict a very considerable expenditure.

The canals are in better conditions, but the public works that have been begun are not nearly completed. The Burgundy canal has already cost twelve millions and will need five more to finish the repairs. This enterprise and that of the Saint-Quentin canal deserve praise. The canal of the Ourcq River [connecting the Seine River with northeastern French waterways], carried out according to an excessively costly plan, requires further expenditures of at least eighteen millions.

Public works in Paris have been subject to the special attention of the government because it saw in them a way of displaying great magnificence in addition to making itself popular. A few of these projects, such as the five slaughterhouses, the wine wholesale warehouses, and the markets will be truly useful. The expenditures for the slaughterhouses alone have been estimated at 12,800,000, of which 7,680,000 has already been paid, with 5,120,000 owing to complete them. As to the markets, no more than 1,200,000 will be needed for completion.

Though other projects for the embellishment of the capital offer less direct advantages, all of them should not, nevertheless, be abandoned. Total expenditures for the above have been estimated at 53,510,000, of which 24,191,000 francs have already been spent. . . . In truth, a part of these expenditures should be cut or can be postponed.

The public treasury almost never underwrote these immense undertakings: the government's role was confined to authorizing the *départements* to raise supplementary taxes to channel into the construction projects that had been decreed. When the government did furnish supplementary funds, these were not drawn from the general treasury of the state, but were rather diverted from the proceeds from special lumbering operations [carried out] by townships or from communal funds deposited in the sinking fund. In this manner eleven millions were provided for prisons and five millions for almshouses. The construction of almshouses will require an additional expenditure of about 8,800,000 francs.

According to this hasty and necessarily incomplete report, one may grasp the situation of the Ministry of the Interior in relation to its diverse functions. The deficit of this ministry cannot as yet be estimated. The information requested from the prefects has not yet been assembled, but a general estimate would place the deficit between forty and fifty millions. The projects that had been begun and that are now suspended would require an even greater sum for their completion. . . .

MINISTRY OF WAR

For the Ministry of War we can only present approximate figures, the accuracy of which cannot be guaranteed. . . . One senses that this disorder was bound to be even greater in the ministry which, if one may say so, was its center and hearth, and which, complex to begin with, was plunged into chaos by the disasters of the last three campaigns. Liquidation commissioners have been ordered to examine the losses incurred in these campaigns and the debts contracted thereby, yet the documents needed for this task have not all been recovered, so that one has to supplement facts by more or less uncertain estimates. . . .

MINISTRY OF THE NAVY

During these last fourteen years the navy has gradually been weakened by the very means used to provide the illusion of strength.

To display a fictitious power along the coasts; to appear to be planning gigantic projects for which the means, however inflated, were inadequate; to view seafaring men only as potential recruits for the land army—such was the system of the previous government which has brought on the destruction of our maritime personnel and the depletion of our naval bases. Warnings by the most sensible men, by the most experienced sailors, even factual evidence, were never able to halt these mad undertakings, these violent measures that belonged to a plan of combination oppressive in its every aspect. Thus in 1804 the plan to invade England was announced ostentatiously. Immediately a port suitable only for fishing trawlers and packet boats was transformed into a vast naval arsenal. Harbor installations were begun on a beach which the tides and winds covered with sand. At great cost, forts, batteries, workshops, storehouses were erected. Thousands of ships were constructed or purchased along every seacoast, as well as along the interior rivers, without considering whether [these ships] could even reach the staging area. Even Paris saw the creation of a navy yard within its walls. Lumber and valuable stores were devoted to building and outfitting a variety of ships that were not even suited to the purpose! And what is left today of all these war preparations? Remnants of a few boats, deplorable accounts which prove that more than 150 millions were sacrificed from 1803 on to create [this flotilla] and then let it decay. Everything that engineering skill and sailors' brave perseverance could do was [indeed] accomplished on the Scheldt River [in present-day Belgium]. Within a short time a large squadron easily navigated a river that had been considered unnavigable for large warships; numerous crews, trained by a competent admiral, supported whenever necessary the land army's operations. And just recently they defended with rare courage the naval base from which their fleet had sailed. . . .

The great works carried out at Cherbourg with so much success, the great Toulon fleet, represent the only useful accomplishments. Elsewhere only mistakes and lack of foresight are conspicuous.

All our naval bases are completely denuded. The immense naval construction that

Louis XVI carefully built up after the peace of 1783 has been squandered. In the course of ill-conceived and ill-organized expeditions during the last fifteen years, France has lost forty-two ships of the line, eight-two frigates, seventy-six corvettes, and sixty-two transports or sloops, which could not be replaced at the cost of 200 millions.

The harbor of Brest, the handsomest, perhaps the best in Europe, where immense fleets may gather in safety and where vast and magnificent facilities exist, has been entirely neglected.

If the naval arsenals are depleted and without munitions, the vessels are even more denuded of real seamen.

The loss of our colonies, the arbitrary measures that were the constant bane of our commerce, the vexations to which fishermen were subjected, the length of the war, the reverses experienced by our fleets, would have been enough to destroy the seafaring population; yet another motive determined the government to pronounce, if one may say so, its absolute extinction.

Our crews, which after the disappearance of our seafaring men had to be recruited by conscription, were organized as front-line regiments. A number of these crews left their ships to fight in German fields and Asturian mountains. Commanded by brave leaders, they helped to uphold the glory of French arms, yet in their encampments they lost their maritime habits. . . .

MINISTRY OF FINANCE

The report on the situation of the Ministry of Finance should, since it is the focal point [for financial operations] shed light on the condition of all the other ministries. Before indicating the results, it is necessary to explain how the former government was able to hide its dealings.

At first glance, the former government's system of government gives the appearance of order and efficiency. Before the beginning of each fiscal year, the Minister of Finance had to combine requests [for funds] by the ministers for the [coming] year's expenditures in order to draw up the budget of outlay. He also had to determine, on the basis of a rough estimate, the account of all taxes and revenues from which the income budget was then determined. These two [sets of] statistics, set up as a balance sheet, constituted the general budget of the state and seemed to promise that by collecting total revenues the outlays of all departments would be defrayed. Yet this balance was really fictitious; the budget, both as to income and to outlay, was distorted by a great many inaccuracies and even some falsifications.

The funds designated as "special," amounting to more than 100 million a year, were not included in the budget. Many extraordinary expenditures were not credited to any ministry. War expenditures were calculated on the basis of [fictitious] manpower, [estimates] far below that of the actual manpower [employed]. One or more drafts would be raised, cavalry mounts, food supplies and public works ordered in the course of a year, without any proportionate increase in budgets. The latter thus became inevitably inadequate, creating a sizeable deficit that increased day by day. Most of the estimated revenues were, moreover, contingent, overestimated, non-collectable, or else only a sum less than the estimated one could [in fact] be collected. Thus the budgets of 1812 and 1813 had a deficit of 312,032,000 francs.

The head of the government was not unaware of these deficits, but he always hoped to make them up either by [the kind of] foreign tribute which his early campaigns had brought in, or by dipping into the special funds, the extrordinary domain finances, the sinking fund, departmental funds, etc. As a result, most of these funds, [originally] not intended for war expenditures, were actually used for them, thus creating a considerable financial deficit. . . . The total of the increase in state indebtedness during these thirten years amounted to the sum of 1,645,469,000 francs.

No doubt such calculations are frightening. Yet the outcome should not be considered an irremediable evil. The Finance Minister will explain to you what sums are subject to immediate repayment, what monies need only to be repaid at the end of a certain period and, finally, what funds simply entail [continued] interest charges. As for us, called as we are merely to present a report on the current state of the kingdom, we have confined ourselves to this distressing task. We have not concealed anything. The accompanying tables bear out with detailed evidence the fact we have summarized. These details will show you at the same time both the disease and the hope for a cure. You will see therein what vitality constantly sustained and renewed France in the midst of her losses, by what means she struggled against ever new disasters. You will be astonished to see how fertile and well cultivated this countryside is, even though it had for so long been exposed to devastation. Though fearful of the government's indebtedness, you will see, on the other hand, substantial capital in private hands that is ready to be funnelled into useful enterprises. Far from despairing about national prosperity, considering all that France has suffered and borne, you may judge for yourself how much can be expected of her under a government whose well-meaning intentions only require her support.

Yet the concerns of this government will not be confined to the reestablishment of a purely material prosperity. Other sources of happiness and glory have been under cruel attack. No less than public wealth can morality escape the baleful influence of a bad government. In this respect [the last government] accentuated evils which the Revolution had brought about. It reestablished religion only to make religion an instrument for its own use.

Public education, subjected to the same dependence, has been unable to respond to the efforts of the respectable body of men who direct it. Their efforts have unceasingly been thwarted by a despotism that sought to dominate all minds in order to enslave all lives unimpeded. National education, to be maintained at the level of European enlightenment, needs to regain a more liberal direction by reverting to principles too long forgotten among us.

Would that one could restore to France those moral habits and that public spirit almost extinguished by cruel misfortunes and long oppression! Noble sentiments have been stifled, generous ideas smothered. Content not only to condemn to inaction the virtues it dreaded, the government stirred up and fomented whatever passions could serve its interests. To extinguish public-spiritedness, it called upon selfish interests. The government closed off all avenues save service in its own behalf. It discouraged all aspirations except those that it alone could satisfy. Boundless ambitions and exaggerated claims were encouraged. Interests and appetites being kept in turmoil, employment became unstable. As almost everyone thought only of improving his status, men lost the qualities proper to their station in life. At last, even the most generous characters had trouble preserving their integrity from every sort of seduction.

Such are the melancholy effects of this corrupting system which today we must fight. We do not conceal its scope. There are periods when peoples, like rulers, need to hear the truth, even though it be mournful and harsh; we have not been afraid to tell it to you. The troubles of the moment are painful, the difficulties great. Much can be expected from [the passage of] time. The nation will feel it necessary to act zealously in hastening the return of its own good fortunes. [The nation's] confidence in her king's intentions, in the enlightenment and wisdom of the two Chambers, will render the government's task less drawn out and onerous. If there were anything that could prevent the prompt realization of these hopes, it would be this restless turbulence seeking to enjoy without delay advantages merely glimpsed; yet your prudence will preserve us from this.

If the taxes were left unpaid, the debts would grow, and our inadequate resources would preclude the diminution of the tax rate. If general unity did not sustain the well-meaning views of our king, useful enterprises would be halted, important improvements suspended, while the impossibility of doing good would increase the evil that has already been done.

While regretting the improvements that must still be postponed, let us enjoy those available to us. Peace is once again opening our harbors. Liberty brings the trader back to his ventures, the worker to his labors; vitality surges in all the members of the body politic. Everyone sees the end of his troubles and glimpses happier destinies. Could we be indifferent to this future peace, after having lived so long with turmoil and anxiety? You will scarcely be insensitive to this, gentlemen. The king also has confidence in his people and their representatives, while France expects everything from their generous agreement. What happier circumstance than that of an assembly that has deserved so well of our country and of a king who wants only to be [the nation's] father. Let us enjoy, gentlemen, this happy reunion. Consider what France expects and what you have already accomplished. May these happy beginnings encourage you in your course, and may the gratitude of your remotest descendants be your emulation, your glory and your reward.

ঙ্গ SECRET MEMORANDUM

Metternich

*Clemens, Prince von Metternich (1773–1859), an imperial knight from
the Rhineland, entered the Habsburg diplomatic service in 1797, rising
to the post of Austrian foreign minister in 1809. Metternich's own
aristocratic and cosmopolitan background was to be reflected in his long
(1809–1848) career as the architect of Austrian (and at times European)
international policies. During Napoleon's ascendancy, Metternich's course
was flexible, running the gamut from appeasement through containment to
out-and-out opposition. In the year after 1815, Metternich stood for
international peace and the repression of any liberal and/or nationalistic
movements that might jeopardize the stability of the multinational state
and the conservative, aristocratic Europe which he served. For the pursuit
of his policies, Metternich relied on maintaining consensus among the
victors over Napoleon (though a chastened France was soon admitted to
this "Concert of Europe"), who dealt with specific problems of common
concern in international conferences or "Congresses." Undermined by the
Greek war of independence, which breached the great-power consensus,
and shattered by the revolutions of 1830, Metternich's dominance survived
in Austria and Germany until 1848.*

Always a diplomat rather than a political theorist, Metternich wrote the
Secret Memorandum *in the fall of 1820 in order to extend his influence
over the Russian Czar, Alexander I. Alexander had originally displayed
vague but persistent liberal leanings out of keeping with the position of the
Autocrat of All the Russias. It was he who in 1815 had founded a sort
of college fraternity for the crowned heads of Europe, the Holy Alliance,
which threatened to get in the way of the more businesslike diplomatic
arrangements that Metternich had envisaged. As Alexander gradually became converted to a mystical conservatism, his inclination in 1820 to send
Russian troops across Europe to crush revolution in Spain was as embarrassing to Metternich as the Russian ruler's liberalism had been earlier.
In his* Memorandum, *the Austrian foreign minister outlined the rational
bases of international conservatism, while flatteringly adopting as his own
Alexander's Holy Alliance of European monarchs. At the same time,
however, Metternich also succeeded in persuading Alexander to renounce
intervention in Spain (which was left to France) and endorse Austrian
suppression of a liberal revolution in southern Italy.*

"L'Europe," a celebrated writer has recently said, "fait aujourd'hui pitié à l'homme d'esprit et horreur à l'homme vertueux." *

It would be difficult to comprise in a few words a more exact picture of the situation at the time we are writing these lines!

Kings have to calculate the chances of their very existence in the immediate future; passions are let loose, and league together to overthrow everything which society respects as the basis of its existence; religion, public morality, laws, customs, rights, and duties, all are attacked, confounded, overthrown, or called in question. The great mass of the people are tranquil spectators of these attacks and revolutions, and of the absolute want of all means of defence. A few are carried off by the torrent, but the wishes of the immense majority are to maintain a repose which exists no longer, and of which even the first elements seem to be lost.

What is the cause of all these evils? By what methods has this evil established itself, and how is it that it penetrates into every vein of the social body?

Do remedies still exist to arrest the progress of this evil, and what are they?

These are doubtless questions worthy of the solicitude of every good man who is a true friend to order and public peace—two elements inseparable in principle, and which are at once the first needs and the first blessings of humanity.

Has there never been offered to the world an institution really worthy of the name? Has truth been always confounded with error ever since society has believed itself able to distinguish one from the other? Have the experiences bought at the price of so many sacrifices, and repeated at intervals, and in so many different places, been all in error? Will a flood of light be shed upon society at one stroke? Will knowledge come by inspiration? If one could believe in such phenomena it would not be the less necessary, first of all, to assure oneself of their reality. Of all things, nothing is so fatal as error; and it is neither our wish nor our intention ever to give ourselves up to it. Let us examine the matter!

THE SOURCE OF THE EVIL

Man's nature is immutable. The first needs of society are and remain the same, and the differences which they seem to offer find their explanation in the diversity of influences, acting on the different races by natural causes, such as the diversity of climate, barrenness or richness of soil, insular or continental position, etc. etc. These local differences no doubt produce effects which extend far beyond purely physical necessities; they create and determine particular needs in a more elevated sphere; finally, they determine the laws, and exercise an influence even on religion.

It is, on the other hand, with institutions as with everything else. Vague in their

Clemens Metternich, "Confusion of Faith," in *Memoirs of Prince Metternich*, ed. Prince R. Metternich (London, 1880–1882), III, 454–476.

* ["Today Europe inspires pity in the man of intelligence, horror in the man of virtue." (*Ed.*)]

origin, they pass through periods of development and perfection, to arrive in time at their decadence; and, conforming to the laws of man's nature, they have, like him, their infancy, their youth, their age of strength and reason, and their age of decay.

Two elements alone remain in all their strength, and never cease to exercise their indestructible influence with equal power. These are the precepts of morality, religious as well as social, and the necessities created by locality. From the time that men attempt to swerve from these bases, to become rebels against these sovereign arbiters of their destinies, society suffers from a *malaise* which sooner or later will lead to a state of convulsion. The history of every country, in relating the consequences of such errors, contains many pages stained with blood; but we dare to say, without fear of contradiction, one seeks in vain for an epoch when an evil of this nature has extended its ravages over such a vast area as it has done at the present time. The causes are natural.

History embraces but a very limited space of time. It did not begin to deserve the name of history until long after the fall of great empires. There, where it seems to conduct us to the cradle of civilisation, it really conducts us to ruins. We see republics arise and prosper, struggle, and then submit to the rule of one fortunate soldier. We see one of these republics pass through all the phases common to society, and end in an almost universal monarchy—that is to say, subjugating the scattered portions of the then civilised world. We see this monarchy suffer the fate of all political bodies: we see its first springs become enfeebled, and finally decay.

Centuries of darkness followed the irruption of the barbarians. The world, however, could not return to barbarism. The Christian religion had appeared; imperishable in its essence, its very existence was sufficient to disperse the darkness and establish civilisation on new foundations, applicable to all times and all places, satisfying all needs, and establishing the most important of all on the basis of a pure and eternal law! To the formation of new Christian States succeeded the Crusades, a curious mixture of good and evil.

A decisive influence was shortly exercised on the progress of civilisation by three discoveries—the invention of printing, that of gunpowder, and the discovery of the New World. Still later came the Reformation—another event which had incalculable effects, on account of its influence on the moral world. From that time the face of the world has changed.

The facilitation of the communication of thoughts by printing; the total change in the means of attack and defence brought about by the invention of gunpowder; the difference suddenly produced in the value of property by the quantity of metals which the discovery of America put in circulation; the spirit of adventure provoked by the chances of fortune opened in a new hemisphere; the modifications in the relations of society caused by so many and such important changes, all became more developed, and were in some sort crowned by the revolution which the Reformation worked in the moral world.

The progress of the human mind has been extremely rapid in the course of the last three centuries. This progress having been accelerated more rapidly than the growth of wisdom (the only counterpoise to passions and to error); a revolution prepared by the false systems, the fatal errors into which many of the most illustrious sovereigns of the last half of the eighteenth century fell, has at last broken out in a country advanced in knowledge, and enervated by pleasure, in a country inhabited by a people whom one can only regard as frivolous, from the facility with which they comprehend and the difficulty they experience in judging calmly.

Having now thrown a rapid glance over the first causes of the present state of society, it is necessary to point out in a more particular manner the evil which threatens to deprive it, at one blow, of the real blessings, the fruits of genuine civilisation, and to disturb it in the midst of its enjoyments. This evil may be described in one word—presumption; the natural effect of the rapid progression of the human mind towards the perfecting of so many things. This it is which at the present day leads so many individuals astray, for it has become an almost universal sentiment.

Religion, morality, legislation, economy, politics, administration, all have become common and accessible to everyone. Knowledge seems to come by inspiration; experience has no value for the presumptuous man; faith is nothing to him; he substitutes for it a pretended individual conviction, and to arrive at this conviction dispenses with all inquiry and with all study; for these means appear too trivial to a mind which believes itself strong enough to embrace at one glance all questions and all facts. Laws have no value for him, because he has not contributed to make them, and it would be beneath a man of his parts to recognize the limits traced by rude and ignorant generations. Power resides in himself; why should he submit himself to that which was only useful for the man deprived of light and knowledge? That which, according to him, was required in an age of weakness cannot be suitable in an age of reason and vigour, amounting to universal perfection, which the German innovators designate by the idea, absurd in itself, of the Emancipation of the People! Morality itself he does not attack openly, for without it he could not be sure for a single instant of his own existence; but he interprets its essence after his own fashion, and allows every other person to do so likewise, provided that other person neither kills nor robs him.

In thus tracing the character of the presumptuous man, we believe we have traced that of the society of the day, composed of like elements, if the denomination of society is applicable to an order of things which only tends in principle towards individualising all the elements of which society is composed. Presumption makes every man the guide of his own belief, the arbiter of laws according to which he is pleased to govern himself, or to allow some one else to govern him and his neighbours; it makes him, in short, the sole judge of his own faith, his own actions, and the principles according to which he guides them.

Is it necessary to give a proof of this last fact? We think we have furnished it in remarking that one of the sentiments most natural to man, that of nationality, is erased from the Liberal catechism, and that where the word is still employed, it is used by the heads of the party as a pretext to enchain Governments, or as a lever to bring about destruction. The real aim of the idealists of the party is religious and political fusion, and this being analysed is nothing else but creating in favour of each individual an existence entirely independent of all authority, or of any other will than his own, an idea absurd and contrary to the nature of man, and incompatible with the needs of human society.

THE COURSE WHICH THE EVIL HAS FOLLOWED AND STILL FOLLOWS

The causes of the deplorable intensity with which this evil weighs on society appear to us to be of two kinds. The first are so connected with the nature of things that no human foresight could have prevented them. The second should be subdivided into two classes, however similar they may appear in their effects.

Of these causes, the first are negative, the others positive. We will place among the first the feebleness and the inertia of Governments.

It is sufficient to cast a glance on the course which the Governments followed during the eighteenth century, to be convinced that not one among them was ignorant of the evil or of the crisis towards which the social body was tending. There were, however, some men, unhappily endowed with great talents, who felt their own strength, and were not slow to appraise the progressive course of their influence, taking into account the weakness or the inertia of their adversaries; and who had the art to prepare and conduct men's minds to the triumph of their detestable enterprise—an enterprise all the more odious as it was pursued without regard to results, simply abandoning themselves to the one feeling of hatred of God and of His immutable moral laws.

France had the misfortune to produce the greatest number of these men. It is in her midst that religion and all that she holds sacred, that morality and authority, and all connected with them, have been attacked with a steady and systematic animosity, and it is there that the weapon of ridicule has been used with the most ease and success.

Drag through the mud the name of God and the powers instituted by His divine decrees, and the revolution will be prepared! Speak of a social contract, and the revolution is accomplished! The revolution was already completed in the palaces of Kings, in the drawing-rooms and boudoirs of certain cities, while among the great mass of the people it was still only in a state of preparation.

It would be difficult not to pause here to consider the influence which the example of England had for a long time exercised on France. England is herself placed in such a peculiar situation that we believe we may safely say that not one of the forms possible to that State, not one of its customs or institutions, would suit any Continental State, and that where we might wish to take them for models, we should only obtain inconvenience and danger, without securing a single one of the advantages which accompany them.

According to the bent of minds in France, at the time of the convocation of the *notables,* and in consequence of the direction which public opinion had received for more than fifty years—a direction which, latterly, had been strengthened and in some sort adapted to France by the imprudent help which her Government had given to the American revolution—all reform in France touching the very foundations of the monarchy was soon transformed into a revolution. What might have been foreseen, and what had been foretold by everybody, the Government alone excepted, was realised but too soon. The French Revolution broke out, and has gone through a complete revolutionary cycle in a very short period, which could only have appeared long to its victims and to its contemporaries.

The scenes of horror which accompanied the first phases of the French Revolution prevented the rapid propagation of its subversive principles beyond the frontiers of France, and the wars of conquest which succeeded them gave to the public mind a direction little favourable to revolutionary principles. Thus the Jacobin propaganda failed entirely to realise criminal hopes.

Nevertheless the revolutionary seed had penetrated into every country and spread more or less. It was greatly developed under the *régime* of the military despotism of Bonaparte. His conquests displaced a number of laws, institutions, and customs; broke through bonds sacred among all nations, strong enough to resist time itself; which is more than can be said of certain benefits conferred by these innovators. From these perturbations it followed that the revolutionary spirit could in Germany, Italy, and later on in Spain, easily hide itself under the veil of patriotism.

Prussia committed a grave fault in calling to her aid such dangerous weapons as secret associations always will be: a fault which could not be justified even by the deplorable situation in which that Power then found itself. This it was that first gave a strong impulse to the revolutionary spirit in her States, and this spirit made rapid progress, supported as it was in the rest of Germany by the system of foreign despotism which since 1806 has been there developed. Many Princes of the Rhenish Confederation were secretly auxiliaries and accomplices of this system, to which they sacrificed the institutions which in their country from time immemorial had served as a protection against despotism and democracy.

The war of the Allies, by putting bounds to the predominance of France, was vigorously supported in Germany by the same men whose hatred of France was in reality nothing but hatred of the military despotism of Bonaparte, and also of the legitimate power of their own masters. With wisdom in the Governments and firmness in principles, the end of the war in 1814 might nevertheless have insured to the world the most peaceful and happy future. Great experiences had been gained and great lessons, which might have been usefully applied. But fate had decided otherwise.

The return of the usurper to France, and the completely false steps taken by the French Government from 1815 to 1820, accumulated a mass of new dangers and great calamities for the whole civilised world. It is to the first of these misfortunes that is partly due the critical state in which France and the whole social body is placed. Bonaparte destroyed in a hundred days the work of the fourteen years during which he had exercised his authority. He set free the revolution which he came to France to subdue; he brought back men's minds, not to the epoch of the 18th Brumaire, but to the principles which the National Assembly had adopted in its deplorable blindness.

What Bonaparte had thus done to the detriment of France and Europe, the grave errors which the French Government have since committed, and to which other Governments have yielded—all these unhappy influences weigh heavily on the world of to-day; they threaten with total ruin the work of restoration, the fruit of so many glorious efforts, and of a harmony between the greatest monarchs unparalleled in the records of history, and they give rise to fears of indescribable calamities to society.

In this memoir we have not yet touched on one of the most active and at the same time most dangerous instruments used by the revolutionists of all countries, with a success which is no longer doubtful. I refer to the secret societies, a real power, all the more dangerous as it works in the dark, undermining all parts of the social body, and depositing everywhere the seeds of a moral gangrene which is not slow to develop and increase. This plague is one of the worst which those Governments who are lovers of peace and of their people have to watch and fight against.

DO REMEDIES FOR THIS EVIL EXIST, AND WHAT ARE THEY?

We look upon it as a fundamental truth, that for every disease there is a remedy, and that the knowledge of the real nature of the one should lead to the discovery of the other. Few men, however, stop thoroughly to examine a disease which they intend to combat. There are hardly any who are not subject to the influence of passion, or held under the yoke of prejudice; there are a great many who err in a way more perilous still, on account of its flattering and often brilliant appearance: we speak of *l'esprit de système;* that spirit always false but indefatigable, audacious and irrepressible, is satisfactory to men imbued with it (for they live in and govern a world created by themselves), but it is so much the more dangerous for the inhabitants of the real world, so different from that created by *l'esprit de système.*

There is another class of men who, judging of a disease by its outward appearance, confound the accessory manifestations with the root of the disease, and, instead of directing their efforts to the source of the evil, content themselves with subduing some passing symptoms.

It is our duty to try and avoid both of these dangers.

The evil exists and it is enormous. We do not think we can better define it and its cause at all times and in all places than we have already done by the word "presumption" (that inseparable companion of the half-educated, that spring of an unmeasured ambition, and yet easy to satisfy in times of trouble and confusion).

It is principally the middle classes of society which this moral gangrene has affected, and it is only among them that the real heads of the party are found.

For the great mass of the people it has no attraction and can have none. The labours to which this class—the real people—are obliged to devote themselves, are too continuous and too positive to allow them to throw themselves into vague abstractions and ambitions. The people know what is the happiest thing for them: namely, to be able to count on the morrow, for it is the morrow which will repay them for the cares and sorrows of to-day. The laws which afford a just protection to individuals, to families, and to property, are quite simple in their essence. The people dread any movement which injures industry and brings new burdens in its train.

Men in the higher classes of society who join the revolution are either falsely ambitious men or, in the widest acceptation of the word, lost spirits. Their career, moreover, is generally short! They are the first victims of political reforms, and the part played by the small number among them who survive is mostly that of courtiers despised by upstarts, their inferiors, promoted to the first dignities of the State; and of this France, Germany, Italy, and Spain furnish a number of living examples.

We do not believe that fresh disorders with a directly revolutionary end—not even revolutions in the palace and the highest places in the Government—are to be feared at present in France, because of the decided aversion of the people to anything which might disturb the peace they are now enjoying after so many troubles and disasters.

In Germany, as in Spain and Italy, the people ask only for peace and quiet.

In all four countries the agitated classes are principally composed of wealthy men— real cosmopolitans, securing their personal advantage at the expense of any order of things whatever—paid State officials, men of letters, lawyers, and the individuals charged with the public education.

To these classes may be added that of the falsely ambitious, whose number is never considerable among the lower orders, but is larger in the higher ranks of society.

There is besides scarcely any epoch which does not offer a rallying cry to some particular faction. This cry, since 1815, has been *Constitution.* But do not let us deceive ourselves: this word, susceptible of great latitude of interpretation, would be but imperfectly understood if we supposed that the factions attached quite the same meaning to it under the different *régimes.* Such is certainly not the case. In pure monarchies it is qualified by the name of "national representation." In countries which have lately been brought under the representative *régime* it is called "development," and promises charters and fundamental laws. In the only State which possesses an ancient national representation it takes "reform" as its object. Everywhere it means change and trouble.

In pure monarchies it may be paraphrased thus:—"The level of equality shall pass over your heads; your fortunes shall pass into other hands; your ambitions, which have been satisfied for centuries, shall now give place to our ambitions, which have been hitherto repressed."

In the States under a new *régime* they say:—"The ambitions satisfied yesterday must give place to those of the morrow, and this is the morrow for us."

Lastly, in England, the only place in the third class, the rallying cry—that of Reform—combines the two meanings.

Europe thus presents itself to the impartial observer under an aspect at the same time deplorable and peculiar. We find everywhere the people praying for the maintenance of peace and tranquillity, faithful to God and their Princes, remaining proof against the efforts and seductions of the factions who call themselves friends of the people and wish to lead them to an agitation which the people themselves do not desire!

The Governments, having lost their balance, are frightened, intimidated, and thrown into confusion by the cries of the intermediary class of society, which, placed between the Kings and their subjects, breaks the sceptre of the monarch, and usurps the cry of the people—that class so often disowned by the people, and nevertheless too much listened to, caressed and feared by those who could with one word reduce it again to nothingness.

We see this intermediary class abandon itself with a blind fury and animosity which proves much more its own fears than any confidence in the success of its enterprises, to all the means which seem proper to assuage its thirst for power, applying itself to the task of persuading Kings that their rights are confined to sitting upon a throne, while those of the people are to govern, and to attack all that centuries have bequeathed as holy and worthy of man's respect—denying, in fact, the value of the past, and declaring themselves the masters of the future. We see this class take all sorts of disguises, uniting and subdividing as occasion offers, helping each other in the hour of danger, and the next day depriving each other of all their conquests. It takes possession of the press, and employs it to promote impiety, disobedience to the laws of religion and the State, and goes so far as to preach murder as a duty for those who desire what is good.

One of its leaders in Germany defined public opinion as "the will of the strong man in the spirit of the party"—a maxim too often put in practice, and too seldom understood by those whose right and duty it is to save society from its own errors, its own weaknesses, and the crimes which the factious commit while pretending to act in its interests.

The evil is plain; the means used by the faction which causes these disorders are so blameable in principle, so criminal in their application, and expose the faction itself to so many dangers, that what men of narrow views (whose head and heart are broken by circumstances stronger than their calculations or their courage) regard as the end of society may become the first step towards a better order of things. These weak men would be right unless men stronger than they are come forward to close their ranks and determine the victory.

We are convinced that society can no longer be saved without strong and vigorous resolutions on the part of the Governments still free in their opinions and actions.

We are also convinced that this may yet be, if the Governments face the truth, if they free themselves from all illusion, if they join their ranks and take their stand on a line of correct, unambiguous, and frankly announced principles.

By this course the monarchs will fulfil the duties imposed upon them by Him who, by entrusting them with power, has charged them to watch over the maintenance of justice, and the rights of all, to avoid the paths of error, and tread firmly in the way of truth. Placed beyond the passions which agitate society, it is in days of trial chiefly that they are called upon to despoil realities of their false appearances, and to show themselves as they are, fathers invested with the authority belonging by right to the heads of families, to prove that, in days of mourning, they know how to be just, wise, and therefore strong, and that they will not abandon the people whom they ought to govern to be the sport of factions, to error and its consequences, which must involve the loss of society. The moment in which we are putting our thoughts on paper is one of these critical moments. The crisis is great; it will be decisive according to the part we take or do not take.

There is a rule of conduct common to individuals and to States, established by the experience of centuries as by that of everyday life. This rule declares "that one must not dream of reformation while agitated by passion; wisdom directs that at such moments we should limit ourselves to maintaining."

Let the monarchs vigorously adopt this principle; let all their resolutions bear the impression of it. Let their actions, their measures, and even their words announce and prove to the world this determination—they will find allies everywhere. The Governments, in establishing the principle of *stability*, will in no wise exclude the development of what is good, for stability is not immobility. But it is for those who are burdened with the heavy task of government to augment the well-being of their people! It is for Governments to regulate it according to necessity and to suit the times. It is not by concessions, which the factions strive to force from legitimate power, and which they have neither the right to claim nor the faculty of keeping within just bounds, that wise reforms can be carried out. That all the good possible should be done is our most ardent wish; but that which is not good must never be confounded with that which is, and even real good should be done only by those who unite to the right of authority the means of enforcing it. Such should be also the sincere wish of the people, who know by sad experience the value of certain phrases and the nature of certain caresses.

Respect for all that is; liberty for every Government to watch over the well-being of its own people; a league between all Governments against factions in all States; contempt for the meaningless words which have become the rallying cry of the factions; respect for the progressive development of institutions in lawful ways; refusal on the part of every monarch to aid or succour partisans under any mask whatever—such are happily the ideas of the great monarchs: the world will be saved if they bring them into action—it is lost if they do not.

Union between the monarchs is the basis of the policy which must now be followed to save society from total ruin.

What is the particular object towards which this policy should be directed? The more important this question is, the more necessary it is to solve it. A principle is something, but it acquires real value only in its application.

The first sources of the evil which is crushing the world have been indicated by us in a paper which has no pretension to be anything more than a mere sketch. Its further causes have also there been pointed out, if, with respect to individuals, it may be defined by the word *presumption,* in applying it to society, taken as a whole, we believe we can best describe the existing evil as the *confusion of ideas,* to which too much generalisation constantly leads. This is what now troubles society. Everything which up to this time has been considered as fixed in principle is attacked and overthrown.

In religious matters criticism and inquiry are to take the place of faith, Christian morality is to replace the Law of Christ as it is interpreted by Christian authorities.

In the Catholic Church, the Jansenists and a number of isolated sectarians, who wish for a religion without a Church, have devoted themselves to this enterprise with ardent zeal: among the Protestant sects, the Methodists, sub-divided into almost as many sects as there are individuals; then the enlightened promoters of the Bible Societies and the Unitarians—the promoters of the fusion of Lutherans and Calvinists in one Evangelical community—all pursue the same end.

The object which these men have in common, to whatever religion they may ostensibly belong, is simply to overthrow all authority. Put on moral grounds, they wish *to enfranchise souls* in the same way as some of the political revolutionists who were not actuated by motives of personal ambition wished to *enfranchise the people.*

If the same elements of destruction which are now throwing society into convulsion have existed in all ages—for every age has seen immoral and ambitious men, hypocrites, men of heated imaginations, wrong motives, and wild projects—yet ours, by the single fact of the liberty of the press, possesses more than any preceding age the means of contact, seduction, and attraction whereby to act on these different classes of men.

We are certainly not alone in questioning if society can exist with the liberty of the press, a scourge unknown to the world before the latter half of the seventeenth century, and restrained until the end of the eighteenth, with scarcely any exceptions but England—a part of Europe separated from the continent by the sea, as well as by her language and by her peculiar manners.

The first principle to be followed by the monarchs, united as they are by the coincidence of their desires and opinions, should be that of maintaining the stability of political institutions against the disorganised excitement which has taken possession of men's minds; the immutability of principles against the madness of their interpretation; and respect for laws actually in force against a desire for their destruction.

The hostile faction is divided into two very distinct parties. One is that of the Levellers; the other, that of the Doctrinaires. United in times of confusion, these men are divided in times of inaction. It is for the Governments to understand and estimate them at their just value.

In the class of Levellers there are found men of strong will and determination. The Doctrinaires can count none such among their ranks. If the first are more to be feared in action, the second are more dangerous in that time of deceitful calm which precedes it; as with physical storms, so with those of social order. Given up to abstract ideas inapplicable to real wants, and generally in contradiction to those very wants, men of this class unceasingly agitate the people by their imaginary or simulated fears, and disturb Governments in order to make them deviate from the right path. The world desires to be governed by facts and according to justice, not by phrases and theories; the first need of society is to be maintained by strong authority (no authority without real strength deserves the name) and not to govern itself. In comparing the number of contests between parties in mixed Governments, and that of just complaints caused by aberrations of power in a Christian State, the comparison would not be in favour of the new doctrines. The first and greatest concern for the immense majority of every nation is the stability of the laws, and their uninterrupted action—never their change. Therefore let the Governments govern, let them maintain the groundwork of their institutions, both ancient and modern; for if it is at all times dangerous to touch them, it certainly would not now, in the general confusion, be wise to do so.

Let them announce this determination to their people, and demonstrate it by facts. Let them reduce the Doctrinaires to silence within their States, and show their contempt for them abroad. Let them not encourage by their attitude or actions the suspicion of being favourable or indifferent to error: let them not allow it to be believed that experience has lost all its rights to make way for experiments which at the least are dangerous. Let them be precise and clear in all their words, and not seek by concessions to gain over those parties who aim at the destruction of all power but their own, whom concessions will never gain over, but only further embolden in their pretensions to power.

Let them in these troublous times be more than usually cautious in attempting real ameliorations, not imperatively claimed by the needs of the moment, to the end that good itself may not turn against them—which is the case whenever a Government measure seems to be inspired by fear.

Let them not confound concessions made to parties with the good they ought to do for their people, in modifying, according to their recognised needs, such branches of the administration as require it.

Let them give minute attention to the financial state of their kingdoms, so that their people may enjoy, by the reduction of public burdens, the real, not imaginary, benefits of a state of peace.

Let them be just, but strong; beneficent, but strict.

Let them maintain religious principles in all their purity, and not allow the faith to be attacked and morality interpreted according to the *social contract* or the visions of foolish sectarians.

Let them suppress Secret Societies, that gangrene of society.

In short, let the great monarchs strengthen their union, and prove to the world that if it exists, it is beneficent, and ensures the political peace of Europe: that it is powerful only for the maintenance of tranquillity at a time when so many attacks are directed against it; that the principles which they profess are paternal and protective, menacing only the disturbers of public tranquillity.

The Governments of the second order will see in such a union the anchor of their salvation, and they will be anxious to connect themselves with it. The people will take confidence and courage, and the most profound and salutary peace which the history of any time can show will have been effected. This peace will first act on countries still in a good state, but will not be without a very decided influence on the fate of those threatened with destruction, and even assist the restoration of those which have already passed under the scourge of revolution.

To every great State determined to survive the storm there still remains many chances of salvation, and a strong union between the States on the principles we have announced will overcome the storm itself.

৺§ SPEECH ON PARLIAMENTARY REFORM

Thomas Babington Macaulay

> *During the early nineteenth century, the middle classes—especially those who acquired their wealth from industry—led a hard-fought struggle to wrest a share of governmental control from the landed barons and squires. A moderate proportion of Western European merchant capitalists were already enjoying some political power, thanks to ancient royal privilege, patrician control of free cities, or marriage and estate alliance with the aristocracy. Yet not until the revolutions of 1830 and 1848 did the industrial bourgeoisie successfully challenge the old order by capturing ministries, parliamentary majorities, or military commands.*
>
> *In England, as early as 1300, some mercantile communities had secured a portion of political responsibility that steadily increased through the grant*

of new constituencies from which representatives to the House of Commons were drawn. This broadening of representation petered out in the seventeenth century, so that by 1750 the situation had already become highly inequitable. After that date the quickening pace of industrialization produced a dramatic population shift from the agricultural south of England to the mineral-rich central and northern shires where the new factories were springing up. By the end of the Napoleonic wars, southern England contained many stagnant towns, and sleepy hamlets in the Midlands were burgeoning into vast metropolises. Throughout these changes, the House of Commons retained its antiquated representational pattern: many declining villages were still endowed with two parliamentary delegates, and one townsite long totally deserted by its inhabitants still sent two representatives to Parliament.

In 1830 many quarters began to clamor for parliamentary reform, reviving an issue that had been submerged during the decades of war with France that opened in 1793. The bitter political battle over the reform bill that began in 1830 lasted more than two years, enlisting unfranchised capitalists and laborers, liberals, socialists, and utilitarians against an obstreperous House of Lords. The Reform Bill, which redressed the balance between north and south and laid down uniform property qualifications for voting, passed only following the threat of mass revolution. In fact, though the Bill extended the franchise to the propertied middle classes, it disappointed many of its supporters by leaving the lower classes as voiceless as before. Yet the precedent for further extension of the suffrage had been set.

A speech by Thomas Babington Macaulay (1800–1859) in support of the Great Reform Bill is reprinted here. Macaulay, perhaps the greatest English historian of the nineteenth century, was then a young man serving his term in Commons. Delivered on the floor of the House, this speech ably summarizes the political objectives and ideals of nineteenth-century liberalism.

It is a circumstance, Sir, of happy augury for the motion before the House, that almost all those who have opposed it have declared themselves hostile on principle to Parliamentary Reform. Two members, I think, have confessed that, though they disapprove of the plan now submitted to us, they are forced to admit the necessity of a

Hansard's Parliamentary Debates (3d series, 1830–1831), II, cols. 1190–1205, 219–229, 232.

change in the representative system. Yet even those gentlemen have used, as far as I have observed, no arguments which would not apply as strongly to the most moderate change as to that which has been proposed by his Majesty's government. I say, Sir, that I consider this as a circumstance of happy augury. For what I feared was, not the opposition of those who are averse to all Reform, but the disunion of reformers. I knew that, during three months, every reformer had been employed in conjecturing what the plan of the Government would be. I knew that every reformer had imagined in his own mind a scheme differing doubtless in some points from that which my noble friend, the Paymaster of the Forces, has developed. I felt, therefore, great apprehension that one person would be dissatisfied with one part of the Bill, that another person would be dissatisfied with another part, and that thus our whole strength would be wasted in internal dissensions. That apprehension is now at an end. I have seen with delight the perfect concord which prevails among all who deserve the name of reformers in this House; and I trust that I may consider it as an omen of the concord which will prevail among reformers throughout the country. I will not, Sir, at present express any opinion as to the details of the Bill; but, having during the last twenty-four hours given the most diligent consideration to its general principles, I have no hesitation in pronouncing it a wise, noble, and comprehensive measure, skilfully framed for the healing of great distempers, for the securing at once of the public liberties, and of the public repose, and for the reconciling and knitting together of all the orders of the State. . . .

The Government has, in my opinion, done all that was necessary for the removing of a great practical evil, and no more than was necessary.

I consider this, Sir, as a practical question. I rest my opinion on no general theory of government. I distrust all general theories of government. I will not positively say that there is any form of polity which may not, in some conceivable circumstances, be the best possible. I believe that there are societies in which every man may safely be admitted to vote. Gentlemen may cheer, but such is my opinion. I say, Sir, that there are countries in which the condition of the labouring classes is such that they may safely be intrusted with the right of electing members of the Legislature. If the labourers of England were in that state in which I, from my soul, wish to see them, if employment were always plentiful, wages always high, food always cheap, if a large family were considered not as an encumbrance but as a blessing, the principal objections to universal Suffrage would, I think, be removed. Universal Suffrage exists in the United States without producing any very frightful consequences; and I do not believe that the people of those States, or of any part of the world, are in any good quality naturally superior to our own countrymen. But, unhappily, the labouring classes in England, and in all old countries, are occasionally in a state of great distress. Some of the causes of this distress are, I fear, beyond the control of the Government. We know what effect distress produces, even on people more intelligent than the great body of the labouring classes can possibly be. We know that it makes even wise men irritable, unreasonable, credulous, eager for immediate relief, heedless of remote consequences. There is no quackery in medicine, religion, or politics which may not impose even on a powerful mind, when that mind has been disordered by pain or fear. It is, therefore, no reflection on the poorer class of Englishmen, who are not, and who cannot in the nature of things be, highly educated, to say that distress produces on them its natural effects, those effects which it would produce on the Americans, or on any other people, that it blinds their judgment, that it inflames their passions, that it makes them prone to believe those who flatter them, and to trust those who would serve them. For the sake, therefore, of the whole society, for the sake of the labouring classes themselves, I hold it to be clearly expedient that, in a country like this, the right of suffrage should depend upon a pecuniary qualification.

But, Sir, every argument which would induce me to oppose Universal Suffrage induces me to support the plan which is now before us. I am opposed to Universal Suffrage because I think that it would produce a destructive revolution. I support this plan because I am sure that it is our best security against a revolution. The noble Paymaster of the Forces hinted, delicately indeed and remotely, at this subject. He spoke of the danger of disappointing the expectations of the nation; and for this he was charged for threatening the House. Sir, in the year 1817, the late Lord Londonderry proposed a suspension of the Habeas Corpus Act. On that occasion he told the House that, unless the measures which he recommended were adopted, the public peace could not be preserved. Was he accused of threatening the House? Again, in the year 1819, he proposed the laws known by the name of the Six Acts. He then told he House that, unless the executive power were reinforced, all the institutions of the country would be overturned by popular violence. Was he then accused of threatening the House? Will any gentleman say that it is parliamentary and decorous to urge the danger arising from popular discontent as an argument for severity; but that it is unparliamentary and indecorous to urge that same danger as an argument for conciliation? I, Sir, do entertain great apprehension for the fate of my country. I do in my conscience believe that, unless the plan proposed, or some similar plan, be speedily adopted, great and terrible calamities will befall us. Entertaining this opinion, I think myself bound to state it, not as a threat, but as a reason. I support this bill because it will improve our institutions; but I support it also because it tends to preserve them. That we may exclude those whom it is necessary to exclude, we must admit those whom it may be safe to admit. At present we oppose the schemes of revolutionists with only one half, with only one quarter of our proper force. We say, and we say justly, that it is not by mere numbers, but by property and intelligence, that the nation ought to be governed. Yet, saying this, we exclude from all share in the government great masses of property and intelligence, great numbers of those who are most interested in preserving tranquillity, and who know best how to preserve it. We do more. We drive over to the side of revolution those whom we shut out from power. Is this a time when the cause of law and order can spare one of its natural allies?

My noble friend, the Paymaster of the Forces, happily described the effect which some parts of our representative system would produce on the mind of a foreigner, who had heard much of our freedom and greatness. If, Sir, I wished to make such a foreigner clearly understand what I consider as the great defects of our system, I would conduct him through that immense city which lies to the north of Great Russell Street and Oxford Street, a city superior in size and in population to the capitals of many mighty kingdoms; and probably superior in opulence, intelligence, and general respectability to any city in the world. I would conduct him through that interminable succession of streets and squares, all consisting of well-built and well-furnished houses. I would make him observe the brilliancy of the shops, and the crowd of well-appointed equipages. I would show him that magnificent circle of palaces which surrounds the Regent's Park. I would tell him that the rental of this district was far greater than that of the whole kingdom of Scotland at the time of the Union. And then I would tell him that this was an unrepresented district. It is needless to give any more instances. It is needless to speak of Manchester, Birmingham, Leeds, Sheffield, with no representation, or of Edinburgh and Glasgow, with a mock representation. If a property tax were now imposed on the principle that no person who had less than a hundred and fifty pounds a year should contribute, I should not be surprised to find that one-half in number and value of the contributors had no votes at all; and it would, beyond all doubt, be found that one-fiftieth part in number and value of the contributors had a larger share of the representation than the other forty-nine fiftieths. This is not government by property. It is government by certain detached portions and fragments of property, selected from the rest, and preferred to the rest, on no rational principle whatever.

To say that such a system is ancient is no defence. My hon. friend, the member for the University of Oxford, challenges us to show that the Constitution was ever better than it is. Sir, we are legislators, not antiquaries. The question for us is, not whether the Constitution was better formerly, but whether we can make it better now. In fact, however, the system was not in ancient times by any means so absurd as it is in our age. One noble Lord has to-night told us that the town of Aldborough, which he represents, was not larger in the time of Edward the First than it is at present. The line of its walls, he assures us, may still be traced. It is now built up to that line. He argues, there-fore, that as the founders of our representative institutions gave members to Aldbor-ough when it was as small as it now is, those who would disfranchise it on account of its smallness have no right to say that they are recurring to the original principle of our representative institutions. But does the noble Lord remember the change which has taken place in the country during the last five centuries? Does he remember how much England has grown in population, while Aldborough has been standing still? Does he consider, that in the time of Edward the First, the kingdom did not contain two millions of inhabitants? It now contains nearly fourteen millions. A hamlet of the present day would have been a town of some importance in the time of our early Par-liaments. Aldborough may be absolutely as considerable a place as ever. But compared with the kingdom, it is much less considerable, by the noble Lord's own showing, than when it first elected burgesses. My hon. friend, the member for the University of Ox-ford, has collected numerous instances of the tyranny which the kings and nobles anciently exercised, both over this house and over the electors. It is not strange that, in times when nothing was held sacred, the rights of the people, and of the representa-tives of the people, should not have been held sacred. The proceedings which my hon. friend has mentioned no more prove that by the ancient constitution of the realm this House ought to be a tool of the King and of the aristocracy, than the Benevolences and the Shipmoney prove their own legality, or than those unjustifiable arrests which took place long after the ratification of the great Charter and even after the Petition of Right, prove that the subject was not anciently entitled to his personal liberty. We talk of the wisdom of our ancestors; and in one respect at least they were wiser than we. They legislated for their own times. They looked at the England which was before them.

They did not think it necessary to give twice as many members to York as they gave to London, because York had been the capital of Britain in the time of Constantius Chlorus; and they would have been amazed indeed if they had foreseen that a city of more than a hundred thousand inhabitants would be left without representatives in the nineteenth century, merely because it stood on ground which in the thirteenth century had been occupied by a few huts. They framed a representative system, which, though not without defects and irregularities, was well adapted to the state of England in their time. But a great revolution took place. The character of the old corporations changed. New forms of property came into existence. New portions of society rose into importance. There were in our rural districts rich cultivators, who were not freeholders. There were in our capital rich traders, who were not livery men. Towns shrank into villages. Villages swelled into cities larger than the London of the Plantagenets. Unhappily while the natural growth of society went on, the artificial polity continued unchanged. The ancient form of the representation remained; and precisely because the form remained, the spirit departed. Then came that pressure almost to bursting, the new wine in the old bottles, the new society under the old institutions. It is now time for us to pay a decent, a rational, a manly reverence to our ancestors, not by superstitiously adhering to what they in other circumstances did, but by doing what they, in our circumstances, would have done. All history is full of revolutions, produced by causes similar to those which are now operating in England. A portion of the community which had been of no account expands and becomes strong. It demands a place in the system, suited, not to its former weakness, but to its present power. If this is granted, all is well. If this is refused, then comes the struggle between the young energy of one class and the ancient privileges of another. Such was the struggle between the Plebeians and the Patricians of Rome. Such was the struggle of the Italian allies for admission to the full rights of Roman citizens. Such was the struggle of our North American colonies against the mother country. Such was the struggle which the Third Estate of France maintained against the aristocracy of birth. Such was the struggle which the Roman Catholics of Ireland maintained against the aristocracy of creed. Such is the struggle which the free people of colour in Jamaica are now maintaining against the aristocracy of skin. Such, finally, is the struggle which the middle classes in England are maintaining against an aristocracy of mere locality, against an aristocracy the principle of which is to invest a hundred drunken potwallopers in one place, or the owner of a ruined hovel in another, with powers which are withheld from cities renowned to the farthest ends of the earth for the marvels of their wealth and of their industry.

But these great cities, says my honourable friend the member of the University of Oxford, are virtually, though not directly, represented. Are not the wishes of Manchester, he asks, as much consulted as those of any town which sends members to Parliament? Now, Sir, I do not understand how a power which is salutary when exercised virtually can be noxious when exercised directly. If the wishes of Manchester have as much weight with us as they would have under a system which should give representatives to Manchester, how can there be any danger in giving representatives to Manchester? A virtual representative is, I presume, a man who acts as a direct representative would act; for surely it would be absurd to say that a man virtually represents the people of Manchester who is in the habit of saying No, when a man directly representing the people of Manchester would say Ay. The utmost that can be expected from virtual representation is that it may be as good as direct representation. If so, why not grant direct representation to places which, as everybody allows, ought, by some process or other, to be represented?

If it be said that there is an evil in change as change, I answer that there is also an evil in discontent as discontent. This, indeed, is the strongest part of our case. It is said that the system works well. I deny it. I deny that a system works well which the people regard with aversion. We may say here that it is a good system and a perfect system. But if any man were to say so to any six hundred and fifty-eight respectable farmers or shopkeepers, chosen by lot in any part of England, he would be hooted down, and laughed to scorn. Are these the feelings with which any part of the government ought to be regarded? Above all, are these the feelings with which the popular branch of the legislature ought to be regarded? It is almost as essential to the utility of a House of Commons that it should possess the confidence of the people, as that it should deserve that confidence. Unfortunately, that which is in theory the popular part of our government, is in practice the unpopular part. Who wishes to dethrone the King? Who wishes to turn the Lords out of their House? Here and there a crazy radical, whom the boys in the street point at as he walks along. Who wishes to alter the constitution of this House? The whole people. It is natural that it should be so. The House of Commons is, in the language of Mr. Burke, a check, not on the people, but for the people. While that check is sufficient, there is no reason to fear that the King or the nobles will oppress the people. But if that check requires checking, how is it to be checked? If the salt shall lose its savour, wherewith shall we season it? The distrust with which the nation regards this House may be unjust. But what then? Can you remove that distrust? That it exists cannot be denied. That it is an evil cannot be denied. That it is an increasing evil cannot be denied. One gentleman tells us that it has been produced by the late events in France and Belgium; another, that it is the effect of seditious works which have lately been published. If this feeling be of origin so recent, I have read history to little purpose. Sir, this alarming discontent is not the growth of a day or of a year. If there be any symptoms by which it is possible to distinguish the chronic diseases of the body politic from its passing inflammations, all those symptoms exist in the present case. The taint has been gradually becoming more extensive and more malignant, through the whole lifetime of two generations. We have tried anodynes. We have tried cruel operations. What are we to try now? Who flatters himself that he can turn this feeling back? Does there remain any argument which escaped the comprehensive intellect of Mr. Burke, or the subtlety of Mr. Windham? Does there remain any species of coercion which was not tried by Mr. Pitt and by Lord Londonderry? We have had laws. We have had blood. New treasons have been created. The Press has been shackled. The Habeas Corpus Act has been suspended. Public meetings have been prohibited. The event has proved that these expedients were mere palliatives. You are at the end of your palliatives. The evil remains. It is more formidable than ever. What is to be done?

Under such circumstances, a great plan of reconciliation, prepared by the ministers

of the Crown, has been brought before us in a manner which gives additional lustre
to a noble name, inseparably associated during two centuries with the dearest liberties
of the English people. I will not say that this plan is in all its details precisely such
I might wish it to be. But it is founded on a great and a sound principle. It takes away
a vast power from a few. It distributes that power through the great mass of the middle
order. Every man, therefore, who thinks as I think is bound to stand firmly by ministers
who are resolved to stand or fall with this measure. Were I one of them, I would
sooner, infinitely sooner, fall with such a measure than stand by any other means that
ever supported a Cabinet.

My hon. friend, the member for the University of Oxford, tells us that if we pass
this law England will soon be a republic. The reformed House of Commons will,
according to him, before it has sat ten years, depose the King and expel the Lords
from their House. Sir, if my hon. friend could prove this, he would have succeeded
in bringing an argument for democracy infinitely stronger than any that is to be found
in the works of Paine. My hon. friend's proposition is in fact this: that our monarchical
and aristocratical institutions have no hold on the public mind of England; that these
institutions are regarded with aversion by a majority of the middle class. This, Sir,
I say, is plainly deducible from his proposition; for he tells us that the representatives
of the middle class will inevitably abolish royalty and nobility within ten years: and
there is surely no reason to think that the representatives of the middle class will be
more inclined to a democratic revolution than their constituents. Now, Sir, if I were
convinced that the great body of the middle class in England look with aversion on
monarchy and aristocracy, I should be forced, much against my will, to come to this
conclusion, that monarchical and aristocratical institutions are unsuited to my country.
Monarchy and aristocracy, valuable and useful as I think them, are still valuable and
useful as means, and not as ends. The end of government is the happiness of the
people; and I do not conceive that, in a country like this, the happiness of the people
can be promoted by a form of government in which the middle classes place no
confidence, and which exists only because the middle classes have no organ by which
to make their sentiments known. But, Sir, I am fully convinced that the middle classes
sincerely wish to uphold the Royal prerogatives and the constitutional rights of the
Peers. What facts does my hon. friend produce in support of his opinion? One fact
only; and that a fact which has absolutely nothing to do with the question. The effect
of this Reform, he tells us, would be to make the House of Commons all-powerful.
It was all-powerful once before, in the beginning of 1649. Then it cut off the head of
the King, and abolished the House of Peers. Therefore, if it again has the supreme
power, it will act in the same manner. Now, Sir, it was not the House of Commons
that cut off the head of Charles the First; nor was the House of Commons then all-
powerful. It had been greatly reduced in numbers by successive expulsions. It was
under the absolute dominion of the army. A majority of the House was willing to take
the terms offered by the King. The soldiers turned out the majority; and the minority,
not a sixth part of the whole House, passed those votes of which my hon. friend speaks,
votes of which the middle classes disapproved then, and of which they disapprove still.

My hon. friend, and almost all the gentlemen who have taken the same side with him in this debate, have dwelt much on the utility of close and rotten boroughs. It is by means of such boroughs, they tell us, that the ablest men have been introduced into Parliament. It is true that many distinguished persons have represented places of this description. But, Sir, we must judge of a form of government by its general tendency, not by happy accidents. Every form of government has its happy accidents. Despotism has its happy accidents. Yet we are not disposed to abolish all constitutional checks, to place an absolute master over us, and to take our chance whether he may be a Caligula or a Marcus Aurelius. In whatever way the House of Commons may be chosen, some able men will be chosen in that way who would not be chosen in any other way. If there were a law that the hundred tallest men in England should be Members of Parliament, there would probably be some able men among those who would come into the House by virtue of this law. If the hundred persons whose names stand first in the alphabetical list of the Court Guide were made Members of Parliament, there would probably be able men among them. We read in ancient history that a very able king was elected by the neighing of his horse; but we shall scarcely, I think, adopt this mode of election. In one of the most celebrated republics of antiquity, Athens, Senators and Magistrates were chosen by lot; and sometimes the lot fell fortunately. Once, for example, Socrates was in office. A cruel and unjust proposition was made by a demagogue. Socrates resisted it at the hazard of his own life. There is no event in Grecian history more interesting than that memorable resistance. Yet who would have officers appointed by lot, because the accident of the lot may have given to a great and good man a power which he would probably never have attained in any other way? We must judge, as I said, by the general tendency of a system. No person can doubt that a House of Commons chosen freely by the middle classes will contain very many able men. I do not say that precisely the same able men who would find their way into the present House of Commons will find their way into the reformed House; but that is not the question. No particular man is necessary to the State. We may depend on it that, if we provide the country with popular institutions, those institutions will provide it with great men. . . .

Turn where we may, within, around, the voice of great events is proclaiming to us, Reform, that you may preserve. Now, therefore, while everything at home and abroad forebodes ruin to those who persist in a hopeless struggle against the spirit of the age; now, while the crash of the proudest throne of the Continent is still resounding in our ears; now, while the roof of a British palace affords an ignominious shelter to the exiled heir of forty kings; now, while we see on every side ancient institutions subverted and great societies dissolved; now, while the heart of England is still sound; now, while old feelings and old associations retain a power and a charm which may too soon pass away; now, in this your accepted time; now, in this your day of salvation, take counsel, not of prejudice, not of party spirit, not of the ignominious pride of a fatal consistency, but of history, of reason, of the ages which are past, of the signs of this most portentous time. Pronounce in a manner worthy of the expectation with which this great debate has been anticipated, and of the long remembrance which it will leave behind. Renew the youth of the State. Save property, divided against itself.

Save the multitude, endangered by its own ungovernable passions. Save the aristocracy, endangered by its own unpopular power. Save the greatest, and fairest, and most highly civilized community that ever existed from calamities which may in a few days sweep away all the rich heritage of so many ages of wisdom and glory. The danger is terrible. The time is short. If this bill should be rejected, I pray to God that none of those who concur in rejecting it may ever remember their votes with unavailing remorse amidst the wreck of laws, the confusion of ranks, the spoliation of property, and the dissolution of social order.

৵ TO THE MEMORY OF THE MARTYRS OF COSENZA

Giuseppe Mazzini

Even though Giuseppe Mazzini (1805–1872) was by training a lawyer and by inclination a man of letters, he really belongs to a breed that was quite novel in the nineteenth century: the professional revolutionary. The son of a middle-class family of Genoa (a city that since 1815 belonged to the Kingdom of Sardinia—or Piedmont), Mazzini became, after 1830, the great apostle of democratic nationalism not only for Italy, but for much of central Europe. Indefatigable as a propagandist for a unitary Italian republic at a time when Italy was only "a geographical expression," Mazzini was equally active as a plotter of insurrections, of what today might be called "national wars of liberation" based on guerilla activity. On the whole, save for a stint as head of the short-lived Roman Republic of 1849, he was notably unsuccessful as a practicing revolutionary. He was more significant as a purveyor of ideas who inspired many of the leaders of the Italian unity movement and who made this goal respectable throughout Western Europe.

The address below was delivered by Mazzini at Milan on July 25, 1848, at a time when the great though unsuccessful national rising in Italy was in progress. The "martyrs of Cosenza" were a small band of Italian revolutionaries, inspired but not directed by Mazzini, who in 1844 had been executed after having led a hopeless uprising against the Kingdom of Naples in southern Italy. By 1848 Mazzini's ideas on nationality in general and Italian unity in particular had already received wide publicity: he simply took the occasion of this anniversary of the execution of a handful of Italian patriots to sum up a doctrine that he had preached since the 1830s.

When I was commissioned by you, young men, to proffer in this temple a few words sacred to the memory of the brothers Bandiera and their fellow-martyrs at Cosenza, I thought that some of those who heard me might exclaim with noble indignation, "Wherefore lament over the dead? The martyrs of liberty are only worthily honoured by winning the battle they have begun; Cosenza, the land where they fell, is enslaved; Venice, the city of their birth, is begirt by foreign foes. Let us emancipate them, and until that moment let no words pass our lips save words of war."

But another thought arose, saying, "Why have we not conquered? Why is it that, whilst we are fighting for independence in the North of Italy, liberty is perishing in the South? Why is it that a war, which should have sprung to the Alps with the bound of a lion, has dragged itself along for four months, with the slow uncertain motion of the scorpion surrounded by a circle of fire? How has the rapid and powerful intuition of a people newly arisen to life been converted into the weary helpless effort of the sick man turning from side to side? Ah! had we all arisen in the sanctity of the idea for which our martyrs died; had the holy standard of their faith preceded our youth to battle; had we reached that unity of life which was in them so powerful, and made of our every action a thought, and of our every thought an action; had we devoutly gathered up their last words in our hearts, and learned from them that Liberty and Independence are one, that God and the People, the Fatherland and Humanity, are the two inseparable terms of the device of every people striving to become a nation; that Italy can have no true life till she be One, holy in the equality and love of all her children, great in the worship of eternal truth, and consecrated to a lofty mission, a moral priesthood among the peoples of Europe,—we should now have had, not war, but victory; Cosenza would not be compelled to venerate the memory of her martyrs in secret, nor Venice be restrained from honouring them with a monument; and we, gathered here together, might gladly invoke their sacred names, without uncertainty as to our future destiny, or a cloud of sadness on our brows, and say to those precursor souls, *Rejoice! for your spirit is incarnate in your brethren, and they are worthy of you.*

The idea which they worshipped, young men, does not as yet shine forth in its full purity and integrity upon your banner. The sublime programme which they, dying, bequeathed to the rising Italian generation, is yours; but mutilated, broken up into fragments by the false doctrines, which, elsewhere overthrown, have taken refuge amongst us. I look around, and I see the struggles of desperate populations, an alternation of generous rage and of unworthy repose; of shouts for freedom, and of formulae of servitude, throughout all parts of our Peninsula; but the soul of the country, where is it? What unity is there in this unequal and manifold movement— where is the Word that should dominate the hundred diverse and opposing counsels which mislead or seduce the multitude? I hear phrases usurping the National omni- potence—"The Italy of the *North—the League of the States—Federative compacts between Princes*," but ITALY, where is it? Where is the common country, the country which the Bandiera hailed as thrice Initiatrix of a new era of European civilisation?

Intoxicated with our first victories, improvident for the future, we forgot the idea

"To the Memory of the Martyrs of Cosenza Executed on the 25th of July 1844," *Life and Writings of Joseph Mazzini* (London, 1891), V, 156–166.

revealed by God to those who suffered; and God has punished our forgetfulness by deferring our triumph. The Italian movement, my countrymen, is, by decree of Providence, that of Europe. We arise to give a pledge of moral progress to the European world. But neither political fictions, nor dynastic aggrandisements, nor theories of expendiency, can transform or renovate the life of the peoples. Humanity lives and moves through faith; great principles are the guiding-stars that lead Europe towards the future. Let us turn to the graves of our martyrs, and ask inspiration of those who died for us all, and we shall find the secret of victory in the adoration of a faith. The angel of martyrdom and the angel of victory are brothers; but the one looks up to heaven, and the other looks down to earth; and it is when, from epoch to epoch, their glance meets between earth and heaven, that creation is embellished with a new life, and a people arises from the cradle or the tomb, evangelist or prophet.

I will sum up for you in a few words this *faith* of our martyrs; their external life is known to you all; it is now matter of history, and I need not recall it to you.

The faith of the brothers Bandiera, which was and is our own, was based upon a few simple uncontrovertible truths, which few indeed venture to declare false, but which are nevertheless forgotten or betrayed by most.—

God and the People.

God, at the summit of the social edifice; the people, the universality of our brethren, at the base. God, the Father and Educator; the people, the progressive interpreter of his Law.

No true society can exist without a common belief and a common aim. Religion declares the belief and the aim. Politics regulate society in the practical realisation of that belief, and prepare the means of attaining that aim. Religion represents the Principle, politics the application. There is but one sun in heaven for all the earth. There is one law for all those who people the earth. It is alike the law of the human being and of collective humanity. We are placed here below, not for the capricious exercise of our own individual faculties—our faculties and liberty are the *means,* not the *end,*—not to work out our own happiness upon earth; happiness can only be reached elsewhere, and there God works for us; but to consecrate our existence to the discovery of a portion of the Divine Law; to practise it as far as our individual circumstances and powers allow, and to diffuse the knowledge and love of it among our brethren.

We are here below to labour fraternally to build up the unity of the human family, so that the day may come when it shall represent a *single sheepfold with a single shepherd,*—the Spirit of God, the Law.

To aid our search after truth, God has given to us tradition—the voice of anterior humanity—and the voice of our own conscience. Wheresoever these accord, is truth; wheresoever they are opposed, is error. To attain a harmony and consistence between the conscience of the individual and the conscience of humanity, no sacrifice is too great. The Family, the City, the Fatherland and Humanity, are but different spheres in which to exercise our activity and our power of sacrifice towards this great aim. God watches from above the inevitable progress of humanity, and from time to time he raises up the great in genius, in love, in thought, or in action, as priests of his truth, and guides to the multitude on their way.

These principles,—indicated in their letters, in their proclamations, and in their conversations,—with a profound sense of the mission entrusted by God to the individual and to humanity, were to Attilio and Emilio Bandiera, and their fellow-martyrs, the guide and comfort of a weary life; and, when men and circumstances had alike betrayed them, these principles sustained them in death, in religious serenity and calm certainty of the realisation of their immortal hopes for the future of Italy. The immense energy of their souls arose from the intense love which informed their faith. And, could they now arise from the grave and speak to you, they would, believe me, address you, though with a power very different from that which is given to me, in counsel not unlike this which I now offer to you.

Love! love is the flight of the soul towards God; towards the great, the sublime, and the beautiful, which are the shadow of God upon earth. Love your family, the partner of your life, those around you ready to share your joys and sorrows; love the dead who were dear to you and to whom you were dear. But let your love be the love taught you by Dante and by us—the love of souls that aspire together; do not grovel on the earth in search of a felicity which it is not the destiny of the creature to reach here below; do not yield to a delusion which inevitably would degrade you into egotism. To love is to give and take a promise for the future. God has given us love, that the weary soul may give and receive support upon the way of life. It is a flower springing up on the path of duty; but it cannot change its course. Purify, strengthen, and improve yourselves by loving. Act always—even at the price of increasing her earthly trials—so that the sister soul united to your own may never need, here or elsewhere, to blush through you or for you. The time will come when, from the height of a new life, embracing the whole past and comprehending its secret, you will smile together at the sorrows you have endured, the trials you have overcome.

Love your country. Your country is the land where your parents sleep, where is spoken that language in which the chosen of your heart blushing whispered the first word of love; it is the home that God has given you, that by striving to perfect yourselves therein, you may prepare to ascend to him. It is your name, your glory, your sign among the people. Give to it your thoughts, your counsels, your blood. Raise it up, great and beautiful as it was foretold by our great men. And see that you leave it uncontaminated by any trace of falsehood or of servitude; unprofaned by dismemberment. Let it be one, as the thought of God. You are twenty-five millions of men, endowed with active, splendid faculties; possessing a tradition of glory the envy of the nations of Europe; an immense future is before you; you lift your eyes to the loveliest heaven, and around you smiles the loveliest land in Europe; you are encircled by the Alps and the sea, boundaries traced out by the finger of God for a people of giants— you are bound to be such, or nothing. Let not a man of that twenty-five millions remain excluded from the fraternal bond destined to join you together; let not a glance be raised to that heaven which is not that of a free man. Let Rome be the ark of your redemption, the temple of your nation. Has she not twice been the temple of the destinies of Europe? In Rome two extinct worlds, the Pagan and the Papal, are superposed like the double jewels of a diadem; draw from these a third world greater than the two. From Rome, the holy city, the city of love (Amor) the purest and wisest among you, elected by the vote and fortified by the inspiration of a whole people, shall dictate the Pact that shall make us one, and represent us in the future alliance of the peoples. Until then you will either have no country, or have her contaminated and profaned.

Love Humanity. You can only ascertain your own mission from the aim set by God before humanity at large. God has given you your country as cradle, and humanity as mother; you cannot rightly love your brethren of the cradle if you love not the common mother. Beyond the Alps, beyond the sea, are other peoples now fighting or preparing to fight the holy fight of independence, of nationality, of liberty; other peoples striving by different routes to reach the same goal,—improvement, association, and the foundation of an Authority which shall put an end to moral anarchy and re-link earth to heaven; an authority which mankind may love and obey without remorse or shame. Unite with them; they will unite with you. Do not invoke their aid where your single arm can suffice to conquer; but say to them that the hour will shortly sound for a terrible struggle between right and blind force, and that in that hour you will ever be found with those who have raised the same banner as yourselves.

And love, young men, love and venerate the ideal. The ideal is the Word of God. High above every country, high above humanity, is the country of the spirit, the city of the soul, in which all are brethren who believe in the inviolability of thought, and in the dignity of our immortal soul; and the baptism of this fraternity is martyrdom. From that high sphere spring the *principles* which alone can redeem the peoples. Arise for the sake of these, and not from impatience of suffering or dread of evil. Anger, pride, ambition, and the desire of material prosperity, are arms common alike to the peoples and their oppressors, and even should you conquer with these to-day, you would fall again to-morrow, but principles belong to the peoples alone, and their oppressors can find no arms to oppose to them. Adore enthusiasm, the dreams of the virgin soul, and the visions of early youth, for they are a perfume of paradise which the soul retains in issuing from the hands of its Creator. Respect above all things your conscience; have upon your lips the truth implanted by God in your hearts, and, while labouring in harmony, even with those who differ from you, in all that tends to the emancipation of our soil, yet ever bear your own banner erect, and boldly promulgate your own faith.

Such words, young men, would the martyrs of Cosenza have spoken, had they been living amongst you; and here, where it may be that, invoked by our love, their holy spirits hover near us. I call upon you to gather them up in your hearts and to make of them a treasure amid the storms that yet threaten you; storms which, with the name of our martyrs on your lips and their faith in your hearts, you will overcome.

God be with you, and bless Italy!

If in France the revolution of 1848 demonstrated the ambiguities of the great revolutionary tradition in dealing with contemporary social problems (see pages 486–501), in Germany the events of the same year undermined the facile ideas concerning the reorganization of Europe according to nationality which men like Mazzini (see pages 465–469) had popularized.

The following debate took place in the summer of 1848 in the German national parliament meeting at Frankfurt am Main. This assembly was the indirect product of the revolutions that had swept aside absolutism in the various individual German states (such as Prussia, Austria, Bavaria, etc.) in March and April, 1848. Elected virtually by manhood suffrage, the parliament convened on May 18 to create a single German national state organized along constitutional principles. This task called for a clear definition of German nationality, particularly in border areas such as Schleswig-Holstein (mostly German-speaking, but ruled by the Danish king), Posen (with a mixed Polish-German population), Bohemia (where Czechs and Germans clashed), and the Tyrol (German-speaking except for a cohesive Italian population in the south).

The conflicting views which such nationality problems evoked were most clearly brought out in the three days' debate beginning on July 24 on the incorporation of a part of the Grand Duchy of Posen (since 1815 under Prussian administration) into an eventual German national state. Formally, the issue before the parliament was whether to accept or reject the recommendations of the parliamentary committee that had studied the problem of Posen for seven weeks before submitting its report. In fact, on July 27, 1848, the recommendations of the committee were accepted by a vote of 342 to 31, with 188 members abstaining or absent.

President   We now turn to the order of the day, namely the discussion of the report of the Committee on International Law, concerning the incorporation of one part of the Grand Duchy of Posen into the German Confederation, the seating of its deputies, as well as the preservation of the nationality of the Poles in West Prussia.

[Here follows the report of the committee.] . . . The following brief exposition may serve to provide a realistic understanding and appreciation of some very compli-

Stenographischer Bericht über die Verhandlungen der deutschen constituirenden National-Versammlung Frankfurt a. M., ed. F. Wigard, II, 1124–1127, 1141–1151, 1163–1169. Translated by Peter Amann.

cated circumstances. Within its present bounds, the Grand Duchy of Posen was created in 1815. In settling claims to his former possessions which the Congress of Vienna recognized as rightful, the king of Prussia obtained a part of the former duchy of Warsaw. The Final Act of the Congress of Vienna of June 9, 1815, included this territorial arrangement by which the formal right of Prussia to the said territory was recognized by the participating powers, that is, by all of Europe. King Frederick William added two of the districts of the portion of the duchy of Warsaw allotted to him to [the province of] West Prussia; the rest he combined with the former district of Netze that had become Prussian at the time of the first partition of Poland. He thus created the Grand Duchy of Posen. In the edict issued at the time he took possession, as well as in his proclamation to the inhabitants of May 15, 1815, the king announced that, in incorporating the province into the Prussian monarchy, the inhabitants would not be forced to surrender their national [identity]. He assured them not only that their personal and property rights [would be preserved], but also [promised] to maintain their religion, [the use] of the Polish language side by side with German, access to all public offices, honors, and distinctions, the appointment of a native-born governor, participation in the constitution which he planned to grant to all his subjects, as well as [the instituting of] a provincial constitution in line with the other provinces of his realm. [The Congress of] Vienna had originally called for freedom [of trade and movement] among the three partitioning powers, but this decision was never put into effect. As a province, the grand duchy was divided into two governing districts of which Posen had seventeen subdistricts and Bromberg nine. In December 1843, the population numbered 790,000 Poles, 420,000 Germans, and almost 80,000 Jews.

In part the Germans are descendants of colonists who immigrated hundreds of years ago and tend to live in the cities, where they constitute the most numerous and prosperous segment of the population. Many towns may be regarded as entirely German, since their Polish population is small or nonexistent. . . . The German population was augmented very considerably when in 1773 Frederick II of Prussia, after detaching the Netze district from Poland, had the Bromberg canal dug at a cost of 1.5 million Thaler. By 1774 this [canal] connected the Vistula to the Oder (and hence to the Elbe) by means of the Brahe, Netze, and Warthe rivers, thus permitting highly important inland shipping. The lands adjoining the Netze, contested for hundreds of years by Poles and Pomeranians, had been left largely uninhabited, as a result of innumerable devastations and because of the marshy terrain. This area was now opened to cultivation and settled by numerous colonists. Gradually many Germans migrated to the grand duchy, buying up relatively inexpensive land, particularly after Prussia, following the 1831 Polish uprising against Russia, had begun systematically to Germanize the province.

According to all reliable reports, the Jews within the grand duchy are thoroughly German, as indeed they want to be. Indisputably they too were originally immigrants from Germany. They spread throughout the grand duchy (as indeed throughout the realm), until they may [nowadays] be found more or less everywhere. The religious toleration formerly prevailing in Poland, as well as the absence of certain qualities among Poles, provided the Jews with a deep-rooted sphere of activity in Poland. As a rule they know both German and Polish, although within the family circle and with their children they speak German.

Thus in all parts of the province Germans are settled, and there are relatively few localities and no extensive areas where Poles and Germans do not live side by side. The German population predominates in the northern and western parts of the province where it borders on West Prussia, the Mark, and Silesia, while in the interior and the eastern parts in the direction of the [Russian] kingdom of Poland the Polish population is numerically dominant. . . . Separated by their nationality, Germans and Poles have never been on intimate terms; indeed, throughout the centuries habitual discord has prevailed. Ever since the first partition of Poland the nobility, as well as all [other] patriotically-minded Poles, have been hostile to the Germans and especially the Prussians. Prussia in particular, by introducing its rigid state and administrative regulations and by seeing to their severe execution, disturbed the Poles' ancient habits and traditional institutions in their most sensitive areas. The peasant, up to this time in a state of servile dependence, gained protection against the arbitrary acts of the nobility, which increased the bitterness of the latter; [yet] the peasants and townsmen also were forced to conform to Prussian regulations which they found highly irksome. The Prussian official [on the other hand] felt slighted because the regulations which he had introduced, administered, and which he held in high esteem, were resisted by the Poles instead of being accepted with gratitude. . . .

As a result of the events of the spring of the current year, there began general agitation among the grand duchy's Poles and, later, among its Germans. The German people, always compassionate towards all unfortunates, had long felt the deep injustice committed by its princes against the Poles. . . . The Germans frankly proffered their hand in brotherhood in order to make up for what their princes had formerly committed. Yet at the very moment that the Poles accepted, the interests and aims of the two nations began to diverge. The Poles thought only in terms of the reestablishment of their old kingdom that was to comprise, at the very least, the territory held before the first partition of 1772. Openly and repeatedly they announced this [objective] which, as far as Prussia and Germany were concerned, extended [the claim] beyond the Grand Duchy of Posen to West Prussia and the whole corridor to East Prussia. The Germans within the grand duchy [on the other hand] thought only of the Poles and not of their territory. They wanted to do justice to the hurt and deeply affronted nationality of the Polish people by contributing to the reestablishment of a free, independent, and national Poland; in any case, they sought to set the Poles, hitherto ruled by Germans, free to establish and rule themselves in accordance with their own nationality. Yet as Germans previously in close union with the Prussian monarchy, they had never considered separating from the latter, and thus essentially from Germany. Nor were they willing to submit to Polish rule against all their inclinations. . . . No matter what the particular circumstances, such sharply clashing views were bound to produce strong tensions between Germans and Poles, at first covertly, then openly. The Poles petitioned the king for the immediate national reorganization of the grand duchy to take place in an orderly and legal manner. . . .

Even before the end of March, many Germans of the Netze district and the western section of the grand duchy armed themselves as they grew increasingly concerned at the possibility of being subjected to Polish rule. While they were willing to extend full recognition to Polish national independence, they called for the division of the grand duchy on the grounds that equity demanded that each should get his own. . . . This national movement of the Germans irritated the Poles to the point where the two nationalities confronted each other with such hostility that not even the best will of the leaders could prevent outbreaks everywhere. A bloody civil war threatened to erupt, and even the numerous Prussian troops that had been concentrated were unable to preserve general order. In order to restore order and carry out the national reorganization of the province under Prussian auspices, General von Willisen was sent to Posen. According to the decision of the ministry, those subdistricts that did not want to join the Polish nationality, particularly those in which Germans predominated, were in any case to retain Prussian organization and administration. General von Willisen's attempt was bound to fail, inasmuch as the Poles clung as firmly to the territorial concept as the Germans did to the national one. Furthermore, the Germans in Posen refused to be governed by the Poles, while the Poles sought to govern the whole of the grand duchy. Finally, the Poles, unable to control their own countrymen who had taken up arms in response to all kinds of promises, could not induce them to disband and go home; their remaining armed detachments had to be dispersed in bloody fighting by regular army units.

In the meantime, on April 6, the Provincial Assembly of Posen by a vote of 26 to 17 rejected the proposal both to incorporate the whole grand duchy into the German Confederation and to elect twelve deputies to the German National Assembly. According to the majority view, the inhabitants, being Poles, did not want to be absorbed into a foreign nationality. The minority, on the other hand, while they did not seek the admission of the whole of the grand duchy into the German Confederation either . . . supported incorporation for the predominantly German subdistricts. They called for the immediate election of five deputies to the German National Assembly by the Provincial Assembly. . . . Numerous petitions, with thousands of signatures constituting undeniable evidence of the state of public opinion among the German inhabitants, reached the king. On April 14 he finally yielded, ordering that the subdistricts of the Netze area and four of the subdistricts of the Posen governing district be excluded from the Polish reorganization. Their incorporation into the German Confederation and the elections to the German parliament were to be initiated. Consequently, on April 22, on Prussia's initiative a session of the German Confederation [Bundestag]* admitted not only the above subdistricts but parts of several other subdistricts into the German Confederation. These comprised a population of 593,390. Soon thereafter the Prussian government was similarly induced to propose the incorporation of the city and fortress of Posen, together with several other subdistricts, that comprised a total population of 273,500, an inclusion voted by the Bundestag on May 2. These two sections were to send twelve deputies to the National Assembly, while the exact determination of the line of demarcation between German and Polish areas was to be reserved for the future. This action marked the irrevocable decision on

* [An assembly of representatives of the governments of the various German states that met at Frankfurt from 1815 to its dissolution by the elected German national parliament in July, 1848. (*Ed.*)]

the part of the Prussian government to divide the Grand Duchy of Posen as created in 1815 into two parts, one organized for the Poles, the other adhering to the German Confederation. . . .

Hence the committee, with only one dissenting vote, makes the following recommendations to the National Assembly:

1   that the unanimous decision by the Bundestag on April 22 and May 2 to follow the Prussian initiative and admit certain parts of the Grand Duchy of Posen into the German Confederation be endorsed; that the twelve deputies elected to the German National Assembly from those parts allotted to Germany, whose credentials had been provisionally accepted, be permanently seated;

2   that the line of demarcation separating Polish from German areas, determined on June 4 of this year by the royal Prussian commissioner General Pfuel, be recognized provisionally; that the final delimitation between the two sections should await further proposals from the Prussian government;

3   that the Prussian government offer a clear-cut declaration guaranteeing the national rights of the Germans in the Polish part of the grand duchy, not only so long as that section is under Prussian administration, but also in the event that the Polish part of Posen should be withdrawn from Prussian administration;

4   that with regard to the petitions concerning West Prussia, the non-German inhabitants of that province should be informed of the National Assembly's resolution of May 31. [The Assembly] granted to all non-German peoples living within the territory of the German Confederation (therefore including these Poles) unrestricted national development and equal treatment with respect to church affairs, education, literature, internal administration, legal matters, and language. . . .

R. Blum   (from Leipzig)   A stranger situation can hardly occur than when a nation which has just gained or is still gaining its freedom is permitted to decide the fate of another nation that is seemingly doomed to destruction. We have in the past probably come to more important decisions than the one before us today. We shall perhaps reach more important ones in the future; yet we shall scarcely ever have to decide a question where the demands of justice tug so strongly and insistently at our heartstrings, possibly creating a conflict between these demands and those of national sentiment. In and of itself, does not misfortune evoke ardent compassion? Is there not an aphorism by a Polish hero—Kosziusko—revered by parties of every shade of opinion, who . . . said that there was no greater sorrow than that of a dying people; for the sorrow common to the whole nation is bequeathed to the survivors down to the last man who alone must bear that sorrow in its entirety. Hence, in viewing these people even without being blind to their deficiencies and errors—for who is blameless? —compassion flowers as one is led to assign them an honorable place in history.

Gentlemen! Let us not forget for how long the Poles constituted a barrier between northern barbarism and western culture. Indeed, let us not forget at this juncture how much we owed them throughout earlier centuries, now that we are all too inclined to see [only] the dark side of these people. Let us not forget that since time immemorial, immigrants admitted to their sanctuary were granted that for which we are still struggling in Germany: nowhere was freedom of conscience so secure as in Poland, and even the Jews, despised and rejected by the world, found a home there. (Several voices: Bravo!) I could offer you still more historical recollections from Poland's past, yet I shall refrain from so doing. However, I must remind those who today are so ready to stress the unfavorable aspects of the Polish people, those who would dispute them every virtue and ascribe to them every vice (Agitation on the Right), that we bear a great share of the guilt.

For the last eighty years, these people have been divided, gagged, and oppressed. We are the ones who have robbed them of their inner resources, their land, their independence, and their freedom. And when he whom for eighty years we have trodden into the dirt appears dirty, do not shift the burden of blame to him. It may well be true that in these long years of subjection and systematic demoralization something has rubbed off on these people that had not been there before. It may be that, step by step, they have sunk lower. Yet in that case our duty to contribute to their resurgence is even clearer because of the part we played in their decline. Thus consciousness of our forefathers' guilt is paired with our compassion for these people. The former we must expiate, since a nation is not like an individual: a nation retains its identity and must atone for sins committed in its name by its former representatives, even without its consent. . . .

What has become of this expiation up to now? In the course of the long period of their oppression, the Poles have from time to time attempted to regain their liberty and to cast off the yoke to which they had been forced to submit. According to the times, this was called heroism or revolution; depending upon the circumstances, the Poles were admired or despised. I do not want to render judgment as to where we stand today. Yet I must say that, judging from what has transpired these last months, there is in any case reason to confess that these people, suppressed for eighty years, have offered to the other peoples of Europe a model of patriotism and irrepressible courage. Had we in this country followed such a course, never would we have sunk to the depth of misery which we reached at the end of the last and the beginning of the present century.

Now that spring has once again come to the peoples, the Poles have sought to take their place in this new dawn. They believed that the hour of rebirth had also struck for them, and believing this they participated in this rebirth wherever and however they were able. Though you might want to point out to them that now and again they have acted hastily and thoughtlessly, at least you recognize the nobility of their impulse. The greater the oppression under which one's country groans and the weaker one's power to redress the balance, the nobler is the impulse to devote one's last strength to the fatherland.

I do not want to accuse here. Were I to do so, I would be committing the same error with which I shall presently charge the report of the committee. However much the heart inclines towards the Poles—and it is a beautiful aspect of the human heart to side with misfortune, even to the point of perhaps idealizing misfortune and downgrading those who oppose it—I shall nonetheless not accuse. I shall accept the chairman's injunction to treat this highly significant European question with consideration and with tact. I do not want to point to the dangers with which Russia threatens us, or to elaborate as to how we may erect a bastion against this danger while purging our guilty consciences. As we are deciding European political affairs here, affairs of the gravest importance not only to our country but to the whole of Europe, I merely want to inquire: What is the principle according to which you are acting? Do you accept a concept of territorial integrity, reflected, for instance, in your attitude toward Schleswig-Holstein, the Slavs and Trieste? Why then did you fail to apply the same principle when a question has come up of another people that happen to include a number of Germans, just as we ourselves include some Danes, Slavs, Italians, and what have you? Or is the concept of nationality your inspiration? Well, in that case be just as fair to the other side: when you partition Posen in order to reclaim Germans, partition Silesia as well and hand over the Slavs to Austria where they belong. Lop off the South Tyrol from Germany! Why, I shall even go further: if your national sentiments are so ardent and if these are your sole guideline, why not free the German Baltic provinces from Russia's sway? Free also the six hundred thousand miserable Germans in Alsace who even have to bear the domination of a republic! (Prolonged applause!) Either one or the other is right; but a policy chosen to fit the convenience of the moment is, in my opinion, no policy at all.

Even here I shall be tactful and say: Possibly after eighty years of oppression it may be necessary that the Poles surrender a part of their soil; possibly there may be a need to draw a line; possibly both freedom and justice dictate just this. In that case you may decide this question only by demonstrating this necessity with all the thoroughness which is such an attractive hallmark of our people. In this report I seek in vain for even the slightest semblance of evidence. I fail to understand how such a report could have been drawn up by and submitted to the representatives of the German people. It contains nothing that has not been taken from newspaper prattle. It contains not one single indication as to where in Posen a sensible frontier should be drawn. Nowhere is there any indication as to the real status of the inhabitants or as to the topographical lay of of the land. Not one table or map to instruct us—nothing! We are to decide by feel, without real understanding, a question that may throw us into a turmoil exceeding anything that life in Europe has seen. . . .

The destiny of peoples cannot be stayed. If the Poles are doomed to surrender a part of their soil and some specified number of Germans, let it come to pass; let them bear this as they have had to bear many a harsh fate before. But let us not persuade them by means of shrapnel; rather, let us have them yield to reason and the urgency [of the situation]. Let us openly convince them before all Europe and only at such time when they shall have begun to regain their nationhood; not now, when they are tied hand and foot, when, instead of negotiating with them, we can only snatch what we claim is ours. . . .

Wilhelm Jordan (from Berlin)   . . . Gentlemen! The European-wide importance which public opinion attributes to our deliberations makes it essential, I would maintain, that we observe an approach differing from that in other instances. I do not believe that we can confine our deliberations about the Posen question within narrow bounds by considering it as a special case, so that by limiting its scope we may reach a decision more easily. I rather believe that after having considered these more restricted aspects of the case, we must take a world historical viewpoint from which the Posen affair should be examined as an episode in the great Polish drama. I openly confess that I would not know how to reach a decision were I to concur with our chairman in refraining completely from any historical examination.

To be able to decide the special aspects of the case under consideration, two principal questions must be answered: (1) Should we recognize the principle of dividing the territory of the grand duchy of Posen in proportion to the two nationalities involved? (2) Should the demarcation line already drawn be approved as the realization of this principle?

With regard to the grand duchy of Posen a very misleading impression is widespread in Europe. The fact that some parts of it have always been Polish in terms of history and inhabitants, while other parts have at times been under Polish rule, explains why up to now all of Posen has quite generally been assumed to be simply Polish. This opinion, as I have said, is completely erroneous. The northern section of Posen, the district of Netze, originally belonged to Pomerania and was only granted to Poland by the Treaty of Thorn, that is, it was conquered by the Poles. Later the Treaty of Warsaw yielded [this section] to Prussia and it has remained in Prussia's possession ever since, except for the brief interim existence of the Duchy of Warsaw. Furthermore, the western sub-districts of Birnbaum, Meseritz, Bomst, and Fraustadt have, as may be gathered from their names, been predominantly German since time immemorial. Other areas, though originally Polish, were Germanized in the course of time until Germans came to predominate there. I shall speak later as to how this took place. In short, it is true that a great part of Posen is at present overwhelmingly German and we must start from this fact.

You know that the revolution in Berlin led to the decision to safeguard the Poles' nationality rights in an unprecedented manner by granting a special constitution to the Polish areas. The Germans felt that they too were entitled to the same treatment. They believed that their nationality should receive recognition and security equal to that granted to the Poles, saying: "It is none of our business to whom some area once belonged. The past cannot have the decisive voice in this case, for it is the living present that has right on its side." Thus they protested against a Polish reorganization of German areas and categorically demanded the secession of the latter from the Polish areas. The government, agreeing with this demand, decided upon such a separation. This has been called a new partition of Poland, though it is nothing more than a recognition of Germany's actual extension eastward, that is, of how far the German tongue and German customs have advanced victoriously.

The question with respect to the line of separation may thus be reduced to another question: Should half a million Germans live under German administration and German officialdom and belong to the great German fatherland? Or, cast off by their fatherland, should they as naturalized foreigners play second fiddle, subjected to another nationality of lesser human worth than the German? Whoever answers "yes" to this last question, whoever maintains that we should hand over the Posen Germans to the Poles to be subjected to Polish administration, is in my view at the very least an unconscious traitor to his own people. (Bravo!)

By answering this question, the other issue is already largely settled. With regard to the line of division that has actually been drawn, one may only inquire whether it be correct, that is, drawn with consideration to the respective weight of the two nationalities. In general, one may say, this principle has been conscientiously observed. Yet as everywhere in public life, the more extreme theoretical consequences have had to be modified to fit the conditions, something which has also occurred in this instance. It was, first of all, inexpedient to create enclaves. Consequently what one may call "national islands" have remained on both sides of the dividing line. Polish sections have had to be incorporated into German territory just as have German districts into Polish areas.

Furthermore, a very important viewpoint could not be neglected, namely, Germany's own security. Were a war to break out, we would be threatened by the loss of our eastern areas unless we retained a strategic defense line within our control. The fulcrum of this strategic defense line, the fortress of Posen itself, demanded no deviation from the principle that had inspired the line of demarcation. Built with ten millions of German money, the city is German by right of a majority of its inhabitants. The gentlemen of the army would be more capable than I in explaining why a fortress is not secured if its lines of communication with other strong points are cut. In such a case, however strong the fortified works, the fortress is as good as lost. Consequently, a few waterways and one road in particular that cross a Polish area were incorporated into the German part, violating in this instance the principle of the line of demarcation. Yet the Prussian government could not and should not have done otherwise. It would have been irresponsible carelessness [on its part], even a breach of duty toward Germany to neglect doing what it did.

With these two questions, gentlemen, the other two are practically solved, dealing as they do with the admission of the German parts of Posen into the German confederation and the permanent seating of the Posen delegation. . . .

You say that political wisdom counsels, justice demands, humanity dictates, the reconstitution of a free Poland. Permit me to examine this reasoning a little more closely. First of all, it has been a commonplace for at least a generation that Germany needs Poland as a first line of defense against Russia, against Asiatic barbarism, as the phrase goes. Gentlemen! It would be pathetic if a people of forty-five million [the Germans], occupying a compact territory in the well-defended center of Europe, required an advance bastion against another people [the Russians], admittedly more numerous by a third, yet so thinly scattered as to paralyze any potential aggressive designs. (Bravo!) . . . It would be a strange misconception indeed, to expect a nation whom we have vanquished in the arts of peace as well as on the battlefield, a nation to whom we dealt the deathblow, a nation that, having counted us among its deadly enemies, should all of a sudden generously forget the whole past to serve as our trusted ally and our bulwark against a people racially akin to them. . . . Even if, all these reasons notwithstanding, we were to free Poland, the great question as to whether Poland could actually achieve its independence from Russia would still remain. I am convinced that it could not. To set Poland free would be either to hand it as a gift to Russia, or, should we demur, to involve us in a war with Russia. . . .

I contend that a policy which calls for freeing Poland regardless of cost is shortsighted and self-effacing, a policy of weakness, a policy of fear, a policy of cowardice. It is high time for us to wake up from a dreamlike altruism which made us enthusiastic about all sorts of nationalities at a time when we ourselves were in servitude and trodden underfoot by all the world. It is high time for us to awaken to a healthy national egoism . . . which on every issue will prefer the welfare and honor of the fatherland. Without such egoism, which the friends of Poland deride so unreservedly, no people can achieve nationhood. "Above all other things, we must be just," they say, "however heavy our sacrifices. We must expiate the weighty guilt of our fathers," their sermon runs, "making good the serious misdeeds in which our princes embroiled us. . . . Even if everything else opposed it, justice demands the restoration of Poland."

Let us look at little more closely at such justice. Let me note, first of all, that I shall forego the purely legalistic argument—though such an argument could be made— that Prussia obtained possessoin of Posen by a treaty made according to the rules. To be honest, the tenets of theoretical [international] law strike me as most pitifully inadequate when they seek to govern the destiny of nations. To rely on them in order to chart the course of peoples is like spinning cobwebs in order to catch eagles. (Agitation on the Left.) No, I admit without subterfuge that our right is none other than the right of the stronger, the right of conquest. The Germans have conquered Polish lands, yet these conquests took place by ways and means that make them irreversible. They are, as has often been observed, not so much conquests of the sword as conquests of the plowshare. It so happens that whereas in the west we were being conquered, in the east we had the great misfortune of doing the conquering ourselves, thus providing whole swarms of German poets with an opportunity to unburden themselves in touching jeremiads about the various nationalities crushed under the German juggernaut. (Laughter on the Right, hissing on the Left.) If we are to be single-mindedly fair, we would not merely have to surrender Posen but half of Germany, for the realm of the Slavs once stretched as far as the Saale River and beyond. Yet as early as the twelfth century, the Germans began their expansion eastward. Saxony and Silesia, Brandenburg, Mecklenburg, Pomerania and the Baltic lands almost as far as the Neva River gradually came into the possession of German colonists, whose conquests were consolidated by force of arms. . . .

The superiority of the German race over most of the Slavic races, with the possible exception of the Russians, is a fact which must be accepted by every impartial observer. Against such facts of natural history, as I call them, decrees conforming to some cosmopolitical sense of justice are quite powerless. . . . Thus I claim that the German conquests in Poland were a necessity of nature. The law of history, differing from what you find in the law books, only recognizes what is a law of nature. One of these proclaims that a people is not entitled to political independence by its mere existence but by the power to maintain a state among other states. The last act of this conquest, the much-decried partition of Poland, was not, as has so often been claimed, the assassination of a people. It was no more than the registration of a death that had already occurred, no more than the burial of a corpse that, being already in the process of dissolution, was unfit to be tolerated among the living. For indeed a people made up of noblemen, Jews, and serfs, reduced to savagery after long years of anarchy, could no longer exist when this kind of freedom became its essential condition of life. . . .

It has often been claimed that Prussia oppressed the Poles. Unfortunately this is not altogether untrue; yet, if oppressed they were, they suffered no more than all of us who had to bear the terrible pressure of a police state. It is a lie to say that Prussia dealt more harshly with the Poles than with the Germans. It never intervened to thwart the development of Polish nationality. In the case of public employment, Polish officials were even decidedly favored. . . . Yet while ten German candidates vied for one opening, one may say in reverse that ten positions awaited one Pole. . . . The Polish educated classes did not have much taste for collaborating in the restoration of their nationality through the workaday, painstaking, practical and prosaic way of the government official. This they left to German seriousness, German hard work, while they preferred to flit abroad, winning friends with their drawing-room manners and their courtly graces. . . .

One needs only to point to what Posen is today and let those speak who, from their own experience, remember what it once was. It was a desert before Prussia got hold of it, much as Cracow * is today. One generation under German administration accomplished what a thousand years of Polish rule failed to do. Admittedly, in this process a great part of the landed wealth passed into German hands. This happened in the world's simplest and most rightful fashion, simply because on the same field the German knows how to grow two to three times as much as the Pole, and because the German used his earnings to best advantage while the Pole lived in poverty. The Poles are still an aristocratic people who consider the Germans' wise thrift and strenuous hard work as signs of a servile disposition, as no more than filthy avarice. . . . It is . . . ridiculous to contend that justice demands the surrender of parts of the country that were once Polish. Did the German clear the forests, drain the swamps, turn the virgin soil, build roads and canals, construct villages and found cities in order to feather new, parasitic nests for the exiled descendants of the many-headed Polish despotism? Is the middle class that owes its origin to German vocational assiduity to be sacrificed once again? Should the marrow of the country be consumed to support a few families of wastrels and mazurka dancers in courtly splendor? (Hissing on the Left; disapproval.) . . .

Prussia is able to give an equally telling answer . . . to the reproach of inhumanity in refusing to free an oppressed people. It is not true that a people have been oppressed. Only an aristocracy that had prevented the mass of its serfs from ever becoming a people has been toppled. Only despots who retained their subjects in a dehumanized condition have been eliminated, and only because of this was [the Prussian government] able to overthrow them. [The Prussian government] laid the basis for a new Polish people, by creating a free peasantry, and this striving, gentlemen, has been recognized by the Poles themselves. Go to Poland and ask the Polish peasant whether he wants to belong to a free Poland or stay with Prussia. "God preserve us from it," he will answer you. "We want to stay with Prussia.". . .

I am not opposing the restoration of Poland as such. Rather do I speak for the only possible kind of restoration that we Germans have already begun and tried out. As much as I totally oppose the restoration of the Polish aristocracy do I favor a restoration of a Polish people who up to now have not existed except in embryo form, nurtured by Germany. As a result of our conquests of Poland, the difficult and enormous

* [Until 1846 an independent Polish city-state. (*Ed.*)]

task of raising this embryo to maturity has fallen upon us Germans. Indeed this task is expiation enough for any odiousness with which the partitions of Poland may have been carried out. Prussia has prepared a cradle for the embryo of a Polish people that it has created, so that [Poland] may develop unimpeded under German protection and safeguarded from the outside world. This is where the Poles ought to prove that they are capable of governing themselves. . . .

Janiszewski (from Posen)   Gentlemen! Accusations against the Poles have been hurled from this rostrum. . . . Some have already been tellingly refuted by earlier speakers; others have been overlooked. Almost all the mistakes of many centuries have been dredged up in order to heap them on the Poles. . . . I could touch upon much of what has been said, but I shall forego to do so except for two points that I cannot ignore.

The first is the accusation of rebellion [that has been levied against us], of [carrying on] a revolution in Posen or a struggle of Pole against German. . . . I draw the gentlemen's attention to a verdict that is still pending and which I do not want to prejudge. The highest Prussian authorities have themselves consented to the creation of a commission to determine the responsibilities. It is to decide whether responsibility for the blood bath is to be borne by the Poles or by the other side. This means that in any case . . . the verdict is in doubt. We are not accused by the authorities. Representatives of the Polish nationality are sitting in the Constituent Assembly in Berlin [that is, the Prussian as against the German national parliament meeting at Frankfurt] instead of being indicted for high treason by the government. It would therefore be well to await the commission's judgment. . . .

The second point upon which I would like to touch was brought up by one of yesterday's speakers who said that the country [Posen] had been conquered by German application and German hard work. I don't want to look too closely into German application and German hard work, yet I do know villages that are worked by Poles and others that are worked by Germans. I do know the whole of the grand duchy of Posen very well indeed, and I am acquainted with rundown German villages as well as with rundown Polish villages. On the contrary, I am acquainted with Polish farms that exceed by far anything that may be found in German hands. I merely draw your attention to the estates owned by General von Chlapowski, by Messrs. Potworowski and Mielzynski, and I challenge anyone to find a German-held estate that is as excellently managed. . . .

Let me get to the issue. Herein, gentlemen, I am aware of a lack of conscious, definite principles. This deficiency has been pointed out by several speakers before me. The proceedings in Holstein and Schleswig have differed from those in Posen. You will therefore forgive me if I decline to start with principles but prefer to confine myself to the concrete, to the given. The question runs as follows: Should the representatives from Posen be permanently seated or not? The decision hinges on whether the grand duchy of Posen may be regarded as part of the German Confederation or not. If this province does not constitute a part of German territory, it can evidently not be represented in a German National Assembly. The two issues are therefore closely connected and indeed inseparable.

Back in 1815 the grand duchy of Posen was granted to the Prussian crown. Bound by the terms of this treaty, the king guaranteed the full preservation of the Polish nationality in this province in a special proclamation. Hence, Posen did not then constitute a part of German federal territory, as the mention and guarantee of Polish nationality attests better than anything else that the province was indeed Polish. This is why even in subsequent years, notwithstanding the notorious system of Germanization, there was no talk of incorporating the province into the German Confederation. This would have been too shameless a breach of the nationality guarantee. Only following the notable March Days in Berlin [the 1848 insurrection which forced the Prussian king to convoke a constituent assembly] did such an idea arise. At that time the Prussian king declared that those provinces of the Prussian monarchy not included within Germany could be incorporated into the German Confedaration, provided this met with their inclination and that they were admitted by the session of the Confederation. Even at this point the Prussian government made no positive claim for itself but left this right to the decision of the popular will.

Following this royal decree, the Polish National Committee immediately dispatched a delegation to the king in Berlin, explaining that as Poles they neither could nor would give up their nationality. They requested that as Prussia adhered to Germany, so Posen as part of the former Polish state should enjoy its own constitution as had been guaranteed in the year 1815. These modest demands were indeed granted. . . . This first expression of the popular will . . . spoke out clearly against including the province within the German Confederation. This expression is even more significant in that its signatories included some Germans as well as Poles. . . . Despite this declaration buttressed by facts, on April 6 the Prussian government laid the question as to whether the grand duchy of Posen did or did not want to be retroactively included in the German Confederation before the [Posen] provincial assembly. By a vote of 26 to 17 the provincial assembly resolved that it did not wish to be incorporated into the German Confederation. Meanwhile the Prussian assembly had decided that Prussia would join Germany, a decision admitted as valid and binding before the law. The decision of the Posen provincial assembly should have been just as lawful and binding. Nonetheless, a minority meeting privately declared the provincial assembly's decision null and void. . . .

Following this illegal private resolution and following . . . petitions, the Prussian government requested incorporation [of German Posen] into Germany. Without considering the justice or injustice of the request, a session of the German Confederation decreed admittance. Gentlemen, these are the facts and the law of the matter. I ask every impartial observer: Is this proceeding lawful, is it just? Did not the government itself make adherence to Germany contingent upon the free expression of the population's desire, only to flout the popular will by requesting annexation [unilaterally]? What was the point, then, of putting the issue to the Posen provincial assembly [in the first place]? Could it be possible that the government officials of the old system, the officials of the police state inspiring the petitions, were considered organs of the popular will? . . . Why was this whole affair rushed through in such haste, in flagrant contradiction to the importance of the matter at hand and the usual circumspection of the German character? The reason for the haste was fear that as the bureaucratic personnel was transferred, the "popular will" would also flee the land. (Applause on the Left.). . .

My constituents, the inhabitants of the subdistricts of Buk and Samter, met on May 30 to lodge a common protest against the election of a representative [to the German Constituent Assembly]. The authorities, however, gave them to understand that this was illegal. As [my constituents] came to realize that any protests would remain fruitless, they grasped the last remaining legal weapon at their disposal: they elected as their deputy a member of the former Polish National Committee who had been in the delegation that had requested [administrative] reorganization from His Majesty, the King. . . . They have sent him here to express their wishes freely and solemnly, namely, that they never requested the annexation of their subdistricts for the simple reason that they were Poles and not Germans. It was therefore impossible to expect them to become Germans. . . .

I have demonstrated to you that the wishes of the population were ignored and that the frontier line accepted by the German Confederation is completely unreliable and in violation of the nationality principle. The report itself bears me out. It specifically notes that 420,000 Germans as against 800,000 Poles lived in the whole of the grand duchy of Posen. Now the German Confederation incorporated a population of 593,000 on April 22, followed by 273,500 on May 2, for a grand total of 866,500. Let us assume —something which is by no means the case, since the two nationalities are intermixed —that the whole compact mass of the German population were packed into just this area. I ask these gentlemen how these districts can be called predominantly German when even they contain 42,000 more Poles than Germans? When one considers, furthermore, that many purely German people are to be found on the other side of this line, these districts must have a Polish majority of at least 100,000. . . . None of this can be justified by recourse to the nationality principle. In its behalf other motives will have to be invoked. . . .

If Germany is to draw this line of demarcation, prettify this as you will, it still remains an act of violence. This act of violence is even more blatant and more grievous to the Poles, coming at a time when peoples and their sacred rights are no longer the object of arbitrary governments. [Violence] is being inflicted at a time when almost all the remaining peoples of Europe are being blessed with a freer existence. Under the pretext of the predominance of a German population, the Poles are being decapitated, so to speak, though they are permitted to survive as an object of derision. Under this pretext the oldest Polish areas to which Poland's ancient history clings are being detached. [The Poles] are deprived of the communities where their educational institutions, the so-called Polish *gymnasia,* are located, until they are left with only the single most ill-equipped school. Everything that is of spiritual value to them is taken away. . . .

The princes, gentlemen, destroyed only what physical force could destroy—only the Polish state and not the nation. . . . Even in their later endeavors, they always shied away from openly proclaiming the Polish provinces to be German. . . . However qualified by "Prussian," "Austrian," or "Russian," the name of Poland at least was always retained. (Great applause.) Is it possible that the remnant is now to be rooted out? . . . Should I accept this? No, I cannot. I cannot accept the irony that a free Germany in the very name of freedom should annihilate the freedom of the Poles! . . .

Gentlemen, let me shed some light on another point upon which many arguments have turned. It is claimed that Germany must protect the Germans living in the grand duchy of Posen and for this purpose carry out this division, this partition. The principle that you owe protection to your brothers will be acknowledged by everyone, gentlemen. . . . Yet however right, true, and humane, you will also agree that correct fundamental principles, when mistakenly or wrongly applied, may do as much harm as false principles. Let us subject this concrete case to closer examination. Let me mention in passing that there are thousands upon thousands of Germans within the grand duchy who do not demand annexation as a means of protection at all. There are other thousands in the grand duchy of Posen today who, though they may be transferred to the Rhineland tomorrow [the reference is to Prussian government officials], are more eager than anyone else in clamoring for this line of demarcation. If we are to get to the bottom of the thing, however, the first question to ask is whether such protection is needed in the present circumstances and, secondly, whether this can be achieved through partition.

The first point . . . hinges on whether the German nationality is endangered in these circumstances, and if so, by what agency. The reorganization proclaimed by the king had been claimed as a threat to the German nationality, and in support of this claim false rumors had been spread throughout the world to the effect that the province was to be separated from the Prussian monarchy. This is fundamentally false, as no one even considered this. It goes without saying that such a course would have turned over both Poles and Germans into Russian hands. Yet only in this way could the hateful claim that the Germans in Posen were to be Polonized be associated with the idea of reorganization. The Poles' petition to the king is in your own hands. Judge for yourselves as to whether it contains anything pointing to the Polonization of the Germans. The only thing that the Poles asked for was an end to the disparity between themselves and all the other subjects within the whole monarchy. They refused to be singled out as subjects to be ruled; they demanded participation in governing themselves. They demanded what cannot be denied to any citizen, namely, [the right] not to be administered by a foreign bureaucracy, not to be discriminated against, not to be Germanized any longer, not to have to purchase these freedoms and rights by renouncing their nationality. In a word, they demanded the restoration of rights that had long been withheld from them, that had always been promised to them, that had always been theirs on paper but never in reality. . . .

Let us assume that the German nationality in Posen really needs the protection of all Germany in addition to that of the king of Prussia. Assuming this, gentlemen, does Germany have no recourse for safeguarding her brethren in the grand duchy of Posen except through an illegal partition of the province? How do you protect your German compatriots in France, England, Russia, and America? And why do you not undertake to partition those countries? (Laughter and applause.) Why not the Baltic provinces where the German population lives much more compactly than in the grand duchy of Posen? Why inflict this only on defenseless Poland? Perhaps because Germans fleeing from the persecutions of their homeland found a refuge there? These Germans lived for hundreds of years among Poles, yet in what way was their nationality offended, in what way was it infringed upon? Did they not remain Germans down to the period when these areas were occupied by the Germans? Did you ever hear these Germans complain of oppression by the Poles? . . .

I want to say something about one specific act—the act of voting. I hereby want to adduce a reason that would tend to invalidate these elections, for at the time of voting the province of Posen was under martial law. . . . Is it possible to proceed with elections of such signal importance in a province groaning under the laws of war, and to carry them out without injury to the participating Polish nationality when in point of fact martial law was uniquely directed against the Poles? Is it possible to hold legal elections at a time when Poles had been arrested and dragged to the fortresses by the hundreds, only to be released without any kind of examination once the elections had terminated? Is it possible to hold a lawful vote when, according to the words of a German eyewitness, Poles were afraid to be seen in the streets of Posen, when the Pole appeared to have been outlawed in his own homeland? (Hear!) . . .

I do not come to you as a beggar. I come armed with my just rights. (Bravo!) I do not appeal for sympathy but for justice, and if this is withheld, gentlemen, then you must admit that no people on earth has had to experience such a bitter deception. . . . And what would be Germany's gain, gentlemen, in forcibly annexing 500,000 to 600,-000 Poles? What can a nation of forty million gain in this way? Nothing trifling, gentlemen! A necessary and inevitable consequence would be for Germany to take 500,000 to 600,000 of its bitterest enemies to its own bosom. For what kind of citizens, gentlemen, can you make of those whom you chain to yourselves by force? . . . You will find that the hearts of men rise up against every injustice. Examine the tortured and horror-filled history of Poland since its partition and you will find that truth written in blood. The Poles have been swallowed, but by God, they have never been digested. (Bravo!) Powerful German states have labored long and persistently to destroy this nationality. What did they accomplish? What glory did they earn? They filled the dungeons, constructed new gallows and, gratuitously, wrote many a page of their own history in human blood, . . . yet without achieving what they had sought.

Gentlemen, do you now want to take over this war of extermination against the Poles? Do you want to assume this role and stake the future of a free Germany upon this bloody road? Do you believe, gentlemen, that the supposed benefits, which you promise that the Poles will derive from annexation, can appease us? Prussia offers the best evidence for that. Gentlemen, we recognize very well indeed the bitter fruits of benefits forced upon us, benefits that have already so often been enumerated for us. We are fed up with advantages that can only be purchased at the highest price in the world, at the cost of our human dignity and our nationality. These are truly no benefits, gentlemen, for such benefits hurt more than a foe's hardest blows. (Bravo on the Left.) An education that can only forge our own chains instead of liberating us must be far more hated and despised than barbarism itself. A policy of justice will indeed be the noblest, yet also the best and withal perhaps the cleverest [policy]. Gentlemen, you are sitting as judges in your own cause. You are to judge between Poles and Germans when you yourselves are Germans. I myself feel and know the sentiment of patriotism, . . . yet you will have to agree that yours is a difficult and slippery role. Nonetheless, I do not despair of obtaining justice. I demand neither sympathy nor compassion nor generosity. I appeal to your virtue, to your sense of righteousness; I appeal to your virtue, to your sense of justice! (Prolonged applause in the Assembly and in the galleries.)

ᴇᴥᴣ DEBATE ON "THE RIGHT TO WORK"

Just as the revolutions of 1848 in Germany showed up the ambiguities of the nationalist tradition (see Debate on Posen, pages 471–486), in France the revolution demonstrated the hollowness of the French revolutionary tradition. In 1848 French political factions of every coloration claimed to be the true heirs of the Great Revolution and were ready to prove their legitimacy by violence if necessary.

This lack of consensus on fundamental issues among politicians, all of whom claimed to be republicans, may be illustrated by the debate on "the right to work" in the French National Assembly. The four representative speeches excerpted here were delivered on September 12, 1848, in the course of a prolonged discussion of the draft of a republican constitution for France submitted by a special parliamentary committee. From September 11 through 14, the discussion centered on an amendment by a left-wing representative, Mathieu (de la Drôme), clearly spelling out every citizen's right to education, a job, and government assistance in case of need—in contrast to the committee's proposal which had evaded any clear-cut commitment. Mathieu's "right to a job" (or "right to work") was the real focus of controversy. The debate ended when his amendment was defeated 596 to 187.

In one sense the issue was closed long before the discussion began, having been decided both by ballots and bullets. In February, 1848, the Paris workers who had overthrown the July Monarchy thought they stood on the threshold of a social revolution. As a down payment they had exacted "the right to work"—a hazy phrase connoting a welfare state if not outright socialism—from a reluctant middle-class Provisional Government. Yet the National Assembly elected in April, 1848, by universal manhood suffrage had not the slightest inclination to permit any redistribution of property or economic power. By June the disillusioned Paris workers had taken to the barricades once again, only to be bloodily crushed by the regular army. The September debate in parliament was therefore only for the record.

Two of the speakers in this selection were men of considerable promi-nence: Alexis de Tocqueville (1805–1859), an aristocrat famed as an analyst of American democracy (see Vol. IV, page 163), was a moderate conservative in French politics, unenthusiastic about the Second Republic; Alexandre Ledru-Rollin (1807–1874), a former Minister of the Interior under the Provisional Government, was the ranking leader of the coalition of democrats and socialists who opposed the conservative parliamentary majority in the National Assembly.

Gauthier de Rumilly   Citizen representatives, if I could believe that we can outlaw poverty and banish all the inequalities that nature herself has ordained by inscribing the three words "Right to Work" into the preamble of our constitution—and such was the argument advanced yesterday by the author of this amendment that I am op-posing—if I agreed with this, I would not hesitate one instant to opt for its adoption. Yet I cannot believe this at all. On the contrary, I can envisage grave dangers should this amendment be adopted, and it is for this reason that I must voice any opposi-tion. . . .

If the amendment simply means to indicate that the republic owes relief to any needy citizens, either by providing work for them within the limits of the state's re-sources or the means of livelihood to those unable to labor and whose families are unable to care for them, then I would claim that the wording [proposed by] the com-mittee should satisfy these aspirations, since the [original] proposal does extend assist-ance in [just] such cases. . . .

"Organization of Labor," "Right to Work"; these are new terms for ideas which are not new and which underline the imprudence of raising insoluble questions. Some time ago an inflexible logician told you, "If you grant me the right to work, you abandon property rights to me." This is where the danger lies. . . . The difference between the proposal of the committee and that of our honorable colleague is the dif-ference between what is possible and what is not. Whatever can be done for the workers should be done. Yet to make promises to them that cannot be kept is nothing other than to deceive them; reason sets limits to all aspirations of fraternity.

If such a right were established by the constitution, how would the state intervene? Of its own free will? No, rather by virtue of an obligation. It will be claimed that un-employment is something that is self-evident, yet there are a thousand different kinds of unemployment. Did we not witness the enrollment in the National Workshops, and should not the past always inculcate its lesson to the future? The great and complex

"Session of the French National Assembly, September 12, 1848," *Le Moniteur universel* (1848), pp. 2415–2419. Translated by Peter Amann.

machine of a civilizing government needs experienced hands. It will drift in the storm unless skillful mariners are at the helm. By tampering with an unfamiliar movement we may move in a direction opposite from that which we had sought, a lack of foresight that may be fatal to the country.

Moral as well as Christian law imposes the duty of helping one's neighbor. Nonetheless, the poor cannot demand this as an obligation nor compel others to acts of charity. Yet what will you accomplish, on the other hand, by securing a universal claim against the state other than to create such an obligation and such a compulsion by means of this right? What! Will the state face new creditors in the name of labor? For every man who has a right is entitled to claim it. This would be no longer a matter of charity, for the charitable act is voluntary. . . . In industrious countries, no one can prevent these industrial crises originating in overproduction. The income of those who are referred to as "the rich" would be used up in vain, as futile as a drop of water in the ocean. Nonetheless, this right would be invoked against the state, for a right is a right.

Thus, however one examines the proposal, whether with regard to the right itself or whether in the light of all its consequences, it is obvious that these consequences cannot be eluded and that they are, as will be shown, bound to be dangerous. Gentlemen, the state will thus have to turn entrepreneur in every industry, to play the provider for all idle workers! Yet the state is endowed with a loftier and nobler function: by stimulating all industries by means of the protection it extends to them—a good system of taxation, [good] legislation, the general direction given to business—the state is enabled to encourage every kind of economic activity. This, gentlemen, is how I see the role of the state with regard to the workers. This is how I envisage general prosperity deriving from everyone's labor.

The state proclaims its respect for property. If the right to work were to be proclaimed, the illusory guarantees granted to property would have to be withdrawn. The time has come to choose between the two, for the consequence of the right to work is communism. To inscribe this right is, willy-nilly, gradually to bring about this consequence, namely the destruction of property. Yet, is not property a fundamental institution within our constitution? Need I go back to its origin? Is it not the fruit of all labor? Agriculture could not have started without private property, for the farmer needs the assurance of being able to gather the fruits of his land. Who among us would deny his faith in the right of property? . . . The road the peoples have travelled toward civilization may be accurately gauged by the degree of security which property enjoys.

Well, then, someone should let me know what the likely effect of the proclamation of the right to work would be, a proclamation, as was once asserted, that would allay disquiet and restore confidence in the country! The effect would be diametrically opposed to this, for it would entail a serious blow to credit, and credit is the stimulus to labor and enterprise. Therefore, if you intimidate property, you are also undercutting labor, [at a time when work] has proved so elusive and is sought after by every diligent man.

It is not true, as was affirmed yesterday, that he who is without possessions is the slave of him who possesses. This is denied by the general progress in consumption that has taken place during these last sixty years. Food production has outstripped population growth. In the period before the great outbreaks of the month of February [1848], per capita food consumption in France was greater than it had been during the previous century. The very quantity of the products essential to meet everyone's needs has grown. The quantity of yard goods, for example, has more than tripled in the last forty years. It therefore cannot be denied that the worker is better fed, better housed, better clothed. . . .

The side effect of every great religious, political, and social movement is to create a profound disturbance of public opinion, giving rise to the most insane ambitions, the most perverse inclinations. The transformation taking place encourages logicians to question the very foundation of society itself; ordinarily they deny [private] property, and under different guises seek the collectivization of goods, the inevitable destruction of labor and savings. There is to be no more responsibility for the individual, for society sees to everything. Yet despite these mad attempts, societies undergo change only by a slow and successive action. By their very mass they resist anyone who has the folly to seek to reconstruct them from top to bottom all of a sudden. If ever there existed a society upon which it would be insane to perform this impossible and perilous experiment of such wholesale reconstruction, it is French society which has undergone a series of renovations in the last sixty years.

French society has emerged victorious though chastened from the terrible struggle of these recent times. In the face of danger it has demonstrated all the mettle of a war-tested nation whose courage is reinforced by the sentiment of being right. . . . The great event of February 24, 1848, has given rise to all kinds of ideas, some correct, others foolish. Reason must be made to prevail in the republic, for the question is not one of spreading ruin but of organizing. There should be no attempt to divide the scattered members of the same family, those who are called workers and those who are called bourgeois. Everybody, that is, all citizens without exception, belong to the people. They are linked in equality and fraternity, invested with the same rights and owing the same [civic] duties.

Common sense is the spirit of democracy. It is this common sense embodied in the nation which must guide us who speak for this intelligent democracy. Let the government and the National Assembly raise high the banner of the republic and scatter the dangerous utopias that have found refuge within its folds. Unfurling this flag and holding it firmly aloft, let them put an end to this anarchy of ideas. Only then will a salutary stimulus to all agricultural and commercial industry make itself universally felt. It will then no longer be necessary to inscribe the right to work in the constitution, for real work will be contributing everywhere to public wealth and prosperity. (Very good! Very good!)

Pelletier Let us not act in such a way that the people will say of the republic what for seventeen years they said of the former king: that his promises were so many lies. This is particularly true of the right to work, which is not, as some seem to believe, a favor that the republic would bestow upon the people, but a just restitution that ought to have been made long ago.

The committee on the constitution, no longer willing to affirm that a job is a citizen's right, has deemed it expedient to change its original draft to declare that "the Republic has an obligation toward the worker within the limits of its resources."

God, in whose presence we shall decree the constitution, created the earth for all men without distinction. If, by means of legislation which at this time need neither be approved nor improved, a few men have privately appropriated the land in order to cultivate it, do they in turn not owe recognition of the right to work to those who own nothing? . . .

What will you tell the children of the poor, the hapless proletarians who, fully obedient toward the laws of your society, will come to you to invoke them in behalf of the family, the fatherland, and property? "I recognize," they will say, "that my share of the original soil is in the possession . . . of those who, coming into the world before me, cleared [the land] and made it fruitful. I acknowledge that those who cleared it enhanced its value and that this new value (all that is really theirs) cannot be separated from the land. Therefore, if they are to enjoy the fruit of their labor or that of their ancestors from whom they have inherited, they are kept from giving me a share of the soil from which I should benefit. I agree to surrender my share to them, . . . to respect their ownership, yet in return do they now owe me my right to work? And in order for this right to be more than a bitter mockery, must they not organize industry and agriculture in such a way that I should be able to find a job in my own country, or obtain, in the absence of work, the means of existence?" (Interruption.) If you want to reply to me, you will be able to come to the rostrum. . . . Will you answer him with Malthus again? . . . Will you say, as Malthus does, that there is no such thing as the right to employment; that man is born into a world already occupied and he is therefore really superfluous on this earth unless the rich happen to need his labor? No, we can no longer be Malthusians. The people would rise in indignation and provide, as it did in February, a formal rebuke to these hateful phrases. . . .

If he [the worker] is without a family, unable to work, you say that you will provide for his support, you will give him the means to live. I acknowledge your good intentions, yet these "means to live" will be no more than charity, and a son of the people ought not to have to live on charity. Alms degrade him who receives them and, besides, this charity will be limited. If it is inadequate, will you tell him, still like Malthus, but this time in the name of the French economists of the Academy of Moral and Political Science [an honorary state-sponsored academic society]: "Workers who go hungry! The state feels an obligation to aid you, but don't forget that you have no right to demand anything. The obligation to assist has no corresponding right. The fundamental principle and the special mission of the state is justice. Although the state also has the sublime yet perilous mission of expressing love and charity toward the people, it must put the reign of justice above anything else. And justice, while respecting man's liberty, may in good conscience leave him to die of hunger. My resources are inadequate. I can offer you only half of what it takes to live. Therefore you shall die, but in dying tender your thanks to me, for even though charity imposed the obligation to give you the little that I have, I had the right to refuse you even this." (Restiveness.)

If the poor son of the people, the luckless proletarian, whom our worm-eaten society can neither employ nor feed, is forced to emigrate—unable to live in the midst of his fellows, among unemployment and the exhausted resources of the republic—leaving you in full possession of the French soil of which he was to have been a beneficiary in his quality of Frenchman, not only are you then his debtor, but, more than that, you rob him of his homeland.

For him, then, there is to be neither family nor homeland nor property. Your social organization has deprived him of all three. Gentlemen, in the name of these inviolable principles, recognize his right to work. . . .

I know this assembly is at loose ends as to how to put this right to employment into operation. Yet this always happens when grave questions must be solved before they have been adequately studied. We cannot, nonetheless, evade the issue by telling the people that nothing would please us more than to consecrate their right to work and to make them happy, but that we shall not do so because we don't know how to secure and organize this right and because we are frightened of the socialists who claim it can be done. The people would answer you: If you don't know how to do something new, go home and give somebody else a chance. (Laughter.) . . .

I raise the social problem before you, not as a philosopher but as a practical man who wants to remain within the limits of what is possible, yet who also wants all that is possible. What is needed and [indeed] the only thing that is acceptable today is a method of social organization that would eliminate misery without causing an immediate disruption in the pattern of society—a social organization [in other words] that would gradually and peaceably lead us to basic reforms, toward the highest social goals.

Here is the problem: For all men who are unemployed, the state must procure work or, in the absence of jobs, the means to live. At the same time, the state should be neither farmer, merchant, nor manufacturer, nor should it hand out alms to the people. . . . This is the social problem I shall try to solve. Should I err, let me be given credit for my good intentions, and let someone with better ideas bring them to this speaker's platform. This is the only way in which we can do our duty.

Allow me to go into some details which will help to clarify my ideas. According to the economists and statisticians, France has six million wage earners, whose salaries amount to about six billion [francs] per year. Of these six million workers, two million live in modest comfort and are able to accumulate very modest savings. Two million exist, that is, they live from day to day, while [the last] two million are indigent.

A voice on the right   And those who get drunk!

Pelletier   Those who get drunk are unhappy. They don't have theaters and concerts! This is the only pleasure left to them!

To these six million wage earners, two million unproductive beggars should be added. . . . Instead of letting them live as they can on public charity, their labor ought to be utilized, bringing the number of workers to eight million.

If, by a simple and easy method that I shall outline, without itself turning industrialist or farmer, the republican government were to organize industry and agriculture in harmony with the common welfare, these eight million men whose product [today] amounts to no more than six billion and who barely consume more than that in spite of all the assistance and alms which pity bestows on them, these eight million men would produce and consume twice, even three times more. . . .

To achieve this, what should be done? Grant joint responsibility for all workers and all industries. In order to invest all workers with joint responsibility, I propose, first of all, that in all French communities, grouped into industrial districts, establishments for the extinction of poverty should be created, just as institutions for the cure of the sick and for sheltering the aged already exist. These establishments, founded by the state in partnership with the local community, would be managed by an administration having the power to collect, as long as it is in the public interest, five per cent of the workers' salaries in return for assuming the responsibility of procuring employment for them or, if no work can be found, means for their existence. . . .

Let us suppose that in all French communities there were to be one or (depending upon the importance of the locality) several such establishments with the task of finding work in order to banish poverty. All idle men, carrying a certificate or booklet indicating their trade and proving that they could be employed within the community, would present themselves there. Each one would address himself to the office in charge of procuring jobs for workers in his trade.

Let us assume a garment-trimming maker who comes to ask for work. Business is slow and the master garment-trimmers of the area have no openings for journeymen. What does one do then? He is given enough to live on, that is, a coupon good for a sum determined by the special rules of of the establishment and always proportionate to food prices. Here is a man who has received an indemnity because he could not be put to work. Who has given him that sum? The state? No, rather the institution supposed to procure employment for him, or, if this is unavailable, means of livelihood. Where has this money been obtained? By drawing on his salary and that of his fellow workers. Has he thus received charity? No, this was actually a fair restitution, or rather, he himself, jointly responsible with all other workers, paid himself. . . .

Indeed, the first idea which should and will occur to the administrators of such establishments is this: Every day four or five hundred workers come to us whom we are obliged to pay because we cannot find work for them. If we were to put them to work, not for the state, as was done in the National Workshops, but for themselves; if we were to found producers' cooperatives instead of putting out money until we go bankrupt, we would collect five per cent of their salaries, and with these inexhaustible resources we could found new associations. . . .

Thus, to lighten our expenditures and to employ a large number of workers who come looking for jobs, we are going to create industrial and agricultural associations based on the principle of mutual responsibility. The workers, formed into a cooperative, remunerated on the basis of piecework wherever possible, chosen by election to this or that managerial post, would participate in the profits in proportion to their work and their skill.

In the countryside we shall have canals dug, rivers diked, mountains reforested, land cleared for cultivation. We shall found agricultural cooperatives.

In the cities, for every ten, twenty, thirty, fifty, a hundred, a thousand, two thousand journeymen shoemakers, tailors, trimming-makers, cutlers, hatters, we shall found cooperatives and open a shoe, hat, trimming, etc., store where we would employ sales-people and capable unemployed men suited to a commercial calling. . . .

What would come of all this?

For all the associated workers, a social position that would be undeniably superior to that provided by individualism today. . . .

All the industrial cooperatives must be mutually responsible for each other; for with-out such responsibility cooperatives face immense dangers and, for the most part, are unlikely to survive. I shall go even further. I say that anyone founding cooperatives without linking them by mutual aid is their greatest opponent, even though he may perhaps be unaware of this.

In the course of a year, as two hundred, five hundred, a thousand, ten thousand cooperating industries, no longer facing present-day anarchical competition, would compete only to further their own interests, few of them would be likely to incur losses.

Yet let us suppose that a few of these cooperatives were to have deficits. What would happen? I have already mentioned that each cooperative would retain one tenth of its profits for an insurance fund to disperse financial liability. If instead of a profit the cooperative were to show a loss at the end of the year, all the members' [wages] would be paid and the losses made good by the insurance fund. Thus, no more losses, no more failures, no more bankruptcies. Credit becomes unlimited, order is no longer threatened, and the republic becomes worthy of its name. . . .

Gentlemen, if you have listened to me, you must understand what good results we may expect from the creation of establishments having the task of procuring work for unemployed citizens or, if jobs are unavailable, of providing means of livelihood.

Not only would they create agricultural projects in our countryside, not only would they found immense cooperatives for all trades, but they would also set up rest homes, as well as homes for disabled civilians, for the aged, for crippled workers unable to labor.

Indigence would disappear immediately. The workers, always able to find jobs or to get enough to live on, would not have to dip into savings. It would therefore become possible for the worker, who always hears you praise the pleasures of owning property, to amass a sufficient sum to buy himself a small estate where he would spend his last days. . . .

Commerce would flourish. Merchants and shopkeepers would sell more and be better paid. Artists and all those made idle by economic depression would have more work than they could handle. Neither professional begging nor begging because of unem-ployment would be possible any longer. If a beggar approached you, you would have the right to tell him: "You have neither money nor a job. Go to such and such a place where you will be given work or something to live on." Thieves will be less numerous; for though some criminals are molded by evil upbringing, there are many others whom poverty turns to crime. These establishments would thus prevent theft and begging. (Laughter.) The people would become freer, happier, purer. We would never hear one of our brothers say that he lacks work or bread. . . .

The February revolution was carried out in the name of liberty, equality, and fra-ternity in order for man to become really free, fraternal, and equal; to end the possibility of riots, bloodshed, civil war, the people must be freed from fear of the morrow. I have shown you the way. If you question its adequacy and know of a better way, your duty is to speak up.

Tocqueville   Citizen representatives, unless I am mistaken, you did not expect me to reply to the last part of the speech you have just heard. It contains the formulation of a complete and complicated system which I shall not counter by propounding another system.

My sole aim at this moment is to discuss the amendment in behalf of which, or should I say in relation to which, the preceding speaker has just spoken. . . .

We do not hide the fact that nothing is gained by putting off problems which lie submerged in the society but which, sooner or later, somehow will break the surface, whether it be by word or deed. . . . Yes, gentlemen, it is necessary that sooner or later this question of socialism which everyone fears and which nobody, up to this point, dares to raise, should finally reach this floor. It is necessary that it be dealt with. It is necessary that we unburden the country of the thought of socialism which has weighed on its breast, so to speak. I confess that my chief reason for coming to the speaker's platform was this need to deal with the question of socialism. It is necessary that we know, that the National Assembly know, that the whole of France know whether or not the February [1848] revolution is a socialist revolution. (Very good!)

This is what has been said, this is what is being repeated. How often did I not hear the cry "Long live the *social* and democratic republic" from behind the June barricades. What is meant by these words? This is the question. It is particularly essential that the National Assembly should settle this issue. (Agitation on the left.)

The Assembly may assume that I do not intend to examine all the various systems which may be designated by this same term, socialism. I merely want to characterize in a few words the recurring features of all these systems. [I shall also inquire] whether the February revolution did indeed seek to achieve such ends.

Unless I am mistaken, gentlemen, the first characteristic of all the systems that go under the name of socialism is the energetic, continuous and immoderate appeal to the material passions of man. (Signs of approval.) . . . A second trait is the assault, sometimes direct, at other times indirect but always continued, on the very principles of private property. In my eyes the third and last trait which marks the socialists of whatever coloring or sect is a deep mistrust of freedom, of human reason. It is a mistrust of the individual left to his own devices simply as a private person. They [socialist doctrines] are all characterized by a continuous, varied, and unceasing attempt to mutilate, shorten, and hinder human liberty in every way. According to their idea, the state should not merely be the directing force of society but the master of every man. What am I saying! His master, his tutor, his pedagogue. (Very good!) That in fear of letting man fail, the state should always take its stand by his side [or] above him, to guide, guard, support, deter him. . . .

As you see, gentlemen, I did not get involved in the details of these systems. I have merely depicted socialism in terms of the principal features by which it can be recognized. Wherever you see these features, you may be sure that socialism can also be found; and wherever you see socialism, you may be certain that these characteristics can be found as well.

Well, gentlemen, what does all this amount to? Is it, as has so often been claimed, the continuation, the complement, the perfection of the French revolution? Is it, as has so often been said, the complement, the natural development of democracy? No, gentlemen, it is neither one nor the other. Call to your minds, gentlemen, the French revolution. Recall this terrible and glorious origin of our modern history. Is it true, as a speaker claimed yesterday, that the French revolution accomplished the great things which have made it world famous by appealing to material sentiments, to the material needs of man? . . .

Do you think that it was by speaking of such things that the revolution could have aroused, animated, mobilized, delivered a whole generation to the hazards of war and a confrontation with death? No, gentlemen, no. It was by speaking of loftier things— of patriotism, of the honor of the homeland, of virtue, of generosity, of self-abnegation, of glory—that great deeds were accomplished. For after all, gentlemen, you may be sure that there is only one secret to making men do great deeds, and that is to appeal to great sentiments. (Very good! Very good!)

And [private] property, gentlemen, [private] property? No doubt the French revolution energetically and cruelly waged war against a certain number of property owners. Yet the principle of property was always respected and honored, was enshrined in the revolutionary constitutions. . . . The French revolution did more than that: not only did the revolution endorse private property but it diffused it by increasing the number of proprietors among the citizens. (Divers exclamations, "That's what we ask!")

Thanks to that, gentlemen, we need not fear today the fatal consequences of the doctrines that the socialists are spreading in the country and even in this hall. It is because the French revolution peopled the country with ten million [proprietors] that there is no danger in permitting such doctrines to be expounded from the rostrum. Though they may no doubt distress society, thanks to the French revolution, such doctrines will never prevail against society and destroy it. (Very good!)

Finally, gentlemen, as to liberty: What strikes me is that although the old regime was sharply at variance with socialist views in many respects, its ideas in the realm of politics were much more akin to those of the socialists than one might suspect. All considered, the old regime was much closer to them than we are. Indeed, the *ancien régime* proclaimed the view that wisdom was confined to the state; that subjects are frail and feeble beings who must be led by the hand or they will stumble or hurt themselves; that it is a good thing unceasingly to hinder, constrain, and restrict individual liberties; that it is necessary to regulate industry, safeguard the quality of products, prevent free competition. On this point the *ancien régime* thought exactly as do the socialists today. And who, I ask you, thought differently? The French revolution!

Gentlemen, what broke all these shackles which in every way paralyzed the free flow of persons, goods, and ideas? What gave back to man the individual dimension which is his true greatness? The French revolution itself. . . .

Gentlemen, is all this great movement of the French revolution supposed to have culminated in the society which the socialists depict with delight, this regulated, regimented, measured society in which the state takes care of everything, where the individual is nothing, where society gathers unto itself, embodies within itself, all power, all life, where man's aim is solely his comfort—this society where enlightenment, where daylight, one might say, will be extinguished? What! Is it for this society of bees or beavers, for this society that is more like a perfect society of animals than of free men, that the French revolution was supposedly undertaken? Is it for this that so many famous men died on the battlefield and on the scaffold, that so much glorious blood drenched the soil? Is it for this that so many passions were inflamed, that so much genius and so many virtues appeared in the world? . . .

No, gentlemen, democracy and socialism are inconsistent. They are not merely different but incompatible. Is the task of democracy perchance to create a more annoying, a more interfering, a more restrictive government than all the others, distinguished solely by the fact that it is elected by the people and would act in its name? But in that case, what would you have accomplished other than to make tyranny legitimate and thereby provide the force and omnipotence it previously lacked? Democracy extends the sphere of individual independence, while socialism restricts it. Democracy credits each man with all that he is worth, while socialism makes each man an agent, an instrument, a cipher. Democracy and socialism are linked by no more than a single word: equality. Yet note the distinction: democracy seeks equality within liberty, while socialism seeks equality in regimentation and serfdom. (Very good! Very good!) Thus the revolution of February must not be a social revolution, and if this is true, one should muster the courage to say so. If it must not become a social revolution, one should have the energy to proclaim this loudly as I myself am doing here. . . . No, the republic of February should be democratic, but it should not be socialist.

A voice on the left Yes, it should! (No! No!—Interruption.)

Tocqueville And if the revolution is not to be socialist, what is it to be?

A member on the left Royalist!

Tocqueville (turning in that direction) It might turn royalist if we were to let you have your way (Lively approval.), but it will not go that way.

Felix Pyat If the misfortune of becoming royalists should happen to us, we would end up where you started out.

Tocqueville If the February revolution is not socialist, what will it be then? Was it, as many people say and believe, purely an accident? Is it to be no more than a change of personnel or of legislation? I do not think so. . . . The reason why I thought revolutions were impending, and indeed the reason why they occurred was this: . . . In total disregard of the most sacred principles spread by the French revolution throughout the world, power, influence, prestige—in a word, life itself—had been confined to fit the very narrow scope of a single class, to the degree that no other country offered a similar example. Even in aristocratic England, even in this England which we often misguidedly set up as a model and an exemplar, the people participated to a considerable extent, however indrectly, in political life. If they themselves did not vote (yet they often did), at least they made their voices heard. They made their will known to those who governed and were linked to them by a reciprocal understanding.

In this country, nothing of the sort. I repeat: All the rights, all the power, all the influence, all the honors, the whole political life was confined to one extremely narrow class. And below—nothing!

Well, this is what gave me the idea that we were on the verge of revolution. I saw what went on within this small privileged class, something that in the long run always happens to small exclusive aristocracies: Civic spirit was waning; corruption increased day by day; intrigue was taking the place of virtue; everything was depreciating, deteriorating.

So much for the top of society.

And what was going on at the bottom? Below the so-called "legal country" [that is, those who paid 200 francs in direct taxes and were thus qualified to vote] was the real people, which was less badly treated than is claimed. . . . The people, existing, so to speak, outside of the whole official framework, lived its own life, more and more detached in mind and heart from those who were supposed to be its leaders. This people gave its mind and heart to those who naturally kept in touch with it. Among the latter, many belonged to those vain utopians of whom we spoke a while ago, while others were dangerous demagogues.

Because I saw these two classes, one small, the other numerous, gradually drifting apart, the latter filled with jealousy, mistrust, and anger, the former heedless to the point of egotism and insensitivity—because I saw these two classes isolated from each other and marching in opposite directions, I said as I had the right to say: The wind of revolution is rising and soon the revolution will be here. (Very good!) . . .

I therefore want the February revolution to have a meaning, a clear, precise, perceptible meaning that shows from the outside for all to see. And what is this meaning? I indicate it in two words: The February revolution must be the true continuation, the real and wholesome execution of what the French revolution had sought. The February revolution must be the realization of our fathers' dreams. (Lively approval.) . . .

This is what the February revolution must be, neither more nor less. The French revolution sought to get rid of classes, though not as far as society is concerned. The French revolution never had the idea of dividing citizens into proprietors and proletarians as you are doing. . . . The French revolution, as I have already told you, never had the ridiculous pretension of creating a power within society that would directly take care of the wealth, the welfare, the well-being of each citizens by substituting the very dubious wisdom of the governors for the practical and responsible wisdom of the governed. The French revolution thought its task was adequately fulfilled in providing every citizen with enlightenment and liberty. (Very good!). . .

Finally, the French revolution had the intention—and it is this intention which has made the revolution not merely sacred but holy in the eyes of the peoples—of introducing charity into politics. . . . The revolution extended, broadened, and raised the conception of the state's duty toward the poor, toward the citizens who suffer. . . . This is what the French revolution sought to do; this is what we ourselves should do. Is there any socialism in this?

On the left   Yes! Yes! There is nothing but that.

Tocqueville   No, this is not socialism but Christian charity applied to politics. . . . Nothing in this gives the workers a claim upon the state; nothing in this forces the state to take the place of private foresight, of private economy, of private honesty. . . . Yes, the February revolution must be Christian and democratic, but it must not be socialist. . . .

Ledru-Rollin   Citizens, the speaker who has just left the rostrum has appealed to the great principles of our glorious French revolution. He has claimed that for our present republic he seeks all that was noble, lofty, and fraternal in the great movement by which our fathers in 1789 and 1793 put their imprint upon the world. This is also what I want. In those times, as he said, external war and internal unrest prevented the principles from being fully realized and put into execution. Such must be our goal today.

After having stated this thesis, he added that the declaration of the right to work is a socialist invention. Socialism, he exclaimed, is the worst thing in the world in being collectivist; in other words, it is the state taking the place of individual liberty and becoming the most horrible of all tyrants. (Very good!) I don't want this any more than he does! (Very good!) And I add that in claiming that it is only in the name of socialism that one may demand the introduction of the right to work into the constitution, he commits the most fundamental error. . . .

The right to work! But as you yourself have said, this was the guiding thought, the constant inspiration of the statesmen of the Convention [the revolutionary assembly in session from 1792 to 1795]. The Right to Work! They inscribed it in the report of one of their most eminent members—in the report of Robespierre. Do you doubt this? Here are his words: "Public assistance is a sacred debt. Society owes a livelihood to unfortunate citizens, either by procuring work for them or by assuring the means of existence to those unable to work." (Varying outcries.). . .

What do you find in this article? Two perfectly distinct concepts: the right to work for the able-bodied and the right to assistance for the disabled, for those who cannot work.

Now, this *double* right is not validated in the current proposal for our modified constitution. You assert that you are not granting the right to work. You simply say that you grant the right to assistance, and these two are entirely different. . . .

The man who begs because he cannot find work (Noise—agitation.) may be arrested by a policeman. He is brought to justice, and there, even though he be innocent and declares that he has vainly looked for work, he is condemned to prison and taken to the workhouse. Is he being treated as a member of the sovereign People? . . . I say that in such a humiliating situation—for, say what you wish, when a man can only eat at the price of being condemned, [his situation is humiliating]—this man may still be your brother, but he is not your equal. You yourself are able to eat without losing face and without being condemned. . . . The Convention was therefore perfectly aware of the profound gulf between work that was honorable and assistance which was humiliating for the able-bodied, and this is why the Convention proclaimed the right to work.

Now I return to my thesis and I say: You have invoked the principles of the great revolution. I invoke its principles. You have asserted that to demand the inclusion of the right to work in the constitution is to surrender to some kind of socialist utopia. I have replied to you: No, in demanding the admission of this right, we make the claim to be the continuators of the great principles of the revolution. (Bravos on the left.) . . .

The only thing we ask is that the principle of liberty, equality, and fraternity be extended to its very limits. As to those who want more than that, or use other means, what difference does it make? This is not the point. What I wanted to demonstrate was that we are not a party of extremists but the true, serious, faithful continuators of the great revolution. (On the left: Very good! Very good!)

Now, gentlemen, I approach the question itself. There are two ways of dealing with this question: with the heart or with the head. With my heart, when every day I meet people in the streets who are in rags, entire familes of vagabonds, when in the country-side I see haggard men and fever-ridden women stretch out their hands. When my heart contracts at this sight and my day remains perturbed, I cry out: "Society is impious. Man has a natural right to live. Let society recognize this by recognizing the right to work, or else!" (Long agitation.)

These impressions which poverty makes on me are, I am sure, shared by you also. Where do we differ? On one point. We claim that a remedy is possible. You claim that misery is the result of I don't know what fatality and that humanity is chained to evil. (No! No!) Yes, this is what you claim, for this has often been said. . . .

Indubitably man is both mind and matter at the same time. Now a while ago I heard someone say, "But the doctrines you are trying to rehabilitate in attempting to appease hunger and misery are materialist doctrines based on the senses.". . . Is there nothing spiritual and idealistic in practicing fraternity toward one's fellow? Does this sentiment no longer evoke the noblest, the purest sympathy in the human heart?

Indeed, when you see the suffering of one of your fellows, when you see, as I did on June 24 [during a Paris working-class uprising] while I was a member of the executive, a man who came to tell me: "I don't want to fight. Yet for the last three days, my wife tells me to fight because we have seven children who have been dying of hunger during these three days." Do you think this man was appealing to my materialism as I listened to him with tears in my eyes? He was appealing to what was most ideal, most lofty within me. Citizens, in providing for the material needs of man you also provide for his soul, for man is both mind and body. You claim that what you want is to meet first of all the needs of the mind. Well, there is your man bending over his loom for twelve hours or toiling under the hot sun for his children's bread. Where is there scope for his mind? How do you expect this man to acknowledge that there is something greater than he? How do you expect this generation, walking, so to speak, in the dust of its predecessors, in a narrowly traced rut, to find time to dream of the splendors of a heaven glistening vainly above his head? (Prolonged agitation.) I say that for the mind to be in charge, to be free, to break the shackles of the senses, the senses themselves must be satisfied.

Thus I cannot draw your distinctions between idealism and materialism. Man is both body and mind. Well, I want the constitution to grant satisfaction to the mind by providing education, to the body by providing the right to work. (Approval on the left.)

Now let us see what reason tells us: "We sympathize with all these evils and would like to remedy them, yet work is in limited supply. Be careful not to transform the state into a general manager and, so to speak, a universal industrialist."

This is not accurate, because this is not what we ask for or what the Convention demanded. Indeed, the Convention said: Property must be diffused. And this doctrine was based on the very nature of things, for France is above all an agricultural country.

This has been her main strength and the concern of all her great statesmen. Industry is secondary. For France industry should be, permit me to say, what your navy is to your military power—an auxiliary but not the central pivot. The Convention therefore sought to have the state extend unfailing protection to the farmer and to agriculture. That is what the Convention demanded and that is what we demand. . . . What I ask is that by extending protection to agriculture and by ennobling it, we send back to it the large number of workers who crowd into our cities and are corrupted by them. (Very good! Very good! We are in agreement!) . . .

We come to ask you to do for France what you have begun to do for Algeria (and for which, by the way, I thank you) ; that is, to create banks, to make loans so that usury may be extinguished, so that the soil may be brought back to its true function, so that agriculture may be freed. If this can be accomplished, you will be able to clear and farm your barrens, your commons, your state lands. When for so many years you would be able to employ so many hands, do not pretend that work is in short supply; for work, as well as consumption, can be more than doubled.

If work is not limited, you should surely inscribe the right to work into the constitution as a matter of both equity and prudence.

Now what answer do I get? I am told that industry must be left free to organize itself. Who indeed seeks to limit this freedom? I? Do I by chance claim that the state should turn manufacturer and producer? I would be insane. Here is my claim: that the state become an intelligent directing force and that—listen well—the state do for this great mass of proletarians what it does for public works—decide where to direct them, in what area to base them, open banks where credit is needed—in a word, that the state use its unique statistical knowledge of the country's forces and resources to determine where they should be employed, that it bring them together or facilitate their association, that it entrust them with the means of production. . . .

Thus I tell you, do not use words lightly. Think carefully, citizens, of our grave and fearful situation. Last February the people did not make a revolution from simple self-interest. . . . When during two months the people came, so to speak, to sing of its love before the City Hall [the seat of the revolutionary government], only an idea sustained them. At this moment the people did not consider its needs, yet if the people did not think of them, it is our own duty to consider them. . . .

In summation, it has been said that the right to work is socialism. I reply: No, the right to work is republicanism in practice. (Very good! Very good!) . . . For how long did you, as well as we, say to the [leaders of the] July revolution [which in 1830 had overthrown the elder branch of the Bourbons and installed the somewhat more liberal Orleans branch]: "Here is the principle; well, apply it now!" The [leaders of the July] revolution resisted, and that is why the July Monarchy fell. (Agitation.)

Let us be more prudent insofar as the right to work is concerned. Let us proclaim it once again because it is equitable and because it is expedient to do so. Inscribe it once again, so that in the annals of humanity we may not seem to go backwards by fifty-five years, so that we may not appear less advanced than our fathers. . . . Inscribe it because the people must obtain [satisfaction] when its demands are just. As early as 1834, in Lyon, it inscribed the slogan, "To live by working or to die by fighting," on its banners [in the course of a large-scale working-class insurrection]. This cry, however sinister and fearsome in the midst of fighting, becomes a guarantee of security when inscribed in our constitution; for this French people is devoted enough to wait, once it has been given this satisfaction, because it is too practical not to grasp that enforcement [of this right] can only be accomplished gradually. Yet, once more, inscribe the principle; for if you close the door to all hope, I am apprehensive that the republic may be fearfully torn asunder. (Prolonged agitation.)

≈§ Part Six

The Advent of Industrialism

↬ STUDIES ON ENGLAND

Léon Faucher

*During the decade following the American War of Independence, a traveler
in search of the shape of things to come would have set out for the
United States. During the revolutionary upheaval of the 1790s he would
have gone to Paris. Within half a century England was to become the
Mecca of such pilgrims. In the 1830s it was England that was being submerged by the wave of the future, as the agricultural backwater of
Lancashire was transformed into an urbanized and industrialized society the
like of which had never been seen in the world. Yet it was widely recognized by that time that this novel phenomenon was not some British
aberration, but the model of a new society that was the destiny of the West.
Thus travelers describing what they had seen in Liverpool and Manchester
around 1840 thought of themselves not merely as reporters, but as social
prophets.*

*The selection below is from the report of one such foreign visitor, the
French journalist Léon Faucher (1803–1854), who made his reputation
by this series of articles on contemporary England published in the widely
respected periodical, the* Revue des Deux Mondes, *in 1844. Faucher,
following the July Revolution of 1830, had abandoned a promising career
as a professor for political journalism. A moderate constitutional monarchist
in tune with the French governing class of his time, he became associated
with economists like Bastiat (see pages 524–525) in advocating laissez faire
and free trade. He was therefore inclined to look favorably upon Great Britain, where these ideas were triumphing. His account and analysis of the
English industrialism which he encountered is thus the work of a friendly,
though not uncritical, observer.*

The epoch in which we live is the age of great cities. The fabulous descriptions of
Thebes, Babylon, Carthage, Syracuse, and even Rome, handed down to us by antiquity,
are today overshadowed by historic realities such as London, Paris, Amsterdam, Vienna,
Naples, Madrid, Berlin, New York, St. Petersburg, and Moscow. In contrast to former
days, capital cities that were once usually crowded with parasitic masses are no longer
alone in gathering inhabitants. Today a laboring population is becoming concentrated

Léon Faucher, *Etudes sur l'Angleterre* (Brussels: Wouters, 1845), pp. 126–130. Translated by
Peter Amann.

in centers of commerce and industry. Work has become the principle of all these asso-ciations: men no longer come together unless it be to produce and to exchange products. As the instruments of production multiply, so do the number of workers.

The population of Europe, after remaining stationary in the course of the last century, has realized immense progress in the last fifty years. Sometimes in spite of war, at other times favored by peace, population has boomed, affecting almost all states. In this movement of expansion the cities have generally gained more than the countryside, while the great cities have outstripped the smaller ones. The natural course of events sees to it that mortality among urban populations exceeds that of rural ones, for peace-able habits and pure air tend to prolong life. Yet the drawing power of massive agglomerations is such that it succeeds in filling any gaps in the ranks by promoting a regular and growing migration from country to city. Attracted by higher salaries, farm-hands are drawn to these vast labor markets, where they are soon transformed into dock or factory workers. While human reproduction, it would seem, is chiefly a rural phenomenon, cities devour men.

This distinctive aspect of our social condition is nowhere more marked than in England. No area of the known world has so great a number of industrious and heavily populated cities. In France, Paris excepted, one may barely cite three or four other cities such as Lyon, Marseille, Bordeaux and Rouen, whose population exceeds one hundred thousand. In Great Britain, Liverpool, Manchester and Glasgow each number about three hundred thousand. Edinburgh, Birmingham, Leeds, Bristol, Shef-field and Newcastle have from one to two hundred thousand. In France in 1836 cities of over ten thousand comprised a population of 3,764,219. In 1831, cities of the same size in Great Britain numbered 4,620,000 inhabitants, despite an overall population barely half that of France. In those years, while only twenty-eight per cent of the population across the Channel was employed in agriculture, in France rural employ-ment still accounted for sixty-eight per cent. According to the census of 1841, the agricultural population of Great Britain has dropped to twenty-two per cent of the total.

The preponderance which today's metropolis has assumed in the two countries may be shown in the following manner: In France from 1801 to 1836 the population of the kingdom increased by twenty-three per cent. During the same interval the population of Marseille grew thirty-two percent, Lille thirty-three per cent, Toulouse fifty-four per cent, Lyon thirty-seven per cent, Le Havre sixty per cent, Paris sixty-six per cent, Reims ninety per cent, Saint-Quentin one hundred, and Saint-Etienne one hundred and fifty per cent. In England from 1811 to 1831 the general population increase amounted to thirty-six per cent. In this space of twenty years the rural population gained only thirty per cent while the total urban population went up fifty-three per cent. The progress is even more striking if one focuses on the major cities: indeed, London grew by forty-two per cent, Edinburgh and Newcastle by sixty, Bristol by sixty-five, Sheffield by seventy, Birmingham by seventy-two, Liverpool by seventy-five, Glasgow by ninety-five and Manchester by one hundred and fifty per cent.

Among all these phenomena, the present state of Lancashire is undoubtedly most noteworthy. In 1801 this county counted a population of 672,565; the census of 1841 noted 1,667,064 inhabitants. Mr. H. Ashworth has observed that, had the population movement in Lancaster conformed to the national pattern, the district would have numbered only 1,125,924 inhabitants in 1841. He concludes therefore that during these last forty years a surplus population must have migrated from the agricultural areas to the commercial and industrial centers. If, moreover, one considers the fact that large cities have a smaller birth rate than rural districts, one must conclude that these migrations must have contributed an even greater contingent.

Lancashire and the manufacturing counties generally have thus created an outlet, a refuge for the overflowing population. Instead of spreading abroad as was the case during the fifteenth and eighteenth centuries, the inhabitants of Great Britain have thus founded these magnificent colonies of wool and cotton where so many idle hands have found work and so much capital an investment. As the *Times* noted the other day, Lancashire has become the poorhouse or, rather, the workhouse of England in the literal sense of the word.

The rural population is not large in Lancashire, today comprising no more than nine per cent of the inhabitants. Everything consists of cities, factories, workshops, offices and construction sites. One cannot take a step without encountering some construction testifying to the triumph of man over nature. Among these marvels, Liverpool and Manchester sum them all up as twin aspects of the same theme.

Nowhere else are the ties uniting commerce to industry so binding. In some respects, Liverpool and Manchester are all of a piece: were one to crumble, the other could not remain standing. There is even more to it than that. These twin cities, symbolizing and personifying human industry at its apogee of production, could not subsist one without the other. Liverpool's trade would never have reached its colossal dimensions but for Manchester's factories that consume its imports while providing the substance for its exports. On the other hand, if the merchants of Liverpool did not ship these products to the four corners of the world, in vain would Manchester rely on its inexhaustible coal fields, accomplish miracles of mechanical invention, breed an industrial race combining audacity with self-control, intelligence with energy. . . .

Once upon a time the growth of cities, as of empires, was a gradual process. [Cities] were the work of centuries and grew by ceaseless accretion. Today, developments are sudden: the tree grows before one's eyes. In less than twenty-five years cities are born, while others see their population double. The world moves at a rapid pace. People, to use the American expression, are always on the go. Disorder is therefore bound to accompany this movement as there is no time for social welfare measures to regulate the course of the evolution. Populations crowd neighborhoods where they lack space and shelter, where, as in the depths of a sewer, disease, physical infection and moral corruption ferment. In time the very underpinnings of the foundation of society are threatened.

All these new or rapidly growing cities display symptoms of this social dislocation. Paris is nothing but one vast hostel whose floating working-class population really has no fixed domicile. Eighty thousand of them pass through the hospitals in any given year. Ten to twelve thousand—one-third of the annual mortality figure—die there. Lyon, an unformed amalgam of three distinct yet intertwined cities, has three police forces and three administrations. The same is true of London and Glasgow. Manchester grew up more or less at random between two parishes, Salford and Chorlton, which today are fused. Only a few years ago, Manchester lacked representation in Parliament, a municipal government, a police force, courts of law. The city was a dependency of Salford, which today is no more than one of its outlying districts.

Modern cities can be classified under three principal headings: [political] capitals, commercial centers and manufacturing cities. Each of these varieties has its distinct influence on the well-being, the activities, the intelligence and the morality of the people who are gathered there. London, Liverpool and Manchester typify the urban populations of the United Kingdom. I have already in passing sketched the physiognomy of London. Liverpool raises similar problems, yet without the admixture of those accidental features which derive from political life or from cosmopolitian habits. It also constitutes the most natural approach to a consideration of the industrial sector of which Manchester is the epitome. . . .

MANCHESTER IN 1844: ITS PRESENT CONDITION AND FUTURE PROSPECTS

There is not perhaps a spot in the whole world where nature offers such abundant facilities for manufacturing labour. Look at Normandy. It abounds in water-power, but it has neither iron nor coals. Manufacturing Flanders has the advantage of coal mines, and of numerous canals, which offer great facilities for speedy transport; but it is a low and flat country, with few or no falls of water, and is situated at a great distance from the grand *entrepôts* of commerce. Alsace possesses a genius for industrial pursuits, as well as for war; but it struggles with scarcity of fuel, and with the distance of the ports whence it procures its raw material, and through which it exports its productions. The same division of natural advantages is to be observed in Switzerland and in Belgium. Zurich must travel three hundred miles for coal, six hundred miles for its raw material, and the same distance for the shipment of its produce. Ghent, the most ancient seat of manufacture in the west of Europe, is alike distant from available water-power, from metallic veins, and from coal mines.

But, in the space of from forty to fifty square miles, from the Ribble to the Mersey, nothing is wanting which nature and man are able to furnish. The chain of hills which shelters it from the north and east winds, gives birth to numerous rivers, or rather rivulets, which, descending rapidly from the summits, and acquiring increased force by continued descent, yield a water-power which supplies a large number of mills. The Irwell alone has nine hundred feet of descent, and of which eight hundred feet are available. Mr. Baines has enumerated three hundred spinning-mills, or dye-works on the banks of this river. A large and rich coal district extends throughout the hundreds of Salford and Blackburn. Iron is abundant in the neighbouring counties of York and Stafford, and also in Wales; and Manchester, the manufacturing metropolis, is only a day's journey from London, and an hour's ride from Liverpool.

Add to this, an incomparable race of men, rude, but not gross, reflective and persevering, inventive, enterprising and indefatigable; appropriating to itself the inventions of others, given to the practical side of things; such a race, in short, as is necessary to forge the weapons of industry. From this richly endowed population have sprung

Léon Faucher, *Manchester in 1844: Its Present Condition and Future Prospects*, trans. J. P. Culverwell (London and Manchester, 1844), pp. 2–3, 6–21, 26–27, 43–48, 50–65, 67–84.

with equal superiority, the artisan, the engineer, the manufacturer, and the merchant. . . .

Strange to say, the inhabitants of Manchester, destined hereafter to cultivate the manufacture of cotton with such unprecedented success, were for a time alarmed at its extraordinary growth, and seemed desirous of checking it in the bud. About 1740, John Kay, the inventor of the fly-shuttle, was driven from his home by persecution, and settled in Paris. In 1768, Hargreaves, discouraged by the indifference of his friends, transferred his invention to Nottingham. In 1779, the workmen paraded the streets and environs of Blackburn, and destroyed the jennies, carding-machines, and every machine driven by horse or water-power. And even the manufacturers, ignorant of the utility of these great inventions, looked favourably upon the rabble, and protected the more violent ones against the rigours of the law. Mr. Peel, (the grandfather of Sir Robert Peel,) having not only suffered the entire demolition of his machines, but having also incurred personal danger, removed to Burton-on-the-Trent, Staffordshire, where he erected a mill; and for many years after this period, there was not a spinning-mill in Blackburn. But what is still more strange is, that after Arkwright had succeeded by a marvellous combination of the various discoveries made in this creative period of the cotton manufacture, in producing yarns superior to any previously known in the markets, the manufacturers of Lancashire combined together to obstruct the sale of them. Arkwright and his partners were thus compelled to extend the sphere of their operations. From spinners they became also weavers. But let Arkwright speak for himself.

> Their first trial was weaving it into stockings, which succeeded; and they soon established the manufacture of calicoes, which promises to be one of the first manufactures in the kingdom. Another still more formidable difficulty arose; the orders for goods which they had received being considerable, were unexpectedly countermanded, the officers of excise refusing to let them pass at the usual duty of threepence per yard, insisting upon the additional duty of threepence per yard as being (Indian) calicoes, though manufactured in England; besides, these calicoes, when printed, were prohibited. By this unforseen obstruction, a very considerable and very valuable stock of calicoes accumulated. An application to the commissioners of excise was attended with no success; the proprietors therefore had no recourse but to ask relief of the Legislature, which, after much money expended, and against a strong opposition of the manufacturers of Lancashire, they obtained. *Arkwright's "Case."*

A few years elapsed, and the same manufacturers, instructed by experience, disputed with this man (who was no longer the barber of Preston, but whom England saluted by the title of Baronet) the property, and also the use of those inventions which had enriched him; and the force of circumstances fixed in Lancashire a manufacture, which the folly of men had exiled.

In every struggle between an individual and a population, the former must necessarily succumb. The men of Manchester eventually gained the victory. After the author of these inventions had enjoyed the exclusive privilege of them for fifteen years, they were, after complicated legal proceedings, made the common property of the public.

And justice wills it thus; men of genius are the product of the country, and of the age in which they live, as much as of their individual efforts, and it is not for their exclusive advantage that Providence has endowed them with those splendid faculties with which they give an impulse to society. And yet on the other hand, we must deplore the ingratitude of public opinion towards Arkwright. He was neither loved nor honoured in the county of Lancaster, and to revenge himself, he gave birth to the competition of Lanarkshire, saying, in allusion to his former state, "that he would find a razor in Scotland, which should shave Manchester."

The competition of Scotland soon manifested itself, although the intervention of Arkwright only accelerated what would otherwise have occurred in the natural course of events. Glasgow had, no less than Manchester, entered into the spirit of this industrial revolution. The county of Lanark had produced a Watt and an Adam Smith, during the period that Lancashire had given birth to Hargreaves, Crompton, and Arkwright, or in other words, whilst the latter county had devised the mechanism for these prodigious results, the former county had supplied the power which should put the mechanism in motion. What then could be more just than that Scotland should receive the spinning-manufacture from Lancashire, in return for the moving power which it had so wonderfully developed?

The unpopularity of Arkwright was not merely of that species which attaches to the career of inventors in general. The men of Lancashire detested in him the excess of those qualities and defects which distinguished their own character in the industrial world. Arkwright was the most complete and absolute type of that race of upstarts who unite to an activity without repose, an ambition without bounds. And it was this character which made him in the estimation of the manufacturers, of his rivals, and of his countrymen, a sort of public enemy. . . .

It was in 1792 that Arkwright formed these projects, which seemed to authorize the greatness and rapidity of his fortune, and at that period, England did not import annually more than from thirty to forty millions of pounds weight of cotton wool; the products of the manufacturer were estimated at from £3,200,000 to £4,000,000, and occupied less than 100,000 hands. His schemes were then considered ambitious, but they certainly did not exceed the bounds of possibility. At the present day, Arkwright would be considered a timid speculator, in presence of the Liverpool capitalists, who operate annually upon more than five hundred millions of pounds, and against whom the manufacturers of Manchester combine, to prevent the artificial rise of cotton. The men of Manchester conduct operations upon the most gigantic scale, such as the imagination can scarcely embrace. I know a spinning-mill in Manchester, which employs 1500 hands, and it has been asserted, that another house in the same town exports annually 30,000 bales of yarns and woollen goods, weighing 15,000 tons, and that it pays upwards of £30,000 for expenses of freight to the port where they are shipped. And a Lancashire manufacturer has exclaimed, inspired by the contemplation of this industrial omnipotence, "Let us have access to another planet, and we will undertake to clothe its inhabitants."

But let us leave these individual examples. What more surprising than the increase of Manchester itself? At the commencement of the present century, Manchester was a town of little dealers and manufacturers who bought unbleached fabrics in Bolton, dyed them, and then hawked them upon horseback, from market to market. Commerce having but little capital, was necessarily limited in its operations The manufacturers lived with extreme economy, and laboured and fared in company with their servants. A brick house was considered quite a luxury. Manufacture was, strictly speaking, scattered in the huts and cottages of the peasants. The weaver was a sort of domestic manufacturer, who bought his yarn when his family was not able to furnish it, and sold it when woven for a price which remunerated him for the labour and outlay which he had incurred. Manufacturers at Manchester were limited to dyeing and dressing, and beyond this the capitalist was nothing more than the Lyons capitalist of the present day, viz. a taker in of goods from the weavers, and a merchant in the disposal of them.

In 1760, the cotton manufacture (concentrated in Lancashire) occupied 40,000 hands, for the most part weavers. Twenty years later, notwithstanding the progress which this manufacture had made, Manchester numbered only 50,000 inhabitants. In 1800, the productive force in this industrial town did not employ more than thirty two steam-engines, equal in all to 430 horses' power.

The humble beginnings of mechanical power in industrial science is well known. The machines in the manufactories were moved by asses, or by horses, and managed by children. Wyatt, the first inventor of spinning by power, employed ten young girls in his establishment at Birmingham, and the first labourers whom Arkwright employed at Nottingham and at Cromford, were young children. The firm of Peel employed as many as 1,000 children. Those formidable engines of industry, which have been compared to the hundred arms of Briareus, had for their management, apprentices from the age of six to twelve years, numbers of whom were eagerly sought in the alms houses and workhouses. Thus is it the orphans and foundlings who have reared with their feeble hands the temple of manufactures, and who have peopled with so teeming a population, the manufacturing districts. . . . This population goes on continually increasing, although each mechanical improvement has the effect of diminishing the number of hands requisite in each department of industry. A single spinner produces more in one day, than he formerly could have done in a year. Mr. Baines has calculated, that 150,000 spinners, tending as many mule jennies, would do as much as forty millions of spinners working with the common spinning-wheel. Since the invention of the self-acting mule and of power-loom weaving, production has continued to increase; for the process is entirely automatic, and the operative has nothing to do but to watch the effects of the moving power.

The progress of production in Lancashire explains the progress of population. Whilst the number of inhabitants for the county increased from 300,000 to 1,660,000, and for Manchester from 40,000 to 306,000, the manufacture of cotton in the kingdom increased from 3,000,000 to 600,000,000 lbs.; and the value of the products increased, notwithstanding the continual reduction of price, from £800,000 to £36,000,000. At the present day, Lancashire possesses three-fifths of the establishments devoted to the spinning and weaving of cotton; and there are more than a hundred factories in the town of Manchester alone.

Nothing is more curious than the industrial topography of Lancashire. Manchester, like a diligent spider, is placed in the centre of the web, and sends forth roads and railways towards its auxiliaries, formerly villages, but now towns, which serve as outposts to the grand centre of industry. The Leeds railway connects Manchester with Oldham, which contains 60,000 inhabitants; also with Bury, Rochdale, and Halifax, each of which numbers from 24,000 to 26,000 souls; the Bolton railway connects it with Bolton, Preston, and Chorley, which together, have more than a hundred factories, and 114,000 inhabitants; on the Sheffield line, a few minutes suffice to reach the establishments of Stalybridge, Ashton, Dukinfield, and Hyde, peopled by more than 80,000 inhabitants; the Birmingham line incorporates with it, so to speak, the 50,000 inhabitants of Stockport; and that of Liverpool connects it with Wigan and Warrington. Thus we have fifteen or sixteen seats of Industry forming this grand constellation.

An order sent from Liverpool in the morning, is discussed by the merchants in the Manchester Exchange at noon, and in the evening is distributed amongst the manufacturers in the environs. In less than eight days, the cotton spun at Manchester, Bolton, Oldham, or Ashton, is woven in the sheds of Bolton, Stalybridge, or Stockport; dyed and printed at Blackburn, Chorley, or Preston, and finished, measured, and packed at Manchester. By this division of labour amongst the towns, and amongst the manufacturers in the towns, and amongst the operatives in the manufactories; the water, coal, and machinery work incessantly. Execution is almost as quick as thought. Man acquires, so to speak, the power of creation, and he has only to say, "Let the fabrics exist," and they exist.

Manchester, which holds under its sway these industrial agglomerations, is itself an agglomeration the most extraordinary, the most interesting, and in some respects, the most monstrous, which the progress of society has presented. The first impression is far from favourable. Its position is devoid of picturesque relief, and the horizon of clearness.

Amid the fogs which exhale from this marshy district, and the clouds of smoke vomited forth from the numberless chimneys, Labour presents a mysterious activity, somewhat akin to the subterraneous action of a volcano. There are no great boulevards or heights to aid the eye in measuring the vast extent of surface which it occupies. It is distinguished neither by those contrasting features which mark the cities of the middle ages, nor by that regularity which characterizes the capitals of recent formation. All the houses, all the streets, resemble each other; and yet this uniformity is in the midst of confusion. On closer examination, however, a certain approximation to order is apparent. Manchester is situated at the confluence of a little river the Irwell, swollen by the waters of the Irk, and of a brook called the Medlock. The Irwell separates Manchester from its principal suburb—the old town which has given its name to the hundred of Salford. On the left bank of the river is another suburb, Chorlton-upon-Medlock, which in 1801, numbered only 675 inhabitants, and which now contains 30,000. The manufactories and machine shops form as it were, a girdle around the town, and follow the courses of the streams. Factories, seven stories in height, rear their lofty fronts along the banks of the Irwell, and along the borders of the canals, which penetrating into the town, form an interior navigation. The waters of the Irk, black and fetid as they are, supply numerous tanneries and dye-works; those of the Medlock supply calico-printing establishments, machine shops, and foundries. The banks of the Irwell, which appear to have been the principal seat of this civilization, still form the centre of it. . . .

From this apparently indifferent combination, there results a great economy both of time and wealth in production. There is perhaps good reason for complaint that too little attention has been paid to the health and convenience of the inhabitants; of the want of public squares, fountains, trees, promenades, and well-ventilated buildings; but it is certain that it would be a difficult task to devise a plan by which the various products of Industry could be more concentrated, or by which the manufactories should be brought nearer to the fuel which feeds them, or more accessible to facilities for disposing of the goods when manufactured. The railways penetrate the town upon immense arcades to the points where it ceases to be inconvenient to load the merchandise upon them, and the canals pass under the streets, and thread their sinuous way in every direction, conveying boat-loads of coal to the doors of the manufactories, and even to the very mouths of the furnaces.

Manchester does not present the bustle either of London or of Liverpool. During the greater part of the day the town is silent, and appears almost deserted. The heavily laden boats glide noiselessly along the canals, not at the feet of palaces, as in Venice, but between rows of immense factories, which divide amongst themselves the air, the water, and the fire. The long trains roll smoothly along the lines of railway, conveying as many multitudes as individuals aforetime. You hear nothing but the breathing of the vast machines, sending forth fire and smoke through their tall chimneys, and offering up to the heavens, as it were in token of homage, the sighs of that Labour which God has imposed upon man.

At certain hours of the day the town appears suddenly animated. The operatives going to, or returning from their work, fill the streets by thousands; or it is perhaps the hour of 'Change, and you see the chiefs of this immense population gathering to one common centre; but even at those times when the inhabitants relax from their arduous duties, and give free course to their feelings, they lose nothing of that serious and angular stiffness, which a too exclusive occupation in industrial pursuits communicates to them.

Dr. W. Cooke Taylor, who visited Lancashire during the commercial crisis of 1841, and who though perhaps somewhat of an optimist, is generally exact, describes in the following terms the impression which Manchester made upon him.

It is essentially a place of business, where pleasure is unknown as a pursuit, and amusements scarcely rank as secondary considerations. Every person who passes you in the street, has the look of thought and the step of haste. Few private carriages are to be seen; there is only one street of handsome shops, and that is of modern date; there are some very stately public buildings, but only one of them is dedicated to recreation, the rest are devoted to religion, charity, science, or business. A modern author has started the theory, that, as certain insects assume the colours and marks of the leaves on which they feed, so the citizens of certain towns offer whimsical analogies to the character of the place in which they dwell. This is, to a considerable extent, true of Manchester. The men are as business-like as the place; and in their character a zeal for religion, charity, and science, is not less conspicuous, than the buildings consecrated to these objects are in the town. I might adduce as proofs, the subscriptions to the fund for building churches, to the Methodist Centenary Fund, to the funds for relieving the citizens of Hamburgh, for erecting the Lancashire Independent College, for supporting the numerous literary and scientific institutions in the town and its neighbourhood; nor will gratitude permit me to omit the hospitable and magnificent reception, given to the members of the British Association at its late meeting in Manchester, though the visit was paid at a season of general depression, and great commercial distress. Were I asked how a stranger could best form a notion of the character of the Manchester Manufacturers, I should recommend him to visit the Exchange of Manchester at the period of "high change;" that is, about noon on a Tuesday. It is the parliament of the lords of cotton—their legislative assembly—which enacts laws as immutable as those of the Medes and Persians; but, unlike every other parliament in the world, very much is done, and very little is said. Nowhere can there be found so practical a comment on the well known line:

'Silence that speaks, and eloquence of eyes.'

Transactions of immense extent are conducted by nods, winks, shrugs, or brief phrases, compared to which the laconisms of the ancient Spartans were specimens of tediousness and verbosity. There is a kind of vague tradition, or rather remote recollection, that a man was once seen to gossip on the Exchange; it was mentioned in the terms one would use if he saw a saraband danced in St. Peter's, or Harlequin playing his antics at the Old Bailey. . . .

These characteristics bespeak the origin of the population. In our manufacturing towns,[1] industry has been grafted upon a pre-existent state of society. Mulhausen was a free town, having political traditions of its own, and which have imparted to its industry a peculiar physiognomy, almost that of a family, or rather of a clan, so much do the inhabitants support and assist each other, and so paternally are the workmen treated. Lyons is a literary and religious as well as an industrial town; the noblesse and the clergy have their distinctive quarters, from which they come to take their share in the working of the munipical arrangements. Rouen belongs as much to the members of the bar as to the manufacturers and landed proprietors. There are present all the elements which concur to form what we call society. But, at Manchester, industry has found no previous occupant, and knows nothing but itself. Every thing is alike, and every thing is new; there is nothing but masters and operatives. Science, which is so often developed by the progress of industry has fixed itself in Lancashire. Manchester has a Statistical Society; and chemistry is held in honour; but literature and the arts are a dead letter. The theatre does nothing to purify and elevate the taste, and furnishes little but what is necessary to attract the crowd habituated to gross pursuits. . . .

If the luxury of equipages and of horses is unknown in Manchester, it does not arise from any economy or austerity of the manufacturers, but from the absence of the higher

---

[1] [*The manufacturing towns of France.* . . .]

classes, who, like the old aristocracy, do not live in the town. The town, strictly speaking, (as Dr. Kay Shuttleworth has remarked before me,) is only inhabited by shop-keepers and operatives; the merchants and manufacturers have detached villas, situated in the midst of gardens and parks in the country. This mode of existence within the somewhat contracted horizon of the family circle, excludes social intercourse, and leads to a local absenteeism. And thus at the very moment when the engines are stopped, and the counting-houses closed, everything which was the thought—the authority—the impulsive force—the moral order of this immense industrial combination, flies from the town, and disappears in an instant. The rich man spreads his couch amidst the beauties of the surrounding country, and abandons the town to the operatives, publicans, mendicants, thieves, and prostitutes, merely taking the precaution to leave behind him a police force, whose duty it is to preserve some little of material order in this pellmell of society. . . .

In Manchester the number of females exceeds very considerably that of males. In a protestant country which rejects religious communities, this disproportion must necessarily induce great irregularity of manners. Nature has ordained that the male births should exceed the female births; because the chances of mortality being greater in the former, the surplus would disappear, and the equilibrium be thus established. Every state of society where the number of females exceeds, or is less than the number of males, will infallibly fall into degradation. Thus the Manufacturing districts, where the women and children prevail, are not in a much better position than the penal colonies of England, in which there are two males for each female, and where promiscuous intercourse is a natural result.

Independently of this circumstance, the manufacturing system, as conducted at the present day, is far from encouraging regularity of conduct.

In congregating so many men, women, and children, together without any other object than Labour, there is full scope for the birth and growth of passions which eventually refuse to submit to constraint, and which end in unbridled license. The union of the sexes, and the high temperature of the manufactories, act upon the organisation like the tropical sun; and puberty is developed before age and education have matured the moral sentiments. The factory girls are strangers to modesty. Their language is gross, and often obscene; and when they do not marry early, they form illicit connexions, which degrade them still more than premature marriage. It is a common occurrence to meet in the intervals of labour, in the back streets, couples of males and females, which the caprice of the moment has brought together. Sometimes they accompany each other to the beer-shop, and thus accustom themselves to a double debauch. All the public inquiries on this subject since 1832, bear witness to this corruption of manners. . . .

The license which reigns in the thick ranks of this population, has arrived at such a height, that statistics are entirely useless, and nothing but personal observation can give a true idea of it. I will here relate an occurrence which has made a deep impression upon me, attesting as it does, a cold formality in matters of debauchery which indicates the absence of the moral sense. Entering into a brothel of the lowest order, I noticed a young female of decent appearance, who appeared to fill the situation of servant. Her orderly deportment presented such a contrast to the cavalier manners of the other inmates of the house, that I desired to know what had induced her to take up her abode in such a place.

The superintendent of Police having had the politeness to put some questions to her, we learnt, (and without the least reason to doubt it,) that this young female, after having worked thirteen hours in a factory, came to assist the mistress of the house in cleaning away the traces of the orgies of the preceding night, and when wanted, to supply the deficiency of the Messalines of the place. Habits of Labour, joined to those of debauch; order, and even decency, in the most abject vice! Is not this a characteristic symptom, as well as a strange monstrosity?

We can easily understand how lax and unstable the ties of family must be, when youth has such commencements. The police reports show that eighty-two persons in 1840, and one hundred and twenty-two in the first six months of 1842, were arrested for having abandoned their infants; a fact which proves that marriage is entered into without any sense of its obligations; and that they reject the contract with the same indifference with which they enter into it. The Report of the Parliamentary Committee of 1834, on drunkenness, mentions some details, by which we may judge of the moral conditions of their homes. "In a single factory, which employed one hundred and seventy hands, and in less than three years, twenty-four married, viz.: thirteen females and eleven males. Amongst the females, one had three children, before she had attained her twenty-second year; four had each two children, before that age; and ten were either mothers or pregnant before marriage. At twelve months from the date of marriage, four had separated from their husbands. Of the whole thirteen, only one could make a shirt for her husband, and only four were capable of mending the house linen. Of the eleven males, four could sign their names, and two could do an addition sum of four cyphers; but all had learnt to play at cards, in the beer-houses."

The thirst for ardent spirits, does not produce the same extent of ravages in Manchester, as it does in Liverpool or in Glasgow; nevertheless, the beer-houses are innumerable; and it is there that the operative spends the few moments of leisure which he enjoys. According to the *Manchester Directory,* for 1840, there were then five hundred and two public-houses, and eight hundred and twelve beer-houses. The numerous dram-shops do not appear to be included in this enumeration, any more than the licensed victuallers, which are four hundred in number. To these we must add the quantities of spirits from the illicit stills of the Irish, and which escape the control, both of the excise and of the police. The progress of drunkenness is indicated by the evidence of Mr. Braidley, who declares, that if the population has doubled, the consumption of gin and whiskey has quadrupled in the same space of time. . . .

Mr. Braidley, whom I have already quoted, states that having stationed himself before a liquor-vault, he counted in the space of forty minutes, no less than one hundred and twelve men, and one hundred and sixty-three women, who went to increase the crowd of customers. This is equal to four hundred and twelve persons per hour; and there are establishments which vend their liquid poison to two thousand persons every evening. The women are perhaps, more given to this brutish drunkenness than the men; and mothers are to be seen sufficiently insensate, or sufficiently denaturalized, to give of the gin to their infants, who thus suck it in with their milk. The passion for liquors, thus gives the death-blow to those family relations, already so seriously shaken by the manufacturing system. That system separates the children from the parents, the husband from the wife; and, when the hours of labour are over, each follows the impulse of his passions; the men go either to the gin-shop or to the beer-house; the women have not the choice, but seek solace in the oblivion produced by the most poisonous liquors.

Of all the buildings in Manchester, these open the earliest in the morning, and close the latest at night. From five or six, A.M., the operatives of both sexes, visit the dram-shops before going to labour. One would think that the manufacturers themselves en-courage this vice of drunkenness; for it is in the public-houses that many of them distribute the wages to their hands; add to which, the payment is made upon the Saturday night, at a time, when being at leisure, the operative yields most easily to the temptations of drink. Still worse, many of the young children receive a bonus of twopence or threepence, in addition to their weekly earnings, which is immediately spent in gin; so that it should seem as though some pains are taken to initiate them into this detestable vice. Is it not thus that the ancients degraded their slaves, from fear lest their reason, being developed, they should aspire to liberty?

For some years the operatives have, with the assistance of the manufacturers, formed mechanics' institutions, which secure to them a place for assembling together, and where they enjoy a library; sometimes they even engage professors to give them lectures upon history, physics, or chemistry. Unhappily, this laudable feature is but very limited in its extent. There are not more than five or six such institutions. The public-house is for the operative, what the public squares were for the ancients. It is there where they meet one another, and where they discuss the topics in which they are interested. Their meetings, whether permanent or accidental; their masonic lodges; their mutual aid societies; their clubs and secret societies, are all held in public-houses. In 1834, there were 30,000 operatives, members of these associations, compelled by their rules, to spend a portion of their payments in drink. Saturday evening and Sunday are the periods of the week devoted to intoxication. Whence this employment of their repose? In what features of the manners or institutions of the country are we to seek for the cause, which induces them to spend in debauchery or idleness, the day which Nature and Religion have consecrated as a respite from daily labour? Let us put out of sight for the moment, the other causes of moral degradation; this of itself, seems a vice inherent in modern society, which manifests itself more conspicuously in Great Britain than elsewhere. We have no longer our national holidays and religious festivals. Athletic games, to which our forefathers had recourse, to exercise and develope the physical powers, are fallen into disuse; and the mystic ceremonies of religious worship, by which, in former times, the soul was borne away from earth, and hovered in celestial regions, have not found favour with the religious in our day. At least in Catholic towns, religious spectacles have given place to scenic representations upon the stage; and the theatre might be made, under the influence of an intelligent government, a powerful means of education. But in Protestant countries, where the bigoted Puritanism of their religion is opposed to all innocent recreation, and admits no other intellectual food upon the Sunday than the Bible, the labouring classes remain sunk in an immoveable stupidity, and know no other relaxation from the *ennui* which afflicts them, than the excitement of drink. Thus, the more rigourously the Sabbath is observed, the more frequented are the public-houses and gin-shops. This holds good as a general rule; and Scotland, for instance, which is infinitely more Puritanical than England, is accordingly the classic ground of Intemperance.

I know nothing more repulsive than this stern and sullen character of the Protestant sects. In proportion to their enthusiasm, they proselyte the soul by violence, and not by the charms of persuasion. It is thus that the stern voice of the fiery Knox succeeded in raising all Scotland in his favour; and the more recent success of the Methodists is to be explained by the same violent excitement. As soon as the sudden excitement is ended, Protestant society is literally cut into two distinct portions. Place yourself in Briggate, at Leeds; Mosley-street, at Manchester; Lord-street, or Dale-street, at Liverpool; of what description are the families you see, walking along in silence, and with a reserved and formal attitude, towards the churches and chapels? You cannot be deceived, they belong almost exclusively to the middle classes. The operatives loiter on the threshold of their cottages, or lounge in groups, at the corners of the streets, until the hour of service is terminated, and the public-houses are opened. Religion is presented to them in such a sombre and gloomy aspect; it succeeds so well in addressing neither the senses, the imagination, nor the heart, that it is no wonder it remains the exclusive patrimony of the rich, and leaves the poorer classes forlorn in a moral desert.

The aristocratic character of society contributes still more to this evil. If the people of Manchester wish to go out upon a fine Sunday, where must they go? There are no public promenades, no avenues, no public gardens; and even no public common. If the inhabitants seek to breathe the pure atmosphere of the country, they are reduced to the necessity of swallowing the dust upon the public highways. Everything in the suburbs is closed against them; every thing is private property. In the midst of the beautiful scenery of England, the operatives are like the Israelites of old, with the promised land before them, but forbidden to enter into it. Aristocracy appropriates to itself the soil, and lives in ease and luxury, yet fears to grant a paltry plot for public recreation to the labourers, who have been the ladder to which they are indebted for their own elevation. Even the cemeteries and the Botanic Gardens, are closed upon the Sunday. What then remains but the brutal diversion of drunkenness? . . .

In the manufacturing districts the operatives are exposed to periodical *crises,* which put a stop to labour, throw whole families out of employment, and produce the same effect that a bad harvest does in the rural districts. Excluding the accidental causes of distress, there yet remains in all the great manufacturing towns a mass of misery which increases from year to year. Notwithstanding the increase of wages and the regularity of employment, Manchester increases in pauperism with its age. In 1833, previous to the operation of the new poor-law, the number of paupers had doubled in Manchester in four years, and the poor-rates had increased from £48,977 to £53,799. The new poor-law, which dates from 1834, and which exercises far more severity in the distribution of relief than the old poor-law, diminished the expenses to £27,645; but the increase soon made its appearance again, and in 1841, they exceeded £40,000. In July, 1843, I found 1,200 paupers in the Manchester workhouse, and in addition to this workhouse, Manchester comprises two other workhouses, that of Salford, and that of Chorlton Union.

The distinctive feature in the distress of Manchester, and that in which the inhabitants resemble very strongly the population of Paris, is the readiness with which they flock to the hospitals whenever illness assails them. In 1831, 27,804 patients received medical aid in the public infirmaries; and in 1840, the number of patients was 42,964, which is equal to one-sixth of the population.

At Paris, half of the population go to the public hospitals and alms-houses to die. At Manchester, half of the births take place in the public charities. To be born into the world, and to quit the world—out of the family, and under the auspices of a public charity, are two features which impeach in an equal degree the state of society.

The extreme poverty in which so many of the operatives live, springs from the same cause which assures to so many others a regular and profitable employment. Manchester being a great labour-mart, must necessarily be a great focus of misery: for if industry, by its immense development presents larger resources, it attracts at the same time a greater number of immigrants, and, consequently a greater competition amongst them for employment. These immigrants flock from all parts of England and Ireland, and thus reduce the remuneration of labour to the minimum necessary for the wants of the most sober, or the most destitute amongst them. And, although board and lodging is more expensive in Manchester than in the neighbouring villages, yet, as a general rule, it may be affirmed, that Manchester is the place where the best workmen are to be found—the best materials to be obtained, and where the lowest wages are paid.

The low scale of remuneration for labour is a feature peculiarly disastrous in a country where great wealth is an element in the social fabric. Let us hear Dr. Kay upon this subject.

> The introduction of an uncivilized race does not tend, even primarily, to increase the power of producing wealth in a ratio by any means commensurate with the cheapness of its labour, and may ultimately retard the increase of the fund for the maintenance of that labour. Such a race is useful only, as a mass of animal organization which consumes the smallest amount of wages. The low price of the labour of such people depends, however, on the paucity of their wants and their savage habits. When they assist the production of wealth therefore, their barbarous habits and consequent moral depression must form part of the equation. They are only necessary to a state of commerce inconsistent with such a reward for labour as is calculated to maintain the standard of civilization. A few years pass and they become burdens to a community, whose morals and physical powers they have depressed; and they then dissipate wealth which they have not accumulated.

Another prolific cause of this misery is the intemperance of the operatives. At Manchester, as at Glasgow, there are numerous families who spend more in gin and whiskey than in bread. At Manchester, as at Paris, it is observed that the best remunerated workmen are not the most decent portion of the operatives; and, as economy doubles the income, it often happens that families, with habits of order and foresight, live better upon ten or twelve shillings per week, than their more improvident neighbours who earn twenty-five to thirty shillings per week. Mr. Chadwick's report furnishes numerous examples of this fact.

Destitution re-acts in its turn; and from being an effect, becomes a fruitful source of intemperance. It is in the poorest parts of the town that the greatest number of spirit vaults are to be found. But nothing impairs the general character of a population more than the fluctuations and changes which mark any considerable portion of it. The immigrant operatives who seek employment in Manchester, do not at all resemble the annual migrants from the provinces to the French capital. These are men and youths who, on the approach of the spring-season, quit their homes to seek employment, for six or seven months, as masons, carpenters, etc., in the buildings of the metropolis. They have houses and families in the country, which they do not abandon without the prospect of a speedy return. Paris is to them only a vast market, whither they direct their steps to earn a little sum of money; and whilst there, they preserve amongst themselves a feeling of clanship, which maintains their self-respect and local character, and keeps them aloof from the vagrant classes of society. The thoughts of a home and family occupy their minds, and keep them from debauchery and dissipation. But the migrators to Manchester are whole families, who wander from town to town, from factory to factory, seeking work, and who have no settled home. These unfortunate operatives live in furnished rooms, where several families are often crowded together in a single bedroom, at the rate of threepence each for bedding. A small and unhealthy lodging is thus much dearer than a separate cottage. Taking their meals in eating-houses, they cannot practise the same economy in their diet, unless, indeed, they adopt the potato regimen of the Irish; and what is still worse for them, their wages are generally lower than what are paid to those parties who are domiciliated, and therefore better known. The Statistical Society states that "in 1836, out of 169,000 inhabitants of Manchester and Salford, 12,500 lived in lodging-houses, and more than 700 slept in cellars with the tenants of these infamous places." This is not all, in these places they meet with beggars, thieves, and prostitutes, and thus these dwelling places are equally dangerous for their morals and their health. Dr. Howard says—

> It seems to be the invariable practice of these *'keepers of fever beds,'* as the proprietors were styled by Dr. Ferriar, to cram as many beds into each room as it can possibly be made to hold; and they are often placed so close to each other that there is scarcely room to pass between them. The scene which these places present at night, is one of the most lamentable description; the crowded state of the beds, filled promiscuously with men, women, and children; the floor covered over with the filthy and ragged clothing they have just put off, and with their various bundles and packages, containing all the property they possess, mark the depraved and blunted state of their feelings, and the moral and social disorder which exists. The suffocating stench and heat of the atmosphere are almost intolerable to a person coming from the open air, and plainly indicate its insalubrity. Even if the place be inspected during the day, the state of things is not much better. Several persons will very commonly be found in bed; one is probably sick, a second is perhaps sleeping away the effects of the previous night's debauch, whilst another is possibly dozing away his time because he has no employment; or is taking his rest now, because he obtains his living by some night-work. In consequence of this occupation during the day the windows are kept constantly closed, ventilation is entirely neglected, and the vitiated atmosphere is ever ready

to communicate its poisonous influence to the first fresh comer, whom habit has not yet rendered insensible to its effects. . . . Where cellars are occuped as lodging-houses, the back room is generally used as the sleeping apartment; and as this has often no window, and can, therefore, only receive air and light through the door opening into the front room, the utter impossibility of ventilation renders the ravages of infectious fevers particularly destructive when they once find entrance. *Sanatory Report.*

The miasms exhaled from such a condensed mass of poverty are a cause of fever and contagion, quite distinct from the putrefaction of animal remains, and from the refuse of the streets. Dr. Howard, one of the most experienced practitioners in Manchester, remarks, that fever rages more in the winter than in the summer; that is, in that portion of the year when the houses of the poor are the most thronged, and when putrefaction goes on more slowly than during summer. In 1832, the cholera ravaged most virulently in these thickly peopled houses. Out of eighteen in a single house, eight were victims to it.

The density of the population is not so great at Manchester as at Liverpool. The town covers a greater extent of surface, and the houses are generally low. The cellars also are far less in demand in Manchester than in Liverpool for the purposes of residence. There are not more than 20,000 persons who live in cellars; scarcely the half of the troglodytes which Liverpool contains. Hence, the ravages of fever are less in the former town. In Liverpool the mortality from fever is 6·78 per cent., whilst in Manchester it is only 5·61 per cent. Until the invasion of the cholera (1832), the sanatory condition of Manchester had never awakened the solicitude of the authorities. At this crisis a board of health was hastily organized; it inspected the habitations of poorer classes, and published a report of the result, drawn up by Dr. Kay, and which made a deep and melancholy impression on the public mind. The report stated, that of 687 streets, 284 were not paved, fifty-three only partially paved; 112 were ill ventilated, and 352 contained heaps of refuse, stagnant pools, ordure, etc. Of 6,951 houses which were visited by the inspectors, 2,565 were infected to such a degree as to require an immediate whitewashing; 960 requiring repair; 1,435 were damp; 452 ill ventilated; and 2,221 were reported as wanting privies. . . .

Manchester, according to the expression of another practitioner, Mr. Roberton, is nothing but an overgrown village, constructed without any plan. Each of the eight townships which form the borough, has its own separate police. With the exception of the centre, where the municipal authority exists, every one can build according to his fancy, and without observing any rule.

The authorities of Manchester devote annually £5,000 to the cleansing of the town. This sum is insufficient, and the organization essentially defective. The first-class streets are cleansed once per week; those of the second class, once per fortnight; and the streets of the third class once a month. As to the courts, alleys, and yards, inhabited by the poorer classes, no means are used to ensure their periodical cleansing. The municipal administration is little less aristocratic at Manchester than at Liverpool, or at London. *There* also, are two towns in one: in the one portion, there is space, fresh air, and provision for health; and in the other, every thing which poisons and abridges existence;

the crowding of cottages and families together; dark and gloomy courts, which are both damp and contagious. It is not, therefore, astonishing that the rate of mortality in Manchester, varies so much amongst the different classes of society. For the professional persons and gentry, the probable duration of life is thirty-eight years; for the shop-keepers, (who inhabit the more narrow and badly cleansed streets,) twenty years only; and for the factory operatives and labouring classes generally, only seventeen years. In the township of Broughton, one of the suburbs, occupied principally by the manufacturers of the town, the mortality amongst the males is one in forty-four and a half; and amongst the females, one in eighty-nine and a half; which gives an average for both sexes, of one in sixty-three. What can be more eloquent than the simple statement of these figures; and is not that an unnatural state of society, in which the manufacturers reserve to themselves, so to speak, the monopoly of existence; in which he lives four times the life of the labourer; in which life is for the mass without virility, and without old age; extending scarcely beyond the threshold of puberty, and perpetuated by a generation of children.

In the manufacturing districts, the number of deaths before the age of twenty, equals the number of deaths which take place before the age of forty; in the non-manufacturing districts, not excepting London. Out of 1,000 infants in the labouring classes, 570 die before they have completed their fifth year. Those who attain to the age of virility, fall into premature old age. No town contains so large a proportion of widows and orphans; and in 435 cases out of 1,000, the father of a family dies of consumption.

The general appearance of the population does not contradict these melancholy statistics. The operatives are pale and meagre in their appearance, and their physiognomy has not that animation which indicates health and vigour. Female beauty is not to be found amongst them, and the declining vigour of the men is replaced by a febrile energy. The officers of the regiments, raised in Lancashire, affirm that the men cannot bear much fatigue. It is evident that the race is degenerating.

The following extract, from the deposition of one Titus Rowbotham, a mechanic, aged fifty-one years, made before a Committee on Manufactures, will furnish full proof of this assertion, and show that the labourers themselves are sensible of their own degradation:—

> When I came to Manchester in 1801, the operatives, like myself, were better fed, better clothed, more moral, and of a more vigorous constitution. The children that are born now are a race much more feeble than their parents. The milk they suck is not so nourishing; their mothers have neither time nor instruction to give to them, and they grow up more vicious and demoralised.

> When I began to work in the cotton manufacture the workmen were not accustomed to that description of labour; they were joiners, carpenters, and colliers, who were induced, by the higher wages which spinning yielded, to abandon their handicraft trades, and become spinners. These men brought their wives with them, women who had been accustomed, like themselves, to outdoor employment. Their children, reared in the manufactories, had much more feeble constitutions, and *the children of these children are more feeble still.* I have the most lively recollection of what passed in my youth. I have before my eyes the images of those

who are now dead as distinctly as though they yet lived. The men that I see now do not at all resemble them. I have seen three generations of operatives. I know men who are of my age, and even younger, (older?) than I, and who have passed their lives in tenting the *mule jenny*. Their intellect is enfeebled and withered like a tree. They are more like grown up children than the race of men I knew formerly. I know many instances of operatives who had, in their youth, the reputation of considerable intelligence, but which has decayed, and soon become extinct with the advance of years; and yet these men are younger than I. The long hours of labour, and the high temperature of the factories, produce lassitude and excessive exhaustion. The operatives cannot eat, and seek to sustain life by the excitement of drink. Some drink beer, and others spirituous liquors. This is the first step; they finish by abandoning themselves to drunkenness and gambling; their health decays, their intellect is depraved, and the money which is spent in such degrading pursuits is abstracted from the food and clothing of their children.

That which the operative here states, respecting the generations which have grown up under his own eyes, will apply with equal force to all the great manufacturing towns. The *wynds* of Glasgow are distinguished by the same destitution and misery which mark Little Ireland, or Gibraltar, in Manchester. The streets of Etaques, at Lille, and the Martainville quarter at Rouen, present (although not on so great a scale) similar scenes of misery and prostitution. The race of manufacturing operatives degenerates upon the Continent just as in Great Britain. They are ricketty in their joints, unfit for arms, and yet agitate the country, but without being able to defend it. There is, in these industrial agglomerations, a feature peculiar to them—I mean that unnatural co-existence between labour and misery, between the excess of vice, and the excess of acitvity. In general, a population is poor only when it is devoid of industry; and its morality is in proportion to its application. Our works on morality are full of axioms destined to put this truth prominently forward; our laws proscribe idleness; and in modern society labour has its altars. I do not wish to contradict this doctrine. I know, too well, that manual labour shuts the door upon physical misery, strengthens the limbs, and tempers the will, in opposing him to the elements, against natural calamities. I know that labour is even the prime law of our existence; but I know, too, that labour may be abused just as much as idleness. The abuse of labour, amongst the people of the north, leads in as direct a road to the degradation of the nations in the north, as the *far niente* of the nations in the south. I could multiply without end, from official documents, proofs of these lamentable results. . . . There are factories in Manchester which are open seventeen hours daily, of which fifteen and a half hours are occupied with effective labour. As to the children in the manufacturing districts, and more especially in Scotland, they recruit the exhaustion of the week's toil, by lying in bed the whole of Sunday. There is no order in the family, and education is a thing unthought of. The mothers, who are working at the *mule jenny* all the day, administer to their infants a preparation of opium, to keep them quiet, or leave them under the care of the younger children; and thus is explained the fact that out of 407 violent deaths, 110 were of children who were burnt or scalded to death. Those who escape these accidental deaths receive no instruction or culture; and in the *wynds* of Glasgow, as well as in Manchester, children are to be seen reduced to a purely animal existence, and without even a name.

Certainly, if there is one nation more than another fitted for labour, that nation is the English; and especially the Lancastrians. Nature has liberally endowed them with an indomitable energy, and with nerves of steel. The Lancashire operative is, indisputably, the best workman on the face of the earth; the best spinner, and the best mechanic. It is he who brings into the field of industry that ingenuity which economises labour, and that active energy which is not surpassed, if indeed equalled, by any other race. But this untiring, this excessive and unceasing energy, carried beyond certain limits, tends to enervate and undermine his frame. Over-working is a malady which Lancashire has inflicted upon England, and which England in its turn has inflicted upon Europe. Manchester is the seat, the concentrated focus of this malady; a malady which is felt in every portion of the kingdom, and which is now interwoven with the habits and constitution of the country. Even its politics are infected with the same evil. The members of the House of Commons devote the day to their private concerns, and consecrate the night to the discussion of public affairs. Add to this the study and the correspondence required from a public character; the attendance at the political clubs; the necessity of being *au fait* upon the hustings, and of saying something *àpropos* upon every imaginable subject, and you will be able to conceive the incessant wear and tear of public life. . . .

The English are not naturally sober, either in their judgments, their appetites, or their conduct. Take them from one extreme and they immediately rebound to the other; and their preachers, who know their character well, cure them of intemperance, by the contrasted extreme of total abstinence. They cannot partake of anything in moderation; they must partake of it to repletion. Their politics are, like their drinks, coarse and stimulating; their ambition without bounds, and their activity without repose. In England, the bow is perpetually on the stretch; and hence the sole danger which can menace such a nation.

ᴥᶘ HARMONIES OF POLITICAL ECONOMY

Frédéric Bastiat

> *To most people in the United States today, the standard view of economic well-being is still that developed by the group of nineteenth-century economists known variously as the "liberal," "classical," "laissez-faire" ("hands-off"), or "Manchester" school. Although initially this view had to contend against the prevailing mercantilist and protectionist views of the eighteenth century (see Adam Smith, pages 221–240), by the mid-nineteenth century the battle was largely won, and the liberal view was firmly*

*established in the popular mind, especially among the independent small
businessmen, where it remains firmly lodged even though the capitalist
system itself has developed beyond these simple individualist and competitive principles. Compared with the scholars' sober formulations,
the popularized version has always resembled a religious faith, at
the same time more extremist than the scholarly view (in its opposition
to all governmental intervention, for example), more ecstatic in its
vision of the providential nature of free competition and the autonomous
economic system, and more dogmatic in the face of opposition.*

*Opposition has not been lacking. Since the early nineteenth century,
socialists of various kinds have mounted an attack against both the pre-
suppositions of laissez-faire theory and the consequences of the economic
systems it attempted to justify. Our selection illustrates both the popularized version of laissez faire and a counterattack against its enemies.
It is from the* Harmonies of Political Economy *by the highly respected
French economist Frédéric Bastiat (1801–1850), who deliberately descended from the heights of scholarly detachment to defend the system
of competition and private property against the "Utopians" and "Communists" like Owen and Cabet, who spoke in the name of equality and
attacked "spoliation" and other alleged evils of the capitalist system.*

Men of Property and leisure!—whatever be your rank in the social scale, whatever step
of the social ladder you may have reached by dint of activity, probity, order, and economy—whence come the fears which have seized upon you? The perfumed but poisoned
breath of Utopia menaces your existence. You are loudly told that the fortune you have
amassed for the purpose of securing a little repose in your old age, and food, instruction, and an outset in life for your children, has been acquired by you at the expense
of your brethren; that you have placed yourselves between the gifts of God and the
poor; that, like greedy tax-gatherers, you have levied a tribute on those gifts, under
the name of Property, of Interest, and of Rent; that you have intercepted the benefits
which the common Father has bestowed on his children, in order to make merchandise
of them. You are called upon for restitution; and what augments your terror is, that
your advocates, in conducting your defence, feel themselves too often obliged to avow
that the usurpation is flagrant, but that it is necessary. Such accusations I meet with a
direct and emphatic negative. You have not intercepted the gifts of God. You have
received them gratuitously, it is true, at the hands of nature; but you have also gratuitously transferred them to your brethren without receiving anything. They have acted
the same way towards you; and the only things which have been reciprocally *compen-*

Frédéric Bastiat, *Harmonies of Political Economy*, trans. P. J. Stirling (2d ed.; Edinburgh:
Oliver and Boyd, n.d.), pp. 218–222, 310–316, 440–443.

sated are physical or intellectual efforts, toils undergone, dangers braved, skill exercised, privations submitted to, pains taken, *services rendered and received.* You may perhaps have thought only of yourselves and your own selfish interest, but that very selfish interest has been an instrument in the hand of an infinitely prescient and wise Providence to enlarge unceasingly among men the domain of Community; for without your efforts all those *useful effects* which you have obtained from nature, in order to distribute them without remuneration among your brethren, would have remained for ever inert. I say *without remuneration,* because what you have received is simply the recompense of your efforts, and not at all the price of the gifts of God. Live, then, in peace, without fear and without misgiving. You have no other property in the world but your right to services, in exchange for other services, by you faithfully rendered, and by your brethren voluntarily accepted. Such property is legitimate, unassailable; no Utopia can prevail against it, for it enters into the very constitution of our being. No theory can ever succeed in blighting or in shaking it.

Men of toil and privations! you cannot shut your eyes to this truth, that the primitive condition of the human race is that of an entire Community,—a perfect Equality,—of poverty, of destitution, and of ignorance. Man redeems himself from this estate by the sweat of his brow, and directs his course towards another Community, that of the gifts of God, successively obtained with less effort,—towards another Equality, that of material prosperity, knowledge, and moral dignity. The progress of men on the road of improvement is unequal, indeed; and you could not complain were the more hurried and precipitate march of the vanguard of progress to retard in some measure your own advance. But in truth it is quite the reverse. No ray of light penetrates a single mind without in some degree enlightening yours. No step of progress, prompted by the conscious possession of property, but is a step of progress for you. No wealth is created which does not tend to your enfranchisement; no capital, which does not increase your enjoyments in proportion to your labour; no acquisition, which does not increase your facilities of acquisition; no Property, which does not tend to enlarge, for your benefit, the domain of Community. The natural social order has been so skilfully arranged by the Divine Architect, that those who are more advanced on the road of civilisation hold out to you, voluntarily or unconsciously, a helping hand; for the order of things has been so disposed that no man can work honestly for himself without at the same time working for all. And it is rigorously true to affirm that every attack upon this marvellous order would on your part be not only a homicide, but a suicide. Human nature is an admirable chain, which exhibits this standing miracle, that the first links communicate to all the others a progressive movement more and more rapid, onwards to the last.

Men of philanthropy! lovers of equality! blind defenders, dangerous friends of the suffering classes, who are yet far behind on the road of civilisation, you who expect the reign of Community in this world, why do you begin by unsettling all interests and shaking all received opinions? Why, in your pride, should you seek to subjugate men's wills, and bring them under the yoke of your social inventions? Do you not see that this Community after which you sigh, and which is to inaugurate the kingdom of God upon earth, has been already thought of and provided for by God himself? Does He want your aid to provide a patrimony for his children? Has He need either of your conceptions or of your violence? Do you not see that this Community is realized more and more every day, in virtue of His admirable decrees; that for the execution of these decrees He has not trusted to your chance services and puerile arrangements, nor even to the growing expression of the sympathetic principle manifested by charity; but that He has confided the realization of His providential designs to the most active, the most personal, the most permanent of all our energies—Self-interest,—a principle imbedded in our inmost nature, and which never flags, never takes rest? Study, then, the social mechanism as it comes from the hand of the Great Mechanician, and you will find that it testifies to a universal solicitude, which far outstrips your dreams and chimeras. You will then, I hope, in place of presumptuously pretending to reconstruct the divine workmanship, be content to admire and to bless it.

I say not that there is no room in this world of ours for reforms and reformers. I say not that mankind are not to call to their service, and encourage with their gratitude, men of investigation, of science, and of earnestness,—hearts faithful to the people. Such are still but too much wanted,—not to overturn the social laws,—but to combat the artificial obstacles which disturb and reverse the action of these laws. In truth, it is difficult to understand why people should keep repeating such commonplaces as this: "Political Economy is an optimist, as far as existing facts are concerned; and affirms that whatever is is right. At the sight of what is evil, as at the sight of what is good, Economists are content to exclaim, *Laissez faire*." Optimists with reference to existing facts! Then we must be ignorant that the primitive condition of man is poverty, ignorance, the reign of brute force! We must be ignorant that the moving spring of human nature is aversion to all suffering, to all fatigue; and that labour being fatigue, the earliest manifestation of selfishness among men is shown in their effort to throw this painful burden on the shoulders of each other! The words cannibalism, war, slavery, privilege, monopoly, fraud, spoliation, imposture, must either have never reached our ears, or else we must see in these abominations the necessary machinery of progress! But is there not in all this a certain amount of wilful misrepresentation, a confounding of all things for the purpose of accusing us of confounding them? When we admire the providential laws which govern human transactions—when we assert that men's interests are harmonious—when we thence conclude that they naturally tend and gravitate towards the realization of relative equality and general progress— it is surely from the play and action of these laws, not from their perturbations and disturbances, that we educe harmony. When we say *laissez faire,* we surely mean, *allow these laws to act,* not, *allow these laws to be disturbed.* According as we conform to these laws or violate them, good or evil is produced; in other words, men's interests are in harmony, provided right prevail, and services are freely and voluntarily exchanged against services. But does this imply that we are ignorant of the perpetual struggle of Wrong against Right? Does this imply that we lose sight of, or approve, the efforts which have been made in all ages, and which are still making, to alter, by force or fraud, the natural equivalence of services? This is exactly when we repudiate as a violation of the natural social laws, as an attack upon property,—for, in our view, the terms, free exchange of services, justice, property, liberty, security, all express the same idea under different aspects. It is not the principle of Property which we contest, but the antagonistic principle of Spoliation. Proprietors of all ranks! reformers of all schools! this is the mission which should reconcile and unite us.

It is time, high time, that this crusade should begin. A mere theoretical war against Property is by no means the most virulent or the most dangerous. Since the beginning of the world there has existed a practical conspiracy against it which is not likely soon to cease. War, slavery, imposture, oppressive imposts, monopolies, privileges, commercial frauds, colonies, right to employment, right to credit, right to assistance, right to instruction, progressive taxation imposed in direct or inverse proportion to our power of bearing it, are so many battering-rams directed against the tottering edifice; and if the truth must come out, would you tell me whether there are many men in France, even among those who think themselves conservative, who do not, in one form or another, lend a hand to this work of destruction?

There are people to whose optics property never appears in any other form that that of a field or a bag of crown-pieces. If you do not overstep sacred landmarks, or sensibly empty their pockets, they feel quite comfortable. But is there no other kind of Property? Is there not the Property of muscular force and intellectual power, of faculties, of ideas—in a word, the Property of Services? When I throw a service into the social scale, is it not my right that it should be held there, if I may use the expression, suspended, according to the laws of its natural equivalence; that it may there form a counterpoise to any other service which my neighbour may consent to throw into the opposite scale and tender me in exchange? The law of common consent agreed to establish a public force for the protection of property thus understood. But in what situation are we placed if this very force assumes to itself the mission of disturbing the equilibrium, under the socialist pretext that liberty gives birth to monopoly, and that the doctrine of *laissez faire* is odious and heartless? When things go on in this way, individual theft may be rare, and may be severely punished, but spoliation is organized, legalized, and erected into a system. Comfort yourselves, Reformers! your work is not yet done—only try to understand what that work really is. . . .

Man has wants which are unlimited—desires which are insatiable. In order to provide for them he has materials and agents which are furnished to him by nature—faculties, instruments, all things which *labour* sets in motion. Labour is the resource which has been most equally distributed to all. Each man seeks instinctively, and of necessity, to avail himself to the utmost of the co-operation of natural forces, of talents natural and acquired, and of capital, in order that the result of this co-operation may be a greater amount of utilities produced, or, what comes to the same thing, a greater amount of satisfaction is acquired. Thus, the more active co-operation of natural agents, the indefinite development of intelligence, the progressive increase of capital, give rise to this phenomenon (which at first sight seems strange)—that a given quantity of labour furnishes an always increasing amount of utilities, and that each man can, without despoiling anyone, obtain a mass of consumable commodities out of all proportion to what his own efforts could have realized.

But this phenomenon, which is the result of the divine harmony which Providence has established in the mechanism of society, would have been detrimental to society, by introducing the germ of indefinite inequality, had there not been combined with it a harmony no less admirable, namely, Competition, which is one of the branches of the great law of human *solidarity*.

In fact, were it possible for an individual, a family, a class, a nation, possessed of certain natural advantages, of an important discovery in manufactures, or of the instruments of production in the shape of accumulated capital, to be set permanently free from the law of Competition, it is evident that this individual, this family, this nation, would have for ever the monopoly of an exceptionally high remuneration, at the expense of mankind at large. In what situation should we be if the inhabitants of the tropical regions, set free from all rivalry with each other, could exact from us, in exchange for their sugar, their coffee, their cotton, their spices, not the equivalent of labour equal to their own, but an amount of labour equal to what we must ourselves undergo in order to produce these commodities under our inclement skies? What an incalculable distance would separate the various conditions of men, if the race of Cadmus * alone could read, if the direct descendants of Triptolemus † alone could handle the plough, if printing were confined to the family of Gutenberg, cotton-spinning to the children of Arkwright, and if the posterity of Watt could alone work the steam engine! Providence has not ordered things thus, but, on the contrary, has placed in the social machine a spring whose power is only less surprising than its simplicity—a spring by the operation of which all productive power, all superiority in manufacturing processes, in a word, all exclusive advantages, slip from the hands of the producer, having remained there, in the shape of exceptional remuneration, only long enough to excite his zeal, and come at length to enlarge the common and gratuitous patrimony of mankind, and resolve themselves into individual enjoyments always progressive, and more and more equally distributed—this spring is *Competition.* We have already seen its economical effects—and it now remains for us to take a rapid survey of its moral and political consequences. I shall confine myself to the more important of these.

Superficial thinkers have accused Competition of introducing *antagonism* among men. This is true and inevitable, if we consider men only in the capacity of producers, but, regarded from another point of view, as consumers, the matter appears in a very different light. You then see this very Competition binding together individuals, families, classes, nations, and races, in the bonds of universal fraternity.

Seeing that the advantages which appear at first to be the property of certain individuals become, by an admirable law of Divine beneficence, the common patrimony of all; seeing that the *natural advantages* of situation, of fertility, of temperature, of mineral riches, and even of manufacturing aptitude, slip in a short time from the hands of producers, by reason of their competition with each other, and turn exclusively to the profit of consumers, it follows that there is no country which is not interested in the advancement and prosperity of all other countries. Every step of progress made in the East is wealth in perspective for the West. Fuel discovered in the South warms the men of the North. Great Britain makes progress in her spinning mills; but her capitalists do not alone reap the profit, for the interest of money does not rise; nor do her operatives, for the wages of labour remain the same. In the long-run, it is the Russian, the Frenchman, the Spaniard; in a word, it is the human race, who obtain equal satisfactions at a less expense of labour, or, what comes to the same thing, superior satisfactions with equal labour.

I have spoken only of the advantages—I might say as much of the disadvantages—

* [Mythical prince responsible for bringing the alphabet to Greece. (*Ed.*)]
† [Semimythical inventor of the plough. (*Ed.*)]

which affect certain nations and certain regions. The peculiar action of Competition is to render general what was before exclusive. It acts exactly on the principle of *Insurance*. A scourge visits the fields of the agriculturist, and the consumers of the bread are the sufferers. An unjust tax is laid upon the vines of France, and this means dear *wine* for all wine-drinkers. Thus, advantages and disadvantages, which have any permanence, only glance upon individuals, classes, or nations. Their providential destination in the long-run is to affect humanity at large, and elevate or lower the condition of mankind. Hence to envy a certain people the fertility of their soil, or the beauty of their harbours and rivers, or the warmth of their sun, is to overlook the advantages in which we are called to participate. It is to contemn the abundance which is offered to us. It is to regret the labour which is saved to us. Hence national jealousies are not only perverse feelings;—they are absurd. To hurt others is to injure ourselves. To place obstacles in the way of others—tariffs, wars, or workmen's strikes —is to obstruct our own progress. Hence bad passions have their chastisement, just as generous sentiments have their reward. The inevitable sanction of an exact distributive justice addresses itself to men's interests, enlightens opinion, proclaims and establishes among men these maxims of eternal truth: that the useful is one of the aspects of the just; that Liberty is the fairest of social Harmonies; and that Honesty is the best Policy.

Christianity has introduced into the world the grand principle of human fraternity. It addresses itself to our hearts, our feelings, our noble instincts. Poliical Economy recommends the same principle to our cool judgment; and, exhibiting the connexion of effects with their causes, reconciles in consoling harmony the vigilant calculations of interest with the inspirations of the sublimest morality.

A second consequence which flows from this doctrine is, that society is truly a *Community*. Messieurs Owen * and Cabet † may save themselves the trouble of seeking the solution of the great *Communist* problem—it is found already—it results not from their arbitrary combinations, but from the organization given by God to man, and to society. Natural forces, expeditive processes, instruments of production, everything is *common* among men, or has a tendency to become so, everything *except pains,* labour, individual effort. There is, and there can be, but one *inequality*—an inequality which Communists the most absolute must admit,—that which results from the inequality of efforts. These efforts are what are exchanged for one another at a price bargained for. All the utility which nature, and the genius of ages, and human foresight, have implanted in the commodities exchanged, we obtain *into the bargain*. Reciprocal remunerations have reference only to reciprocal efforts, whether actual under the name of Labour, or preparatory under the name of Capital. Here then is Community in the strictest sense of the word, unless we are to pretend that the personal share of enjoyment should be equal, although the quota of labour furnished is not so, which indeed would be the most iniquitous, the most monstrous, of inequalities,—I will add, the most fatal; for it would not destroy Competition—it would only give a retrograde action. We should still compete, but the Competition would be a rivalry of idleness, stupidity, and improvidence.

* [Robert Owen (1771–1858): English utopian Socialist. (*Ed.*)]
† [Etienne Cabet (1788–1856): French utopian Communist. (*Ed.*)]

In fine, the doctrine—so simple, and, as we think, so true—which we have just developed, takes the great principle of human *perfectibility* out of the domain of declamation, and transfers it to that of rigorous demonstration. This internal motive, which is never at rest in the bosom of the individual, but stirs him up to improve his condition, gives rise to the progress of art, which is nothing else than the progressive co-operation of forces, which from their nature call for no remuneration. To Competition is owing the concession to the community of advantages at first individually obtained. The intensity of the labour required for the production of each given result goes on continually diminishing, to the advantage of the human race, which thus sees the circle of its enjoyments and its leisure enlarging from one generation to another, whilst the level of its physical, intellectual, and moral improvement is raised; and by this arrangement, so worthy of our study and of our profound admiration, we behold mankind recovering the position they had lost.

Let me not be misunderstood, however. I do not say that all fraternity, all community, all perfectibility, are comprised and included in Competition. I say only that Competition is allied and combined with these three great social dogmas—that it forms part of them, that it exhibits them, that it is one of the most powerful agents of their realization.

I have endeavoured to describe the general effects of Competition, and consequently its benefits, for it would be impious to suppose that any great law of nature should be at once hurtful and permanent; but I am far from denying that the action of Competition is accompanied with many hardships and sufferings. It appears to me that the theory which has just been developed explains at once those sufferings, and the inevitable complaints to which they give rise. Since the work of Competition consists in *levelling,* it must necessarily run counter to all who proudly attempt to rise above the general level. Each producer, in order to obtain the highest price for his labour, endeavours, as we have seen, to retain as long as possible the exclusive use of an *agent,* a *process,* or an *instrument,* of production. Now the proper mission and result of Competition being to withdraw this exclusive use from the individual, in order to make it *common* property, it is natural that all men, in their capacity of producers, should unite in a concert of maledictions against *Competition.* They cannot reconcile themselves to Competition otherwise than by taking into account their interests as consumers, and regarding themselves, not as members of a coterie or a corporation, but as men. . . .

I repeat that I do not deny or ignore, on the contrary I deplore as much as any one can, the sufferings attendant on Competition; but is this any reason for shutting our eyes to its advantages? And it is all the more consoling to observe these advantages, inasmuch as I believe Competition, like all the great laws of nature, to be indestructible. Had it been otherwise, it would assuredly have succumbed to the universal resistance which all the men who have ever co-operated in the production of commodities since the beginning of the world have offered to it, and more especially it would have perished under the *levée en masse* of our modern reformers. But if they have been foolish enough to attempt its destruction, they have not been strong enough to effect it.

And what progressive principle, I would ask, is to be found in the world, the beneficent action of which is not mingled, especially in the beginning, with suffering and misery? The massing together of human beings in vast agglomerations is favourable to boldness and independence of thought, but it frequently sets private life free from the wholesome restraint of public opinion, and gives shelter to debauchery and crime. Wealth and leisure united give birth to mental cultivation, but they also give birth to pride and luxury among the rich, and to irritation and covetousness among the poor. The art of printing brings home knowledge and truth to all ranks of society, but it has brought also afflicting doubt and subversive error. Political liberty has unchained tempests and revolutions, and has modified the simple manners of primitive nations, to such a degree as to induce thinking men to ask themselves whether they would not have preferred tranquillity under the cold shade of despotism. Christianity herself has cast the noble seed of love and charity into a soil saturated with the blood of martyrs.

Why has it entered into the designs of Infinite Goodness and Justice that the happiness of one region or of one era should be purchased at the expense of the sufferings of another region or of another era? What is the Divine purpose which is concealed under this great law of *solidarity,* of which Competition is only one of the mysterious aspects? Human science cannot answer. What we do know is this, that good always goes on increasing, and that evil goes on diminishing. From the beginning of the social state, such as conquest had made it, when there existed only masters and slaves, and the inequality of conditions was extreme, the work of Competition in approximating ranks, fortunes, intelligences, could not be accomplished without inflicting individual hardships, the intensity of which, however, as the work proceeded, has gone on diminishing, like the vibrations of sound and the oscillations of the pendulum. To the sufferings yet in reserve for them, men learn every day to oppose two powerful remedies—namely, *foresight,* which is the fruit of knowledge and experience; and *association,* which is organized foresight. . . .

To watch over the public security.

To administer common property.

To levy taxes.

Such I believe to be the legitimate circle within which Government functions ought to be circumscribed, and to which they should be brought back if they have gone beyond it.

This opinion, I know, runs counter to received opinions. "What!" it will be said, "you wish to reduce Government to play the part of a judge and a police-officer! You would take away from it all initiative! You would restrain it from giving a lively impulse to learning, to arts, to commerce, to navigation, to agriculture, to moral and religious ideas; you would despoil it of its fairest attribute, that of opening to the people the road of progress!"

To people who talk in this way, I should like to put a few questions.

Where has God placed the motive spring of human conduct, and the aspiration after progress? Is it in all men? or is it exclusively in those among them who have received, or usurped, the delegated authority of a legislator, or the patent of a placeman? Does every one of us not carry in his organization, in his whole being, that boundless, restless principle of action called *desire?* When our first and most urgent wants are supplied, are there not formed within us concentric and expansive circles of desires of an order more and more elevated? Does the love of arts, of letters, of science, of moral and religious truth, does a thirst for the solution of those problems which concern our present and future existence, descend from collective bodies of men to individuals, from abstractions to realities, from mere words to living and sentient beings?

If you set out with this assumption—absurd upon the face of it—that moral energy resides in the State, and that the nation is passive, do you not place morals, doctrines, opinions, wealth, all which constitutes individual life, at the mercy of men in power?

Then, in order to enable it to discharge the formidable duty which you would intrust to it, has the State any resources, of its own? Is it not obliged to take everything of which it disposes, down to the last penny, from the citizens themselves? If it be from individuals that it demands the means of execution, individuals have realized these means. It is a contradiction, then, to pretend that individuality is passive and inert. And why have individuals created these resources? To minister to their own satisfactions. What does the State do when it seizes on these resources? It does not bring satisfactions into existence, it *displaces* them. It deprives the man who earned them in order to endow a man who has no right to them. Charged to chastise injustice, it perpetrates it.

Will it be said that in displacing satisfactions it purifies them, and renders them more moral?—that the wealth which individuals had devoted to gross and sensual wants the State has devoted to moral purposes? Who dare affirm that it is advantageous to invert violently, *by force,* by means of spoliation, the natural order according to which the wants and resires of men are developed?—that it is moral to take a morsel of bread from the hungry peasant, in order to bring within the reach of the inhabitants of our large towns the doubtful morality of theatrical entertainments?

And then it must be remembered, that you cannot displace wealth without displacing labour and population. Any arrangement you can make must be artificial and precarious when it is thus substituted for a solid and regular order of things reposing on the immutable laws of nature.

There are people who believe that by circumscribing the province of Government you enfeeble it. Numerous functions and numerous agents, they think, give the State the solidity of a broader basis. But this is pure illusion. If the State cannot overstep the limits of its proper and determinate functions without becoming an instrument of injustice, of ruin, and of spoliation—without unsettling the natural distribution of labour, of enjoyments, of capital, and of population—without creating commercial stoppages, industrial crises, and pauperism—without enlarging the proportion of crimes and offences—without recurring to more and more energetic means of repression—without exciting discontent and disaffection,—how is it possible to discover a guarantee for stability in these accumulated elements of disorder?

You complain of the revolutionary tendencies of men, but without sufficient reflection. When in a great country we see private services invaded and converted into public services, the Government laying hold of one-third of the wealth produced by the citizens, the law converted into an engine of spoliation by the citizens themselves, thus impairing, under pretence of establishing, the equivalence of services—when we see population and labour displaced by legislation, a deeper and deeper gulf interposed between wealth and poverty, capital, which should give employment to an increasing population, prevented from accumulating, entire classes ground down by the hardest privations—when we see Governments taking to themselves credit for any prosperity which may be observable, proclaiming themselves the movers and originators of everything, and thus accepting responsibility for all the evils which afflict society,—we are only astonished that revolutions do not occur more frequently, and we admire the sacrifices which are made by the people to the cause of public order and tranquillity.

But if laws and the Governments which enact laws confined themselves within the limits I have indicated, how could revolutions occur? If each citizen were free, he would doubtless be less exposed to suffering; and if, at the same time, the feeling of responsibility were brought to bear on him from all sides, how should he ever take it into his head to attribute his sufferings to a law, to a Government which concerned itself no farther with him than to repress his acts of injustice and protect him from the injustice of others? Do we ever find a village rising against the authority of the local magistrate?

The influence of liberty on the cause of order is sensibly felt in the United States. There, all, save the administration of justice and of public property, is left to the free and voluntary transactions of the citizens; and there, accordingly, we find fewer of the elements and chances of revolution than in any other country of the world. What semblance of interest could the citizens of such a country have in changing the established order of things by violence, when, on the one hand, this order of things clashes with no man's interests, and, on the other, may be legally and readily modified if necessary?

But I am wrong. There are two active causes of revolution at work in the United States—slavery and commercial restriction. It is notorious that these two questions are constantly placing in jeopardy the public peace and the federal union. Now, is it possible to conceive a more decisive argument in support of the thesis I am now maintaining? Have we not here an instance of the law acting in direct antagonism to what ought to be the design and aim of all laws? Is not this a case of law and public force sanctioning, strengthening, perpetuating, systematizing, and protecting oppression and spoliation, in place of fulfilling its legitimate mission of protecting liberty and property? As regards slavery, the laws says, "I shall create a force, at the expense of the citizens, not to maintain each in his rights, but to annihilate altogether the rights of a portion of the inhabitants." As regards tariffs, the law says, "I shall create a force, at the expense of the citizens, not to ensure the freedom of their bargains and transactions, but to destroy that freedom, to impair the equivalence of services, to give to one citizen the liberty of two, and to deprive another of liberty altogether. My function is to commit injustice, which I nevertheless visit with the severest punishment when committed by the citizens themselves without my interposition."

It is not, then, because we have few laws and few functionaries, or, in other words, because we have few public services, that revolutions are to be feared; but, on the contrary, because we have many laws, many functionaries, and many public services. Public services, the law which regulates them, the force which establishes them, are from their nature never neutral. They may be enlarged without danger, on the contrary with advantage, when they are necessary to the vigorous enforcement of justice; but carried beyond this point they are so many instruments of legal oppression and spoliation, so many causes of disorder and revolutionary ferment.

Shall I venture to describe the poisonous immorality which is infused into all the veins of the body politic, when the law thus sets itself, upon principle, to indulge the plundering propensities of the citizens? Attend a meeting of the national representatives when the question happens to turn on bounties, encouragements, favours, or restrictions. See with what shameless rapacity all endeavour to secure a share of the spoil,— spoil which, as individuals, they would blush to touch. The very man who would regard himself as a highway robber, if, meeting me on the frontier and clapping a pistol to my head, he prevented me from concluding a bargain which was for my advantage, makes no scruple whatever in proposing and voting a law which substitutes the public force for his own, and subjects me to the very same restriction at my own expense. In this respect, what a melancholy spectacle France presents at this very moment! All classes are suffering, and in place of demanding the abolition for ever of all legal spoliation, each turns to the law, and says, "You who can do everything, you who have the public force at your disposal, you who can bring good out of evil, be pleased to rob and plunder all other classes, to put money in my pocket. Force them to come to my shop, or pay me bounties and premiums, give my family gratuitous education, lend me money without interest," etc.

It is in this way that the law becomes a source of demoralization, and if anything ought to surprise us, it is that the propensity to individual plunder does not make more progress, when the moral sense of the nation is thus perverted by legislation itself. . . .

ఆర్ TRAFFIC

John Ruskin

John Ruskin (1819–1900) came from a highly religious background. He was denied the toys and pastimes of a normal childhood, and family reading was mostly confined to the Bible. Quite possibly it was in reaction to such sternness that he developed his affinity for the color and joys of art and literature, specializing in imaginative analyses of medieval and renaissance architecture. By the time he was forty he had a considerable reputation as an art historian, yet he abandoned this field as frivolous for what seemed of deeper concern, the increasing materialism accompanying the spread of industrialization. From 1860 to his death, he concentrated on economics and politics, plunging every year into ever more eccentric plans to free man from deadening labor. The last of his fortune was spent in promoting utopian cooperative communities of farmer-craftsmen. Despite the foredoomed failure of the efforts of his last years, he was an important figure in Victorian England, because the volume of his works inspired a great popular interest in art and literature, and his social

criticism, together with that of Thomas Carlyle and Matthew Arnold, en-
couraged thoughtful reaction against the assumption that industrial society
was self-perfecting.

"Traffic," presented below, was originally delivered as a public lecture.
In April, 1864, he was invited to the northern industrial town of Bradford
to advise its merchant and industrial princes on the planning of a pro-
posed stock exchange. His reputaion as an architectural critic made him a
logical choice and was intended to add tone to the project. Instead of
technical advice, what the good entrepreneurs of Bradford got was
this most disturbing sermon. The essay still stands as an extremely cogent
and provocative expression of man's exasperation with the modern world.

My good Yorkshire friends, you asked me down here among your hills that I might talk to you about this Exchange you are going to build: but, earnestly and seriously asking you to pardon me, I am going to do nothing of the kind. I cannot talk, or at least can say very little, about this same Exchange. I must talk of quite other things, though not willingly;—I could not deserve your pardon, if, when you invited me to speak on one subject, I *wilfully* spoke on another. But I cannot speak, to purpose, of anything about which I do not care; and most simply and sorrowfully I have to tell you, in the outset, that I do *not* care about this Exchange of yours.

If, however, when you sent me your invitation, I had answered, "I won't come, I don't care about the Exchange of Bradford," you would have been justly offended with me, not knowing the reasons of so blunt a carelessness. So I have come down, hoping that you will patiently let me tell you why, on this, and many other such occasions, I now remain silent, when formerly I should have caught at the opportunity of speaking to a gracious audience.

In a word, then, I do not care about this Exchange—because *you* don't; and because you know perfectly well I cannot make you. Look at the essential conditions of the case, which you, as business men, know perfectly well, though perhaps you think I forget them. You are going to spend £30,000, which to you, collectively, is nothing; the buying a new coat is, as to the cost of it, a much more important matter of consideration to me, than building a new Exchange is to you. But you think you may as well have the right thing for your money. You know there are a great many odd styles of architecture about; you don't want to do anything ridiculous; you hear of me, among others, as a respectable architectural man-milliner; and you send for me, that I may tell you the leading fashion; and what is, in our shops, for the moment, the newest and sweetest thing in pinnacles.

John Ruskin, "Traffic," in *Selections from the Works of Ruskin*, ed. Chauncey B. Tinker (Boston, 1908), pp. 277–304.

Now, pardon me for telling you frankly, you cannot have good architecture merely by asking people's advice on occasion. All good architecture is the expression of national life and character; and it is produced by a prevalent and eager national taste, or desire for beauty. And I want you to think a little of the deep significance of this word "taste"; for no statement of mine has been more earnestly or oftener controverted than that good taste is essentially a moral quality. "No," say many of my antagonists, "taste is one thing, morality is another. Tell us what is pretty: we shall be glad to know that; but we need no sermons—even were you able to preach them, which may be doubted."

Permit me, therefore, to fortify this old dogma of mine somewhat. Taste is not only a part and an index of morality;—it is the ONLY morality. The first, and last, and closest trial question to any living creature is, "What do you like?" Tell me what you like, and I'll tell you what you are. Go out into the street, and ask the first man or woman you meet, what their "taste" is; and if they answer candidly, you know them, body and soul. "You, my friend in the rags, with the unsteady gait, what do *you* like?" "A pipe and a quartern of gin." I know you. "You, good woman, with the quick step and tidy bonnet, what do you like?" "A swept hearth, and a clean tea-table; and my husband opposite me, and a baby at my breast." Good, I know you also. "You, little girl with the golden hair and the soft eyes, what do you like?" "My canary, and a run among the wood hyacinths." "You, little boy with the dirty hands, and the low forehead, what do you like?" "A shy at the sparrows, and a game at pitch farthing." Good; we know them all now. What more need we ask?

"Nay," perhaps you answer; "we need rather to ask what these people and children do, than what they like. If they *do* right, it is no matter that they like what is wrong; and if they *do* wrong, it is no matter that they like what is right. Doing is the great thing; and it does not matter that the man likes drinking, so that he does not drink; nor that the little girl likes to be kind to her canary, if she will not learn her lessons; nor that the little boy likes throwing stones at the sparrows, if he goes to the Sunday school." Indeed, for a short time, and in a provisional sense, this is true. For if, resolutely, people do what is right, in time they come to like doing it. But they only are in a right moral state when they *have* come to like doing it; and as long as they don't like it, they are still in a vicious state. The man is not in health of body who is always thinking of the bottle in the cupboard, though he bravely bears his thirst; but the man who heartily enjoys water in the morning, and wine in the evening, each in its proper quantity and time. And the entire object of true education is to make people not merely *do* the right things, but *enjoy* the right things:—not merely industrious, but to love industry—not merely learned, but to love knowledge—not merely pure, but to love purity—not merely just, but to hunger and thirst after justice.

But you may answer or think, "Is the liking for outside ornaments,—for pictures, or statues, or furniture, or architecture,—a moral quality?" Yes, most surely, if a rightly set liking. Taste for *any* pictures or statues is not a moral quality, but taste for good ones is. Only here again we have to define the word "good." I don't mean by "good," clever—or learned—or difficult in the doing. Take a picture by Teniers, of sots quarrelling over their dice; it is an entirely clever picture; so clever that nothing in its kind has ever been done equal to it; but it is also an entirely base and evil picture.

It is an expression of delight in the prolonged contemplation of a vile thing, and delight in that is an "unmannered," or "immoral" quality. It is "bad taste" in the profoundest sense—it is the taste of the devils. On the other hand, a picture of Titian's, or a Greek statue, or a Greek coin, or a Turner landscape, expresses delight in the perpetual contemplation of a good and perfect thing. That is an entirely moral quality—it is the taste of the angels. And all delight in art, and all love of it, resolve themselves into simple love of that which deserves love. That deserving is the quality which we call "loveliness"—(we ought to have an opposite word, hateliness, to be said of the things which deserve to be hated) ; and it is not an indifferent nor optional thing whether we love this or that; but it is just the vital function of all our being. What we *like* determines what we *are,* and is the sign of what we are; and to teach taste is inevitably to form character.

As I was thinking over this, in walking up Fleet Street the other day, my eye caught the title of a book standing open in a bookseller's window. It was—"On the necessity of the diffusion of taste among all classes." "Ah," I thought to myself, "my classifying friend, when you have diffused your taste, where will your classes be? The man who likes what you like, belongs to the same class with you, I think. Inevitably so. You may put him to other work if you choose; but, by the condition you have brought him into, he will dislike the other work as much as you would yourself. You get hold of a scavenger or a costermonger, who enjoyed the Newgate Calendar for literature, and 'Pop goes the Weasel' for music. You think you can make him like Dante and Beethoven? I wish you joy of your lessons; but if you do, you have made a gentleman of him:—he won't like to go back to his costermongering."

And so completely and unexceptionally is this so, that, if I had time to-night, I could show you that a nation cannot be affected by any vice, or weakness, without expressing it, legibly, and for ever, either in bad art, or by want of art; and that there is no national virtue, small or great, which is not manifestly expressed in all the art which circumstances enable the people possessing that virtue to produce. Take, for instance, your great English virtue of enduring and patient courage. You have at present in England only one art of any consequence—that is, iron-working. You know thoroughly well how to cast and hammer iron. Now, do you think, in those masses of lava which you build volcanic cones to melt, and which you forge at the mouths of the Infernos you have created; do you think, on those iron plates, your courage and endurance are not written for ever,—not merely with an iron pen, but on iron parchment? And take also your great English vice—European vice—vice of all the world—vice of all other worlds that roll or shine in heaven, bearing with them yet the atmosphere of hell—the vice of jealousy, which brings competition into your commerce, treachery into your councils, and dishonour into your wars—that vice which has rendered for you, and for your next neighbouring nation, the daily occupations of existence no longer possible, but with the mail upon your breasts and the sword loose in its sheath; so that at last, you have realized for all the multitudes of the two great peoples who lead the so-called civilization of the earth,—you have realized for them all, I say, in person and in policy, what was once true only of the rough Border riders of your Cheviot hills—

They carved at the meal
With gloves of steel,
And they drank the red wine through the helmet barr'd;—

do you think that this national shame and dastardliness of heart are not written as legibly on every rivet of your iron armour as the strength of the right hands that forged it?

Friends, I know not whether this thing be the more ludicrous or the more melancholy. It is quite unspeakably both. Suppose, instead of being now sent for by you, I had been sent for by some private gentleman, living in a suburban house, with his garden separated only by a fruit wall from his next door neighbour's; and he had called me to consult with him on the furnishing of his drawing-room. I begin looking about me, and find the walls rather bare; I think such and such a paper might be desirable—perhaps a little fresco here and there on the ceiling—a damask curtain or so at the windows. "Ah," says my employer, "damask curtains, indeed! That's all very fine, but you know I can't afford that kind of thing just now!" "Yet the world credits you with a splendid income!" "Ah, yes," says my friend, "but do you know, at present I am obliged to spend it nearly all in steel-traps?" "Steel-traps! for whom?" "Why, for that fellow on the other side the wall, you know: we're very good friends, capital friends; but we are obliged to keep our traps set on both sides of the wall; we could not possibly keep on friendly terms without them, and our spring guns. The worst of it is, we are both clever fellows enough; and there's never a day passes that we don't find out a new trap, or a new gun-barrel, or something; we spend about fifteen millions a year each in our traps, take it altogether; and I don't see how we're to do with less." A highly comic state of life for two private gentlemen! but for two nations, it seems to me, not wholly comic. Bedlam would be comic, perhaps, if there were only one madman in it; and your Christmas pantomime is comic, when there is only one clown in it; but when the whole world turns clown, and paints itself red with its own heart's blood instead of vermilion, it is something else than comic, I think.

Mind, I know a great deal of this is play, and willingly allow for that. You don't know what to do with yourselves for a sensation: fox-hunting and cricketing will not carry you through the whole of this unendurably long mortal life: you liked pop-guns when you were schoolboys, and rifles and Armstrongs are only the same things better made: but then the worst of it is, that what was play to you when boys, was not play to the sparrows; and what is play to you now, is not play to the small birds of State neither; and for the black eagles, you are somewhat shy of taking shots at them, if I mistake not.

I must get back to the matter in hand, however. Believe me, without further instance, I could show you, in all time, that every nation's vice, or virtue, was written in its art: the soldiership of early Greece; the sensuality of late Italy; the visionary religion of Tuscany; the splendid human energy and beauty of Venice. I have no time to do this to-night (I have done it elsewhere before now); but I proceed to apply the principle to ourselves in a more searching manner.

I notice that among all the new buildings that cover your once wild hills, churches and schools are mixed in due, that is to say, in large proportion, with your mills and mansions; and I notice also that the churches and schools are almost always Gothic, and the mansions and mills are never Gothic. Will you allow me to ask precisely the meaning of this? For, remember, it is peculiarly a modern phenomenon. When Gothic was invented, houses were Gothic as well as churches; and when the Italian style superseded the Gothic, churches were Italian as well as houses. If there is a Gothic spire to the cathedral of Antwerp, there is a Gothic belfry to the Hôtel de Ville at Brussels; if Inigo Jones builds an Italian Whitehall, Sir Christopher Wren builds an Italian St. Paul's. But now you live under one school of architecture, and worship under another. What do you mean by doing this? Am I to understand that you are thinking of changing your architecture back to Gothic; and that you treat your churches experimentally, because it does not matter what mistakes you make in a church? Or am I to understand that you consider Gothic a pre-eminently sacred and beautiful mode of building, which you think, like the fine frankincense, should be mixed for the tabernacle only, and reserved for your religious services? For if this be the feeling, though it may seem at first as if it were graceful and reverent, you will find that, at the root of the matter, it signifies neither more nor less than that you have separated your religion from your life.

For consider what a wide significance this fact has: and remember that it is not you only, but all the people of England, who are behaving thus, just now.

You have all got into the habit of calling the church "the house of God." I have seen, over the doors of many churches, the legend actually carved, "*This* is the house of God and this is the gate of heaven." Now, note where that legend comes from, and of what place it was first spoken. A boy leaves his father's house to go on a long journey on foot, to visit his uncle: he has to cross a wild hill-desert; just as if one of your own boys had to cross the wolds to visit an uncle at Carlisle. The second or third day your boy finds himself somewhere between Hawes and Brough, in the midst of the moors, at sunset. It is stony ground, and boggy; he cannot go one foot further that night. Down he lies, to sleep, on Wharnside, where best he may, gathering a few of the stones together to put under his head;—so wild the place is, he cannot get anything but stones. And there, lying under the broad night, he has a dream; and he sees a ladder set up on the earth, and the top of it reaches to heaven, and the angels of God are ascending and descending upon it. And when he wakes out of his sleep, he says, "How dreadful is this place; surely this is none other than the house of God, and this is the gate of heaven." This PLACE, observe; not this church; not this city; not this stone, even, which he puts up for a memorial—the piece of flint on which his head has lain. But this *place;* this windy slope of Wharnside; this moorland hollow, torrent-bitten, snow-blighted! this *any* place where God lets down the ladder. And how are you to know where that will be? or how are you to determine where it may be, but by being ready for it always? Do you know where the lightning is to fall next? You *do* know that, partly; you can guide the lightning; but you cannot guide the going forth of the Spirit, which is that lightning when it shines from the east to the west.

But the perpetual and insolent warping of that strong verse to serve a merely ecclesiastical purpose is only one of the thousand instances in which we sink back into gross Judaism. We call our churches "temples." Now, you know perfectly well they are *not* temples. They have never had, never can have, anything whatever to do

with temples. They are "synagogues"—"gathering places"—where you gather yourselves together as an assembly; and by not calling them so, you again miss the force
of another mighty text—"Thou, when thou prayest, shalt not be as the hypocrites are;
for they love to pray standing in the *churches*" [we should translate it], "that they
may be seen of men. But thou, when thou prayest, enter into thy closet, and when
thou hast shut thy door, pray to thy Father"—which is, not in chancel nor in aisle, but
"in secret."

Now, you feel, as I say this to you—I know you feel—as if I were trying to take
away the honour of your churches. Not so; I am trying to prove to you the honour
of your houses and your hills; not that the Church is not sacred—but that the whole
Earth is. I would have you feel, what careless, what constant, what infectious sin
there is in all modes of thought, whereby, in calling your churches only "holy," you
call your hearths and homes "profane"; and have separated yourselves from the
heathen by casting all your household gods to the ground, instead of recognizing, in
the place of their many and feeble Lares, the presence of your One and Mighty Lord
and Lar.

"But what has all this to do with our Exchange?" you ask me, impatiently. My
dear friends, it has just everything to do with it; on these inner and great questions
depend all the outer and little ones; and if you have asked me down here to speak
to you, because you had before been interested in anything I have written, you must
know that all I have yet said about architecture was to show this. The book I called
The Seven Lamps was to show that certain right states of temper and moral feeling
were the magic powers by which all good architecture, without exception, had been
produced. *The Stones of Venice* had, from beginning to end, no other aim than to
show that the Gothic architecture of Venice had arisen out of, and indicated in all
its features, a state of pure national faith, and of domestic virtue; and that its Renaissance architecture had arisen out of, and in all its features indicated, a state of
concealed national infidelity, and of domestic corruption. And now, you ask me what
style is best to build in, and how can I answer, knowing the meaning of the two
styles, but by another question—do you mean to build as Christians or as Infidels?
And still more—do you mean to build as honest Christians or as honest Infidels? as
thoroughly and confessedly either one or the other? You don't like to be asked such
rude questions. I cannot help it; they are of much more importance than this Exchange
business; and if they can be at once answered, the Exchange business settles itself in a
moment. But before I press them farther, I must ask leave to explain one point clearly.

In all my past work, my endeavour has been to show that good architecture is
essentially religious—the production of a faithful and virtuous, not of an infidel and
corrupted people. But in the course of doing this, I have had also to show that good
architecture is not *ecclesiastical*. People are so apt to look upon religion as the business
of the clergy, not their own, that the moment they hear of anything depending on
"religion," they think it must also have depended on the priesthood; and I have had
to take what place was to be occupied between these two errors, and fight both, often
with seeming contradiction. Good architecture is the work of good and believing men;
therefore, you say, at least some people say, "Good architecture must essentially have
been the work of the clergy, not of the laity." No—a thousand times no; good archi-

tecture has always been the work of the commonalty, *not* of the clergy. "What," you say, "those glorious cathedrals—the pride of Europe—did their builders not form Gothic architecture?" No; they corrupted Gothic architecture. Gothic was formed in the baron's castle, and the burgher's street. It was formed by the thoughts, and hands, and powers of labouring citizens and warrior kings. By the monk it was used as an instrument for the aid of his superstition; when that superstition became a beautiful madness, and the best hearts of Europe vainly dreamed and pined in the cloister, and vainly raged and perished in the crusade,—through that fury of perverted faith and wasted war, the Gothic rose also to its loveliest, most fantastic, and, finally, most foolish dreams; and in those dreams, was lost.

I hope, now, that there is no risk of your misunderstanding me when I come to the gist of what I want to say to-night;—when I repeat, that every great national architecture has been the result and exponent of a great national religion. You can't have bits of it here, bits there—you must have it everywhere or nowhere. It is not the monopoly of a clerical company—it is not the exponent of a theological dogma —it is not the hieroglyphic writing of an initiated priesthood; it is the manly language of a people inspired by resolute and common purpose, and rendering resolute and common fidelity to the legible laws of an undoubted God.

Now, there have as yet been three distinct schools of European architecture. I say, European, because Asiatic and African architectures belong so entirely to other races and climates, that there is no question of them here; only, in passing, I will simply assure you that whatever is good or great in Egypt, and Syria, and India, is just good or great for the same reasons as the buildings on our side of the Bosphorus. We Europeans, then, have had three great religions: the Greek, which was the worship of the God of Wisdom and Power; the Mediaeval, which was the worship of the God of Judgment and Consolation; the Renaissance, which was the worship of the God of Pride and Beauty: these three we have had—they are past,—and now, at last, we English have got a fourth religion, and a God of our own, about which I want to ask you. But I must explain these three old ones first.

I repeat, first, the Greeks essentially worshipped the God of Wisdom; so that whatever contended against their religion,—to the Jews a stumbling-block,—was, to the Greeks—*Foolishness.*

The first Greek idea of deity was that expressed in the word, of which we keep the remnant in our words *"Di*-urnal" and *"Di*-vine"—the god of *Day,* Jupiter the revealer. Athena is his daughter, but especially daughter of the Intellect, springing armed from the head. We are only with the help of recent investigation beginning to penetrate the depth of meaning couched under the Athenaic symbols: but I may note rapidly, that her aegis, the mantle with the serpent fringes, in which she often, in the best statues, is represented as folding up her left hand, for better guard; and the Gorgon, on her shield, are both representative mainly of the chilling horror and sadness (turning men to stone, as it were), of the outmost and superficial spheres of knowledge—that knowledge which separates, in bitterness, hardness, and sorrow, the heart of the full-grown man from the heart of the child. For out of imperfect knowledge spring terror, dissension, danger, and disdain; but from perfect knowledge, given by the full-revealed Athena, strength and peace, in sign of which she is crowned with the olive spray, and bears the resistless spear.

This, then, was the Greek conception of purest Deity; and every habit of life, and every form of his art developed themselves from the seeking this bright, serene, resistless wisdom; and setting himself, as a man, to do things evermore rightly and strongly; not with any ardent affection or ultimate hope; but with a resolute and continent energy of will, as knowing that for failure there was no consolation, and for sin there was no remission. And the Greek architecture rose unerring, bright, clearly defined, and self-contained.

Next followed in Europe the great Christian faith, which was essentially the religion of Comfort. Its great doctrine is the remission of sins; for which cause, it happens, too often, in certain phases of Christianity, that sin and sickness themselves are partly glorified, as if, the more you had to be healed of, the more divine was the healing. The practical result of this doctrine, in art, is a continual contemplation of sin and disease, and of imaginary states of purification from them; thus we have an architecture conceived in a mingled sentiment of melancholy and aspiration, partly severe, partly luxuriant, which will bend itself to every one of our needs, and every one of our fancies, and be strong or weak with us, as we are strong or weak ourselves. It is, of all architecture, the basest, when base people build it—of all, the noblest, when built by the noble.

And now note that both these religions—Greek and Mediaeval—perished by falsehood in their own main purpose. The Greek religion of Wisdom perished in a false philosophy—"Oppositions of science, falsely so called." The Mediaeval religion of Consolation perished in false comfort; in remission of sins given lyingly. It was the selling of absolution that ended the Mediaeval faith; and I can tell you more, it is the selling of absolution which, to the end of time, will mark false Christianity. Pure Christianity gives her remission of sins only by *ending* them; but false Christianity gets her remission of sins by *compounding for* them. And there are many ways of compounding for them. We English have beautiful little quiet ways of buying absolution, whether in low Church or high, far more cunning than any of Tetzel's trading.

Then, thirdly, there followed the religion of Pleasure, in which all Europe gave itself to luxury, ending in death. First, *bals masqués* in every saloon, and then guillotines in every square. And all these three worships issue in vast temple building. Your Greek worshipped Wisdom, and built you the Parthenon—the Virgin's temple. The Mediaeval worshipped Consolation, and built you Virgin temples also—but to our Lady of Salvation. Then the Revivalist worshipped beauty, of a sort, and built you Versailles and the Vatican. Now, lastly, will you tell me what *we* worship, and what *we* build?

You know we are speaking always of the real, active, continual, national worship; that by which men act, while they live; not that which they talk of, when they die. Now, we have, indeed, a nominal religion, to which we pay tithes of property and sevenths of time; but we have also a practical and earnest religion, to which we devote nine-tenths of our property and sixth-sevenths of our time. And we dispute a great deal about the nominal religion: but we are all unanimous about this practical one; of which I think you will admit that the ruling goddess may be best generally described as the "Goddess of Getting-on," or "Britannia of the Market." The Athenians had an "Athena Agoraia," or Athena of the Market; but she was a subordinate type of their goddess, while our Britannia Agoraia is the principal type of ours. And all your great architectural works are, of course, built to her. It is long since you built a great cathedral; and how you would laugh at me if I proposed building a cathedral on the top of one of these hills of yours, taking it for an Acropolis! But your railroad mounds, vaster than the walls of Babylon; your railroad stations, vaster than the temple of Ephesus, and innumerable; your chimneys, how much more mighty and costly than cathedral spires! your harbour-piers; your warehouses; your exchanges!—all these are built to your great Goddess of "Getting-on"; and she has formed, and will continue to form, your architecture, as long as you worship her; and it is quite vain to ask me to tell you how to build to *her;* you know far better than I.

There might, indeed, on some theories, be a conceivably good architecture for Exchanges—that is to say, if there were any heroism in the fact or deed of exchange which might be typically carved on the outside of your building. For, you know, all beautiful architecture must be adorned with sculpture or painting; and for sculpture or painting, you must have a subject. And hitherto it has been a received opinion among the nations of the world that the only right subjects for either, were *heroisms* of some sort. Even on his pots and his flagons, the Greek put a Hercules slaying lions, or an Apollo slaying serpents, or Bacchus slaying melancholy giants, and earthborn despondencies. On his temples, the Greek put contests of great warriors in founding states, or of gods with evil spirits. On his houses and temples alike, the Christian put carvings of angels conquering devils; or of hero-martyrs exchanging this world for another: subject inappropriate, I think, to our manner of exchange here. And the Master of Christians not only left His followers without any orders as to the sculpture of affairs of exchange on the outside of buildings, but gave some strong evidence of His dislike of affairs of exchange within them. And yet there might surely be a heroism in such affairs; and all commerce become a kind of selling of doves, not impious. The wonder has always been great to me, that heroism has never been supposed to be in any wise consistent with the practice of supplying people with food, or clothes; but rather with that of quartering one's self upon them for food, and stripping them of their clothes. Spoiling of armour is an heroic deed in all ages; but the selling of clothes, old, or new, has never taken any colour of magnanimity. Yet one does not see why feeding the hungry and clothing the naked should ever become base businesses, even when engaged in on a large scale. If one could contrive to attach the notion of conquest to them anyhow! so that, supposing there were anywhere an obstinate race, who refused to be comforted, one might take some pride in giving them compulsory comfort! and, as it were, *"occupying* a country" with one's gifts, instead of one's armies? If one could only consider it as much a victory to get a barren field sown, as to get an eared field stripped; and contend who should build villages, instead of who should "carry" them! Are not all forms of heroism conceivable in doing these serviceable deeds? You doubt who is strongest? It might be ascertained by push of spade, as well as push of sword. Who is wisest? There are witty things to be thought of in planning other business than campaigns. Who is bravest? There are always the elements to fight with, stronger than men; and nearly as merciless.

The only absolutely and unapproachably heroic element in the soldier's work seems to be—that he is paid little for it—and regularly: while you traffickers, and exchangers, and others occupied in presumably benevolent business, like to be paid much for it— and by chance. I never can make out how it is that a *knight*-errant does not expect to be paid for his trouble, but a *pedlar*-errant always does;—that people are willing to take hard knocks for nothing, but never to sell ribands cheap; that they are ready to go on fervent crusades, to recover the tomb of a buried God, but never on any travels to fulfil the orders of a living one;—that they will go anywhere barefoot to preach their faith, but must be well bribed to practise it, and are perfectly ready to give the Gospel gratis, but never the loaves and fishes.

If you chose to take the matter up on any such soldierly principle; to do your commerce, and your feeding of nations, for fixed salaries; and to be as particular about giving people the best food, and the best cloth, as soldiers are about giving them the best gunpowder, I could carve something for you on your exchange worth looking at. But I can only at present suggest decorating its frieze with pendant purses; and making its pillars broad at the base, for the sticking of bills. And in the innermost chambers of it there might be a statue of Britannia of the Market, who may have, perhaps advisably, a partridge for her crest, typical at once of her courage in fighting for noble ideas, and of her interest in game; and round its neck, the inscription in golden letters, "Perdix fovit quae non peperit." [1] Then, for her spear, she might have a weaver's beam; and on her shield, instead of St. George's Cross, the Milanese boar, semi-fleeced, with the town of Gennesaret proper, in the field; and the legend, "In the best market," and her corslet, of leather, folded over her heart in the shape of a purse, with thirty slits in it, for a piece of money to go in at, on each day of the month. And I doubt not but that people would come to see your exchange, and its goddess, with applause.

Nevertheless, I want to point out to you certain strange characters in this goddess of yours. She differs from the great Greek and Mediaeval deities essentially in two things —first, as to the continuance of her presumed power; secondly, as to the extent of it.

1st, as to the Continuance.

The Greek Goddess of Wisdom gave continual increase of wisdom, as the Christian Spirit of Comfort (or Comforter) continual increase of comfort. There was no question, with these, of any limit or cessation of function. But with your Agora Goddess, that is just the most important question. Getting on—but where to? Gathering together—but how much? Do you mean to gather always—never to spend? If so, I wish you joy of your goddess, for I am just as well off as you, without the trouble of worshipping her at all. But if you do not spend, somebody else will—somebody else must. And it is because of this (among many other such errors) that I have fearlessly declared your so-called science of Political Economy to be no science; because, namely, it has omitted the study of exactly the most important branch of the business—the study of *spending*. For spend you must, and as much as you make, ultimately. You

---

[1] *"We have brought our pigs to it."*

gather corn:—will you bury England under a heap of grain; or will you, when you have gathered, finally eat? You gather gold:—will you make your house-roofs of it, or pave your streets with it? That is still one way of spending it. But if you keep it, that you may get more, I'll give you more; I'll give you all the gold you want—all you can imagine—if you can tell me what you'll do with it. You shall have thousands of gold-pieces;—thousands of thousands—millions—mountains, of gold: where will you keep them? Will you put an Olympus of silver upon a golden Pelion—make Ossa like a wart? Do you think the rain and dew would then come down to you, in the streams from such mountains, more blessedly than they will down the mountains which God has made for you, of moss and whinstone? But it is not gold that you want to gather! What is it? greenbacks? No; not those neither. What is it then—is it ciphers after a capital I? Cannot you practise writing ciphers, and write as many as you want? Write ciphers for an hour every morning, in a big book, and say every evening, I am worth all those noughts more than I was yesterday. Won't that do? Well, what in the name of Plutus is it you want? Not gold, not greenbacks, not ciphers after a capital I? You will have to answer, after all, "No; we want, somehow or other, money's *worth*." Well, what is that? Let your Goddess of Getting-on discover it, and let her learn to stay therein.

2d. But there is yet another question to be asked respecting this Goddess of Getting-on. The first was of the continuance of her power; the second is of its extent.

Pallas and the Madonna were supposed to be all the world's Pallas, and all the world's Madonna. They could teach all men, and they could comfort all men. But, look strictly into the nature of the power of your Goddess of Getting-on; and you will find she is the Goddess—not of everybody's getting on—but only of somebody's getting on. This is a vital, or rather deathful, distinction. Examine it in your own ideal of the state of national life which this Goddess is to evoke and maintain. I asked you what it was, when I was last here;—you have never told me. Now, shall I try to tell you?

Your ideal of human life then is, I think, that it should be passed in a pleasant undulating world, with iron and coal everywhere underneath it. On each pleasant bank of this world is to be a beautiful mansion, with two wings; and stables, and coach-houses; a moderately-sized park; a large garden and hot-houses; and pleasant carriage drives through the shrubberies. In this mansion are to live the favoured votaries of the Goddess; the English gentleman, with his gracious wife, and his beautiful family; always able to have the boudoir and the jewels for the wife, and the beautiful ball dresses for the daughters, and hunters for the sons, and a shooting in the Highlands for himself. At the bottom of the bank, is to be the mill; not less than a quarter of a mile long, with a steam engine at each end, and two in the middle, and a chimney three hundred feet high. In this mill are to be in constant employment from eight hundred to a thousand workers, who never drink, never strike, always go to church on Sunday, and always express themselves in respectful language.

Is not that, broadly, and in the main features, the kind of thing you propose to yourselves? It is very pretty indeed seen from above; not at all so pretty, seen from below. For, observe, while to one family this deity is indeed the Goddess of Getting-on, to a thousand families she is the Goddess of *not* Getting-on. "Nay," you say, "they have all their chance." Yes, so has every one in a lottery, but there must always be the same number of blanks. "Ah! but in a lottery it is not skill and intelligence which take the lead, but blind chance." What then! do you think the old practice, that "they should take who have the power, and they should keep who can," is less iniquitous, when the power has become power of brains instead of fist? and that, though we may not take advantage of a child's or a woman's weakness, we may of a man's foolishness? "Nay, but finally, work must be done, and some one must be at the top, some one at the bottom." Granted, my friends. Work must always be, and captains of work must always be; and if you in the least remember the tone of any of my writings, you must know that they are thought unfit for this age, because they are always insisting on need of government, and speaking with scorn of liberty. But I beg you to observe that there is a wide difference between being captains or governors of work, and taking the profits of it. It does not follow, because you are general of an army, that you are to take all the treasure, or land, it wins; (if it fight for treasure or land;) neither, because you are king of a nation, that you are to consume all the profits of the nation's work. Real kings, on the contrary, are known invariably by their doing quite the reverse of this,— by their taking the least possible quantity of the nation's work for themselves. There is no test of real kinghood so infallible as that. Does the crowned creature live simply, bravely, unostentatiously? probably he *is* a King. Does he cover his body with jewels, and his table with delicates? in all probability he is *not* a King. It is possible he may be, as Solomon was; but that is when the nation shares his splendour with him. Solomon made gold, not only to be in his own palace as stones, but to be in Jerusalem as stones. But, even so, for the most part, these splendid kinghoods expire in ruin, and only the true kinghoods live, which are of royal labourers governing loyal labourers; who, both leading rough lives, establish the true dynasties. Conclusively you will find that because you are king of a nation, it does not follow that you are to gather for yourself all the wealth of that nation; neither, because you are king of a small part of the nation, and lord over the means of its maintenance—over field, or mill, or mine,— are you to take all the produce of that piece of the foundation of national existence for yourself.

You will tell me I need not preach against these things, for I cannot mend them. No, good friends, I cannot; but you can, and you will; or something else can and will. Even good things have no abiding power—and shall these evil things persist in victorious evil? All history shows, on the contrary, that to be the exact thing they never can do. Change *must* come; but it is ours to determine whether change of growth, or change of death. Shall the Parthenon be in ruins on its rock, and Bolton priory in its meadow, but these mills of yours be the consummation of the buildings of the earth, and their wheels be as the wheels of eternity? Think you that "men may come, and men may go," but—mills—go on for ever? Not so; out of these, better or worse shall come; and it is for you to choose which.

I know that none of this wrong is done with deliberate purpose. I know, on the contrary, that you wish your workmen well; that you do much for them, and that you desire to do more for them, if you saw your way to such benevolence safely. I know that even all this wrong and misery are brought about by a warped sense of duty, each of you striving to do his best; but, unhappily, not knowing for whom this best should be done. And all our hearts have been betrayed by the plausible impiety of the modern economist, telling us that, "To do the best for ourselves, is finally to do the best for others." Friends, our great Master said not so; and most absolutely we shall find this world is not made so. Indeed, to do the best for others, is finally to do the best for ourselves; but it will not do to have our eyes fixed on that issue. The Pagans had got beyond that. Hear what a Pagan says of this matter; hear what were, perhaps, the last written words of Plato,—if not the last actually written (for this we cannot know), yet assuredly in fact and power his parting words—in which, endeavouring to give full crowning and harmonious close to all his thoughts, and to speak the sum of them by the imagined sentence of the Great Spirit, his strength and his heart fail him, and the words cease, broken off for ever. They are at the close of the dialogue called *Critias,* in which he describes, partly from real tradition, partly in ideal dream, the early state of Athens; and the genesis, and order, and religion, of the fabled isle of Atlantis; in which genesis he conceives the same first perfection and final degeneracy of man, which in our own Scriptural tradition is expressed by saying that the Sons of God inter-married with the daughters of men, for he supposes the earliest race to have been in-deed the children of God; and to have corrupted themselves, until "their spot was not the spot of his children." And this, he says, was the end; that indeed "through many generations, so long as the God's nature in them yet was full, they were submissive to the sacred laws, and carried themselves lovingly to all that had kindred with them in divineness; for their uttermost spirit was faithful and true, and in every wise great; so that, in *all meekness of wisdom, they dealt with each other,* and took all the chances of life; and despising all things except virtue, they cared little what happened day by day, and *bore lightly the burden* of gold and of possessions; for they saw that, if *only their common love and virtue increased, all these things would be increased together with them;* but to set their esteem and ardent pursuit upon material possession would be to lose that first, and their virtue and affection together with it. And by such reasoning, and what of the divine nature remained in them, they gained all this greatness of which we have already told; but when the God's part of them faded and became ex-tinct, being mixed again and again, and effaced by the prevalent mortality; and the human nature at last exceeded, they then became unable to endure the courses of for-tune; and fell into shapelessness of life, and baseness in the sight of him who could see, having lost everything that was fairest of their honour; while to the blind hearts which could not discern the true life, tending to happiness, it seemed that they were then chiefly noble and happy, being filled with an iniquity of inordinate possession and power. Whereupon, the God of Gods, whose Kinghood is in laws, beholding a once just nation thus cast into misery, and desiring to lay such punishment upon them as might make them repent into restraining, gathered together all the gods into his dwelling-place, which from heaven's centre overlooks whatever has part in creation; and having assembled them, he said"—

The rest is silence. Last words of the chief wisdom of the heathen, spoken of this idol of riches; this idol of yours; this golden image, high by measureless cubits, set up where your green fields of England are furnace-burnt into the likeness of the plain of Dura: this idol, forbidden to us, first of all idols, by our own Master and faith; for-bidden to us also by every human lip that has ever, in any age or people, been ac-counted of as able to speak according to the purposes of God. Continue to make that forbidden deity your principal one, and soon no more art, no more science, no more pleasure will be possible. Catastrophe will come; or, worse than catastrophe, slow mouldering and withering into Hades. But if you can fix some conception of a true human state of life to be striven for—life, good for all men, as for yourselves; if you can determine some honest and simple order of existence; following those trodden ways of wisdom, which are pleasantness, and seeking her quiet and withdrawn paths, which are peace;—then, and so sanctifying wealth into "commonwealth," all your art, your literature, your daily labours, your domestic affection, and citizen's duty, will join and increase into one magnificent harmony. You will know then how to build, well enough; you will build with stone well, but with flesh better; temples not made with hands, but riveted of hearts; and that kind of marble, crimson-veined, is indeed eternal.